The Counts of Tripoli a[...]
in the Twelfth Century

The county of Tripoli in what is now North Lebanon is arguably the most neglected of the so-called 'crusader states' established in the Middle East at the beginning of the twelfth century. The present work is the first monograph on the county to be published in English, and the first in any western language since 1945. What little has been written on the subject previously has focused upon the European ancestry of the counts of Tripoli: a specifically Southern French heritage inherited from the famous crusader Raymond IV of Saint-Gilles. Kevin Lewis argues that past historians have at once exaggerated the political importance of the counts' French descent and ignored the more compelling signs of its cultural impact, highlighting poetry composed by troubadours in Occitan at Tripoli's court. For Lewis, however, even this belies a deeper understanding of the processes that shaped the county. What emerges is an intriguing portrait of the county in which its rulers struggled to exert their power over Lebanon in the face of this region's insurmountable geographical forces and its sometimes bewildering, always beguiling diversity of religions, languages and cultures. The counts of Tripoli and contemporary Muslim onlookers certainly viewed the dynasty as sons of Saint-Gilles, but the county's administration relied upon Arabic, its stability upon the mixed loyalties of its local inhabitants, and its very existence upon the rugged mountains that cradled it. This book challenges prevailing knowledge of this little-known crusader state and by extension the medieval Middle East as a whole.

Kevin James Lewis completed a doctorate in History at the University of Oxford, where he produced a thesis on aspects of the 'crusader' county of Tripoli during the twelfth century, under the supervision of Professor Christopher Tyerman. Previously he studied at Cardiff University's Centre for the Crusades, taught by Professors Helen Nicholson, Peter Edbury and Denys Pringle. More recently he held a Past & Present Postdoctoral Fellowship at the Institute of Historical Research, University of London.

Rulers of the Latin East

Series editors

Academics concerned with the history of the Crusades and the Latin East will be familiar with the various survey histories that have been produced for this fascinating topic. Many historians have published wide-ranging texts that either seek to make sense of the strange phenomenon that was the Crusades or shed light upon the Christian territories of the Latin East. Such panoramic works have helped to generate enormous interest in this subject, but they can only take their readers so far. Works addressing the lives of individual rulers - whether kings, queens, counts, princes or patriarchs - are less common and yet are needed if we are to achieve a more detailed understanding of this period.

This series seeks to address this need by stimulating a collection of political biographies of the men and women who ruled the Latin East between 1098 and 1291 and the kingdom of Cyprus up to 1571. These focus in detail upon the evolving political and diplomatic events of this period, whilst shedding light upon more thematic issues such as: gender and marriage, intellectual life, kingship and governance, military history and inter-faith relations.

The Counts of Tripoli and Lebanon in the Twelfth Century

Sons of Saint-Gilles

Kevin James Lewis

Routledge
Taylor & Francis Group
LONDON AND NEW YORK

First published 2017 by Routledge

2 Park Square, Milton Park, Abingdon, Oxfordshire OX14 4RN
52 Vanderbilt Avenue, New York, NY 10017

Routledge is an imprint of the Taylor & Francis Group, an informa business

First issued in paperback 2019

British Library Cataloguing-in-Publication Data
A catalogue record for this book is available from the British Library

Library of Congress Cataloging-in-Publication Data
Names: Lewis, Kevin James, 1987– author.
Title: The counts of Tripoli and Lebanon in the twelfth century : sons of Saint-Gilles / Kevin James Lewis.
Description: Milton Park, Abingdon, Oxon ; New York, NY : Routledge, 2017. | Includes bibliographical references and index.
Identifiers: LCCN 2016047794| ISBN 9781472458902 (hardback : alkaline paper) | ISBN 9781315609911 (ebook)
Subjects: LCSH: Tripoli, Counts of. | Toulouse, Counts of. | Tripoli (Lebanon)—History. | Tripoli (Lebanon)—Biography. | Nobility—Lebanon—Tripoli—Biography. | French—Lebanon—Tripoli—Biography. | Lebanon—Kings and rulers—Biography. | France—Kings and rulers—Biography. | Power (Social sciences)—Lebanon—Tripoli—History—To 1500. | Tripoli (Lebanon)—Politics and government.
Classification: LCC D194 .L49 2017 | DDC 956.92—dc23
LC record available at https://lccn.loc.gov/2016047794

ISBN: 978-1-4724-5890-2 (hbk)
ISBN: 978-0-367-88055-2 (pbk)

Typeset in Baskerville
by Swales & Willis Ltd, Exeter, Devon, UK

For my parents

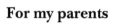

Contents

Illustrations

Figures

Map

Preface

It has been more than seventy years since the publication of the last full monograph on the county of Tripoli, despite the intervening decades witnessing a huge upsurge in publications on the crusades and the Latin East. This book is intended to go some way towards redressing this imbalance, shedding light upon the most neglected of crusader states while also contributing to Syrian and Lebanese history more broadly. The present work is based loosely upon my doctoral thesis completed at the University of Oxford in 2014, which was entitled *Rule and Identity in a Diverse Mediterranean Society: Aspects of the County of Tripoli during the Twelfth Century*. The structure, focus and much of the content of the earlier piece is radically different from that of *The Counts of Tripoli and Lebanon in the Twelfth Century*. Whereas the thesis was structured thematically and comprised a handful of focused case studies, the present work has been arranged chronologically and takes a much more holistic approach to the subject. The book therefore is hopefully more accessible to those who have not spent a good few years contemplating what took place in the shadow of Mount Lebanon some nine centuries ago.

Kevin James Lewis
London, July 2016

Acknowledgements

In the course of researching and writing both a thesis and a book on the county of Tripoli, I have incurred debts of gratitude to many individuals and organisations. I am grateful to the staff and students of Cardiff University (2005–9), Merton College, Oxford (2010–12), and Hertford College, Oxford (2012–14), for providing stimulating intellectual environments during my time first as an undergraduate and eventually as a doctoral student. Particular thanks are owed to Hertford and the Drapers' Company, for awarding me a Senior Scholarship (2012–14); the Arts and Humanities Research Council, for awarding a doctoral research grant (2012–13); the Institute of Historical Research and Past and Present, for awarding a Postdoctoral Research Fellowship (2014–15); and the Council for British Research in the Levant, for providing a scholarship to study Arabic in Jordan (2012). Although the thesis and the book are very much different beasts, my debt of gratitude to these sources of support throughout my years of doctoral research endures.

I would like to thank the staff at the following libraries, archives and museums: numerous institutions in Oxford, particularly the Bodleian, the History Faculty Library, the Oriental Institute Library, the Ashmolean Museum and the college libraries of Merton, Magdalen and St Hugh's; the British Library; Cardiff University's Arts and Social Studies Library; the Library of the School of Oriental and African Studies, University of London; the National Library of Malta, Valletta; and the Biblioteca Apostolica Vaticana.

I have been fortunate to meet countless experts in my chosen field and it would be impractical to list all those who have provided advice, support and constructive criticism. Particular thanks must be addressed to the following: Michael Athanson, Betty Binysh, Paul Brand, Andrew Buck, Damien Carraz, Anna Chrysostomides, Peter Edbury, Ian Forrest, Huw Grange, Bernard Hamilton, Catherine Holmes, Michael Jeffreys, Hugh Kennedy, Max Lau, Gregory Lippiatt, Nicholas Morton, Helen Nicholson, André Penafiel, Jonathan Phillips, Denys Pringle, John Pryor, Yousif Qasmiyeh, Hugh Reid, Theresa Vann and Mark Whittow.

Liz Mincin deserves a special mention, for help with Greek and for providing huge quantities of encouragement over the past few years.

My doctoral supervisor, Dr Christopher Tyerman, was and is an inexhaustible source of knowledge, wisdom and advice. Without his unfailing patience and clarity of thought, this book would be much the poorer.

Finally, I would like to thank my parents, to whom *The Counts of Tripoli and Lebanon in the Twelfth Century* is dedicated. Without them and their constant support, it is safe to say that the book would not have existed. Needless to say, I alone am to blame for the errors within.

Abbreviations

AA	Albert of Aachen, *Historia Ierosolimitana: History of the Journey to Jerusalem*, ed. Susan B. Edgington (Oxford, 2007)
AK	Anna Komnene, *The Alexiad*, trans. E. R. A. Sewter and Peter Frankopan (London, 2009)
BD	Bahā᾽ al-Dīn bin Shaddād, *Sīrat Ṣalāḥ al-Dīn: «al-sīra al-yūsufiyya»*, ed. Jamāl al-Dīn al-Shayyāl (Cairo, 1962)
BMB	*Bulletin du Musée de Beyrouth*
CCSSJ	*Le Cartulaire du Chapitre du Saint-Sépulcre de Jérusalem*, ed. Geneviève Bresc-Bautier (Paris, 1984)
CDRG	*Codice Diplomatico della Repubblica di Genova dal DCCCCLVIII al MCLXIII*, ed. Cesare Imperiale di Sant'Angelo, 3 vols (Rome, 1936–42)
CGOH	*Cartulaire général de l'Ordre des Hospitaliers de S. Jean de Jérusalem (1100–1310)*, ed. J. Delaville le Roulx, 4 vols (Paris, 1894–1906)
CHR	*The Catholic Historical Review*
Cont.	*La continuation de Guillaume de Tyre (1184–1197)*, ed. M. R. Morgan, Documents relatifs à l'histoire des Croisades publiés par l'Académie des Inscriptions et Belles-Lettres 14 (Paris, 1982)
D.Jerus.	*Die Urkunden der lateinischen Könige von Jerusalem*, ed. Hans Eberhard Mayer, 4 vols, Monumenta Germaniae Historica: Diplomata Regum Latinorum Hierosolymitanorum (Hannover, 2010)
DOP	*Dumbarton Oaks Papers*
EHR	*The English Historical Review*
Eracles	'L'Estoire de Eracles empereur et la conquest de la terre d'Outremer: C'est la continuation de l'estoire de Guillaume archevesque de Sur', in *Recueil des Historiens des Croisades: Historiens Occidentaux*, vol. 2, pp. 1–481
GF	*Gesta Francorum et aliorum Hierosolimitanorum*, ed. Heinrich Hagenmeyer (Heidelberg, 1890)
IA	Ibn al-Athīr, *Al-kāmil fī al-tārīkh*, ed. C. J. Tornberg, rev. ed., 12 vols + index (Beirut, 1965–7)
IJ	Ibn Jubayr, *Riḥla*, ed. William Wright and M. J. de Goeje (Leiden, 1907)

ʿImād	ʿImād al-Dīn al-Iṣfahānī, *Kitāb al-fatḥ al-qussī fī al-fatḥ al-qudsī*, ed. Carlo de Landberg (Leiden, 1888)
IQ	Ibn al-Qalānisī, Abū Yaʿlā Ḥamza, *History of Damascus, 363–555 a. h., by Ibn al-Qalānisī from the Bodleian Ms. Hunt. 125, being a continuation of Hilâl al-Sâbi*, ed. H. F. Amedroz (Leiden, 1908)
JV	James of Vitry, *Historia orientalis*, ed. Jean Donnadieu (Turnhout, 2008)
MGH SS	*Monumenta Germaniae Historica: Scriptores*, 39 vols (Hanover, 1826–)
PT	Petrus Tudebodus, *Historia de Hierosolymitano Itinere*, ed. John Hugh Hill and Laurita L. Hill, Documents relatifs à l'histoire des croisades publiés par l'Académie des Inscriptions et Belles-Lettres 12 (Paris, 1977)
RA	Raymond of Aguilers, *Le « Liber » de Raymond d'Aguilers*, ed. John Hugh Hill and Laurita L. Hill, Documents relatifs à l'histoire des croisades publiés par l'Académie des Inscriptions et Belles-Lettres 9 (Paris, 1969)
RHC Ar	*Recueil des Historiens des Croisades: Documents Arméniens*, 2 vols (Paris, 1869–1906)
RHC Oc	*Recueil des Historiens des Croisades: Historiens Occidentaux*, 5 vols (Paris, 1844–95)
RHC Or	*Recueil des Historiens des Croisades: Historiens Orientaux*, 5 vols (Paris, 1872–1906)
RRH	*Regesta Regni Hierosolymitani (MXCVII–MCCXCI)*, ed. Reinhold Röhricht (Innsbrück, 1893)
RRH Add.	*Regesta Regni Hierosolymitani (MXCVII–MCCXCI): Additamentum*, ed. Reinhold Röhricht (Innsbrück, 1904)
Usāma	Usāma bin Munqidh, *Usāmah's Memoirs entitled* Kitāb al-Iʿtibār, ed. Philip K. Hitti (Princeton, NJ, 1930)
WT	William of Tyre, *Chronicon*, ed. R. B. C. Huygens, 2 vols, Corpus Christianorum Continuatio Mediaevalis 63–63A (Turnhout, 1986)

Introduction

Sons of Saint-Gilles

The Frankish county of Tripoli was not historically important, at least in the traditional sense. Its counts won no particularly great military victories beyond the conquest of the county itself and commissioned no great works of literature. The county's archives were sacked in an epoch long past and their contents erased from history. Only paint flaking off forgotten church walls, once-mighty fortresses gutted by the fires of modern wars, and crumbling manuscripts in distant libraries stand testament to the fact that the county and its inhabitants existed at all. Yet the study of the county and its rulers is important in that it raises a number of hitherto unasked and unanswered questions regarding the development both of the so-called 'crusader states' and of Lebanon and Syria more generally. Though small, the county's history encapsulates the principal forces that shook and shaped the Latin East as a whole.

The county was not simply the product of European crusaders, but grew amid the verdant valleys of Lebanon, the forbidding heights of the Alawite mountains and the fertile plains that lay between. It was in this Syro-Lebanese context that the counts of Tripoli sought to establish their rule. In many ways, the manifold pressures on the counts were greater than those faced by other Frankish rulers. True, the threat of invasion seems to have been slighter because hostile forces preferred crossing the Jordan into the southern kingdom of Jerusalem, or the Orontes into the northern principality of Antioch, rather than over the mountains that cradled the county. However, the kings of Jerusalem and princes of Antioch did not face the same cultural complexity as in the Lebanon region, which made it all the harder for the counts to negotiate and enforce the terms of their power.

The demographic complexity of the county was unmatched anywhere else in the crusader states. Within the county could be found the spiritual descendants of the Byzantine Empire and the Fāṭimid Caliphate, two empires that had shared the region a generation before, leaving behind the Christian Orthodox Melkites who pledged allegiance to the Byzantine emperor and the Shīʿa Muslims who remembered the Fāṭimid caliphs in their Friday prayers. Other religious groups were unique to Lebanon specifically. There were the Maronite Christians, many of whom supported the Roman Catholic crusaders on the basis of a somewhat mythologised shared history. These lived alongside Ethiopian, Nestorian and 'Jacobite' Syrian Orthodox Christians. Nearby were the Druze, who worshipped the Fāṭimid caliph al-Ḥākim (r. 996–1021) as divine. Two further radical Shīʿa groups that had split from the Fāṭimid caliphate during caliphal succession crises were the Nuṣayrīs or Alawites, who gave their sect's name to the mountain where they lived north of the Frankish county, and the notorious Nizārīs, who sought refuge in the same region and came to be known as the 'Assassins'. Even the counts themselves, who never forgot that they were descended in the male line from European crusaders, had Armenian blood coursing through their veins by the middle of the twelfth century. The counts thus faced a bewildering array of identities in this contested space, not least within themselves.

Much previous scholarship on the Latin East has focused upon its institutions, drawing upon such texts as John of Ibelin's *Livre des Assises*, William of Tyre's *Historia Ierosolimitana* and various surviving pieces of cartulary evidence. Throughout the present work, many such traditional sources are challenged and shown to be unreliable at best. At the highest level, the very concept of the crusader states as independent and clearly demarcated polities is cast into doubt, with these polities depicted as having been subject to much greater constitutional change than previously thought. It is not simply the conclusions of previous historians that are contested, but also the methodological assumptions underpinning them. The present monograph also engages with a much broader range of sources and themes than has been attempted in previous historiography, primarily by incorporating a greater quantity of evidence drawn from both Arabic sources and under-utilised western sources such as Occitan poetry.[1] In so doing, many obscure issues relating to how the counts ruled over and lived within this unique society are illuminated.

The present work is arranged chronologically and divided into five chapters. Chapter 1 focuses on two rulers: William Jordan of Cerdanya and Bertrand of Toulouse, rival claimants to what would become the county of Tripoli after the death of the crusader Raymond IV of Saint-Gilles and Toulouse in 1105. Chapters 2 and 3 concern the reigns of Count Pons and his son Raymond II respectively. Chapters 4 and 5 both deal with a single count: Raymond III, whose reign was by far the longest, arguably the most complex and easily the best documented – not to mention most debated. Raymond IV of Saint-Gilles himself, the first self-professed 'count of Tripoli', does not receive his own chapter or indeed much special attention at all beyond what is absolutely necessary for the purpose of setting the scene. It has been deemed wise to omit him from the present work since most of his life was spent in the west or else participating in the First Crusade at a time when the very existence of the county of Tripoli had yet to be imagined. As such, the structure of this present work questions

Jean Richard's influential belief that the county of Tripoli was primarily the product of Raymond IV's 'action personnelle'.[2] More than one person determined the county's existence and fate.

Historiography

Few historians have produced works that deal with the Latin East as a whole. A notable and recent exception is Malcolm Barber, whose accomplished synthesis of existing literature on the crusader states has quickly established itself as a principal reference work.[3] Another example is Bernard Hamilton's study of one aspect of the entire Latin East: its ecclesiastical structure.[4] Most historians have studied one crusader state to the exclusion of the others, with the majority of these focusing their efforts upon the kingdom of Jerusalem.[5] There are three main reasons for this overriding fascination with the kingdom: the greater abundance of sources for the kingdom compared to the other crusader states; the special fascination of contemporary narrators and modern historians with Jerusalem and the Holy Land, of which Tripoli was not truly part;[6] and the considerable efforts made by scholars such as Prawer and Kedar, working in the modern state of Israel, which lies entirely within the boundaries of the former kingdom.[7] No other state occupying what was once the Latin East – the kingdom of Jordan and the republics of Syria, Lebanon, Egypt and Turkey – enjoys such a prolific indigenous 'school' of crusade historians.

The principality of Antioch has been neglected when compared to Jerusalem, but has enjoyed some historiographical attention nonetheless. The first and most comprehensive study of the principality itself was Claude Cahen's *La Syrie du Nord*, in which the author stressed the need to place the principality within its local Syrian context, challenging the prevailing tendency of historians to treat the Latin East as if merely an offshoot of contemporary French society.[8] Although Cahen later rejected calls for his thesis to be republished because he had come to disagree with many of its arguments, it remains the uncontested authority on the principality of Antioch.[9] Cahen's is still one of the most capable demonstrations of the use of Arabic alongside western languages in a crusades-related study, even after the emergence of two further monographs and numerous articles in more recent years.[10]

The county of Edessa, which fell after fewer than fifty years, has received a somewhat disproportionate amount of historiographical attention. The Armenian historian Ter-Gregorian Iskenderian produced a lengthy study as early as 1915, followed four decades later by Robert Nicholson's biographical study of Count Joscelin I.[11] More recently, Monique Amouroux-Mourad produced a brief monograph on the county's history and society, while MacEvitt's study of interactions between Latin and eastern Christians has at its core an analysis of the county's foundation.[12]

Turning to the county of Tripoli itself, it quickly becomes clear that it has been the most neglected of the four original crusader states. Marshall Baldwin completed a doctoral thesis at Princeton University in 1934, intended to be a biographical study of Count Raymond III.[13] This work was divided into two parts, the first dealing with Raymond's political career in the kingdom of Jerusalem and the second being an overview of the economic, demographic and ecclesiastical context of the county. Baldwin promptly published the first half with minimal revisions as a book.[14] Until the later years of the twentieth century, this was a major influence upon modern historians' views of the political crises that wracked the kingdom of Jerusalem prior to Saladin's conquests in the 1180s. Much of the second part of Baldwin's thesis was reworked as a separate research article.[15] Baldwin's output as a whole is marked by a frequently naïve and uncritical use of Latin and French sources, rendering his thesis and subsequent publications largely descriptive.

The only monograph dedicated solely to the county, rather than to its most famous ruler, remains Richard's *Le comté de Tripoli sous la dynastie toulousaine* (1945). As its title suggests, this compact survey deals predominantly with the county from the perspective of the western Europeans who conquered and settled the region, particularly the southern French Raymond IV of Saint-Gilles and his descendants, and explains many of its historical and social phenomena through this 'Provençal' lens. Richard owes a personal and intellectual debt to René Grousset, who suggested the topic to Richard, and thus Richard's work is framed as a complement to Grousset's expansive *Histoire des Croisades et du royaume franc de Jérusalem.*[16] In Grousset's grand theory, the Latin East was a microcosm of contemporary 'France', with each state defined by the origins of its founders and early rulers. The kingdom of Jerusalem was dominated by Lotharingians under Godfrey of Bouillon and Baldwin I, and the principality of Antioch was Norman due to Bohemond of Taranto and Tancred of Lecce; the short-lived county of Edessa shared the kingdom of Jerusalem's early Lotharingian identity, whereas the county of Tripoli had a 'Provençal' character derived from Raymond IV of Saint-Gilles and his progeny.[17] Richard strives to corroborate Grousset's somewhat neocolonialist theory by using it to explain the county of Tripoli's independence from its Latin Christian neighbours and by stressing the distinctiveness of its 'Provençal' identity. Richard equates the constitutional relationship between the counts of Tripoli and the kings of Jerusalem with the relationship between the rulers of the 'grands fiefs autonomes de la France' – including the house of Tripoli's cousins in Toulouse – and the Capetian kings of France.[18] The implication is that a distinct 'Provençal' or 'Toulousan' distaste for social hierarchies explains why the counts of Tripoli did not accept the king of Jerusalem's authority in the same way as did, for example, the princes of Galilee or lords of Tiberias in the kingdom of Jerusalem.

Since 1945 the county and its rulers have failed to attract much historical interest. Richard has continued to lead the way with irregular publications on the subject. Initially, these were annexes to his original monograph, such as his article on Raymond of Saint-Gilles's early attempts to establish his rule in North Syria or his speculative localisation of toponyms mentioned in medieval sources on the basis of modern Lebanese place-names.[19] In 1963, he contributed to a collection of articles on the historical relationship between the south of France and the Islamic world, providing a restatement and abridgement of his previous work insofar as it concerned direct contact between the dynasties of Tripoli and Toulouse.[20] Some two decades later he returned to the county, going beyond the *dynastie toulousaine* to explain the baronial insurrections against the count-princes of the *dynastie antiochénienne* in the thirteenth century, blaming the revolts upon the latter's arbitrary power over the composition of the High Court.[21]

For some decades, Richard's research focused mainly on the Latin Christian barons, having devoted only a cursory section of his original monograph to 'les indigènes'.[22] One of his studies attempted to address this shortcoming by discussing the place of local Christians in the governance of the county.[23] More recently he has provided an overview of those aspects of the county's history that can be termed 'eastern', from local intermediaries to religious demographics, although this paper suffers from being more descriptive than analytical.[24] Finally, in a volume dedicated to the county of Tripoli as an 'état multiculturel et multiconfessionnel', Richard has returned to the Frankish barons, providing a synthesis and elaboration of his long career studying this particular subject.[25]

Alongside Richard, a number of other historians have dealt with aspects of the county's history. The collection of articles *Le comté de Tripoli: État multiculturel et multiconfessionnel* represents the published proceedings of a conference held in Beirut in 2002 – primarily a collaboration between France's Université Paul Valéry-Montpellier III and Lebanon's Université Saint-Esprit de Kaslik.[26] Although meagre compared to the huge output of the Israeli school, archaeological and historical research conducted by Lebanese scholars has been fairly continuous since the mid-twentieth century, as a perusal of locally published journals and locally organised conference proceedings demonstrates.[27] The contributors to the Montpellier-Kaslik volume specifically make a few salient points, which have been used accordingly. It must be said that the collection generally focuses only on the Christian groups of the county – particularly the Armenians and the Maronites – to the exclusion of the Muslims, and some of the contributions seem shallow and redundant. Furthermore, it is doubtful whether the collection can be classified as truly independent of Richard, who provides a preface and an article, and to whose work one of the editors explicitly affiliates the volume.[28]

Other studies relevant to the county include Marie-Bernadette Bruguière's comparison of inheritance customs in the counties of Toulouse and Tripoli.[29] As part of a broader exploration of the crusading movement's impact upon Provençal society, Damien Carraz has discussed the county of Tripoli as 'un enracinement éphémère' of Provençal settlement, although this is based largely on Richard's conclusions.[30] As part of his general study of the fortunes of the Porcelet family of Arles in Provence, Martin Aurell supplies a survey of those members of this family who settled in the county soon after the First Crusade, again heavily reliant upon Richard.[31] More firmly independent works include brief papers by Jonathan Riley-Smith on the ecclesiastics in Raymond of Saint-Gilles's company at Tripoli, and by Thomas Asbridge on Raymond's failed attempts to destabilise Bohemond of Taranto's rule in North Syria during the First Crusade.[32] Robert Irwin's brief discussion of the final decades of the county in the thirteenth century as told in Arabic sources should be read alongside Richard's simultaneously published paper on the *dynastie antiochénienne*, shedding additional light upon baronial discontent in these final years as well as upon Mamluk grand strategy.[33] Hans Mayer dedicates two chapters of his *Varia Antiochena* to subjects of direct relevance to the county, namely the succession to the county after the death of Raymond III in 1187, and Genoese forged documents from both Tripoli and Antioch in the early thirteenth century.[34] Wolfgang Antweiler's careful prosopography of Tripoli's ecclesiastics tends only to confirm the conclusions of previous scholarship relating to the operation of the Latin Church in the crusader states, although it is a helpful reference work.[35]

Provençal or Occitan?

What should be apparent is that the vast majority of literature on the county of Tripoli has focused upon the western heritage of the counts as the principal driving force behind its history. It is not altogether unreasonable and certainly not surprising that much past scholarship has had an Occidentalist thrust. As this book makes clear – not least in its title – the twelfth-century counts of Tripoli never forgot their European ancestry as direct descendants of the famous crusader Count Raymond IV of Saint-Gilles (= Raymond I of Tripoli). In 1132 Raymond's grandson, Count Pons of Tripoli, described himself in a charter as 'Pons, from the counts of Saint-Gilles'.[36] As Shagrir has noted, many settlers in the east retained toponymic by-names that evoked places of ancestral or personal origin in Europe, reflecting a strong and enduring attachment to their ancestral homeland.[37] Pons's own son Raymond II again stressed this western ancestry when he confirmed his father's charter ten years later as 'Raymond, son of Count Pons of Saint-Gilles [*sic*]'.[38] Later still, the great chronicler-archbishop William of Tyre made a special effort to emphasise Count Raymond III's direct patrilineal descent from his legendary great-great-grandfather, Raymond of Saint-Gilles.[39] As Dunbabin has shown, the French [*sic*] aristocracy of the twelfth century found justification for their particular dynastic identities in the genre of genealogy, incorporating heroic deeds by the crusaders alongside the likes of the Trojans, King Arthur and Charlemagne.[40] William's genealogy of Raymond must be seen in this light.

Arabic authors too preserved the Tripolitan counts' Saint-Gilles title. From the very beginning they called Raymond IV of Saint-Gilles simply '*Ṣanjīl*'.[41] Ibn al-Qalānisī once referred to Raymond as 'the son of Saint-Gilles' (*ibn Ṣanjīl*).[42] Raymond's son Bertrand of Tripoli also bore the Saint-Gilles title in Arabic accounts, even if the authors in question tended to confuse him more than any other, perhaps due to the brevity of his reign (1109–12); Ibn al-Qalānisī named him erroneously 'Raymond, son of (Raymond of) Saint-Gilles' (*Raymund bin Ṣanjīl*).[43] The emphasis on the name of Saint-Gilles extended into the reign of Bertrand's son Pons, whom Ibn al-Qalānisī dubbed 'Pons *Ṭalūlā*, son of Bertrand of Saint-Gilles'.[44] It is likely that the perplexing word *Ṭalūlā* is a garbled form of Toulouse (Latin *Tolosa*).[45] If so, this would represent a rare reference to Pons's specifically Toulousan heritage alongside his identification with Saint-Gilles. This is all the more significant, because no western source suggests that the counts of Tripoli retained a claim to Toulouse beyond Bertrand's death in 1112, with an anomalous exception being a highly dubious, sixteenth-century manuscript of the *Lignages d'Outremer*, which described Raymond II as 'count of Tripoli and Toulouse'.[46]

The continued presence of the Saint-Gilles title, and perhaps also that of Toulouse, in relation to Pons is arguably more significant than the use of the same in reference to his predecessors, since Pons was the first count of Tripoli never to have been count of Saint-Gilles and Toulouse – William Jordan of Cerdanya (r. 1105–9) excepted. Even after Pons's death, the Saint-Gilles name did not disappear altogether from Arabic texts. Ibn al-Athīr called Raymond III 'Raymond, son of Raymond, the man of Saint-Gilles', thus including both him and his father Raymond II under the label *Ṣanjīl*.[47] It is from this Arabic usage that the present book derives its subtitle *Sons of Saint-Gilles*. This choice was made deliberately to evoke the main argument pursued here that the counts of Tripoli were westerners in name and self-perception, yet worked within a distinctly Syro-Lebanese framework. By including the vital local context, the aim has been to avoid the restricted approach of some previous historians, who have concentrated on the superficial and distant at the expense of the fundamental and local.

There are other reasons to qualify what earlier historians have written on the county of Tripoli. Richard's and Grousset's suggestion that the county's principal defining quality was its domination by 'Provençal' settlers is perhaps too simple a generalisation. Tripoli lacked a monopoly on southern French settlers in Syria,[48] but equally significant is the fact that the very term 'Provençal' is imprecise. Certainly the term 'provinciales' and its cognates appear throughout the so-called 'eyewitness' chronicles of the First Crusade, including the *Historia* of the 'Provençal' Raymond of Aguilers, when their authors were describing Raymond IV of Saint-Gilles's contingent.[49] Nevertheless, this usage can be confusing and should be clarified. The modern definition of Provence is narrow, extending from Arles in the west to Nice in the east, whereas in the medieval context the term *provinciales* was frequently applied to people living anywhere within the old Roman *Provincia*, which included the ecclesiastical province of Narbonne and thus Languedoc and even Toulouse.[50] Raymond of Aguilers himself recognised the potential for confusion, taking the time to inform his readers that 'everyone from Burgundy, the Auvergne, Gascony and Languedoc are called Provençals'.[51]

Raymond of Saint-Gilles was accompanied by numerous crusaders from beyond modern Provence. Albert of Aachen described two distinct ethnolinguistic groups who followed Raymond of Saint-Gilles and Adhémar of Le Puy: Provençals (*Prouinciales*) and Gascons (*Wascones*).[52] One derivative source referred to Provençaux (*Provincels*), Gascons (*Gascoinz*), men of Pierrefort in the Auvergne (*ces de Pierrefort*) and Aragonese (*Arragonçois*).[53] Some of Raymond's followers were named individually in the sources. For example, Gaston IV of Béarn – a lordship on the frontier between Gascony, Languedoc and Aragon – brought his skill in siege warfare to Raymond's army.[54] Bernard Raymond of Béziers, Languedoc, died in a battle on 29 December 1097.[55] Raymond Pilet and Raymond, viscount of Turenne in the Limousin, captured Tortosa on behalf of Count Raymond in 1098.[56] It thus seems appropriate to jettison the term 'Provençal' in favour of 'Occitan', a term that more accurately captures the geographical breadth of Raymond's main recruitment grounds and also indicates the main source of unity for this expansive region, namely the use of the Romance vernacular of *langue d'oc*, in contradistinction to the *langue d'oïl* spoken in northern France.[57] An alternative term, more common in Francophone scholarship but less evocative of the region's linguistic distinctiveness, is the Midi.

Notes

1 A comprehensive analysis and evaluation of the sources used in the present work can be found in Appendix 1.

2 Jean Richard, *Le comté de Tripoli sous la dynastie toulousaine (1102–1187)*, Bibliothèque archéologique et historique 39 (Paris, 1945), p. 9.

3 Malcolm Barber, *The Crusader States* (London, 2012).

4 Bernard Hamilton, *The Latin Church in the Crusader States: The Secular Church* (London, 1980).

5 For example: Reinhold Röhricht, *Geschichte der Königreichs Jerusalem (1100–1291)* (Innsbrück, 1898); John L. La Monte, *Feudal Monarchy in the Latin Kingdom of Jerusalem, 1100 to 1291* (Cambridge, MA, 1932); Jean Richard, *Le Royaume Latin de Jérusalem* (Paris, 1953); Joshua Prawer, *Histoire du Royaume Latin de Jérusalem,*

2 vols (Paris, 1969–70); Joshua Prawer, *The Latin Kingdom of Jerusalem: European Colonialism in the Middle Ages* (London, 1972); Jonathan Riley-Smith, *The Feudal Nobility and the Kingdom of Jerusalem, 1174–1277* (London, 1973); A.V. Murray, *The Crusader Kingdom of Jerusalem: A Dynastic History 1099–1125* (Oxford, 2000).

6 See Chapter 3.

7 Ronnie Ellenblum, *Crusader Castles and Modern Histories* (Cambridge, 2007), pp. 60–1.

8 Claude Cahen, *La Syrie du Nord à l'époque des croisades et la principauté franque d'Antioche* (Paris, 1940).

9 Cf. Claude Cahen, 'Préface à la réimpression de sa thèse', *Arabica* 43.1 (1996), pp. 85–8.

10 Cf. Hans Eberhard Mayer, *Varia Antiochena. Studien zum Kreuzfahrerfürstentum Antiochia im 12. und frühen 13. Jahrhundert*, Monumenta Germaniae Historica: Studien und Texte 6 (Hannover, 1993); Thomas S. Asbridge, *The Creation of the Principality of Antioch, 1098–1130* (Woodbridge, 2000); *East and West in the Medieval Eastern Mediterranean: Antioch from the Byzantine Reconquest until the End of the Crusader Principality*, ed. Krijnie Ciggaar *et al.*, 2 vols, Orientalia Lovaniensia Analecta 147, 199 (Leuven, 2006–13).

11 D. Ter-Gregorian Iskenderian, *Die Kreuzfahrer und ihre Beziehungen zu den armenischen Nachbarfürsten bis zum Untergange der Grafschaft Edessa* (Leipzig, 1915); R. L. Nicholson, *Joscelyn I, Prince of Edessa*, Illinois Studies in the Social Sciences 34.4 (Urbana, IL, 1954).

12 Monique Amouroux-Mourad, *Le comté d'Edesse 1098–1150* (Paris, 1988); Christopher MacEvitt, *The Crusades and the Christian World of the East: Rough Tolerance* (Philadelphia, 2008), *passim.*

13 Marshall Whithed Baldwin, *Raymond III of Tripoli (1140–87) and the Fall of the Kingdom of Jerusalem*, 2 vols (Unpublished Ph.D. thesis: Princeton University, 1934).

14 Marshall Whithed Baldwin, *Raymond III of Tripolis and the Fall of Jerusalem (1140–1187)* (Princeton, NJ, 1936).

15 Marshall Whithed Baldwin, 'Ecclesiastical Developments in the Twelfth Century Crusaders' State of Tripolis', *The Catholic Historical Review* (*CHR*) 22.2 (1936), pp. 149–71.

16 Richard, *Le comté*, pp. i, ii, vi.

17 René Grousset, *Histoire des Croisades et du royaume franc de Jérusalem*, 3 vols (Paris, 1934–6), vol. 1, *passim.*

18 Richard, *Le comté*, pp. 35, 43, 45, 47 and *passim.*

19 Jean Richard, 'Note sur l'archidiocèse d'Apamée et les conquêtes de Raymond de Saint-Gilles en Syrie du nord', *Syria* 25.1–2 (1946–8), pp. 103–8; Jean Richard, 'Questions de topographie tripolitaine', *Journal Asiatique* 236 (1948), pp. 53–9.

20 Jean Richard, 'Les Saint-Gilles et le comté de Tripoli', *Islam et chrétiens du Midi (XIIe-XIVe s.)*, Cahiers de Fanjeaux 18 (Toulouse, 1983), pp. 65–75.

21 Jean Richard, 'Les comtes de Tripoli et leurs vassaux sous la dynastie antiochénienne', in *Crusade and Settlement: Papers read at the First Conference of the Society for the Study of the Crusades and the Latin East and presented to R. C. Smail*, ed. Peter W. Edbury (Cardiff, 1985), pp. 213–21.

22 Richard, *Le comté*, pp. 85–8.

23 Jean Richard, '*Cum omni raisagio montanee* . . . À propos de la cession du Crac aux Hospitaliers', in *Itinéraires d'Orient: Hommages à Claude Cahen*, ed. Raoul Curiel and Rika Gyselen, Res Orientales 6 (Burs-sur-Yvette, 1994), pp. 187–92.

24 Jean Richard, 'Affrontement ou confrontation? Les contacts entre deux mondes au pays de Tripoli au temps des Croisades', *Chronos* 2 (1999), pp. 7–25.

25 Jean Richard, 'Les familles féodales franques dans le comté de Tripoli', in *Le comté de Tripoli: Etat multiculturel et multiconfessionnel (1102–1289)*, ed. Gérard Dédéyan and Karam Rizk (Paris, 2010), pp. 7–30.

26 *Le comté de Tripoli: Etat multiculturel et multiconfessionnel (1102–1289)*, ed. Gérard Dédéyan and Karam Rizk (Paris, 2010).

27 *Bulletin du Musée de Beyrouth* (*BMB*) 1–36 (1937–86); *De Toulouse à Tripoli: Itinéraires de cultures croisées*, ed. Edgar Weber *et al.* (Toulouse, 1997). See also: Ḥassān Salamé-Sarkis, *Contribution à l'histoire de Tripoli et de sa région à l'époque des croisades: problèmes d'histoire, d'architecture et de céramique*, Bibliothèque archéologique et historique 106 (Paris, 1980).

28 Jean Richard, 'Préface', in *Le comté*, ed. Dédéyan and Rizk, pp. 1–2; Karam Rizk, 'Avant-propos', in *Le comté*, ed. Dédéyan and Rizk, p. 5.

29 Marie-Bernadette Bruguière, 'Un precedent à la loi salique? L'exclusion des femmes dans la maison de Toulouse et de Tripoli', *Mémoires de l'Académie des Sciences, Inscriptions et Belles-Lettres de Toulouse* 141 (1979), pp. 141–52.

30 Damien Carraz, *L'Ordre du Temple dans la basse vallée du Rhône (1124–1312): Ordres militaires, croisades et sociétés méridionales*, Collection d'histoire et d'archéologie médiévales 17 (Lyon, 2005), pp. 79–81.

31 Martin Aurell, *Une famille de la noblesse provençale au Moyen Âge: les Porcelet* (Avignon, 1986), pp. 147–52.

32 Jonathan Riley-Smith, 'Raymond IV of St Gilles, Achard of Arles and the Conquest of Lebanon', in *The Crusades and their Sources: Essays presented to Bernard Hamilton*, ed. John France and William G. Zajac (Aldershot, 1998), pp. 1–8; T. Asbridge, 'The Principality of Antioch and the Jabal as-Summāq', in *The First Crusade: Origins and Impact*, ed. Jonathan Phillips (Manchester, 1997), pp. 142–51.

33 Robert Irwin, 'The Mamlūk Conquest of the County of Tripoli', in *Crusade and Settlement*, ed. Edbury, pp. 246–9.

34 Mayer, *Varia*, pp. 184–202, 203–17.

35 Wolfgang Antweiler, *Das Bistum Tripolis im 12. und 13. Jahrhundert. Personengeschichtliche und strukturelle Probleme*, Studia humaniora 20 (Düsseldorf, 1991).

36 Pontius ex comitibus Sancti Egidii. Cl. Devic and J. Vaissète, *Histoire Générale de Languedoc avec des notes et les pièces justificatives*, 2nd ed., 16 vols (Toulouse, 1872–1904), vol. 5, no. 551, col. 1055; *Regesta Regni Hierosolymitani (MXCVII–MCCXCI)*, ed. Reinhold Röhricht (Innsbrück, 1893) (*RRH*), no. 211.

37 Iris Shagrir, 'The Medieval Evolution of By-naming: Notions from the Latin Kingdom of Jerusalem', in *In Laudem Hierosolymitani: Studies in Crusades and Medieval Culture in Honour of Benjamin Z. Kedar*, ed. Ronnie Ellenblum, Jonathan Riley-Smith and Iris Shagrir (Aldershot, 2007), p. 59.

38 Raymundus, Pontii comitis Sancti Egidii filius. Devic and Vaissète, *Histoire*, vol. 5, no. 551, col. 1054; *RRH*, no. 211.

39 William of Tyre, *Chronicon*, ed. R. B. C. Huygens, 2 vols, Corpus Christianorum Continuatio Mediaevalis 63–63A (Turnhout, 1986) (WT), vol. 2, pp. 966–77.

40 Jean Dunbabin, 'Discovering a Past for the French Aristocracy', in *The Perception of the Past in Twelfth-Century Europe*, ed. Paul Magdalino (London, 1992), pp. 1–14.

41 See, for example: Al-ʿAẓīmī, Muḥammad bin ʿAlī al-Ḥalabī, *Tārīkh ḥalab*, ed. Ibrāhīm Zaʿrūr (Damascus, 1984), pp. 361, 362; Ibn al-Qalānisī, Abū Yaʿlā Ḥamza, *History of Damascus, 363–555 a. h., by Ibn al-Qalānisī from the Bodleian Ms. Hunt. 125, being a continuation of Hilâl al-Sâbi*, ed. H. F. Amedroz (Leiden, 1908) (IQ), pp. 143, 146, 147.

42 IQ, p. 140.

43 Raymund bin Ṣanjīl. IQ, p. 163. See also: Ibn al-Athīr, *Al-kāmil fī al-tārīkh*, ed. C. J. Tornberg, rev. ed., 12 vols + index (Beirut, 1965–67) (IA), vol. 10, p. 475. Cf. IQ, pp. 167, 169, 174, 177.

44 Bunḍ [corr. (P)unṣ] Ṭalūlā bin Badrān al-Ṣanjīlī. IQ, p. 240. Cf. IQ, pp. 185, 197.

45 Cf. Ibn al-Qalānisī, Abū Ya'lā Ḥamza, *The Damascus Chronicle of the Crusades: Extracted and Translated from the Chronicle of* Ibn al-Qalānisī, trans. H. A. R. Gibb (London, 1932), pp. 221, 222.
46 Rymondo [*sic*], conte de Tripoli e de Tolosa. *Lignages d'Outremer*, ed. Marie-Adélaïde Nielen, Documents relatifs à l'histoire des croisades publiés par l'Académie des Inscriptions et Belles-Lettres 18 (Paris, 2003), p. 160. See also: *Lignages*, pp. 49–50.
47 Raymund bin Raymund al-Ṣanjīlī. IA, vol. 11, pp. 419, 526.
48 See Chapter 2.
49 Marcus Bull, 'Overlapping and Competing Identities in the Frankish First Crusade', in *Le Concile de Clermont de 1095 et l'Appel à la Croisade: Actes du Colloque Universitaire International de Clermont-Ferrand (23–25 juin 1995) organisé et publié avec le concours du Conseil Régional d'Auvergne* (Rome, 1997), p. 210; A. V. Murray, 'National Identity, Language and Conflict in the Crusades to the Holy Land, 1096–1192', in *The Crusades and the Near East*, ed. Conor Kostick (London, 2011), p. 117; Léan Ní Chléirigh, '*Gesta Normannorum*? Normans in the Latin Chronicles of the First Crusade', in *Norman Expansion: Connections, Continuities and Contrasts*, ed. Keith J. Stringer and Andrew Jotischky (Farnham, 2013), p. 213.
50 Edouard Baratier, 'Marquisat et comtés en Provence', in *Histoire de la Provence*, ed. Edouard Baratier (Toulouse, 1969), pp. 134–5; Elisabeth Magnou-Nortier, *La société laïque et l'Église dans la province ecclésiastique de Narbonne (zone cispyrénéenne) de la fin du VIIIe à la fin du XIe siècle*, Publications de l'Université de Toulouse-Le Mirail A.20 (Toulouse, 1974), pp. 63–7; Jean-Pierre Poly, *La Provence et la Société féodale (879–1166): Contribution à l'étude des structures dites féodales dans le Midi* (Paris, 1976), pp. v–vi.
51 Omnes de Burgundia et Alvernia/Arvenia et Gasconiam [corr. Gasconia] et Gotti [corr. Gothia, i.e. Languedoc] Provinciales appellantur. Raymond of Aguilers, *Liber*, ed. John Hugh Hill and Laurita L. Hill, Documents relatifs à l'histoire des croisades publiés par l'Académie des Inscriptions et Belles-Lettres 9 (Paris, 1969) (RA), p. 52.
52 Albert of Aachen, *Historia Ierosolimitana: History of the Journey to Jerusalem*, ed. Susan B. Edgington (Oxford, 2007) (AA), p. 200.
53 'Li Estoire de Jerusalem et d'Antioche', in *Recueil des Historiens des Croisades: Historiens Occidentaux*, 5 vols (Paris, 1844–95) (*RHC Oc*), vol. 5, p. 627.
54 RA, p. 145.
55 RA, p. 51.
56 *Gesta Francorum et aliorum Hierosolimitanorum*, ed. Heinrich Hagenmeyer (Heidelberg, 1890) (*GF*), pp. 426–8; Petrus Tudebodus, *Historia de Hierosolymitano Itinere*, ed. John Hugh Hill and Laurita L. Hill, Documents relatifs à l'histoire des croisades publiés par l'Académie des Inscriptions et Belles-Lettres 12 (Paris, 1977) (PT), p. 129.
57 Linda M. Paterson, *The World of the Troubadours: Medieval Occitan society, c. 1100–c. 1300* (Cambridge, 1993), pp. 1–4; Xavier de Planhol, *An Historical Geography of France*, trans. Janet Lloyd, Cambridge Studies in Historical Geography 21 (Cambridge, 1994), pp. 123–9; J. Salvat, 'Provençal ou occitan?' *Annales du Midi* 66.3 (1954), pp. 229–41. But cf. Linda M. Paterson, 'Was there an Occitan Identity in the Middle Ages?' in her *Culture and Society in Medieval Occitania* (Farnham, 2011), §I, pp. 4–5.

1 The succession of cousins

Counts Raymond I (1103–5), William Jordan (1105–9) and Bertrand (1109–12)

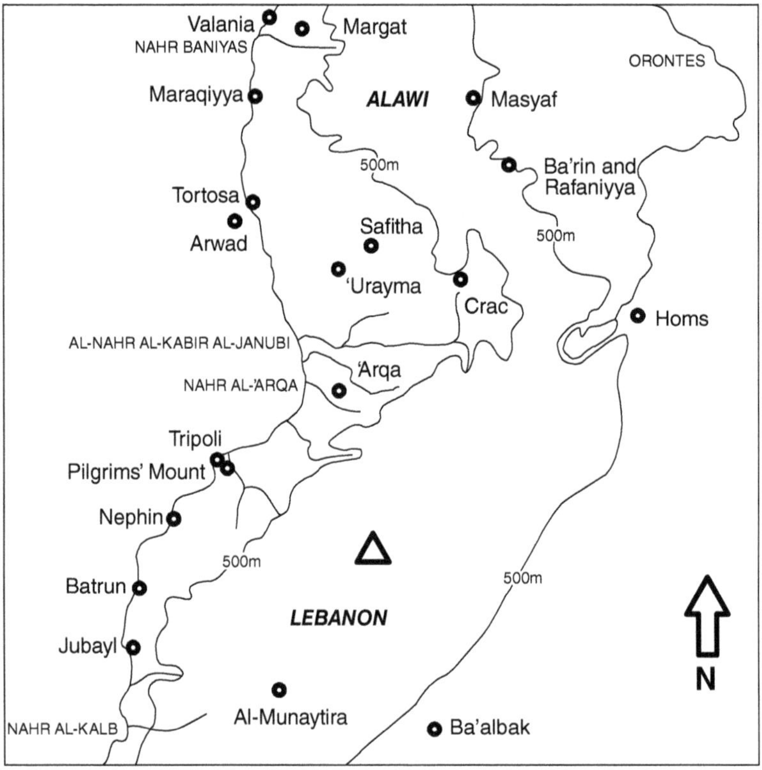

Map 1.1 The county of Tripoli

Introduction

On 28 February 1105, Count Raymond IV of Saint-Gilles and Toulouse – one of the greatest magnates in the kingdom of France and a leading figure on the First Crusade (1095–9) – died in dramatic circumstances, crashing through a roof into a burning building. He had been using this elevated

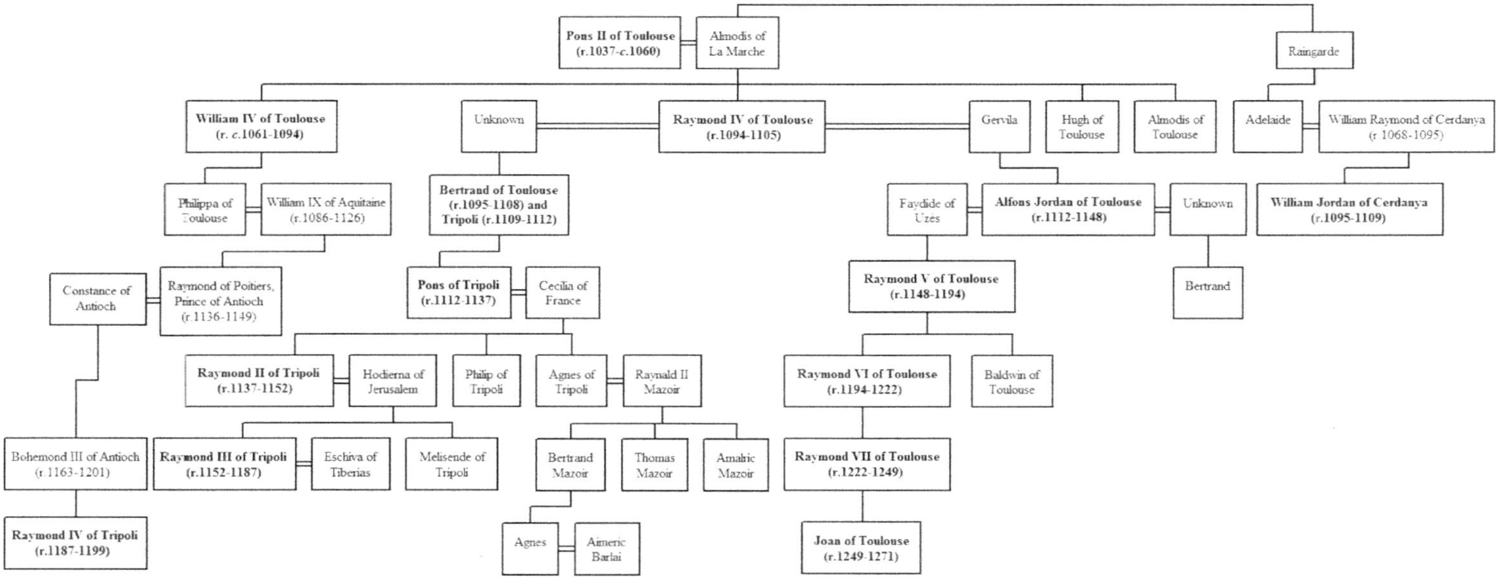

Figure 1.1 Select genealogy of the counts of Toulouse and Tripoli

position to survey a battle fought outside the gates of Tripoli, which he had been besieging in earnest for approximately two years. Although he never lived to see Tripoli in Christian hands, he has nonetheless received much of the credit for establishing the county of Tripoli, the fourth and final of the 'crusader states' to emerge in the Levant during and after the First Crusade. Raymond was the first crusader to call himself 'count of Tripoli' and it is from him that his successors are numbered in modern convention. The old count was the progenitor of the so-called 'Toulousan dynasty', who ruled the county for some eight decades. In this chapter, Raymond's career and legacy as they relate to Tripoli specifically are put into better perspective. An aspect of this task involves clarifying his contribution to the establishment of the county vis-à-vis the achievements of his successors. Another facet is to question what historians have traditionally assumed about the development of the Latin East in the earliest period of its history. Jean Richard believed that the county of Tripoli owed its very existence to Raymond's 'action personnelle', but the reality was far more complex than a question of individual agency.[1]

Diplomacy and religion

At the time of Raymond's death the siege of Tripoli was proving to be long and arduous, in part due to a complex local political legacy. The city had been governed by a local Twelver Shīʿa Muslim dynasty, the Banū ʿAmmār, ever since *c.*1070 when this family of *qāḍīs* (Islamic religious judges) had achieved *de facto* autonomy from the Ismāʿīlī Fāṭimid caliphate based in Cairo. The Fāṭimids had lost their grip on much of Syria at this time due to a series of so-called 'calamities', not least the military ascendancy of the Saljūq Turks.[2] Yet the Saljūqs' own hold on Syria was inconsistent. True, their achievement had been impressive: building a vast empire from Central Asia to Asia Minor that incorporated Persia, the wealthiest part of the Islamic world at the time in terms of both actual finances and ancient cultural legacy. Saljūq rule was legitimised through a blend of ancestral nomadic steppe traditions, the Perso-Islamic court culture of Baghdad and the often reluctant, inconstant support offered by the ʿAbbāsid caliph, complete with his genealogical ties to the Arab tribes from which Islam had originated. On a practical level, provinces were established and local governors were empowered centrally to enable the administration of this vast realm. Despite this, the Saljūq empire nevertheless remained a fundamentally decentralised territory, where ostensible titles and hierarchies were less important than the office-holders' personal relationships to the sultan and where government varied greatly from region to region.[3] Köhler has argued that, in the absence of consistent central authority, a 'constellation of powers' came into being in Saljūq Syria, with governance and power effectively devolved to the level of city-states – Tripoli key among them.[4]

The political fragmentation of Syria has long been regarded as a crucial factor in the astounding success of the First Crusade. Just as interesting as the straight military victories were the lengths local rulers were willing to go in terms of using diplomacy to save themselves from the crusaders. In Tripoli, Jalāl al-Mulk bin ʿAmmār (r. 464/1072–492/1099) was quick to make self-serving alliances of convenience with the crusaders as soon as they arrived in the region. A Latin priest, likely in Raymond of Saint-Gilles's entourage, named Ebrard arrived in Tripoli on a diplomatic mission as early as 1097.[5] In fact the crusaders had sent diplomatic missions to other Muslim powers as early as 1095–6 (AH 489).[6] Although the outcome of Ebrard's mission is unknown, Latin chronicles report that Jalāl al-Mulk sent numerous envoys to the crusader armies bearing gifts, seeking desperate peace treaties and even offering the crusaders their own public market within Tripoli itself. In so doing, the *qāḍī* clearly hoped to retain Tripoli itself, together with a handful of neighbouring towns including ʿArqa and Jubayl.[7] The most obvious indication of Jalāl al-Mulk's underlying motives came when he offered the crusaders an old Muslim man, whose job was to guide them through the difficult mountain roads to the south towards Jerusalem and away from Tripoli.[8]

Latin chroniclers who were present on the expedition seized upon Jalāl al-Mulk's somewhat obsequious diplomacy with enthusiasm, exaggerating it for political and religious aims. Raymond of Saint-Gilles's chaplain, Raymond of Aguilers, claimed that the *qāḍī* had specifically requested his lord's standards and seals to demonstrate his submission to the count and to gain him some protection against the other crusaders. As Jalāl al-Mulk erected the Toulousan banner over his city and castles, Raymond wrote proudly that 'from that time the count's reputation was such that it seemed to surpass the reputations of all who went before'.[9] The story should not be taken at face value, as it was likely crafted deliberately to combat a humiliating passage in the *Gesta Francorum*, in which the commander of the Muslim forces at Antioch had allegedly asked for a crusader banner in the desperate hope of receiving protection. Upon learning that he had been sent Raymond of Saint-Gilles's, he returned it and requested Bohemond of Taranto's standard instead.[10]

Perhaps the most incredible claim regarding Jalāl al-Mulk's diplomacy was recorded in the *Gesta Francorum* and by Peter Tudebode. Purportedly this Twelver Shīʿite *qāḍī* and heir to the Fāṭimid governors of old had offered to receive baptism and convert to Christianity if the crusaders helped him against the Fāṭimid caliph al-Mustaʿlī (r. 1094–1101).[11] Historians have doubted that this offer and others like it were actually made during the First Crusade, or at least made with any sincerity.[12] The idea that the 'pagan' Muslims were always on the brink of conversion to Christianity was a *topos* in medieval Latin literature.[13] That said, there may be more to this story than mere Christian propaganda and wishful thinking. For one thing, Tripoli's independence from the Fāṭimids looked to be at risk. The Fāṭimid caliphate had seen its power withdraw rapidly from Syria in the 1060s and 1070s but a time of reconquest had dawned following the appointment to the vizierate of Badr al-Jamālī, a *mamlūk* ('slave') of Armenian descent and a veteran of Syrian wars, in 1073/74 (AH 466).[14] Badr al-Jamālī's son al-Afḍal Shāhanshāh had succeeded him in 1094 and had pursued equally aggressive policies. That Jalāl al-Mulk sought to preserve his city's autonomy from this worrying Fāṭimid resurgence is not surprising.

As for the offer of baptism specifically, it seems reasonable enough to assume the *qāḍī* did not actually desire to become a Christian. The obvious presence of fear, not to mention diplomatic convenience, raises doubts as to his sincerity. From an ecclesiastical perspective, the canonical validity of something uncomfortably close to a coerced baptism – forbidden by the Church – is similarly dubious.[15] Yet it is possible that Jalāl al-Mulk did offer to be baptised without actually intending to convert. Surprisingly, the act of baptism was not synonymous with conversion to Christianity in medieval Syria. Many Christian practices, among them baptism, lingered in populations converted to Islam for centuries before and after the crusades – a remarkable demonstration of ritual continuity and syncretism.[16] Ibn Taymiyya, an Islamic polemicist in the thirteenth century, condemned Muslims – especially 'ignorant women' (*juhhāl al-nisā'*) – who took part in bathing and ablutions, particularly upon Christian festivals such as Epiphany, the so-called 'Festival of Baptism' (*'īd al-ghiṭās*).[17] Also in the thirteenth century, James of Vitry observed how Muslims led their children to the famous shrine of Tortosa in the north of the county of Tripoli in order to be baptised, simply because they believed that this ritual conferred longer lives and cures to illnesses.[18] In other words, they did not believe that baptism made their children Christian, but rather made them healthier.

In the mid-twelfth century, the Jacobite bishop John of Mardē recognised that the intention behind such Muslim participation in baptismal rites was problematic and he was duly concerned that a sacrament was being abused in such a superstitious way. Interestingly, John did not suggest the outright prohibition of the practice, but rather hoped to regulate it by introducing a new form of baptism for Muslims entitled the 'baptism of St John', which did not confer entry to the Church and would be liturgically distinct from the Christian sacrament, thereby sparing the latter from abuse.[19] It is not known if Christian priests widely adopted the baptism of St John, although a recent analyst believes that the custom of non-Christians seeking baptism, with no intent to convert, must have been 'very widespread' at the time to garner such a response.[20]

The observation that Muslims did not necessarily regard baptism as synonymous with conversion to Christianity – apostasy from Islam – is obviously significant and runs counter to current historiographical thinking. It is already known that many Syrian Muslims underwent baptism after the arrival of the crusaders, and historians have uniformly agreed that, as long as each alleged instance can be verified, such acts should be read as signs of genuine religious conversion.[21] Baptism became an increasingly key part of Latin attitudes and policy towards the Muslims in the twelfth and early thirteenth centuries, alongside the growing interest in conversion more generally.[22] In light of the identifiable practice of Muslims seeking baptism for superstitious motives, this policy was evidently flawed. Nor should modern historians be so quick to dismiss the possibility that Muslim rulers at the time of the First Crusade did indeed undergo or offer to undergo baptism without also intending to become Christian. If many Muslims were already requesting and receiving baptism from local Christian priests at the time, then the promises made to accept baptism in the face of crusader armies seem less incredible, if rather less significant when attempting to evaluate the crusaders' success as missionaries.

Through his various offers of gold, travel advice, alliances and baptism, Jalāl al-Mulk succeeded in convincing the crusaders to move southwards. Although Raymond of Saint-Gilles was already calling for Tripoli to be besieged at this early juncture, the majority of the crusaders – particularly the 'paupers' and religious mystics – were impatient to reach Jerusalem to complete their belated pilgrimage. Raymond's own chaplain evidently sided with the pious pilgrims against his lord, describing various miracles that took place to convince the travellers to abandon Tripoli and continue towards the Holy City. These fantastic signs included an apparition of St George and the dramatic discovery by a priest named Peter Desiderius of a stockpile of relics at the church of St Leontios.[23] This unidentified site was possibly a remnant of the great Late Antique shrine to this Roman soldier-saint, martyred in Tripoli sometime between the years AD 70 and AD 79.[24] The crusaders would soon adopt the distinctly Syro-Lebanese devotion to equestrian military saints – SS George and Leontios being fine examples – and brought such cults back to the west, where they proved to be one of the First Crusade's most enduring cultural legacies in Europe.[25]

In the meantime, the crusaders departed Tripoli laden with relics and dreams of Jerusalem. Jalāl al-Mulk did not enjoy his hard-won breathing space for long; he died shortly afterwards, around the same time that the crusaders first conquered Jerusalem – 15 July 1099 – and then defeated the Fāṭimid vizier al-Afḍal at Ascalon on 12 August 1099.[26] The *qāḍī* of Tripoli was succeeded by his brother, Fakhr al-Mulk Abū 'Alī bin 'Ammār (r. 492/1099–501/1108). The city of Tripoli continued to enjoy a period of respite under Fakhr al-Mulk as the reluctant pilgrim Raymond of Saint-Gilles found himself embroiled in a volatile dispute with his fellow crusader, Godfrey of Bouillon, who was elected 'advocate of the Holy Sepulchre' and perhaps even 'king' of Jerusalem.[27] Raymond allegedly wished to acquire the 'kingdom' (*regnum*) for himself, jealous that Godfrey had effectively usurped the prime position of authority.[28]

The considerable Fāṭimid threat demonstrated at Ascalon, however, seems to have made Raymond realise the error or perhaps the futility of his ways. Subsequent to the Frankish victory, Raymond prudently chose to withdraw from Jerusalem and spent a few years attempting to establish himself in North Syria. The count had embarked on a course of action that would lead him ultimately back to Tripoli.

Ambition in the north

Raymond's attempts to carve out a northern lordship inevitably brought him into conflict with Bohemond of Taranto and Tancred of Lecce. These Normans had been two of Raymond's greatest rivals on the First Crusade and had since proclaimed themselves princes of Antioch – the city over which their dispute with the count of Saint-Gilles had first arisen. The original plan during the First Crusade had been to conquer the city from the Saljūqs and restore it to Byzantine control in accordance with an oath sworn to Emperor Alexios I Komnenos at Constantinople in 1097. By summer 1098 relations between the Greeks and the Latins had worsened to the point that Bohemond had thought it reasonable to claim the city as his own. Count Raymond had objected, perhaps because he genuinely respected the oath to Alexios, or perhaps because he too wanted Antioch for himself. From the conquest of the city in June 1098 until Bohemond's eventual victory over Raymond in January 1099, an awkward situation had prevailed with Bohemond and Raymond each controlling different sectors of the metropolis. Third parties were careful to remain neutral in what was a tense situation, with the Genoese explicitly refusing to pick sides.[29] Nor was this rivalry confined to Antioch itself. The surrounding region of North Syria had belonged to the Byzantine duchy (*doukate*) of Antioch before the Saljūq invasions and it is likely that Emperor Alexios had promised this *doukate* in its entirety to Bohemond at the start of the First Crusade.[30] Yet such agreements had been respected neither by the rebellious Bohemond nor by the envious Raymond. In late 1098 Raymond had attempted to impose his authority over the strategically important region of Jabal al-Summāq in the hope of countering Bohemond's powerbase at Antioch. Tensions soon flared in the city of Maʿarrat al-Nuʿmān, which the crusaders had conquered in December of that year. As Bohemond and Raymond had been vying for control of the city, it was effectively divided into antagonistic Norman-controlled and Provençal-controlled sections for a number of weeks.[31]

By early 1099 Raymond had lost his various holdings in Antioch and Maʿarrat al-Nuʿman to Bohemond, yet his return to the Norman-held territories of the north after the battle of Ascalon served only to reignite the Norman–Provençal enmity. Most controversially, Raymond quickly set himself up as Emperor Alexios's deputy in the city of Latakia. The count had earlier secured Latakia in 1098 with a combined fleet from the Low Countries and Provence, before restoring it to Alexios, who had maintained control of this port throughout the feuding of Bohemond and Raymond further inland.[32] Between 1099 and 1101, Raymond acted as Alexios's lieutenant in Syria, ruling over a 'principauté byzantino-provençale' centred on Latakia.[33] During this time, Raymond treated Latakia as his base of operations, leaving his wife Elvira of Castile and familiars there while he travelled to Constantinople to meet new crusaders from the west in 1101.[34]

Raymond's governance of Latakia surely galled Bohemond. The Byzantine stance by the late 1090s was that Bohemond, although still *doux* in theory, had failed to respect imperial suzerainty in Antioch and had thus negated his right to hold the *doukate* in its entirety. The famous Treaty of Devol, which Emperor Alexios would force Bohemond to sign in 1108, broke with earlier tradition by alienating from the Norman-held *doukate* all those lands that the empire controlled, either directly or via Raymond of Saint-Gilles. These included Latakia, Jabala and Valania, which were later incorporated into the principality of Antioch, as well as Tortosa, Maraqiyya and the island of Arwād, which eventually formed the northern marches of the county of Tripoli.[35] Of course the agreement at Devol was still a few years away and even then was quickly forgotten. Certainly in 1099 then imperial opposition could do nothing to discourage Bohemond or his successor Tancred from viewing Latakia and the other alienated territories as rightful parts of what would eventually become a Latin principality loosely modelled on the Byzantine prototype.[36] Indeed, a great scandal erupted in 1099 precisely because of Bohemond's persistent attacks on Byzantine-held Latakia. It was only thanks to the intervention of the newly appointed papal legate Daimbert of Pisa and Raymond of Saint-Gilles himself that the prince of Antioch was evicted from the city.[37]

Ironically, Raymond's Latakian principality was not brought to an end by the Normans of Antioch but by the Byzantine emperor, who ordered his Latin lieutenant to surrender it to imperial representatives in 1101.[38] Alexios nevertheless found Raymond other work to do for him. In the same year, the count commanded a body of imperial troops and turcopoles in support of the so-called Crusade of the Faint-Hearted, comprising men who had either fled the First Crusade, such as Stephen of Blois, or never joined it at all, such as Raymond's nephew-in-law Duke William IX of Aquitaine. The expedition was intended to consolidate Christian gains against the Saljūqs in Anatolia, yet met with disaster. Raymond only narrowly escaped, limping back to Constantinople to face the indignant Alexios.[39]

Worse was still to come. After departing Constantinople for Syria, Raymond was captured by one of Tancred's men, Bernard the Foreigner. Although framed as punishment for Raymond's perceived culpability for the disastrous outcome of the 1101 crusade, the arrest was surely motivated more by the long-running political conflict between Raymond and the Normans. Tancred took this opportunity to force Raymond to swear an oath to stop attempting to take land anywhere to the north of Acre.[40] Shortly thereafter Tancred seized from the Greeks two of Raymond's former powerbases: Latakia and the ancient city of Apamea (Āfāmiyyā) in the Syrian interior.[41] The fledgling principality of Antioch was moving still further towards realising the limits of the old Byzantine *doukate*, which had traditionally comprised both of these cities.

With his independent and Byzantine-sponsored adventures alike leading only to failure, Raymond finally found himself back at Tripoli in 1103, where he began to assail the city, assembling an army 'from various places and kingdoms' in Europe.[42] This has perplexed some historians, as it would appear to signal that Raymond had broken his oath to Tancred to remain south of Acre.[43] It is possible that Albert of Aachen – the one author to record Raymond's promise to Tancred but also a man who never visited the east and was entirely reliant on hearsay[44] – made the easy mistake of confusing Arabic ʿAkkā (Latin *Acra*) with ʿArqa (*Archas*), the small town just north of Tripoli. The significance of this becomes clear when it is considered that ʿArqa happened to mark the southern border of the old Byzantine *doukate* and thus the ultimate ambitions of the princes of Antioch in this direction. This frontier has sometimes been equated with the 'Great Southern River' (al-Nahr al-Kabīr al-Janūbī), a river that was once the Eleutherus of Biblical Antiquity and today serves as the international border between the republics of Lebanon and Syria.[45] There can be little doubt that the crusaders were aware of this old border, shared by the Byzantines and the Fāṭimids from the late tenth century to the second half of the eleventh. For one thing, it is likely that when negotiating with the crusaders and obliging them to swear their famous oaths to him, Alexios Komnenos intended for the First Crusade to conquer and restore only those lands that had belonged to the empire before the Saljūq invasions, a mere few years previously.[46] These lands likely comprised Antioch, Latakia and other territories north of ʿArqa, but not Jerusalem, Tripoli or anywhere else to the south.

Interestingly, the Fāṭimid Muslims also helped to inform the crusaders that Syria had recently been divided into two spheres: northern Byzantine and southern Shīʿite. Moved by their common interest in defeating the Sunnī Saljūqs, the Fāṭimids had sent envoys to meet the Franks at Antioch in 1097, praising the crusaders' miraculous victories against the Turks won in the service of 'Jesus the son of the Virgin Mary'.[47] This is an intriguing approximation of the Arabic 'Jesus son of Maryam' (ʿĪsā bin Maryam) and acknowledges the shared Islamo-Christian belief in the virgin birth.[48] In response to these remarkably friendly Muslim ambassadors, the crusaders had sent some of their own envoys back to Egypt, intending to settle a 'friendly alliance' with their leader.[49] Raymond of Aguilers later detailed the terms offered by the crusader embassy sent from Antioch:

> If he [al-Afḍal] gave us aid to Jerusalem or returned to us Jerusalem with its appurtenances, we would return to him all his cities, which the Turks had taken from him, when we captured them. Other cities of the Turks, which had not been part of his kingdom, we would share with him if we captured them with his aid.[50]

Köhler believes this to be a reliable account of serious diplomatic intent on the part of the crusaders and the Fāṭimids.[51] The content of this agreement suggests that the Latin crusaders offered the Fāṭimids terms that were remarkably similar to, perhaps even modelled upon, the terms agreed and enshrined in oath between the crusaders and the Byzantine emperor at Constantinople some months previously. It suggests that the crusaders at this point viewed their main political goal as the restoration of the pre-Saljūq status quo in agreement with the Byzantines and Fāṭimids, with the one exception being the Latins' insistence upon Christian control over Jerusalem.

In the event, the crusaders' negotiations with both the Byzantines and the Fāṭimids broke down, although the relationship with the Fāṭimids crucially became antagonistic only when the Franks reached ʿArqa, entering what Raymond of Aguilers called 'their land' (*terram suam*).[52] The crusaders' arrival at ʿArqa represented their penetration into the Fāṭimid 'sphere of influence', which surprised the Fāṭimids greatly because they were still working on the assumption that the Franks were mere Byzantine mercenaries, concerned only with the reconquest of the formerly Byzantine north.[53] The crusaders' insistence on reaching and controlling southerly Jerusalem proved the real sticking point for negotiations with the Fāṭimids, who had managed to reconquer the city from the Saljūqs as recently as 1098. Al-Afḍal was only willing to allow the crusaders to visit Jerusalem in controlled groups of no more than two or three hundred at a time, with the added condition that they would promptly exit his territories after performing their devotions. However, the crusaders stubbornly refused to yield their claim to Jerusalem, boldly telling the Fāṭimid envoys that they would take 'Babylon' (Cairo) itself if they were not given the Holy City.[54] This impasse eventually led to war and the crusaders' victory over the Egyptians at Ascalon. What is relevant here is that the old border at ʿArqa clearly retained political and diplomatic significance even during the First Crusade.

As for Tripoli, it had never been part of the Byzantine *doukate* of Antioch but rather the Fāṭimid caliphate. It had not been under Byzantine control since 645, although it had been constantly reconnoitred by resurgent imperial forces since the tenth century. The Fāṭimids had invested a great deal into preserving their northernmost city by constructing impressive defences and by maintaining a permanent garrison there in the mid-eleventh century.[55] This military stalemate at Tripoli came to be the effective border between the Byzantine Empire and the Fāṭimid Caliphate at this time.[56]

Evidently it remained relevant as a concept even after the advent of the Saljūqs and then crusaders had challenged the rule of Greeks and Egyptians alike. When Raymond of Saint-Gilles besieged Tripoli in 1103, perhaps in accordance with an oath sworn to Tancred to remain south of ʿArqa, the count was likely following a territorial and political framework set by this eleventh-century precedent.

The siege of Tripoli and the Pilgrims' Mount

Despite the differences that had emerged between the Franks and the Byzantines, Emperor Alexios continued to provide Raymond with support when the count decided to besiege Tripoli in 1103, perhaps hoping that a friendly presence there would help him to reclaim the greater prize of Antioch. Upon initiating the siege, Raymond and his men built a new fortress to overlook the city, affording them protection while harrying and restricting their enemies.[57] According to Anna Komnene, the Byzantine *doux* of Cyprus provided logistical and material support in the building of this castle, no doubt explaining the rapidity of its construction.[58] The fort was built upon a section of high ground and was dubbed the 'Pilgrims' Mount' by the crusaders and their descendants.[59] The Pilgrims' Mount directly faced Tripoli's sole land gate and thus blockaded the one road into the city – a bridge that spanned a section of the Qādīshā river now known as Nahr Abū ʿAlī after Fakhr al-Mulk Abū ʿAlī bin ʿAmmār himself, Tripoli's last ʿAmmārid ruler.[60]

As the siege progressed, the crusader camp at the increasingly fortified Pilgrims' Mount grew into a permanent suburb. There was born a new crusader society, complete with a flourishing economy and plentiful churches – some of which survive today, albeit converted into mosques after the Mamluk conquest.[61] It was at the Pilgrims' Mount that Raymond began to rule the territory around Tripoli: issuing charters and even perhaps minting his own coins.[62] William of Tyre explained how Raymond collected an annual tribute from the locals and ruled 'as if he already possessed the city without dispute'.[63] By 1103, Raymond even went by the presumptuous title 'count of Tripoli, by the grace of God' – a direct challenge to the beleaguered ʿAmmārid *qāḍī*, Fakhr al-Mulk, who still held the city itself.[64] At the same time, Raymond took to styling himself 'the most excellent leader of the Christian army in Syria' throughout the siege of Tripoli.[65] Clearly Raymond viewed himself as still fighting the First Crusade – a war that many modern historians would claim had ended half a decade before.[66] This represented a continuation of his unfulfilled ambition to be recognised as the crusade's overall leader back in the 1090s and, although now restricted to the Lebanon region, this grandiose title surely helped him recruit more of those crusaders who had failed for whatever reason to participate in the original expedition. Thus did the ranks of those besieging Tripoli swell under Raymond's auspices.

Figure 1.2 The Citadel of Saint-Gilles, Tripoli © Denys Pringle

Raymond's claim to Tripoli was strengthened further by his appointment of Albert, the abbot of St Erard in Provence, as Latin bishop to the city's long-vacant episcopal see.[67] Back in 1098, Raymond had elevated the priest Peter of Narbonne to the see of Apamea (Āfāmiyyā) and Albara (al-Bāra) without any direct ecclesiastical approval.[68] Thus by the time he reached Tripoli, the count had already demonstrated a flagrant disregard for the high principles of the ongoing Gregorian Reform movement. The long but controversial tradition of lay investiture was set to be customary throughout the Latin East even into the thirteenth century.[69] As with his appointment of Peter of Narbonne to Apamea, it may well be that Raymond envisaged that Bishop Albert would act as his deputy in matters of governance on those occasions when the count was absent from Tripoli. After the count's death in 1105, however, Albert would travel west, where he would participate in an ecclesiastical council concerning the Peace of God held at the cathedral of Mende in Lozère, Languedoc. This particular incident was recorded by a hagiographer, excited by the supposedly miraculous discovery of the lower jawbone of St Privat that took place on this occasion.[70] Albert is described in this curious text as an 'archbishop', which led Richard to propose that Raymond of Saint-Gilles had even sought to create a metropolitan see at Tripoli, independent of the archbishop of Tyre – as yet unconquered although set to become part of the kingdom of Jerusalem in due course.[71] This theory is tantalising but it rests upon what could easily be a copyist's error in the one surviving fourteenth-century copy of the lost twelfth-century original of this text.[72] The evidence therefore is simply insufficient. In all likelihood, the bishop of Tripoli never styled himself archbishop, at Mende or anywhere else.

As the crusader town of Pilgrims' Mount grew further and the besiegers entrenched themselves more deeply, the Muslims of Tripoli naturally grew more anxious and desperate. Fakhr al-Mulk watched impotently as the parasitical crusader suburb spread and strangled his city. The *qāḍī* initially followed his brother and predecessor Jalāl al-Mulk in seeking a diplomatic solution to the Frankish threat. An early truce between Fakhr al-Mulk and Raymond of Saint-Gilles, which had temporarily delayed the eventual full siege, had been established as early as 1101–2 (AH 495), conditional upon the payment of a ransom of money and horses.[73] In 1105, the two men concluded a seven-year armistice. By the terms of this agreement, Raymond would hold Tripoli's expanding suburbs, but would both respect Fakhr al-Mulk's right to rule Tripoli itself and guarantee safe unbroken passage for travellers and supplies to and from the city. Unfortunately for this particular peace process, the truce was broken soon after when a disgruntled Tripolitan made an attempt on Raymond's life with a poisoned dagger.[74]

With the failure of the diplomatic route, the increasingly hard-pressed Fakhr al-Mulk launched an assault against the Pilgrims' Mount in 1105. This was neither the first such raid nor the first of these to fail in achieving its main objective of dislodging the crusader siege. As early as 1099, a particularly bloody skirmish had broken out in the midst of Jalāl al-Mulk's desperate negotiations. The Christians had defeated the Muslim soldiers, whose dismembered bodies floated back into the city via its Umayyad-era aqueduct, befouling the population's drinking water.[75] In 1105 the defeated Muslims did nevertheless have some consolation, as they managed to set fire to a number of structures in the crusader camp. Upon one of these buildings stood Raymond of Saint-Gilles himself.

The death of a crusader

As he surveyed the skirmish in 1105, Raymond was apparently unaware of the flames eating away at the structure beneath his feet. Eventually the roof collapsed, plunging Raymond down into the smoke and heat below. He was dragged to safety but never recovered.[76] True, Raymond had once been a fearsome warrior with an equally fearsome reputation. When his son Alfons Jordan later headed to Syria to fight in the Second Crusade, the Franks and Muslims expected much of him simply because of his father's reputation.[77] The castle Raymond built on the Pilgrims' Mount remains a lasting testament to his military achievements, still known to Tripolitans today as the Citadel of Saint-Gilles (*Qalʿat Ṣanjīl*).[78] An Arab poet in his service even composed a poetic verse or *qaṣīda* in his honour, following his victory over the Fāṭimid vizier al-Afḍal at the battle of Ascalon:

> You have rendered the religion of the Messiah victorious with your sword,
> For to God belongs your achievement, the blessing of Saint-Gilles.
> And people have never heard of something narrated
> As shamefully as the defeat of al-Afḍal.[79]

Through his patronage of this poet, Raymond showed himself happy to practise self-aggrandisement in Arabic as well as Latin.

By 1105, Raymond's great martial achievements were behind him, for he was old. He had been in his sixties when he had joined the First Crusade a decade before, which may explain his famous commitment to remain and die in the east, rather than return home to his extensive lands in Toulouse and Provence.[80] In his younger days perhaps his body could have resisted the shock and injury of falling into a burning building, yet this proved impossible at seventy years of age. Ten days after his fall, on 28 February, Raymond died. Ibn al-Athīr claimed that his body was brought to Jerusalem for burial, which would accord with the general belief among Christians at the time that the Holy City was the most desirable place to be laid to rest.[81] Albert of Aachen, however, insisted that Raymond was interred at the Pilgrims' Mount, his base of operations for the three years prior to his death.[82] Indeed, archaeologists have identified an octagonal structure at the heart of Tripoli's citadel, which they believe may be a purpose-built tomb for the count and his progeny, based on the round aedicule of Jerusalem's Holy Sepulchre.[83] The count's grave was located in what was probably a chapel donated by Raymond to the canons of the Holy Sepulchre in the very year of his death. This had been a mosque prior to the crusaders' arrival, but Raymond himself had described in polemical language how it had been converted into Christian use:

> A certain house on the Pilgrims' Mount, which already now has become a worthy and everlasting dwelling place for God, all heinous ceremony of heathenism having thenceforth been driven off.[84]

It was fitting that a man such as Raymond, who had dedicated the later stages of his life to crusading, was buried amid such a material testament to Christianity's triumph over Islam.

Enter William Jordan

The arrangements for Raymond's burial were among the least of the concerns he left to his followers. As was so often the case in the Middle Ages, the most pressing question concerned his succession. Raymond left behind two known sons. One of these he had managed to sire at the Pilgrims' Mount, in spite of the ongoing siege and his own advancing years. Named Alfons Jordan, the child was born to Raymond's second wife, Elvira of León and Castile, in 1103.[85] Although this two-year-old infant was conveniently located within his late father's Syrian headquarters, he was far too young to rule. A group of Provençal barons, led by William of Montpellier, recognised this and escorted Alfons back to the west by ship, where they were to protect the boy and raise him to adulthood.[86]

Raymond's other son, Bertrand, was certainly of age, having been born *c.*1068.[87] Raymond had apparently left Bertrand in the west when he departed on the First Crusade, relying on his son to govern his domains in his absence.[88] This was no mean feat, as Raymond had gained control over a vast area following the death of his brother William IV of Toulouse, stretching from Provence in the east to Toulouse in the west and from Le Puy in the north to the Pyrenees in the south.[89] Bertrand seems to have struggled to keep his father's lands together. With Raymond absent, Bertrand soon found himself preyed upon by various regional rivals and so the Toulousan empire began to crumble. The most immediate threat to Bertrand's rule came from the neighbouring duchy of Aquitaine. In the 1080s or 1090s, Duke William IX of Aquitaine had married William IV's daughter Philippa – Raymond of Saint-Gilles's niece and Bertrand's first cousin. Philippa strongly believed that Toulouse should have passed to her either upon her father's death or upon her uncle's departure for the

Figure 1.3 The tomb of Count Raymond I of Tripoli (= Raymond IV of Saint-Gilles and Toulouse) © Denys Pringle

First Crusade. Her new husband was only too happy to press these claims as soon as Count Raymond had left for Syria. Most dramatically, William IX and Philippa seized Toulouse itself in 1098 and began issuing charters as the 'count and countess of Poitou and Toulouse'.[90] During this time, the couple had their only son, the future William X of Aquitaine, who was appropriately dubbed 'the Toulousan'.[91] Bertrand managed to regain his city in 1100, but the house of Aquitaine never forgot Philippa's claim. William and Philippa would seize Toulouse once again in 1114, this time from Bertrand's half-brother Alfons Jordan, and were to hold it until 1119.[92] Decades later still, Eleanor of Aquitaine would perpetuate the belief that her family had the right to rule Toulouse, influencing both of her husbands – King Louis VII of France and Henry II of England – and her son Richard I of England.[93]

Bertrand's position was not helped by the doubt that hung over his legitimacy. In 1076, Pope Gregory VII had excommunicated Raymond of Saint-Gilles for his consanguineous marriage to Bertrand's mother, although the count remained stubbornly committed to this union in the face of canon law.[94] This marital irregularity apparently inspired the rumour recorded by William of Malmesbury that Bertrand was illegitimate – 'a son born of a mistress'.[95] The pope's forceful dissolution of Raymond's marriage had retroactively rendered his son illegitimate in the eyes of many, who were encouraged all the more to challenge Bertrand's right to rule. As far as Raymond of Saint-Gilles's eastern inheritance at Tripoli was concerned, Bertrand was thus on the wrong side of the Mediterranean and far too preoccupied by political turbulence closer to home to succeed his father immediately.

With Raymond's sons either unsuitable or unavailable, command of his army and lands in Syria fell to Count William Jordan of Cerdanya, one of his followers and his first cousin once removed.[96] Cerdanya was a tiny Pyrenean lordship, which both the Occitan counts of Toulouse and the Catalan counts of Barcelona had claimed with varying degrees of success throughout the eleventh century.[97] The exact situation upon the eve of the First Crusade is unclear, but it is likely that Raymond of Saint-Gilles's energetic rule over an unusually large swathe of territory had reinforced the Toulousan claim to Cerdanya at Barcelona's temporary expense.

Historians have tended to overlook William Jordan's contribution to the formation of the county of Tripoli, perhaps because he was an exception to the otherwise straightforwardly patrilineal succession of counts who would rule in an unbroken chain from Raymond of Saint-Gilles in 1103 to Raymond III of Tripoli in 1187. More importantly, his career in the east is poorly documented. It is not even clear when William Jordan first arrived in Syria. No reliable source identifies him as a participant in the First Crusade, with his initial appearance in the Latin chronicles coming in 1105, followed only by the occasional mention thereafter.[98] William of Malmesbury evidently conflated him with the infant Alfons

Jordan.[99] Arabic accounts are similarly unhelpful. Ibn al-Qalānisī erroneously believed that the count of Cerdanya – 'al-Sardānī' – was 'the son of (Raymond of) Saint-Gilles's sister' (*ibn ukht ṣanjīl*).[100] Al-ʿAẓīmī skipped William Jordan altogether, simply writing that Raymond was succeeded immediately by his 'son' – that is to say, Bertrand.[101]

Modern historians have failed to clarify the situation any further. Richard seems to think that William Jordan arrived only in 1105, just in time to be granted command after Raymond's death.[102] By contrast, Riley-Smith has included William Jordan among his list of 'near-certain' participants in the First Crusade, which he somewhat imprecisely defines as having extended from 1096 to 1103.[103] He brings forth two sources as evidence of William's presence on the First Crusade, although both are dubious. One is a plenary indulgence granted by Pope Urban II to a group of Pyrenean counts, the count of Cerdanya included, if they fought against the Muslims of Asia.[104] This source does not indicate when the counts were expected to set out, or even whether the counts were to follow Urban's encouragement to fight in Asia or nearby Spain. The other piece of evidence is the surviving fragment of the late twelfth-century Occitan epic of the First Crusade, the *Canso d'Antioca,* which includes 'lo com de Sardana' in Adhémar of Le Puy's train at the siege of Antioch.[105] This late source, with its clear aim being to aggrandise local noble families, naturally invites suspicion.

Against these questionable pieces of evidence, there is a hitherto-neglected charter in which Bertrand of Saint-Gilles confirmed certain donations to the church of St Sernin of Toulouse made by his cousin and political rival Philippa.[106] The charter can be dated as early as *c.*1100, soon after Bertrand had reclaimed Toulouse from the usurper Philippa and her husband William of Aquitaine.[107] Crucially, Bertrand's confirmation was witnessed by none other than Count William Jordan of Cerdanya.[108] Devic and Vaissète concluded that William Jordan had supported Bertrand in seizing back Toulouse.[109] This in turn suggests that William Jordan remained in the west for at least a few years after the departure of Raymond of Saint-Gilles for the Holy Land in 1096. Regrettably, it is impossible to be more precise than to say William Jordan headed to Syria between *c.*1100 and 1105.

Confusion also hangs over William Jordan's exact role after Raymond of Saint-Gilles's death. Some have suggested that he did not succeed Raymond in truth, merely acting as regent on behalf of the underage heir Alfons Jordan.[110] There is no certain evidence to suggest that William Jordan adopted the title 'count of Tripoli', as Raymond had done. Little Alfons would later return to Syria as a man in the 1140s, perhaps with the ambition of reclaiming his Lebanese patrimony.[111] Nevertheless, there is reason to suspect that William Jordan saw himself as more than a caretaker: no less than Raymond of Saint-Gilles's true successor in Syria. True, he may never have styled himself count of Tripoli, but he did assume the old count's claims to supreme command of the First Crusade by adopting the grandiose title 'leader of the Christian army'.[112] William also issued confirmations of Raymond's acts. He stated unequivocally in one such document that he had 'succeeded Raymond in the *honor* (of Tripoli) by hereditary law'.[113] According to Albert of Aachen, William Jordan succeeded Raymond 'by blood inheritance'.[114] Albert went on to write that William Jordan himself claimed that he acquired his Syrian lands from Raymond 'in hereditary succession'.[115] Interestingly William Jordan used this argument against Raymond's own son Bertrand when the latter eventually arrived at Tripoli a few years later. Nor was William Jordan without sympathisers and allies. The Byzantines were content to acknowledge William Jordan's rule, sending an envoy to convince him to reconfirm the oath to Emperor Alexios, which his late cousin had faithfully observed until the last.[116] When William Jordan himself died in mysterious circumstances in 1109, the crusaders at the siege of Tripoli split into two camps: those who were pleased and those who mourned.[117] This suggests that he was not viewed unanimously as a simple regent turned unwelcome usurper.

William Jordan's achievement

Whatever William Jordan's exact legal status, historians have given the count of Cerdanya short shrift in terms of his actual achievements; the patchy nature of surviving evidence and the brevity of his reign do not excuse them entirely. William of Tyre, for example, stressed how William Jordan continued Raymond's work at the Pilgrims' Mount with diligence, energy and valour.[118] In fact, the main reason William Jordan failed to conquer Tripoli was a lack of adequate naval support, which had also prevented Raymond of Saint-Gilles from doing the same. The old city of Tripoli was located on a small outcrop of land protruding into the Mediterranean. When the Persian Nāṣir Khusraw visited Tripoli in the 1040s, he described it as a four-sided city with only one wall facing the land and three facing the sea, pounded by the waves.[119] The twelfth-century Arab geographer Al-Idrīsī wrote that 'the sea grabs the town from three directions'.[120] With the city thus arrayed, all a besieging army could hope to do without a navy was to blockade Tripoli on its land facing, as indeed the citadel on the Pilgrims' Mount succeeded in doing. Yet this alone would never be sufficient.

Between the beginning of the siege in 1103 and the eventual fall of the city in 1109, the Fāṭimids kept the city supplied with regular maritime shipments. Albert of Aachen recorded how Raymond of Saint-Gilles had only failed to take the city because the inhabitants had received continuous supplies and reinforcements from Fāṭimid ports.[121] Al-ʿAẓīmī recorded how a Fāṭimid fleet had arrived at Tripoli to reinforce it in 1103/4 (AH 497) and had apparently encountered no real opposition, despite the Frankish siege.[122] The same situation prevailed under William Jordan and nothing captures his frustration better than Albert of Aachen's report that the count had tried but failed to prevent a Fāṭimid navy from taking shelter in Tripoli's harbour one night in 1105.[123] Why this particular navy was allegedly returning to Egypt from Jaffa via northerly Tripoli is a mystery, but William's impotence is clear. ʿAmmārid Tripoli could also rely on its own small domestic fleet in addition to the Fāṭimid navy. The Tripolitans were sufficiently capable to launch amphibious raids on the city's immediate hinterland in 1102/3 (AH 496), attempting to kill and drive out the peasantry in the hopes of depopulating and thus starving Frankish-held territory.[124] The same Tripolitan sailors later fought off a Byzantine flotilla bringing supplies to the Franks in 1105/6 (AH 499) – even managing to capture a ship and its full complement of crew in the process.[125] It seems then that the Tripolitan fleet went unchallenged by the forces of the land-bound Christian siege.

With Tripoli practically unassailable for as long as the crusaders lacked overwhelming naval support, William Jordan focused his energies on conquering the surrounding land, pushing into the Syrian interior. His deeds in this respect deserve greater emphasis than they have traditionally received. After all, it was during his time as commander at Tripoli that the *qāḍī* Fakhr al-Mulk became so desperate as to go on a tour of the Islamic Middle East in 1107/8 (AH 501), seeking help from various sources including the Sunnī 'Abbāsid caliph in Baghdad, the Sunnī Saljūq sultan also in Baghdad and the temperamental Saljūq *atābak* of Damascus, Ṭughtakīn.[126] Unfortunately for Fakhr al-Mulk, no help was forthcoming from these quarters and the power vacuum his absence left in Tripoli rendered his own city highly vulnerable to internal as well as external pressures. A popular revolt against Fakhr al-Mulk – perhaps led by his own cousin – restored the city to Fāṭimid control a year before it was to fall to the crusaders.[127] Fakhr al-Mulk was thus forced into exile and ʿAmmārid Tripoli, which had prospered as an independent city-state for a generation, was no more.

Arguably William Jordan's greatest achievement was to capture the town of ʿArqa in March/April 1109 (Shaʿbān 502). ʿArqa had already been weakened by a political dispute after its *mamlūk*-governor had rebelled against his master, Fakhr al-Mulk bin ʿAmmār of Tripoli, allegedly because the besieged *qāḍī* could no longer provide him with the supplies he needed to hold out against the Franks. Thus the *mamlūk* had sought help from Ṭughtakīn of Damascus, only to be murdered by a disgruntled subordinate named Isrāʾīl who presumably remained loyal to Shīʿa Tripoli.[128] Meanwhile, William Jordan had been preparing to conquer ʿArqa for years by devastating the crops around the town; this had only exacerbated the lack of supplies, further plunging the populace into starvation. Finally, the count of Cerdanya won a battle in the field against Ṭughtakīn and the relief force requested by ʿArqa's former *mamlūk*-governor. This victory gave William Jordan the room and impetus to take the fortress of ʿArqa by storm.[129] Ṭughtakīn received some consolation, as William Jordan agreed to hand over the treacherous Isrāʾīl in return for the release of a Frankish prisoner who had been imprisoned in Damascus for seven years.[130]

ʿArqa went on to become one of the main Frankish settlements in the county of Tripoli, proving to be militarily useful and economically profitable. Richard describes it as 'la clef de Tripoli', by virtue of its recurrent strategic importance in battles fought throughout the crusader period.[131] Al-Idrīsī praised its great affluence and a Latin contemporary called the town 'almost impregnable' (*fere inexpugnabilem*).[132] ʿArqa even acquired some dubious religio-historical importance in the eyes of some Franks, with the chronicler Ernoul making an obvious but seemingly unique etymological pun: claiming that it was the site where Noah built his Ark – a distortion of an established tradition associating Noah with Lebanon, attested in both eastern and Latin sources of the period.[133]

To put William Jordan's conquest of ʿArqa into greater perspective, it is worth considering past attempts to take this strategically important fortified town. During the First Crusade, ʿArqa had witnessed important negotiations between the crusaders and the Fāṭimids but had also been subject to a lengthy, bloody and ultimately abortive siege in April–May 1099, in which the chronicler Raymond of Aguilers's knightly co-author Pons of Balazun lost his life.[134] It was also where Raymond of Saint-Gilles suffered humiliation by association when his charge, the mystic Peter Bartholomew, died following a trial by fire to ascertain the veracity of the famous Holy Lance of Antioch.[135] It had largely been this embarrassment that had obliged Raymond to abandon the siege. ʿArqa continued to resist permanent crusader occupation for another decade. Count Raymond failed to take it in the three or so years he spent besieging Tripoli, just 14 miles to the south-west. Thus William Jordan's success, where the First Crusade and his more famous predecessor had failed, is a fine demonstration of the contribution he made to the establishment of what would become the county of Tripoli, qualifying Richard's emphasis on Raymond of Saint-Gilles's 'action personnelle'.[136]

Albert of Aachen was particularly ebullient about the consequences of ʿArqa's capture, writing that William Jordan and his soldiers then proceeded to use the town as a base from which they 'took possession of the whole region, assaulting as far as Damascus day by day'.[137] ʿArqa is not particularly close to Damascus, some 70 miles as the crow flies. Moreover, the two locales are separated by the Lebanon and Anti-Lebanon mountain ranges, which themselves are split by the Biqāʿ valley. Other than Albert's vague testimony, there is no evidence to suggest that William Jordan ever went anywhere near Damascus. One might be tempted to conclude that Albert either got carried away in reporting this Christian victory, or – as an author who wrote from second-hand gossip and never actually visited Syria – simply did not know the geography of the region well enough to provide flawless descriptions.

Despite the confusion, an Arabic eyewitness to William Jordan's raids into the Syrian interior offers evidence that loosely supports Albert's account. Usāma, famous scion of the Syrian Munqidh clan, could still recall decades after the event how the men of his family had struggled with William Jordan of Cerdanya (*al-Sardānī*) near their hometown of Shayzar, fighting two skirmishes in 1108 alone.[138] Although the Munqidhid ruler of Shayzar – Usāma's uncle – had sued for peace with Raymond of Saint-Gilles as the armies of the First Crusade had marched down the Orontes valley in 1099, the count of Toulouse had never actually conquered the city and apparently never returned.[139] It is true that William Jordan also failed to conquer Shayzar, but his willingness and ability to maintain pressure on this relatively distant Muslim stronghold, seemingly forgotten by his predecessor, remains notable. He also managed to exact tribute from some of the eastern Christian farmers living nearby. As Count Pons of Tripoli would later note, 'Count William was accustomed to take bezants from the cattle of Syrians working in villages' – some of which were located 'in the land of Rafaniyya' only a few miles from Shayzar.[140]

Shayzar was located on the Orontes, which leads back to Albert of Aachen's reference to Damascus. The Old Testament names two rivers said to pertain to Damascus: the *Pharpar* or *Farfar* and the *Albana* or *Abana*.[141] More recent exegetical theory holds that the Albana should be identified with al-Nahr al-Baradā (the Cold River) and the Pharpar with either one of the Baradā's distributaries: the Nahr Tawrā (the aptly named Torah River) or al-Nahr al-Aʿwaj (the Crooked River) respectively.[142] Nevertheless, medieval Latin authors misidentified the Albana as the Nahr al-ʿArqa (*fluvius Archados*), which flowed just south of ʿArqa itself.[143] Crucially, they – Albert of Aachen included – routinely identified the Farfar with the Orontes.[144] For example, in March 1181 Count Raymond III of Tripoli would donate land to the Hospitallers as far as the river Orontes, or rather 'as far as the river that we commonly dub the *Fer*'.[145] This misidentification was compounded by the fact that the Arabs of the region seem to have referred to a location on the Orontes by the colloquial name *Jisr al-Ḥadīd*, 'bridge of iron', even before the First Crusade, in reference to a local legend.[146] Clearly influenced by the locals they met, the chroniclers of the First Crusade translated this into Latin as the *Pons Farreus*, which in turn strengthened the association of the Orontes with the Farfar.[147]

That the Orontes was identified with the Farfar – a supposed 'river of Damascus' – is obviously relevant to Albert of Aachen's claim that William Jordan fought 'as far as Damascus'. Conceivably, Albert of Aachen heard from one of his oral sources that William Jordan was engaged in skirmishes near Shayzar, that is to say along the Farfar. Personally unfamiliar with Syrian geography, he would have turned to his Biblical knowledge to conclude that William Jordan was fighting near Damascus. His account of William's actions was more a confused distortion than an outright exaggeration or error.

Far from being an ineffective and obscure footnote in the history of Tripoli's Latin rulers, William Jordan played an important part in consolidating Frankish rule over the region that would later become the county. His active efforts in pushing his fledgling domain as far as the Orontes is significant because it laid the groundwork for the county's theoretical limits. As historians have long recognised, the Franks regarded the Orontes as the county's eastern border with the Muslim emirates of Hama and Homs, even if this was not always reflected in reality.[148] When Raymond III mentioned the Orontes in March 1181, he implied that his theoretical – if not actual – property rights only extended up to the Orontes.[149] The equation of the Orontes with the county's eastern boundary was arguably William Jordan's greatest legacy.

Enter Bertrand

William Jordan was unable to enjoy his fledgling lordship for long, since he was soon forced to refocus his energies against a foe from an unexpected quarter – his former lord and ally in the west, Bertrand of Saint-Gilles. It is not entirely clear why Bertrand chose to head east in 1108. Perhaps Bertrand was forced out by the same men led by William of Montpellier, who had escorted his younger half-brother Alfons Jordan across the Mediterranean, from Tripoli to Toulouse. Indeed, Richard posits that the lingering doubts over Bertrand's legitimacy had entirely undermined his authority to rule, leaving Alfons Jordan the sole legitimate heir to Raymond IV's western domains.[150] A more benign proposal and one no less credible is that Bertrand simply wished to head east to follow in his father's footsteps, longing for the adventure and spiritual fulfilment that a crusade promised. He had spent years in the west, no doubt hearing of his father's exploits in Syria from the hundreds of Occitan crusaders who had returned home. William of Montpellier and his associates, bringing with them the young Alfons Jordan, are perhaps the best known. Not only would these men have brought tales of adventure on crusade, but the arrival of Bertrand's younger brother – far from being a threat to his rule – may well have offered the count the opportunity to offload his responsibilities in the west in favour of entering the service of God in the east.

A monk of the priory of La Chaise-Dieu, just north of Le Puy, recorded how Bishop Albert of Tripoli sent Raymond of Saint-Gilles's famous stockpile of relics gathered and plundered during the First Crusade back to this western priory upon the old count's death. Although this is entirely possible in light of Albert's attendance at the council of Mende *c.*1105–7, some caution is necessary. The monastic author of La Chaise-Dieu also claimed that Albert himself had been a monk of La Chaise-Dieu and, upon his departure for the east, had been one of the first priors of the small affiliated house of Privezac in Rouergue. This seems to contradict the more reliable evidence that Albert had been abbot of St Erard. This author had an evident desire to exaggerate the role of his own abbey of La Chaise-Dieu in the First Crusade elsewhere in his narrative, writing that Raymond of Saint-Gilles's special devotion to St Robert had led him to take the cross at his tomb.[151] It would therefore be wise to treat the claims of this hagiographical text with more scepticism than some historians have done.[152] Nevertheless, if the story of Raymond's relics is true, then the arrival of such a vast collection of his late father's religious treasures in Occitania may well have inspired Bertrand all the more to set out on crusade.

Whatever the true reason for Bertrand's departure, depart he did. His was no small expedition and he managed to recruit a large number of crusaders. According to Albert of Aachen, Bertrand left the port of Saint-Gilles with forty ships loaded with 4,000 soldiers, plus additional sailors. He then sailed east to Genoa, where a further eighty galleys presumably crewed in similar fashion to their Provençal counterparts swelled the navy still further.[153] The Genoese had had some time to prepare for an expedition eastwards, having received a missive from William Jordan seeking their assistance at Tripoli soon after the death of Raymond of Saint-Gilles many months earlier.[154] The Genoese were not alone in lending their support to Bertrand's crusade. William of Malmesbury added that Bertrand also received support from the Pisans, allegedly because they were kin to his Lombard wife.[155] From Genoa, the fleet hugged the northern Mediterranean coastline round into Byzantine waters, putting into the port of Almyros, where the crusaders seized necessary supplies by force. As soon as he heard about this latest intrusion, Alexios Komnenos sent an envoy to meet Bertrand. The envoy carried with him a familiar demand: that the count swear the customary oath of loyalty to Alexios Komnenos, in line with the precedent established by his father over a decade previously and confirmed by William Jordan rather more recently.[156] The Byzantines were presumably unconcerned with the potential for dispute between Bertrand and William Jordan, as long as neither rejected the emperor's nominal supremacy.

From Byzantium, the Provençal–Genoese fleet sailed to Syria. Here Bertrand began to unsettle the emerging Latin East, primarily by dredging up his own father's unsuccessful claims to various cities and lands. As soon as he arrived at the port of Saint-Symeon in the fledgling principality of Antioch, he re-ignited his father's grudge with the Norman Tancred of Lecce – now prince of Antioch – by demanding the restoration of the property briefly held by Raymond in the north during the First Crusade. This included part of Antioch itself. Bertrand's aggressive diplomacy achieved nothing with the impassive Tancred.[157] Thus the count sailed south to Tortosa, which he reached in March 1109. Tortosa was the first major site in the future county of Tripoli to have been conquered by the crusaders, long before other settlements such as Jubayl, 'Arqa or Tripoli itself. As early as 1098, two of Raymond's followers, Raymond Pilet and Raymond of Turenne in the Limousin, had taken the city after a relatively easy siege, offering it to their lord immediately afterwards.[158] One of the earliest visitors to the east, the English pilgrim Saewulf, made special note of the fact that 'Duke' Raymond ruled Tortosa *c.*1102.[159] After the First Crusade, it seems to have been integrated into Raymond's short-lived Byzantine protectorate of Latakia. Albert of Aachen claimed that the old count only remained in Syria at all to protect Tortosa, Latakia and his other holdings against the jealous Normans – contrary to the tradition that he had piously sought to die in the east as a pilgrim.[160] It would seem that Raymond briefly lost control of Tortosa, since Fulcher of Chartres and William of Tyre both claimed that the count (re-)conquered the city in 1101, with the help of those who had survived the ill-fated Anatolian Crusade earlier that year.[161]

Tortosa's importance was not simply military, but also lay in its status as an episcopal city with a famous shrine – the most important in the whole patriarchate of Antioch.[162] Latin Christian and Arab Muslim authors alike wrote that the city's cathedral had been the first church founded in honour of the Virgin Mary by St Peter and his fellow Apostles.[163] Indeed, James of Vitry recorded that the Church was held in greater honour than all other churches dedicated to the Virgin and was frequented by many people – both Christian and Muslim – expecting miracles and favours, 'from the infancy of the primitive Church until today'.[164] Purported Apostolic origins notwithstanding, very little is known about the shrine's true antiquity. It is possible that it had been operational prior to the First Crusade. Enlart noted a tradition attesting to its existence as early as AD 387.[165] The shrine at Tortosa was perhaps preserved or reinvigorated by the Byzantine occupation of Tortosa from the second half of the tenth century up until the Saljūq invasions of the late eleventh, when the city represented the empire's southernmost outpost along the border with the Fāṭimids. It may even have been under this more recent period of Byzantine rule that the shrine was created in the first place. It has been argued that the nearby Marian shrine of Ṣaydnāyā was founded not under Emperor Justinian, as tradition would have it, but rather more recently, in 1059.[166] The Chronicle of Amadi reported that there was a sacred icon at Tortosa during the crusader period, which had been taken to Cyprus by 1308, presumably to escape the Mamluks.[167] This icon may have had Byzantine origins, as did the more famous one at Ṣaydnāyā.

By the time Bertrand arrived, the city had passed into the hands of William Jordan, together with Raymond of Saint-Gilles's other possessions in the east, either 'by hereditary law' or by William Jordan's opportunism in the absence of any legitimate heir. What William Jordan did with it in the years of his short reign is unclear, but whoever governed it in his stead in early 1109 made no move to block Bertrand from landing there, where he dined and rested overnight without trouble. Come the morning, Bertrand opened a dispute by despatching an envoy to William Jordan, making the twin demands that the count of Cerdanya yield to him 'the land of Camolla' (*terram de Camolla*) and also show him his 'friendship and service' (*amiciciam et obsequium*).[168] In terms of the latter, Bertrand likely wished to remind his former ally in the west of the loyalty he owed the house of Toulouse. Indeed, 'friend' (*amic*) was one of the vague terms used to describe the retainers of lords within the loose, quasi-feudal social hierarchy of contemporary Occitania, where there was often the expectation of mutual assistance and loyalty, if not obligatory vassalic service *per se.*[169]

More curious is Bertrand's insistence upon acquiring 'the land of Camolla'. Many historians have grappled with the meaning of this enigmatic toponym. Richard thinks it was a reference to Homs, which leads him to conclude that the early counts of Tripoli viewed this inland Syrian city and not Tripoli itself as the ultimate goal of their conquests.[170] After all, why else would Bertrand demand the land of Homs rather than the land of Tripoli? Certainly Homs is referred to as *Camolla,* or approximates such as *Chamela,* in many contemporary texts.[171] Moreover, Albert of Aachen claimed that William Jordan had inherited from Raymond of Saint-Gilles not the land of Tripoli, but the 'land and cities [*sic*] of Homs'.[172] Homs's Muslim ruler, Janāḥ al-Dawla, had submitted himself to Raymond of Saint-Gilles during the First Crusade.[173] Henceforth the counts expected to receive tribute from Homs – something they made sure to exact whenever they had the requisite military strength, even if they never succeeded in occupying it. Paying this protection money to the Franks clearly rankled with the Muslims of Homs. As early as 1101/2 (AH 495), Janāḥ al-Dawla united with Fakhr al-Mulk bin ʿAmmār of Tripoli and the two men led their combined forces against Raymond of Saint-Gilles, then based at Tortosa. However, the Muslims were swiftly defeated and Janāḥ al-Dawla was reduced to paying tribute once more.[174] Worse was to come a year later, when Janāḥ al-Dawla was assassinated on 2 May 1103 (22 Rajab 496). Raymond acted quickly, arriving at Homs to exact tribute just three days later.[175] Raymond's successors tended to be less active than he in pursuing their perceived rights in Homs, but his great-grandson Raymond II still enjoyed fishing rights in the nearby lake as late as the 1140s.[176]

Throughout the twelfth century, Homs was effectively an unstable frontier town, subject to frequent political turmoil. Governance passed back and forth between local and distant Muslim rulers and the city found itself regularly assailed by crusader armies and raiding parties – sometimes seeking to conquer, more often to collect tribute. Its location on two important routes through Syria – between Damascus and Aleppo along the Orontes valley, and between Frankish and Muslim territory through the so-called Homs Gap that split the Nuṣayrī and Lebanon mountains – ensured that every serious attempt at consolidating rule in the area inevitably turned on Homs. Certainly Richard argues that the

Homs Gap alone was the defining feature of the county of Tripoli's eastern border – the place through which trade and armies flowed and thus could be controlled.[177] Indeed, the city's placement on the Orontes ensured that the counts of Tripoli equated it with the easternmost limits of their power, as in a document of 1184 in which Raymond III noted that Homs lay 'on the side of the river beyond the limits of Christianity', while his lands were on the nearer side.[178] At the same time, Homs's location on a regional crossroads guaranteed that no single power could hold it for long without also dominating the vast network of trade, travel and communication, of which Homs itself was the nexus.

Homs's strategic value is clear, but not all historians agree with Richard on the precise detail that Bertrand was demanding Homs itself in 1109. It is far from certain that *Camolla* and its approximates were synonymous with Homs alone. One of the lesser settlements within the county of Tripoli was Lo Camel (*Kaʾīma* or *Kamliyya*), located near Crac des Chevaliers (*Ḥiṣn al-Akrād*).[179] Usually it is obvious in the contemporary sources whether *Camolla* stood for Homs, Lo Camel or some other site, but not always. Moreover, there is a very strong possibility that *Camolla* referred to the entire Buqayʿa plain. This was located between Tripoli and Tortosa, being the principal plain in the future county of Tripoli and a vital source of crops – the second most important being the neighbouring ʿAkkār plain to the south-east. Elsewhere in his narrative, Albert of Aachen described the Buqayʿa as 'the valley of Camels', perhaps in reference to the camels bred there.[180] The Buqayʿa stretches almost as far as Homs, where the crusaders first entered the plain during the First Crusade, so it seems most probable that Bertrand was not claiming the city of Homs but rather the territory of the Buqayʿa more broadly, from the Gap of Homs to the Mediterranean. This would explain why William Jordan was said to hold the 'cities of Camolla' and not the *city* of Homs.[181]

Faced with Bertrand's overbearing demands, William Jordan chose to seek an unlikely alliance against this new arrival, rather than yield to his former lord. Thus, he requested help from Tancred, the same Norman prince of Antioch who had been at loggerheads with the Occitan crusaders ever since the First Crusade. William Jordan even agreed to serve Tancred as 'his knight' (*miles suus*) in return for assistance against Bertrand. Tancred enthusiastically accepted the offer, hoping to expand his principality still further and perhaps to annex Tripoli itself.[182] No doubt Tancred also held a personal grudge after Bertrand had tried to claim Antioch itself. Bertrand's presence posed a similar threat to Tancred as to William Jordan, permitting the two former rivals to discover a mutual enemy.

William Jordan apparently abandoned the Pilgrims' Mount to coordinate a joint attack with Tancred against Bertrand at Tortosa, although Bertrand managed to evade this by heading south – presumably by sea – to Tripoli. He immediately stole command of the siege from the absent William Jordan and sent an appeal for help to King Baldwin I of Jerusalem, promising his allegiance to the monarch just as his rival had offered his to Tancred.[183] This must have goaded Tancred in particular, since the prince of Antioch had suffered at the hands of the king of Jerusalem before, when Baldwin and his predecessor Godfrey had conspired years before to push Tancred out of his first lordship in the Latin East: the principality of Galilee in the kingdom of Jerusalem.[184] Factions were quickly forming as Bertrand's arrival threatened to cast the whole of the Latin East into civil war, little more than a decade after its birth.

The council of Tripoli (1109)

With open conflict between the Franks looming, King Baldwin intervened personally to settle what boiled down to a dispute over the inheritance of Raymond of Saint-Gilles. The king called a council to be held at the ongoing siege of Tripoli, ostensibly concerned to avoid a damaging conflict that would serve only to expose the embryonic Frankish settlements to Muslim attack. Baldwin also hoped to curtail Tancred of Antioch's growing power, since the king took the opportunity to condemn the prince for seizing land both in Tripoli via William Jordan and in the county of Edessa. The atmosphere outside Tripoli was tense, to say the least. Tancred had to restrain an enraged William Jordan from going forth to attack Bertrand, heedless of Baldwin's attempts at seeking a peaceful resolution. When Tancred and William Jordan did reach the council, they brought an estimated force of 700 cavalrymen. Baldwin matched them with 500 cavalrymen and at least another 500 footsoldiers brought from the south, not to mention the thousands of Occitan and Genoese crusaders led by Bertrand. Soon after, a large body of Edessan soldiers arrived to swell the number of combatants still further.[185] The Arab author Ibn al-Qalānisī was fairly well-informed about the dispute at the heart of the council, which suggests that this huge event made an impact even on the Franks' Muslim neighbours.[186] With these disparate Frankish factions gathered, the council must have seemed a tinderbox of loyalties and perceived injustices waiting for a spark.

In the end, the council succeeded in that open war was averted, but the precise details of the settlement reached at Tripoli are not entirely clear. According to Fulcher of Chartres, Bertrand's claim to the county was based on 'hereditary right' – despite William Jordan's earlier claims to the same. For his part, the count of Cerdanya now argued that he had earned the right to rule Tripoli because he had been trying to take it for so long.[187] This should not be dismissed as a weak or irrelevant notion, since right of conquest underpinned property ownership in other conquered regions in the Middle Ages, including England from 1066 right up to the early fourteenth century.[188] Indeed, the verdict at Tripoli proved fairly balanced, acknowledging that both claimants deserved satisfaction. Albert of Aachen wrote that Bertrand was to receive those lands occupied by his father upon his death, namely the Pilgrims' Mount and by extension Tripoli itself. Meanwhile, William Jordan was to receive those lands that he had conquered since Raymond's death, thus forming a lordship based around ʿArqa and extending eastwards towards Homs, Shayzar and Damascus.[189] Albert made no explicit mention of Tortosa's fate. It might have been thought that Tortosa would have gone to Bertrand on the basis that it had once belonged to his father, were it not for William of Tyre's later elaboration clarifying that this city was earmarked for William Jordan while Jubayl – another city absent from Albert's telling – was given to Bertrand.[190] The latter town was described by Caffaro as being 'of the district of Tripoli'.[191] It is William of Tyre's more comprehensive account that Richard accepted, as seems a reasonable judgement.[192] William went on to add that William Jordan and Bertrand were to hold their two lordships – effectively the northern and southern halves of what would become known as the county of Tripoli – as vassals of Tancred and Baldwin respectively.[193]

Asbridge describes the council of Tripoli as a disappointment for Tancred, who failed to secure Tripoli through his proxy, William Jordan.[194] This interpretation may be disputed, since Tancred's status as William Jordan's suzerain was at least now confirmed, giving him control over what had once been the *theme* of Tortosa – the southernmost district of the Byzantine *doukate* of Antioch prior to the Saljūq invasions and Alexios Komnenos's meddling in the Treaty of Devol. The very fact that Tortosa was granted to William Jordan and thus Tancred of Antioch, rather than to Bertrand and Baldwin of Jerusalem, indicates something very significant but hitherto ignored. The ruling reached at the council of Tripoli did not distribute Raymond of Saint-Gilles's inheritance according to the claims of his two self-professed heirs as much as it conformed to the same pre-Saljūq status quo that had divided the Levant into a northern and southern sphere – Byzantine and Fāṭimid respectively – half a century before the First Crusade. Almost exactly a decade after the first crusaders had met the Fāṭimid ambassadors at the old border of ʿArqa, this town once again came to mark a frontier, as the southernmost point of William Jordan's new lordship of ʿArqa-Tortosa and thus the principality of Antioch. In fact, the difference between the Byzantine–Fāṭimid border of the eleventh century and this new frontier was minor; the former had likely been at al-Nahr al-Kabīr al-Janūbī, north of ʿArqa, while the latter was marginally further south at Nahr al-ʿArqa, just south of ʿArqa itself. Was the resemblance between the Fāṭimid-Byzantine border of the mid-eleventh century and the settlement reached outside Tripoli in 1109 merely the product of coincidence or a conscious attempt at imitation on the part of the crusaders? This must be left to speculation. In either case, the bipartite division of the conquered territories as decided at Tripoli was set to influence the politics of the early Latin East for years to come.

The four crusader states?

It is worth taking a moment from the present narrative to consider the broader implications of the settlement at Tripoli in 1109 when attempting to understand the Latin East as a whole, specifically the internal borders between the so-called 'crusader states'. Surprisingly, modern historians have paid little attention to the formation of the crusader states in the years immediately after the First Crusade, tacitly trusting in William of Tyre's influential description of the Latin East's internal borders:

> The whole region of the Latins of the East was divided into four principalities. The first from the south was the kingdom of Jerusalem, having its beginning at the stream between Byblos (Jubayl) and Beirut – maritime cities of the province of Phoenicia – and its end in the desert beyond Daron towards Egypt. The second was the county of Tripoli towards the north, having its beginning at the aforesaid stream and its end at the stream between Maraclea (Maraqiyya) and Valania (Bāniyās), likewise maritime cities. The third was the principality of Antioch, which having its beginning from the same river extended right up to Tarsus of Cilicia towards the West. The fourth was the county of Edessa, which from the forest called *Marrith* extended east beyond the Euphrates.[195]

This quadripartite schema outlining four 'principalities' was repeated by later medieval historians, including Burchard of Mount Sion and Marino Sanudo, who clarified that the river between Jubayl and Beirut – the county of Tripoli's southern border – was specifically the 'Dog River' (*Nahr al-Kalb*) while the river between Maraqiyya and Valania – the county's northern limits – was the 'River of Valania' (*Nahr Bāniyās*).[196] As is clear, William's borders are primarily rivers, suggesting a conceptual linearity that challenges some of the conclusions emanating from the historiographical debate on medieval frontiers: specifically that no such political or national boundaries existed between medieval 'states'.[197] Despite the protestations of Ellenblum and others, it is clear from this passage that linear borders were relevant to William of Tyre on some level, otherwise he would not have bothered to record them at all.

Most historians have neglected the narrative context of the passage, seeking to use William's chronicle only as 'a quarry for historical information', disregarding its strengths and weaknesses as a structured and integrated whole.[198] William's aim in writing this specific passage was not to provide a definitive guide to the borders of the Latin East, which could be applied to the entire twelfth century, but to set the scene for one particular moment: intense competition between the great lords for the military support offered by the participants of the Second Crusade arriving in 1148.[199] There is no implication here that the borders of the Latin East had been set as such immediately after the First Crusade or that they had remained immutable since. After all, William was writing between *c.*1170 and 1184, so is hardly a reliable source for the earliest phase of Frankish settlement, decades earlier.[200]

Historians have made no real attempt to question *why* the Latin East should have been quadripartite in form or if it was always so. Little if any room is left for a gradual process of state-building following the First Crusade. Perhaps the most influential elaboration of William's four-state model is Grousset's; he saw the Latin East in rather colonialist terms as a microcosm of contemporary 'France', divided according to the origins of each crusader state's founders and early rulers. Jerusalem and Edessa are thus viewed as Lotharingian, Antioch as Norman and Tripoli as 'Provençal'.[201] Later historians have tended to confirm Grousset's model, with Richard in particular arguing that the county of Tripoli was only independent of its neighbours at Antioch and Jerusalem because of the distinctly 'Provençal' identity of its ruling dynasty and Frankish settlers.[202]

By trusting in William's framework, historiography has become compartmentalised. Most studies have been of individual 'crusader states' – principally the kingdom of Jerusalem – in almost complete isolation from one another.[203] Compartmentalisation and a bias towards Jerusalem have meant that even those historians who do acknowledge a gradual process of state formation nevertheless work towards William's quadripartite model as a teleological endpoint. Tibble's examination of the formative years of the kingdom of Jerusalem provides a pertinent case study. Tibble traces the attempts of the early kings of Jerusalem to intensify their authority over their vassals and would-be vassals, bringing them steadily into the fold of an increasingly integrated realm. He restricts his analysis to areas like the principality of Galilee over which this royal policy was ultimately successful: the kingdom of Jerusalem as later conceived by William of Tyre. He considers royal successes but not royal failures to integrate into the kingdom other regions, including the county of Tripoli.[204] Nor is Tibble alone in adopting this *a posteriori* approach. Mayer's various studies on the early development of the kingdom's lesser lordships are predicated upon the knowledge that these lordships would one day become part of the realm.[205] It could be said that Tibble and Mayer have studied an anachronistically conceived 'kingdom of Jerusalem in waiting', in much the same way that Bull accuses historians of medieval France of having focused too often on 'France in waiting' to the exclusion of sometime domains of the *rex Francorum* – such as Flanders and Catalonia – which were not later incorporated into modern France.[206]

This same sort of anachronistic approach can be discerned in studies focusing on the county of Tripoli. La Monte saw Tripoli as 'a fief of Jerusalem' occupying 'a position, legally as geographically, midway between the practically independent Antioch in the north and the fiefs south of the Nahr-el-Kalb, which were directly dependent upon the king of Jerusalem, such as Galilee, Jaffa and Montreal'.[207] Yet Mayer and Tibble have already shown that the latter were not always as firmly under royal authority as they would ultimately become, so this comparison is of limited use. Richard explicitly rejects La Monte's implication that contemporaries regarded Tripoli as part of the kingdom in any real sense. Instead, he sees the relationship between the king of Jerusalem and the count of Tripoli as one defined by 'vassalité limitée' – conceived more in personal than territorial terms – which in any case was quickly eroded by Tripoli's distinct southern Frenchness.[208] Fink takes a view directly opposite to Richard's, writing that 'the county of Tripoli remained a fief of the southern kingdom' and thus fully part of its history.[209] Despite their differences, these historians share the belief that the relationship between the county and the kingdom – whatever it might have been – was essentially unchanging from the Christian conquest of Tripoli in 1109 until Saladin's invasions in 1187–8, with the border set permanently at the location identified by William of Tyre – Nahr al-Kalb. Only Edbury has hinted at the possibility of constitutional change occurring at a relatively late point, observing that Tripoli 'had passed out of the king of Jerusalem's *mouvance* by the middle years of the twelfth century, and most people seem to have regarded it as totally independent'.[210]

To be sure, William of Tyre's framework does find corroboration in other sources, although only those that date from the late twelfth and thirteenth centuries. Ernoul stated unequivocally that 'neither the land of Tripoli nor that of Antioch is part of the kingdom'.[211] Arguably the most persuasive yet neglected evidence is a letter sent by ʿImād al-Dīn al-Iṣfahānī to the *dīwān* of Baghdad, recording Saladin's conquests in the late 1180s. ʿImād al-Dīn described the frontiers of the 'crusader states' – excluding long-lost Edessa – in a way highly reminiscent of William's description:

> Now delivered to us was all of the kingdom of Jerusalem, demarcated towards Egypt by al-ʿArīsh and in the direction of the *Ḥijāz* [western Arabia] by Karak and Shawbak. It comprises the coastal land up to the outermost districts of Beirut. Nothing remained of this kingdom except Tyre. Conquered also was all of the province of Antioch and all of its strongholds, which belonged to the Franks and Armenians, and it is demarcated from the remotest part of the land of Jabala and Latakia to the land of the son of Leon [Cilician Armenia under Leon II]. There remained Antioch alone and a few of its fortresses. There remained no land, of which the districts were not conquered and which was generally not overwhelmed in terms of what had been its situation, except Tripoli, for nothing was conquered of it except the city of Jubayl.[212]

This extract alone confirms that the 'crusader states' did exist as identifiable, conceptual and political units by the late twelfth century, recognised even by an author working in a very different linguistic and literary tradition.

There is, however, contradictory evidence. The thirteenth-century legalist John of Ibelin asserted that the county had been one of the four great baronies of the kingdom in the twelfth century on the basis that it – unlike the alternative candidate of Transjordan – possessed its own constable and marshal and owed the service of a full hundred knights to the crown.[213] Richard rejects John's claim on the basis that his work is a late authority, probably written *c.*1265.[214] It is certainly reasonable to dismiss John of Ibelin on the grounds of his late context, writing long after the events of 1187 when much of the kingdom had been conquered and the county had been integrated dynastically with the principality of Antioch. Edbury suggests that John of Ibelin only included the county as one of the baronies in order to denigrate his thirteenth-century rival Philip of Montfort, lord of militarily weak Transjordan, and to flatter his ally, Bohemond III of Tripoli (= Bohemond VI of Antioch).[215] Yet if John is to be set aside for his late context, then so too should Ernoul and his contrary assertion that Tripoli was not part of the realm. Although a small part was apparently written around the end of the 1180s, the Chronicle of Ernoul in its surviving form cannot date any earlier than 1227 or 1231. With both of these texts post-dating the foundation of the crusader states by roughly a century, both must be discarded as reliable indicators of the formative period of the early Latin East.

The bipartite Latin East

In fact, a handful of sources from the formative period of the Latin East do survive, offering a remarkably divergent picture. The settlement reached at the council of Tripoli in 1109 is one such example, partitioning the Latin East into two. Crucially, corroboration of this bipartition of the Latin East – split somewhere between Tripoli and Tortosa – can be found in various parallel texts. Most striking is a document claiming to record a decision made by Bishop Adhémar of Le Puy, papal legate on the First Crusade and close ally of his fellow Occitan magnate, Raymond of Saint-Gilles. Allegedly, the legate had enacted a division of the territory to be conquered by the crusaders sometime 'after the capture of Antioch' in December 1097 and before the legate's death in August 1098.[216] Hagenmeyer attempted to date the text more precisely to one of three *concilia* held by the crusader princes and clergy at Antioch around this time, specifically the one on 3 July 1098.[217] The decree now exists only in one of the four surviving copies of the cartulary of the canons of the Holy Sepulchre, probably copied *c.*1230–9 (during the Christian reoccupation of Jerusalem) from a lost twelfth-century version composed before Saladin's conquest in 1187:[218]

> After the capture of Antioch, the bishop of Le Puy and legate of the Apostolic See, making use of the nobility in a wise council, set the limit for the kingdom of Jerusalem and the principality of Antioch at the

> river that flows between Tripoli and Tortosa, decreeing that Jerusalem would possess by perpetual right all the land from the southern part right up to the river and Antioch would equally obtain that which lies on the other side of the river.[219]

As with William of Tyre's borders, the identity of the river in this passage is unclear. It could be Nahr Abū Mūsā or, as Röhricht suggested, Nahr al-ʿArqa (the crusaders' Albana).[220] Indeed, an anonymous author in the mid-twelfth century, known as Pseudo-Fretellus, indicated the latter as the northern border of the kingdom of Jerusalem according to a similarly bipartite conception of the Latin East.[221] This identification by Pseudo-Fretellus seems to recall – perhaps unwittingly – the council of Tripoli, which took the decision to set the border between the domains of William Jordan and Bertrand somewhere between ʿArqa and Tripoli, in the rough vicinity of Nahr al-ʿArqa. This in turn raises the possibility that a plan to re-impose a bipartite political order on the Levant, inspired by the eleventh-century precedent and contemporary ambitions of the Byzantines and Fāṭimids, was current among the crusaders from the days of Adhémar of Le Puy and the First Crusade right up to the council of Tripoli in 1109. After all, Adhémar, more than most crusaders, had been attuned to Byzantine strategic goals for re-establishing imperial rule in North Syria, which he had hoped to achieve – in co-operation with the Byzantines themselves – right up until his death.[222] It is conceivable then that he could have at least inspired the decree attributed to him.

Most pertinent here is the fact that the county of Tripoli, as outlined in William of Tyre's quadripartite description of the Latin East, simply does not exist in the bipartite division of territory indicated in the supposed 'Adhémar decree' and hinted at some years later by Pseudo-Fretellus. What would become the county's northern half is placed in the principality of Antioch and its southern half, including the city of Tripoli itself, in the kingdom of Jerusalem. Equally significant to observe is that the earliest crusader-settlers actually attempted to make this theoretical partition of conquered land a reality. As early as 1100, Godfrey of Bouillon had claimed Tripoli for his fledgling Jerusalemite domain by offering the Venetians half of the spoils of the city if they assisted him in conquering it, even before Raymond of Saint-Gilles had initiated his siege at the Pilgrims' Mount.[223] This particular element of Godfrey's plans did not come to fruition but his intent to take Tripoli for his own realm was clear. Indeed, it could be argued that the contentious partition of territory proposed by King Baldwin I at the council of Tripoli in 1109 indicated a deliberate return to a royal policy of territorial division, including Jerusalemite dominance over Tripoli specifically, which had been first articulated a decade before and pursued unsuccessfully by Godfrey of Bouillon.

The precise division at Nahr al-ʿArqa was proposed at Tripoli in 1109 yet never realised, due to a tragedy that struck one of the key players when William Jordan died in suspicious circumstances soon after the council. The sources do not agree on the culprit. Albert of Aachen and Caffaro identified the guilty party as William's squire.[224] Fulcher of Chartres claimed that the murderer was unknown but that the death polarised opinion among the Latins.[225] Ibn al-Qalānisī blamed an anonymous Frank, whom William Jordan was inexplicably intending to attack in a field near ʿArqa.[226] Decades later, William of Tyre felt bold enough to make the obvious connection to Bertrand, albeit with the prudent disclaimer that this was an unsubstantiated rumour.[227] Whoever the culprit was, Bertrand certainly benefited. It might have been expected that all of William Jordan's possessions would have reverted to his lord Tancred, but Albert of Aachen wrote that it was Bertrand who received 'Arqa and the rest of William's conquests.[228] On at least one occasion, Bertrand was too enthusiastic in securing William Jordan's former possessions, since he was later obliged to restore some property, which the count of Cerdanya had previously given to the canons of the Holy Sepulchre; Bertrand's restoration was done for the benefit of William Jordan's conveniently departed soul.[229]

Whatever befell William Jordan, the aftermath of his death did not abrogate the plan for a bipartite Latin East completely, but simply modified it. Although he took ʿArqa, Bertrand did not seize anything north of al-Nahr al-Kabīr al-Janūbī. This was primarily because Tancred himself moved quickly to occupy Tortosa immediately after William Jordan's death.[230] Asbridge describes this action as an attempt to establish a 'buffer zone against the county of Tripoli', yet it may be more appropriate to describe it as an action aimed against the kingdom of Jerusalem – including the city of Tripoli – rather than the county *per se*.[231] Around the same time, Tancred forced the rulers of Shayzar to pay him tribute and seized Ḥiṣn al-Akrād – later corrupted into Latin as *Crat* or, more famously, French *Crac des Chevaliers* – again north of al-Nahr al-Kabīr al-Janūbī.[232] Raymond of Saint-Gilles had reconnoitred this fort during the First Crusade, with the result that Ṭughtakīn of Damascus had agreed that its residents would henceforth pay tribute to the Franks. This had not been enough for Raymond, who had attacked it *c.*1102/3 (AH 496) but had been unable to take it before he was distracted by the opportunity presented at Homs by the murder of its governor, Janāḥ al-Dawla. According to Ibn ʿAsākir and the derivative Ibn al-Furāt, the Muslim commander at Ḥiṣn al-Akrād ultimately chose to surrender to Tancred voluntarily because he preferred him to Raymond's son Bertrand, who was then away besieging Beirut with King Baldwin.[233] Indeed, there is evidence that Tancred was much more inclined to tolerate Muslim client rulers, than were some of his fellow crusaders.[234] For example, he offered to allow Fakhr al-Mulk bin ʿAmmār to hold 'Jubayl' (corr. 'Jabala') as an Antiochene 'fief' (*al-iqṭāʿ*), shortly after the latter's eviction from Tripoli – a gift refused by the proud *qāḍī* in favour of exile in Muslim lands.[235]

Historians have failed to realise that a two-state view of the early Latin East existed in the minds of contemporaries, partly because those few who have noted the curious Adhémar decree at all have tended to doubt its provenance and value. A rare exception is Röhricht, who briefly mentioned this text and mounted no challenge to its veracity, but also failed to offer any explanation for why the internal borders of the crusader states evidently shifted at some later point to the configuration given by William of Tyre.[236] Hagenmeyer assumed that the decree as it survives must have been adapted or composed wholesale at a later date, for the simple reason that mention is made of the 'kingdom' (*regnum*) of Jerusalem, which had yet to be established upon Adhémar's death.[237]

Cahen advanced the most sophisticated theory on this point, believing that the decree in its entirety was probably a later forgery. He suggests that it was written for the use of Patriarch Bernard of Antioch, who hoped to justify to Pope Paschal II at the council of Benevento in February 1113 the extension of the Antiochene patriarchate as far south as Tortosa, which had been incorporated into the principality of Antioch through Tancred's actions after the council of Tripoli.[238] This places the text into the context of the long-running controversy over ecclesiastical borders in the Latin East, revolving around the particular question of the archbishopric of Tyre's ecclesiastical loyalties. Although Tyre had been part of the patriarchate of Antioch in the former Byzantine tradition, the papacy took the decision in the early twelfth century to bind the ecclesiastical boundaries to the *de facto* political boundaries established by the Franks after the First Crusade. The outcome was that the province of Tyre was henceforth bisected, with its southern dioceses in the kingdom of Jerusalem – Acre, Sidon, Beirut and Tyre itself – realigned under the patriarchate of Jerusalem and its northern dioceses in what would become the county of Tripoli – Tortosa, Jubayl and Tripoli – rendered direct dependents upon the patriarch of Antioch. Clergymen on both sides contested this awkward reality throughout the twelfth century, agreeing that the archdiocese of Tyre should be reunited into one integral whole, but differing on its patriarchal allegiance. A definitive and lasting resolution was never achieved, it proving impossible to satisfy both sides.[239]

Negotiations over the borders of the Church were drawn out and disputed fiercely by both ecclesiastical and secular rulers. Most relevant to Cahen's argument is that the supposed 'Adhémar decree' in its only surviving form is accompanied by Pope Paschal's decree at Benevento, clarifying the papacy's position in response to a delegation from the prince and patriarch of Antioch.

> Whilst Pope Paschal was celebrating a council at Benevento, envoys were sent across from the patriarch and prince [Roger][240] of Antioch, who in the same council demanded that the rights of the church of Antioch be restored. To these he gave a response of this sort: 'We are not accustomed to answer quickly regarding the management of churches,

> but to your petition, because of the length you have come and the long road by which you expect to return, we ought not to delay in being prepared to respond. Venerable Pope Urban, of holy memory, when he celebrated a council for a most crowded congregation in Clermont and encouraged the road to Jerusalem, is remembered and known to have decreed that whichever princes could conquer provinces or cities, once the rituals of the Gentiles had been eliminated, the restored churches would extend to (the limits of) their rule.'[241]

In short, military conquest defined the Church's borders. If Cahen was right to link the Adhémar decree with Benevento, then there would be only a narrow timeframe in which the text could have been written, between 1109 and 1113.

Beguiling as Cahen's theory is, questions remain. Although he clearly believed the text to be no more than a reflection of Antiochene pleading at Benevento, he did not consider or explain why this supposed forgery actually advocated a reduction in the extent of the patriarchate of Antioch, by pushing the border north of Tripoli itself. After all, Patriarch Bernard of Antioch had already subordinated Bishop Albert of Tripoli to himself, *c.*1104. He or his successor would later appoint a suffragan bishop to southerly Jubayl between *c.*1128 and 1138, and their successors would continue to lay claim to the entirety of the traditional archdiocese of Tyre – including dioceses south of Jubayl in the kingdom of Jerusalem properly – steadily into the 1130s, and even as late as the 1190s.[242] The Adhémar decree describes a border that matches neither the theoretical ambitions of the patriarch of Antioch at the time, nor the actual network of suffragan bishops he was actively working to establish south of Tortosa. It is also a mystery why a division that allegedly supported Antiochene claims and was supposedly irrelevant within a few short years of Benevento should have ended up in a thirteenth-century copy of the cartulary of the canons of the Holy Sepulchre, close associates of the patriarch of Jerusalem.[243]

Moreover, if the Adhémar decree truly is a forgery to justify Antioch's acquisition of Tortosa after the council of Tripoli, then it is curious that Pope Paschal's ruling at Benevento lacks any special reference to this city. In none of his extant letters on the same subject did the pope give any indication that he knew where the patriarchal borders of Antioch and Jerusalem actually were.[244] Indeed, neither the record of Benevento nor the various papal letters mention any city in the county of Tripoli and like Adhémar's decree omit the county's very existence. The whole debate surrounding Paschal's bull was predicated upon the assumption that the state-patriarchates of Jerusalem and Antioch shared a disputed border but a border nonetheless – something flatly contradicting William of Tyre's later conception, in which they are separated from one another by the intervening county of Tripoli. The broader implication is that Tripoli and the future county's other settlements were viewed either as part of the patriarchate and kingdom of Jerusalem or as part of the patriarchate and principality of Antioch, not something separate.

At the very least, Cahen's theory may explain why Adhémar's supposed decree recorded the border between the kingdom and principality according to the *de facto* frontier established after the council of Tripoli. It may also be reasonable to posit that Adhémar of Le Puy did not really write the decree attributed to him, which may indeed be a forgery written at some point after the establishment of the *regnum* of Jerusalem and perhaps even after the council of Tripoli. The main weakness with Cahen's argument in this respect is that he did not have in mind King Baldwin's actual ruling at the council of Tripoli, which placed the border around Nahr al-ʿArqa, but rather its untidy implementation, when opportunistic manoeuvring on the part of the rivals Bertrand and Tancred after William Jordan's death had pushed the division of the Latin East to al-Nahr al-Kabīr al-Janūbī. Cahen's objections do not explain why the council of Tripoli should have set the border in the region between Tortosa and Tripoli in the first place. As already seen, Albert of Aachen's legalistic argument that Bertrand simply inherited his father's former lands does not make sense in light of William of Tyre's claim that Tortosa – once held by Raymond of Saint-Gilles – went to William Jordan. This conundrum can only be solved if one assumes that the delegates at the council of Tripoli had in mind the Byzantine–Fāṭimid precedent of the mid-eleventh century. Doubts over the Adhémar decree itself do not preclude the possibility that it and the council of Tripoli reflected this older precedent.

Thanks to Bertrand's promise to become King Baldwin's man in 1109, the county of Tripoli would for the time being exist only as the northernmost fief of Jerusalem. Moreover, it was to have a territorial extent much reduced from what later historians in the vein of William of Tyre would recognise, deprived as it was of the lands north of al-Nahr al-Kabīr al-Janūbī, including Tortosa and Ḥiṣn al-Akrād seized by Tancred. The emergence of the county of Tripoli and the Latin East as modern historians know them would have to wait at least another decade.[245]

The fall of Tripoli and its aftermath

The resolution of the brewing conflict over Raymond of Saint-Gilles's Syrian legacy, thanks as much to King Baldwin's proactive intervention as to William Jordan's suspicious death, permitted a concerted Frankish assault on Tripoli. The council of Tripoli, as well as offering a solution to a serious dispute, conveniently brought together a substantial proportion of the total forces available to the Latin East – from Jerusalem, Antioch and Edessa – to conclude this lengthy siege, alongside those crusaders who had previously fought under the late William Jordan and also those who had only recently arrived with Bertrand. Most important was the strong Italian showing in this joint force. Bertrand's Genoese and Pisan fleet finally allowed the hitherto-impregnable maritime city to be stormed effectively 'by land and by sea'.[246] Albert of Aachen, Fulcher of Chartres and William of Tyre all reported that the beleaguered inhabitants of Tripoli surrendered the city peacefully, fearful of the coalescence of disparate Christian factions and particularly the Pisans and Genoese. With the surrender accepted, the Christian army subsequently entered and garrisoned the city, occupying it thoroughly.[247]

Despite its evident importance, the dating of Tripoli's capture is unclear and Albert of Aachen failed to give a precise date at all. Arabic authors mostly agreed on 12 July (11 Dhū al-Ḥijja).[248] Fulcher of Chartres dated the fall to 26 June 1109, but did so through a poetic allusion too obscure even for William of Tyre, who erroneously dated the event to 10 June.[249] In support of Fulcher, however, there is a document issued by Count Bertrand, apparently after the conquest, in which he granted land in Tripoli to the Genoese out of gratitude for their assistance. The document was given on the sixth day before the Kalends of July – that is, 26 June.[250]

The indigenous population of Tripoli suffered somewhat in the immediate aftermath of the crusader conquest. Ibn al-Qalānisī recorded how, upon the capture of the city in 1109, the Franks acquired the books of Tripoli's 'House of Learning' (*dār ʿilm-hā*) and private libraries, with a later tradition claiming that they were destroyed.[251] No Latin source records the theft or destruction of Tripoli's books, but the suspicion and contempt reserved for Arabic texts is evident in Albert of Aachen's vitriolic description of books at Antioch a decade previously. 'Countless codices' were found after the rout of Kurbughā in 1098 but were dismissed entirely and destroyed because they supposedly contained 'the sacrilegious rites of the Saracens, Turks and other peoples and also the abominable songs of seers and soothsayers, written with accursed characters'.[252]

The crusader conquest had a specifically human impact upon Tripoli's intellectual life. Following the city's fall and the destruction of its once-prestigious House of Learning, most of the Arabic intelligentsia – the *ʿulamāʾ* – were displaced. Many can be found subsequently as refugees in the service of neighbouring Muslim rulers. Ibn al-Khayyāṭ was a poet who had served the Muslim rulers of Tripoli and who went on to write some of the earliest and fiercest anti-Frankish, pro-*jihād* poetry in Damascus, perhaps drawing on his personal experiences of Frankish cruelty during Tripoli's long siege.[253] Another notable poet was Ibn Munīr al-Ṭarābulusī ('the Tripolitan'), a Shīʿite who was born in Tripoli in 1080–1 (AH 473) and spent his early years there before achieving fame for his fine verses and infamy for his controversial lifestyle in Damascus and Aleppo, dying *c.*1152 (AH *c.*547).[254] A further refugee was 'an elderly man of the people of Tripoli' (*shaykh min ahl ṭarābulus*) who developed ingenious incendiary devices at the siege of Tyre in 1111, two years after the capture of his hometown.[255]

The household of the Munqidh family at Shayzar provided refuge to some of the exiled Tripolitan *litterati* in the early twelfth century.

The scandalous poet Ibn Munīr al-Ṭarābulusī once stayed at Shayzar as a guest of the Munqidhids.[256] Around the same time, the family employed at least two further Tripolitan intellectuals: an esteemed grammarian by the name of Abū ʿAbd Allāh al-Ṭulayṭulī ('of Toledo'?) – formerly the director of Tripoli's destroyed House of Learning – who went on to tutor the famous Usāma bin Munqidh, and an accomplished copyist by the name of Yānis who produced two complete copies of the Qurān for Usāma's father.[257] Fakhr al-Mulk bin ʿAmmār, former Islamic *qāḍī* of Tripoli, had sought refuge and been warmly received in Shayzar for a brief time after his own forced departure from his home, perhaps remembering how his brother had hosted ʿAlī bin Munqidh (d. 475/1082–3) in Tripoli many years before.[258] The other Tripolitan scholars may have followed Ibn ʿAmmār, as he had undoubtedly patronised *ʿulamāʾ* in the past, but upon their arrival at Shayzar had found the Munqidhid emir to be a suitably generous, not to mention more secure alternative to the exiled *qāḍī*, who soon headed to Damascus. In short, the case of Tripoli demonstrates well the truth of Kedar's conclusion that the arrival of the Franks resulted in 'the disappearance of [the Islamic] intellectual elite' from the areas they conquered, leaving only a parochial 'secondary elite' of village *shaykhs* and *imāms* to cater to the local Muslims' spiritual needs.[259]

Despite the great tragedy that had befallen the Shīʿa of Tripoli, caution should be exercised when assuming that the crusader conquest marked a complete break with the past, at least in terms of demographics. The inhabitants of Tripoli were apparently not massacred en masse by the crusaders in 1109. It is thought that such an infamously cruel policy was implemented in other cities captured around this time, especially Jerusalem, although there is an ongoing debate between modern historians as to whether or not the First Crusade stimulated atrocities that went beyond the routine slaughters expected and commonly encountered in medieval warfare.[260] Later Arab and Latin chroniclers certainly believed that the residents of at least one of the cities in the county of Tripoli had fallen victim to a massacre, namely Tortosa, where the Muslims were systematically slaughtered or else enslaved.[261] Mayer thinks that Tripoli's population fell victim to a similar tragedy, although there is no reliable evidence to support this.[262] Albert of Aachen described how Fāṭimid reinforcements were caught hiding in an underground shelter and subsequently executed by King Baldwin, after a local Muslim woman divulged the location of these soldiers to some Frankish thugs who were torturing her in the hope of seizing her riches.[263] Of course, these hidden soldiers were foreign military personnel, not natives of the city, and Albert's strange story was probably no more than a garbled retelling of the arrival of a Fāṭimid fleet eight days too late to save Tripoli.[264] Indeed, the tortured woman received back all of her stolen possessions and buildings, which itself suggests some tolerance of Muslims owning property in the city.[265] The only reliable contemporary to claim that there was a massacre of the populace was Fulcher of

Chartres, who reported how the unruly 'minores Ianuensium' instigated a small-scale slaughter against the wishes of the commanders.[266] It seems unlikely that Fulcher's accidental, Genoese-led slaughter was on the same scale witnessed wherever the policy was deliberately implemented by the commanders.

Not even hostile Muslim contemporaries reported a massacre at Tripoli, although they did claim that the city and its people were captured and enslaved 'by the sword' (*bi-al-sayf*).[267] Ibn al-Athīr did report a systematic massacre of the rural population in the vicinity of Tripoli, albeit not one conducted by the invading Franks, but by the besieged *qāḍī* Fakhr al-Mulk bin ʿAmmār, who had hoped to depopulate the countryside and thus starve out the besieging crusaders.[268] Abū al-Fidāʾ and Sibṭ bin al-Jawzī claimed that the crusaders did kill (*qatalū*) as well as enslave the residents upon the city's capture, as did Matthew of Edessa within three decades of the event and an anonymous Syriac chronicler over a century afterwards, but these generally late sources are often derivative, laced with obvious embellishments, internal contradictions and factual inaccuracies.[269]

The comparatively peaceful takeover makes it likely, then, that the population of Tripoli was largely unaffected by the crusader conquest. Supposedly some of the poorer residents (*al-fuqarāʾ*) of Tripoli left the city during the siege, although the richer ones remained and even the poor could have returned after the surrender.[270] A striking testament to the number of indigenous people who chose to continue living in Tripoli under Frankish rule is the fact that James of Vitry, French-born bishop of Acre in the early thirteenth century, was forced to hire a translator when he visited Tripoli in 1221 because the main language spoken there remained Arabic (*lingua sarracena*) after more than a century of Latin rule.[271]

Of course, this is not to say that the Muslims of Tripoli enjoyed religious freedom after the crusader conquest. A generation before the First Crusade, in 1047, the Persian Nāṣir Khusraw claimed that his fellow Shīʿite Muslims made up the entire population of Tripoli.[272] William of Tyre recorded that, following the fall of Tripoli in 1109, the Franks offered these Muslims a choice: to depart in peace without their properties and possessions, or to retain them under Christian rule 'under a fixed payment, paid to the lord count annually'.[273] This is surely an example of the widely attested Frankish practice of inverting the customary *jizya* poll tax levied by Islamic governments on non-Muslim monotheists, Christians included.[274] A few decades later, Ibn Jubayr used the exact term *jizya* when noting with disdain how the Muslims near Tibnīn in the kingdom of Jerusalem were obliged to pay the poll tax.[275] In the kingdom of Sicily, the *jizya* was levied on Muslims and Jews and was again referred to by its Arabic term, even in official documents produced by the Christian government.[276] Evidently this inverted *jizya* was not a significant enough burden to force all of Tripoli's Muslims to leave their homes, if many did at all. Wilbrand of Oldenburg indicated in 1212 – after approximately 100 years of Christian rule – that Tripoli 'had very many inhabitants, Christian, Jewish and Saracen'.[277]

The *jizya* was not the only insult suffered by the Muslims of Tripoli. It was common throughout the Latin East for Islamic religious buildings to be refitted for Christian use as a triumphalist sign of Christianity's victory, and vice versa.[278] Bahā' al-Dīn reported that Saladin's first act after reconquering Jerusalem in 1187 was to remove the huge cross placed on the Dome of the Rock back when the city had been conquered by the Christians in 1099.[279] Tripoli was no exception to the process of post-conquest Christianisation, as demonstrated by the chapel of the Holy Sepulchre at the Pilgrims' Mount, built on the site of a former mosque.[280] The city's great Friday mosque was apparently converted into a Latin cathedral, dedicated to the Virgin Mary.[281] This may well be identical with the suitably grand 'king's mosque' (*regis bafumaria*) mentioned in a Latin document dated 26 June 1109, a matter of days after the Frankish conquest.[282] The cathedral was later rebuilt entirely in the European Romanesque style typical of the twelfth century, as is evident from the surviving *spolia* reused in a mosque built on the site much later by the Mamluk Sultan Khalīl (r.1290–3).[283]

Jubayl, Genoa and Islam

To the south of Tripoli lay the future county's third episcopal city, Jubayl. This was known to the crusaders by the Semitic loanword *Gibelet* or by the Ancient Greek toponym *Byblos*, by which it appears in the Old Testament.[284] The date of the Christian conquest is uncertain, occurring within either a few weeks or a few years of the fall of Tripoli in June 1109. The chronology of Jubayl's capture is muddled primarily by the fact that both Latin and Arab authors confused this city with northerly Jabala, which was later incorporated into the principality of Antioch.[285] William of Tyre and Ibn al-Qalānisī claimed that Jubayl was conquered around the same time that Tripoli was captured. According to these authorities, the Genoese sailors took Jubayl during a lull in the siege of Tripoli, with Ibn al-Qalānisī adding that the town's Muslim inhabitants were subsequently mistreated and deprived of their possessions.[286]

Against these sources, Albert of Aachen claimed that Raymond of Saint-Gilles, who had been resident in Tortosa at the time, had requested the aid of a large Genoese and Pisan fleet in conquering Jubayl (*Gibeloth*) as early as March 1104. These Italians had sailed east as pilgrims to Jerusalem – some years prior to the Italian fleet that had sailed with Count Bertrand in 1108 – and had wintered at Raymond's former base of Latakia. Raymond had then suggested that they go to Jubayl to exterminate the local Muslims and replace them with Christians. The Italians agreed and proceeded to attack the city by sea, while Raymond blockaded it by land. Albert implied that little time passed before the city fell. The city and its citizens were then 'handed over and subjugated into the hands of Raymond'.[287] Al-ʿAẓīmī also claimed that the Franks took the town 'by truce' (*bi-l-amān*) around the same time, in 1103/4 (AH 497).[288] One man who might be expected to have known the exact date was the Genoese Caffaro, who implied that the city fell in 1104. Raymond of Saint-Gilles had allegedly given a third of Jubayl to the Genoese out of gratitude, while retaining two-thirds for himself.[289]

Ibn al-Athīr similarly placed the event in 1103/4 (AH 497), noting that the Franks seized Muslim property in the city through torture and other punitive measures.[290] His sources clearly confused him, as he wrote later that Tancred of Antioch did not capture Jubayl until immediately after the conquest of Tripoli in 1109. His tangled account nevertheless helps to clarify the situation, as he also claimed that Tancred drove Fakhr al-Mulk bin ʿAmmār, exiled lord of Tripoli, out of Jubayl at this time.[291] Yet he had previously claimed that Ibn ʿAmmār, having found himself evicted from Tripoli by the pro-Fāṭimid revolt that had occurred during his diplomatic mission to Sunnī lands, had subsequently set himself up in his second city, Jabala.[292] In other words, if Tancred did not drive Fakhr al-Mulk out of Jabala until 1109, then it is marginally more likely that Jubayl was the city that fell in 1104.[293]

This assessment is far from certain and it is entirely possible that both Jabala and Jubayl were unstable during these first few years, changing hands regularly. After all, Anna Komnene claimed that the Byzantine military seized Jabala as early as 1100, but this city had presumably been reacquired by the Muslims generally and Fakhr al-Mulk specifically by 1109.[294] Moreover, one gets the impression when reading the contemporary accounts that the definition of a conquest could stretch from wholesale occupation to the mere payment of tribute. In other words, the sources may not present inaccurate and contradictory evidence as much as they offer *incomplete* accounts of the shifting alliances and land exchanges of this turbulent period.

Jubayl's significance within the county of Tripoli was that it became Genoa's principal colony in the Latin East in the twelfth century. Despite the fact that the Genoese crusaders were allied with Raymond of Saint-Gilles and his son Bertrand, they evidently regarded Jubayl as belonging to the commune of Genoa itself. According to Caffaro, Count Bertrand was so grateful to the Genoese for their assistance in conquering Tripoli that he gave them an entire third of this city, together with the two-thirds of Jubayl originally retained by his father in 1104. For reasons unclear, Bertrand soon reneged upon this generous offer and ejected the Genoese from his new capital. Fortunately for the Genoese, they now held the entirety of Jubayl and apparently refused to concede any authority there to Bertrand. Henceforth the Genoese placed the town in the care of their representatives, namely the crusaders Hugh Embriaco and Ansaldo Corso. Although Ansaldo held the original one-third of Jubayl granted by Raymond of

Saint-Gilles in 1104 and continued to do so for some indeterminate length of time after 1109, it was Hugh who was to enjoy the lion's share of Jubayl, receiving the two-thirds that had previously belonged to the late count and had been conceded by Bertrand in his short-lived burst of largesse.[295] In the long term it was also Hugh whose family was to settle there, becoming and remaining Jubayl's local Frankish seigneurial dynasty until the thirteenth century.

From 1109, then, the commune of Genoa and its Syrian representatives enjoyed exclusive control over the entirety of Jubayl and thus collected its revenues wholesale, which made it distinctly more profitable than the comparatively restricted Genoese quarters in cities such as Acre.[296] This should not be underestimated. Jubayl was one of the county's leading ports, second only to Tripoli itself. Indeed, Marino Sanudo reported that 'the port of Jubayl had a chain'.[297] Although such devices were used in harbours across the Mediterranean to control ships' access and egress for the sake of both security and taxation, this is the only definite reference to one having been used in the county of Tripoli. This chain alone implies regular, profitable taxation. As far as politics are concerned, it would appear that Jubayl remained effectively independent of the rest of the county of Tripoli until the mid-twelfth century.[298] This observation, like the realisation that many crusaders anticipated a bipartite rather than quadripartite Latin East, challenges historians' traditional understanding of the shape and limit of the county of Tripoli at this early stage.

Concerning the fate of Jubayl's Muslim inhabitants, it seems that they suffered at least as much as their co-religionists in Tripoli did. If anything, the stories of torture, plunder and extermination in Jubayl suggest a worse fate still. Although the Latins guaranteed the safety of the Muslim citizens of Jubayl upon the city's conquest, Ibn al-Qalānisī wrote that they subsequently mistreated the inhabitants and seized their property.[299] Those who chose or were able to stay saw their religious freedoms curtailed. Just as mosques were converted into churches, public ceremonial in the county – as throughout the Latin East – ceased to be Islamic and became Christian. Jubayl offers a particularly striking demonstration of this. According to ʿImād al-Dīn, the eventual return of Muslim rule to Jubayl on 4 August 1187 (27 Jumādā I AH 583) was accompanied by widespread rejoicing among the Muslim populace, largely because Islam could be celebrated in public once again. Through poetry, this author juxtaposed the welcome return of Islamic rectitude with the equally satisfactory expulsion of perceived Christian corruption:

> Most of the people of Sidon, Beirut and Jubayl were earnest Muslims, surrendered to habitation with the Franks, but then they experienced honour after humiliation and surpassed abundance after scarcity; the good news proved true and the pulpits sang; the shame of the churches was purified and the assembly of Fridays was proclaimed publicly;

> the Qurān was recited and Satan was enraged; the (church) bells fell silent and the (Christian) laws became void; the Muslims elevated their own leaders and discovered their souls.[300]

The right to pray openly and loudly figures prominently in ʿImād al-Dīn's poetry. Kedar observes that it would not be until the Council of Vienne (1311–12) that the Latin Church would formally forbid the *adhān*, the Muslim call to prayer, in Christian territories.[301] More generally, he argues that Islam was not universally supressed throughout the Latin East.[302] Nevertheless, it would appear that the local authorities in Jubayl at least did choose to suppress this and other open expressions of Islam.

Also clear from ʿImād al-Dīn's poem is that the Christians not only repressed the public celebration of Islam, but replaced it with Christianity. His particular mention of bells is an under-appreciated dynamic of Christian rule over Muslims during the crusader period. Ever since the so-called Covenant of ʿUmar in the earliest period of Islamic history, Muslim authorities had prohibited the loud and public use of bells and *semantra* by Christian *dhimmīs* lest they drown out the *adhān*, which sent the unambiguous message that Islam was to be the dominant religion.[303] James of Vitry made special note of the use of the Maronites' use of percussive wooden *semantra* in lieu of bells, which were presumably quieter and more tolerable to Muslims.[304] ʿImād al-Dīn's account of how bells replaced the *adhān* in Jubayl, only for the situation to be reversed again in the 1180s, shows that Muslims under crusader rule were aggrieved at what bells represented: an inversion of the traditional Islamic socio-religious hierarchy, an aural accompaniment to the inverted fiscal *jizya*.

Jubayl was not the only town at this time where bells or their absence were a key expression of the supremacy of one religion over another. Archaeological evidence attests to the fact that the Franks introduced bells elsewhere. Copper carillon bells from the Frankish period were discovered in 1906 at Bethlehem, together with organ pipes.[305] Part of the bell-tower of the cathedral of Tripoli survives, incorporated into the Mamluk Grand Mosque's minaret, while the former Cistercian monastery of Belmont has the only fully surviving Frankish bell-tower in the former Latin East, dating to the second half of the twelfth century or the mid-thirteenth.[306] It is very likely that other extant churches, such as that of Enfeh (Nephin), possessed bell-towers in the Frankish period.[307]

Although the suppression of Islam seemed a cruel injustice to local Muslims, it should be noted that other indigenous groups welcomed the crusaders' promotion of Christianity. The early modern Maronite Christian patriarch, Isṭifān al-Duwayhī (1630–1704), claimed that the Christians of Mount Lebanon had been confident enough under crusader rule to replace their wooden *semantra* with 'bells of copper' (*ajrās min nuḥās*) as early as 1112.[308] Centuries before, the Melkite deacon

Sulaymān al-Ashlūḥī had written a poetic lament for the fall of Tripoli to the Mamluks in 1289, an event through which he had seemingly lived. Sulaymān's poem takes the reader on a tour of the abandoned, crumbling edifices of the crusaders' Tripoli of old, which could still be seen on the shoreline after the Mamluks had abandoned it in favour of 'new' Tripoli.[309] Sulaymān recalled a lost time when these evocative ruins were alive with public Christian ceremonial, complete with readings from Scripture, elaborate sung liturgies and the billowing fragrance of censers.[310] This poem survived in a Maronite manuscript composed two centuries removed from the Mamluk conquest of Tripoli, attesting to the enduring and pan-Christian appeal of such nostalgic longing for a time when Christians ruled the area. Sulaymān's verses mourning the Muslims' repression of Christianity in Tripoli are ironically reminiscent of ʿImād al-Dīn's earlier joy that Islam had finally been restored to Jubayl after a period of Christian oppression.

The Christian sources, like their Islamic equivalents, may be doubted for their evident polemical quality. Certainly al-Duwayhī, like other Maronite clerics in the seventeenth century, was writing to argue that the Maronites had always been faithful and orthodox allies of the Roman Church – in terms of practice as well as doctrine – at a time when he and other Maronite leaders had a particular interest in allying with Catholic Europeans – especially the French – against the Ottoman Turks.[311] Indeed, James of Vitry noted as late as the thirteenth century that the use of *semantra* remained one of the regrettable signs that the Maronites had not abandoned certain superficial eastern practices and were thus not wholly united with the Roman Church.[312] Nevertheless, archaeological and art historical evidence does suggest that Frankish rule played a part in liberating local Christians from some of the more restrictive consequences of Islamic government. In particular, the crusaders lifted the traditional Islamic prohibition on the construction of new churches, which served as the 'catalyst' to a 'well-documented resurgence in Christian chapel construction and painting programmes' in this region, the so-called 'Syrian Renaissance'.[313] The crusader conquest of the Lebanon region was neither wholly bad nor wholly good for the region's indigenous inhabitants, varying from religion to religion and from place to place.

The Jerusalemite fief

Returning to Tripoli itself, the fall of this city meant the removal of an important centre of Muslim resistance to the crusaders, which had prevailed through war and diplomacy for almost exactly a decade after the fêted conquest of Jerusalem. Yet there was still much work for the crusaders to do. Bertrand's earlier promise to pay homage to King Baldwin – made at the height of his dispute with William Jordan and Tancred – still held, and the count was obliged to confirm his fealty as the king's 'liege man' (*homo ligius*) after the siege. This personal bond between count and king remained valid in theory until at least the days of Bertrand's great-grandson Raymond III.[314] This oath ought to be viewed in conjunction with those contemporary texts that divide the Latin East territorially between Jerusalem and Antioch, drawing the border between Tripoli and Tortosa. Thus, the county of Tripoli at this point should not be regarded as a separate 'crusader state', but rather the kingdom of Jerusalem's northernmost fief – albeit extending only as far as ʿArqa and al-Nahr al-Kabīr al-Janūbī, where the principality of Antioch began.

Given the county's constitutional status at this early stage, it is unsurprising that Bertrand's most prominent acts in the years immediately following 1109 were performed in the service of the king. Bertrand accompanied the king on a number of military expeditions during his short reign, namely the sieges of Beirut and Sidon in 1110, a close call with the Damascene army near Tiberias in 1111 and the relief of the principality of Antioch's eastern frontier, also in 1111.[315] It is notable that the two captured cities of Beirut and Sidon lay between Tripoli and the rest of the kingdom, and their capture can be seen as efforts to unite the county and the remainder of the realm. In fact, Bertrand was the one to suggest the conquest of Beirut, specifically because of the obstacle it posed to travellers between Tripoli and the south.[316]

Bertrand did not see unmitigated success at the expense of the Muslims. Richard believes that the county's expansion slowed sharply from 1109 onwards, due to the Tripolitan army's numerical weakness at the time.[317] This was perhaps the result of warriors returning home to Europe after the fall of Tripoli, just as earlier crusaders had left Syria soon after the conquest of Jerusalem. A shortage of Frankish settlers ensured that the rulers of the Latin East would always lack the strength sufficient to protect their lands. Thus, the count of Tripoli began to suffer military defeats and was obliged to make peace with his Muslim neighbours, in direct contrast with the confident bellicosity of William Jordan. Following a victory at al-Raḥba on the Euphrates, the Saljūq warlord Āq Sunqur al-Bursuqī headed west, where he joined forces with Ṭughtakīn of Damascus and won a victory against the Franks of Tripoli in 1109, shortly after the fall of Tripoli itself.[318] Soon afterwards, Bertrand established a peace treaty with Ṭughtakīn. The terms of this were that the Franks would receive a third of the produce of the fruitful Biqāʿ valley, while the Muslims would take the rest.[319] This was one of many similar agreements – *condominia* in Latin, *munāṣafāt* in Arabic – reached between Muslim and Frankish rulers at the time, with the aim being to share the revenue of disputed borderlands.[320] Militarily speaking, they were admissions of stalemate.

Alongside his suzerain at Jerusalem and his enemy at Damascus, Bertrand also had to contend with his ally at Constantinople – Alexios Komnenos – and his rival at Antioch, Tancred. It would appear that Bertrand continued to maintain the anti-Norman, pro-Byzantine stance first assumed by his father during the First Crusade. In late 1111, Alexios Komnenos sought to launch yet another military campaign against Tancred. In preparation for this expedition that never came, Alexios sent a mission of envoys, led by the *doux* Manuel Boutoumites, to request that Bertrand lend his support against Tancred. The count agreed, evidently preferring to maintain close ties with the distant Byzantine emperor than to foster a friendship with his fellow Latin Christian to the north. Satisfied, the Byzantine ambassadors sailed south to meet with the king of Jerusalem. As testament to the trust they were willing to place in Bertrand, the Greeks deposited money for safekeeping with the Latin bishop of Tripoli, fearing that King Baldwin and other Frankish rulers – Bertrand excepted – would be tempted to seize it otherwise.[321] Bertrand had thrown his lot in with the Byzantines and war with the Normans loomed.

Conclusion

Tripoli *c.*1050 was the fulcrum in an epic imperial struggle: the key bastion in the Fāṭimid Caliphate's defence against the Byzantine Empire in North Syria. In a few short decades, it had become the northernmost outpost of the newly established Frankish county of Tripoli, a dependency of Jerusalem and the frontline in an encroaching war between the Byzantines and the Normans. A vital part in this transformation was performed by Count Raymond IV of Saint-Gilles but there were many other decisive players. Not least of these was William Jordan of Cerdanya, whose persistence at Tripoli and confidence in driving the crusader conquest deep into the Syrian interior served as the benchmark for future counts of Tripoli. There were also profound trends that proved difficult to buck. Trilateral negotiations between the crusaders, the Byzantines and the Fāṭimids during the First Crusade ensured that the memory of a bipartite Levant in the pre-Saljūq period of the mid-eleventh century was not forgotten, even by the crusaders who gradually rejected the active influence of the Byzantines and Fāṭimids themselves. William Jordan's willingness to subordinate himself to Tancred, followed by Bertrand's parallel oath to King Baldwin, opened the way for the disparate and amorphous Latin conquests to be moulded into a clear emulation of this very eleventh-century precedent. Much later, William of Tyre would allege that there were four great crusader lordships, but his influential outline failed to capture the fluidity of political reality in the early years of crusader settlement. Contemporaries would have observed instead the gradual emergence of two politics on the Syrian coast, as yet unaware that they would later be driven apart by the appearance of a third. Between 1109 and early 1112, Bertrand was count of Tripoli, but not yet ruler of an independent 'crusader state'.

Notes

1 Cf. Richard, *Le comté*, p. 9.
2 H. A. R. Gibb, 'The Caliphate and the Arab States', in *A History of the Crusades*, ed. Kenneth M. Setton, 6 vols (Madison, WI, 1969–89), vol. 1, p. 94.
3 A. C. S. Peacock, *The Great Seljuk Empire* (Edinburgh, 2015), *passim.*
4 Michael A. Köhler, *Alliances and Treaties between Frankish and Muslim Rulers in the Middle East: Cross-Cultural Diplomacy in the Period of the Crusades*, trans. P. M. Holt and Konrad Hirschler (Leiden, 2013), pp. 8–20.
5 RA, p. 117.
6 Carole Hillenbrand, *The Crusades: Islamic Perspectives* (Edinburgh, 1999), pp. 44–5.
7 *GF*, pp. 423–4, 436, 438–9; PT, pp. 128, 132–3; RA, pp. 106–7, 125; AA, pp. 386–8.
8 AA, pp. 388–90.
9 Erat eo tempore tantum nomen comitis, ut nullius umquam nomini priorum inpar esse videretur. RA, p. 107.
10 *GF*, pp. 379–80.
11 *GF*, pp. 438–9; PT, pp. 128, 132–3.
12 For example: John France, 'The First Crusade and Islam', *The Muslim World* 67.4 (1977), p. 254; Ahmad Hoteit, 'Les différentes communautés de Tripoli et leur attitude envers les croisés', in *De Toulouse à Tripoli: Itinéraires*, ed. Weber *et al.*, pp. 45–6.
13 Adam Knobler, 'Pseudo-Conversions and Patchwork Pedigrees: The Christianization of Muslim Princes and the Diplomacy of Holy War', *Journal of World History* 7 (1996), pp. 182, 197 and *passim.*
14 Paul E. Walker, *Exploring an Islamic Empire: Fatimid History and its Sources* (London, 2002), pp. 65–8; Gibb, 'The Caliphate', pp. 93–4.
15 Benjamin Z. Kedar, *Crusade and Mission: European Approaches toward the Muslims* (Princeton, NJ, 1984), pp. 62–4, 68–70, 72–4.
16 F. W. Hasluck, *Christianity and Islam under the Sultans*, 2 vols (Oxford, 1929), vol. 1, pp. 31–4; Speros Vryonis, *The Decline of Medieval Hellenism in Asia Minor and the Process of Islamization from the Eleventh through the Fifteenth Century* (Berkeley, CA, 1971), pp. 371–2; Jack Boulos Victor Tannous, *Syria Between Byzantium and Islam: Making Incommensurables Speak. Volume 1* (Unpublished Ph.D. thesis: Princeton University, 2010), pp. 453–4.
17 Ibn Taymiyya, *Iqtiḍā' al-ṣirāṭ al-mustaqīm mukhālafat aṣḥāb al-jaḥīm*, ed. Muḥammad Ḥāmid al-Fiqī (Cairo, 1950), p. 227 and *passim*; Alexandra Cuffel, 'From Practice to Polemic: Shared Saints and Festivals as "Women's Religion" in the Medieval Mediterranean', *Bulletin of the School of Oriental and African Studies* 68.3 (2005), p. 410.
18 James of Vitry, *Historia orientalis*, ed. Jean Donnadieu (Turnhout, 2008) (JV), p. 206. See also: James of Vitry, *Lettres de Jacques de Vitry (1160/1170–1240), évêque de Saint-Jean-d'Acre*, ed. R. B. C. Huygens (Leiden, 1960), no. 2, p. 94; Wilbrand of Oldenburg, 'Journey to Syria, Lesser Armenia, Cyprus, and the Holy Land (1211–1212): A New Edition', ed. Denys Pringle, *Crusades* 11 (2012), p. 121.
19 Jōḥannān of Mardē, 'Canons', in *The Synodicon in the West Syrian Tradition*, ed. Arthur Vööbus, 2 vols, Corpus Scriptorum Christianorum Orientalium 375–6 (Louvain, 1975–6), vol. 1, p. 246.
20 Tannous, p. 474.
21 Bernard Hamilton, 'Knowing the Enemy: Western Understanding of Islam at the Time of the Crusades', *Journal of the Royal Asiatic Society of Great Britain and Ireland*, 3rd series, 7.3 (1997), p. 380; Alex Mallett, *Popular Muslim Reactions to the Franks in the Levant, 1097–1291* (Farnham, 2014), pp. 106–7.
22 Kedar, *Crusade and Mission*, pp. 68–70, 73. Cf. Köhler, *Alliances*, pp. 34–6, 39–40, 42–3.
23 RA, pp. 131–4.

24 Jean Maurice Fiey, 'Un grand sanctuaire perdu? Le Martyrion de Saint Léonce à Tripoli', *Le Muséon: Revue d'études orientales* 95.1–2 (1982), pp. 77–98.
25 Mat Immerzeel, 'Divine Cavalry: Mounted Saints in Middle Eastern Christian Art', in *East and West in the Crusader States: Context – Contacts – Confrontations*, ed. Krijnie Ciggaar, Herman Teule *et al.*, Orientalia Lovaniensia Analecta, 75, 92, 125 (Leuven, 1996–2003), vol. 3, pp. 265–86.
26 Al-ʿAẓīmī, *Tārīkh ḥalab*, p. 360.
27 Jonathan Riley-Smith, 'The Title of Godfrey of Bouillon', *Bulletin of the Institute of Historical Research* 52.125 (1979), pp. 83–6.
28 RA, p. 152.
29 *RRH*, no. 16.
30 Jonathan Shepard, 'When Greek meets Greek: Alexius Comnenus and Bohemond in 1097–98', *Byzantine and Modern Greek Studies* 12 (1988), pp. 217–27; Klaus-Peter Todt, 'Antioch and Edessa in to [*sic*] so-called Treaty of Deabolis (September 1108)', *ARAM* 11–12 (1999–2000), pp. 490–501; Jean-Claude Cheynet, 'The Duchy of Antioch during the Second Period of Byzantine Rule', in *East and West: Antioch*, vol. 1, pp. 15–16. But cf. John H. Pryor and Michael J. Jeffreys, 'Alexios, Bohemond, and Byzantium's Euphrates Frontier: A Tale of Two Cretans', *Crusades* 11 (2012), pp. 31–79.
31 Asbridge, 'The principality', pp. 142–51.
32 AA, p. 478.
33 Richard, *Le comté*, pp. 10–12.
34 Fulcher of Chartres, *Historia Hierosolymitana (1095–1127)*, ed. Heinrich Hagenmeyer (Heidelberg, 1913) (FC), pp. 320–1; WT, vol. 1, p. 466.
35 Anna Komnene, *The Alexiad*, trans. E. R. A. Sewter and Peter Frankopan (London, 2009) (AK), pp. 392–3.
36 Todt, 'Antioch and Edessa', pp. 498–501.
37 AA, pp. 476–8, 480–5.
38 AK, p. 317.
39 AA, pp. 594–616; AK, pp. 319–20; WT, vol. 1, pp. 466–7.
40 AA, p. 632.
41 WT, vol. 1, pp. 481–2.
42 A diuersis locis et regnis. AA, p. 680.
43 AA, p. 633 n. 72.
44 Susan Edgington, 'The First Crusade: Reviewing the Evidence', in *The First Crusade*, ed. Phillips, pp. 62–3.
45 Warren Treadgold, *A History of the Byzantine State and Society* (Stanford, CA, 1997), map 14, p. 531; Mark Whittow, *The Making of Orthodox Byzantium, 600–1025* (Basingstoke, 1996), map xiv, pp. 312–13; Peter Frankopan, *The First Crusade: The Call from the East* (London, 2012), p. xv; 1 Maccabees 11:7, 12:30. Latin Christian authors wrongly identified the Eleutherus as the river Leontes (Līṭānī), which flows between Beirut and Tyre. Burchard of Mount Sion, 'Descriptio Terrae Sanctae', in *Peregrinatores Medii Aevi Quatuor*, ed. J. C. M. Laurent, 2nd ed. (Leipzig, 1873), pp. 25–6.
46 Paul Magdalino, *The Byzantine Background to the First Crusade* (Toronto, 1996), pp. 36–7.
47 Ihesum Marie virginis filium. RA, p. 58; Jean Flori, *Pierre l'Ermite et la première croisade* (Paris, 1999), 352–4.
48 Qurān 3.47, 19.20–22.
49 Fędus amiciciam. RA, p. 58.
50 Si faceret nobis auxilium a Ierusalem, vel redderet nobis Iherusalem, cum pertinenciis suis, redderemus nos ei omnes civitates suas quas Turci ei abstulerant cum caperemus eas. Alias autem civitates Turcorum, quę de regno eius non fuerunt, si cum auxilio eius caperentur, inter nos partiremur. RA, pp. 109–10.

51 Köhler, *Alliances*, pp. 46–7, 51–3.
52 RA, pp. 109–10.
53 Köhler, *Alliances*, pp. 53, 47; Flori, *Pierre l'Ermite*, pp. 354–5, 397–9.
54 RA, p. 110.
55 Nāṣir Khusraw, *Nāṣer-e Khosraw's Book of Travels (Safarnāma)*, trans. W. M. Thackston, Persian Heritage Series 36 (Albany, 1986), p. 13.
56 Treadgold, *History*, 507; Jean-Claude Cheynet, 'La conception militaire de la frontière orientale (IXe–XIIIe siècle)', in *Eastern Approaches to Byzantium: Papers from the Thirty-third Spring Symposium of Byzantine Studies, University of Warwick, Coventry, March 1999*, ed. Antony Eastmond (Aldershot, 2001), pp. 60, 62.
57 AA, p. 680.
58 AK, 317–18.
59 WT, vol. 1, pp. 485–6.
60 Anis Chaaya, 'Les fortifications des entrées du château Saint-Gilles de Tripoli', *Archaeology & History in the Lebanon* 26–27 (2007–8), p. 141.
61 Mathias Piana, 'From Montpèlerin to Ṭarābulus al-Mustajadda: The Frankish-Mamluk Succession in Old Tripoli', in *Egypt and Syria in the Fatimid, Ayyubid and Mamluk Eras, VI: Proceedings of the 14th and 15th International Colloquium Organized at the Katholieke Universiteit Leuven in May 2005 and May 2006*, ed. U. Vermeulen and K. D'Hulster, Orientalia Lovaniensia Analecta 183 (Leuven, 2010), pp. 307–54.
62 *RRH*, nos 38, 44, 48; *Cartulaire de l'Abbaye de Saint-Victor de Marseille*, ed. Guérard, 2 vols (Paris, 1857), vol. 2, no. 802; Devic and Vaissète, *Histoire*, vol. 5, no. 420, cols 791–3; *Le Cartulaire du Chapitre du Saint-Sépulcre de Jérusalem*, ed. Geneviève Bresc-Bautier (Paris, 1984) (*CCSSJ*), no. 79; C. J. Sabine, 'The Billon and Copper Coinage of the Crusader County of Tripoli, *c.*1102–1268', *The Numismatic Chronicle*, 7th series, 20 (1980), p. 75.
63 Quam si urbem ipsam sine contradictore possideret. WT, vol. 1, p. 486.
64 Comes [. . .] gratia Dei Tripolitanus. Jean Richard, 'Le chartrier de Sainte-Marie Latine et l'établissement de Raymond de Saint-Gilles à Mont-Pèlerin', in *Mélanges d'histoire du Moyen Âge dédiés à la mémoire de Louis Halphen* (Paris, 1951), pp. 607–8, 610; Richard, 'Les Saint-Gilles', p. 68.
65 Christianę militię excellentissimus princeps in partibus Syrię. *CCSSJ*, no. 79; *RRH*, no. 48.
66 Cf. Jonathan Riley-Smith, *The First Crusaders, 1095–1131* (Cambridge, 1997), pp. 8–9.
67 William of Malmesbury, *Gesta Regum Anglorum: The History of the English Kings, Volume I*, ed. R. A. B. Mynors, Rodney M. Thomson and Michael Winterbottom (Oxford, 1998), p. 700; 'De Miraculis S. Roberti, Auctore Bertrando monacho Casæ-Dei', ed. Labbe, in *Acta Sanctorum Aprilis*, ed. Godefridus Henschenius and Davidus Papebrochius, 3 vols (Antwerp, 1675), vol. 3, p. 330; Richard, *Le comté*, pp. 17, 59; Hamilton, *Latin Church*, pp. 25, 122; Antweiler, pp. 29–30.
68 See Chapter 2.
69 Antweiler, pp. 244–5; Hamilton, *Latin Church*, pp. 135–6.
70 *Les Miracles de Saint Privat suivis des opuscules d'Aldebert III, évêque de Mende*, ed. C. Brunel (Paris, 1912), pp. xix, 37; Antweiler, p. 30.
71 Richard, *Le comté*, p. 59.
72 *Les Miracles de Saint Privat*, pp. i-ii, xxxix; John Gordon Rowe, 'The Papacy and the Ecclesiastical Province of Tyre (1100–1187)', *Bulletin of the John Rylands Library* 43 (1960–1), p. 163; Antweiler, pp. 30–1.
73 IA, vol. 10, p. 344.
74 IQ, p. 147; William of Malmesbury, *Gesta Regum*, p. 700.
75 RA, p. 125; PT, pp. 130–1.
76 IA, vol. 10, pp. 411–12.
77 WT, vol. 2, p. 756. See Chapter 3.

78 Nina Jidejian, *Tripoli through the Ages* (Beirut, 1980), p. 59.

79 Naṣarta bi-sayf-ka dīn al-masīḥ

fa-li-llāh darru-ka mann ṣanjilī [*sic*]
wa-mā sama'a al-nās fīmā ruwī
bi-aqbaḥ min kasrat al-afḍal.

Mujīr al-Dīn, *Kitāb al-uns al-jalīl bi-tārīkh al-quds wa-al-khalīl*, 2 vols (Cairo, 1866), vol. 1, p. 273.

80 Riley-Smith, *First Crusaders*, p. 19.

81 IA, vol. 10, p. 412; Riley-Smith, *First Crusaders*, p. 29.

82 AA, p. 680. Cf. WT, vol. 1, pp. 496–7.

83 Paul Deschamps, 'Raymond de Saint-Gilles et sa sépulture au château de Tripoli (Liban)', in *Etudes de civilisation médiévale (IXe-XIIe siècles). Mélanges offerts à Edmond-René Labande à l'occasion de son départ à la retraite et du XXe anniversaire du C.E.S.C.M. par ses amis, ses collègues, ses élèves* (Poitiers, 1974), pp. 212–16; Denys Pringle, 'The Church of the Holy Sepulchre in the Castle of Tripoli (Mont-Pèlerin)', in *Egypt and Syria in the Fatimid, Ayyubid and Mamluk Eras V: Proceedings of the 11th, 12th and 13th International Colloquium Organized at the Katholieke Universiteit Leuven in May 2001, 2002 and 2003*, ed. U. Vermeulen and K. D'Hulster, Orientalia Lovaniensia Analecta, 169 (Leuven, 2007), pp. 168–76. Cf. Salamé-Sarkis, pp. 64–83.

84 Domum quandam in Monte Peregrino, quę domus antiquo tempore immundis paganorum supersticionibus dedita fuerat, quatinus, omni gentilitatis nefario ritu inde profugato, jam nunc Deo dignum fieret perpetuum habitaculum. *CCSSJ*, no. 79; *RRH*, no. 48.

85 WT, vol. 1, p. 486; William of Malmesbury, *Gesta Regum*, p. 700.

86 William of Malmesbury, *Gesta Regum*, p. 700.

87 Etienne Léon Lamonthe-Langon, *Biographie toulousaine*, 2 vols (Paris, 1823), vol. 1, p. 61.

88 Riley-Smith, *First Crusaders*, p. 138.

89 John Hugh Hill and Laurita Lyttleton Hill, *Raymond IV, Count of Toulouse* (Syracuse, 1962), pp. 7–19.

90 Willelmi comitis Pictavensis & Tolosae [. . .] Philippia Tolosana atque Pictavensis comitissa. Devic and Vaissète, *Histoire*, vol. 5, nos 399, 400, cols 753–6. See also: Devic and Vaissète, *Histoire*, vol. 3, pp. 542–4; Bruguière, pp. 144–5.

91 Ralph V. Turner, *Eleanor of Aquitaine: Queen of France, Queen of England* (London, 2009), p. 61.

92 Devic and Vaissète, *Histoire*, vol. 3, pp. 622–3, 648–9. Cf. Bruguière, pp. 145–6.

93 Bruguière, p. 146; Richard Benjamin, 'A Forty Years War: Toulouse and the Plantagenets, 1156–96', *Historical Research* 61 (1988), pp. 270–83.

94 H. E. J. Cowdrey, *Pope Gregory VII, 1073–1085* (Oxford, 1998), p. 341.

95 Ex una pelicum [*sic*] filium natum. William of Malmesbury, *Gesta Regum*, p. 696. Cf. Richard, *Le comté*, p. 5.

96 WT, vol. 1, p. 497.

97 Thomas N. Bisson, 'The Rise of Catalonia: Identity, Power, and Ideology in a Twelfth-Century Society', in his *Medieval France and Her Pyrenean Neighbours: Studies in Early Institutional History* (London, 1989), pp. 127–30.

98 FC, pp. 484–5; AA, pp. 710, 774; WT, vol. 1, p. 497.

99 Willelmum peregrinum. William of Malmesbury, *Gesta Regum*, p. 700.

100 IQ, p. 163. Cf. IA, vol. 10, pp. 400, 475.

101 Al-'Aẓīmī, *Tārīkh ḥalab*, p. 362.

102 Richard, *Le comté*, p. 5.

103 Riley-Smith, *First Crusaders*, p. 225.

104 *Papsturkunden in Spanien, Vorarbeiten zur Hispania Pontificia, I. Katalanien, II. Urkunden und Regesten*, ed. Paul Kehr (Berlin, 1926), no. 23.
105 *The* Canso d'Antioca*: An Occitan Epic Chronicle of the First Crusade*, ed. Carol Sweetenham and Linda M. Paterson (Aldershot, 2003), pp. 198, 199, 355.
106 Devic and Vaissète, *Histoire*, vol. 5, no. 408.i, col. 767. See also: Devic and Vaissète, *Histoire*, vol. 5, no. 400, cols 754–6.
107 Bruguière, p. 145.
108 Devic and Vaissète, *Histoire*, vol. 5, no. 408.i, col. 767.
109 Devic and Vaissète, *Histoire*, vol. 3, pp. 543–4.
110 Richard, *Le comté*, p. 5; Marie-Luise Favreau-Lilie, *Die Italiener im Heiligen Land vom ersten Kreuzzug bis zum Tode Heinrichs von Champagne (1098–1197)* (Amsterdam, 1989), 116.
111 See Chapter 3.
112 Christianȩ militiȩ ductor. *CCSSJ*, no. 79; *RRH*, no. 48.
113 Hereditario jure in honorem successit. *CCSSJ*, no. 79; *RRH*, no. 48.
114 Hereditario sanguine. AA, p. 710.
115 In hereditatem. AA, p. 780.
116 AK, p. 320.
117 FC, pp. 531–2.
118 WT, vol. 1, p. 497.
119 Nāṣir Khusraw, p. 12.
120 Al-baḥr ya'khudhu-hā min thalāthat awjuh. Al-Idrīsī, *Opus Geographicum sive «Liber ad eorum delectationem qui terras peragrare studeant»*, ed. E. Cerulli *et al.*, 2nd ed. (Leiden, 1971–84), p. 372.
121 AA, p. 680.
122 Al-ʿAẓīmī, *Tārīkh ḥalab*, p. 362.
123 AA, p. 710.
124 IA, vol. 10, pp. 365–6.
125 IA, vol. 10, p. 412.
126 IQ, pp. 160–1.
127 IQ, p. 161; IA, vol. 10, p. 454.
128 IA, vol. 10, pp. 467–8.
129 AA, p. 774; IA, vol. 10, p. 468.
130 IA, vol. 10, p. 468.
131 Richard, *Le comté*, p. 21.
132 Al-Idrīsī, p. 373; Pseudo-Fretellus, 'Tractatus de Locis circa Hierusalem', in Melchior de Vogüé, *Les Eglises de la Terre Sainte* (Paris, 1860), p. 421.
133 Ernoul, *Chronique d'Ernoul et de Bernard le Trésorier*, ed. L. de Mas Latrie (Paris, 1871), p. 62. Cf. Ibn Khurdādhba, *Kitāb al-masālik al-mamālik*, ed. M. J. de Goeje, Bibliotheca Geographorum Arabicorum 6 (Leiden, 1889), p. 76; Ibn Jubayr, *Riḥla*, ed. William Wright and M. J. de Goeje (Leiden, 1907) (IJ), p. 281; Yāqūt bin ʿAbd Allāh al-Ḥamawī, *Muʿjam al-buldān*, 5 vols (Beirut, 1955–7), vol. 4, p. 177; Wilbrand of Oldenburg, p. 120; Peregrine Horden and Nichols Purcell, *The Corrupting Sea: A Study of Mediterranean History* (Oxford, 2000), p. 56; René Dussaud, *Topographie historique de la Syrie antique et médiévale* (Paris, 1927), p. 402.
134 RA, pp. 35, 107.
135 AA, p. 378.
136 Cf. Richard, *Le comté*, p. 9.
137 Totam regionem usque Damascum expugnantes de die in diem inuaserunt. AA, p. 774.
138 Usāma bin Munqidh, *Usāmah's Memoirs entitled* Kitāb al-Iʿtibār, ed. Philip K. Hitti, Princeton Oriental Texts 1 (Princeton, NJ, 1930) (Usāma), p. 50.
139 *GF*, pp. 415–16.

140 Wilelmus comes solebat accipere [bisantios] de bubus Surianorum in [. . .] villis laborantium [. . .] in terra de Rafania. *Cartulaire général de l'Ordre des Hospitaliers de S. Jean de Jérusalem (1100–1310)*, ed. J. Delaville le Roulx, 4 vols (Paris, 1894–1906) (*CGOH*), vol. 1, nos 79, 82; *RRH*, nos 108, 118.
141 2 Kings 5:12.
142 'Abana', in *The Encyclopædia Britannica*, 11th edn, 29 vols (Cambridge, 1910–11), vol. 1, p. 6.
143 John of Würzburg, 'Peregrinatio', in *Peregrinationes Tres: Saewulf, John of Würzburg, Theodericus*, ed. R. B. C. Huygens (Turnhout, 1994), p. 104; Theoderich, 'Descriptio', in *Peregrinationes Tres*, ed. Huygens, pp. 194–5; Pseudo-James of Vitry, 'Historiae Orientalis Liber Tertius', in *Gesta Dei per Francos*, ed. Jacques Bongars (Hanover, 1611), vol. 1, p. 1127.
144 See, for example: AA, p. 190; *GF*, p. 415.
145 Ad usque flumen quod vulgariter Fer nuncupamus. *CGOH*, vol. 1, no. 596; *RRH*, no. 602.
146 Cahen, *La Syrie*, 134 n. 3.
147 See, for example: *GF*, p. 239.
148 E. G. Rey, *Les colonies franques de Syrie aux XIIme et XIIIme siècles* (Paris, 1883), pp. 356–7.
149 *CGOH*, vol. 1, no. 596; *RRH*, no. 602.
150 Richard, *Le comté*, p. 5.
151 'De Miraculis S. Roberti', p. 330; Pierre Roger Gaussin, *L'Abbaye de la Chaise-Dieu (1043–1518)* (Paris, 1962), pp. 142, 217.
152 Antweiler, pp. 27–9. Cf. Hill and Hill, *Raymond IV*, p. 3; Gaussin, pp. 131–2, 141–2, 217; Riley-Smith, *First Crusaders*, p. 150.
153 AA, p. 776.
154 Caffaro of Caschifellone, 'De Liberatione Ciuitatum Orientis Liber', in *Annali Genovesi di Caffaro e de' suoi continuatori dal MXCIX al MCCXCIII*, ed. Luigi Tommaso Belgrano, 5 vols (Genoa, 1890–1929), p. 122.
155 William of Malmesbury, *Gesta Regum*, p. 700. See Chapter 2.
156 AA, p. 776.
157 AA, pp. 776–8.
158 *GF*, pp. 426–8; PT, p. 129; AA, p. 376.
159 Saewulf, 'Peregrinatio', in *Peregrinationes Tres*, ed. Huygens, p. 75.
160 AA, p. 484.
161 FC, pp. 433–5; WT, vol. 1, pp. 467–8, 475.
162 Hamilton, *Latin Church*, p. 143.
163 JV, p. 206; James of Vitry, *Lettres*, no. 2, pp. 93–4; Burchard of Mount Sion, p. 30; William of Nangis, *Chronique latine de Guillaume de Nangis, de 1113 à 1300, avec les continuations de cette chronique, de 1300 à 1368*, ed. H. Géraud, 2 vols (Paris, 1843), vol. 1, p. 118; 'Gesta Episcoporum Halberstadensium', ed. Ludwig Weiland, *Monumenta Germaniae Historica: Scriptores* (*MGH SS*), 39 vols (Hannover, 1826–), vol. 23, p. 119; Wilbrand of Oldenburg, p. 121; Al-Dimashqī, *Nukhbat al-dahr fī ʿajāʾib al-barr wa-al-baḥr*, ed. A. F. Mehren (Jubayl, 2008), pp. 207–8.
164 Usque hodie . . . ab infantia primitive Ecclesie. JV, p. 206.
165 Camille Enlart, *Les Monuments des Croisés dans le Royaume de Jérusalem*, 2 vols (Paris, 1925–8), vol. 2, p. 403. But cf. Baldwin, 'Ecclesiastical Developments', p. 158.
166 Paul Devos, 'Les premières versions occidentales de la légende de Saïdnaia', *Analecta Bollandiana* 65 (1947), pp. 271–2; Bernard Hamilton, 'Our Lady of Saidnaiya: an Orthodox Shrine Revered by Muslims and Knights Templar at the Time of the Crusades', in *The Holy Land, Holy Lands, and Christian History: Papers read at the 1998 Summer Meeting and the 1999 Winter Meeting of the Ecclesiastical History Society*, ed. R. N. Swanson, Studies in Church History 36 (Woodbridge, 2000), pp. 208–9.

167 *Chroniques d'Amadi et de Strambaldi*, ed. René de Mas Latrie, 2 vols (Paris, 1891–3), vol. 1, p. 292. See also: Rey, *Les colonies*, pp. 286–7.
168 AA, pp. 778–80.
169 Paterson, *World*, pp. 24, 69–70 and *passim*.
170 Richard, *Le comté*, pp. 17–18.
171 For example, see: *CGOH*, vol. 1, nos 144, 676, 801, 804.
172 Terram et ciuitates de Camolla. AA, p. 710.
173 RA, pp. 106–7; IA, vol. 10, p. 278.
174 Sibṭ bin al-Jawzī, 'Extraits du Mirât ez-Zèmân', *Recueil des Historiens des Croisades: Historiens Orientaux*, 5 vols (Paris, 1872–1906) (*RHC Or*), vol. 3 pp. 524–5. Cf. IQ, pp. 140–1; IA, vol. 10, p. 344.
175 Kamāl al-Dīn, *Zubdat al-ḥalab min tārīkh ḥalab*, ed. Sāmī al-Dahhān, 3 vols (Damascus, 1951–68), vol. 2, pp. 146–7. But cf. IQ, p. 142.
176 *RRH*, no. 212; *CGOH*, vol. 1, no. 144.
177 Richard, *Le comté*, pp. 1–3.
178 Que citra flumen sunt a finibus Christianitatis. *CGOH*, vol. 1, no. 676; *RRH*, no. 637. See also: *CGOH*, vol. 1, nos 801, 804; *RRH*; *Regesta Regni Hierosolymitani (MXCVII-MCCXCI): Additamentum*, ed. Reinhold Röhricht (Innsbrück, 1904) (*RRH Add.*), nos 651a, 651b.
179 Richard, 'Questions', p. 54 n. 1; *CGOH*, vol. 1, nos 79, 82, 1096; vol. 2, nos 2094, 2184, 2280; *RRH*, nos 108, 118, 759, 1057, 1102; *RRH Add.*, no. 1079a; Jonathan Riley-Smith, 'The Templars and the Castle of Tortosa in Syria: An Unknown Document concerning the Acquisition of the Fortress', *The English Historical Review* (*EHR*) 84.331 (1969), p. 285. Cf. *CGOH*, vol. 1, no. 589; *RRH*, no. 595. Earlier, Richard had identified Lo Camel with al-Akma – located perhaps near Tortosa or perhaps near ʿArqa and the Lebanon foothills. Richard, *Le comté*, pp. 2, 94. Cf. IQ, p. 162; Ibn al-Qalānisī, trans. Gibb, p. 88 n. 1.
180 Uallem que dicitur Camelorum. AA, p. 376; Paul Deschamps, *Les Châteaux des Croisés en Terre Sainte*, 3 vols (Paris, 1934–73), vol. 1, p. 110. Cf. AA, p. 780 n. 13.
181 Ciuitates de Camolla. AA, p. 710.
182 AA, p. 780; Asbridge, *Creation*, pp. 115–16.
183 AA, p. 780.
184 Steven Tibble, *Monarchy and Lordships in the Latin Kingdom of Jerusalem 1099–1291* (Oxford, 1989), pp. 7, 11–12.
185 AA, pp. 780–2.
186 IQ, p. 163.
187 FC, p. 529.
188 Michael T. Clanchy, *From Memory to Written Record: England 1066–1307*, 3rd ed. (Oxford, 2013), pp. 23–45.
189 AA, p. 782.
190 WT, vol. 1, p. 508.
191 De districto Tripoli. Caffaro, 'De Liberatione', p. 120.
192 Richard, *Le comté*, pp. 5, 31.
193 WT, vol. 1, p. 508.
194 Asbridge, *Creation*, pp. 116–17.
195 Orientalis enim Latinorum tota regio quattuor princip[at]ibus erat distincta. Prius enim ab austro erat regnum Ierosolimorum, initium habens a rivo qui est inter Biblium et Beritum, urbes maritimas provincie Phenicis, et finem in solitudine que est ultra Darum, que respicit Egyptum; secundus erat versus septentrionem comitatus Tripolitanus, a rivo supradicto habens initium, finem vero in rivo qui est inter Maracleam et Valeniam, urbes similiter maritimas; tercius erat principatus Antiochenus, qui ab eodem rivo habens initium usque in Tarsum Cilicie versus occidentem protendebatur, quartus erat comitatus Edessanus, qui ab ea silva, que dicitur Marrith, in orientem ultra Eufraten protendebatur. WT, vol. 2, p. 756.

196 Burchard of Mount Sion, pp. 27, 31; Marino Sanudo, 'Liber Secretorum Fidelium Crucis', in *Gesta Dei per Francos*, ed. Jacques Bongars (Hanover, 1611), vol. 2, pp. 244–5; Deschamps, *Les Châteaux*, vol. 1, p. 15 n. 4. Cf. Rey, *Les colonies*, p. 357; Deschamps, *Les Châteaux*, vol. 1, p. 15; vol. 3, p. 7.

197 Ronnie Ellenblum, 'Were there Borders and Borderlines in the Middle Ages? The Example of the Latin Kingdom of Jerusalem', in *Medieval Frontiers: Concepts and Practices*, ed. David Abulafia and Nora Berend (Aldershot, 2002), pp. 105–19; Ellenblum, *Crusader Castles*, pp. 118–45; Nora Berend, 'Preface', in *Medieval Frontiers*, ed. Abulafia and Berend, pp. x–xv, at xiv; Ralph W. Brauer, *Boundaries and Frontiers in Medieval Muslim Geography*, Transactions of the American Philosophical Society 85.6 (Philadelphia, 1995), pp. 1–69. Cf. Denys Pringle, 'Castles and Frontiers in the Latin East', in *Norman Expansion*, ed. Stringer and Jotischky, pp. 233–9; Bernard S. Bachrach, 'Review Article: Medieval Identity: People and Place', *The International History Review* 25 (2003), p. 870.

198 P. W. Edbury and John Gordon Rowe, *William of Tyre: Historian of the Latin East* (Cambridge, 1990), p. 1.

199 WT, vol. 2, pp. 756–7.

200 Edbury and Rowe, *William*, p. 26.

201 Grousset, *Histoire*, vol. 1, *passim*.

202 Richard, *Le comté*, *passim*. See also: Hans Eberhard Mayer, 'The Latin East, 1098–1205', in *The New Cambridge Medieval History. Volume IV: c. 1024–c. 1198. Part II*, ed. David Luscombe and Jonathan Riley-Smith (Cambridge, 2004), pp. 644, 647, 649.

203 See Introduction.

204 Tibble, *Monarchy*, *passim*.

205 H. E. Mayer, 'Carving Up Crusaders: The Early Ibelins and Ramlas', in *Outremer: Studies in the History of the Crusading Kingdom of Jerusalem Presented to Joshua Prawer*, ed. B. Z. Kedar, H. E. Mayer and R. C. Smail (Jerusalem, 1982), pp. 101–18; Hans Eberhard Mayer, 'The Origins of the Lordships of Ramla and Lydda in the Latin Kingdom of Jerusalem', *Speculum* 60.3 (1985), pp. 537–52.

206 Marcus Bull, 'Introduction', in *France in the Central Middle Ages 900–1200*, ed. Marcus Bull (Oxford, 2002), pp. 5–6.

207 La Monte, *Feudal Monarchy*, p. 188.

208 Richard, *Le comté*, pp. 35, 43.

209 Harold S. Fink, 'The Foundation of the Latin States, 1099–1118', in *A History of the Crusades*, ed. Setton, vol. 1, p. 398.

210 Peter W. Edbury, *John of Ibelin and the Kingdom of Jerusalem* (Woodbridge, 1997), p. 166.

211 La tiere de Triple ne d'Antioce n'est mie dou roiaume. Ernoul, p. 27.

212 Alān fa-qad khallaṣa jamīʿ mamlakat al-quds, wa-ḥaddu-hā fī samt miṣr min al-ʿarīsh, wa-ʿalā ṣawb al-ḥijāz min al-karak wa-al-shawbak, wa-tashtimal ʿalā al-bilād al-sāḥiliyya ilā muntahā aʿmāl bayrūt, wa-lam yabaq min hadhihi al-mamlaka illā ṣūr. wa-futiḥa ayḍan jamīʿ iqlīm anṭākiyya wa-muʿāqil-hā allatī li-l-firanj wa-al-arman, wa-ḥaddu-hu min aqṣā bilād jabala wa-al-lādhiqiyya ilā bilād ibn lāʿūn, wa-baqīt anṭākiyya bi-mufrad-hā, wa-al-quṣīr min ḥuṣūn-hā, wa-lam yabaq min al-bilād allatī lam-tuftaḥ aʿmāl-hā, wa-lam taḥull ʿamman kānat ʿalay-hi ḥāl-hā, siwan ṭarābulus, fa-inna-hā lam yuftaḥ min-hā illā madīnat jubayl. Abū Shāma, *Kitāb al-rawḍatayn fī akhbār al-dawlatayn al-nūriyya wa-al-ṣalāḥiyya*, ed. Ibrāhīm Shams al-Dīn, 4 vols-in-2 (Beirut, 2002), vol. 4, p. 34.

213 John of Ibelin, *Le Livre des Assises*, ed. Peter W. Edbury, The Medieval Mediterranean: Peoples, Economies and Cultures, 400–1500, 50 (Leiden, 2003), p. 600.

214 Richard, *Le comté*, p. 33; Jean Richard, 'Pairie d'Orient latin: les quatre baronnies des royaumes de Jérusalem et de Chypre', *Revue historique de droit français et étranger*, 4th series, 28 (1950), p. 73; Edbury, *John*, p. 193.

215 Edbury, *John*, pp. 166, 193.
216 Post captam antiochiam. *CCSSJ*, no. 89.
217 FC, p. 741 n. 35.
218 Vatican City, Biblioteca Apostolica Vaticana, MS Vat. lat. 7241; *CCSSJ*, p. 12.
219 Post captam antiochiam podiensis ep[is]c[opus] sedis ap[osto]lice legatus, prudenti optimatu[m] usus co[n]silio, ier[oso]limitano regno & antiocheno p[ri]ncipatui t[er]minu[m] posuit, fluium [corr. fluuium] sc[i]l[ice]t q[ui] t[ri]polim & tortosam int[er]fluit: decerne[n]s ut ier[usa]l[e]m om[n]em t[er]ra[m] a parte aust[ra]li usq[ue] ad eunde[m] fluuium iure p[er]henni posside[re]t. Et antiochia ex alt[er]a fluminis parte iacentem nich[il]ominus obtineret. Vat. lat. 7241, fol. 3v. Cf. *CCSSJ*, no. 89.
220 Röhricht, *Geschichte*, p. 99 n. 1.
221 Pseudo-Fretellus, 'Tractatus', p. 432. See Chapter 2.
222 Frankopan, *First Crusade*, p. 170.
223 *Die Urkunden der lateinischen Könige von Jerusalem*, ed. Hans Eberhard Mayer, 4 vols, Monumenta Germaniae Historica: Diplomata Regum Latinorum Hierosolymitanorum (Hannover, 2010) (*D.Jerus.*), vol. 1, no. *9; Monachus Anonymus Littorensis, 'Historia de Translatione Sanctorum Magni Nicolai Terra Marique Miraculis Gloriosi', *RHC Oc*, vol. 5, p. 272; *RRH*, no. 31; Favreau-Lilie, *Die Italiener*, pp. 78–9; Elena Bellomo, 'The First Crusade and the Latin East as Seen from Venice: The Account of the *Translatio sancti Nicolai*', *Early Medieval Europe* 17.4 (2009), p. 428.
224 AA, p. 786; Caffaro, 'De Liberatione', p. 123.
225 FC, pp. 531–2.
226 IQ, p. 163.
227 WT, vol. 1, p. 508.
228 AA, p. 786.
229 *CCSSJ*, no. 86.
230 Richard, *Le comté*, p. 31.
231 Asbridge, *Creation*, p. 65.
232 IQ, p. 167.
233 Ibn al-Furāt, *Ayyubids, Mamlukes and Crusaders*, ed. U. Lyons and M. C. Lyons, 2 vols (Cambridge, 1971), vol. 1, pp. 182–3.
234 Benjamin Z. Kedar, 'The Subjected Muslims of the Frankish Levant', in *Muslims under Latin Rule, 1100–1300*, ed. James M. Powell (Princeton, NJ, 1990), p. 151.
235 IQ, p. 164.
236 Röhricht, *Geschichte*, p. 99.
237 FC, p. 741 n. 35.
238 Cahen, *La Syrie*, pp. 315–16. See also: Richard, *Le comté*, p. 45 n. 1.
239 Rowe, 'The Papacy', pp. 160–89; Hamilton, *Latin Church*, pp. 26–28, 66.
240 Vatican City, Biblioteca Apostolica Vaticana, MS Vat. lat. 1345, fol. 214v; *Acta Pontificum Romanorum Inedita*, ed. J. von Pflugk-Harttung, 2 vols (Stuttgart, 1880–84), vol. 2, no. 247.
241 Pascali papa ap[ud] b[e]n[e]uentu[m] [con]ciliu[m] celebrante, ab antiocheno pat[ri]archa & p[ri]ncipe nu[n]cii tr[a]nsmissi s[un]t, q[ui] in eodem co[n]cilio antiochene iura ecc[lesi]e s[ibi] restitui postulauer[un]t. Quib[us] hui[us]modi dedit responsu[m]. No[n] solem[us] de t[ra]ctatib[us] ecc[lesiarum] cito responde[re], S[ed] petit[i]o[n]i u[est]re q[uia] de longe uenistis, & longa uia uos expectat reddit[ur]os: n[on] est differend[um] q[uod] habem[us] paratu[ru]m responde[re]. S[an]c[t]e memorie uen[er]abil[is] Vrbanus p[a]p[a], q[ua]n[do] [con]ciliu[m] pop[u]lossime (sic) [con]gregationi i[n] mo[n]te claro celebrauit, uiamq[ue] ier[oso]limitana[m] suscitauit: decreuisse memorat[ur] & scit[ur], q[uod] q[ui][cun]q[ue] p[ri]ncipes

p[ro]ui[n]cias [ue]l ciuitates sup[er] gentiles [con]q[ui]rerent, eliminatis gentiu[m] ritib[us], eo[rum] principatibus ecclesie restitute p[er]tinerent. Vat. lat. 7241, fol. 3v. Cf. *CCSSJ*, no. 89. See also: FC, pp. 739–42.

242 Rowe, 'The Papacy', pp. 160–89; Hamilton, *Latin Church, passim.*

243 *CCSSJ*, p. 12.

244 FC, pp. 742–5. See also: WT, vol. 1, pp. 537–40.

245 See Chapter 2.

246 Terra marique. William of Malmesbury, *Gesta Regum*, p. 700.

247 AA, pp. 782–4; FC, pp. 532–3; WT, vol. 1, pp. 509–10.

248 W. B. Stevenson, *The Crusaders in the East: A Brief History of the Wars of Islam with the Latins in Syria During the Twelfth and Thirteenth Centuries* (Cambridge, 1907), p. 57.

249 FC, pp. 533, 534 n. 14; WT, vol. 1, p. 510.

250 *D.Jerus.*, vol. 1, no. 35; *Codice Diplomatico della Repubblica di Genova dal DCCCCLVIII al MCLXIII*, ed. Cesare Imperiale di Sant'Angelo, 3 vols (Rome, 1936–42) (*CDRG*), vol. 1, no. 24; *RRH*, no. 55; FC, p. 534 n. 14.

251 IQ, p. 163. Cf. Baldwin, 'Ecclesiastical Developments', pp. 154–5; Emmanuel Sivan, *L'Islam et la Croisade: Idéologie et Propagande dans les Réactions Musulmanes aux Croisades* (Paris, 1968), p. 29.

252 Codices uero innumerabiles [. . .] in quibus sacrilegi ritus Sarracenorum, Turcorum, quarumque gentium inscripti erant, et nefanda carmina ariolum et aruspicum cum caracteribus execrabilibus. AA, p. 336.

253 Carole Hillenbrand, 'The First Crusade: The Muslim Perspective', in *The First Crusade*, ed. Phillips, p. 70.

254 Ibn Khallikān, *Wafayāt al-a'yān*, ed. Iḥsān 'Abbās, 8 vols (Beirut, 1968–72), vol. 1, pp. 156–60.

255 IA, vol. 10, pp. 488–9.

256 Ibn Khallikān, *Wafayāt*, vol. 3, p. 124.

257 Usāma, pp. 208–9.

258 IQ, pp. 164–5; Al-'Aẓīmī, *Tārīkh ḥalab*, p. 364; Ibn Khallikān, *Wafayāt*, vol. 3, p. 410.

259 Benjamin Z. Kedar, 'Some New Sources on Palestinian Muslims Before and During the Crusades', in *Die Kreuzfahrerstaaten als multikulturelle Gesellschaft*, ed. Hans Eberhard Mayer, Schriften des Historischen Kollegs, Kolloquien, 37 (Munich, 1997), p. 133.

260 Kedar, 'Subjected Muslims', pp. 143–4; Konrad Hirschler, 'The Jerusalem Conquest of 492/1099 in the Medieval Arabic Historiography of the Crusades: From Regional Plurality to Islamic Narrative', *Crusades* 13 (2014), pp. 37–76.

261 IA, vol. 10, p. 344; WT, vol. 1, p. 468.

262 Hans E. Mayer, 'Latins, Muslims and Greeks in the Latin Kingdom of Jerusalem', *History* 63 (1978), p. 180.

263 AA, pp. 784–6.

264 IQ, p. 164; IA, vol. 10, pp. 475–7.

265 AA, p. 786.

266 FC, p. 533.

267 IQ, p. 163; IA, vol. 10, p. 476.

268 IA, vol. 10, pp. 365–66.

269 Abū al-Fidā', *Kitāb al-mukhtaṣar fī akhbār al-bashar (al-Tārīkh)*, 4 vols (Cairo, 1907), vol. 2, p. 224; Sibṭ bin al-Jawzī, 'Extraits', p. 527; Matthew of Edessa, 'Extraits de la chronique de Matthieu d'Édesse', *Recueil des Historiens des Croisades: Documents Arméniens*, 2 vols (Paris, 1869–1906) (*RHC Ar*), vol. 1, p. 90; *Anonymi Auctoris Chronicon ad A.C. 1234 pertinens*, trans. J.-B. Chabot *et al.*, 2 vols, Corpus Scriptorum Christianorum Orientalium 109, 354 (Louvain, 1965–74), vol. 2, p. 45.

270 IA, vol. 10, p. 412.
271 James of Vitry, *Lettres*, no. 2, p. 93.
272 Nāṣir Khusraw, p. 13.
273 Sub certa pensione, domino comiti annuatim persolvenda. WT, vol. 1, p. 510. Cf. FC, p. 532.
274 Jonathan Riley-Smith, 'The Survival in Latin Palestine of Muslim Administration', in *The Eastern Mediterranean Lands in the Period of the Crusades*, ed. P. M. Holt (Warminster, 1977), p. 13; Kedar, 'Subjected Muslims', pp. 168–70.
275 IJ, p. 301.
276 Jeremy Johns, *Arabic Administration in Norman Sicily: The Royal Dīwān* (Cambridge, 2002), pp. 34–8; Alex Metcalfe, *Muslims and Christians in Norman Sicily: Arabic Speakers and the End of Islam* (London, 2003), pp. 34–6.
277 Plurimos habens inhabitatores, Christianos, Iudeos et Sarracenos. Wilbrand of Oldenburg, p. 120.
278 Kedar, 'Subjected Muslims', pp. 161–2.
279 Bahā' al-Dīn bin Shaddād, *Sīrat Ṣalāḥ al-Dīn: «al-sīra al-yūsufiyya»*, ed. Jamāl al-Dīn al-Shayyāl (Cairo, 1962) (BD), p. 82.
280 See above under 'The death of a crusader'.
281 *CGOH*, vol. 1, no. 210; *RRH*, no. 275.
282 *CDRG*, vol. 1, no. 24; *RRH*, no. 55.
283 Jidejian, *Tripoli*, pp. 60, 75–6, 77, figs 99–100, 102, 105; Pierre Coupel, 'Trois petites églises du comté de Tripoli', *BMB* 5 (Paris, 1941), p. 44 n. 1.
284 Ezekiel 27:9; 1 Kings 5:18.
285 AA, p. 670 n. 55.
286 WT, vol. 1, pp. 508–09; IQ, p. 143.
287 [Urbs] cum ciuibus suis in manu ipsius Reimundi tradita et subiugata est. AA, p. 670.
288 Al-'Aẓīmī, *Tārīkh ḥalab*, p. 362.
289 Caffaro, 'De Liberatione', p. 120.
290 IA, vol. 10, p. 372.
291 IA, vol. 10, p. 476.
292 IA, vol. 10, p. 454.
293 See also: AA, p. 670 n. 55.
294 AK, p. 327.
295 Caffaro, 'De Liberatione', pp. 119–20, 122–4.
296 See Chapter 4.
297 Gibeletū portum habet [. . .] cum catena. Marino Sanudo, 'Liber Secretorum', p. 85.
298 See Chapter 2.
299 IQ, p. 143.
300 'Imād al-Dīn al-Iṣfahānī, *Kitāb al-fatḥ al-qussī fī al-fatḥ al-qudsī*, ed. Carlo de Landberg (Leiden, 1888) ('Imād), p. 42; Abū Shāma, *Kitāb al-rawḍatayn*, vol. 3, p. 208.
301 B. Z. Kedar, '*De Iudeis et Sarracenis*: On the Categorization of Muslims in Medieval Canon Law', in *Studia in honorem ementissimi cardinalis Alphonsi M. Stickler*, ed. R. I. Castillo Lara (Rome, 1992), p. 211.
302 Kedar, 'Subjected Muslims', pp. 139–40, 160–2.
303 Antoine Fattal, *Le Statut Légal des non-Musulmans en pays d'Islam* (Beirut, 1958), pp. 203–7, 210.
304 JV, p. 318. See also: Burchard of Mount Sion, p. 92.
305 Adrian J. Boas, 'The Frankish Period: A Unique Medieval Society Emerges', *Near Eastern Archaeology* 61.3 (1998), pp. 165, 166.

306 Camille Enlart, 'L'abbaye cistercienne de Belmont en Syrie', *Syria* 4.1 (1923), p. 10; Coupel, 'Trois petites églises', p. 44; A. C. Breycha-Vauthier, 'Deir Balamand: Témoin de Cîteaux en terre libanaise', *BMB* 20 (1967), p. 15; Jidejian, *Tripoli*, pp. 60, 61, 75–6, figs 89, 105; Camille Asmar, *L'Abbaye de Belmont dite Deir el Balamend*, BMB 25 (Paris, 1972), p. 29.
307 Coupel, 'Trois petites églises', pp. 44, 45 fig. 9.
308 Iṣṭifān al-Duwayhī, *Tārīkh al-azmina*, ed. Buṭrus Fahd, 3rd ed. (Beirut, 198–), p. 104.
309 See Conclusion.
310 Ray Jabre-Mouawad, 'Un témoin melkite de la prise de Tripoli par les Mameluks (27 avril 1287)', in *Studies on the Christian Arabic Heritage in Honour of Father Prof. Dr. Samir Khalil Samir S.I. at the Occasion of his Sixty-Fifth Birthday*, ed. Rifaat Ebied and Herman Teule, Eastern Christian Studies 5 (Leuven, 2004), pp. 149–56.
311 Kamal S. Salibi, *Maronite Historians of Mediæval Lebanon* (Beirut, 1959), *passim*; Robert W. Crawford, 'William of Tyre and the Maronites', *Speculum* 30.2 (1955), p. 223.
312 JV, p. 318. See also: Burchard of Mount Sion, p. 92.
313 Balázs Major, *Medieval Rural Settlements in the Syrian Coastal Region (12th and 13th centuries)*, 2 vols (Unpublished Ph.D. thesis: Cardiff University, 2008), vol. 1, p. 169; Erica Cruikshank Dodd, *Medieval Painting in the Lebanon* (Wiesbaden, 2004), pp. 5–8; Mat Immerzeel, *Identity Puzzles: Medieval Christian Art in Syria and Lebanon* (Leuven, 2009), pp. 25–6, 175.
314 WT, vol. 1, p. 510.
315 FC, pp. 534–6, 549–57; AA, pp. 786–8, 792, 804–8; IQ, pp. 167–8, 174; WT, vol. 1, pp. 515–16, 520–1.
316 AA, pp. 786, 804. See Chapter 2.
317 Richard, *Le comté*, p. 18.
318 Al-ʿAẓīmī, *Tārīkh ḥalab*, p. 364.
319 IQ, p. 165.
320 Köhler, *Alliances*, pp. 312–19.
321 AK, pp. 402–3.

2 The forging and freedom of the county

Count Pons (1112–37)

Introduction

On 3 February 1112, Count Bertrand of Tripoli died of a sudden illness.[1] Bertrand was probably born in the late 1060s so would have been in his early forties at the time of his death.[2] Bertrand was neither as long-lived as his father nor as successful. His political aspirations had been forever strangled by rivals, both in Toulouse, where William IX of Aquitaine had evicted Bertrand from his own city, and in Tripoli, where another William – William Jordan – had threatened to plunge the Latin East into a civil war in order to reject Bertrand's demands. Bertrand ruled Tripoli without rival for only three years and even then he had to dance to the tune played by his new lord, King Baldwin. Meanwhile the prince of Antioch continued to occupy lands that Bertrand saw as rightfully his on account of his father's claims dating back to the First Crusade, including territory that would later become part of the county of Tripoli – most notably Tortosa and the future Crac des Chevaliers.

It thus fell to Bertrand's young son Pons to recover some of the confidence and political success that Raymond of Saint-Gilles had once enjoyed. Pons's career had one key advantage over his father's, in that his reign in Tripoli was not cut short by a premature death; in fact it proved to be the second longest of any of the Toulousan counts of Tripoli. In this respect, Pons would be surpassed only by his grandson Raymond III (1152–87). The long reigns of Pons and Raymond III would also be the most eventful in the county's history. Both counts oversaw radical changes in Tripoli's relationship with its neighbours, particularly the kingdom of Jerusalem. Due to his controversial involvement in the downfall of the kingdom, Raymond has attracted rather more attention from historians than has Pons. Despite this, there is a strong case to view Pons as the more important, at least as far as the county itself is concerned.

In many ways, the county of Tripoli owed its very existence as an independent polity to Pons and the remarkable stability of his reign. In the twenty-five years of his rule, Pons saw three kings of Jerusalem, three counts of Edessa and seven princes and regents of Antioch come and go. Dynastic instability should not be overlooked, for it was one of the main reasons why lesser lordships such as Hebron or Galilee never achieved the status of independent 'crusader state', as did the county of Tripoli under Pons.[3] Indeed, Pons himself led rebellions against two separate kings of Jerusalem. As will be demonstrated, it was also largely the county's specific geographical circumstances, nestled amid the mountains of Lebanon, that meant Pons proved so much more successful than other lords when it came to securing autonomy for his new-born polity.

Maternal ambiguity

There is no reason to doubt that Pons was Bertrand's biological son, but the identity of his mother is disputed. Curiously, the only chroniclers to attempt an identification of Pons's mother both lived in the Norman world – Orderic Vitalis in Normandy itself and William of Malmesbury in England. It is a mystery why these men, living on the far side of Latin Christendom, should be the best sources for Pons's parentage. Unfortunately, the two authors also offer only contradictory accounts. Orderic claimed that Pons was born to Helen, the daughter of Duke Odo I of Burgundy.[4] Meanwhile, William claimed that Pons's mother was an otherwise anonymous niece of the redoubtable Lombard marchioness Matilda of Tuscany.[5] Allegedly, Pons's grandfather Raymond of Saint-Gilles had married his son Bertrand to this niece as part of his grand territorial strategy – seeking to protect the eastern flanks of his possessions in Provence, presumably by providing his son Bertrand with dower lands in Lombardy and by securing an alliance with the great Matilda.[6]

There is no wholly convincing evidence in favour of one woman over the other. In the days when the reconstruction of the past was little more than an antiquarian pursuit, such technical points of aristocratic genealogy greatly exercised proto-historians. The seventeenth-century French Jesuit Philippe Labbe tried to reconcile the two accounts by suggesting that Bertrand had married twice: first to the anonymous Lombard woman in an unknown year and then to Helen of Burgundy in June 1095.[7] The great eighteenth-century monk-historians of Languedoc, Claude Devic and Joseph Vaissète, proposed that Bertrand had married his first wife in 1088, only for her to die soon after without issue and thus allow for the second marriage, which resulted in Pons. Devic and Vaissète rejected the baseless claim made by some of their contemporaries that the mysterious first wife was Adelaide, daughter of the local viscount Raimond-Bernard Trencavel and Ermengarde of Carcassonne. They also refused to accept that this first wife's aunt was indeed the famous Matilda of Tuscany, since they could not see how her fairly distant lands would have provided strategic protection to Bertrand's discrete Provençal domain, as William of Malmesbury claimed.[8]

It should be stressed that there is little in the way of firm primary evidence to support even the speculative theory that Bertrand was married twice, other than the contradictions in the sources themselves. Orderic Vitalis did note that Helen of Burgundy remarried after Bertrand's death, which would suggest that she outlived Bertrand.[9] Herein may lie a clue. According to Albert of Aachen, Pons inherited Tripoli 'from his *parents*' (*a parentibus*) upon his father's death.[10] The implication is that Pons's mother lived long enough to reach Syria with her husband and infant son. This in turn would imply that the woman in question was Helen, not the Lombard.

Yet even this conclusion is in doubt, and other accounts undermine the suggestion that Bertrand ever married Helen of Burgundy. According to Orderic Vitalis, Helen later married William III Talvas, count of Ponthieu, and bore him many children, including Guy II, later count of Ponthieu.[11] In the *Gesta Normannorum Ducum*, no mention is made of Pons and it is alleged that Helen and William of Ponthieu had 'two sons and just as many daughters'. However, the text's accompanying claim that Helen had previously married the duke of Burgundy – her father – casts doubt on this testimony.[12] The *Gesta Normannorum Ducum* was contradicted further by Chibnall, who identified a total of six sons and one daughter from the union of Helen and William, all appearing in a charter of 1127.[13] The modern genealogical reference work *Europäische Stammtafeln* ascribes to Helen and William no fewer than eleven children.[14] Nothing is known of later ties between Pons and his purported half-siblings, or indeed between the houses of Tripoli and Ponthieu more generally. Guy II of Ponthieu would later accompany Louis VII on the Second Crusade only to die at Ephesus in December 1147, before the king reached Tripoli where Pons's son Raymond II then ruled.[15] In short, nothing beyond Orderic's word itself suggests that Bertrand was ever married to Helen, or that Helen was Pons's mother.

By contrast, there are good reasons the view the Lombard woman as a stronger candidate. According to William of Malmesbury, Bertrand's marriage to his Lombard wife explains why, during his crusade of 1108–9, he was able to secure naval support from Pisa, as the Pisans were allegedly his wife's kinsmen.[16] William's account is corroborated by a curious slip in Albert of Aachen's account of Bertrand's crusade, when he describes the count of Toulouse having joined his Provençal fleet to a Genoese fleet at Pisa.[17] Edgington assumes this was a simple mistake, with the chronicler confusing Genoa for Pisa.[18] It is just as credible that Albert knew that Bertrand had stopped at Pisa, attracted there by his bonds of kinship and the military support these promised. Surely it is reasonable then to assume that Bertrand's Lombard woman was with him at the time and not some thirteen years in her grave. If it was the Lombard woman, not Helen of Burgundy, who accompanied Bertrand to Syria, then it was presumably the same woman who was the mother from whom Pons inherited Tripoli.

Raymond of Saint-Gilles had also had political cause to arrange a marriage alliance with Matilda of Tuscany, as William of Malmesbury suggested. Both Raymond and Matilda had been closely associated with the anti-imperial camp that had coalesced around Pope Gregory VII in the 1080s. In 1076, the pope had excommunicated Raymond for his consanguineous marriage – the cause of Bertrand's purported retroactive illegitimacy – but by the 1080s, Gregory was seeking Raymond's support against the western Emperor Henry IV, by flattering him and reminding him of his former love for St Peter. Raymond reciprocated, swearing fealty to the pope at the tomb of St Peter in Rome – agreeing to protect the pope's interests and becoming one of the so-called 'faithful of St Peter'. Meanwhile, Matilda was one of the staunchest supporters of the anti-imperialist Gregorian Reform movement, as demonstrated by her politics, military activities and intellectual patronage. Like Raymond, Matilda was willing even to accompany Pope Gregory on the mooted proto-crusade of 1074.[19]

This anti-imperial, pro-papal milieu is crucial. Technically speaking, Provence was held by Raymond as an imperial fief, not as a 'French' fief as was the case with his western territories in Toulouse and the Languedoc. Therefore, Raymond shared Matilda's concern that the state-building ambitions of Henry IV and the Salian dynasty more broadly represented a threat to baronial autonomy. The papal cause – including participation in the First Crusade – served as a convenient rallying cry and ideological fig leaf for these primarily political concerns. That Raymond and Matilda saw benefit in strengthening their loose affiliation with a formal marriage alliance would not be surprising. Moreover, Bertrand himself was no mere pawn in this, since he had already declared himself an open supporter of the Gregorian papacy by the 1080s.[20] In doubting the plausibility of Bertrand's Lombard wedding, Devic and Vaissète supposed that a strategic alliance to protect Provençal lands had to involve nearby contiguous buffer lands, which Matilda was simply unable to provide. However, alliances of mutual defence – in this case against Emperor Henry – were not necessarily predicated on such a strictly territorial view. It seems likely then that Bertrand did marry Matilda's niece as part of a broader alliance against Henry IV sweeping the southern imperial fringe from Provence to Tuscany. At the same time, a reasonable, albeit tentative conclusion is that Bertrand never actually married Helen of Burgundy, let alone fathered by her a legitimate heir.

Pons's minority

In their attempts to establish Pons's parentage, William of Malmesbury's modern editors have assumed that Pons must have been of a relatively advanced age in order to inherit Tripoli from his father.[21] Males in the Latin East, or at least the kingdom of Jerusalem in the thirteenth century, reached their majority and could thus inherit at fifteen.[22] In other words, it would have been necessary for Pons to have been born in 1097 or earlier in order to have reached his majority by his father's death in 1112. Yet this reasoning neglects a crucial piece of evidence, which reveals that Pons's reign began with a minority. The Muslim chronicler Ibn al-Qalānisī, who also happens to be the only author in any language to provide a specific date for Count Bertrand's death, explicitly insisted that Pons was too young to rule in February 1112. He described Pons as 'a small boy' (*ṭifl ṣaghīr*). He was so young, in fact, that the courtiers of Tripoli – described as Pons's 'bondsmen' or 'guardians' (*kuffal*), 'adherents' or 'lords' (*aṣḥāb*) – were obliged to reach a special agreement with Tancred of Antioch, whereby they 'made him one of Tancred's knights' (*ja'alū-hu min khayl-hi*).[23] In other words, Pons did not begin his reign as a grown man, which necessitated a period of regency.

Ibn al-Qalānisī is alone in depicting the beginning of Pons's reign as a minority in such clear language, but circumstantial evidence does support his claim. William of Tyre confirmed that Pons – still a mere 'adolescent' (*adolescens*) – was in Tancred's service (*in sui obsequio*) at the time of the latter's own death in December 1112.[24] In Pons's ancestral home of Occitania, medical theory held that males reached adolescence (*adolescentia*) around the age of fourteen.[25] William of Malmesbury corroborated that Pons was a very young man at the start of his reign, referring to him as both '*adolescens*' and '*ephebus*' in quick succession.[26] Of course, Pons was never described in the Latin sources as a mere 'boy' (*puer*) and could hardly have become one of Tancred's knights in 1112 if he truly remained an infant.

Pons was probably no more than a couple of years shy of fourteen in February 1112, having reached adolescence but not yet his legal majority at fifteen.[27] Therefore he had presumably not been born in Syria; rather, he was brought east, likely during his father's crusade in 1108–9. This conclusion is strengthened still further by the apparent brevity of Pons's time spent as a minor in Antioch, first under Tancred and then under his successor Prince Roger, following Tancred's death in December 1112. Pons accompanied Roger in the Antiochene–Tripolitan force that marched south to aid Baldwin I of Jerusalem against Mawdūd, the Saljūq atabeg of Mosul who had invaded Frankish lands in late June 1113. Baldwin had called upon Roger and Pons for help, but had evidently grown impatient waiting for these reinforcements and had attempted to attack Mawdūd's forces alone near a bridge on the road to Tiberias, where the king's army met with defeat. Roger and Pons candidly criticised Baldwin for his impetuosity upon their eventual arrival.[28]

As Albert of Aachen and William of Tyre recounted this sequence of events, they strongly implied that Pons acted only in concert with Roger. Even Ibn al-Qalānisī confirmed that Pons had accompanied Roger rather than having acted independently.[29] Most telling is Fulcher of Chartres's account of the same campaign, in which he stated quite clearly that Baldwin had summoned Roger but made no mention whatsoever of Pons.

All Fulcher had to say was that 'part of the people of Tripoli had already united with the royal army' *before* Roger's arrival and that these were the ones who joined their voices to Roger's in criticising Baldwin's impatience.[30] Pons remained nowhere to be seen, perhaps suggesting that these Tripolitan commanders were the 'guardians and lords' who ruled in the young count's stead. Pons was probably present within Roger's entourage while the host of Tripoli itself was being led by his barons and deputies – the very men who had sent the young count to Antioch. As late as summer 1113, Tripoli apparently remained without its count.

By 1115 at the latest, Pons's minority had finally ended with the count taking up residence in Tripoli, where he could now exercise his rule in full. In this year, an army of Latin Christians led by King Baldwin I of Jerusalem and another of Damascene Muslims led by Ṭughtakīn of Damascus joined forces to aid Prince Roger against a Turkish invasion of the principality of Antioch, led by Bursuq of Hamadān. In the complex political world of the Levant in the early twelfth century, Bursuq's appearance gave the Franks and the Damascenes a mutual enemy. Unlike the defeat suffered in 1113, the combined forces were able to drive the Turks off without bloodshed near Sarmīn, on the principality of Antioch's eastern marches.[31] According to Walter the Chancellor's narration, Prince Roger had written to both the king of Jerusalem and the count of Tripoli, implying that Pons was no longer present at the court of Antioch but in Tripoli.[32] As chancellor of Antioch itself, Walter can surely be trusted on this point. Indeed, it is worth noting that Walter at no point in his chronicle placed Pons in Antioch, which may suggest that the young count had left before the beginning of the chancellor's narrative on 29 November 1114.

The regency committee

Pons's minority is remarkable, not so much for its brevity, but for those who governed in his stead. The 'guardians and lords' who ruled Tripoli for the first year or two of Pons's reign are anonymous in Ibn al-Qalānisī's account.[33] Richard quite reasonably concluded that these mysterious figures were the county's 'grands barons'.[34] A search for continuity among the men who attended both Pons and his father before him reveals some likely candidates. Most prominent is Roger, the county's constable. He appeared alongside the young Pons in one of Bertrand's charters, issued in 1110 or 1111.[35] Roger had probably accompanied Bertrand and his family on the crusade of 1108–9, although very few of the participants in this expedition have been identified.[36] Roger continued to appear in Tripolitan documents after Pons's succession, first in 1117 and again in 1127.[37] Roger was presumably 'the officer constable' (*al-muqaddam kund iṣṭabl*) who accompanied Pons on a raid into the fertile Biqāʿ valley sometime between 16 May 1116 and 4 May 1117 (AH 510). According to Ibn al-Qalānisī, the two men only narrowly evaded capture at the hands of an unexpected force from Damascus and Mosul.[38] The *condominium* settlement reached between Bertrand and Ṭughtakīn in 1109, allowing the Franks to take one-third of the produce from the Biqāʿ valley, was apparently an insufficient guarantee of protection.[39]

As constable, Roger was the most important secular figure in the county after the count himself. He was effectively the count's lieutenant, commanding the army in his absence. This rank was all the more important in the Latin East, where heightened military pressures inflated the role beyond that of the ministerial seneschal, who enjoyed greater prominence in western states. Certainly Roger's name always headed those secular witness lists in which he appeared – second only to the comital family. One of the county's forts, Le Puy du Connétable (modern Qalʿat al-Msaylḥa), likely acquired its name from having once belonged to Roger himself, further demonstrating his personal prestige within Tripolitan society.[40] The loyal constable surely took a leading role in the county's administration and military affairs during Pons's minority.

Roger did not govern alone, since Ibn al-Qalānisī made it quite clear that Pons had many officers and guardians. A perusal of witness lists from this period reveal a number of possible figures. These include the secular Udalard of *Pontiano* and Pons of *Grilione*, who witnessed Count Bertrand's 1110/11 charter alongside Roger and the young Pons. They probably originated from Catalonia and Occitania, where the names Udalard and Pons were respectively popular. Among their fellow witnesses can also be found numerous clergymen, including Bishop Albert of Tripoli, Archbishop Peter of Āfāmiyyā (Apamea) and al-Bāra (Albara), and the visiting bishop of Béziers.[41] It is known that clerics played an important part ruling other areas of the early Latin East, not to mention throughout the Latin Christian world more generally. Indeed, Peter of Apamea-Albara had first been appointed archbishop in 1098 specifically to act as Raymond of Saint-Gilles's deputy in the region, lest it be seized back by the local Muslims or stolen by his great rival Bohemond of Taranto. Peter had proven himself perfectly capable of fulfilling all the responsibilities expected of him, including overseeing defensive arrangements, and he continued to hold his position even after Tancred of Antioch effectively disenfranchised Raymond and the Provençals of this territory in 1102.[42] Although Āfāmiyyā itself was henceforth to lie firmly within the principality of Antioch, its archbishop continued to exercise authority over one of the county of Tripoli's four bishoprics – easternmost Rafaniyya. Similarly, when Raymond appointed Albert as bishop of Tripoli *c.*1103, he very likely envisaged that the former abbot would assist him in the governance of the Pilgrims' Mount and eventually Tripoli. The participation of Peter and Albert in the government of the county in 1112 would thus come as no surprise at all.

Anna Komnene's account of this period may offer some corroboration of ecclesiastical governance in Tripoli. It will be remembered that

Byzantine envoys seeking an alliance with the Tripolitans in early 1112 had left money in the care of Count Bertrand and Bishop Albert of Tripoli before heading south to meet King Baldwin of Jerusalem.[43] When these imperial ambassadors returned to Tripoli, they found that Bertrand was dead. Worse, his son and the same bishop refused to return the money, eventually yielding only after the Byzantines threatened to cut off the vital supply link between Cyprus and Tripoli.[44] Given that Pons was evidently still in Tripoli and had yet to head north to Antioch, it would seem that this diplomatic crisis took place very soon after Bertrand's death, when negotiations with Tancred for his wardship of Pons were yet to be finalised. Moreover, Anna's testimony strongly implies that Bishop Albert had no small measure of influence over the young count and Tripoli's administration.

That a group of officers and not an individual ruled the county at this time is significant in itself. Alone it suggests that Pons's mother, whoever she might have been, did not act as regent, as Hodierna of Jerusalem later did on behalf of Pons's grandson, Raymond III.[45] Nor did any individual male figure step up to assume sole command. It might be thought that a lesson had been learned after William Jordan – perhaps intended initially as a mere regent – had attempted to claim the fledgling county for himself as Raymond's *de facto* heir. Such governance by committee also had a highly relevant precedent, which was so recent for there to be chronological overlap. This was when a similar group of courtiers governed the western possessions of the house of Toulouse on behalf of Pons's infant uncle, Alfons Jordan, after William of Montpellier had brought him to Europe in 1105 and after his half-brother Bertrand had headed eastwards in 1108.[46] According to William of Malmesbury, William of Montpellier and Raymond of Saint-Gilles's other former followers took charge of Alfons's protection and upbringing.[47] This was a long-term arrangement, since Alfons did not come into his majority until *c.*1118.

Undoubtedly the officers of Tripoli would have known of the situation in the west, perhaps modelling their own arrangement upon it. For one thing, William of Montpellier had been with the crusaders at Tripoli before returning west in 1105 and was presumably well known to those of Bertrand's followers who had not headed east from Europe until 1108 – men such as Roger the constable. Generally speaking, contact between Tripoli and Occitania remained fairly frequent in the early years of Pons's reign, remembering of course that Bishop Albert had only recently returned from the council of Mende.[48] Although Pons was the first count of Tripoli never to rule in the west, either in Toulouse and Saint-Gilles or in Cerdanya, he nonetheless held property in his ancestral homeland. As late as 1132, Pons still held property in the county of Velay, where the First Crusade's legate, Adhémar of Le Puy, had once been bishop. These possessions were not all enumerated, yet included fishing rights (*piscaria*) in the River Loire. It is not at all clear why Pons held property in the west or how he could have benefited from such distant holdings, but it seems likely that comital agents helped to manage them. Pons later surrendered his western holdings to the church of Le Puy in 1132 and, when Pons's son Raymond II later confirmed his father's donation in 1142, Count Robert III of Auvergne acted as an intermediary between the count of Tripoli and his ecclesiastical benefactors in Velay, bringing the confirmation itself to the west.[49] Jonathan Phillips has shown how channels of communication between the Latin East and the west remained alive and active throughout the twelfth century.[50] That the counts of Tripoli maintained property on both sides of the Mediterranean for decades after the First Crusade – probably with the help of the count of Auvergne – vividly underlines this point. Moreover, such trans-Mediterranean connectedness makes it all the more likely that the two regency committees of Toulouse (1108–*c.*1118) and Tripoli (1112–*c.*1113) operated in full knowledge of each other.

Occitan–Norman rapprochement

It should not be thought that Tripoli's regency committee simply conducted business as usual. In fact, the barons proactively set the county on a radically different path from the one it had been following since at least 1109, if not earlier still. By enrolling Pons as one of Tancred's knights, the guardians brought to an end the long-running and acrimonious dispute between the Occitan crusaders and the Normans.[51] Since the infamous spats between Raymond of Saint-Gilles and Bohemond of Taranto during the First Crusade, the Occitans and Normans had had a strained relationship at best, divided from one another by culture and language – the Normans speaking *langue d'oïl* and the Occitans *langue d'oc.* Indeed, Huizinga saw in such mutual hostility on crusade an early demonstration of a conscious proto-nationalist sentiment in the Middle Ages.[52] The Norman Ralph of Caen claimed that the 'Provençals' (*Provinciales*) were as different from the Normans (*Franci*), 'as much as a hen is to a duck', for they were less bellicose, plainer in their garb and fonder of food than the allegedly austere Normans.[53]

Count Raymond's actions on behalf of the Byzantines after the First Crusade had continued to stoke anti-Norman sentiment among the Occitan crusaders. William Jordan's and Bertrand's willingness to acknowledge Emperor Alexios Komnenos's suzerainty over what had been the southern *themes* of the duchy of Antioch – including Tortosa – only served to perpetuate this. William Jordan, who had temporarily allied with Tancred in 1109, had been forced into this arrangement out of necessity rather than choice after the Byzantines had received Bertrand's loyalty. Crucially, William Jordan's brief truce with Tancred did little to end the grave hostility between the Occitans of Tripoli and the Normans of Antioch. It is important to remember that, upon his death, Count Bertrand himself had been planning to aid the Byzantines in a war against Prince Tancred.[54]

Given such enduring tension, it is somewhat surprising that the predominantly Occitan ruling committee of Tripoli chose to seek a rapprochement with the Norman prince of Antioch in 1112. After all, the very men who sent Pons to Antioch were the same who had struggled against the Normans alongside Bertrand and perhaps even Raymond of Saint-Gilles and William Jordan. Nor was this simply a case of reversing Occitan–Norman hostility, since it was also concomitant upon their implicit rejection of the earlier alliance with the anti-Norman Byzantines. Additionally, it is perplexing that Pons should not have been sent to serve out his minority under King Baldwin of Jerusalem, who was theoretically his and Tripoli's direct suzerain. Why then should the late Bertrand's former followers – Pons's guardians – have changed tack so dramatically and so rapidly, moving Tripoli closer to Antioch and further from both Jerusalem and Constantinople?

Richard assumes that the Tripolitans were pushed towards Antioch by the increasingly onerous demands made of them by Emperor Alexios and King Baldwin. By aligning with the Normans and thereby rejecting the mooted military alliance with the Byzantines against Antioch, the Tripolitans desired to terminate or to diminish their dependence upon the Byzantine empire.[55] The implication is that Pons's guardians had decided that imperial support from Constantinople was not worth a Latin civil war in North Syria, even one waged against their long-term rivals. Indeed Pons – under the influence of Bishop Albert – had not only refused to return the gold left in his father's care by the Byzantine ambassadors in 1112, but had attempted at the same time to avoid reconfirming the fealty previously sworn to Emperor Alexios by his father and grandfather.[56] After 1112, Tripoli's relationship with Byzantium would hold little practical relevance and be intermittent at best.[57]

As for the king of Jerusalem, Richard also believes that the Tripolitans were growing weary of Baldwin's demands on their stretched military resources, as exhibited by the numerous campaigns in which Count Bertrand had been expected to participate during his short reign.[58] Bertrand's death offered the Tripolitans an opportunity to weaken their allegiance to Baldwin by acquiring a new allegiance to Tancred: a 'feudal' counterweight to Jerusalem's domineering influence. It is worth adding that the king had represented a somewhat unwelcome influence over Count Bertrand. Although Godfrey of Bouillon had apparently expected Tripoli to form part of his realm, Baldwin I had been unable to exercise any direct authority over this city until 1109 – partly because it had remained in Muslim control and partly because Raymond of Saint-Gilles and William Jordan had viewed themselves as independent 'commanders of the Christian army'. In 1109, however, the occasion to enforce the royal prerogative had presented itself to Baldwin, when he had called the council of Tripoli to decide between the competing claims of Bertrand and William Jordan. At this point the king had managed to split the late count

Raymond's lands into a northern and southern half, rendering the latter – including Tripoli – a firmly Jerusalemite fief.[59] In this respect he had followed exactly the same policy already implemented to consolidate his power in the south, where he had integrated such quasi-independent crusader lordships as the principality of Galilee into his expanding kingdom, first by intervening in their internal affairs at times of dynastic weakness and then by dividing them into a smaller, weaker and more manageable parcels.[60] The Occitan crusaders at Tripoli had already seen their autonomy curtailed by the king during the succession crisis of 1109 and must have feared further erosion of their power in 1112, when the county again seemed ripe for royal intervention in the wake of Count Bertrand's sudden death and the minority of his only son.

In 1112, the future of the Toulousan dynasty itself rested on a knife's edge, not just in Syria but also in the west. Here the guardians of the infant Alfons Jordan faced a familiar enemy, William IX of Aquitaine, who was set to invade Toulouse for a second time in 1114.[61] Simultaneously Count Raymond-Beranger III of Barcelona posed a threat to Provence and the areas around Carcassonne.[62] The house of Toulouse thus faced eviction and even extinction on both sides of the Mediterranean. This is the context for understanding the Tripolitans' decision to seek a rapprochement with Tancred in 1112. William Jordan had once sought Tancred's help against the threat posed to his very right to rule by Bertrand and King Baldwin. Ironically, Bertrand's former followers now found themselves having to do much the same. For his part, Tancred himself had been a victim of arbitrary royal policy in the recent past, first forced out of Galilee *c.*1099–1101 and later curtailed in both Tripoli and Edessa at the council of Tripoli in 1109.[63] Tancred thus understood the Tripolitans' fear of further royal interference and knew first hand the impact it could have on one's career, which gave the Normans and the Occitans common cause in 1112.

Tancred was clearly keen to seal the alliance with the Tripolitans, because he sweetened the deal by offering them the lands that had been so contentious in 1109, namely the city of Tortosa, the town of Maraqiyya and the fortresses of Ṣāfīthā (later the Templars' Chastel Blanc) and Ḥiṣn al-Akrād (Crac des Chevaliers). Tancred gave these back to the Tripolitans, although not fully; rather he 'enfeoffed' (*aqṭaʿa*) Pons with them.[64] Thus the Tripolitans could be content that lands once held by Raymond and William Jordan had been restored, while Tancred could be content that he retained suzerainty over them as the young count's liege lord.

Pons was soon to receive a second boon when Tancred, lying on his deathbed in December 1112, arranged for the count to be betrothed to Tancred's own soon-to-be-widowed Cecilia, daughter of King Philip I of France.[65] According to William of Malmesbury, Tancred arranged for his wife's marriage to Pons because he saw the young man's great potential to be of benefit to the Christians and a cause of ruin for the Turks.[66]

The significance of this union, beyond furthering the Occitan–Norman rapprochement, was that the Toulousan dynasty had now acquired the important symbol of royal blood. Decades later, William of Tyre would emphasise Count Raymond III's descent from the French crown via Cecilia when justifying the count's regency of Jerusalem in 1174.[67] More immediately and prosaically, Count Pons benefited by acquiring Cecilia's dowry lands in the principality of Antioch, namely the fortresses of Arzghān and al-Rūj in the Orontes valley.[68] Both Arzghān and al-Rūj would prove critical to Pons's rebellion against King Fulk some twenty years later.[69] More importantly, a 'Provençal outpost' had already been established at al-Rūj during the First Crusade by one of Raymond of Saint-Gilles's followers, Peter of Roaix.[70] Thus, at least one more of the Toulousan dynasty's claimed holdings in the principality of Antioch was restored through the Norman–Occitan rapprochement of 1112, removing yet another point of contention standing between friendlier relations.

According to Albert of Aachen, Pons's and Cecilia's wedding was celebrated in Tripoli in summer 1115 upon King Baldwin's advice, following the campaign against Bursuq of Hamadān.[71] In truth, Baldwin probably did no more than give his consent to the betrothal already agreed by Tancred and the Tripolitans, acting as Pons's theoretical suzerain. This delay of almost two years was most likely due to Pons's minority. Contemporary canon law allowed a man to marry at fourteen, but it might have been deemed prudent to wait until Pons came into his full inheritance at fifteen.[72] Of course, there is also the possibility that the king prevaricated because he was uneasy at the consolidation of the Tripolitan–Antiochene alliance this union represented, which was beginning to undermine his own seigneurial claims over Pons and Tripoli. Baldwin's loyal chaplain, Fulcher of Chartres, rather inexplicably failed to mention the marriage, despite confirming that the king did go to Tripoli at this time.[73] The royalist Fulcher may not have approved of this union if it threatened the king's authority. As far as the Tripolitans were concerned, however, Baldwin had nothing to offer them or Pons in 1112, certainly when compared to the generosity of Tancred, and if anything the king actually loomed as a potential threat to their autonomy, hence their seeking of a new and closer relationship with Antioch despite previous tensions.

The persistence of a bipartite Latin East

With Tancred's grant of lands north of ʿArqa to Pons in fief in 1112, only three years after the council of Tripoli in 1109, the crusader-settlers were again redrawing the map of the emergent Latin East. Certainly Richard believes that Tancred's enfeoffment of Pons was a critical development in the early history of the county of Tripoli, as it brought to a definitive end the brief period between 1109 and 1112 when the county of Tripoli – or rather its southern half under the rule of Bertrand – was a true 'fief hiérosolymitain'. Now that Pons controlled both the Antiochene fiefs of the north and the Jerusalemite fiefs of the south, his domain filled the area that William of Tyre would later define to be the county of Tripoli – its northern border located between Maraqiyya and Valania and its southern border between Jubayl and Beirut.[74] According to Richard, any indication subsequent to this point that the county remained part of the kingdom of Jerusalem or the principality of Antioch, or indeed anything other than a truly autonomous polity in and of itself, should be written off as an irrelevant and inconsequential relic of these three short years.[75] The two 'crusader states' of Antioch and Jerusalem had been driven apart by the emergence of a third: independent Tripoli.

Richard's interpretation deserves some further evaluation. Pons's acquisition of Antiochene fiefs was significant for the political landscape of the Latin East, but these lands were not immediately integrated fully with his Jerusalemite holdings, thereby creating a new 'crusader state' wholly independent of both Antioch and Jerusalem. Rather, the agreement in 1112 did no more than to give the count of Tripoli *personal* lands within the principality of Antioch, which were regarded as something separate from – albeit contiguous with – his Jerusalemite lands in the south. In 1174, Raymond III of Tripoli would marry Eschiva of Tiberias, but his county of Tripoli and her principality of Galilee did not become one unit.[76] Later still, the principality of Antioch and the county of Tripoli were united under one dynasty only to remain largely separate in an administrative sense.[77] The case of Normandy and England after 1066 offers a more general and familiar medieval parallel of two states united dynastically but divided administratively.

The kings of Jerusalem and their courtiers continued to view Tripoli as part of their realm for at least a decade after 1112, regardless of Pons's new Antiochene fiefs. Just as his father Bertrand had done, Pons assisted his liege King Baldwin on numerous military expeditions and often acted only on his explicit instruction.[78] Fulcher of Chartres did not bother to mention the Tripolitans at all in his description of the joint Christian–Muslim campaign against Bursuq of Hamadān in 1115, listing only three distinct contingents: Jerusalem, Antioch and Damascus.[79] As already seen, Pons and the Tripolitans did participate in this campaign, so their absence from Fulcher's list here is curious, unless the county was still regarded as a Jerusalemite fief with an essentially discrete Antiochene annex. Walter the Chancellor confirmed the king's enduring authority over the count by writing that Pons had only headed north to fight Bursuq in the first place after Baldwin had commanded him to do so.[80]

Fulcher later wrote an epitaph for Baldwin I after the king's death in 1118, in which the monarch was said to have been personally responsible for capturing a number of important cities along the coast of Syria, including Tripoli.

Acre, Caesarea, Beirut, also Sidon,
He took by force from the atrocious native enemies.
Next, the lands of the Arabs or rather those lands that touch the Red Sea,
He brought under his authority and subdued to obedience.
And he captured Tripoli, but also oppressed Arsūf no less,
And many more besides he rendered tributaries.[81]

No mention is made of Count Bertrand's role in capturing Tripoli and no indication is given that this city was in any way different from the other cities brought under the king's authority. It must be noted that all of Baldwin's conquests listed here lay south of the important boundaries of al-Nahr al-Kabīr al-Janūbī and Nahr al-ʿArqa, suggesting the persistence of the bipartite scheme observed in sources ever since the First Crusade.

A deed issued in the name of Count Pons himself in February 1117, recording a donation to the Venetians, was unusual in that it was dated by the number of years served in office by the current bishop of Tripoli and, most relevantly, by the number of years served by King Baldwin I.[82] Richard argues that the document was written in Venice by the recipients who, as 'étrangers au comté', did not know that it was independent of Jerusalem.[83] The fact that the authors may have been foreign is not sufficient cause to dismiss this evidence. It seems strange that the Venetians could have been so misinformed, since it is well known that they were in regular contact with the Latin East throughout this period and, as this very document indicates, had a permanent presence in Tripoli itself. At the very least it suggests that the county's political status vis-à-vis the kingdom appeared ambiguous to contemporaries.

Arguably the most convincing evidence to demonstrate that many still regarded the Syrian coast as having been divided into just two spheres long after 1112 is a relatively late passage in a recension of the itinerary of the pilgrim Fretellus: 'Twelve milestones from Tripoli, towards the east, is the Albana, the river of ʿArqa (Nahr al-ʿArqa), at which limit begins the kingdom of Jerusalem.'[84]

This survives in a manuscript dated to the 1150s, but the original source it enhances was written sometime around 1137.[85] By claiming that the kingdom of Jerusalem's northern border was at Nahr al-ʿArqa, rather than al-Nahr al-Kabīr al-Janūbī, it conforms precisely to the settlement reached at Tripoli in 1109, prior to William Jordan's death and also Bertrand's subsequent acquisition of ʿArqa itself.[86]

The weight of early evidence therefore suggests that the Frankish coast of the Latin East continued to be viewed as a bipartite territory – tripartite with the inclusion of landlocked Edessa – just as it had in the first decade after the First Crusade, with Count Pons himself possessing discrete but contiguous fiefs in the principality of Antioch and kingdom of Jerusalem respectively. It is therefore necessary to look later than 1112 for the point at which the county of Tripoli and thus the Latin East as a whole took the form recognisable from William of Tyre's account. What is already clear is that the county of Tripoli must have lain at the very heart of the resultant border changes.

The question of Jubayl

The important theme emerging from this discussion is that the county of Tripoli in the early twelfth century was not the clearly defined state that historians recognise when reading sources dating from the mid-twelfth century and later. Nor was the county's lack of coherence at this time merely the result of its constitutional division between an Antiochene north and a Jerusalemite south. Pons enjoyed only piecemeal control over his lands, particularly in the Jerusalemite half where one of the principal settlements, Jubayl, remained stubbornly beyond his direct authority. Although the council of Tripoli in 1109 had ruled that this port-city should belong to Bertrand, the subsequent spat between the count of Tripoli and Jubayl's Genoese caretakers, led by the Embriaci family, had effectively rendered the town autonomous of comital authority.[87] Although free of the count's power, it is important not to imagine Jubayl as a Genoese 'colony' in the modern sense. Phillips and Hall have observed that the way in which the Embriaci as a family took full control of the city fit a general pattern seen right across the Mediterranean, from Jubayl in Syria to Almería in Iberia, whereby Genoa's conquests were all effectively 'privatised' in the hands of individuals. This crucially spared the commune itself any direct commercial risk or political responsibility.[88]

There is little evidence that the Embriaci softened their refusal to acknowledge the count's authority during the reign of Bertrand's son, with a representative from Jubayl – Lord Hugh Embriaco – appearing in only one charter from this period.[89] Meanwhile, charters issued by the Embriaci themselves imply a sense of Genoese exceptionalism in Jubayl and its environs. In 1135 Adele, the widow of Hugh Embriaco of Jubayl, donated to the canons of the Holy Sepulchre an annual payment of twelve bezants and 120 *rotula* of oil to be levied from the town of Nephin. Adele's document bears a witness list composed exclusively of figures unknown to comital witness lists of the period. In fact, the document was issued 'by the command of the lady and her son [Hugh's heir in Jubayl], William Embriaco', with no reference whatsoever to the count of Tripoli.[90]

Perhaps most striking is the vexing issue of the Church in Jubayl. The earliest mention of a Latin bishop of Jubayl comes only in 1133, when Pope Innocent II – an ally of Genoa at the time – confirmed Bishop Romanus in office. Although Richard assumed that a bishop was appointed to Jubayl immediately after the city's conquest by the crusaders, it is the opinion of both Rowe and Hamilton that the diocese remained vacant as late as the 1120s and even the 1130s, when the patriarch of Antioch initiated a reshuffle of his vast territory, creating also the sees of Tortosa and

Rafaniyya, *inter alia*.[91] This was probably in response to Jerusalem's controversial acquisition of the traditionally Antiochene archdiocese of Tyre in 1124, which threatened the northern patriarch's prerogatives in the Tripolitan sees of Tortosa, Tripoli and Jubayl, not to mention those of Beirut, Acre, Sidon and Tyre itself in the kingdom of Jerusalem proper.

Subsequent to the see's belated resurrection, the bishops of Jubayl remain obscure figures, even if not quite to the extent Cahen believed.[92] As is often the case with the Latin East, the most prominent bishops of Jubayl are found in the thirteenth century. For example, Bishop Vassal led the way in establishing the Cistercian abbey of St Sergius in the 1230s.[93] Either Vassal himself or one of his predecessors had an intellectually pretentious streak, insisting in the 1210s that people call his episcopal city by its Greek Biblical name of Byblos rather than the 'vulgar' Gibelet, which was the Franks' Romance corruption of Semitic Gebal (Hebrew) or Jubayl (Arabic).[94] Indeed, Latin authors consistently referred to the city in the ecclesiastical although not secular sense as Byblos, which suggests this classical titular style was an entrenched custom. Clearly not all bishops of Jubayl were learned classicists, however, with one condemned by Pope Innocent IV in 1243 for being profoundly uneducated and effectively illiterate.[95]

Despite the eclectic mix of men who sat the episcopal throne of Jubayl in the thirteenth century, it remains the case that their twelfth-century forerunners are largely unknown. Prior to 1187, they appear mainly as addressees of papal bulls, mostly subject to demands that they and the other Tripolitan bishops respect the authority of the archbishop of Tyre and thus the patriarch of Jerusalem rather than the patriarch of Antioch.[96] Throughout Pons's reign and the twelfth century as a whole the bishops of Jubayl never witnessed a single document in the county, whether issued by the count of Tripoli or the lord of Jubayl. This is all the more striking when compared to the other bishops in the county. No bishop of Jubayl appeared alongside the bishops of Tripoli, Tortosa and Rafaniyya when they gathered on 8 February 1127 and twice in 1132, nor when the bishops of Tripoli and Rafaniyya witnessed a charter in December 1139.[97] Jubayl's bishop was similarly absent from two subsequent gatherings in 1142, when the archbishop of Albara-Apamea represented his vacant suffragan see of Rafaniyya, and a third in 1145, when just the bishops of Tortosa and Tripoli witnessed a comital charter.[98] Graham Loud's belief that Otto of Freising met the bishop of Jubayl at the papal court in Rome to discuss the fall of Edessa and the plight of the Latin East in 1145 is mistaken, as the original Latin refers to *Gabulensem episcopum* – that is, the bishop of Jabala.[99] Indeed, the bishops of Jubayl may have adopted the pretentious customary toponym 'Byblos' precisely in order to avoid this common source of confusion.

It may be that the bishops of Jubayl failed to participate regularly in the county's affairs because their see was unusually impoverished, as both Wilbrand of Oldenburg and James of Vitry noted.[100] Jubayl was arguably the smallest of the four dioceses, lacking the fertile plains and resultant tithe revenues of the north. Indeed, Tripoli and Tortosa were actually conglomerations of multiple dormant dioceses due to the fact that the Latin population in the county was too small to justify re-establishing every single bishopric found in the ancient ecclesiastical lists. As William of Tyre explained, the see of Tripoli comprised the ancient diocese of Tripoli itself and also those of ʿArqa, Batrūn[101] and Orthosias (*Artusca*),[102] while Tortosa incorporated Tortosa, the nearby island of Arwād and Maraqiyya. Meanwhile, Jubayl was a lone see with no dependents.[103] Rafaniyya was also a solitary diocese, but was compensated somewhat by being the only Latin bishopric covering the vast area of the county's eastern marches, beginning around Crac and extending up to Homs.

Of course, it seems surprising that the bishops of Jubayl could have been so poor, given the valuable trade flowing through the city's port. Another reason why the bishops of Jubayl remained apart from the county's other clergy for much of the twelfth century may be because they were associated so closely with Jubayl's isolationist Genoese lords. The connection to Genoa could explain why Jubald, bishop-elect of Jubayl, appeared as the only representative from the county of Tripoli alongside various secular and ecclesiastical witnesses from the kingdom of Jerusalem in a charter issued in Acre by the city's bishop *c.*1167.[104] Genoa had control of its own quarter in Acre, which was the commune's second greatest Syrian outpost after Jubayl itself, and the commune's interest in the city was set to grow in the later twelfth and thirteenth centuries.[105] Perhaps then Jubald was more inclined to appear in Acre rather than Tripoli, which had never had a Genoese quarter due to Count Bertrand's controversial decision to rescind this particular promise in 1109.[106]

Yet even this explanation has its limits. Many decades later in February 1186, Raymond Embriaco of Jubayl issued a document that was witnessed by the bishop of Tripoli but not by Jubayl's own chief cleric.[107] By this point the Embriaci had warmed to the idea of a closer relationship with the central government at Tripoli, which explains the bishop of Tripoli's presence. Where then was the bishop of Jubayl? Taking into account both the see's poverty and the Genoese dominance of Jubayl in general, it may simply be that the Embriaci had been unwilling to endow the cathedral and diocese sufficiently to allow for the emergence of a strong bishop, for political or financial reasons. Jubayl itself had initially been promised in its entirety to the church of St Lawrence of Genoa.[108] St Lawrence's was understood to represent the commune of Genoa as a whole but was also the mother-church of Genoa's far-flung colonies, Jubayl included. If ecclesiastical matters in Jubayl and elsewhere were generally directed by the chapter of St Lawrence's, then it might not have been deemed a priority for there to have been a bishop of Jubayl at all. This frames Jubayl as something of a Genoese 'peculiar' in ecclesiastical terms, existing beyond the ordinary church hierarchy of the Latin East.

Mack believes that the fine and ornate crusader cathedral still standing in Jubayl is testament to the Embriaci lords' willingness to spend money on beautifying their church and city.[109] The most impressive element of this structure – the surviving baptistery – dates to *c.*1200.[110] This was after the point at which Mack believes the Embriaci to have accepted their place in local Syro-Frankish society.[111] Therefore, this does not challenge the proposal here that the earlier Embriaci might have been reluctant to grant the bishops of Jubayl too much money and freedom. For the Embriaci, the chief value of having a bishop in Jubayl may have been to prevent the city being integrated into the 'super-diocese' of Tripoli, together with ʿArqa, Batrūn and Orthosias. After all, the Embriaci were keen to resist Tripoli's dominance in the secular sphere. Maybe the bishopric of Jubayl was not constituted permanently at all in the twelfth century, with bishops occasionally appointed on a somewhat *ad hoc* basis in response to specific needs, hence their irregular appearances in the sources and their lack of involvement in the quotidian administration of either the county of Tripoli generally or Jubayl specifically.

Genoese, Occitan and 'Frankish' identity

The most recent scholarship on the Genoese in the Latin East suggests that the Embriaci of Jubayl remained aloof from the other permanent crusader-settlers until the mid-twelfth century. By the 1160s, the third generation had started to identify more with their fellow Syrian-born aristocratic 'Franks' and less with their Italian cousins back in Genoa.[112] This question of settler identity is an important one. Historians have spilt much ink dissecting the meaning of the word 'Frank' in a crusader context. The First Crusade was partially conceived as a pan-Frankish expedition, a resurrection of past Carolingian glory, in which all participants were able to become 'Franks', even if they were not Frankish in the strict ethnic, linguistic, historic or geographic senses.[113] True, Godfrey of Bouillon was said to be descended from Charlemagne, but it was a comparative stretch for Ralph of Caen to call his fellow Normans – descendants of Scandinavians who had entered the Frankish realm *after* the Carolingian golden age – '*Franci*'.[114] Most relevantly, 'Frankishness' seems to have become the predominant identity for the crusader-settlers throughout the Latin East, uniting them against their indigenous subjects and neighbours in a legal as well as cultural sense.[115]

Arabic authors, aware of the 'Franks' (*ifranj*, sg. *franjī*) since the Carolingian period itself, now used the term to distinguish the Latin crusaders from their erstwhile Byzantine allies, known as 'Romans' (*al-Rūm*).[116] For the Arabs, the crusaders all spoke one 'Frankish language' (*lugha franjiyya*), seemingly oblivious to the subtle differences between the crusaders' Latin and their various Romance vernaculars. Bahāʾ al-Dīn bin Shaddād praised a Byzantine envoy who could speak Arabic, Greek and 'Frankish' (*al-franjiyya*).[117] Only rarely did Arab authors indicate the existence of sub-categories of 'Frank' and never did they isolate the 'Provençals'.[118] Indeed, the lead Occitan crusader, Raymond of Saint-Gilles, was explicitly called 'Saint-Gilles the Frank' (*ṣanjīl al-franjī*).[119] Arabic authors did, however, choose to distinguish the Italians from the 'Franks'. Ibn al-Qalānisī provided early Arabic corroboration of this observation, by distinguishing between 'the Franks and the Genoese' (*al-ifranj wa-al-janawiyy*[*ūn*]) in his description of Bertrand of Saint-Gilles's arrival in Syria in 1109.[120] As is known from Albert of Aachen, Bertrand had brought men from the Provençal port of Saint-Gilles as well as Genoese, but it is clear that Ibn al-Qalānisī, writing a few years later, saw no difference between Provençals and Franks, only between Franks and Genoese.[121] Despite Richard's insistence on Tripoli's distinctly 'Provençal' character, the Occitan identity was not strong enough to impact upon contemporary Arabic accounts in the same way that Italo-Genoese identity did.

The Latins themselves were rather more aware of the distinct Occitan identity in the earliest period of crusader settlement. Even during the First Crusade some doubted whether the Occitans were truly 'Franks', given their seemingly peculiar cultural mores. Worst of all, they spoke *langue d'oc* – a Romance dialect that was closer to Catalan and Castilian than *langue d'oïl*. Thus many chroniclers of the First Crusade distinguished the southern French from the (other) Franks by terming them 'Provençals'.[122] Authors continued to apply the 'Provençal' label to Occitan settlers in the Latin East, even if it ultimately proved less enduring than the Embriaci's Italo-Genoese identity. In 1119, Count Pons accompanied King Baldwin to lend assistance to the principality of Antioch against Ilghāzī of Mārdīn, although they arrived too late to save Prince Roger from defeat and death at the Battle of the Field of Blood (*Ager Sanguinis*). According to Walter's account of the events surrounding this catastrophe, Pons did not lead the 'Tripolitans' *per se* but rather the 'Provençals' (*provinciales*).[123]

It may be that Pons, who presumably spoke *langue d'oc*, was envisaged as fulfilling a leadership role in an ethnic or linguistic sense rather than a territorial: that is, a 'ruler of the Provençals' in the Latin East as a whole, deputised to the king of Jerusalem. Mayer notes that the king of Jerusalem from 1115 onwards styled himself 'king of the Latins', thereby constructing a kingdom exclusive to one particular religio-linguistic caste: a Latin Christian *Staatsvolk* that implicitly excluded people of other groups, including Muslims but also Greek and Syrian Christians.[124] Was it the case that, around the same time that the king of Jerusalem became king of the Latins, so too did Count Pons become 'count of the Provençals', ruling over a specifically Occitan *Staatsvolk*?

Not all Occitans lived within the county of Tripoli. Many of low social status seem to have settled in the kingdom of Jerusalem, perhaps attracted to its heightened sanctity and prestige as the 'true' Holy Land.[125] In 1156 names familiar to the Midi, such as Pons of Provence, Aimery of Poitiers and Peter the Catalan, dominated a list of the burgess inhabitants of Mahumeria (al-Bīra), one of the 'new towns' established by the canons of the Holy Sepulchre.[126] By the thirteenth century, Acre had a 'Provençal street'.[127] Prawer suspected that the burgesses of the Latin East were disproportionately of Occitan stock because they had easier and cheaper access to the Syrian-linked ports of Provence than their counterparts elsewhere in Europe.[128] This observation is clearly significant, as it suggests that the county of Tripoli was not unique among the crusader states for having a high proportion of Occitan settlers. Since the county did not monopolise 'Provençal' settlement, then the 'Provençals' who followed Pons in 1119 may well have been drawn from elsewhere within the Latin East, bound loosely to the count by shared culture and language, which in turn made it pragmatic for Pons to lead them into battle.

Conversely, just as the county was not the only area in Latin Syria with high proportions of Occitan settlers, so too was the county itself not exclusively or homogeneously Occitan. The indigenous population, the Genoese and other Italian settlers, and also French-dominated religious orders all ensured that this was not the case. According to pseudo-Fretellus in the second quarter of the twelfth century, Tripoli was '*provincialium civitas*'.[129] Modern translators have rendered this 'the city of the provincials' or, more awkwardly, 'a city of people of the province'.[130] Technically correct, these misleading and clunky translations should be jettisoned in favour of 'city of the Provençals'. In other words, the *city* of Tripoli was dominated by Occitans, but the *county* was not necessarily so. It will be remembered that this same author also believed that Tripoli was the northernmost city of the kingdom of Jerusalem and not the capital of an independent crusader state.[131] At a time of such fluidity in terms of political borders, it is perhaps not surprising that the settlers within the county would have defined themselves primarily in non-territorial terms, as a diffuse Occitan *Staatsvolk* or a Genoese colony, for example. The county of Tripoli as historians imagine it – a well-defined Occitan crusader state – did not yet exist, if indeed it ever was to.

Slide to autonomy

The first decade of Pons's reign must be understood in a context of fluid borders and identities. He ruled over a patchwork polity, with non-Occitan and Occitan settlers alike owing theoretical allegiances to a diverse range of earthly powers, including the Byzantine emperor, the king of Jerusalem, the prince of Antioch and – in the specific case of the Embriaci at Jubayl – the commune of Genoa. It was at this time, when the very structure of the Latin East remained negotiable, that Pons moved to assert his autonomy, creating in the process the county of Tripoli as William of Tyre and modern historians would come to recognise it.

The separation of the county of Tripoli – that is, the southern half, discrete from the Antiochene fiefs – from the kingdom of Jerusalem was a long road, but one marked by distinct milestones. One such event was the council of Nablus held on 23 January 1120, which aimed to reform morals in the kingdom of Jerusalem after a period of famine and war and was attended by all the secular and ecclesiastical magnates of the kingdom including the new king, Baldwin II (r. 1118–31).[132] Although Mayer has argued that the council ought to be regarded partly as a secular '*parlement*' or '*Reichsversammlung*' on account of lay participation, it was effectively a church synod, dealing primarily with ecclesiastical and moral matters and presided over by the patriarch of Jerusalem.[133] In regard to Tripoli, neither the count nor the bishops attended.

Attendance at the council was restricted to those who lived in the patriarchate of Jerusalem. It might be thought then that the Tripolitans absented themselves from Nablus because they sided with the Antiochene interpretation of the Tyre dispute, believing that they owed allegiance to the patriarch of Antioch and not to the patriarch of Jerusalem. Yet it will be recalled that this was not a purely ecclesiastical issue, since Pope Paschal II had rendered the patriarchal and secular borders of the Latin East coterminous at the council of Benevento in 1113.[134] The secular borders were henceforth determined pragmatically by whichever territories the prince of Antioch and king of Jerusalem were able to conquer respectively. Given that Fulcher of Chartres had described King Baldwin I as the conqueror of Tripoli only a few years before Nablus, Tripoli should have been regarded as part of the kingdom and thus the patriarchate of Jerusalem.[135] Fulcher was certainly not ignorant of Paschal's decree, since he copied into his chronicle Paschal's bull of 1111, which had pre-empted Benevento by binding the patriarchal borders of Jerusalem to the king's conquests.[136]

The county of Tripoli's dioceses were central to the Tyre dispute. The Tripolitan sees of Tripoli, Jubayl and Tortosa all became direct suffragans of the patriarch of Antioch in the Latin period, captured as they were before the metropolitan see of Tyre itself in 1124.[137] Although Pope Paschal had offered the elegant solution of linking patriarchal borders to secular conquests, the patriarch of Antioch had refused to accept this, seeing it as a diminution of his patriarchate.[138] Even before Benevento, Patriarch Bernard had stepped in to subordinate to himself the first Latin bishop of Tripoli, Albert of St Erard, evidently jealous of his rights.[139] That Albert's successor, Bernard I (r. *c.*1117–*c.*1128), did not attend Nablus suggests that he sided with the Antiochene claims over his see and thus rejected both the Jerusalemite view and the papal ruling. The theoretical intertwining of ecclesiastical territory and secular conquest at this time meant that there was a crucial secular element to the Tripolitans' absence from Nablus. Just as the bishop was rejecting Tripoli's place within the patriarchate of Jerusalem, so too was Count Pons denying Tripoli's position within the kingdom of Jerusalem. Perhaps this is why the royalist Fulcher of Chartres rather mysteriously chose not to record the council of Nablus at all, as it would have involved admitting that the king of Jerusalem was losing his grip on Tripoli.

By failing to attend the council of Nablus, Pons excluded himself from one of the most important formative moments in the history of the Latin East. The council was the first point at which all of the nobles of the kingdom came together to agree on a set of common regulatory codes. After the council, its disciplinary regulations were sent out across the patriarchate of Jerusalem, where they were still found in church archives when William of Tyre was writing decades later.[140] This entire process, both the symbolic gesture of gathering together and the real action of establishing common legislation, would have contributed to the development of a 'Jerusalemite' identity and the consolidation of patriarchal and therefore royal authority over what had previously been little more than a group of disparate lordships loosely associated by varying relationships with the king. The count of Tripoli, who had been regarded previously as a member of this loose confederation of royal vassals, was no longer a part of it.

The council of Nablus seems to signal a process similar to that which had occurred a couple of centuries before in England, whereby the Anglo-Saxon king had gone from being viewed as the (theoretical) king of Britain, to being viewed as the (practical) king of just England.[141] George Molyneaux has described this process in sociological terms, utilising Michael Mann's sociological opposition of 'extensive' and 'intensive' power. Extensive power is widely recognised but loosely implemented, while intensive power is narrowly acknowledged but comprehensively applied.[142] It could be said that the king of Jerusalem enjoyed extensive power over a broadly defined kingdom of Jerusalem – including Tripoli – in the 1100s and 1110s, but failed to intensify this anywhere other than the comparatively narrow territory described by William of Tyre, which is to say only as far north as Beirut. The county of Tripoli did not become independent so much as fail to be integrated under the king's intensifying authority.

Given the importance of Nablus, it is probably not a coincidence that soon after the council concluded tensions between the king of Jerusalem and the count of Tripoli flared up, almost to the point of bloodshed. Fulcher of Chartres recorded that in 1122, 'Count Pons refused him [the king of Jerusalem] obedience, as his father Bertrand had initiated'. Intending to avenge the contempt shown by Pons, Baldwin gathered his army at Acre and marched north to Tripoli, carrying with him no less a relic than the True Cross. Open war was only averted and peace established through the mediation of nobles on both sides.[143] This event was of some significance, even warranting a passing mention from one later Arabic chronicler, Kamāl al-Dīn of Aleppo, who wrote that the king was engaged 'in a litigation' (*fī ḥakūma*) with the count.[144]

One key difficulty in discerning Pons's motives here is Fulcher of Chartres's royalist bias in reporting the incident. According to Fulcher, it was Pons who was brought to reason.[145] Evidently in Fulcher's opinion, royal suzerainty over Tripoli was right and proper, whereas Tripolitan independence was irrational. For Fulcher to provide any actual reason for Pons's rebellion would be to acknowledge a possible shortcoming in royal overlordship and to provide Pons's actions with some justification. Fulcher instead depicted the rebellion as baseless and spontaneous.[146] The similarly royalist William of Tyre later expanded upon the apparent spontaneity of the rebellion by blaming an anonymous adviser.[147] William's intention may have been to remove the stain of anti-royalism from the grandfather of his friend, sometime patron and two-time regent of the kingdom, Raymond III.

It is likely that Pons's act of disobedience began as a refusal to support the king on one of his many military expeditions. Richard suggested that Pons rebelled because, although he had at first tolerated the king's frequent demands for military assistance, he had grown increasingly impatient and no longer saw the necessity of royal support, especially as he personally had been more closely tied to the prince of Antioch since 1112.[148] Richard's theory may seem credible on first inspection. However, in 1122 Antioch was governed by none other than Baldwin II, who had held the position of regent since Prince Roger's death at the Field of Blood in 1119.[149] It is thus impossible to agree with Richard that Pons felt it safe to reject royal authority on the grounds that the prince of Antioch – a vacant position in 1122 – would provide necessary military support. Pons was in fact politically isolated at this time. Baldwin II was ruling both Jerusalem and Antioch, while the king's own former county of Edessa was being ruled by Joscelin, who was personally dependent on the king. Indeed, Fulcher of Chartres waxed lyrical about the king's assumption of the regency of Antioch, writing that Baldwin was now lord of all the lands 'from Egypt to Mesopotamia', implicitly including Antioch and Edessa as well as Jerusalem and Tripoli.[150] He added proudly that, 'up until this point, [Baldwin] had appeared as king of the Jerusalemites alone, but with the death of Prince Roger of Antioch, he had been made king of the Antiochenes, with the addition of a second kingdom'.[151]

Given the political situation, Babcock and Krey reasonably suggested that Pons's rebellion in 1122 was in response to an active attempt by Baldwin to consolidate his rule in Tripoli: the seditious count being the only obstacle to the king becoming 'real ruler of all the Latin states in Syria' and thereby founding a 'Latin empire'.[152] Certainly Fulcher's account of Pons's rebellion hints that royal supremacy over the Latin East was the main issue at stake here. The whole event was framed in these terms by Baldwin himself when he brought with his army the True Cross, the most potent political symbol available to the kings of Jerusalem, other than perhaps the Holy Sepulchre itself.[153] The relic was deployed primarily in times of desperation, but also in offensive campaigns aimed at 'the acquisition of territory which would be incorporated into the kingdom': a category into which Murray groups the Tripoli incident.[154] Gerish has argued that 'no court writer used the True Cross to legitimize royal power'.[155] Yet this is exactly what Baldwin's use of it against Count Pons implies, being in fact the only recorded time that the relic was used against a Latin Christian.[156]

Only a few years earlier, Count Pons had been a firm ally of the king of Jerusalem, assisting him on military expeditions. Just three years before his rebellion, Fulcher of Chartres had described Pons as one of the 'allies of the glorious [True] Cross'.[157] Why should the early 1120s have witnessed such a stark reversal in Pons's loyalties, first with the count's absence from Nablus and then with his open rebellion two years later? The answer may be revealed if the county of Tripoli is treated not as an independent state but as a constituent part of the kingdom, affected by the political rhythms of the realm in much the same way as other lordships. The death of King Baldwin I in 1118 had brought about a period of internal crisis for the kingdom. The barons of the kingdom had divided into two camps over who should succeed Baldwin, with one group – the 'legitimists' – backing his brother and appointed heir, Eustace III of Boulogne, who was far away in the west, and the other – the 'pragmatists' – supporting his cousin Baldwin of Edessa, who was already conveniently in the east. Internal political chaos in Jerusalem was avoided only because Eustace decided to remain in Europe rather than press his claims in the east. However, King Baldwin II's rule was henceforth overshadowed by doubts over his legitimacy and undermined by discontent among certain barons.[158]

Murray notes simply that the crisis over Baldwin II's legitimacy was an opportune time for Pons's rebellion.[159] However, this treats Pons as if he was already the ruler of an independent crusader state, rather than one of the barons of the kingdom, over which royal power had not yet intensified fully. Pons may well have been one of the 'legitimists', which would explain why he apparently believed that his father's oath to King Baldwin I back in 1109 had not transferred to the 'pretender' Baldwin II a decade later. After all, William of Tyre's assertion that Pons was breaking 'from the oath to which he was obliged to be loyal' should not necessarily be read as an oath that Pons personally had sworn.[160] This may also be the reason why Pons chose not to attend the council of Nablus, which had been an early attempt to demonstrate the realm's unity under the newly crowned Baldwin II. In turn, Pons's pointed absence from Nablus probably made Baldwin himself feel obligated to act so forcefully against Pons in 1122.

Although Fulcher implied that Pons's rebellion came to naught, there is some indication that Pons's surrender to Baldwin did not halt Tripoli's move away from royal authority. Fulcher wrote that peace was assured through the intervention of nobles present on 'both' (*utrinque*) sides.[161]

Perhaps the questions over Baldwin's legitimacy forced the king to pay heed to his nobles, as he was unable to attempt military action against Pons lest it spark a civil war across the entire kingdom between legitimists and pragmatists. The outcome of this pacific approach was that Pons was apparently not forced to submit formally to royal authority. Had Pons been forced to reaffirm his subordination to the king of Jerusalem, Fulcher would surely have reported it, yet the chaplain wrote simply that Baldwin and Pons 'were made friends'.[162] Conceptually speaking, 'friendship' may have been associated with the weaker social bonds present in contemporary Occitania.[163] After all, it had been friendship and not fealty *per se* to which Bertrand of Toulouse had appealed in his attempt to secure William Jordan's loyalties in 1109.[164] Only the derivative and unreliable Lisiard of Tours elaborated the account to claim that Pons swore a renewed oath formally in 1122.[165] In short, Baldwin did not use violence to push the matter of fealty, probably because he viewed the loss of one lordship, Tripoli, as preferable to the potential loss of many more seditious legitimist domains, closer to the heart of his realm.

After Pons's rebellion, the county of Tripoli emerges in the sources as an increasingly independent and distinct polity, with relations between the count and the king of Jerusalem finally approximating Richard's concept of 'vassalité limitée'.[166] Pons and his successors continued to assist the king or his army in joint military expeditions throughout the twelfth century. It is after 1122 that Richard's judgement that the counts' participation in such campaigns was motivated more by a sense of 'solidarité chrétienne [. . .] entre Francs' than by the obligations of strict vassalage starts to be valid.[167] Matthew of Edessa recorded that Pons recognised Baldwin II's supremacy in 1126 upon the arrival of Bohemond II of Antioch in the east, but so did Bohemond himself as well as Joscelin of Edessa.[168] This and other subsequent instances of the king of Jerusalem acting as *primus inter pares* among the rulers of the Latin East were mere mementoes of the failed project that was the king's 'Latin empire'.

The fall of Tyre

From the early 1120s onward, contemporary chroniclers acknowledged that the count of Tripoli and the Tripolitans formed a discrete unit in war, not simply the 'Provençal' part of the royal army. A prime example of this relates to Pons's involvement in the capture of Tyre on 29 June 1124. William of Tyre wrote that various banners were erected over the conquered city as a sign of victory, with the king's standard over the city gate, the Venetian doge's banners over the so-called Green Tower and the count of Tripoli's distinct flag over the tower of '*Tanaria*'.[169] If William's late account can be trusted, then the fact that Pons erected his own banner set apart from the royal standard further suggests that the county of Tripoli now had its own distinct political identity.

Pons's participation in the capture of Tyre demonstrated his and his county's growing status within the Latin East in a multitude of other ways beyond the symbolism of banners. It might come as a surprise that Pons was aiding the kingdom of Jerusalem just two years after his rebellion, but it is understandable given the 'solidarité chrétienne' that had superseded the earlier notions of Jerusalem's direct primacy over Tripoli. Moreover, the controversial Baldwin II was conveniently absent, having been captured by the Artuqid Balak of Mārdīn in 1123.[170] As the king languished in prison, it fell to the patriarch of Jerusalem to oversee the siege of Tyre, aiming to take advantage of the recent arrival of a large Venetian fleet commanded by the doge of Venice, Domenico Michele.[171] At the siege of Tyre, Pons came into his own, by now in his mid-twenties and effectively the highest-ranking secular magnate present.

The capture of Tyre had long been a strategic objective of the Franks. Pons's father had helped Baldwin I in the ultimately unsuccessful siege of this city over a decade earlier and Tyre's hinterland had been occupied by Jerusalemite forces for a number of years before the siege of 1124.[172] Tyre's great importance was evident in the twin spheres of trade and warfare. Back in 1113, Baldwin I had established a truce with Mas'ūd, emir and governor of Tyre, to ensure that the highways were safe for travellers and merchants.[173] Clearly the stability of Tyre was important to both Muslim and Christian traders and nothing could be more stable from the Christian perspective than Christian control of the city.

Tyre's military importance primarily lay in the naval sphere. After the fall of Tripoli in 1109, followed by Beirut and Sidon in 1110, Tyre represented the northernmost port available to the Fāṭimid caliphate – a safe haven where ships could shelter from adverse weather and enemy fleets while taking on supplies and fresh water. The successive loss of these cities to the crusaders led to the progressive diminution of Fāṭimid naval power.[174] In this context, the conquest of Tyre would surely have seemed about as important to Pons – ruler of Tripoli, a city routinely subject to Fāṭimid maritime raids – as it was to the kingdom of Jerusalem proper. The further Frankish dominance of trade routes and the further pacification of the seas would have presented obvious benefits to the economic wellbeing and military security of Tripoli, which accrued its wealth from the broader rhythms of Levantine trade.

Tyre ultimately derived its importance in maritime trade and naval strategy from its geography, which was remarkably similar to Tripoli's. Latin and Greek pilgrims openly compared the two cities, noting that both were built 'in the sea' upon narrow rocky promontories, leaving only their eastern facings exposed to the land while the waves surrounded them to the north, south and west.[175] The peninsulas of Tripoli and Tyre served as natural breakwaters against the thrashing of the Mediterranean. In the case of Tyre, the city had originally been an island until Alexander the Great had connected it to the mainland by constructing an artificial causeway during his siege of the city in 332 BC.[176] Ibn al-Athīr described Tyre as 'like the palm of a hand in the sea with the forearm joined to the mainland, with the sea on both sides of the forearm and with battle only possible on the forearm'.[177] During Saladin's siege of this city in 1187, Frankish naval supremacy proved instrumental in preserving this 'hand' of Tyre.[178] It was just as crucial when the Franks were first seeking to capture the city back in 1124. This was where the Venetians proved so important. Just as Italian fleets had been key to the conquest of Tripoli, the Venetians' arrival gave the Franks of Syria the vital ability to blockade Tyre on its maritime facings, as well as its considerably shorter land frontage.

According to William of Tyre, Pons was summoned to the siege by the nobles of the realm. The count brought with him an impressive retinue, his arrival enhancing the Christians' courage greatly and plunging the beleaguered Muslims into the depths of despair.[179] Curiously, Pons's grand entrance is lacking from Fulcher of Chartres's earlier account. Perhaps Fulcher still smarted over Pons's repudiation of royal authority, or perhaps William of Tyre simply chose to embellish the count's role in order to enhance the ancestral reputation of his grandson Raymond III. William went on to emphasise Pons's contribution throughout the siege, particularly in the division of labour. The bulk of the army had fairly passive duties, with most of the Venetians left to invest the city and to protect the siege engines while their fleet was sent south to counter a possible naval attack from Egypt. Meanwhile, Pons was entrusted to lead the Frankish cavalry and salaried footsoldiers (*stipendiarii pedites*) on a sortie to intercept a relief force led by Ṭughtakīn of Damascus. Pons was accompanied by William of Bures, the king's constable and the secular administrator of the realm. Damascene resolve collapsed in the face of this formidable strike force and Ṭughtakīn chose to retreat back to Damascus rather than risk attacking.[180]

Before long, even Fulcher of Chartres was describing Pons as one of the principal Frankish leaders. During the siege, the absent Count Joscelin I of Edessa sent to the Christians at Tyre the head of Baldwin II's captor Balak, who had been decapitated during a battle. The besieging Christian forces were so pleased to receive this gruesome trophy that Pons elevated the messenger – Joscelin's squire – to the rank of knighthood.[181] That Pons conducted the dubbing ceremony demonstrates his seniority at this point. As if to underline the count's status, Fulcher wrote that it was Pons 'of course' (*nempe*) who promoted the squire.[182] It is true that the Jerusalemite chroniclers Fulcher of Chartres and William of Tyre sometimes strove to assert Pons's theoretical subordination to Jerusalemite interests in the siege of Tyre. William stressed that Pons remained 'always obedient to the patriarch and other princes [of Jerusalem] as if one of the low-born'.[183] However, the consistent impression is that Pons was far more than a subservient young follower of Jerusalemite whims. The count of Tripoli had become one of the greatest lords in Frankish Syria and an active personality not to be dismissed lightly. In summarising Pons's contribution to the siege of Tyre, Fulcher of Chartres rather limply described the count as the kingdom's 'most faithful helper', in contradistinction to the people of Antioch who did not even bother to turn up.[184] The king's 'Latin empire' was over before it had even begun.

Tyre finally fell to the Christians on 29 June, after which the crusaders' various banners were flown over the city.[185] It is hard to ascertain exactly what the conquest meant from a Tripolitan perspective since Pons apparently acquired nothing of permanence in the city. The acquisition of Tyre probably did help to enrich and secure Tripoli in an indirect sense, as the effective range of the Fāṭimid fleet was pushed south to Ascalon. There would not be another recorded Muslim naval attack on Tripoli until 1151.[186] At the same time as providing enhanced security, the conquest of Tyre may have helped to consolidate the separation of Tripoli from the kingdom in an economic sense. Prior to 1124, the only gold mint in operation in the Latin East was Tripoli's, where the crusaders issued what they called 'bezants' but were in fact imitations of Fāṭimid *dīnārs*, a handful of which survive.[187] The kingdom was content with Tripoli's mint and did not seek to continue minting gold coins at other conquered Fāṭimid sites, including Acre and Beirut. After 1124, however, the crusaders did begin to mint coins at Tyre, with Ibn Khallikān reporting that these were inscribed with the caliph's name.[188] In fact, controversy would later ensue in the 1250s, when Pope Innocent IV's legate observed that these imitation coins even bore the Islamic creed (*al-shahāda*): 'there is no God but God, Muḥammad is His messenger'.[189]

The minting of gold coins at Tyre may well have been a pragmatic response to the changed political circumstances since Tripoli's conquest in 1109.

Figure 2.1 Twelfth-century 'crusader' imitation *dīnār* minted at Tripoli (Metcalf no. 485) © Ashmolean Museum, University of Oxford

In the early 1120s, the court of Jerusalem could no longer regard the mint at Tripoli as the realm's property, hence the decision to strike *dīnārs* in Tyre – a more secure Jerusalemite possession. Yet the same development may have had the side-effect of consolidating Tripoli's move beyond the realm. Just as the count of Tripoli felt confident enough to act autonomously of the king of Jerusalem, so too was the kingdom of Jerusalem no longer reliant upon the northern city of Tripoli for its invaluable gold coinage. Following the precedent of the council of Nablus, Jerusalemite power had been intensified and concentrated still further in the southern territories of the realm, at the expense of the king's rapidly evaporating influence over the far-flung county of Tripoli.

Wars in the east

Little is known of Pons's activities – or indeed Tripolitan affairs more broadly – in the years immediately following the capitulation of Tyre. This is primarily a problem arising from the sources, or rather the lack thereof. Walter the Chancellor's history ends in 1122 and Fulcher of Chartres's chronicle terminates abruptly in 1126. William of Tyre's chronicle remains the only major narrative for the next few decades but is regrettably patchy and unreliable for the period between 1127 and 1165.[190] What is known of Pons's reign throughout most of the 1120s and the early 1130s is necessarily piecemeal, reconstructed from the odd reference in narrative evidence or else from charters. Pons continued to take part in military engagements, although William of Tyre only recorded those that involved the Jerusalemites. Less than a year after the capture of Tyre, Pons participated in a joint Frankish expedition led by the recently emancipated King Baldwin II against a familiar enemy, Bursuq of Hamadān. In 1125, Bursuq attacked the principality of Antioch once again and managed to capture the town of Cafarda (Kafartāb) and to besiege Hasar (Aʿzāz), before the Christians intercepted and defeated him on 11 June 1125.[191] All four 'crusader states' – Jerusalem, Tripoli, Antioch and Edessa – contributed to this alliance, evoking again the 'solidarité chrétienne' that inspired Latin co-operation in this period.

In 1126, this sense of Christian solidarity served to benefit the county of Tripoli directly. Back in October 1115, Ṭughtakīn of Damascus had conquered Rafaniyya, the county of Tripoli's easternmost bishopric and arguably its least secure settlement – subject to frequent assault and occupation by neighbouring Muslim powers.[192] Pons's grandfather, Raymond of Saint-Gilles, had first reconnoitred the city in early 1099 during the First Crusade, when it was described as a well-populated settlement in a fertile area brimming with crops.[193] As early as April 1105, Ṭughtakīn of Damascus had conquered Rafaniyya back from the crusaders, slaughtering its Frankish inhabitants and burning their newly built castle.[194] No doubt Ṭughtakīn was taking advantage of Raymond of Saint-Gilles's death at the

Pilgrims' Mount just two months earlier. Raymond's immediate successor, William Jordan, retained enough authority in the region to extract tribute from local villagers living nearby but apparently did not control the town itself.[195] His rival and successor tried to reconquer Rafaniyya in 1109 and again a year later when he was assisted by King Baldwin I, but neither of these assaults proved successful.[196] Sometime in the next few years, the Latins of Tripoli did secure Rafaniyya once more, although it is unclear if credit for this should go to Bertrand, Pons or the intervening regency committee. When Ṭughtakīn conquered it yet again in 1115, this constituted Pons's earliest known defeat.

Some eleven years later, Pons finally found the time and resources to launch a serious attempt to reconquer Rafaniyya for Christendom. Fulcher of Chartres wrote that Pons requested assistance from Baldwin II, who was duly 'moved' (*motus*) and agreed to help, with the siege of Rafaniyya beginning on 13 March 1126.[197] This latest siege shows signs of being a major affair compared to previous ones, which were probably opportunistic assaults. As they had done elsewhere, including at Tripoli twenty years before, the Christians in 1126 built a siege fortress a short distance from Rafaniyya, to offer protection to their own soldiers and to blockade the target city more intensively. This they called Montferrand. Like the Pilgrims' Mount at Tripoli, Montferrand serves as a perfect example of what Joshua Prawer identified as the earliest stage in the pattern of 'crusader colonisation': the construction of a 'strong point' in which the Franks could take refuge and pursue various occupations.[198] In addition to building Montferrand, which was set to be the centre of abortive attempts at Frankish settlement in the area, the Christians used their stone throwers to subject Rafaniyya to a relentless eighteen-day barrage, after which the city's inhabitants finally surrendered on 31 March 1126.[199]

What is especially interesting about the fall of Rafaniyya is that Pons received the city back in its entirety. King Baldwin simply returned to Jerusalem, apparently without enjoying any tangible reward for his efforts.[200] As William of Tyre elaborated, Baldwin was doing no more than 'faithfully seeing to the common business of the Christian people'.[201] To put it another way, Christian solidarity alone motivated Baldwin, not the desire to aid a former vassal and certainly not any wish to extend his own royal authority back to the county of Tripoli. Of course, Rafaniyya – north of al-Nahr al-Kabīr al-Janūbī and a suffragan of the archbishop of Apamea rather than Tyre – lay beyond the kingdom and patriarchate of Jerusalem, even in the widest possible conception of these territories. Therefore, Baldwin had no theoretical claim to this distant city whatsoever, even had the setbacks to his exercise of extensive power never occurred in the early 1120s. Rafaniyya was subsequently part of the comital demesne, as it probably had been during earlier periods of Frankish occupation.[202]

Following the capture of Rafaniyya, Pons's next known military action came in November 1129 when a joint Latin expedition headed for

Damascus. The background to this lay in an embassy to Europe led by Hugh of Payns, first master of the Templar military order, in 1128. The aim of this trip had been partly to secure official recognition for this novel religious order from the magnates gathered at the Council of Troyes, but also to recruit crusaders for Baldwin II of Jerusalem's planned Damascene campaign. A third objective may have been to add weight to ongoing negotiations with Count Fulk V of Anjou, who was the court of Jerusalem's preferred candidate to marry King Baldwin's eldest daughter, the princess Melisende.[203] Hugh of Payns was able to inspire a significant number of European volunteers to travel to Syria, including Count Fulk, which made the 1129 crusade one of the largest since the First Crusade. When it came to the actual march on Damascus, the army was led by barons drawn predominantly from the Latin East, including Pons, King Baldwin, Prince Bohemond II of Antioch and Count Joscelin I of Edessa. Despite high hopes and numerous troops, the Christian army was soon undone and forced to retreat before reaching Damascus. William of Tyre blamed poor discipline, a timely Damascene assault, terrible weather and the Christians' sins.[204] This proved to be Pons's last recorded offensive action against the Muslims. His reign to date had been illustrious, at least judged by the standards of his peers, but with less than a decade remaining his fortunes were set to shift radically.

Waves of sedition

Ten years after his rebellion against King Baldwin II in 1122, Pons found himself in opposition to another controversial king of Jerusalem: the same Count Fulk of Anjou who had first visited Syria in 1129 during the abortive crusade against Damascus.[205] Although the expedition itself had proven ill-fated, Fulk had agreed to marry Princess Melisende nonetheless. The subsequent union had allowed the count of Anjou to secure the throne of Jerusalem after King Baldwin's death in 1131. As king, Fulk soon made himself unpopular among the barons of the kingdom and the Latin East more generally. For one, he excluded Melisende – his wife and the fount of his legitimacy – from the government of the realm.[206] Fulk also disinherited many of the established nobles of the kingdom of Jerusalem and some in the principality of Antioch so as to replace them with his own loyal posse of Angevins. This naturally angered those veterans who had served under Baldwin I and Baldwin II.[207] Murray observes that the wave of baronial discontent that greeted Fulk's policies was in some ways similar to the opposition encountered by Baldwin II in the 1110s and 1120s.[208] It thus comes as no great surprise that Pons rebelled against Fulk in similar circumstances to those in which he had rebelled against Baldwin.

The precise form of Pons's second rebellion was that he, William of Ṣahyūn (modern Qalʿat Ṣalāḥ al-Dīn),[209] and Count Joscelin II of Edessa lent their support to Princess Alice of Antioch's attempt to seize the principality of Antioch following the death of her father Baldwin II and the succession of her brother-in-law King Fulk.[210] This likely occurred sometime after Baldwin's death on 21 August 1131 and very probably in summer 1132.[211] Pons, Alice and their allies were not the only ones to revolt during the tumultuous early years of Fulk's reign. Within the kingdom of Jerusalem proper, Hugh II of Jaffa would revolt in 1134, in what was perhaps the most dramatic case of a Jerusalemite baron openly declaring himself an enemy of the crown.[212] Enmity had gradually grown between Hugh and Fulk until the former felt obliged to go to war.

Many of the kingdom's barons had initially sympathised with the popular lord of Jaffa, nursing not a few grievances of their own against the king. However, the realm's baronage supposedly turned against Hugh after he made the great blunder of allying with the Fāṭimid Muslims of Ascalon against Fulk.[213] As Michael Köhler has shown, alliances with Muslims were remarkably common practice for the rulers of the Latin East, who shared their local Islamic counterparts' concern with retaining their petty lordships at all costs against encroaching great powers – Islamic sultanates and Christian empires alike.[214] Yet, whereas alliances with Muslims against Muslims appear to have been wholly uncontroversial affairs, it remained the case that alliances against fellow Christians – pragmatic though they may be – sat awkwardly with the ideology of crusading holy war that lingered always in the arsenal of would-be political rivals or critics. It was into this category that Hugh's alliance with the Fāṭimids fell, inviting the public outrage that undermined his cause and proved most expedient to Fulk.

William of Tyre, who was only a child at the time, provided the sole detailed account of Hugh's rebellion. He explained the conflict as having resulted from King Fulk's jealousy over a suspected affair between the young and attractive count of Jaffa and Queen Melisende, Hugh's cousin, without explaining how this private matter led to a fully fledged civil war.[215] As Mayer notes, this is clearly unsatisfactory. Instead, he points to Fulk's two unpopular strategies of disenfranchising Melisende and disinheriting veterans – particularly those of Norman descent or upbringing, like Hugh of Jaffa himself.[216] Even Ibn al-Qalānisī in Damascus was aware that Fulk was an unpopular ruler responsible for throwing the Frankish territories into discord.[217]

Returning to Alice's revolt, this and Hugh's rebellion should not be viewed in isolation simply because they occurred on different sides of the Latin East's supposed political borders. There were certainly intriguing parallels. It is likely that Pons was motivated to join Alice's rebellion for at least one of the two reasons that inspired Hugh, namely discontent with Fulk's arbitrary and unwelcome rule over both the kingdom of Jerusalem and the Latin East more generally. Perhaps Pons was concerned that Fulk's willingness to disinherit others threatened to undermine the baronial class of the entire Latin East. As in 1122, the king of Jerusalem's power was paradoxically reaching great heights at the same time that his reign was being challenged openly. Pons's rebellion in 1122 coincided with a period when royal authority threatened to engulf the county within a 'Latin empire', with Baldwin II both king of Jerusalem and regent of Antioch. Similarly, his alliance with Alice in 1132 came at a moment when Fulk was ruling Jerusalem as king and Antioch as regent.[218] Fear of the king's power seems a more satisfactory, not to mention consistent explanation than William of Tyre's cynical claim that Alice simply bribed Pons and others into lending their support.[219]

Pons may also have been motivated by the second reason that drove Hugh into sedition, namely Fulk's treatment of his own wife. Historians reading William of Tyre's sensationalist gossip of Melisende's marital infidelity have been quick to see Hugh as a defender of the queen's rights. However, they have been surprisingly slow to note that Pons also had his own reasons to contest Fulk's attempts to minimise the queen's involvement in the running of the kingdom. Most obviously he was allied to Melisende's sister Alice, although another tie bound Pons to Melisende: his son Raymond's marriage to another of the queen's sisters, Hodierna. No source records exactly when this marriage took place, but Hodierna was born *c.*1115–17 and may have been betrothed as early as 1127.[220] The actual wedding was probably delayed due to her extreme youth and she did not give birth to her eldest child, the future Count Raymond III, until 1140.[221] It is very possible that negotiations for Hodierna's betrothal to Raymond began in the aftermath of Pons's rebellion against the princess's father, King Baldwin II, in 1122. Such a marriage may have been envisaged as an act of reconciliation between the houses of Tripoli and Jerusalem after such an acrimonious dispute. If Pons did choose to make a stand against Fulk on the basis of his treatment of his daughter-in-law's sister, then he did so despite the fact that his own wife Cecilia was Fulk's half-sister via their controversial mother, Bertrade of Montfort. William of Tyre observed this with some incredulity, but this would hardly be the only time a medieval family was rent apart by internecine squabbling.[222]

Sharing many political and personal concerns with Pons in the early 1130s, Hugh of Jaffa himself may have seen the count of Tripoli as an inspiration – a man who had successfully asserted his independence from royal authority in 1122 and who had dared to do the same again a decade later. For one thing, Mayer suspects that Hugh was actively plotting with Princess Alice against Fulk in 1134, after Alice's and Pons's rebellion but before his own.[223] On a more subtle level, Pons may have served as a revolutionary precedent to Hugh in a titular sense. In the years preceding 1134, Hugh had taken to styling himself 'count' (*comes*) and even 'prince' (*princeps*) and 'consul' of Jaffa, although the royal chancery insisted on referring to him as mere 'lord' (*dominus*). Mayer believes that such titular self-aggrandisement was significant specifically because it recalled the 'independent counts' of Tripoli and Edessa, not to mention the wholly autonomous prince of Antioch, the sometimes seditious prince of Galilee and Fulk – former count and consul of Anjou – himself.[224]

It is rather ironic that the title of 'count' should have been so controversial and powerful a symbol in the rejection of royal power. After all, 'count' (*comes*) had originally meant 'companion' of the early medieval Frankish kings and emperors, and was thus an implicitly subordinate title. By the twelfth century, however, this had changed. The counts of Tripoli and Edessa were the only two widely recognised *comites* in the Latin East at this time.[225] After Hugh's fruitless rebellion, there were no counts of Jaffa until the domain was united to that of Ascalon in the early 1150s, when it became officially a 'county' under a member of the royal family itself – Fulk's second son, Amalric.[226] Amalric's wife Agnes of Courtenay insisted on retaining the prestigious title of 'countess' even after she and Amalric were obliged to divorce, lest the kingdom's barons refuse to recognise Amalric's right to succeed his brother Baldwin III in 1163.[227] Of course, the counts of Tripoli had not acquired their title through a deliberate exercise in self-aggrandisement, as Hugh of Jaffa tried to do. Rather, they were simply counts because the first self-professed *comes Tripolitanus*, Raymond I, was already a count in his own right as count of Toulouse and Saint-Gilles. The counts of Tripoli may have been fairly restrained in their titular ambitions, but their association with challenging royal authority seems to have inspired other would-be revolutionaries.

Hugh's evocation of powerful, independent or semi-independent rulers demanded a strong response from King Fulk, who was able to besiege Jaffa in the wake of Hugh's controversial alliance with the Fāṭimids. Hugh surrendered and agreed to go into exile for three years, after which he was to be readmitted to the kingdom by way of reconciliation. Ultimately, the disinherited Hugh felt compelled to return into permanent voluntary exile in Apulia, after suffering an unprovoked attack on the streets of Jerusalem at the hands of a man who sought King Fulk's favour.[228] Mayer delivers a compelling summary of Fulk's motives in suppressing Hugh when he writes that 'under no circumstances could the King tolerate the creation of yet another independent crusader state in the Latin East at the expense of the kingdom'.[229]

A narrow road to independence

Returning to Alice's revolt, the significance of Pons's involvement goes far beyond the count's later and indirect influence upon Hugh of Jaffa. The events of 1132 reveal most vividly the reason *why* – not simply *when* – the county of Tripoli was able to move inexorably towards independence, while other potential crusader states – the lordship of Jaffa, for instance, or the principality of Galilee – remained subject to royal power and never gained full autonomy. Pons's first major act during Alice's rebellion, and the one that seemingly brought his rebellious sentiments into the open, was to refuse Fulk and his army passage through the county of Tripoli. This occurred when the king was travelling north to assist elements of the

Antiochene nobility against Princess Alice. Denied the land route, Fulk was forced to bypass the county entirely: travelling by sea up to the northern port of Saint Symeon, where he was given command of the entire principality by the Antiochene nobles.[230]

Richard observes that kings of Jerusalem had traversed the county on their way to Antioch numerous times previously, which leads him to question why Fulk took the sea route on this occasion. Was it because the count had the legal right to deny access, perhaps according to 'la nature du contrat féodal' agreed with Count Bertrand back in 1109, or because the king simply did not have the time to impose his royal prerogative by force? Richard suggests the latter to be more likely, as Fulk did eventually force Pons into submission, albeit not in the county of Tripoli itself but in the principality.[231] This neglects an important factor in this whole affair, namely the role played by local geography. The reason why Pons's blockade against King Fulk proved so effective was because the count was able to make use of the restrictive mountain pass that connected the county of Tripoli with the rest of the kingdom of Jerusalem. This exceedingly narrow road hugged the coast, running between the steep slopes of Lebanon to the east and the Mediterranean to the west. The path crossed the Dog River (Nahr al-Kalb), which lay between Beirut and Jubayl – the very point where William of Tyre would later draw the border shared by the kingdom of Jerusalem and the county of Tripoli.[232]

Contemporary authors regularly observed the obstacle posed to travellers by the Beirut–Jubayl road, especially when detailing how the armies of the First Crusade had followed it. Peter Tudebode described the road south of Tripoli as 'tight and steep'.[233] The anonymous author of the *Gesta Francorum* wrote that 'we crossed through the mountain, in which is an exceedingly narrow road, and in that place we thought that enemies lying in wait would find us'.[234] Due to the dangers of this road, the crusaders' local allies offered guidance. Desperate for the crusaders to move on from his city of Tripoli, the *qāḍī* Jalāl al-Mulk bin ʿAmmār had provided them with safe passage through the mountains, led by an old Muslim guide who was familiar with the area. In Albert of Aachen's words, this man led the crusaders through 'a road twisted through the constricted straits of the mountain, so tight a path that only barely might one man after another, one animal after another, march'.[235] According to Fulcher of Chartres, Fakhr al-Mulk bin ʿAmmār later warned the southbound Baldwin I of Edessa in 1100 of various 'Saracens' who were hiding in a 'narrow path next to the sea on the public road'.[236] In Fulcher's words, 'if pre-warned enemies wanted to block travellers, by no means could 100,000 knights pass, as long as 100 or even 60 armed men on lookout held that entrance forcefully against them'.[237]

So important was this road that its narrowest stretch, right where it crossed the Dog River, had its own special toponym: the aptly-named 'Dog Pass' (*Passus Canis*).[238] As contemporaries knew, the constriction of the

Passus Canis made it very easy for any party to restrict access to unwelcome travellers. In the decades prior to 1132, great effort was made to overcome the difficulties in communicating and travelling between the kingdom of Jerusalem and the county of Tripoli. In the early 1110s, King Baldwin I of Jerusalem and his loyal servant Bertrand of Tripoli had joined forces to conquer the Fāṭimid-held settlements of Beirut and Sidon, which lay between the realm's core and the outlying county.[239] The participants in these early campaigns showed a distinct awareness of the problems caused specifically by geographical obstacles. When Bertrand travelled south to help King Baldwin besiege Beirut, he chose to sail south from Tripoli in order to avoid the dangerous land route of the *Passus Canis*. Indeed, the count had been the one to recommend the conquest of Beirut in the first place, observing that the city posed an obstacle to travellers 'on a road right where the mountains descend into the abyss of the sea'.[240] As he strove to connect his county to the rest of a rapidly expanding realm, Bertrand could not have predicted the irony that two decades later his own son would use the *Passus Canis* to reject royal power.

The border between the county and the kingdom, which once did not exist at all, came to be set at the *Passus Canis*. This was initially a *de facto* geographical obstacle, which distinguished the county from the kingdom and vice versa in the pragmatic sense of making it difficult to travel between the two. The earliest Frankish settlers tried their best to overcome this natural barrier, refusing to compromise on their territorial vision of a Latin East bisected north of Tripoli. When the count of Tripoli later acquired cause to dissociate himself from the king of Jerusalem, he sensibly took advantage of the strategic opportunity presented by the *Passus Canis*. He certainly used it against King Fulk in 1132 and it is wholly plausible that he had used it against King Baldwin II a decade before. Thus, a narrow mountain pass gradually ceased to be a mere inconvenience and came to be viewed as a firm, consolidated, political reality. The emergence of this border marked the transformation of the county of Tripoli into a discrete polity – a 'crusader state'. Meanwhile, the more exposed fiefs south of the Dog River enjoyed no such geographical protection and thus were steadily more intensively ruled by Jerusalem's central royal government.

Changes to the north

Medievalists often forget that the incidents they describe and analyse were grounded in a certain place, as well as a certain time. Pons's rebellion in 1132 showcases this perfectly, because it was so heavily dependent upon the count's manipulation of local Lebanese geography. Nor was the *Passus Canis* the only topographic feature to shape the course of events in 1132. After Fulk reached Saint Symeon and began to deal with Alice's rebellion in person, he soon encountered the count of Tripoli once again. It will be remembered that Pons held possessions in the principality of Antioch by virtue of his marriage to Cecilia, Prince Tancred's widow. These were the dower fortresses of Arzghān and al-Rūj. In 1132, Pons used both of these as operational bases, from which he harried King Fulk and his Antiochene allies throughout the rebellion.[241] He also seems to have extended his influence in the eastern marches of the principality by conquering the small fortress of Ḥiṣn Salamiyya – east of the Orontes and roughly equidistant between Homs and Hama.[242]

Unlike before, when Fulk could postpone judgement on Pons by sailing around the county, now nothing held him back. Fulk's army clashed with Pons's near al-Rūj, and after a hard-fought battle, Fulk emerged victorious. Pons managed to escape, but many of his men were captured and led in chains to Antioch.[243] This conflict was no small affair, entering even the annals of Arab contemporaries. Al-ʿAẓīmī of Aleppo wrote that 'the army of Antioch attacked the army of Tripoli' sometime between 23 November 1131 and 11 November 1132 (AH 526).[244] According to this same author, 'fighting between the Franks continued until some of them were killed' in AH 527 – the same year Ibn al-Qalānisī reported an unusually major and violent dispute between the Franks in Muḥarram (11 November to 10 December 1132).[245] The Arabic evidence suggests that the conflict was longer than William of Tyre's condensed account would imply: perhaps beginning in summer 1132, but continuing into early winter.

Fulk's harsh treatment of the Tripolitans was not the first time that he had dealt sternly with rebels. The former count of Anjou had an extensive track record of subjecting unruly vassals to his authority, having quashed a number of rebellions back in the west in order to make Anjou one of the most centralised and autocratic grand lordships within the entire kingdom of France.[246] It would only be another couple of years until Fulk reduced Hugh of Jaffa to obedience as well, rendering Jaffa a royal fief. Given Fulk's severity in such cases of sedition, it is perhaps surprising that Pons emerged as unscathed as he did from his defeat at the king's hands. His men were humbled, imprisoned and in some cases killed, but the count himself did not lose Tripoli in the same way that Hugh lost Jaffa. Nor did Pons share Hugh's fate of exile. Although Fulk's suppression of rebels elsewhere had afforded him opportunities to extend or consolidate his power, there is no indication that he required the defeated Pons to reaffirm the allegiance he had once owed to the king of Jerusalem for the county.[247]

In fact, Fulk allowed Pons a surprising degree of latitude after his second rebellion, and Tripoli itself became something of a refuge for dissident anti-royalists in the years to come. Following his participation in Hugh of Jaffa's later revolt, the Jerusalemite Ralph of Fontanelli took refuge at the court of the anti-Angevin Alice of Antioch in Latakia, appearing there in 1134 and 1135.[248] Subsequently he went to Tripoli, appearing with Pons's son Raymond II in 1142 and 1145, after which it seems he never returned to the kingdom.[249] It is entirely possible that Ralph first went to Tripoli during the lifetime of Raymond's rebellious father, who was no friend to Fulk. Tripoli's emerging position as a political refuge just beyond the border of the kingdom makes it comparable to other medieval 'fringes', such as similarly mountainous Wales, where outcasts from the Anglo-Norman political system could often be found.[250]

Fulk's failure or reluctance to restore royal rule over Tripoli in 1132 may suggest either that he was overstretched enough as king of a fractious kingdom and regent of a disputed principality, or that the crown of Jerusalem now recognised tacitly the county of Tripoli's *de facto* independence. After all, Fulk's predecessor Baldwin II had set a weak precedent by agreeing to become no more than Pons's 'friend'. At the same time, the importance of peace in and of itself should not be ignored, especially in the wider context of the Latin East, where much effort was expended to keep the Franks united against the Muslims who surrounded them. William of Tyre emphasised that peace was restored in 1132 in a fashion similar to the resolution in 1122, through the third-party mediation of 'assiduous men and loyal expounders of peace'.[251] Fulk's decision not to enforce traditional Jerusalemite claims to Tripoli was a sensible conciliatory policy, with the king willing to compromise in order to keep the count of Tripoli sweet and thus to restore harmony to the crusader states, lest their mutual enemies to the east took advantage of their internal chaos. It will be remembered that both al-ʿAẓīmī and Ibn al-Qalānisī took an interest in this very public dispute, which proves that word of Christian disunity was already spreading among local Muslims with potentially damaging consequences.

Just as one part of the reconciliation after 1122 may have been the marriage of Baldwin II's daughter Hodierna to Pons's son Raymond II, so too does it seem likely that the peace of 1132 closely preceded a second marriage of political convenience. In 1132, it was the turn of Pons's daughter Agnes – named for her maternal grandmother, Agnes of Kiev. As is clear from later charter evidence, Agnes of Tripoli married Raynald II Mazoir. The first record of this union can be dated no earlier than 1151, but the marriage presumably had taken place much earlier than this, since Agnes must have been quite advanced in age by this point. Her own father died some two decades before this and she herself died *c.*1165, having borne her husband a number of children.[252] Moreover, she and her two brothers, the future Count Raymond II and his obscure younger brother Philip of Tripoli, had already been old enough to witness their father's charters by the early 1140s.[253]

A closer consideration of Agnes's husband suggests that she was possibly married to him in the aftermath of Pons's rebellion against King Fulk. Raynald was the son of Raynald I Mazoir, a pre-eminent figure in the early principality of Antioch who held the position of constable – viewed by some historians as no less than the prince's deputy.[254] By the mid-twelfth century, the Mazoirs ruled the city of Valania and the castle of Margat on the southern border of the principality of Antioch, together with the town of Maraqiyya in the northern county of Tripoli, which had perhaps formed part of Agnes's dowry.[255] It is of course possible that this union was contracted without reference to King Fulk, but it seems more than coincidence that, when the king departed North Syria after crushing Pons and his fellow rebels in 1132, he entrusted the governance of the principality of Antioch to none other than Raynald I Mazoir.[256] Moreover, al-Rūj and Arzghān – the two castles used by Pons to harass Fulk's troops in 1132 – also seem to have passed to the Mazoirs at this time as further enhancements to Agnes's dowry. It will be remembered that the two forts had only come into Pons's hands in the first place by virtue of his marriage to Prince Tancred's widow Cecilia.[257] William of Tyre made it clear that Pons's use of these strongholds during Alice's rebellion had greatly outraged Fulk's allies among the Antiochene nobility.[258] Thus, it was entirely in Fulk's interests to arrange for Agnes to marry Raynald II. This union helped to pacify the count of Tripoli by making a suitable match for his daughter, while ensuring that the barons of Antioch were also happy: content that the key border forts of al-Rūj and Arzghān were now safely in the hands of one of their own rather than a volatile 'foreigner' like the count of Tripoli.

Indeed, it seems that Fulk punished Pons only for those rebellious acts he performed in the principality of Antioch, while continuing to respect the count's rights in the county of Tripoli. This raises the question as to why the barons of Antioch were so aggrieved by Pons's actions in the north. After all, Arzghān and al-Rūj were not Pons's only Antiochene fiefs and should be viewed alongside Tortosa, Ḥiṣn al-Akrād and all the other lands the count had acquired from Prince Tancred in 1112. Interestingly, the latter all lay south of the river of Valania (Nahr Bāniyās), which served as the county of Tripoli's border with the principality of Antioch, according to William of Tyre.[259] It would appear that this northern border, like its southern counterpart at the *Passus Canis,* only emerged in the years between 1112 and 1132. Furthermore, the northern frontier was shaped – in the north as in the south – by local geographical circumstances, specifically another narrow road threading its way between the mountains and the sea.

Just as the *Passus Canis* came to mark the effective territorial limits of the kingdom of Jerusalem and county of Tripoli at the very point where the slopes of Lebanon met the Mediterranean, so too did the coastal road between Maraqiyya and Valania – passing under the shadow of Jabal al-Nuṣayriyya and the Mazoir-held fortress of Margat, donated to the Hospitaller Order in 1186 – come to divide the county from the principality of Antioch. As with the *Passus Canis,* contemporaries routinely observed how tight the northern road was and the difficulties this presented to travellers. In 1307, the Armenian Hayton of Gorgios wrote that the pass was difficult to traverse on account of its narrow width and that any hostile forces could block access to travellers with ease.[260] Over a century earlier, ʿImād al-Dīn al-Iṣfahānī described the passage of Saladin's army from Maraqiyya to Valania in 1188 following the sultan's invasion of the county of Tripoli and principality of Antioch. His is arguably the best account of the difficulties encountered when navigating this northern mountain road:

> Our journey to Jabala on the coast went under the castle of Marqab (Margat), which is a fortress of the Hospitallers on the highland: an elevated place and lofty watchtower, narrow of road, difficult to obtain, but it was unavoidable to traverse that strait and to follow that road.[261]

This account provided the basis for Ibn al-Athīr's note that 'the road [under Margat] is a narrow defile, through which none pass except one after the other'.[262] This is remarkably similar to Albert of Aachen's description of men passing '*homo post hominem*' through the *Passus Canis*.[263]

Geographically speaking, the Margat Pass was not as restrictive as the *Passus Canis* and there is no obvious incident when any count of Tripoli used it to refuse entry to the princes of Antioch, as Pons did to King Fulk in the south. Perhaps the princes were simply less active than the kings in pursuing the intensification of their rule in what would become the county of Tripoli, making such resistance unnecessary. Nonetheless, the reaction of the Antiochene nobility to Pons's actions in 1132 suggests that the Margat Pass was similar to the *Passus Canis* in that it too helped to distinguish the county from the principality in a *de facto* sense, before William of Tyre immortalised the border in his chronicle. The nobles of the 1130s cared only about bringing to an end Pons's use of fiefs north of Margat; neither they nor their ally Fulk seem to have concerned themselves with humbling the count south of this line. These nobles felt no resentment at Pons's ongoing possession of his Antiochene lands at Tortosa, Ṣāfīthā, Maraqiyya and Ḥiṣn al-Akrād. In fact, they were even willing to allow Pons a dynastic union with the Mazoirs of Margat, right on the border, as a means of getting him to surrender Arzghān and al-Rūj. Raynald II's marriage to Agnes of Tripoli basically created for Antioch's benefit a buffer zone straddling the border with the county of Tripoli – stretching from Valania and Margat in the principality, down as far as Maraqiyya within the county proper.

The foregoing suggests an inversion of the situation in the south, where the king of Jerusalem found it increasingly difficult to extend his power into the county. In the north, Pons evidently struggled to stretch his own authority *beyond* the county. Whether power was projected inward or outward, the geographical circumstances of the Levantine coastal strip were exercising a real and powerful influence upon the ongoing crystallisation of political power in the county of Tripoli and the Latin East more generally. Pons's fiefs between al-Nahr al-Kabīr al-Janūbī and

Nahr Bāniyās were now regarded as something apart from those that lay further north still, while his fiefs to the south had separated from the kingdom of Jerusalem. These two formerly discrete clusters, united under the count of Tripoli's *personal* rule, were henceforth to be viewed as an integral, *territorial* whole. Out of the geographical exigencies of the *Passus Canis* and the Margat Pass, Pons's reign had seen the birth of the county of Tripoli as it would be recognised by William of Tyre and modern historians alike.

Defeat, sedition and the counter-crusade

Fulk's victory over Pons in 1132 failed to restore Jerusalemite authority over Tripoli, but nonetheless marked the beginning of a sharp decline in the county's military fortunes. William of Tyre was keen to diminish the consequences of this inter-Christian conflict and wrote only that Fulk *captured* Tripolitan soldiers, making no explicit reference to the deaths one would expect from open battle.[264] Muslim observers lacked William's sensitivity in reporting how Fulk and Pons shed Christian blood, with both al-ʿAẓīmī and Ibn al-Qalānisī writing candidly that 'some were killed'.[265] Exact figures are impossible to ascertain, but evidently there was significant loss of life – certainly notable enough to attract the attention of these external Arab reporters.

The counts of Tripoli had lacked a military force sufficient to make permanent offensive gains at the expense of neighbouring Islamic powers since late 1109, when Count Bertrand had been forced to establish *condominia* with the Muslims of Damascus.[266] Pons had participated in a handful of aggressive expeditions during his reign, but in these he had either been supported by allies – as in the Latin-Damascene campaign against Bursuq of Hamadān in 1115, or Hugh of Payns's crusade in 1129 – or been fighting his fellow Latins, as in his war with King Fulk in 1132. Richard observes how Pons was the first count of Tripoli never to attack the nearby town of Homs.[267] Pons's most aggressive act was to seize Rafaniyya in 1126, yet this represented merely the reconquest of a city that had remained out of his control for more than a decade, so was more a belated defensive action than anything.[268] Fulk's crushing of Pons in 1132 could only have hurt the already weakened state of the county's military.

The following five years witnessed a succession of military catastrophes for the county of Tripoli, no doubt precipitated by Pons's damaging defeat in 1132. In October 1133, a large force of Türkmens from the north, led by ʿImād al-Dīn Zankī, raided Tripoli itself and some neighbouring fortifications. These invaders ripped through the county, killing and capturing many Franks, seizing booty and animals. Pons led an army to intercept the Türkmens on the county's eastern frontier, near Rafaniyya, but suffered a major and bloody defeat. The few survivors, led by Pons himself, sought refuge in his new fortress of Montferrand, where they quickly found themselves besieged by the Turkic raiders. The situation seemed dire, but Pons was allegedly able to slip out with a small retinue and headed for Tripoli, where he was able to send a letter to King Fulk, then at Acre, seeking assistance. This support was duly provided and the Jerusalemite relief force met the Türkmens in battle. The battle effectively amounted to a stalemate, with the Franks retreating to Rafaniyya and the Turks choosing to withdraw back to their own lands, deprived of a comprehensive victory.[269] Although their accounts differ on a few minor details, both Ibn al-Qalānisī and William of Tyre insisted that the Tripolitans were reliant upon Jerusalemite aid, provided by Pons's recent enemy Fulk. Indeed, according to William, Fulk offered help only because his half-sister and Pons's wife Cecilia – *not* Pons himself, who remained trapped in Montferrand in this version of the story – had come to Sidon from Tripoli and beseeched him in person.[270] Clearly, a sense of familial co-operation had recovered from the crisis of 1132, testament to the more conciliatory tone struck in its aftermath.

Of course, reconciliation could never resurrect the men of Tripoli who had been killed by Fulk's army. The Templar-instigated crusade of 1129 was the last offensive military expedition in which Count Pons is known to have taken part, but the heavy defeat at Montferrand in 1133 was certainly not his last catastrophe. According to Richard, the 1130s saw the county enter a new phase in its history, defined by permanent Muslim reconquest.[271] Notably, this coincided with a period of significant political and ideological change within Islamic Syria. The years 1118–46 saw the political classes of Muslim Syria and Egypt begin to act upon the anti-crusader, 'jihadist' rhetoric that had been hitherto confined to disgruntled intelligentsia.[272] Moreover, Zankī's entry into formerly independent Aleppo in 1128, a major coup in Damascus in 1135 and a resurgent Byzantine empire under John II Komnenos meant – in one way or another – that the Franks now had fewer options for mutually beneficial alliances with local Muslim powers and instead faced greater hostility.[273] Had Tripoli's military strength not been sapped by the fruitless civil war with King Fulk, perhaps prospective Muslim invaders would have been less tempted to act upon their ideological motives, and their raiding would have been less damaging.

Frankish military weakness and external Muslim aggression were compounded by a third factor, internal indigenous sedition. As the county was suffering defeat after defeat, the local peoples of the county and its immediate surroundings were becoming a cause for concern among the Latin ruling caste. The most dramatic development in this respect was the rise of the Nizārī 'Assassins', a sect of Ismāʿīlī Shīʿites who had split from the mainstream Fāṭimids over the succession to the caliph al-Mustanṣir (r. 1036–94). The autocratic vizier al-Afḍal had settled the dispute in favour of the late caliph's son al-Mustaʿlī, but the proto-Assassins had favoured the caliph's own alleged choice, namely another son named Nizār – whence came the title 'Nizārī'.[274] At first the Nizārīs had enjoyed a level of support throughout the caliphate that was far from negligible. However, the sect failed to secure power within the Fāṭimid realm, and their attempts to convert the Sunnī-dominated cities of Syria through itinerant preaching proved just as unsuccessful, coming under intense pressure from the governments of Damascus and Aleppo. They were subsequently obliged to seek refuge in Jabal al-Nuṣayriyya – the Alawite mountains between the emergent county of Tripoli and principality of Antioch – where they were relatively safe from both Sunnī and mainstream Shīʿa persecution.[275] In doing so, they followed a pattern regularly identifiable in the course of Islamic history, whereby political and religious outcasts from central society and government have found asylum in relatively inaccessible mountains.[276]

The Nizārīs were successful at entrenching themselves in Jabal al-Nuṣayriyya specifically because they were able to encourage the local populace to participate in violent uprisings against the Frankish rule that had begun to be established there in the years immediately after the First Crusade. The inhabitants of the mountains were predominantly other radical Shīʿites – followers of the Nuṣayrī (ʿAlawī) sect that gave the region its name.[277] Crucially, much of the seditious Shīʿa activity in Jabal al-Nuṣayriyya took place in the 1130s. According to al-ʿAẓīmī, the people of the unidentified settlement of Baḥrāʾ led an indigenous revolt, seizing the fortress of Bikisrāʾīl from Raynald I Mazoir (*al-Māzwīr*) in 1130/1 (AH 525).[278] By 1132/3 (AH 527), a Nizārī missionary named Abū al-Fatḥ had managed to take Qadmūs, which was to become one of the Nizārīs' principal strongholds.[279] Prince Bohemond II of Antioch had acquired this just four years previously.[280] In 1135, another uprising – this time unsuccessful – occurred at Balāṭunus.[281] The future centre of the informal Nizārī polity was Maṣyāf, which came under their control in 535/*c.*1140.[282] These places were all located in the principality of Antioch, although bordered on the county of Tripoli (as defined by William of Tyre). In fact, some were former tributaries to the counts of Tripoli. Shortly after the First Crusade, Ṭughtakīn of Damascus had agreed that the residents of Maṣyāf would henceforth pay a regular tribute to Raymond of Saint-Gilles, based then at nearby Tortosa.[283] This arrangement was presumably terminated by the Assassin takeover, if not before.

Even if the Assassin-controlled sites did not directly threaten the integrity of the county of Tripoli, they were of strategic significance more generally, especially in terms of linking the Latin-controlled Mediterranean coastline in the west to the disputed Orontes valley in the east. The Alawite mountains had been a fairly passive region in the earliest years of the twelfth century, with its Nuṣayrī residents rendered tributary to Frankish rule. During the First Crusade, the region had been safe enough for Christian armies to pass through without difficulty. Peter Tudebode recorded how the crusaders led by Raymond of Saint-Gilles had taken Rafaniyya (*Caphaliam*) and then crossed 'through a high and immense mountain into the Buqayʿa valley'.[284]

It is significant that they travelled across Jabal al-Nuṣayriyya rather than the less forbidding Homs Gap to the south, which would later become the strategic lynchpin of the county of Tripoli's eastern frontier – guarded from 1142 by the Hospitaller stronghold of Crac des Chevaliers. The Alawite hills quickly became dangerous territory, however, not because of their geography, but their hostile inhabitants. Towards the end of the crusader period, Burchard of Mount Sion felt it prudent to warn that these locals were all that made the mountain forbidding to Christian travellers, since it was 'neither very high nor inaccessible, as some say'.[285] Fear had elevated Jabal al-Nuṣayriyya.

As time passed, the Assassins' territories would crystallise to the point that contemporaries came to recognise a sharply demarcated border between their Shīʿa lordship and the county of Tripoli. Burchard of Mount Sion reported how this was demarcated by a long line of boundary stones, with crosses carved into them on the Christian side and daggers on the Nizārī side.[286] The transformation of the Alawite mountains into a hornets' nest of Nizārī sedition had serious ramifications for the effective exercise of Frankish power both in and through this region. For one thing, the deterioration of travel and communication through the mountains likely contributed to the growing isolation of the county from the principality of Antioch. These difficulties compounded the purely geographical difficulties associated with the Margat Pass. Shīʿa agitation in the Jabal al-Nuṣayriyya also made it more difficult for the counts of Tripoli to hold onto their eastern frontier. It was surely no coincidence that the county's principal military difficulties in the 1130s centred upon Rafaniyya, which the influx of Nizārī uprisings had cut off from the heartlands of the county of Tripoli.[287]

Christian control over the county's eastern frontier, along the Orontes, weakened noticeably around this time. The recurrent threat to Rafaniyya was not the only danger associated with this increasingly destabilised region. Usāma bin Munqidh described how a large group of some 700 to 800 Frankish pilgrims travelled along the road from the south via Rafaniyya to Āfāmiyyā, probably sometime between the Christian capture of Rafaniyya in 1126 and its eventual conquest by Muslim forces in 1137. Unfortunately for the pilgrims, they got lost after leaving Rafaniyya and ended up at Islamic Shayzar, where they were captured and slaughtered by the residents of the town, including Usāma's father and uncles.[288] Some scholars have suggested that the Munqidhids were Twelver Shīʿa, or perhaps Shīʿa-sympathising Sunnīs.[289] Whatever the case, the Munqidhids were neither Nizārī nor Nuṣayrī, so their brutal treatment of Christian pilgrims on the county's eastern frontier was a sign of the penetration of anti-Frankish sentiment into the local populace more broadly, whether Shīʿa specifically or Muslim more generally.

In an atmosphere of growing unrest in the countryside, it is no surprise that relations between the Franks and even their closest indigenous subjects grew steadily more fraught. Back when the crusaders had first entered the region, they had found it immediately necessary to employ local intermediaries, if only for the sake of conducting diplomacy or navigating unfamiliar terrain. The best-known among these servants and aides among the Christian and Muslim communities were the *ruʾasāʾ* (sg. *rayyis/raʾīs*), who were literally 'chiefs' or 'headmen'. Many of them can be found in surviving documentation from across the Latin East, under such latinised terms as *raisii.* Their exact functions varied considerably. For example, the county of Tripoli was unique among crusader states for its 'petty kings' (*reguli*) – seemingly identical with the Maronite mountain chieftains (*muqaddamūn*) who have been such a quintessential and instrumental feature of Lebanese history.[290]

In the case of the *ruʾasāʾ* of cities like Tripoli, these were high-ranking men of state, just as they had been before the crusader conquest and as they indeed remained in contemporary Islamic cities such as Aleppo and Damascus.[291] Usāma bin Munqidh provides a characteristically lively and human account of one *raʾīs* of Tripoli named Yūnān who was a native Syrian Christian (*naṣrānī*). This man assisted one of Usāma's slaves, who was returning home from Damascus to Shayzar in late summer 1131, but found his way disrupted by Zankī's campaigns against Homs and Hama. This forced the slave to make a significant diversion, via Baʿalbak and Tripoli, where he met Yūnān. The *raʾīs* first provided Usāma's *mamlūk* with a mule for hire, then escorted him in person part of the way from Tripoli to Shayzar. Finally, after departing briefly, he returned to warn a large gang of robbers on the mountain road to leave the man alone.[292] That Yūnān's authority extended far beyond the city limits of Tripoli and was respected even by mountain highwaymen are significant demonstrations of his power and prestige.

Despite this, Tripoli's *raʾīs* was very much reliant upon the Latin count's favour. In a particularly dramatic yet neglected passage, the Aleppan chronicler al-ʿAẓīmī recorded that 'the count of Tripoli (Pons) killed the city's *raʾīs*' sometime between November 1132 and October 1133 (AH 527).[293] This is only known time in the whole history of the Latin East that a *raʾīs* was executed and, regrettably, al-ʿAẓīmī made no attempt to explain why Pons ordered this. It did, however, closely follow Pons's defeat at the hands of Zankī's Türkmens and also occurred at the height of the Nizārī-Nuṣayrī rebellions. Did Pons suspect the *raʾīs* of treachery? Was the executed *raʾīs* the same *raʾīs* Yūnān who had shown himself overly familiar with local Shīʿa-sympathising Muslims by helping Usāma's *mamlūk* just two years earlier?[294] Such questions must go unanswered due to a lack of firm evidence, but the picture is very much one of rapidly eroding trust between Franks and the indigenous population – an increasing Latin paranoia coinciding with and perhaps driven by the sharp reversal in the county's military fortunes.

In the later stage of Pons's career, he faced more than enough difficulties with military defeat and internal sedition, but his worsening situation was exacerbated still further with a reduction in the amount of contact between his Lebanese county and his ancestral Occitan homeland. Throughout the siege of Tripoli, southern French contingents regularly accompanied Counts Raymond, William and Bertrand. A handful – most notably Bishop Albert of Tripoli – visited Occitania in return.[295] For a few years after the siege and into Pons's reign, Occitan clergy in particular continued to visit the court of Tripoli. In 1115, Bishop Berengar of Orange, acting as papal legate, advised Bishop Pons of Tripoli on the surrender of certain tithes to the Hospital.[296] On 9 December 1125, Bishop Pons of Le Puy and Abbot Berengar of St Feliu, Catalonia, oversaw the settlement of a dispute over tithes between Philip, cantor of Tripoli, and the early Hospitallers.[297] Berengar of St Feliu remained in the county for at least a few more months, appearing in a witness list on 14 March 1126.[298] After this, however, visiting Occitan clergy were no longer readily apparent in the county of Tripoli.

No Occitan visitors to the county can be identified with certainty between 1126 and 1132, when Pons chose to surrender all of his possessions in the county of Velay to the local bishop, Umberto of Le Puy.[299] It is not known if Pons's surrender of his western rights, the decline in identifiable Occitan visitors and the military defeats of the 1130s were interlinked. For one thing, it is impossible to tell whether Pons's donation of Velay came before or after his humiliation by King Fulk. Nevertheless, reasoned speculation would suggest that the phenomena were indeed related. As Phillips has argued, the rulers of the crusader states were heavily reliant upon the aid provided by their cousins and co-religionists in the west, and this aid largely took the form of manpower.[300] If Tripoli and Occitania were no longer as closely intertwined as they once had been, it may be that fewer crusaders and settlers from that region were arriving to bolster the county's ranks. The paucity of documentary evidence for both the county of Tripoli and the south of France precludes any definite judgements. At the very least, it remains suggestive that Pons chose to yield his western property at the same time he was facing manifold difficulties in the east, colouring the 1130s as a time of diminishing circumstances right across the board. The increasingly beleaguered Pons no longer found it feasible to maintain a presence on both sides of the Mediterranean as his predecessors had done.

In early 1137, Tripoli's problems coalesced, precipitating the greatest threat to the county's very existence since the First Crusade. In March of that year, the Muslim ruler of Damascus, Bazwāj, led an army deep into the county, penetrating as far as the Pilgrims' Mount, right up to the gates of the capital. This was the closest a Muslim army had been to the city of Tripoli since its capture in 1109, representing well the trough into which the county's military strength had slumped. Initially Count Pons took a passive approach, sheltering behind his city walls in the presumed hope that this was a mere temporary raiding party, but the audacity of Bazwāj in approaching Tripoli itself demanded a response. Thus, the count and his army sallied forth to meet the Muslim army in the field. The weakness and desperation of the Tripolitan army at this juncture are indicated by the fact that even the city's bishop Gerald participated, although his exact role – as an active fighter, which would have contradicted Gregorian values, or as a source of spiritual encouragement and thus an enhancement to morale – is unknown.[301]

The ensuing battle ended in disastrous defeat for the Christians. According to William of Tyre, few nobles fell, but both the count and bishop were captured. Meanwhile, a large number of non-noble 'men of middling status' – perhaps footsoldiers – were killed. The bishop was soon released, apparently because the Muslims did not recognise him as he was presumably dressed in secular military garb. The count was not as fortunate. He was killed in captivity, with William of Tyre attributing this not to his Muslim captors *per se*, but rather to some unexplained treachery on the part of the 'Syrians' – that is, local Christians – living on Mount Lebanon.[302] Pons's eventful life was at an end, the count overcome by internal indigenous sedition as much as by external Muslim aggression. Tripoli itself was spared, as Bazwāj was evidently unable or unwilling to press his advantage. The Damascene army returned home, attacking a number of Frankish forts on the way, including that of Wādī Ibn al-Aḥmar and another at a region named al-Kūra.[303] The latter is an area near Tripoli, which even today contains plentiful archaeological remains of eastern Christian churches – the very places where those accused of betraying Pons were accustomed to worship. Pilgrims returning from the east at the end of 1137 brought word of Pons's death in battle with the 'pagans' to Orderic Vitalis in Normandy, who was to mourn the death of this famous Christian hero.[304] Pons's defeats in the last years of his reign were evidently not enough to tarnish the illustrious reputation he had earlier won in the eyes of even the most distant of observers.

Conclusion

Pons's reign, if measured in terms of military and political success, can be traced as an arc, beginning and ending with nadirs of uncertainty and weakness between which a zenith rises with the count's fortunes. When his father died in early 1112, the county of Tripoli was a proto-lordship of small extent split in two by the principality of Antioch and the kingdom of Jerusalem, in accordance with the initial expectations of the Byzantine- and Fāṭimid-inspired crusaders. With Count Bertrand's sudden death and the succession of his underage son, it seemed likely that Tripoli's fate was to be integrated still further into the crystallising kingdom of Jerusalem, as its northernmost city. Worse still, the prospect loomed that Raymond of Saint-Gilles's dynasty would be disinherited, in Syria and in the west. Through a combination of savvy negotiations with Tancred of Antioch on the part of Pons's guardians, Pons's own persistence in rebelling against royal authority and – perhaps most importantly – the geographical exigencies of the region, the dynasty was preserved and the county's very existence renegotiated as an independent 'crusader state'. In hindsight, one wonders if Pons's firm stand against external rulers like King Baldwin II, erstwhile allies like King Fulk and local subjects like the *raʾīs* of Tripoli was wholly advisable, given the disasters that eventually befell him in the 1130s. Nevertheless, by the time of Pons's death, it was clear that his reign had been pivotal in changing the very configuration of the Latin East. By pointedly ignoring the king of Jerusalem's pretensions at Nablus and by taking advantage of local geographical circumstances, Pons had carved out a practically independent lordship for himself, one that had been neither intended nor anticipated by the earliest crusader-settlers. Jean Richard wrote that the county of Tripoli owed its very existence to the 'action personnelle' of Raymond IV.[305] In fact, the county of Tripoli, as understood by later generations of historians from William of Tyre to the present day, was the creation of his grandson.

Notes

1 IQ, p. 181; Richard, *Le comté*, p. 6 n. 2. Cf. Grousset, *Histoire*, vol. 2, p. 889.
2 Lamonthe-Langon, *Biographie toulousaine*, vol. 1, p. 61.
3 Tibble, *Monarchy*, pp. 9–10, 12.
4 Orderic Vitalis, *Historia Æcclesiastica*, ed. Marjorie Chibnall, 6 vols (Oxford, 1969–80), vol. 6, p. 430.
5 William of Malmesbury, *Gesta Regum*, p. 700.
6 William of Malmesbury, *Gesta Regum*, p. 696.
7 Philippe Labbe, *Tableaux genealogiques de la maison royale de France. Et des six Pairies Laïques; Bourgogne, Normandie, Guyenne, Tolose, Flandre, Champagne*, 2nd ed. (Paris, 1664), p. 464.
8 Devic and Vaissète, *Histoire*, vol. 3, pp. 474–5, 600–1. Cf. Rodney M. Thomson and Michael Winterbottom, *William of Malmesbury, Gesta Regum Anglorum: The History of the English Kings, Volume II. General Introduction and Commentary* (Oxford, 1999), pp. 346–7; Richard, *Le comté*, p. 6.
9 Orderic Vitalis, *Historia*, vol. 6, p. 430.
10 AA, p. 854.
11 Orderic Vitalis, *Historia*, vol. 6, p. 430.
12 Duos filios et totidem filias. *Gesta Normannorum Ducum*, ed. Elisabeth M. C. Van Houts, 2 vols (Oxford, 1992–5), vol. 2, p. 266.
13 Orderic Vitalis, *Historia*, vol. 6, p. 431 n. 6; *Calendar of Documents Preserved in France, Illustrative of the History of Great Britain and Ireland. Vol. I. A.D. 918–1206*, ed. J. Horace Round (London, 1899), no. 970.
14 *Europäische Stammtafeln: Stammtafeln zur Geschichte der Europäischen Staaten. Neue Folge, Band III, Teilband 4: Das Feudale Frankreich und sein Einfluss auf die Welt des Mittelalters*, ed. Detlev Schwennicke, (Marburg, 1989), Tafel 638.
15 WT, vol. 2, p. 749.
16 William of Malmesbury, *Gesta Regum*, p. 700.
17 AA, p. 776.
18 AA, p. 776 n. 7.
19 Riley-Smith, *The First Crusade and the Idea of Crusading* (London, 2003), pp. 6–8; Cowdrey, *Pope Gregory VII*, pp. 341–2.

20 Cowdrey, *Pope Gregory VII*, pp. 342–3.
21 Thomson and Winterbottom, *William of Malmesbury*, pp. 346–7.
22 John of Ibelin, *Le Livre*, p. 377.
23 IQ, p. 181.
24 WT, vol. 1, p. 522.
25 Paterson, *World*, p. 298.
26 William of Malmesbury, *Gesta Regum*, p. 700.
27 Cf. Devic and Vaissète, *Histoire*, vol. 3, pp. 585–6.
28 WT, vol. 1, pp. 523–4. See also: AA, pp. 840–2.
29 IQ, pp. 184–5.
30 Pars quoque gentis Tripolitanae iam exercitui regio conglobata. FC, p. 570.
31 AA, p. 854.
32 Walter the Chancellor, *Bella Antiochena*, ed. Heinrich Hagenmeyer (Innsbrück, 1896), p. 67.
33 IQ, p. 181.
34 Richard, *Le comté*, p. 40.
35 *RRH*, no. 58.
36 Cf. Riley-Smith, *First Crusaders*, p. 242.
37 *RRH*, nos 84, 118.
38 IQ, p. 197. Ibn al-Qalānisī confused Pons with his father Bertrand (*Badrān*).
39 IQ, p. 165.
40 Richard, *Le comté*, pp. 48–50.
41 *CCSSJ*, no. 86; *RRH*, no. 58.
42 Richard, 'Note', pp. 103–6; Jonathan Riley-Smith, 'The Latin Clergy and the Settlement in Palestine and Syria, 1098–1100', *CHR* 74.4 (1988), pp. 547–8; Asbridge, 'The principality', pp. 146–7.
43 See Chapter 1.
44 AK, pp. 403–6.
45 See Chapter 4.
46 Devic and Vaissète, *Histoire*, vol. 3, pp. 618–19. See Chapter 1.
47 William of Malmesbury, *Gesta Regum*, p. 700.
48 See Chapter 1.
49 *RRH*, no. 211; Devic and Vaissète, *Histoire*, vol. 5, no. 551.i, cols 1054–5. While visiting on this occasion, Count Robert also witnessed Raymond's famous donation to the Hospitallers in 1142. *RRH*, no. 212; *CGOH*, vol. 1, no. 144. See Chapter 3.
50 Jonathan Phillips, *Defenders of the Holy Land: Relations Between the Latin East and the West, 1119–1187* (Oxford, 1996), *passim*.
51 Asbridge, *Creation*, pp. 122–3
52 Johan Huizinga, 'Patriotism and Nationalism in European History', in his *Men and Ideas: History, the Middle Ages, the Renaissance*, trans. James S. Holmes and Hans van Marle (London, 1960), pp. 108–9. See also: Bull, 'Overlapping', pp. 208–10; Murray, 'National identity', pp. 117–19.
53 Quantum anati gallina. Ralph of Caen, *Tancredus*, ed. Edoardo D'Angelo (Brepols, 2011), pp. 58–9.
54 See Chapter 1.
55 Richard, *Le comté*, p. 40.
56 AK, p. 406.
57 Richard, *Le comté*, p. 30. Cf. Isabelle Augé, 'Les Comnènes et le comté de Tripoli: une collaboration efficace?' in *Le comté*, ed. Dédéyan and Rizk, p. 145.
58 Richard, *Le comté*, pp. 31–2.
59 See Chapter 1.
60 Tibble, *Monarchy*, pp. 7–8, 20 and *passim*.
61 Devic and Vaissète, *Histoire*, vol. 3, pp. 622–3, 648–9.
62 Devic and Vaissète, *Histoire*, vol. 3, pp. 609, 611–12.

63 Hans E. Mayer, 'Etudes sur l'histoire de Baudouin 1er roi de Jérusalem', in his *Mélanges sur l'histoire du royaume latin de Jérusalem* (Paris, 1984), p. 11; Tibble, *Monarchy*, pp. 7, 11–12; Asbridge, *Creation*, pp. 115–19.
64 IQ, p. 181.
65 WT, vol. 1, p. 522.
66 William of Malmesbury, *Gesta Regum*, p. 700.
67 WT, vol. 2, pp. 966–7. See Chapter 5.
68 WT, vol. 2, p. 636; Cahen, *La Syrie*, pp. 105, 158–9, 279, 350. Prince Tancred held al-Rūj in 1111, a year before he gave it to Pons via Cecilia. FC, pp. 553–4.
69 See below under 'Changes to the north'.
70 *GF*, pp. 233–4; Thomas Asbridge, *The First Crusade: A New History* (Oxford, 2004), p. 148.
71 AA, p. 854.
72 W. Onclin, 'L'Âge requis pour le mariage dans la doctrine canonique médiévale', in *Proceedings of the Second International Congress of Medieval Canon Law: Boston College, 12–16 August 1963*, ed. Stephan Kuttner and J. Joseph Ryan (Vatican City, 1965), pp. 239–40.
73 FC, p. 584.
74 Richard, *Le comté*, p. 45 n. 1.
75 Richard, *Le comté*, pp. 9–43.
76 Cf. Richard, *Le comté*, p. 72.
77 For example: *CGOH*, vol. 3, no. 3020.
78 AA, p. 854; WT, vol. 1, p. 530; Walter the Chancellor, *Bella*, pp. 67–8.
79 FC, pp. 582–3.
80 Walter the Chancellor, *Bella*, pp. 67–8.
81 Accon, Caesaream, Berytum, necne Sidonem
Abstulit infandis hostibus indigenis.
Post terras Arabum vel quae tangunt mare Rubrum,
Addidit imperio, subdidit obsequio.
Et Tripolim cepit, sed et Arsuth non minus ursit,
Pluraque praeterea fecit honore rata. FC, p. 614.
82 *Urkunden zur Älteren Handels- und Staatsgeschichte der Republik Venedig mit Besonderer Beziehung auf Byzanz und die Levante vom Neunten bis zum Ausgang des Fünfzehnten Jahrhunderts*, ed. G. L. F. Tafel and G. M. Thomas, 3 vols (Vienna, 1856–7), vol. 1, no. 36; *RRH*, no. 84.
83 Richard, *Le comté*, p. 36.
84 Duodecimo miliario a Tripoli, contra Orientem Albana fluvius Archados, a quo modo incipit regnum Jerusalem. Pseudo-Fretellus, 'Tractatus', p. 432.
85 Pseudo-Fretellus, 'Tractatus', pp. 408–9.
86 See Chapter 1.
87 See Chapter 1.
88 Martin Hall and Jonathan Phillips, *Caffaro, Genoa and the Twelfth-Century Crusades*, Crusade Texts in Translation 24 (Ashgate, 2013), p. 36.
89 *RRH*, no. 118; *CGOH*, vol. 1, no. 82.
90 Jussu dominę et filii ejus, Willelmi Ebriaci. *CCSSJ*, no. 84; *RRH*, no. 161. Cf. *CCSSJ*, no. 85.
91 Rowe, 'The Papacy', pp. 163–5, 173, 177–8; Hamilton, *Latin Church*, p. 28. Cf. Richard, *Le comté*, p. 58.
92 Cahen, *La Syrie*, p. 323.
93 See Chapter 4.
94 Wilbrand of Oldenburg, p. 119.
95 *Les Registres d'Innocent IV publiés ou analysés d'après les manuscrits originaux du Vatican et de la Bibliothèque Nationale*, ed. E. Berger, 4 vols (1884–1919), no. 57; Hamilton, *Latin Church*, p. 229.

96 *CCSSJ*, no. 105; WT, vol. 2, p. 647; *CDRG*, vol. 2, no. 152; *RRH*, nos 175, 184, 580.
97 *CGOH*, vol. 1, no. 82; vol. 2, no. VII; *RRH*, nos 118, 191, 211; *RRH Add.*, no. 142a.
98 *CGOH*, vol. 1, nos 144, 160; *RRH*, nos 211, 212, 236.
99 Graham A. Loud, 'Some Reflections on the Failure of the Second Crusade', *Crusades* 4 (2005), p. 5; Otto of Freising, 'Chronica sive Historia de Duabus Civitatibus', ed. Adolf Hofmeister, in *Monumenta Germaniae Historica: Scriptores rerum Germanicarum*, 78 vols (Hanover, 1871–2007), vol. 45, pp. 363–5.
100 Wilbrand of Oldenburg, p. 119; James of Vitry, *Lettres*, no. 2, p. 93.
101 Batrūn was a coastal town of middling importance in the county of Tripoli, of a similar rank to ʿArqa – greater than minor settlements like Maraqiyya, albeit eclipsed by the great cities of Tripoli and Tortosa, even Jubayl. Burchard of Mount Sion would later describe it as formerly 'opulent' (*opulenta*), although bemoaned the fact that it had been 'totally destroyed' (*funditus* [. . .] *destructa*) by *c.*1280. Burchard of Mount Sion, p. 27.
102 Orthosias – *Artusca* or *Artussia* in the Latin sources, Arḍ Arṭūsī (Lebanon) today – has left little trace in the written record for the crusader period and was reduced to being a small village and a mere parish, never to recover its former episcopal status. Jean Richard, 'Le comté de Tripoli dans les chartes du fonds des Porcellet', *Bibliothèque de l'école des chartes* 130.2 (1972), pp. 349–50; *CGOH*, vol. 1, no. 72; *RRH*, no. 107.
103 WT, vol. 2, p. 649.
104 *CCSSJ*, no. 141; *RRH*, no. 435.
105 Merav Mack, *The Merchant of Genoa: The Crusades, the Genoese and the Latin East, 1187–1220s* (Unpublished PhD thesis: University of Cambridge, 2003), pp. 117–18, 121–2, 136–42.
106 See Chapter 1.
107 *CGOH*, vol. 1, no. 782; *RRH*, no. 648.
108 *D.Jerus.*, vol. 1, no. 35; *CDRG*, vol. 1, no. 24; *RRH*, no. 55.
109 Mack, *Merchant*, pp. 122–3.
110 Enlart, *Les Monuments*, vol. 2, p. 123.
111 See below under 'Genoese, Occitan and "Frankish" identity'.
112 Mack, *Merchant*, pp. 128–32.
113 Flori, *Pierre l'Ermite*, pp. 168–70; Murray, 'National Identity', pp. 116–17; Bull, 'Overlapping', pp. 195–211.
114 See, for example: Ralph of Caen, *Tancredus*, p. 58.
115 Alan V. Murray, 'Ethnic Identity in the Crusader States: The Frankish Race and the Settlement of Outremer', in *Concepts of National Identity in the Middle Ages*, ed. Simon Forde, Lesley Johnson and Alan V. Murray (Leeds, 1995), pp. 61–6.
116 Luboš Kropáček, 'Les *Ifrandj* dans les sources arabes', in *Clovis: histoire & mémoire, II: Le baptême de Clovis, son écho à travers l'histoire*, ed. Michel Rouche (Paris, 1997), p. 467; Hillenbrand, 'The First Crusade', p. 136.
117 BD, p. 133.
118 Ibn al-Athīr knew of 'the Germans' (*al-almān*), not as a distinct category, but 'a type of Frank' (*al-nawʿ min al-firanj*). Ibn al-Athīr, *Al-tārīkh al-bāhir fī al-dawla al-atābakiyya bi-l-mūṣul*, ed. ʿAbd al-Qādir Aḥmad Ṭulaymāt (Cairo, 1963), p. 88.
119 For example: IA, vol. 10, p. 343.
120 IQ, p. 163.
121 AA, p. 776.
122 Bull, 'Overlapping', p. 210; Murray, 'National identity', p. 117. See Introduction.
123 Rex [. . .] comitemque cum Prouincialibus [. . .] imperauit. Walter the Chancellor, *Bella*, p. 96.
124 Mayer, 'Latins, Muslims and Greeks', pp. 175–6. See also: Ellenblum, *Crusader Castles*, p. 131.
125 See Chapter 3.

126 *CCSSJ*, no. 117; *RRH*, no. 302; Denys Pringle, 'Magna Mahumeria (al-Bīra): the Archaeology of a Frankish New Town in Palestine', in *Crusade and Settlement*, ed. Edbury, p. 147.
127 Rue des/z Prouensaus. *D.Jerus.*, vol. 3, nos 799, 819.
128 Joshua Prawer, *Crusader Institutions* (Oxford, 1980), pp. 382–3.
129 Pseudo-Fretellus, 'Tractatus', p. 432.
130 Pseudo-Fretellus, *Fetellus (Circa 1130 A.D.)*, trans. J. R. MacPherson, Palestine Pilgrims' Text Society 5 (London, 1892), p. 52; John Wilkinson, *Jerusalem Pilgrimage 1099–1185*, Works Issued by the Hakluyt Society, 2nd series, 167 (London, 1988), p. 210.
131 Pseudo-Fretellus, 'Tractatus', p. 432.
132 WT, vol. 1, pp. 563–4.
133 Hans Eberhard Mayer, 'The Concordat of Nablus', *Journal of Ecclesiastical History* 33.4 (1982), pp. 531–3; Benjamin Z. Kedar, 'On the Origins of the Earliest Laws of Frankish Jerusalem: The Canons of the Council of Nablus, 1120', *Speculum* 74.2 (1999), pp. 310–31.
134 See Chapter 1.
135 FC, p. 614; Rowe, 'The Papacy', p. 167.
136 FC, p. 745.
137 Rowe, 'The Papacy', pp. 160–89.
138 See Chapter 1.
139 Rowe, 'The Papacy', p. 163; Hamilton, *Latin Church*, p. 25.
140 WT, vol. 1, p. 563.
141 George Molyneaux, 'Why Were Some Tenth-Century English Kings Presented as Rulers of Britain?' *Transactions of the Royal Historical Society* 21 (2011), pp. 59–91.
142 Michael Mann, *The Sources of Social Power. Volume 1: A History of Power from the Beginning to AD 1760*, new ed. (Cambridge, 2012), p. 7 and *passim*.
143 Comes, Pontius nomine [. . .] recusans ei [Baldwin II] obsequi, uti Bertrannus pater eius fecerat. FC, pp. 647–8.
144 Kamāl al-Dīn, *Zubdat al-ḥalab*, vol. 2, p. 204.
145 FC, p. 648.
146 Verena Epp, *Fulcher von Chartres. Studien zur Geschichtsschreibung des ersten Kreuzzuges*, Studia humaniora 15 (Düsseldorf, 1990), p. 268.
147 Pacis inimicus. WT, vol. 1, p. 566.
148 Richard, *Le comté*, pp. 31–2.
149 WT, vol. 1, p. 562.
150 Ab Aegypto [. . .] usque Mesopotamiam. FC, p. 635.
151 Sicut enim huc usque Hierosolymorum rex singulariter exstiterat, ita, mortuo principe Antiocheno Rogero, Antiochenorum rex addito altero regno efficitur. FC, pp. 634–5.
152 William of Tyre, *A History of Deeds Done Beyond the Sea*, trans. E. A. Babcock and A. C. Krey, 2 vols (New York, 1976), vol. 2, pp. 54 n. 14, 539 n. 55.
153 FC, p. 648; A. V. Murray, '"Mighty Against the Enemies of Christ": The Relic of the True Cross in the Armies of the Kingdom of Jerusalem', in *The Crusades and Their Sources*, ed. France and Zajac, pp. 218–19. Cf. Deborah Gerish, 'The True Cross and the Kings of Jerusalem', *The Haskins Society Journal* 8 (1996), pp. 137–42.
154 Murray, 'Mighty', p. 223.
155 Gerish, 'True Cross', p. 149.
156 Murray, 'Mighty', p. 234. Murray erroneously identifies the count as Bertrand.
157 Socii gloriosae crucis. FC, p. 630.
158 Alan V. Murray, 'Baldwin II and His Nobles: Baronial Factionalism and Dissent in the Kingdom of Jerusalem, 1118–1134', *Nottingham Medieval Studies* 38 (1994),

pp. 60–85; Hans Eberhard Mayer, 'The Succession to Baldwin II of Jerusalem: English Impact on the East', *Dumbarton Oaks Papers* (*DOP*) 39 (1985), pp. 139–47.

159 Murray, 'Baldwin II', p. 67; Murray, *Crusader Kingdom*, p. 134.

160 De iure fidelitatis tenebatur impendere. WT, vol. 1, p. 566.

161 FC, p. 648.

162 Amici facti sunt. FC, p. 648.

163 Paterson, *World*, pp. 69–70.

164 See Chapter 1.

165 Lisiard of Tours, 'Secunda Pars Historiae Iherosolimitanae', in *RHC Oc*, vol. 3, p. 579.

166 Richard, *Le comté*, p. 35.

167 Richard, *Le comté*, pp. 34–5, 37–8.

168 Matthew of Edessa, 'Extraits', p. 147.

169 WT, vol. 1, p. 601.

170 FC, pp. 658–9; WT, vol. 1, p. 567.

171 FC, pp. 695–6; WT, vol. 1, p. 593.

172 WT, vol. 1, pp. 601–2. See Chapter 1.

173 IQ, pp. 188–9.

174 John H. Pryor, *Geography, Technology, and War: Studies in the Maritime History of the Mediterranean, 649–1571* (Cambridge, 1988), pp. 114–25; Yaacov Lev, 'The Fatimid Navy and the Crusades, 1099–1171', in *Tropis II: 2nd International Symposium on Ship Construction in Antiquity, Delphi, 1987: Proceedings*, ed. Harry E. Tzalas (Athens, 1990), pp. 257–8.

175 Wilbrand of Oldenburg, p. 120; Burchard of Mount Sion, p. 28; John Phocas, *The Pilgrimage of Joannes Phocas in the Holy Land (In the Year 1185 A.D.)*, trans. Aubrey Stewart, Palestine Pilgrims' Text Society 5 (London, 1889), p. 10. See Chapter 1.

176 Ned Stafford, 'How geology came to help Alexander the Great', *Nature*. Uploaded 14 May 2007. Accessed 17 August 2014. http://www.nature.com/news/2007/070514/full/news070514-2.html

177 Al-madīna ka-al-kaff fī al-baḥr, wa-al-sāʿid muttaṣal bi-al-barr wa-al-baḥr min jānibay al-sāʿid, wa-al-qitāl inna-mā huwa fī al-sāʿid. IA, vol. 11, p. 554.

178 IA, vol. 11, pp. 554–5.

179 WT, vol. 1, p. 594.

180 WT, vol. 1, p. 596.

181 FC, pp. 726–7; WT, vol. 1, pp. 598–9.

182 FC, p. 727.

183 Domino patriarche et aliis principibus tanquam unus de vernaculis obediens semper [. . .] ob reverentiam domini comitis. WT, vol. 1, p. 599.

184 Adiutor fidelissimus. FC, p. 739.

185 WT, vol. 1, p. 601.

186 See Chapter 3.

187 It is possible that imitation *dīnār*s were later minted at Acre, but probably not until some years after the city's conquest in 1104. Louis Blancard, *Le besant d'or sarrazinas pendant les croisades: Etude comparée sur les monnaies d'or, arabes et d'imitation arabe, frappées en Egypte et en Syrie, aux XIIme et XIIIme siècles* (Marseille, 1880), pp. 20, 36.

188 Ibn Khallikān, *Wafayāt*, vol. 5, p. 301.

189 *Les Registres d'Innocent IV*, ed. Berger, no. 6336; Blancard, *Le besant*, p. 28. See also: Kevin James Lewis, 'Medieval Diglossia: The Diversity of the Latin Christian Encounter with Written and Spoken Arabic in the "Crusader" County of Tripoli, with a Hitherto Unpublished Arabic Note from the Principality of Antioch (MS, AOM 3, Valletta: National Library of Malta, no. 51v)', *Al-Masāq: Islam and the Medieval Mediterranean* 27.2 (2015), pp. 141–4.

190 See Appendix 1.
191 FC, pp. 761–7; WT, vol. 1, pp. 604–6.
192 IQ, p. 192.
193 *GF*, pp. 418–19. Note that the author named Rafaniyya '*Kephaliam*'.
194 IQ, p. 148.
195 *CGOH*, vol. 1, nos 79, 82; *RRH*, nos 108, 118.
196 Richard, *Le comté*, pp. 19–20.
197 FC, pp. 795–6.
198 Joshua Prawer, 'Colonization Activities in the Latin Kingdom of Jerusalem', *Revue belge de philologie et d'histoire* 29 (1951), pp. 1066–82.
199 FC, 798–9; IQ, p. 216.
200 FC, p. 799.
201 Populi christiani communibus fideliter obtemperans negociis. WT, vol. 1, pp. 610–11.
202 Richard, *Le comté*, carte 6.
203 Phillips, *Defenders*, pp. 19–43; Malcolm Barber, *The New Knighthood: A History of the Order of the Temple* (Cambridge, 2012), pp. 11–19.
204 WT, vol. 1, pp. 620–2.
205 WT, vol. 1, p. 620.
206 Hans Eberhard Mayer, 'Studies in the History of Queen Melisende of Jerusalem', *DOP* 26 (1972), pp. 98–113.
207 Hans Eberhard Mayer, 'Angevins *versus* Normans: The New Men of King Fulk of Jerusalem', *Proceedings of the American Philosophical Society* 133 (1989), pp. 1–25; Orderic Vitalis, *Historia*, vol. 6, pp. 390–2.
208 Murray, 'Baldwin II', pp. 60–85.
209 Hugh Kennedy, *Crusader Castles* (Cambridge, 1994), pp. 8485.
210 WT, vol. 2, pp. 635–6.
211 William of Tyre, trans. Babcock and Krey, vol. 2, p. 55 n. 15.
212 For dating, see: Mayer, 'Studies', pp. 104–5.
213 WT, vol. 2, pp. 651–3.
214 Köhler, *Alliances*, passim.
215 WT, vol. 2, p. 652.
216 Mayer, 'Studies', pp. 98–113; Mayer, 'Angevins', pp. 1–25.
217 IQ, p. 233.
218 William of Tyre, trans. Babcock and Krey, vol. 2, p. 54 n. 14; Thomas Asbridge, 'Alice of Antioch: A Case Study of Female Power in the Twelfth Century', in *The Experience of Crusading. Volume Two: Defining the Crusader Kingdom*, ed. Peter W. Edbury and Jonathan Phillips (Cambridge, 2003), pp. 37–8.
219 WT, vol. 2, p. 636.
220 Hans Eberhard Mayer, *Bistümer, Klöster und Stifte im Königreich Jerusalem* (Stuttgart, 1977), p. 253.
221 Raymond III was twelve in 1152. See Chapter 3.
222 WT, vol. 2, p. 636.
223 Mayer, 'Studies', pp. 104–5.
224 Mayer, 'Studies', p. 108 n. 31a; Mayer, 'Carving', pp. 110–12; Mayer, 'The Origins', p. 544.
225 There may also have been counts of Marash and al-Athārib (*Cereph*) in the principality of Antioch. Orderic Vitalis, *Historia*, vol. 6, p. 124; *Les Archives, la Bibliothèque et le Trésor de l'Ordre de Saint-Jean de Jérusalem à Malte*, ed. J. Delaville le Roulx, Bibliothèque des Ecoles françaises d'Athènes et de Rome 32 (Paris, 1883), no. 19, p. 98. Cf. Mayer, *Varia*, p. 67; George T. Beech, 'The Crusader Lordship of Marash in Armenian Cilicia, 1104–1149', *Viator* 27 (1996), pp. 44–5; Andrew D. Buck, *The Principality of Antioch and its Frontiers in the Twelfth Century* (Woodbridge, 2017), pp. 132–5, 142–3.

226 Mayer, 'Studies', pp. 108 n. 31a, 175–6.
227 Bernard Hamilton, *The Leper King and His Heirs: Baldwin IV and the Crusader Kingdom of Jerusalem* (Cambridge, 2000), p. 26 and n. 22.
228 WT, vol. 2, pp. 653–5.
229 Mayer, 'Studies', p. 108 n. 31a.
230 WT, vol. 2, p. 636.
231 Richard, *Le comté*, pp. 35–6. See below under 'Changes to the north'.
232 See Chapter 1.
233 Per artam viam et arduam. PT, p. 133.
234 Transivimus [. . .] per montem, in quo est via nimis angusta, et illic putavimus inimicos insidiantes nobis invenire. *GF*, pp. 440–41.
235 Uia reflexa per angustas fauces montis tam arta semita [. . .] ut uix homo post hominem, animal post animal incederet. AA, p. 388.
236 Meatus artissimus [. . .] iuxta mare in via publica. FC, pp. 355–8.
237 Si hostes praemuniti viantibus prohibere voluerint, nullatenus C milia militum transire poterunt, quin C aut LX viri armati introitum illum violenter contra illos obtineant exspectantes. FC, p. 358.
238 Burchard of Mount Sion, p. 27; Marino Sanudo, 'Liber Secretorum', p. 245; *CGOH*, vol. 3, no. 3396.
239 See Chapter 1.
240 A montanis uiam exhibet iuxta litus abyssi maris descendentibus. AA, pp. 786, 804.
241 WT, vol. 2, p. 636.
242 Al-ʿAẓīmī, *Tārīkh ḥalab*, p. 384.
243 WT, vol. 2, pp. 636–37.
244 Awqaʿa ʿaskar anṭākiyya bi-ʿaskar ṭarābulus. Al-ʿAẓīmī, *Tārīkh ḥalab*, p. 384.
245 Waqʿ bayna al-firanj ḥattā qutila baʿḍ-hum baʿḍan. Al-ʿAẓīmī, *Tārīkh ḥalab*, p. 385. Cf. IQ, p. 236.
246 Mayer, 'Studies', p. 104.
247 Richard, *Le comté*, p. 32.
248 *RRH*, nos 148, 150; *RRH Add.*, no. 151a; Mayer, 'Angevins', pp. 16–17.
249 *RRH*, nos 212, 236.
250 David Crouch, 'A Norman "conventio" and Bonds of Lordship in the Middle Ages', in *Law and Government in Medieval England and Normandy: Essays in honour of Sir James Holt*, ed. George Garnett and John Hudson (Cambridge, 1994), p. 310 n. 31.
251 Per viros industrios et fidelis pacis interpretes. WT, vol. 2, p. 637.
252 *CGOH*, vol. 1, no. 201; *RRH Add.*, no. 270a. Agnes lived until at least 1165, appearing in documents up until that point. *RRH*, no. 347; *RRH Add.*, no. 419a; *Codice diplomatico del Sacro Militare Ordine Gerosolimitano oggi di Malta*, ed. Sebastiano Paoli, 2 vols (Lucca, 1733), vol. 1, no. 163, p. 206; *CGOH*, vol. 1, no. 341. She and Raynald had a number of children, including a son named Bertrand – presumably after Agnes's paternal grandfather, Bertrand of Tripoli – who ruled Margat after his father. *CGOH*, vol. 1, nos 341, 457, 546, 613, 763, 783, 786, 809; vol. 4, nos 595*bis.*, 624*bis.*; *Documents concernant les Templiers extraits des archives de Malte*, ed. J. Delaville le Roulx (Paris, 1882), no. 6; *RRH*, nos 521, 560, 568, 609, 612, 630, 647, 649, 652; *RRH Add.*, nos 419a, 535b, 611a, 611b, 626a, 644a, 650a; Chandon de Briailles, 'Lignages d'Outre-Mer: les seigneurs de Margat', *Syria* 25.3–4 (1946), pp. 243–6. Agnes had apparently died by c.1175, when a document issued by her widower husband referred to her living in the past tense. *Inventaire de pièces de Terre Sainte de l'ordre de l'Hôpital*, ed. J. Delaville le Roulx (Paris, 1895), no. 123, p. 27; *RRH Add.*, no. 535b. Via Bertrand, Agnes would have a granddaughter named after her, who sought to

move to Tripoli, her ancestral home, in 1239. *RRH*, no. 896; *RRH Add.*, nos 1088a, 1093b; de Briailles, 'Lignages', pp. 246–8. See also: *Lignages*, pp. 118–19.
253 *RRH*, nos 211, 212; Devic and Vaissète, *Histoire*, vol. 5, no. 551.i, cols 1054–5; *CGOH*, vol. 1, no. 144.
254 Cahen, *La Syrie*, p. 452.
255 Jochen Burgtorf, 'The Hospitaller Lordship of Margat', in *East and West: Antioch*, vol. 2, pp. 12, 14.
256 WT, vol. 2, p. 637.
257 Cahen, *La Syrie*, 537–8.
258 WT, vol. 2, p. 636.
259 See Chapter 1.
260 Hayton of Gorgios, 'Flos Historiarum Terre Orientis', ed. C. Köhler, *RHC Ar*, vol. 2, p. 360.
261 ʿImād, p. 134.
262 Al-ṭarīq maḍīq lā yasluku-hu illā al-wāḥid baʿda al-wāḥid. IA, vol. 12, p. 7.
263 AA, p. 388.
264 WT, vol. 2, p. 637.
265 Al-ʿAẓīmī, *Tārīkh ḥalab*, p. 385; IQ, p. 236.
266 See Chapter 1.
267 Richard, *Le comté*, pp. 17–18.
268 See above under 'Wars in the east'.
269 IQ, p. 240. Cf. WT, vol. 2, p. 638.
270 WT, vol. 2, p. 638. See also: Richard, *Le comté*, p. 34.
271 Richard, *Le comté*, p. 24.
272 Sivan, *L'Islam*, pp. 39–56; Hillenbrand, *Crusades*, pp. 116–67.
273 Köhler, *Alliances*, pp. 104–21.
274 Bernard Lewis, 'The Sources for the History of the Syrian Assassins', *Speculum* 27.4 (1952), p. 480.
275 Bogdan Smarandache, 'The Franks and the Nizārī Ismāʿīlīs in the Early Crusade Period', *Al-Masāq* 24.3 (2012), pp. 226–31; Bernard Lewis, 'Sources', p. 484.
276 Xavier de Planhol, *Minorités en Islam: géographie politique et sociale* (Paris, 1997), pp. 83–91 and *passim*.
277 Little is known of the Nuṣayrīs themselves during the Frankish period, although they may be identical with the mysterious, fiercely anti-Christian '*Uannini*' who lived near ʿArqa and Crac des Chevaliers. Burchard of Mount Sion, pp. 29, 90; Major, *Medieval Rural Settlements*, vol. 1, pp. 254–6.
278 Al-ʿAẓīmī, *Tārīkh ḥalab*, p. 383. Cf. Cahen, *La Syrie*, p. 353.
279 Al-ʿAẓīmī, *Tārīkh ḥalab*, p. 385.
280 Al-ʿAẓīmī, *Tārīkh ḥalab*, p. 381.
281 Cahen, *La Syrie*, pp. 170–1, 353.
282 Smarandache, 'Franks', p. 231.
283 Ibn al-Furāt, *Ayyubids*, vol. 1, p. 182.
284 Per altam et immensam montaneam [. . .] in vallem Dessem. PT, 127.
285 Non multum alta nec inaccessibilia, ut quidam dicunt. Burchard of Mount Sion, pp. 29, 30.
286 Burchard of Mount Sion, p. 90.
287 See Chapter 3.
288 Usāma, pp. 129–30. Usāma himself did not claim to have been present. This may suggest that this particular incident took place during the period after Usāma's exile from Shayzar in June 1131. Usāma's father was frail in his old age, explaining why he had stayed at Shayzar while Usāma's uncles, who returned in time to finish off the Frankish pilgrims, were on a military expedition. Usāma's father died on 30 May 1137, not long after Raymond II became count of Tripoli

and not long before Zankī captured Rafaniyya in July. Usāma bin Munqidh, *The Book of Contemplation: Islam and the Crusades*, trans. Paul M. Cobb (London, 2008), pp. xxv–xxvi.

289 Claude Cahen, *Orient et Occident au temps des Croisades* (Paris, 1983), pp. 81–2; Robert Irwin, 'Usamah ibn Munqidh: An Arab-Syrian Gentleman at the Time of the Crusades Reconsidered', in *The Crusades and Their Sources*, ed. France and Zajac, p. 78 and n. 36; Usāma bin Munqidh, *An Arab-Syrian Gentleman and Warrior in the Period of the Crusades: Memoirs of Usāmah ibn-Munqidh (*Kitāb al-I'tibār*)*, trans. Philip K. Hitti (New York, 2000), p. 14. Cf. Paul M. Cobb, *Usama ibn Munqidh: Warrior-Poet of the Age of Crusades* (Oxford, 2005), pp. 73–4.

290 Joshua Prawer, 'Social Classes in the Crusader States: The "Minorities"', in *A History of the Crusades*, ed. Setton, vol. 5, p.103; Richard, '*Cum omni*', pp. 188–92. See: Kevin Lewis, 'Medieval Diglossia', pp. 126–30.

291 Axel Havemann, 'The Vizier and the Ra'īs in Saljuq Syria: The Struggle for Urban Self-Representation', *International Journal of Middle East Studies* 21.2 (1989), pp. 233–40.

292 Usāma, pp. 79–80.

293 Qatala qūmiṣ aṭrābulus ra'īs-hā. Al-'Aẓīmī, *Tārīkh ḥalab*, p. 385.

294 Neither Yūnān nor the anonymous and perhaps identical executed *ra'īs* appears in the list of twelfth-century *ru'asā'* compiled by Richard, whose use of Usāma was minimal. Richard, *Le comté*, p. 87.

295 See Chapter 1.

296 *RRH*, no. 78; *Codice diplomatico*, ed. Paoli, vol. 1, no. 2, pp. 269–70.

297 *RRH*, no. 107; *CGOH*, vol. 1, no. 72.

298 *RRH Add.*, no. 113b; *CGOH*, vol. 1, no. 75.

299 Devic and Vaissète, *Histoire*, vol. 5, no. 551.i, cols 1054–5; *RRH*, no. 211.

300 Phillips, *Defenders*, pp. 1, 8, 12 and *passim*.

301 WT, vol. 2, p. 661.

302 WT, vol. 2, p. 661. See Chapter 3.

303 IQ, pp. 258, 262.

304 Orderic Vitalis, *Historia*, vol. 6, pp. 494–6.

305 Richard, *Le comté*, p. 9.

3 Military decline and matrimonial discord

Count Raymond II (1137–52)

Introduction

Raymond II's reign began and was to end in bloodshed. Forty years had passed since the First Crusade had stormed into Syria, shattering what little Muslim opposition had stood against it. Now the heirs and usurpers of those Muslim leaders who had failed so dramatically in the 1090s and 1100s were gathering their forces, uniting the fractured Islamic world by treaty or by sword. The days when the Franks of Syria could actively dictate the terms of surrender were over; their military policies became ever more reactive as the frequency and confidence of Muslim raids into Christian lands increased. The kingdom of Jerusalem still posed a very real threat to Islam, as its later invasions of Egypt were to show, but the northern crusader states during Raymond II's reign could muster none of the military strength necessary to overcome those Muslims who now overran their former territories. The principality of Antioch had been weakened even before Raymond II succeeded his father in 1137 – as early as the Battle of the Field of Blood in 1119 – and its time as a credible northern counterweight to the influence of the kingdom of Jerusalem was over.[1] Regarding the county of Edessa, this outlying state would be erased entirely from the map before the end of Raymond's life.

As for Tripoli itself, Raymond II has hitherto escaped close scrutiny. Jean Richard dedicated less of his 1945 monograph to Raymond II than to any of the other counts of Tripoli, excepting only William Jordan.[2] This is due largely to the fact that William of Tyre's narrative is notoriously imprecise and sparse for the middle years of the twelfth century.[3] The relative brevity of Raymond's fifteen-year reign (1137–52) in large part explains why his life lacks the breadth and depth of evidence available for his father Pons and his son Raymond III. What is remarkable is that Raymond II left only a few more traces in the written record than did his short-lived predecessors, William Jordan and Bertrand, and in truth achieved rather less than they did. Nevertheless, there is much more to be said than an uncritical regurgitation of William of Tyre's piecemeal account, or a series of apologies for inadequate evidence. Most notable is a selection of sources from both the Latin West and the Arabic-speaking world, which have been neglected by past historians but together allow an overdue reappraisal of Raymond's career and the events he witnessed, acted upon and – for the most part – mishandled.

Treachery on the mountain

Raymond II had one advantage over his father, which is that he came to power as an adult. There was no minority in 1137 as there had been in 1112. Raymond's precise age in 1137 is unknown but his parents had been married since at least 1115, so he could easily have been in his early twenties. Indeed, the exact term used by William of Tyre to describe him around the time of his accession was 'adolescent' (*adolescens*), which implies an age of at least fifteen years – the likely age of majority in the Latin East.[4] There seems little reason to accept Richard's supposition that Raymond remained in his minority until 1140.[5]

Raymond's relative maturity was small consolation for the serious problems he encountered from his first day as count. Tripoli and the Latin East as a whole were being buffeted by the changing tide of the military situation in Syria, as the descendants of the first crusaders struggled to increase, consolidate or even hold their lands in the face of increasing Muslim aggression, led primarily in the north by the warlord ʿImād al-Dīn Zankī of Mosul (d. 1146). Raymond entered the fullness of his power when the county itself was at risk of extinction in the throes of the worst crisis it had faced since its initial establishment. Raymond's father had died in a clash with the Muslims of Damascus, and Raymond himself, supported only by the diminished forces of his county, could hardly hope to exact his revenge upon the most powerful city of Islamic Syria. Thus it was that he turned to a softer target.

William of Tyre wrote that Count Pons had not been killed by the Damascenes in battle, but in captivity, allegedly because a group of 'Syrians' (*Surianis*) living on Mount Lebanon had betrayed him.[6] Little is known about these 'Syrians' and Latin authors consistently used the very term *Suriani*, together with its cognates, in reference to local Christians. Of course, this remains imprecise given the sheer variety of eastern Christians who lived in the Latin East and were routinely identified as 'Syrians', including pro-Byzantine Melkites, pro-Latin Armenians, the so-called Jacobites (non-Chalcedonian Syrian Orthodox) and the dyophysite Nestorians.[7] Because the 'Syrians' who supposedly betrayed Pons lived in Lebanon, Kamal Salibi was inclined to identify these Christians in particular as members of that most quintessentially Lebanese sect – the Maronite Church.[8] This might be justified on the basis that William of Tyre identified the Maronites as a 'certain nation of Syrians'.[9] However, James of Vitry believed that the *Suriani*, the Maronites, the Jacobites and the Nestorians were all discrete groups, implying that the term *Suriani* primarily referred to Melkites.[10] A few decades later, the medieval French translation of the Hospitallers' General Chapter at Acre in 1265 rendered *Suriani* as *Nestorin*.[11]

The fact is that Lebanon had an even greater diversity of Christian sects in the Middle Ages than it does now, with the Maronites only coming to dominate the region at the expense of other communities – including Jacobites, Nestorians and Ethiopians – in the early modern period.[12] It is likely that the Franks in the twelfth century actually had more regular contact with the Jacobites, who populated the lower foothills and many of the county's coastal towns, than with the Maronites, who predominantly lived on the higher summits of Mount Lebanon, especially between Jubayl and Beirut.[13] For example, William of Oldenburg recorded that the 'Syrians' (*suriani*) living in Nephin produced excellent wine for their Frankish overlords.[14] Interaction between the Franks and the low-altitude Syrian Christians extended beyond the economic sphere to the religious. A surviving church near Batrūn, now known as Sayyīdat al-Kharā'ib (Our Lady of the Ruins), had a double-naved structure, which Dodd and Nordiguian suggest may indicate the coexistence of multiple rites – Latin and some form of eastern Christian – in the same building.[15] Numerous other surviving churches both on the coast and inland along the Q̱ādīshā valley exhibit 'crusader' features, primarily in the content and style of surviving wall paintings.[16] This valley, terminating at Tripoli itself near the neighbouring al-Kūra district where Count Pons lost his life, was thick with Christian churches and monasteries of varying sects in the Middle Ages – as attested by Burchard of Mount Sion.[17] Archaeological evidence thus challenges Prawer's classic argument that the Latins mostly avoided settling in rural areas, preferring the greater security of cities and fortresses.[18]

Not all rural areas were equal as far as the Franks were concerned. As Ellenblum has argued, the Franks in the kingdom of Jerusalem were much more likely to interact with and live alongside eastern Christians in historically sedentary regions than with Muslims inhabiting historically nomadised areas.[19] In the county of Tripoli, relations between the Latins and the locals were determined more by altitude than sedentarisation. James of Vitry wrote that the heights of Lebanon were 'in a land rarely explored'.[20] Significantly, the Maronites were concentrated in the stretch of territory between Jubayl and Beirut where Lebanon came closest to the sea. This was the very same area that proved consistently difficult for Frankish communication and travel between the county of Tripoli and the kingdom of Jerusalem, with the consequence that the two polities inexorably grew apart.[21] No wonder then that the Franks did not encounter the Maronites in their own homes and villages as routinely as they did the Jacobites, Nestorians and Melkites of the coast.

The Maronites were not the only group to be sheltered and isolated by Lebanon's steep slopes. The Druze were followers of a uniquely Lebanese sect that believed the Fāṭimid caliph al-Ḥākim to be divine.[22] They were separated from the Franks still further, living on the far side of Lebanon where the Russian pilgrim Abbot Daniel warned of 'infidels' who posed a serious threat to travellers.[23] The Franks proved remarkably ignorant of the Druze, with James of Vitry knowing only that they followed both 'the law of Muḥammad' and 'their own secret law' – the latter of which permitted them to break with traditional Islamic norms, such as abstention from eating pork.[24]

Returning to the Maronites specifically, the foregoing discussion of Lebanon's geography is not to say that the Latins had no dealings with the Maronites in the way that they did with the Jacobites and Melkites. Rather, such interactions took a different form. In the centuries preceding the crusades, the Maronites had managed to use their position on the forbidding Lebanese heights in order to resist much of the interferences in their way of life that other non-Muslim *dhimmī* groups had to endure under Islamic governments.[25] For example, Islamic law ruled that Christian groups had to wear some form of distinctive clothing, traditionally a woollen belt known as a *zunnār*.[26] Interestingly, Burchard of Mount Sion noted that Syrian Christians continued to wear this belt even under Frankish rule, becoming the only way the Latins could distinguish them from the Muslims.[27]

A more significant burden upon *dhimmī* groups under Islam was that they were demilitarised. By contrast, the Maronites had managed to retain their arms. Testament to this are the numerous Latin chroniclers who praised the Maronites' martial prowess, which was often deployed alongside Frankish armies. William of Tyre observed that the Maronites regularly served the Latin Christians in military matters.[28] James of Vitry noted the Maronites' particular expertise as archers.[29] Modern historians have regarded this Maronite military service as having contributed greatly to the county of Tripoli's defence, which in turn elevated their standing in the eyes of the Franks.[30]

At the same time, the Maronites' rare ability to defend themselves violently if necessary afforded them some further measure of autonomy, first under the Muslims and then under the Franks. Richard and Salibi believed that the Maronites' prominent military function allowed them to be integrated without much difficulty into the Franks' 'established feudal system', with their peasants becoming serfs and their chieftains becoming *reguli* (*ru'asā'*).[31] Indeed, Prawer and Richard believed that the very term *reguli* – 'petty kings' – set the Maronite *muqaddams* apart from the near-synonymous *raisii* of the other religious minorities in the Latin East, rendering them more like the Franks' equals than their subjects: reflecting the strong and distinctly Lebanese tradition of *montagnard* autonomy.[32] Secular independence was matched by ecclesiastical autonomy. According to William of Tyre, the Maronites retained their own church hierarchy, including patriarch and bishops, even after most agreed to unite themselves to Rome after 1181.[33] Thus they became the first 'Uniate' church – a distinctive communion within the predominantly Latin-rite Roman Catholic Church – and remained so to the present day.[34] Of course, the fact that the Maronites retained such independence over their lives and territories, as compared to other, more dependent Christian communities, underlines just how little this particular group was affected by the Franks on a day-to-day basis and vice versa.

It would appear from Latin and Arabic sources that there were two settlements that served as the principal arenas for contact between the Franks of Tripoli and the Maronites. These were al-Munayṭira to the south of Lebanon and Bsharrī to the north. Surviving evidence indicates that al-Munayṭira was the only Frankish settlement within the county of Tripoli to be located deep within Lebanon itself, specifically on a road crossing the mountain between Jubayl and Baʿalbak. The Franks seemingly used this route to launch raids into the Biqāʿ valley on the far side of Lebanon, as in 1116/17 and 1175.[35] Muslim armies occasionally did the same, albeit in reverse. Thus Nūr al-Dīn would lead an army westwards from the Biqāʿ to seize al-Munayṭira in the mid-1160s, occupying it for a brief while.[36] Al-Munayṭira was one of the county's lesser fiefs, with two Frankish lords – Bernard and William – recorded in the late twelfth and thirteenth centuries.[37] Some Latins lived there permanently and it was the home of an infamously barbaric Frankish physician, whose fondness for brutal amputations and senseless head operations was immortalised by Usāma bin Munqidh.[38] According to the late-medieval Maronite poet Jibrāʾīl bin al-Qilāʿī (1447–1516), Maronites lived in the vicinity of al-Munayṭira as well, with one 'chieftain' (*muqaddam*) named Kāmil describing himself as 'a knight of the king [*sic*] of Jubayl' (*fāris malik jubayl*), joining his lord in raids on Baʿalbak.[39] Ibn al-Qilāʿī's descriptions of *muqaddamūn* like Kāmil of al-Munayṭira are surely exaggerated for literary effect and anachronistic political motives, but Kamal Salibi nevertheless believed that such 'legendary figures' were based on real historical 'prototypes'.[40] Ibn al-Qilāʿī's account suggests that the Maronites of al-Munayṭira lay within the orbit of the lords of Jubayl, which is corroborated by William of Tyre's claim that most Maronites lived in the diocese of Jubayl.[41]

As for Bsharrī, this settlement was located among the countless Christian villages of the Qādīshā valley and seems to have been dominated by Maronites. In the Mamluk period, Bsharrī and other settlements in the Qādīshā valley were inextricably linked with Tripoli, as their inhabitants would migrate to Tripoli's rural hinterland during the winter season and sell their produce in the city's many markets.[42] There is no reason to doubt that this seasonal migration occurred under Latin rule as well. Crucially, Bsharrī was recognised as a Frankish lordship within the county's feudal structure. Latin lords of Bsharrī (*de Bus*[*s*]*arra*) are recorded between 1145 and 1205.[43] It seems then that Bsharrī, alongside al-Munayṭira, was one of the few places where the Latins and Maronites were in contact on a regular quotidian basis. Of course, it is worth noting that such interaction was not always harmonious. In the 1230s, the Maronites of al-Munayṭira would rebel against the lord of Jubayl.[44] Around the same time, Bsharrī also became for the Maronites a hotbed of controversial anti-Frankish sedition.[45]

Historians for a long time sought to downplay the complexities of the relationship between the Franks and the Maronites, preferring to emphasise co-operation over conflict. This was largely for early modern political reasons, linked to a shared interest of the Europeans and Maronites to ally together against the Ottomans. The first author to state that the local 'Syrians' who assisted Raymond of Saint-Gilles in the initial conquest of Syria and Lebanon were Maronites specifically was the influential Maronite patriarch and Roman Catholic apologist Isṭifān al-Duwayhī in the seventeenth century. Al-Duwayhī's attempts to frame Maronite history as one of orthodox continuity and loyalty to the Roman Church against all the odds led him to deflect criticism for supposedly dishonourable actions as well as to claim responsibility for more edifying ones. Thus, wary of William of Tyre's explicit claim that the 'Syrians' of Lebanon had betrayed Pons in 1137, al-Duwayhī chose to attribute this crime to the Türkmens instead.[46]

Ironically, had al-Duwayhī not been so keen to equate Lebanese 'Syrians' with Maronites specifically, then his assertion that the Türkmens killed Pons would have been unnecessary. The location of Pons's defeat and death in the lowland region of al-Kūra suggests the involvement of Jacobites and Nestorians rather than mountain-dwelling Maronites. Moreover, although the Maronites did not have as consistent a friendship with the Latins as al-Duwayhī and others have tried to depict, it was actually the low-altitude Syrian Christians who had the greatest cause in the 1130s to resent the Franks and Pons specifically. Only a few years before, *c.*1133, the late count had killed one of their own, the *raʾīs* of Tripoli, probably out of suspicion of his loyalties.[47]

Tensions between the Latins and the indigenous Christians were exacerbated greatly by Raymond II's response to his father's death. According to William of Tyre, the young count mustered the few knights who remained to him and marched up the hills into Lebanon. How far they got is unclear, but they presumably focused their attentions on the nearby Jacobite- and Nestorian-dominated foothills, rather than the Maronite settlements in the more forbidding heights. The Franks rode into Christian villages and attacked the inhabitants viciously, capturing men, women and children alike and leading them back to Tripoli in chains. Here the young count had most if not all of them tortured to death in public.[48] Any who survived this brutal display may well have been enslaved. The imposing castles that survive even today in what was once the Latin East were often built by forced labour. In the early 1240s, a workforce consisting of 'a multitude of workers and of slaves' – perhaps Muslim prisoners – managed to rebuild the castle of Ṣafad in less than three years.[49] The famous Persian Muslim poet Sa'dī, whose poetry now adorns the United Nations building in New York, remembered how, around the same time Ṣafad was rebuilt, he had been taken prisoner at Acre and then forced by his Frankish captors to dig ditches at Tripoli alongside 'Jews' (*juhūdān*).[50] Why these Jews should have been put to forced labour is unclear, but their presence indicates that Muslims and Syrian Christians were not the only local people to suffer punishment and persecution under the Franks.

As for Raymond II's behaviour specifically, what seems to modern sensibilities a shocking act of violence committed against an unwitting civilian populace – collective punishment for a rumoured crime – met with William of Tyre's high praise. Writing at a remove of many decades, the archbishop believed that the public tortures and executions meted out to the Lebanese Christians had been just punishment for the alleged betrayal of Count Pons. Moreover, he claimed that Raymond's raid on the villagers provided 'the first lessons of his martial courage'.[51]

Cut off and cut down

It was easy enough for the grief-stricken Raymond to vent his anger on local Christians, even given the dilapidated state of the Tripolitan military, but he was soon to face a much more serious challenge, which he proved unable to meet. In July 1137, only a few short months after the soldiers of Damascus had shattered the Tripolitan army and killed many of its men including the count himself, 'Imād al-Dīn Zankī attacked the county from the north-east.[52] According to William of Tyre, it was specifically because Zankī had learned of Pons's crushing defeat and death a few months before that he chose to attack the county at this juncture. As William vividly put it, 'the entire region was destitute of military forces'.[53]

Following the same course taken during his first invasion of the county in 1133, Zankī focused his attentions on the region around Rafaniyya and Montferrand. These two settlements had become ever more isolated from the Frankish coastline after the establishment of the Nizārīs in Jabal al-Nuṣayriyya throughout the 1130s.[54] Zankī had initially been attacking Muslim-held Homs on the county's eastern frontier, but seeing how hard a nut this was to crack, he chose to divert his attention against the more vulnerable Christian settlements.[55] Kamāl al-Dīn later claimed that Zankī only chose to attack the Franks at Montferrand because they had been planning to lend their assistance to the *atābak* of Homs, who was a client of Damascus at the time.[56] Given that the Christians of Tripoli had recently suffered a grievous defeat at the hands of the Damascenes and were now much reduced in terms of military strength, it seems hard to believe they pursued such an actively interventionist policy. Indeed, it is more plausible to assume that Kamāl al-Dīn interpolated the story of Homs's collusion with the Franks in order to justify Zankī's transparently grasping attack upon his fellow Muslims – hardly appropriate behaviour for a man who later received the largely retrospective and posthumous mantle of *mujāhid*.[57]

Count Raymond, confronted with this imposing Muslim army within his lands and all too aware of the depleted ranks of his own military, sent messengers to his uncle, King Fulk of Jerusalem, desperately seeking help just as his own mother – Fulk's sister – had done four years previously on behalf of his father.[58] As before, the king came to Tripoli's aid, enacting an emergency levy of cavalrymen and footsoldiers from the kingdom.[59] This incident underlines again that the county was no longer regarded as a true part of the realm. William of Tyre made it clear that Fulk was moved by an avuncular solicitude for his nephew and also by a 'paternal concern for the needs of all Christians', and not by any seigneurial obligation to a vassal. William also referred to Rafaniyya as being both 'in Tripolitan territory' and 'in foreign parts'.[60] This turn of phrase is one of the earliest implications that the county of Tripoli was something distinct from the *regnum* and also that it now incorporated the formerly Antiochene fief of Rafaniyya, thereby spanning the old border near ʿArqa.

No sooner had the king reached the 'foreign' county of Tripoli than he received an urgent communiqué from Prince Raymond of Antioch, who faced an altogether different threat to his lands: John II Komnenos, son of the Byzantine emperor Alexios and technically co-emperor with him since 1092. Like his father, who had died in 1118, John was fixated on regaining Antioch for the empire and in 1137 chose to lay siege to it. That he was willing to resort to a show of force shows exactly how important Antioch was to imperial grand strategy in the region. Caught off-guard by the disturbing coincidence of Zankī's invasion of the county of Tripoli and John Komnenos's siege of Antioch, Fulk had no option but to call an impromptu crisis meeting with his senior advisors and Count Raymond. They soon reached the consensus that a two-stage plan was necessary: first to defeat the Muslims at Montferrand, 'which seemed easy enough' (*quod leve satis videbatur*), and then to head north to confront the Byzantines. The combined armies of Jerusalem and Tripoli thus proceeded eastwards to Montferrand with what would soon prove to be misplaced optimism.[61]

As soon as Zankī heard that Christian reinforcements were marching to the relief of Montferrand, he lifted the siege and headed to intercept them. What followed was disaster for the Christians. Zankī demonstrated his supreme ability as a general by killing and capturing all of the Christian footsoldiers and most of their knights.[62] Kamāl al-Dīn estimated the number of Frankish dead at 2,000, with many more captured.[63] Raymond of Tripoli himself was thrown into captivity, while Gaufrid Chatpalu, the brother of Count Joscelin I of Edessa, was killed. Fulk fled with his entourage and took refuge in Montferrand, joining the very same people whom he had come to save. Worse was that in this rout the king lost all of the supplies intended for both his army and the beleaguered inhabitants of Montferrand.[64] The Franks were now in extremely dire straits.

According to William of Tyre, the Christians suffered this savage defeat for three reasons. First was that the Christians were simply 'devoid of divine favour', evoking the common medieval belief that there was a causal link between religious worth and military success. William's second explanation was less supernatural and certainly shrewder, with the archbishop observing fairly that Zankī was 'an extremely wise man, possessing much experience of military matters'.[65] His third reason is arguably the most intriguing, as he claimed that the Franks had been led by their guides down treacherously narrow mountain paths, which had made it exceedingly difficult for them to defend themselves against the Muslims. William claimed that 'it was doubtful whether this was done through error or malice' on the part of the guides.[66]

Who these guides were is unclear, but William's account implies strongly that they were locals of some description. Were they Christians who smarted over Raymond's treatment of their fellows a few weeks previously? Were they, as Richard suggests, the increasingly seditious Nuṣayrī inhabitants of the very mountains between Tripoli and Rafaniyya, which the Franks were foolhardily trying to traverse?[67] In any case, the incident shows how the Latins' prospects in the county of Tripoli were narrowing dramatically. They could no longer trust their indigenous subjects to provide the assistance necessary to defend their once-sprawling and highly mountainous territories effectively. Just as the count of Tripoli was no longer able to extend his power over Mount Lebanon and the *Passus Canis* into the kingdom of Jerusalem, or over Jabal al-Nuṣayriyya and the Margat Pass into the principality of Antioch, so too were he and his allies now unable to cross the same mountains safely in order to check their Muslim rivals. The days when William Jordan had extended his reach up to the Orontes valley were but a distant memory.

The Latin East on the brink

With the count in captivity and the king besieged, desperate pleas for help were sent to Antioch, Jerusalem and Edessa. Assistance was soon forthcoming. Raymond of Antioch abandoned his own besieged city to aid the king, while Joscelin II of Edessa, Baldwin of Marash and Patriarch William I of Jerusalem all rushed to lend assistance.[68] However, the situation worsened further as soon as these reinforcements set out. Bazwāj of Damascus was no friend to Zankī, yet seized the opportunity presented by his rival's invasion of the county of Tripoli. With the departure of both the king and patriarch of Jerusalem in quick succession, Bazwāj invaded the kingdom of Jerusalem. His army ravaged the undefended and unfortified city of Nablus, plundering it, enslaving its inhabitants and burning it to the ground.[69] With Bazwāj's invasion of the realm, three of the four crusader states were now under direct threat. As Phillips puts it, the 'Latin East was [. . .] simultaneously assailed by three hostile powers':

John Komnenos in the principality of Antioch, Bazwāj in the kingdom of Jerusalem and Zankī in the county of Tripoli.[70] Less than forty years after the First Crusade, one could be forgiven for assuming that the brief experiment of Latin Christian rule in Syria and the Holy Land had already reached its end.

As it happened, the Latin East was to survive this crisis, thanks to the irony of having too many enemies, who were each as hostile towards one another as they were towards the Franks. Zankī had initially assumed a distinctly leisurely air while besieging Montferrand, which he seems to have intended to starve into submission rather than take by force. Usāma bin Munqidh had travelled the short distance from Shayzar to participate in this siege and recalled later how Zankī had organised impromptu horseraces to pass the time, insistently borrowing – and never returning – Usāma's own prized Frankish horse for this very purpose.[71] As Zankī became aware of the various forces coalescing in Syria, he was soon obliged to abandon such pleasant diversions, instead adopting a real sense of urgency. According to William of Tyre, Zankī was disturbed by the Latin relief forces approaching his position, but his greatest concern was the threat posed by the Byzantine emperor, whom he assumed was in Syria to fight Muslims rather than to restate the old imperial claim to Antioch.[72]

Zankī's concern over Emperor John's intentions was a reasonable fear. Ibn al-Qalānisī confirmed that John had already sent an envoy to Zankī in May and had indeed marched from Antioch towards Montferrand in August, apparently wishing to support the Franks against the Muslims on this occasion.[73] The emperor had certainly not forgotten his dispute with Prince Raymond, who would later return to Antioch after the threat from Zankī had dissipated, only to find the city still under Byzantine siege.[74] That ownership of Antioch remained a contentious issue between the Latins and the Greeks even at this crucial juncture had serious consequences. With the benefit of hindsight, Kamāl al-Dīn praised God for this inter-Christian squabble, as it had prevented a timely and united response to Zankī's invasion.[75] Of course, this was far from clear at the time. Syrian Muslims other than Zankī also quite sensibly assumed that the Byzantines posed more of a threat to them than to the Franks. The citizens of Aleppo went to special lengths to fortify their city against a feared Byzantine atack.[76]

With Frankish reinforcements approaching from all directions and with the largest Byzantine expeditionary force to enter Syria for a generation looming, Zankī chose to bring his siege of Montferrand to a rapid conclusion. Despite the pressures upon him, Zankī was unwilling to retreat empty-handed as he had done in 1133. He knew that time was of the essence, but was also aware that the Franks trapped in Montferrand itself were entirely cut off from events in the outside world. He skilfully turned this lack of intelligence to his advantage. Zankī shrewdly offered the Franks very generous terms of surrender, knowing that they would accept them, unaware of how close at hand reinforcements were. These terms included the freeing of all Christian captives – Raymond II foremost – and also safe passage from the fortress for the king and his men. In return, the desperate Franks agreed to give Zankī Montferrand, neighbouring Rafaniyya and 50,000 *dīnār*s.[77] Zankī had Montferrand demolished, lest the Franks reoccupy it, and magnanimously gave the surrendering King Fulk a robe of honour.[78] The bruised and broken Latin Christian army marched back to safer territory in the county of Tripoli, apparently retracing their steps over the Alawite slopes from Rafaniyya to ʿArqa. It was only when they arrived here that Fulk, Raymond and their men realised that they had been duped. Gathered in the fields near ʿArqa were the relief forces from Edessa and Antioch. The king was annoyed that these reinforcements had been so tantalisingly close, yet accepted that this latest war with Zankī was over. The defeated Franks all headed for their homes elsewhere in the Latin East, without a thought of returning eastwards to reclaim Rafaniyya.[79]

The threat posed by Zankī was no longer an immediate one, but purchasing this respite had come at a high cost. Rafaniyya was not a major settlement within the county of Tripoli, blighted as it was by constant military insecurity as it passed back and forth between Christian and Muslim control in the years from 1099 to 1137.[80] Rafaniyya's local inhabitants would continue to suffer from political instability even after Zankī's conquest. Petty local rivalries were as important in this respect as the passage of armies and holy wars. The Muslim lord of Rafaniyya and the emir of Hama had a long-standing enmity, which could sometimes spill over into violence. Despite the town's evident weakness, Rafaniyya and its loss were nonetheless important. Since at least 1126, it had formed part of the comital demesne.[81] Symbolically it had been one of the county's four episcopal cities and the only one not to be embroiled in the wrangling over the archdiocese of Tyre. Its bishop seems to have lived the remainder of his days in Tripoli, appearing there in 1139, and a successor was never appointed.[82] As late as the 1220s, the Hospitallers launched raids against nearby Montferrand (Baʿrīn), perhaps in the hope of a much-belated reconquest.[83] Such attempts worried the local Muslim powers, but the Hospitallers' ambitions ultimately proved in vain, for Rafaniyya and Montferrand were never again in Frankish control. Hindsight thus teaches that, with Zankī's conquest of 1137, the county of Tripoli had suffered its first permanent loss of territory and its north-eastern frontier had been pushed irretrievably westwards beyond the Nuṣayrī mountains.

Byzantine pretensions

For most of the Latins, withdrawal to their respective domains meant returning to comparative safety – a retreat from the cliff's edge upon which Zankī's invasion had placed them. Prince Raymond of Antioch, however, still had to deal with the Byzantine emperor and his ongoing siege of the principality's capital.[84] Clearly King Fulk no longer thought it worth his time to continue north to Antioch. Knowing he could not hope to resist the full strength of the empire in battle, Raymond chose the diplomatic route. The prince agreed to pledge his fealty to John Komnenos and to allow him unfettered access to Antioch itself, while the emperor agreed to allow Raymond and his successors to hold North Syria in his stead. This included Antioch and the Muslim-held cities of Aleppo, Shayzar, Hama and Homs, on the understanding that the emperor was able to conquer them in a planned invasion of Syria.[85]

It is clear that John and Raymond continued to view the Latin principality of Antioch as a direct continuation of the eleventh-century Byzantine *doukate*. William of Tyre wrote that the emperor would 'restore' (*restitueret*) Aleppo, Homs and the other Muslim cities of North Syria to the prince.[86] Neither Raymond nor his Norman predecessors had ever actually held these, so the only grounds for this interpretation were legal, theoretical and based on half-forgotten precedent. John's father Alexios had promised Aleppo to Bohemond I of Antioch as one of the terms of the Treaty of Devol in 1108, which in turn was based on the territorial precedent set by the former Byzantine *doukate*.[87] It is clear, then, that Byzantine and Antiochene strategy was still being shaped by the bipartite Levant of the pre-Saljūq period. Perhaps this is why pseudo-Fretellus, writing a decade or so after 1137, believed that there remained only two crusader states – Jerusalem and Antioch – divided at Nahr al-ʿArqa.[88]

That the Byzantines remained committed to an increasingly irrelevant partition of territory may explain a curious incident during John Komnenos's time in Syria. According to Niketas Choniates, the emperor chose to attack the Muslim cities in the region as a favour to the prince of Antioch and, crucially, the count of Tripoli – both of whom he regarded as his 'liegemen'.[89] The precise terminology employed by Niketas Choniates for 'liege' – *ligion* (λιγιον) – would seem to denote a stronger seigneurial relationship between the emperor and the count of Tripoli than previously seen. The term is clearly a borrowing from Latin *ligius*, which first appeared in Greek literature as *lizion* (λίζιον) in Anna Komnene's account of the Treaty of Devol in reference to Bohemond I of Antioch.[90] The presence of such a loanword amid the learned Attic Greek of Anna Komnene should come as little surprise, since the Byzantines regularly used alien social concepts and rituals such as the oath of fealty in their dealings with their many foreign allies and mercenaries, including both Franks and Turks.[91]

Importantly, the Byzantines did not apply the precise term *ligion/lizion* to dealings with all of their allies and clients. According to John Pryor, Anna only ever used it when describing Bohemond's relationship to her father the emperor. By contrast, Bohemond's fellow crusaders, including Raymond of Saint-Gilles, William Jordan, Bertrand of Saint-Gilles and Pons of Tripoli, were merely *douloi tou basileos* (*δουλοι του βασιλέως*) – 'servants of the emperor' – which placed them within the empire's established political cosmology. Pryor thus thinks that Anna's use of the neologism *lizios* indicates that there was a different, stronger bond between Alexios and Bohemond than between Alexios and the other crusaders.[92] This in turn supports the prevailing belief among modern historians that the Byzantine emperors prioritised their re-establishment of direct imperial rule over Antioch (and probably Edessa), but remained content with a vaguer, informal recognition of loose suzerainty over the southern crusader states.[93]

Returning to Niketas Choniates, his use of *ligios* in reference to the count of Tripoli seems somewhat more perplexing. If the Byzantine emperor now regarded Raymond II of Tripoli as a 'liegeman' on an equal footing with the prince of Antioch, then 1137 might at first appear to represent a discernible intensification of imperial claims over Tripoli. This would seem wholly inexplicable given Pryor's thesis that the Byzantines treated the counts of Tripoli, together with the kings of Jerusalem, rather differently to the princes of Antioch. It might therefore be tempting to assume that Niketas Choniates – a late authority writing a century afterwards – simply got his facts wrong, at best confusing the count of Tripoli for the count of recently Byzantine Edessa. Neither William of Tyre nor John Kinnamos, both near-contemporary with events, made mention of Tripoli's submission to the emperor on this occasion – except perhaps the latter's vague allusion to other Franks 'who inhabited the region'.[94]

Neglected Greek evidence may yet substantiate Niketas Choniates's account. Within a short time of the events in 1137, a handful of poets at the court of John Komnenos wrote propagandist verses to celebrate the emperor's many achievements in his Syrian campaign. Theodore Prodromos (*c.*1100–*c.*1165) applauded 'how Tripoli was made subject'.[95] Similarly, in an oration directed largely against the arrogance of the Latins – 'Kelts' – Michael Italikos (*c.*1090–*c.*1157) praised the fact that 'the Phoenician lords' were now 'subject from afar' to the emperor.[96] If any Latin was to be described as a Phoenician lord, then the count of the ancient Phoenician city of Tripoli was the obvious choice.[97] This surely corroborates Niketas's report that Raymond of Tripoli did reconfirm his allegiance to the Byzantines in 1137. Indeed, it is known that the poems of Prodromos and Italikos were among Niketas's sources, making his narrative that much more reliable than its late composition date might otherwise suggest.[98]

Why, then, should John Komnenos have been so interested in the county of Tripoli and the Lebanon region more generally in 1137, exceeding the restricted Antioch-focused ambitions of his father a couple of decades previously? For one thing, political changes since the time of Alexios Komnenos had ensured that the county of Tripoli now extended north into former territories of the Byzantine *doukate* of Antioch such as Tortosa and Maraqiyya.[99] Although Tripoli itself lay south of the old border, it was nevertheless ruled by a man who held Antiochene lands. Count Raymond, as lord of the formerly Byzantine *themes* of Tortosa and Maraqiyya, was now as much a part of the imperial political hierarchy as the prince of Antioch, albeit less prestigious. The Franks had themselves reshaped the political borders of Syria and were already accepting that the eleventh century's bipartite Levant was a thing of the past, replaced by four distinct 'crusader states' – not to mention neighbouring Muslim powers – at least in a *de facto* sense. Was it also the case that the Byzantines were choosing to forget the past?

The Latin conquest of the Levantine coastline had also transformed, perhaps expanded the Byzantine *oikoumene* in other, subtler ways. According to Ibn al-Qilāʿī, a twelfth-century Maronite chieftain (*muqaddam*) named Kisrā travelled to Constantinople to pay homage to the Byzantine emperor, who duly dubbed him 'king of Mount Lebanon' (*malik jabal lubnān*). Whatever the meaning of this vague and probably exaggerated title, it is likely that the renewed contact between the Maronites and Byzantines at this time was stimulated by the Frankish conquest of Lebanon, which had helped to open the region to the wider Christian world. Indeed, Kisrā is described as if he himself was a crusader, with a cruciform sword-hilt and a cross on his armour, while the emperor is described with the distinctly Latinate loanword '*imbirādūr*' (*imperator*) as well as the familiarly Arabic '*malik al-rūm*' (king of the Romans).[100] For the first time in perhaps centuries, the Byzantine conception of empire again stretched to include Mount Lebanon. The way in which the Franks had radically, if gradually, changed the territorial framework of the Levant continued to exert an influence on the Byzantines, if only by uncoupling their ambitions from eleventh-century precedent. John's son Manuel I Komnenos would later make the bold claim that even the southerly kingdom of Jerusalem was 'part of his empire'.[101]

John Komnenos's mooted invasion of Muslim Syria finally came in 1138 after the emperor had spent the winter in Cilicia.[102] Had it been successful in capturing the promised cities of Aleppo, Shayzar, Hama and Homs, the map of the Latin East would have been altered once again. For one thing, had Prince Raymond become the Byzantine client-ruler of Homs, the county of Tripoli would have been enclosed almost entirely on its eastern frontier by a much-enhanced principality of Antioch. Only the county's near-impermeable border running across Mount Lebanon would have remained as a front open to further territorial growth at the expense of Islam. In practice, the county would have become like the Iberian lordships of León, Catalonia and Portugal, which saw their borders with Islam gradually sealed off by the conquests of their Christian neighbours during the Reconquista – at once granting them greater protection against Muslim invasion while curtailing opportunities for future expansion.

At first it seemed that John's grand expedition into Syria, supported by Prince Raymond of Antioch and Count Joscelin II of Edessa, was destined to succeed when the emperor conquered Hama and Kafarṭāb. Regrettably for both the Franks and the Byzantines, John Komnenos's expedition faltered at its first major obstacle, the city of Shayzar. John Kinnamos explained that the city was simply impregnable.[103] Certainly the imposing Saljūq-era citadel at its heart remains today as a monument to the town's heavy medieval fortifications.[104] William of Tyre, however, laid the blame on the Christians themselves, specifically Prince Raymond and Count Joscelin. The archbishop praised John Komnenos for his efforts, but claimed that his young Latin allies had simply been unwilling to put in the necessary work, preferring instead to procrastinate by playing games and gambling – medieval vices that appear remarkably often in crusading chronicles.[105] In the end, the emperor gave up on the Franks, reached a deal with the local Muslims and withdrew, having achieved very little.[106] William, who framed much of his narrative in such a way as to show how profitable co-operation with the Byzantines could be if handled correctly, presented this farcical affair as a sober warning to those who failed to appreciate or foster good relations with the Greeks.[107]

Medieval outsourcing

With the county of Tripoli weakened severely by the events of the 1130s, stretching back at least to Fulk's bloody victory over Pons in 1132, and with its eastern frontier still exposed to Muslim invasion after the disappointing failure of John Komnenos's Syrian war, Count Raymond II became increasingly dependent upon external military aid, as his actions in the 1140s would demonstrate. Already the count had failed to assist John Komnenos and his Latin allies in the campaign against Shayzar, which Lilie blames on Tripolitan military weakness.[108] In the first half of the 1140s, Raymond carried out perhaps the most far-reaching action of his entire reign by granting most of the county's eastern domains – much of this having been lost to the Zankids in 1137 – to the military religious order of the Hospital of St John.[109]

The donation charter's dating clause clearly reads 1142, but has nonetheless caused some confusion among historians. The document's modern editor Delaville le Roulx, together with Reinhold Röhricht, favoured the date given in the document itself.[110] Richard originally agreed, only to correct it to 1144 on the grounds that the chancellor responsible for this charter was Peter, who does not seem to have taken up his office until at least 1143.[111] By 1994, however, Richard had begun to express doubts that his amendment was correct after all.[112] With the charter itself and the majority of its modern analysts pointing to 1142, this is the date used here. Indeed, the charter was witnessed by Robert III, count of Auvergne, who seems to have been visiting Syria.[113] While in the east, Robert also took responsibility for carrying another charter with him back to the west. This was Raymond II's 1142 confirmation of his father's earlier surrender of rights in the county of Velay in 1132.[114] It seems unlikely that Robert would have stayed in the east for two years to witness the donation to the

Hospitallers in 1144, so it seems quite reasonable to assume that this did also occur in 1142 after all.

Raymond's donation included the recently conquered settlements of Rafaniyya and Montferrand, with Raymond perhaps hoping that the Hospitallers would be able to recover them. Secular rulers elsewhere were known to make such donations to the military orders in the hope that these sworn brothers would succeed where they had failed. Just a year before in 1141, Alfonso I of Aragon had promised the Hospitallers the Muslim-held city of Tortosa in south Catalonia, although in this case the Order appears to have shown 'little willingness to take the bait'.[115] In addition to Rafaniyya, Raymond's donation included a few minor and obscure settlements such as *Mardabech* (unidentified) and *Lacum* (al-Akūn), but also Ḥiṣn al-Akrād – 'the fortress of the Kurds'. Latin scribes would soon corrupt the final syllable of this Arabic toponym, dubbing the castle *Cratum*.[116] Through mutations of orthography, Crat became Crac, which in turn would become known to the modern reader as Crac des Chevaliers, recalling the monastic knights who made this their principal fortification in Syria.

Historians have long been in agreement that Raymond was motivated to give away so much because of the ascendance of Zankī and particularly the disasters of 1137, which had seen the loss of Rafaniyya and the county's army decimated.[117] The count even agreed to reimburse those secular lords who had their lands transferred to the Hospital, with 600 bezants going to William of Crat and 1,000 bezants to Gislebert of Puylaurens and his wife.[118] In this generosity, Riley-Smith sees the government's 'anxiety [. . .] to hand over its responsibilities for these frontier marches'.[119]

Andrew II of Hungary would visit Crac in 1218, evocatively describing it as 'the key to Christian land'.[120] Andrew's metaphor captured well the castle's immense strategic value, dominating the Buqayʿa plain and east-west travel through this area. Arab geographers vividly illustrate its importance. Abū al-Fidāʾ noted that it lay a single march from Homs in one direction and Tripoli in the other.[121] From its unparalleled vantage point, al-Dimashqī claimed that it was possible to see the Mediterranean coast to the west and the Muslim cities of Baʿalbakk and Damascus to the south.[122] This was partly an exaggeration, at least as far as Baʿalbakk and Damascus were concerned, but the statement makes clear the strategic value of the site.

The fortress itself would endure for centuries as the greatest monument to the Frankish period in the Levant and is known to Syrians today as the tautological Qalʿat al-Huṣn (Castle of the Fort). Its magnificence surpasses other crusader remains, even Jerusalem's Church of the Holy Sepulchre or Acre's medieval streets. The castle would survive numerous Muslim assaults in the Frankish period, culminating in its conquest by the Mamluk sultan Baybars in 1271. In the sixteenth century, the Ottomans arrived to take the castle from the Mamluks. The fortress had thus endured centuries of war by the time the young T. E. Lawrence described it in 1910 as 'perhaps the best preserved and most wholly admirable castle in the world'.[123] Decades later still in 2006, the United Nations Educational, Scientific and Cultural Organisation (UNESCO) would enrol Crac as a World Heritage Site, although this was not enough to save it from mortar shells and air-to-ground missiles, which ripped through the castle's interior during 2012–14, causing serious damage. In the 1140s, of course, such destruction lay far in the future. So too, in fact, did the bulk of the construction. What constitutes the formidable castle today was built largely in the thirteenth century. One must therefore imagine Crac des Chevaliers in 1140 as a smaller fort, built by the Muslims and subject to minimal renovation since the First Crusade.[124]

The chief beneficiary of Raymond's donation was the Hospitaller Order, which remained as undeveloped in the 1140s as the castle itself. The Hospital of St John had been founded in the 1070s by Amalfitan merchants led by the enigmatic Gerard as a hospice for pilgrims in late-Fāṭimid Jerusalem. Like other Latin religious organisations in eleventh-century Jerusalem, such as the Hospital's sister foundation, St Mary Latina, this small institution expanded rapidly after the First Crusade conquered the Holy City, receiving donations from people across Latin Christendom. Crucially, the Order's military responsibilities were a later addition to their duties of administering hospices and medical care. Indeed, the Order's militarisation may have followed the example set by another early crusader religious organisation, the more militant Templars established by Hugh of Payns. The Hospitallers only gradually became more militant from the 1130s and 1140s and this process was to continue for years to come, until it eventually eclipsed the Order's hospitaller duties.[125]

Historians are broadly correct to see Raymond II's donation of 1142 as a watershed moment in the history of the county of Tripoli, when its count gave away vast swathes of his territory, not to mention significant liberties in war and finances. The land given in 1142 would henceforth serve as the core of a practically independent, ecclesiastical state within a state.[126] Yet this discussion of the 1142 donation must be qualified with the awareness that Raymond himself could not have known just how significant his act would later prove to be. After all, the Hospitallers' domain in the east of the county only reached its thirteenth-century peak after many years of receiving additional grants of land and privileges, from the counts of Tripoli and their vassals. Furthermore, Raymond's decision to transfer much of the defensive burden of the county's eastern frontier to an organisation that, for all its presumed wealth at this early stage, had only recently acquired a military function must have seemed a risky experiment. This, of course, underlines how desperate the count and his courtiers must have been at this time. Although Baldwin and Riley-Smith argued that the liberties granted to the Order allowed them to build a semi-autonomous 'state within a state' centred on Crac, Richard believed that Count Raymond had expected rather that the Hospitallers would serve him in the same way as was expected of secular lords, working alongside him and owing some loose allegiance.[127] The later expansion of the Hospitallers' power and prestige, largely at the expense of Tripoli's secular government, was by no means foreseeable in 1142.

It is also worth observing that Raymond's grand donation was not wholly novel in the county's history, even if it was undeniably set apart by its size, character and long-term significance. Raymond's predecessors had already given the Hospital a generous amount of land and power. The Hospital had a house at the Pilgrims' Mount as early as 1100–15 and a series of documents in the 1110s and 1120s confirmed numerous earlier donations to the Order, with some allegedly stretching back as far as Raymond of Saint-Gilles and most concentrated within the county's eastern marches. These donations included the granting of tithes in the bishoprics of Tripoli and ʿArqa,[128] the receipts of a tax levied from farmers living near Rafaniyya, toll-collecting rights at the gates of Tripoli itself, vineyards and villages in the plains of ʿAkkār and Buqayʿa, other properties near ʿArqa and Crac and a hospice for the poor to be built in or around Rafaniyya.[129] The latter is particularly intriguing, given that this hospice was apparently being constructed shortly before hundreds of pilgrims were killed on the road between Rafaniyya and Āfāmiyyā.[130] Historians of the military orders have not previously linked this particular event to the militarisation of the Hospitallers but it is surely worthy of consideration. This tragedy reflects the deteriorating security in the east of the county during the 1130s, which no doubt demonstrated to all – not least the Hospitallers – that hospices alone were no longer enough to protect the pilgrims travelling through this region. The growing need to bear arms to protect their pilgrim charges likely convinced the Hospitallers of the need to militarise as an institution and also showed Raymond II the potential value of entrusting them with greater responsibilities for securing the eastern frontier, where they already had fairly extensive property and thus local knowledge.

Raymond's donation in 1142 granted the Hospitallers a huge amount of power and influence, which continued to grow until the very end of Latin rule in the region. It also placed upon them a huge burden. When thinking of the Hospitaller lordship at Crac, it is often easy to envisage a domain with clear territorial integrity and well-defined limits – an ecclesiastical enclave bordering on the county of Tripoli proper to the west and the Islamic emirate of Homs to the east.[131] In truth, Hospitaller control within this area was piecemeal. The count did surrender the grand stronghold of Crac, but many lesser settlements within its orbit remained in his control and in the hands of lesser landholders such as the bishop of Tortosa. Balázs Major has recently explained the rationale behind the count's ostensible generosity in pragmatic economic terms: 'renouncing the costly castles was much easier than giving up prosperous villages'.[132] In other words, donations such as Raymond's were something of a mixed blessing for the Hospital. Although it is tempting to admire the imposing ruins of Crac today, such edifices were drains on resources – as heavy a burden on the county's budget as on its military policy. For Raymond, the 'loss' of Crac must have felt liberating in no small way.

Crusade, competition and kinship

In 1144, Zankī's ascendancy in North Syria led him to capture Edessa, which in turn sent shockwaves reverberating throughout Latin Christendom. People for whom the glorified triumph of the First Crusade lingered on the threshold between living memory and legend struggled to understand why God had seemingly abandoned them in favour of supposed infidels. Charismatic preachers, not least the Cistercian Bernard of Clairvaux, attempted to explain what had happened and settled upon the medieval trope of sinful decadence. The generation of the First Crusade had deserved their astounding victories, as worthy and pious Christians, but their sons and grandsons had failed to live up to such high standards, falling into old habits of sin and complacence. Like a firm yet loving father, God had chastised the current generation of Christians by allowing the Muslims to take Edessa, although not without offering them the opportunity to redeem themselves in a new holy war. Such was the logic behind the Second Crusade, launched in 1145 by Bernard Clairvaux's former protégé, Pope Eugenius III. The Second Crusade managed to recruit an even wider selection of people than had the first, including the two most prestigious monarchs in contemporary Europe, King Conrad III of Germany and King Louis VII of France.[133]

Since the First Crusade, stories had circulated about the astonishing achievements of its participants and unsurprisingly their sons and grandsons were keen to live up to the precedent set by their noble ancestors.[134] Nothing was so vivid a reminder of these pioneering crusaders than the offspring they had left to rule in the east, who were now the cousins of the very Europeans setting out on the Second Crusade. As the new generation of crusaders began to arrive in Syria – and in some cases before they had even left Europe – they each received entreaties for help from these eastern relatives. The competition between the Latin barons of Syria for such invaluable military assistance was fierce. William of Tyre criticised how each of the rulers of the crusader states – Jerusalem, Antioch, Tripoli and Edessa – selfishly sought aid only to expand his own domain to the detriment of others.[135] Although the Second Crusade had been launched specifically to assist Edessa, this was quickly forgotten. William revealed his own bias, clearly believing that the northern lords' appeals for help threatened to distract the crusaders from what he thought to be their rightful mission: to serve only the kingdom of Jerusalem, ruled jointly by Queen Melisende and her son King Baldwin III since the death of King Fulk in 1143.

The greatest risk to Jerusalem's hopes of harnessing the Second Crusade lay in the kinship networks that bound the arriving westerners to their cousins living elsewhere in the Latin East. William of Tyre described at some length Prince Raymond of Antioch's attempts to convince his nephew-in-law King Louis VII of France to stay and assist him in North Syria, although the king soon left when he heard rumours that the prince was seducing his queen, Eleanor of Aquitaine.[136] After this incident, the Jerusalemite court were all the more concerned that Raymond of Tripoli – another of Louis's cousins via the king's aunt and count's mother Cecilia – would also make sentimental appeals to family bonds and delay Louis still further. The patriarch of Jerusalem was thus dispatched 'to the Tripolitan parts' in order to steal the king away from Count Raymond, escorting him swiftly southwards. Such language served to underline that the county was now effectively 'foreign territory' as far as the kingdom's government was concerned. It is no wonder that it was at this point in his narrative that William of Tyre famously described the crusader states as having been divided into four distinct entities, in a fashion much more explicit than any author had done previously.[137] It would appear then that the unusually intense competition between Latin rulers during the Second Crusade did much to crystallise political borders that previously had been acknowledged only implicitly and applied somewhat inconsistently.

In terms of the actual competition for assistance, the Jerusalemites had an unfair advantage over their rivals. According to William of Tyre, the arriving crusaders largely ignored the pleas of the northern rulers, flocking to Jerusalem en masse 'out of reverence for the venerable places, the love and devotion of which drew all people more'.[138] It is not uncommon for modern historians to write as if medieval Christians regarded the whole area conquered by the First Crusade and subsequently occupied by the Frankish settlers as the Holy Land. In fact, most visitors to the Latin East had a much more restricted understanding of the limits of this geographical space. James of Vitry asserted that the river Dan and town of Caesarea Philippi (Bāniyās) marked the northern extent of the Promised Land.[139] This derived from the phrase 'from Dan to Beersheba', which is the Old Testament's most common definition of the northern and southern extent of Israel.[140] In one of his letters, James bemoaned that from where he lived in Acre he could see the Holy Land but was not himself in it.[141] The same sentiment would surely have applied to the county of Tripoli, further north still. In the 1280s, Burchard of Mount Sion implied that Tortosa was the northernmost part of the Holy Land, thereby incorporating the whole county of Tripoli.[142] However, he contradicted himself elsewhere by asserting like James of Vitry that relatively southerly Acre 'was never part of the Holy Land'.[143]

The county of Tripoli, the principality of Antioch and the county of Edessa, as well as Acre and the northern provinces of the kingdom of Jerusalem, all lay beyond the confines of the Promised Land proper.

True, the county had a small handful of shrines. The shrine of St Leontios outside Tripoli itself failed to recoup the great prestige it had enjoyed in Late Antiquity, barely enduring centuries of Islamic rule only to be plundered by Raymond of Saint-Gilles's army in 1099 and to have its relics sent to Occitania by Bishop Albert of Tripoli in 1105.[144] Towards the middle of the twelfth century, Tripoli received its first Latin-specific shrine: the tomb of a pilgrim-turned-hermit named Radulph, who began his eremitical life in one of the many communities in the principality of Antioch's so-called Black Mountain. Upon John Komnenos's siege of Antioch in 1137, Radulph moved to Tripoli where he would practise extreme asceticism until his death in 1142. His burial site outside the city soon became a site where miraculous cures were experienced by 'many' (*multis*). The life of this figure was recorded within Carmelite sources, which is appropriate given the Carmelites' own origins in the same twelfth-century eremitical milieu.[145] There is nothing to suggest that Radulph himself was a Carmelite, but it seems that they acquired his posthumous legacy. Perhaps they also maintained his tomb and shrine, which may be identical with a still-standing former Carmelite church in Tripoli, built of Roman and Byzantine *spolia* and later converted into a Mamluk mausoleum: the Ṭaynāl mosque.[146]

Latin Christians believed Nahr al-ʿArqa to be the so-called Abana, one of the two rivers of Damascus mentioned in Scripture.[147] Some also claimed it to be the place where the second-century Christian martyr and soldier-saint Eustace had lost his wife and children.[148] This particular detail may have originated among the local Christians living near Tripoli. Soldier saints were extremely popular among Lebanese Christians and many such cults – including that of St Eustace – travelled west after the crusaders encountered them for the first time.[149] The ʿArqa variant of this legend could thus be one of the county of Tripoli's few surviving literary legacies. To what extent St Eustace was venerated in the county itself is unknown.

Other sites in the county were of even less religious significance or else more obscure still. The first-century Flavius Josephus had located the famous Sabbatikon river, which flowed only on the Sabbath, between ʿArqa and Rafaniyya.[150] It seems doubtful that any Latins tried to identify this antique curiosity with any particular river, although Fulcher of Chartres thought it appropriate to cite Josephus's account when describing Count Pons's siege of Rafaniyya in 1126.[151] The region around Tripoli itself was dense with streams rushing down from Lebanon, being where the Qādīshā river and its numerous distributaries entered the sea. Consequently, the area from Tripoli down to Tyre was known to the Latins as Lebanon's 'fountain of gardens', referenced by King Solomon in his Song of Songs.[152] This particular book of Scripture gave the county another minor site, the 'mount of leopards', which could be found just outside of Tripoli. According to Burchard of Mount Sion, there was a cave nearby, which was venerated by local Muslims as the tomb of the Prophet

Joshua (Yūsha‘ bin Nūn), although Burchard himself thought it was actually the tomb of Noah's grandson Canaan.[153] Posterity has favoured the Muslim view and Joshua's tomb can be visited today in what is now the al-Menyeh district of Tripoli.

Other Old Testament prophets had their tombs in the vicinity of the county of Tripoli. Jews, Muslims and local Christians believed that the site of the prophet Noah's tomb was at Karak Nūḥ.[154] Few if any Latins seem to have visited this site, most likely because it was in an area dominated by Muslims and Druze. Wilbrand of Oldenburg came closest, but even he was forced to rely on indirect testimony, writing merely that 'it was said' (*dicuntur*) that Noah was buried there.[155] Despite Latin ignorance, Noah/Nūḥ was broadly popular throughout the Lebanon region at this time, most likely because the frequent flooding that blighted the area in the Middle Ages put people in mind of the Biblical Deluge.[156] Arab geographers claimed that Noah lived in Saḥr, a village near Homs in the mountains, whence the Deluge supposedly began to pour forth.[157] Many medieval Muslims believed that Noah's Ark had set forth from Mount Lebanon.[158] These local legends evidently penetrated western tradition. Ernoul made the unique claim that Noah's Ark had been built at ‘Arqa, making an obvious yet erroneous etymological pun.[159] With the notable exception of Karak Nūḥ, there is no proof that such diluvial sites attracted any serious religious commemoration, either in the county of Tripoli or just beyond its borders.

The county of Tripoli simply lacked any kind of sacred geography that could ever compete with the hallowed ground and scores of shrines – great and small – to be found in the kingdom of Jerusalem. Mount Lebanon and Jubayl were jointly famous for their role in producing and shipping the timber used for the Temple of Solomon and the Cross of Christ.[160] There was, however, little reason to visit Lebanon's famous cedars, of which only a few still stood by the Middle Ages, when one could more easily head to the Holy City and see the Temple and the Cross themselves. As the arriving crusaders in 1148 demonstrated, Jerusalem would always attract disproportionate interest compared to its neighbours, which translated into a much higher volume of pilgrims. In 1126, a Provençal pilgrim named Bernard William of *Fraxino* (La Garde-Freinet) died in Tripoli, but only because he was 'on the Jerusalem pilgrimage'.[161] In the particular case of the Second Crusade, Jerusalem's more sacred landscape resulted in the kingdom's receipt of more military aid. If Tripoli was not the Holy Land, then dying to defend it would have had less merit for crusaders. The resentment felt by the other great lords when confronted by the Jerusalemite monopoly on crusader support in 1148 not only confirmed that the Latin East was now split into four discrete 'crusader states', but led them to shun the king's subsequent, ill-advised expedition against Damascus. Neither the count of Tripoli, the prince of Antioch nor the count of Edessa would assist their southern neighbour in this upcoming campaign.

The belated return of a son of Saint-Gilles

With their great fame and large followings, King Louis and King Conrad have traditionally been the crusaders to attract the most attention from historians. Yet contemporaries also recognised the contribution offered by other participants, among them Count Alfons Jordan of Toulouse – Raymond of Saint-Gilles's youngest son, who had been born at the Pilgrims' Mount in 1103, before having been shipped off to the west upon his father's death in 1105.[162] After attaining his majority *c.*1119, Alfons quickly set about re-strengthening his father's realm after the misfortunes it had suffered during the past two decades, largely due to the aggression of Aquitaine and Barcelona. In 1125, Alfons managed to neutralise one of the greatest threats to the Toulousan domain by agreeing a peace treaty with Raymond-Berengar III of Barcelona. The count of Toulouse conceded eastern Provence, which was technically a part of the Holy Roman Empire, and retained everything west of the Rhône – that is, the 'French' territories.[163] Alfons's achievements were such that he left a lasting legacy in Occitania, where his own name became a rallying cry for supporters of his grandson Raymond VI of Toulouse (r. 1194–1222) in the thirteenth-century Albigensian war.[164]

The Second Crusade was to be Alfons's third great pilgrimage and his most adventurous, following two earlier ones to Santiago de Compostela.[165] Although Alfons had spent the vast majority of his life in the west, it was only natural that he would hope to return one day to Syria, the land of his birth. His desire to go to the east was surely intensified further by the example set by his father – a man who, like Syria itself, lay beyond Alfons's own memory, but whose repute was legendary. The Second Crusade provided Alfons with the ideal opportunity to fulfil his personal, religious and familial ambitions. He evidently felt comfortable enough in his past achievements to absent himself from Occitania, which he seems to have left in the hands of his barons and underage son, the future Raymond V of Toulouse (r. 1148–94).

As befitted Alfons's enduring reputation in the south of France, people at the time expected the count of Toulouse to make a considerable contribution to the greatest military expedition for a generation. According to William of Tyre, many Franks hoped Alfons would exhibit the 'auspicious and fruitful omen of his father'.[166] Alfons clearly impressed his enemies as well, striking fear into the Muslims of Syria. The count of Toulouse was one of only three crusaders to be named individually in Ibn al-Qalānisī's account of the Second Crusade, alongside Louis and Conrad.[167] The great reputation of Alfons's father, Raymond *Ṣanjīl*, was no less a part of the Arab Islamic history of the First Crusade than of the Christian. In the event, however, the Muslims were relieved and Christian hopes dashed when Alfons died of poisoning – or so it was alleged – almost as soon as he reached the Holy Land, landing in Acre but expiring at Caesarea Maritima on the road to Jerusalem.[168]

Despite Alfons's unexpected death, his expedition represented the largest wave of Occitan crusaders to head east since his half-brother Bertrand's crusade of 1108, if not the First Crusade itself. Since the early reign of Count Pons, very few visitors from the south of France are known to have visited the county of Tripoli. Robert III of Auvergne, who was present in 1142 to manage the surrender of the house of Tripoli's possessions in the county of Velay, is one notable exception. Identifying Alfons's followers individually is difficult, given the dilapidated state of evidence for the south of France prior to the thirteenth century. Charters are the best sources for the departure of Provençal knights, such as Raymond and William of Les Baumes.[169] The names of a handful of other Occitan participants are also known, including Raymond Trencavel, the viscount of Béziers and Agde, Hugh VII of Lusignan, count of La Marche, and Pons of Meynes in Languedoc.[170] One possible participant was the troubadour Jaufré Rudel, who legend says fell in love with Countess Hodierna of Tripoli without ever seeing her. A thirteenth-century biography of Rudel claims that he sailed to Tripoli, dying in the countess's arms.[171] This perhaps gave rise to Richard's otherwise unsubstantiated claim that most of the Provençal crusaders landed at Tripoli during the Second Crusade, while Alfons himself landed at southerly Acre.[172]

Alfons's most important follower, at least as far as the history of the county of Tripoli is concerned, was his illegitimate son Bertrand. After his father's sudden death, Bertrand continued to fulfil his crusader's vow. Kamāl al-Dīn reported that he participated in the siege of Damascus, making him the only confirmed Occitan participant in this particular event.[173] Despite initial success, the assault on Damascus ended in failure, as the crusaders proved unable to take the city and were thus forced into a peace treaty. The westerners in the army were outraged, believing that the city was spared only because the Syrian Franks had accepted a bribe from the 'infidel' Muslims. The disappointed Europeans returned home, hereafter viewing their cousins in the Latin East with sourness and suspicion.[174]

Scandal at ʿUrayma

Most of the embittered crusaders sailed for Europe as soon as they could, their hopes of reliving the glories of the First Crusade dashed. Bertrand of Toulouse, however, did not depart peacefully from Syria and his next appearance in the written record shows him embroiled in a more personal controversy, as he came into conflict with his own cousin, Count Raymond II of Tripoli. After the crusaders' surrender at Damascus, Bertrand headed north into the county of Tripoli, where he purportedly seized and held ʿUrayma – a fortress in the north between ʿArqa and Tortosa. According to Arabic authors, Bertrand took this castle as the first step towards achieving his greater ambition of capturing Tripoli itself from Raymond II.[175]

The events surrounding this development constitute the most shocking scandal to hit the county thus far.

Richard believes that Bertrand's capture of 'Urayma was part of a grander scheme dreamt up by his father Alfons, who had intended to take the county of Tripoli from Count Raymond on the curious grounds of porphyrogeniture – a system of succession favouring those sons born after their father's reign began, even at the expense of elder sons born earlier.[176] It was only on this basis that Alfons – born after his father Raymond of Saint-Gilles had claimed the title of 'count of Tripoli' – could argue the stronger case for his inheritance of the county against the descendants of his elder brother Bertrand (I) of Tripoli. Richard theorises that Alfons wished to give the county of Tripoli to his illegitimate son, while leaving the county of Toulouse to his legitimate heir, the future Raymond V. Although Alfons died before realising this ambition, Bertrand (II) remained committed to the implementation of his father's plan, laying claim to what he now believed to be his rightful inheritance, just as his uncle – another purportedly illegitimate usurper by the same name, Bertrand (I) – had ousted William Jordan back in 1109.

Richard's theory is beguiling. Less certain is his proposal that Count Raymond II of Tripoli, aware of this looming threat, acted pre-emptively to have Alfons poisoned at Acre, lest he succeed in the intended coup. According to Richard, this crime gave Bertrand the added motive of seeking vengeance for his father's murder.[177] The only contemporary to blame Count Raymond explicitly for poisoning Alfons at Acre was the anonymous author of a thirteenth-century Syriac chronicle. According to this account, Raymond suspected that Alfons intended to claim his rights in the county of Tripoli and even went to meet his cousin at Acre, where he evidently felt obliged to murder him.[178] The Syriac author did not go so far as to verify that Alfons did indeed have designs on Tripoli. Moreover, it is hardly the most reliable piece of evidence, so some scepticism about Raymond's involvement in Alfons's death is surely advisable.

William of Tyre wrote that no culprit for Alfons's murder was ever identified and the prudent archbishop chose not to speculate.[179] Fortunately for historians, other Latin authors did make accusations. The Premonstratensian continuator of the chronicle of Sigebert of Gembloux blamed an anonymous '*regina*'.[180] Although Richard believes Raymond II to have been the culprit, he nevertheless makes the suggestion that Sigebert's continuator had in mind Eleanor of Aquitaine, queen of France. It must be admitted that Eleanor was conveniently present in the east at the time of Alfons's death, being in the entourage of her crusading husband, Louis of France. She was also an active claimant to the county of Toulouse through her grandmother Philippa, Alfons's cousin and wife to William IX of Aquitaine.[181]

Despite the case against Eleanor, not all have agreed with Richard's interpretation. Bruguière observes that Alfons had a legitimate heir, his son Raymond V, so it would have been difficult even at the time to think that Eleanor hoped to inherit Toulouse simply by having the count murdered.[182] Moreover, Richard seems to have been unaware that the medieval chronicler William of Nangis elaborated the original account by identifying the queen specifically as *regina Jerosolymorum* – Queen Melisende of Jerusalem.[183] Mayer, who also seems not to have read William of Nangis, reaches the same conclusion independently, observing that the original author – Sigebert's continuator – had himself been a fierce critic of Melisende elsewhere. Mayer even gives Melisende a motive in poisoning Alfons, namely to protect her brother-in-law's possessions in Tripoli, remembering of course that her younger sister Hodierna was married to Count Raymond II.[184] This may be true, although Sigebert's continuator and William of Nangis wrote instead that Melisende simply wished to prevent Alfons from performing a 'great act', implying that the queen had some nefarious, undisclosed reason to undermine the Second Crusade.[185] One might speculate that she wished failure on her son, King Baldwin III, for whom the expedition was a vital project and with whom she had hardly the healthiest relationship.[186]

It is impossible to know for certain the guilty party and, in truth, Alfons was probably not poisoned at all, even if his death, like the deaths of many a medieval magnate, inevitably led to rumours of conspiracy. These rumours certainly never reached Arab authors, who were otherwise well-informed about the scandal at ʿUrayma. Ibn al-Qalānisī knew that Alfons had died, but did not mention poison.[187] Medieval sea travel, on cramped ships with limited fresh water supplies, would hardly have been conducive to good health. Stumbling ashore, likely seasick and dehydrated, into the rising heat of a late Palestinian spring may well have brought on symptoms in Alfons easily mistaken for poisoning, not least death. If so, Alfons was not the only victim of the risks of travel during the Second Crusade. Ibn al-Qalānisī hinted at what was probably the true cause of Alfons's passing when he noted that a huge number of anonymous Franks, including 'some of their kings', died of disease and hunger, as well as war.[188] A biography of one of Alfons's supposed followers, the troubadour Jaufré Rudel, explicitly said that Rudel 'took ill in the ship' and died soon after landing at Tripoli.[189]

Arguably more controversial than Alfons's rumoured poisoning was the fate suffered by his son Bertrand at ʿUrayma. Raymond II was clearly desperate to remove this latest threat to his perilous reign, yet still lacked the military might to contest these newly-arrived crusaders. There may have been a scent of rebellion in the air as well. It is far from certain that Bertrand and his crusaders took ʿUrayma by force and it is possible that its obscure Frankish lord had voluntarily welcomed Bertrand into his stronghold. Perhaps the lord agreed with the logic that Alfons Jordan and his line, not Bertrand (I) and his heirs, were Tripoli's rightful lords. Certainly no secular lord of ʿUrayma was ever recorded again after the crisis of 1148.[190]

Lacking the military strength to retake ʿUrayma himself, Raymond chose to do something that would offend many of his fellow Franks: namely seek assistance from Muslims. According to Kamāl al-Dīn and Ibn al-Athīr, the troubled count wrote a 'letter' (*kitāb*) to two of the principal Muslim rulers in the region, Zankī's son Nūr al-Dīn of Mosul and Muʿīn al-Dīn of Damascus. Raymond permitted these Muslims to enter his county unfettered and to seize ʿUrayma, capturing in the process Bertrand and his entire entourage, which apparently included 'his mother' – presumably Alfons Jordan's mistress, rather than the late count's legal wife, Faydide of Uzès.[191]

William of Tyre seems to have been embarrassed by this whole affair and chose not to record it at all. William's apparent distaste for alliances with Muslims, at least when directed against other Christians, is reflected by his censuring of other, similar incidents. The best examples are his condemnation of Alice of Antioch for attempting to secure an alliance with Zankī of Mosul in 1130, supposedly against the barons of the principality and her father Baldwin II, and his similar criticism of Hugh II of Jaffa for allying with the Muslims of Aleppo against King Fulk in 1134.[192] Ironically, William's treatment of such inter-faith co-operation as taboo or outrageous was not necessarily characteristic of the politico-military strategy employed by most of his co-religionists in Syria. As Köhler has shown, the uncompromising ideologies of holy war – crusade and armed *jihād* – made little impact upon the political and military policies of local Muslim and Frankish rulers in twelfth-century Syria. Pragmatism ruled and alliances were forged regularly with little regard for religion, as long as the independence of local petty rulers – kings of Jerusalem and emirs of Damascus, among others – could be secured against the ambitious foreign imperialists, both of the Islamic East and Egypt and of the Christian West and Byzantium.[193]

That William chose to excise Raymond II's alliance with Nūr al-Dīn entirely from his narrative shows either that the archbishop was one of a few Levantine Franks to have felt genuine disgust at such Muslim–Christian joint ventures, or else that he merely recognised the potential damage that knowledge of this apparently common Syrian practice might have had upon his readers in the west. As when he chose not to speculate about Alfons's alleged poisoning, William was surely aware that the reputation of the Syrian Franks was still reeling from the bitter recriminations of their western cousins that circulated in Europe after the Second Crusade's acrimonious end. William partly intended to use his chronicle to recruit crusaders to assist the kingdom of Jerusalem, so reminding westerners of the questionable way in which the Syrian Franks had behaved during and immediately after the expedition of 1148 would hardly have helped his case.[194] Moreover, William must have been sensitive to the reputation of the house of Tripoli specifically, writing at a time when Raymond III seemed to him the best hope for the kingdom of Jerusalem. William clearly viewed discretion as vital to the long-term security and prosperity of his threatened homeland, regardless of his true feelings towards pragmatic military alliances with local Muslims.

Despite William's attempts to suppress the incident, a trace of Raymond II's betrayal of his cousin did slip into his narrative. The archbishop noted later that 'Bertrand, the natural son of the count of Saint-Gilles' had been released from Aleppo over a decade later in 1159, along with various other Christian prisoners following negotiations between the Byzantine emperor Manuel Komnenos and Nūr al-Dīn.[195] This is all that is known of Bertrand's captivity after 1148 and there is no record of him after his release in 1159.

William was not the only contemporary author to attempt to control information about what was otherwise a scandalous conspiracy. Ibn al-Qalānisī of Damascus also refrained from mentioning the alliance between Raymond and Nūr al-Dīn. He did mention the capture of 'Urayma, but depicted it as if it had been the result solely of Nūr al-Dīn's own initiative.[196] Elisséeff has suggested that the 'Urayma incident was an early example of Nūr al-Dīn's enthusiasm for the counter-crusading *jihād*.[197] Mallett has argued otherwise, suggesting that Nūr al-Dīn was concerned only with local strategic ambitions – reminiscent of Köhler's central argument – until he assumed the image of a *mujāhid* for largely political reasons in the 1150s.[198] Be that as it may, Ibn al-Qalānisī's reticence when he was writing more or less contemporaneously with events suggests a concern on his part to depict Nūr al-Dīn as a righteous Muslim ruler, acting only in opposition to and never alongside the Franks. Did Ibn al-Qalānisī, like William of Tyre, struggle with the tension between lofty ideology and simple pragmatism?

Just as William of Tyre was aware of how the siege of Damascus had soured relations between the Syrian and European Latins, so too was Ibn al-Qalānisī personally cognisant of the same event's irreparable effect on relations between Damascus itself and the Franks. Sivan sees the Second Crusade as having signalled the beginning of a new phase of the counter-crusade in Damascus, as the Muslims of this city realised that the Latin Christians were a serious threat, more pressing than their petty rivalries with their co-religionists.[199] Even Köhler admits that the Second Crusade inspired a degree of popular enthusiasm for *jihād* in Damascus that risked destabilising the local Syrian system of atomised powers that had so far preserved the Franks against their more numerous, yet deeply divided Muslim neighbours.[200] If Ibn al-Qalānisī had reminded his readers of Nūr al-Dīn's willingness to co-operate with the count of Tripoli, even against a Christian, this would have gone against the prevailing trend of public opinion in Damascus. Presumably later Muslim authors, namely Kamāl al-Dīn and Ibn al-Athīr, did incorporate the account that Raymond had requested the assistance of Nūr al-Dīn, because the latter's reputation and the specific nature of Zankid-era opposition to the Franks were no longer current concerns.

Interestingly, Raymond was not the only one accused of betraying Bertrand at ʿUrayma. Sigebert's continuator and the derivative William of Nangis once again implicated Queen Melisende. Crucially, they gave the queen an accomplice on this occasion: not her brother-in-law Count Raymond, but her own sister, the countess Hodierna. These Latin authors recorded the whole affair from Alfons's arrival in the east to Bertrand's capture as follows:

> Count Alfons of Saint-Gilles with a naval army landed in Palestine. Since it was hoped that he would perform a great act, he was poisoned wickedly by the treachery – so it is said – of the queen of Jerusalem and he died at Palestinian Caesarea. Then his adolescent son [Bertrand], fearing for himself, entered a certain castle [ʿUrayma] belonging to his cousin [Raymond II], but by the treachery of the same queen with a sister was captured by the Turks.[201]

Historians have previously read the phrase 'with a sister' (*cum sorore*) as if the sister in question was Bertrand's, captured with him and his other followers. These same historians have then constructed surprisingly elaborate narratives about this young woman, whose very existence is unsubstantiated. Devic and Vaissète claimed that Nūr al-Dīn made the sister his wife, while Richard claimed that he entered her into his 'harem'.[202] Bruguière suggests – again with no proof – that the sister became Nūr al-Dīn's favourite wife, birthing his son and heir Ismāʿīl al-Malik al-Ṣāliḥ. In this fanciful interpretation, this was why Raymond III would later seek to support al-Malik al-Ṣāliḥ – his supposed second cousin once-removed – against Saladin in 1174.[203] Together, these scholars have failed to appreciate that the regrettable ambiguity of the original Latin also allows for the much more likely reading that the sister was Hodierna, who was not captured *with* Bertrand, but actively plotted *with* Melisende. Hodierna had motive, as she obviously stood to lose much from Bertrand's attempted coup against her husband's domain.

As a political actor, historians have long failed to give Hodierna the attention she deserves, preferring to focus upon her more famous and better-documented sisters, Melisende of Jerusalem and Alice of Antioch, whom Mayer describes as equally 'domineering and given to politicking'.[204] Yet Hodierna too followed what was clearly a family tradition of female political agency. Another demonstration of this came a decade after the ʿUrayma incident. In 1157, Queen Melisende of Jerusalem intervened illicitly in the election of the patriarch of Jerusalem to ensure that her preferred candidate, her own chaplain Amalric of Nesle, was chosen, despite his alleged incompetence. This event proved highly controversial for the way in which the queen flouted the Gregorian ideals of investiture in a supposedly reformed Church. Crucially, she was supported in her interference 'with the efforts and advice of both Lady Hodierna, countess of Tripoli, Lady Melisende's sister, and Lady Sybil, countess of Flanders, sister to the Lord King'.[205]

For centuries, Hodierna's role in this incident was obscured by an unfortunate instance of haplography – when a copyist's eyes accidentally skip words or whole lines.[206] William of Tyre's nineteenth-century editors suspected they were dealing with the work of a drowsy medieval copyist, but erroneously concluded that Sybil alone supported Melisende.[207] Indeed, this was the solution taken by William's thirteenth-century French translator, which would suggest that the mistake crept into the manuscript tradition at a very early stage.[208] Later historians were more willing to accept that a third woman was involved, but most assumed that the sister in question was Melisende's youngest, the nun Yveta, due to links between her religious house at Bethany, St Lazarus, and Countess Sybil.[209] Wisely, in hindsight, Mayer preferred to use the vague term 'ladies of the royal family' when referring to Melisende's co-conspirators.[210] No historian correctly assumed that Hodierna was the sister involved until the rediscovery of the most complete manuscript of William of Tyre's chronicle. It is now apparent that Hodierna was just as willing as her sisters to involve herself in the key political affairs of the time.

Assuming that Hodierna and Melisende did arrange Bertrand's capture in 1148, then this would have given William of Tyre further cause to suppress information about the scandal. He was always quick enough to condemn Alice of Antioch for her alliance with Nūr al-Dīn's father in 1130, but this conformed with his abiding, even misogynist dislike of this ambitious woman.[211] William could not invite criticism of Hodierna for the same reason that he had to defend her husband – their son had become William's politician of choice by the 1170s and 1180s. William was rather more protective still of Melisende's reputation. Although she had been no more retiring than her sister Alice, the archbishop recognised that she represented dynastic continuity and thus stability for the kings of Jerusalem in the twelfth century.[212] Attacks on her were attacks on the very royal family to which William dedicated much of his life's service. That she was evidently accused – falsely or otherwise – of murder and treachery in 1148 is proof enough that her reputation required defending, but there was more. Bernard of Clairvaux, chief preacher of the Second Crusade and Europe's most influential figure more broadly, felt compelled to write a didactic letter to Melisende, in which he advised her on governance in a way that portrayed her very femininity as an obstacle to overcome.[213] With such commentators expressing their concern that Jerusalem was effectively controlled by a woman, William of Tyre would have felt obliged to portray Melisende in the most favourable light possible. This, of course, gave him another reason to omit any mention of the crisis at ʿUrayma.

Consequences in Occitania and Tripoli

Richard concluded that the whole scandal during the Second Crusade led to an irrevocable breakdown of relations between Occitania and Tripoli.

In his opinion, this is why there was an apparent scarcity of Occitan visitors to the county after 1148. This in turn explains why Raymond II's successor, Raymond III, was later forced to rely upon non-Occitan settlers like Plivain, the Pisan lord of Batrūn from *c.*1180, to replace extinct Occitan families in the county. Another related consequence of this acrimonious incident was that no member of the house of Toulouse came forward to claim Tripoli when Raymond III died without issue in 1187.[214] Richard claimed with finality that Alfons Jordan was the 'last crusader to arrive from Toulouse', adding that the scandal of his death was such that the whole 'Toulousan and Provençal region turned away from crusading in the second half of the twelfth-century'.[215] Richard's interpretation would thus have it that Raymond II, or at least his wife, sacrificed the long-term prosperity of his county, his dynasty and the whole crusading movement in return for the short-term gain of eliminating Bertrand.

Of course, if Richard's theory is correct, then it seems odd that no Latin source directly implicates Raymond II in the death of Alfons Jordan or the capture of Bertrand, and only indirectly accuses him of any wrongdoing at all via a vague reference to his wife and sister-in-law. Furthermore, it could be argued that the regularity of Occitan–Tripolitan contact had already dropped off before the Second Crusade. Count Pons had already been forced to abandon his property in the county of Velay in 1132 – an act confirmed by Raymond II in 1142.[216] Prior to this, the last confirmed Occitan visitor had been Bishop Pons of Le Puy in December 1125, accompanied by the Catalan abbot Berangar of Sant Feliu.[217]

A handful of Occitans were still finding their way to Tripoli within a few years of the Second Crusade, but it is wrong to think this ceased with the controversy of 1148. For one, Occitania simply did not 'turn away from crusading' after the Second Crusade. Troubadour enthusiasm for the Holy Land only emerged around the time of the Second Crusade and continued long after, with many of these poets expressing deep concern over the lack and failure of crusading expeditions throughout the following century.[218] Carraz observes that *individual* Provençal pilgrimages to the Holy Land never ceased, even if their participation in the great expeditions subsequent to the Second Crusade was slight.[219] It is not known how many of these pilgrims went to the county of Tripoli, as opposed to the Holy Land proper, but at least one, the troubadour Peire Vidal, would seek out Raymond III of Tripoli specifically.[220] As Richard himself observed in one of his more recent works, the heirs of the counts of Toulouse claimed to be the legitimate heirs of the county of Tripoli as late as 1259.[221]

Conversely, travel in the opposite direction, from Tripoli to Occitania, was restored soon after Alfons's death, or else never suffered a break. Various men with the by-name 'of Tripoli' can be found scattered across the breadth of Occitania from Provence to Gascony, spanning a date range between 1167 at the latest and 1295 at the earliest.[222] Some of these individuals had probable links to identifiable families in the county of Tripoli.

A certain 'Peter of Tripoli' (*Petrus/Peiro de Tripol*) appeared in Puylaurens in Languedoc between 1178 and 1204.[223] Even Richard is aware of this individual, believing him to be a returning – perhaps disinherited – member of the so-called family of Puylaurens, who appear as lords of Gibelacar (*Jabal 'Akkār*) in the county of Tripoli between 1117 and 1151.[224] Peter's appearances in the west after 1148 surely presents a challenge to Richard's own theory that contact between Tripoli and Occitania had ceased by this point.

Another possible visitor from Tripoli – this time neglected by Richard – was William *de Sivra*, who was in Saint-Gilles in 1157.[225] William was very possibly a member of Tripoli's *de Siura* family, likely named after Ṣūrāt, a settlement some four miles to the east of Batrūn.[226] Richard believes that they were of fairly humble stock, who rose through the ranks of Tripolitan society to be knights by the end of the twelfth century.[227] The volume of Tripolitans in Occitania after 1148 suggests that more were heading westwards than were travelling eastwards, perhaps to escape the worsening security of the county itself, although one must be wary of the distorting effect of poor source survival for the east. What is clear is that contact between Occitania and the county did not come to an abrupt halt with the Second Crusade, or even after the extinction of Tripoli's Toulousan dynasty in 1187.

The Templars of Tripoli

With Bertrand thrown into captivity, the most immediate threat to Raymond II's rule at Tripoli was gone. The Muslims responsible for taking 'Urayma clearly departed the scene quite rapidly, making no discernible attempt to hold the fortress. It was, after all, located deep within the county, on the Christian-controlled side of the Alawite mountain, which prevented the extension of Islam westwards into Christendom just as it effectively precluded Frankish rule stretching any further east. Count Raymond was back in control of 'Urayma, but he still faced an insurmountable problem in that he apparently lacked the resources to repair it or to hold it against any future invasion or rebellion. He thus turned to his one remaining option, to gift it to a military religious order in the hopes that the brother-knights could afford to carry out necessary renovations and to defend it in perpetuity, thereby preserving the integrity of what remained of the county of Tripoli.

Raymond may have been aware that his and his father's donations to the Hospital of St John had been somewhat over-generous, if unavoidable given the circumstances. With much of the county's eastern marches in their control, the count may have felt he was running the risk of saving his county from the Muslims, only to lose it to the Hospitallers. This could explain why Raymond had decided to give 'Urayma to the Hospitallers' great rivals, the Templars, by the early 1150s – shortly after Bertrand's capture.[228] The Templars had come into contact with the count of Tripoli at a fairly early stage in their development, when their founder and first master, Hugh of Payns, had campaigned with Count Pons in an ill-fated attempt on Damascus in 1129.[229] Despite this, they were rather slow to enter the county of Tripoli on a permanent basis. Whereas the Hospitallers had been established in the county since at least the 1110s, there is no definite proof that the Templars had possessions in the county until 1152. In April/May of this year (Muḥarram AH 547), Nūr al-Dīn had again invaded the poorly defended county. His army took prisoners, burned castles and captured the cathedral city of Tortosa, which he garrisoned.[230] This destructive raid was perhaps in revenge for a large-scale Frankish raid into the Biqāʿ valley in December 1151 (Ramaḍān AH 546), which had been repelled by the Muslim governor of Baʿalbakk only after the Franks had already seized scores of human captives and livestock.[231] No doubt Nūr al-Dīn also timed his invasion to coincide with the chaotic civil war then raging between Baldwin III and his mother Melisende in the kingdom of Jerusalem. Fortunately for the Latins, Nūr al-Dīn apparently did not stay long at Tortosa. However, neither the local lord, Raynard of Maraqiyya, nor Count Raymond of Tripoli found they had the funds to repair the damage done to the city. It was thus transferred first to the local bishop and then, when this cleric could not afford the cost, to the Templars. These warrior monks were a convenient choice, as they already seem to have been in control of the neighbouring castle of Ṣāfīthā (Chastel Blanc).[232]

Why were the Templars so much slower to enter the county than the Hospitallers? The Hospital may have had an advantage in Tripoli, since the Hospitallers already enjoyed special favour in the counts' homeland of Occitania – thanks in part to a spurious legend linking their founder, Blessed Gerard, to Provence.[233] Indeed, the Order had a smattering of houses, property and brethren in Provence and Toulouse even before Count Bertrand (I) had left on crusade in 1108.[234] Meanwhile, although the Templars later proved popular in Provence, this did not come until they received the patronage of Count Alfons Jordan in 1134.[235] The Tripolitans' ancestral preference for the Hospitallers could have been compounded by the Templars' own close relationship with Pons's rival Baldwin II of Jerusalem. The king had helped the Templars in their early days, not least by supporting them at the Church councils of Nablus in 1120 and Troyes in 1129 and by giving them their headquarters in Jerusalem *c.*1119.[236] This was al-Aqṣā mosque: believed by Muslims to be the holiest site in Jerusalem, being the 'farthest sanctuary' to which Muḥammad travelled on his Night Journey.[237] The occupying Latins believed it to be the stables of the Old Testament king Solomon, whose Temple – actually the Umayyad Dome of the Rock built over the same site – lay within a short distance, hence the Templars' name. The Templars' early association with the king may have been unattractive to the anti-royalist Pons, who had pointedly absented himself from the council of Nablus, at which the Templars' vocation was first properly discussed.[238]

Thus, the Templars had had to wait for Pons's son Raymond, who was of course married to Baldwin II's daughter Hodierna. According to one fanciful Occitan tale, Countess Hodierna had the love-struck troubadour Jaufré Rudel buried in the Templar house in Tripoli after he died in her arms in 1148.[239] As Nicholson has observed, this detail links the story to the emerging trope of the Templars as 'hosts and undertakers for wandering knights' in Arthurian romance.[240] Yet, it may also hint subtly at a continuing association between the brothers of the Temple and the family of Baldwin II. Perhaps Hodierna was the first to introduce the Templars to the county of Tripoli.

Once they had arrived in the county, the knights went on to enjoy an illustrious history there. Tortosa quickly became the Templars' main headquarters in the county. At some point, the Templars would also take control of the nearby island of Arwād, which was fated to be the Templars' very last outpost in Syria, surrendering to the Mamluks only as late as 1303.[241] As for Ṣāfīthā, this stronghold became the Templars' answer to nearby Crac des Chevaliers and indeed probably enjoyed many of the same privileges, including the right to act beyond the count's direct authority. The Templars also had a strong presence in the countryside around Tortosa. The local bishop agreed to give them unbridled authority over most of the rural parishes of his diocese from 1152 onwards.[242] Although surviving source evidence today is weighted heavily towards the Hospitallers, Balázs Major suspects that Templar properties in the county rivalled those of the Hospital.[243]

The passing of Edessa

When Zankī conquered Edessa back in 1144, this did not bring to an immediate end this most isolated of crusader states. Joscelin II of Edessa managed to salvage something of his former county in 1146, by launching a daring and opportunistic raid on Edessa itself to capitalise on Zankī's recent death. The count managed to take his city back and hold it for a few years. The late warlord's son Nūr al-Dīn, however, retook the city for the final time in 1150, throwing Joscelin into prison and, as in 1144, openly slaughtering the city's Christian inhabitants – Franks and Armenians alike – in the streets.[244]

With Joscelin imprisoned indefinitely and with many of his men incarcerated or killed, his wife Beatrice decided to sell what remained of the shattered county, namely the few surviving fortresses in its westernmost limits, centred on Turbessel. The buyer was Emperor Manuel Komnenos, who had succeeded his father John in 1143. Manuel presumably saw the purchase as an overdue restoration of Byzantine rule to what had been the *doukate* of Edessa,[245] and he promptly garrisoned the remaining forts with imperial troops. This transfer was apparently conditional upon the king of Jerusalem's consent, recalling the southern monarch's former links to the county in the days of Baldwin I and Baldwin II, or else his half-forgotten extensive power as the Latin East's ruler *primus inter pares.* Thus, Baldwin III headed north to meet Manuel for the sake of ratifying the sale.[246] William of Tyre's narrative is notoriously unreliable for the mid-twelfth century and this particular event is extremely difficult to date, but it probably occurred as early as August 1150.[247]

Baldwin III relied heavily upon Count Raymond of Tripoli throughout the surrender and evacuation of the county of Edessa. The king had recently suffered a major setback in his own realm, as a sizeable chunk of the southern nobility had refused his summons.[248] These were those lords who had sided with Baldwin's mother Melisende against the king in what was rapidly becoming the most serious constitutional crisis ever to hit the kingdom of Jerusalem. The king could hardly shirk his responsibilities in negotiating the liquidation of the county of Edessa, so instead headed 'to the Tripolitan regions' to seek Raymond's help. The count of Tripoli agreed and so he and a number of his knights joined the king's party on the journey north to meet the Byzantines.[249] Recalling the role the county of Tripoli had played as a marginal refuge for political outcasts from the kingdom proper in the preceding two decades, following the rebellions of Alice of Antioch and Hugh of Jaffa, it is striking to see the king of Jerusalem himself exiled and forced to rely upon the realm's ambiguously loyal northern neighbour.[250]

On the day the transfer was to be formalised, Baldwin, Raymond and their attendant noblemen – together with some magnates from Antioch for good measure – met with the Greeks. Upon completion of the necessary diplomatic and ceremonial niceties, the king and count led a huge train of mournful Christian refugees – both Latin and Armenian – from the former county of Edessa to the relative safety of the southern Frankish lordships, with Baldwin in the van and Raymond and the royal constable, Humphrey of Toron, the rear.[251] MacEvitt has theorised that the Latins of the county of Edessa had shown only 'rough tolerance' to their Armenian subjects in the first half of the twelfth century. This policy consisted of shifting, *ad hoc* alliances of convenience with individual Armenian warlords, together with a pragmatic avoidance of thorny doctrinal issues between the Latin and Armenian churches.[252] Zankī's massacre of Edessan Christians of every stripe seems to have forced the two communities closer.

William of Tyre reported that the Edessan refugees were led to Antioch, although it is conceivable that some of these headed further south, even to Tripoli.[253] It is known that there were Armenian communities in the Lebanon region at this time.[254] On a more sentimental level, the countess of Tripoli at the time was herself half-Armenian; Hodierna's mother was the Armenian Morphia of Melitene, who had married Baldwin II during his time as count of Edessa. Did Hodierna feel any particular solicitude for these exiles? Regrettably, traces of the Armenian men, women and children who once followed King Baldwin, tramping southwards from their homes, have proved no more enduring than the county of Edessa itself.

The maritime frontier

Since the crusaders' capture of Fāṭimid ports in the first quarter of the twelfth century, culminating with Tyre in 1124, the Ismā'īlī Shī'a of Egypt had posed less of a direct threat to Tripoli than had their Sunnī Saljūq rivals in the Syrian interior. Nevertheless, there was still life in the declining caliphate. Ibn al-Qalānisī wrote that an unusually large Egyptian fleet ravaged the coastal towns of the Franks in June/July 1151 (Rabī' I AH 546). The Fāṭimid sailors killed and captured many people, seized much booty and destroyed Latin and Byzantine Christian ships caught by surprise in the harbours. The fleet sailed on a northerly trajectory, beginning with Jaffa and Acre, then up the Syrian coast to pillage Tyre, Beirut and finally Tripoli.[255]

William of Tyre did not specifically mention this incident, but he did observe that this was a time of increased naval activity on the part of the Egyptians, whose land operations had been impeded greatly by the Franks' refortification of Gaza in 1149–50, entrusted to the Templars.[256] At the same time, the Christians were intensifying their pressure on Ascalon, the one major Levantine port still in Fāṭimid hands. Even this was destined to fall to the Franks in 1153. Showing strategic acuity, William identified the heightened strain on Muslim Ascalon as another factor that had forced the Fāṭimids to invest in their navy in the early 1150s. One particular flotilla built at this time supposedly had as many as seventy galleys (*galee*) and an indeterminate number of troop transports and supply ships.[257] It is surely no coincidence that Ibn al-Qalānisī counted exactly seventy warships in the fleet that raided Tripoli and other coastal cities in 1151.[258]

The Franks of Tripoli were spared any long-term Fāṭimid occupation. The attack, although damaging, did not translate into permanent conquest. Moreover, the fleet of 1151 seems to have been exceptional and was certainly the last attested occasion on which the Fāṭimids threatened their former possession of Tripoli directly, by land or by sea. The next Egyptian naval assault on Tripoli would not be until 1180: directed by Saladin, the man who was to abolish the Fāṭimid caliphate.[259]

The second council of Tripoli and the return of royal authority

By the 1150s, the prevailing opinion was that the county of Tripoli was no longer part of the kingdom of Jerusalem or the principality of Antioch in the strict sense. The bickering between the rulers of the crusader states during the Second Crusade had underlined that much. This is not to say that the county's historic relationship with its neighbours had been forgotten. Sometime *c.*1150, pseudo-Fretellus – or at least his copyist – thought it still appropriate to place the boundary between the kingdom of Jerusalem and the principality of Antioch at Nahr al-'Arqa.[260] In the late twelfth or early thirteenth century, Ernoul still felt it necessary to clarify to his readers that 'the county of Tripoli is not part of the kingdom', implying some lingering confusion among contemporaries.[261] The old arrangement of the Latin East even continued to have some intermittent relevance. In 1145, both the prince of Antioch and the king of Jerusalem had felt it necessary to put their seals of approval on Raymond II's 1142 donation of Crac des Chevaliers and its surroundings to the Hospital.[262] This newly created ecclesiastical domain spanned the old border between the principality and kingdom at Nahr al-ʿArqa (or al-Nahr al-Kabīr al-Janūbī) and the donation's significance was evidently such that the half-forgotten prerogatives of Antioch and Jerusalem were briefly resurrected.[263] It is in light of the persistent memory of the county's dependent status within the early Latin East that the so-called 'second council of Tripoli' must be understood.

Sometime after April or May 1152,[264] King Baldwin III of Jerusalem summoned a gathering at Tripoli, which William of Tyre would call a 'general court'. The king invited to his council the nobility of both Antioch and Jerusalem, although no mention was made of the barons of the county of Tripoli itself – either because of a traditional adherence to a bipartite state-system or more likely because their attendance at a major event in their own capital required no invitation. Patriarch Aimery of Antioch was also invited, together with all his suffragans, presumably including the bishops of the county's three remaining sees – Tripoli, Tortosa and Jubayl. The delegates at Tripoli in 1152 discussed 'state affairs', which likely included Nūr al-Dīn's recent occupation of Tortosa and the Fāṭimid raid up the coast, although William of Tyre chose not to detail these or the vast majority of other matters. Instead, the archbishop focused his attention on the council's main objective, which was to force Raymond of Antioch's widow Constance, the heiress of the principality of Antioch, into marrying one of a string of suitors. King Baldwin, who was Constance's first cousin as well as the senior magnate in the Latin East, had carefully selected each of these hopefuls from the ranks of the Jerusalemite nobility. He was deeply anxious to avoid yet another damaging dynastic crisis in the principality, which had seen its rulers die prematurely far more than the other crusader states. Most recently, Prince Raymond had died in his thirties at the battle of Ināb in 1149, sparking a political and military crisis made all the more worrying by the subsequent and final loss of the county of Edessa.[265] The principality of Antioch was all that remained to defend Frankish North Syria and in 1152 it was entering its third year without a prince.

Aiding Baldwin in his attempt to control Constance's future were two of the princess's aunts, the king's own mother Queen Melisende and her sister Hodierna of Tripoli. In the event, however, nobody – man or woman – was able to convince Constance to marry. All attempts at persuasion failed and so the disappointed participants began to leave Tripoli for home. William of Tyre chose to blame this failure upon the princess's alleged aversion to marriage and her desire to live an independent life, as well as the interference of Patriarch Aimery, who supposedly wished to prevent the creation of a new prince, lest he restrict the cleric's own ambitions.[266] Certainly the latter was a reasonable fear; Aimery would later suffer grievously at the hands of Constance's eventual choice of husband, Raynald of Châtillon.

What is most remarkable about the council is the fact that King Baldwin was able to call and hold it in Tripoli at all. Mayer argues that the king's summoning of this meeting was a formal act.[267] The legalist John of Ibelin, writing almost exactly a century later, claimed that the king of Jerusalem could hold court freely anywhere in the realm, whether or not the lord of the location in question permitted it.[268] Richard recognised that this posed a problem to his thesis that the county was never a true part of the realm, so he suggested that the king enjoyed the right to hold court even in the lands of those '*grands vassaux*' whose bonds to Jerusalem were attenuated at best, including the count of Tripoli.[269] This view is based on the assumption that the county's constitutional relationship to the kingdom of Jerusalem was largely static and unambiguously understood by contemporaries. This does not allow for the possibility that there were differing political interpretations at play in 1152 – such as the increasingly outdated view that Tripoli was part of the kingdom – or that change in legal interpretation could have occurred subsequent to this. John of Ibelin partly based his law-code on precedents he was able to find in twelfth-century sources, meaning that his rulings ought not to be treated as prescriptive so much as descriptive. Perhaps John based his law about the king's rights to hold court partly on his reading of William of Tyre's description of the 1152 council, remembering of course that John believed – probably for the wrong reasons – that Tripoli was indeed one of the realm's baronies.[270]

Richard's static interpretation of the county's constitutional status extended to his viewing of Baldwin III's calling of the 1152 council as a demonstration of the exact same royal prerogative that had allowed Baldwin I to summon a similar gathering at Tripoli back in 1109 in order to settle the bitter dispute between William Jordan and Bertrand.[271] In other words, the king of Jerusalem's hypothetical, limited and *unchanging* suzerainty over Tripoli was all that was required to justify the actions of both kings, despite the intervening half-century. In truth, much had changed in Tripoli's relationship to the crown. In 1109, Baldwin I had sought to determine the fate of Tripoli itself, imposing his authority over a territory widely believed to be part of his kingdom and subject to his extensive power. By contrast, in 1152 Baldwin III was seeking to settle an issue only indirectly related to the county, which had since become distinct from the realm proper. There was no hint of restoring direct Jerusalemite rule to Tripoli in 1152.

The contemporary context and thus meaning of the king's actions in 1152 inevitably differed from his predecessor's intervention in 1109, but the second council was nevertheless intended to be a significant demonstration of royal authority. Baldwin III had recently won a victory against his own mother in the kingdom of Jerusalem. Tense years of division in the realm had finally culminated in a brief but violent civil war between the two parties, erupting on Easter Sunday (30 March) 1152 and ending in victory for the king by 20 April. Mayer thus interprets Baldwin's holding of the council of Tripoli only a few weeks after the queen's surrender as a deliberate display of his triumph. The king sought to proclaim his suzerainty over his mother – who was in attendance at the council despite her recent defeat – and her rebellious partisans, who had abandoned Baldwin when he had needed their help in negotiating the surrender of the county of Edessa two years previously. Mayer also suspects Baldwin of hoping to resurrect the traditional role once played by the king of Jerusalem as 'arbiter of the whole Latin East' – interfering with the succession to the principality of Antioch at a council held in Tripoli. Indeed, this is why the choice of Tripoli itself was of import, deliberately recalling the first council summoned by the first Baldwin back in 1109 to arbitrate over Tripolitan and also Antiochene and Edessan affairs.[272] Baldwin III and those whom he obliged to meet at Tripoli in 1152 could not have failed to realise that the king was indeed seeking to evoke the symbolic precedent of 1109, even if all present – Baldwin included – accepted that there was now a gaping practical divide between the monarch's intensive kingdom of Jerusalem and what had been an extensive 'Latin empire'.

Matrimonial strife

Constance's resistance to a hypothetical marriage was not the only matrimonial crisis to hit the council of Tripoli in 1152. The union of Count Raymond and Countess Hodierna was proving just as problematic as it entered what was probably its twentieth year. According to William of Tyre, Queen Melisende had travelled north to see her niece Constance and also to settle a severe dispute that had arisen between her sister and brother-in-law: 'an enmity born from marital jealousy'.[273] William chose not to disclose the underlying reasons for this strife but enough is known of Hodierna and her husband to make speculation possible. For one thing, Raymond's tenure as count of Tripoli had been disappointing to say the least, marked by failure more than success. His countess, however, was a king's daughter and sister to two of the leading politicians of the age, Melisende of Jerusalem and Alice of Antioch. Moreover, Hodierna herself was an active political agent, as demonstrated by her purported involvement in the betrayal of Bertrand of Toulouse in 1148 and her confirmed participation in the patriarchal election of 1157. She was to prove just as prominent in the early years of her son's reign.[274]

William of Tyre's exceedingly brief summary of Raymond II's reign, written at least two decades after the council, serves as testament to the count's lacklustre career as contrasted against his wife's high social status. The archbishop failed to note even one of Raymond's deeds as count, emphasising instead the fact that his wife was one of King Baldwin II's daughters. As William put it, Raymond III was 'on his father's side of lesser rank'.[275] The inequality of status that lay at the heart of Raymond II's and Hodierna's marriage was compounded by its inversion of the traditional gender hierarchy of the Middle Ages. Raymond must have felt this all the more acutely in the unique circumstances of 1152. If Raymond envied Hodierna's standing in high society, then it is no surprise that tensions flared up at the council of Tripoli, when she and her immediate royal family – principally her nephew Baldwin III and sister Melisende – were dominating affairs. Raymond himself, meanwhile, seems to have done little if anything at the council, marginalised in his own patrimony.

As if the contrast between husband and wife in the socio-political sphere was not enough, rumours were circulating that Hodierna had been unfaithful. The Byzantine author John Kinnamos reported that doubts hung over the parentage of Raymond's and Hodierna's daughter Melisende of Tripoli, who was suspected of being the illegitimate product of some dalliance, presumably her mother's.[276] Count Raymond's jealousy was to be stoked still further by gossip. Assuming the legend has any truth to it, Hodierna's beauty was already common knowledge in the west by the time of the Second Crusade. Jaufré Rudel supposedly fell in love with her upon hearing stories of her told by returning pilgrims. The story of this as told by the troubadour's thirteenth-century biographer is worth producing here in full:

> Jaufré Rudel of Blaye was a very noble man, the prince of Blaye. He fell in love with the countess of Tripoli without seeing her due to the very good and courteous things that he heard said about her by pilgrims who were coming from Antioch [*sic*]. He composed about her many songs with good tunes, albeit with poor words. And because of the desire to see her he took the cross and set to sea, but a sickness seized him in the ship and he was brought to Tripoli into a hospice near death. This was made known to the countess and she came to him, to his bed, and took him in her arms. He realised that she was the countess and immediately regained his senses and praised God that He had sustained his life until he had seen her. He then died in the arms of the countess. She then had him buried with great honour in the house of the Temple and on the same day she became a nun due to the sorrow that she felt for his death.[277]

There is no consensus regarding the historical veracity of this account, in whole or in part. Certainly the *vida*'s claim that Hodierna took the habit in the 1140s or later is unsubstantiated, although it did give rise to the similarly unfounded and confused belief that Hodierna's daughter Melisende became a nun.[278] Nevertheless, the basic fact that Rudel travelled east on the Second Crusade is seemingly confirmed by another piece of evidence, a song by the prolific troubadour Marcabru dated *c.*1147–8.[279] If it was truly the case that pilgrims were accustomed to gossiping of Hodierna's beauty, then this may have exacerbated Raymond's jealousy at the rumours that young Melisende was another man's daughter.

Hodierna would not be the first woman in history to fall victim either to rumours of infidelity or to the overactive sexual fantasies of men, which have both often served to undermine female power. R. Howard Bloch has proposed that the literary genre of 'Distant Love', as pioneered by Rudel, was an expression of 'medieval misogyny', which served to subordinate women by objectifying and silencing them – reduced to voiceless, over-idealised subjects.[280] Similarly, Lambert has observed that the thirteenth-century French translator of William of Tyre's chronicle added qualities of beauty and sexual virtue to the archbishop's original description of Hodierna's sister, Queen Melisende. William had originally ignored her physical features to emphasise that she was in fact a politically able and intelligent woman, yet the translator's emphasis upon her physicality and sexuality served to constrain her achievements within a 'private sphere' by diluting her 'public effectiveness'.[281]

Figure 3.1 Jaufré Rudel dies in Countess Hodierna's arms (BnF, Ms Français 854, 121v) © Bibliothèque nationale de France

Even William of Tyre himself reported accusations that Queen Melisende had engaged in an affair with Hugh II of Jaffa, which some at the time believed was why the self-appointed 'count' had gone to war with her husband, King Fulk, in the early 1130s.[282] In truth, this most likely concealed the true reason for Hugh's rebellion, that he and other barons were outraged by how the king was effectively disenfranchising Melisende.[283] In light of Melisende's long history of open conflict with husband and son alike, Raymond of Tripoli perhaps feared that his wife posed a similar potential danger to his own power. Just as Hugh of Jaffa had been willing to ally with local Muslims in order to defend Melisende's rights, so too had Hodierna shown herself happy to ally with Nūr al-Dīn to oust the pretender Bertrand from 'Urayma in 1148. Moreover, Hodierna was of mixed Latin-Armenian ancestry at a time of growing suspicion among the Latins as to the true loyalties of eastern Christians. Raymond II's attitudes to his wife were thus shaped by a blend of social, gender and ethnic anxieties.

It would seem that the various tensions between the count and countess of Tripoli damaged their marriage beyond repair. Queen Melisende's attempts to reconcile Raymond and Hodierna ultimately failed, so she decided instead to take her sister back to Jerusalem. Such a drastic act proved that this was no minor tiff. As Hodierna and Melisende headed south from Tripoli, Count Raymond set out in the opposite direction, escorting Princess Constance part of the way to Antioch. After a while, Raymond left Constance's train and turned back south for home, followed by Radulf of Merlo – one of the princess's spurned suitors who had made a last-ditch attempt to win Constance's hand and thus the principality.[284] Unbeknown to these two men travelling together with their respective marital woes, worse lay ahead of them.

A brutal death, a brutal response

Raymond, Radulf and their entourages reached Tripoli together, passing through the gate that separated the barbican from the city wall proper. As they did so, they were suddenly set upon by a group of Nizārī Assassins, who viciously attacked the Franks where they stood. Three men died 'miserably' (*miserabiliter*): Radulf, one of his knights and Count Raymond himself.[285] This was not the first demonstration of the Nizārīs' much-feared tactics, but it was the first recorded time in history that Latin Christians fell victim to such an ambush. It would not be the last, as subsequent events would show. A Jewish visitor from Spain, Benjamin of Tudela, would soon write that the Assassins were at war with the Franks and with the count of Tripoli specifically, no doubt having heard of Raymond II's shocking fate a decade earlier.[286] The Nizārīs and the Franks had had fitful alliances in the second quarter of the twelfth century, sharing a common enemy in the Sunnī Zankids, but the audacious murder of the count of Tripoli signalled a new, more antagonistic phase in these relations. [287]

Why should Count Raymond have been targeted in particular? What had he done to deserve the dubious honour of being the Assassins' first Latin victim? No contemporary source provides a clear motive to this seemingly random act of violence but historians have recently developed a beguiling explanation, based upon Raymond's military policies. Hamilton writes that the Assassins had 'no quarrel with the Christians', except perhaps Raymond's recent establishment of the Templars at Tortosa following Nūr al-Dīn's invasion in 1152, the very same year as his death. Both Bernard Hamilton and Bernard Lewis theorise that the Templars posed a real threat to the Nizārīs because they were unusually resistant to the Assassins' 'scare tactics', while the Nizārīs remained themselves 'peculiarly vulnerable' to the Templars. The linked phenomena of Templar resistance and Assassin weakness were attributable to the Templars' distinctive organisational and vocational qualities. Murder only works as a political weapon in the short term if the intended target can be removed, and in the long term if the survivors are capable of fear. However, the Templars' monastic structure allowed them to replace murdered officers with rapid ease, unlike the achingly slow and vulnerable hereditary replenishment of secular dynasties. Thus the short-term impact of murder was mitigated. Moreover, since the brothers of the Temple were expected to seek and welcome martyrdom, even an individual Templar's fear of death was to be repressed.[288] Thus the long-term psychological effect was neutralised. By *c.*1173, the Templars had proven so effective against the Assassins that they had managed to cow the Nizārīs into paying a considerable annual tribute.[289]

The Assassins certainly had reason to fear the expansion of the Templars on the boundaries of their territory. Smarandache has elaborated this observation that the Templars were encroaching on Assassin lands by arguing that Raymond's death came at a time when the Franks were first becoming aware of the Nizārīs as a distinct group of Muslims and reconfiguring the defence of their states accordingly. This defensive reconfiguration in the county of Tripoli was shaped primarily by Raymond II's considerable donation of lands to the military orders, not simply the Templars at Tortosa but also the Hospitallers around Crac des Chevaliers, located on what had become a frontier between the Franks and the Assassins.[290] It will be remembered that the Assassins had greatly expanded their territory in the Nuṣayrī mountains since the 1130s, driving a wedge between the heartlands of the county of Tripoli and its eastern extremities – the very lands donated to the Hospital in 1142.[291] Judged by the interpretations of Hamilton and Smarandache, the assassination of Raymond II was for the Nizārīs an act of pre-emptive self-defence, lest the new military orders impact too greatly upon their Syrian operations. Unable to make an impact on the unusually resistant Templars and Hospitallers themselves, the Assassins chose to attack the more vulnerable target of Count Raymond. Neither of his children had yet attained their majorities, so his death could easily have precipitated yet another of the Latin East's many dynastic crises – exposing the inherent weakness of secular government at the time.

Count Raymond's death came as an understandable shock to the Franks. This one murderous act by Muslims presaged a frenzy of Latin Christian violence against the indigenous people of Tripoli. As William of Tyre reported, the 'people' – the Latin Christian element – flew to arms and killed 'whomever appeared foreign to us [*sic*] in language or appearance', in the hopes of finding the perpetrators.[292] Following earlier precedent, the Franks' suspicion of the local Syrians erupted in violence, again with little if any distinction made between the various religious groups that comprised the broad category of 'non-Frank'. It is doubtful that many, if any, genuine Nizārīs suffered during this Frankish riot. It is not even clear if the Assassins directly responsible for the murder were caught or killed. By contrast, it is certain that many other indigenous inhabitants and visitors of Tripoli did suffer. In the end, the brutal attacks upon the locals only ceased thanks to the timely intervention of King Baldwin, who had remained in Tripoli after his council to partake of some gambling. Disturbed by the uproar in the city, the king was evidently wise enough to recognise that the misdirected violence achieved nothing.[293] The reign of Count Raymond II ended as it had begun, with the peaking of inter-communal hostility and the consequent spilling of his Syrian subjects' blood.

Conclusion

Whereas Raymond's father had overseen the county's move to independence, and whereas his own son would later rise to prominence in the kingdom of Jerusalem, Raymond II died with few achievements to his name. His most significant acts were either of dubious repute – for example his massacre of the Christians of Lebanon in 1137 – or themselves a sign of weakness, most notably the transfer of vast swathes of strategically important lands to the military orders. It cannot be denied that Raymond did at least try to hold on to the lands his predecessors had first conquered and forged into an independent crusader state, but he seems to have been unable to build much upon these past achievements. Rather, he became ever more desperate to cling on to what he had even to the point of betraying one of his own blood during the Second Crusade.

The broad trend of Raymond's career was a continuation of what had become apparent in the last few years of his father's life: military decline in the face of an increasingly confident and motivated Islamic opposition. This led Raymond to trust ever more in the emerging institution of the military religious order, outsourcing much of the defence of the county to the Hospitallers and Templars. Just as external threats seemed more serious than ever, so too did internal sedition appear at times to be a matter of some concern, as the count had learned from personal experience even while his own heavy-handed governance had likely served only to exacerbate this. Meanwhile, Raymond's shortcomings in the military and political spheres were thrown into relief by the achievements of his wife. Most countesses of Tripoli suffered the fate of relative obscurity, but Raymond's bride – Princess Hodierna of Jerusalem – surely eclipsed her husband. Indeed, Raymond was ultimately fated to die with the recriminations of Hodierna and her indomitable sister Melisende still ringing in his ears. Ironically, Hodierna herself fared little better in posterity, her political ambitions soon forgotten as she was reduced to being the beautiful yet voiceless target of a distant stranger's affections. Rudel's infatuation endured even to the modern period, forming the subject of a French operetta by Edmond Rostand in the nineteenth century and a joke in one of P. G. Wodehouse's novellas in the twentieth.[294] What was to be remembered of Tripoli under Raymond II and Hodierna was not the political and military achievements seen under earlier counts, but lustful, exotic and even farcical fantasies.

Notes

1 Asbridge, *Creation*, pp. 214–16 and *passim*.
2 Richard, *Le comté*, *passim*.
3 See Appendix 1.
4 WT, vol. 2, pp. 662, 663–5; La Monte, *Feudal Monarchy*, p. 51.
5 Richard, *Le comté*, p. 47 n. 5.
6 WT, vol. 2, p. 661.
7 Baldwin, 'Ecclesiastical Developments', p. 153.
8 Kamal S. Salibi, 'The Maronites of Lebanon under Frankish and Mamluk Rule (1099–1516)', *Arabica* 4.3 (1957), p. 295. Cf. Grousset, *Histoire*, vol. 2, pp. 67–9.
9 Natio quedam Syriorum. WT, vol. 2, p. 1018.
10 JV, p. 276. See also: Hamilton, *Latin Church*, pp. 159–60.
11 *CGOH*, vol. 3, no. 3180.
12 Hanan Charaf and Anis Chaaya, 'Syriac Cult Places in Wadi Qadisha in Lebanon', in *Ideologies as Intercultural Phenomena: Proceedings of the Third Annual Symposium of the Assyrian and Babylonian Intellectual Heritage Project, Held in Chicago, USA, October 27–31, 2000* (Milan, 2002), pp. 46, 48, 49.
13 WT, vol. 2, p. 1018; Jean Charaf, 'Les Maronites et le comté de Tripoli d'après Duwayhi: essai critique', in *Le comté*, ed. Dédéyan and Rizk, pp. 60–3; Olivia Olmo, 'Les chrétiens orientaux dans le comté de Tripoli: localisation et positions sociales', in *Le comté*, ed. Dédéyan and Rizk, p. 168.
14 Wilbrand of Oldenburg, p. 120.
15 Dodd, *Medieval Painting*, pp. 26–8; Lévon Nordiguian, 'La chapelle de Saydet Al-Kharayeb à Kfâr Heldâ (Caza de Batrûn)', in *Le comté*, ed. Dédéyan and Rizk, pp. 105–7. Cf: Denys Pringle, *The Churches of the Crusader Kingdom of Jerusalem: A Corpus*, 4 vols (Cambridge, 1993–2009), vol. 1, no. 89, p. 206.
16 For example, see: Mat Immerzeel, 'Medieval Wall Paintings in Lebanon: Donors and Artists', *Chronos* 10 (2004), pp. 8, 16–17, 18, 29, 30.
17 Burchard of Mount Sion, p. 28.
18 Cf. Prawer, 'Colonization', pp. 1063–118; Prawer, *Latin Kingdom*, pp. 66–7; Major, *Medieval Rural Settlements*, vol. 1, pp. 22, 81, 243, 258–60, 261, 263; Ahmad Hoteit, 'Influence des Croisades sur les diverses Communautés religieuses libanaises',

in *Die Folgen der Kreuzzüge für die orientalische Religionsgemeinschaft: Internationales Kolloquium vom 16.-18.10.1996 in Halle/Saale*, ed. W. Beltz (Halle-Saale, 1996), p. 67.

19 Ronnie Ellenblum, *Frankish Rural Settlement in the Latin Kingdom of Jerusalem* (Cambridge, 1998).

20 In terra rarissime reperiuntur. JV, p. 338.

21 See Chapter 2.

22 Philip K. Hitti, *Origins of the Druze People and Religion: With Extracts from Their Sacred Writings* (New York, 1928), pp. 26–32.

23 Abbot Daniel, *The Pilgrimage of the Russian Abbot Daniel in the Holy Land. 1106–1107 A.D.*, trans. C. W. Wilson, Palestine Pilgrims' Text Society 4 (London, 1895), p. 30. See also: de Planhol, *Minorités*, pp. 70–83.

24 Machometi lex [. . .] lex alia occulta. JV, p. 150. See also: James of Vitry, *Lettres*, no. 2, p. 95.

25 de Planhol, *Minorités*, pp. 59–70 and *passim*.

26 Fattal, *Le Statut*, pp. 96–110.

27 Burchard of Mount Sion, p. 89.

28 WT, vol. 2, p. 1018.

29 JV, p. 314

30 Richard, *Le comté*, p. 88; Baldwin, 'Ecclesiastical Developments', p. 153; Salibi, 'Maronites', pp. 294–5.

31 Richard, *Le comté*, pp. 86–8; Salibi, 'Maronites', pp. 291–2. See Chapter 2.

32 Prawer, 'Social Classes', p. 103; Richard, '*Cum omni*', pp. 188–92; *CGOH*, vol. 1, no. 144; *RRH*, no. 212.

33 WT, vol. 2, pp. 1018–19. See Chapter 5.

34 Hamilton, *Latin Church*, pp. 207–8.

35 Richard, *Le comté*, pp. 3, 19.

36 IA, vol. 11, p. 322. See Chapter 4.

37 *CGOH*, vol. 1, no. 676; *Documenti sulle Relazioni delle Città Toscane coll'Oriente Cristiano e coi Turchi fino all'anno MDXXXI*, ed. Giuseppe Müller (Florence, 1879), I, no. 49, pp. 79–80; *Tabulae Ordinis Theutonici*, ed. Ernest Strehlke (Berlin, 1869), no. 82, p. 65; *RRH*, nos 637, 758, 1068; Richard, *Le comté*, p. 76 and n. 2. Cf. Richard, *Le comté*, p. 55.

38 Usāma, pp. 132–3.

39 Jibrāʾīl bin al-Qilāʿī, 'Madīḥa ʿalā jabal lubnān', in his *Zajaliyyāt*, ed. Baṭrus al-Jamīl, Uṣūl wa-marājiʿ tārīkhiyya 2 (Beirut, 1982), pp. 92–4.

40 Salibi, 'Maronites', pp. 293–4.

41 WT, vol. 2, p. 1018.

42 Salibi, 'Maronites', pp. 295, 296.

43 *CGOH*, vol. 1, no. 160; *RRH*, nos 236, 807; Richard, *Le comté*, p. 76 and n. 2.

44 Jibrāʾīl bin al-Qilāʿī, 'Madīḥa', pp. 99–100.

45 Salibi, 'Maronites', pp. 295, 296.

46 Jean Charaf, 'Les Maronites', pp. 58–60, 67–8.

47 See Chapter 2.

48 WT, vol. 2, p. 661.

49 Multitudo operariorum et sclavorum. R. B. C. Huygens, 'Un nouveau texte du traité "De constructione castri Saphet"', *Studi Medievali*, 3rd series, 6.1 (1965), p. 382.

50 Muṣliḥ al-Dīn Saʿdī Shīrāzī, *The Gulistan (Rose Garden)*, ed. and trans. Wheeler M. Thackston (Bethesda, MD, 2008), p. 63. My thanks go to Elizabeth Binysh for bringing this particular morsel to my attention.

51 Hec prima virtutis sue rudimenta. WT, vol. 2, pp. 661–2.

52 IQ, p. 258.

53 Regionem quoque universam militaribus destitutam auxiliis. WT, vol. 2, p. 663.

54 See Chapter 2.
55 IQ, p. 258.
56 Kamāl al-Dīn, *Zubdat al-ḥalab*, vol. 2, pp. 261–2.
57 Hillenbrand, *Crusades*, pp. 112–16.
58 See Chapter 2.
59 WT, vol. 2, pp. 663–64.
60 Paterno more pro universis christiani populi necessitatibus debitam gerens sollicitudinem [. . .] in finibus Tripolitanis [. . .] in exteris regionibus. WT, vol. 2, pp. 663–4, 667.
61 WT, vol. 2, p. 664.
62 WT, vol. 2, pp. 664–5.
63 Kamāl al-Dīn, *Zubdat al-ḥalab*, vol. 2, p. 261.
64 WT, vol. 2, p. 665.
65 Gratia destituti divina [. . .] vir sagacissimus et rei militaris multam habens experientiam. WT, vol. 2, p. 664.
66 Errore an malicia dubium est. WT, vol. 2, p. 664.
67 Richard, *Le comté*, p. 88.
68 WT, vol. 2, pp. 665–6; IQ, p. 259; John Kinnamos, *Deeds of John and Manuel Comnenus*, trans C. M. Brand (New York, 1976), p. 23.
69 WT, vol. 2, pp. 666–7.
70 Phillips, *Defenders*, p. 68.
71 Usāma, p. 46.
72 WT, vol. 2, p. 669.
73 IQ, p. 260.
74 WT, vol. 2, pp. 670–1.
75 Kamāl al-Dīn, *Zubdat al-ḥalab*, vol. 2, p. 262.
76 IQ, p. 263.
77 WT, vol. 2, p. 669; IQ, p. 259.
78 Kamāl al-Dīn, *Zubdat al-ḥalab*, vol. 2, p. 262.
79 WT, vol. 2, pp. 669–70.
80 See Chapter 2.
81 Richard, *Le comté*, carte 6. See Chapter 2.
82 *CGOH*, vol. 2, no. VII; *RRH*, no. 191; Hamilton, *Latin Church*, p. 39.
83 IA, vol. 12, p. 488.
84 Cf. John Kinnamos, *Deeds*, pp. 23–4.
85 WT, vol. 2, pp. 670–1. Cf. John Kinnamos, *Deeds*, p. 24; Niketas Choniates, *O City of Byzantium, Annals of Niketas Choniatēs*, trans. Harry J. Magoulias (Detroit, 1984), p. 16.
86 WT, vol. 2, p. 671.
87 AK, p. 393. See Chapter 2.
88 Pseudo-Fretellus, 'Tractatus', p. 432.
89 Niketas Choniates, *Historia*, ed. Jan-Louis van Dieten, Corpus Fontium Historiae Byzantinae 11 (Berlin, 1975), p. 27. Cf. Niketas Choniates, *O City*, trans. Magoulias, p. 16.
90 Anna Komnene, *Alexias*, ed. Diether R. Reinsch and Athanasios Kambylis, 2 vols, Corpus Fontium Historiae Byzantinae 40.1–2 (Berlin, 2001), vol. 1, p. 414; AK, p. 386; J.H. Pryor, 'The oaths of the leaders of the First Crusade to Emperor Alexius I Comnenus: Fealty, Homage – πίστις, δουλεία', *Parergon: Bulletin of the Australian and New Zealand Association for Medieval & Renaissance Studies*, new series, 2 (1984), pp. 130–1.
91 Jonathan Harris, *Byzantium and the Crusades* (London, 2003), p. 28.
92 Pryor, 'The oaths', pp. 131–2.
93 John L. La Monte, 'To What Extent was the Byzantine Empire the Suzerain of the Latin Crusading States?' *Byzantion* 7 (1932), pp. 256–7; Harris, *Byzantium*, p. 80;

Ralph-Johannes Lilie, *Byzantium and the Crusader States 1096–1204*, trans. J. C. Morris and Jean E. Ridings (Oxford, 1988), pp. 69–70; Richard, *Le comté*, p. 30.
94 John Kinnamos, *Deeds*, p. 24. Cf. Richard, *Le comté*, pp. 28–9.
95 Theodore Prodromos, Poem 11, line 168, in *Theodore Prodromos: historische Gedichte*, ed. Wolfram Hörandner (Vienna, 1984), p. 258.
96 Michael Italikos, 43, lines 17–18, in *Michel Italikos lettres et discours*, ed. Paul Gautier (Paris, 1972), p. 260.
97 My thanks go to Max Lau for bringing these poems to my attention and providing English translations.
98 Alicia Simpson, *Niketas Choniates: A Historiographical Study* (Oxford, 2013), pp. 230–1.
99 See Chapter 2.
100 Jibrāʾīl bin al-Qilāʿī, 'Madīḥa', p. 93; Salibi, 'Maronites', p. 292.
101 Imperii participem. WT, vol. 2, p. 855.
102 WT, vol. 2, p. 674.
103 John Kinnamos, *Deeds*, p. 24.
104 Cristina Tonghini, *Shayzar I: The Fortification of the Citadel* (Leiden, 2012).
105 WT, vol. 2, p. 675; Elizabeth Lapina, 'Gambling and Gaming in the Holy Land: Chess, Dice and Other Games in the Sources of the Crusades', *Crusades* 12 (2013), pp. 121–32.
106 WT, vol. 2, pp. 675–6.
107 Edbury and Rowe, *William*, pp. 130–50.
108 Lilie, *Byzantium*, p. 120.
109 *CGOH*, vol. 1, no. 144; *RRH*, no. 212.
110 *CGOH*, vol. 1, 116; *RRH*, 53.
111 Richard, *Le comté*, pp. 36, 49, 53, 56, 62, 69 and *passim*. Cf. Richard, *Le comté, addenda et errata*.
112 Jean Richard, '*Cum omni*', p. 187.
113 *CGOH*, vol. 1, no. 144; *RRH*, no. 212.
114 Devic and Vaissète, *Histoire*, vol. 5, no. 551.i, cols 1054–5; *RRH*, no. 211. See Chapter 2.
115 H. J. A. Sire, 'The Character of the Hospitaller Properties in Spain in the Middle Ages', in *The Military Orders: Fighting for the Faith and Caring for the Sick*, ed. Malcolm Barber (Aldershot, 1994), pp. 23–4.
116 Jean Richard, '*Cum omni*', p. 187.
117 Baldwin, 'Ecclesiastical Developments', p. 163; Richard, *Le comté*, p. 63; Jonathan Riley-Smith, *The Knights of St. John in Jerusalem and Cyprus*, c. *1050–1310* (London, 1967), pp. 55–6.
118 *CGOH*, vol. 1, no. 144; *RRH*, no. 212.
119 Riley-Smith, *Knights of St. John*, p. 56.
120 Terre clavem christiane. *CGOH*, vol. 2, no. 1602; *RRH*, no. 908.
121 Abū al-Fidāʾ, *Kitāb taqwīm al-buldān*, ed. J. T. Reinaud and W. Mac Guckin de Slane (Paris, 1840), p. 259.
122 Al-Dimashqī, *Nukhbat*, p. 208.
123 T. E. Lawrence, *Crusader Castles*, ed. Denys Pringle (Oxford, 1988), p. 77.
124 Deschamps, *Les Châteaux*, vol. 1, *passim*.
125 Jonathan Riley-Smith, *The Knights Hospitaller in the Levant, c.1070–1309* (Basingstoke, 2012), pp. 16–22, 27–37; Helen Nicholson, *The Knights Hospitaller* (Woodbridge, 2001), pp. 2–13.
126 Baldwin, 'Ecclesiastical Developments', pp. 163–4; Richard, *Le comté*, p. 66; Riley-Smith, *Knights Hospitaller*, pp. 29–30; Nicholson, *Knights*, p. 11.
127 Richard, *Le comté*, p. 66. Cf. Baldwin, 'Ecclesiastical Developments', pp. 163–4; Riley-Smith, *Knights of St. John*, p. 56.
128 The reference to *Archarum episcopatu* alongside *episcopatu Tripolis* is a curious anachronism, since ʿArqa was an ancient see that remained dormant and vacant

under the Franks. It was never resurrected and was instead placed under the jurisdiction of the bishop of Tripoli. WT, vol. 2, p. 649.

129 Anthony Luttrell, 'The Earliest Hospitallers', in *Montjoie: Studies in Crusade History in Honour of Hans Eberhard Mayer*, ed. Benjamin Z. Kedar, Jonathan Riley-Smith, and Rudolf Hiestand (Aldershot, 1997), pp. 53–4.

130 Usāma, pp. 129–30. See Chapter 2.

131 See, for example: Richard, *Le comté*, carte 4.

132 Major, *Medieval Rural Settlements*, vol. 1, p. 166.

133 Jonathan Phillips, *The Second Crusade: Extending the Frontiers of Christendom* (London, 2007).

134 Jonathan Riley-Smith, 'Family Traditions and Participation in the Second Crusade', in *The Second Crusade and the Cistercians*, ed. Michael Gervers (New York, 1992), pp. 101–5.

135 WT, vol. 2, pp. 756–7.

136 WT, vol. 2, pp. 754–5.

137 Ad partes [. . .] Tripolitanas. WT, vol. 2, p. 756. See Chapter 1.

138 Ob reverentiam locorum venerabilium, quorum amor et devotio omnes trahebant amplius. WT, vol. 2, pp. 756–7.

139 JV, pp. 190–2. See also: Burchard of Mount Sion, pp. 20–1.

140 Judges 20:1; 1 Samuel 3:20; 2 Samuel 3:10, 17:11, 24:2, 24:15; 1 Kings 4:25; 1 Chronicles 21:2; 2 Chronicles 30:5. Cf. Numbers 34:1–15, Ezekiel 47:13–20.

141 James of Vitry, *Lettres*, no. 2, pp. 89–90.

142 Burchard of Mount Sion, p. 31.

143 Nunquam fuit de terra sancta. Burchard of Mount Sion, p. 23; Aryeh Grabois, 'Christian Pilgrims in the Thirteenth Century and the Latin Kingdom of Jerusalem: Burchard of Mount Sion', in *Outremer*, p. 293.

144 See Chapter 1.

145 Benjamin Z. Kedar, 'Gerard of Nazareth: A Neglected Twelfth-Century Writer in the Latin East: A Contribution to the Intellectual and Monastic History of the Crusader States', *DOP* 37 (1983), pp. 58, 66, 74.

146 Jidejian, *Tripoli*, pp. 60, 86–7, figs 150–7.

147 2 Kings 5:12. See Chapter 1.

148 Theoderich, 'Descriptio', pp. 194–5; Pseudo-James of Vitry, 'Historiae Orientalis Liber Tertius', p. 1127. But cf. Jacobus a Voragine, *Legenda Aurea Vulgo Historia Lombardica Dicta*, ed. Th. Graesse, 2nd ed. (Leipzig, 1850), p. 714.

149 Kirk Ambrose, *The Nave Sculpture of Vézelay: The Art of Monastic Viewing* (Toronto, 2006), pp. 45–6.

150 Flavius Josephus, *The Jewish War*, ed. and trans. H. St. J. Thackeray, 3 vols, The Loeb Classical Library: Josephus 2–3 (London, 1961), vol. 3, pp. 534–5.

151 FC, pp. 796–7.

152 Fons [h]ortorum. Wilbrand of Oldenburg, p. 120; JV, pp. 188, 198; Canticles 4:15. Cf. Baldwin, 'Ecclesiastical Developments', pp. 151–2.

153 Mons leopardorum. Burchard of Mount Sion, p. 28; Canticles 4:8.

154 ʿAlī bin Abī Bakr al-Harawī, *Kitāb al-Ishārāt ilā Maʿrifat al-Ziyārāt*, ed. Josef W. Meri, Studies in Late Antiquity and Early Islam 19 (Princeton, NJ, 2004), p. 21; IJ, p. 281; Al-Dimashqī, *Nukhbat*, p. 199; Yāqūt, *Muʿjam al-buldān*, vol. 4, p. 453; Josef W. Meri, *The Cult of Saints among Muslims and Jews in Medieval Syria* (Oxford, 2002), pp. 245, 246.

155 Wilbrand of Oldenburg, p. 120.

156 Horden and Purcell, p. 56; Dussaud, *Topographie*, p. 402.

157 Yāqūt, *Muʿjam al-buldān*, vol. 2, p. 158. Cf. Al-Harawī, p. 25; IJ, p. 212.

158 Ibn Khurdādhba, *Kitāb al-masālik*, p. 76. Cf. IJ, p. 212.

159 Ernoul, p. 62.

160 Ezekiel 27:9; 1 Kings 5:18; Wilbrand of Oldenburg, p. 119; Ernoul, p. 204.

161 In Jherosolimitana peregrinatione. *CGOH*, vol. 1, no. 75.
162 See Chapter 1.
163 Jean Dunbabin, *France in the Making, 843–1180*, 2nd ed. (Oxford, 2005), p. 300.
164 Andrew Roach, 'Occitania Past and Present: Southern Consciousness in Medieval and Modern French Politics', *History Workshop Journal* 43 (1997), p. 6.
165 Devic and Vaissète, *Histoire*, vol. 3, p. 756.
166 Faustum et felix omen patris. WT, vol. 2, p. 756.
167 IQ, p. 297; Richard, *Le comté*, p. 6 n. 4.
168 WT, vol. 2, p. 756. Cf. IQ, p. 300.
169 Carraz, p. 75.
170 Devic and Vaissète, *Histoire*, vol. 3, p. 754; *Biographies des troubadours: textes provençaux des XIIIe et XIVe siècles*, ed. J. Boutière and A. H. Schutz, 2nd ed. (Paris, 1973), pp. 16–17, 19 n. 4; Poly, *La Provence*, p. 321 n. 25.
171 *Biographies*, ed. Boutière and Schutz, p. 17; Kevin James Lewis, 'Countess Hodierna of Tripoli: From Crusader Politician to "Princesse Lointaine"', *Assuming Gender* 3.1 (2013), pp. 10–16.
172 *Biographies*, ed. Boutière and Schutz, p. 17; Richard, *Le comté*, p. 6.
173 Kamāl al-Dīn, *Zubdat al-ḥalab*, vol. 2, p. 292.
174 WT, vol. 2, pp. 761–8.
175 Kamāl al-Dīn, *Zubdat al-ḥalab*, vol. 2, p. 292; IA, vol. 11, p. 131. See: Kennedy, *Crusader Castles*, pp. 70–1.
176 Richard, *Le comté*, pp. 7, 46. See also: Carraz, p. 112; Köhler, *Alliances*, pp. 160–1. But cf. Bruguière, p. 148.
177 Richard, *Le comté*, p. 7.
178 *Anonymi Auctoris Chronicon*, vol. 2, pp. 87, 111, 119.
179 WT, vol. 2, p. 756; Richard, *Le comté*, p. 6.
180 'Continuatio Praemonstratensis', in 'Sigeberti Gemblacensis Chronographia', ed. L. C. Bethmann, *MGH SS*, vol. 6, p. 454.
181 Richard, *Le comté*, p. 6; Bruguière, p. 146. Cf. Richard, 'Les Saint-Gilles', p. 70.
182 Bruguière, p. 147.
183 William of Nangis, *Chronique*, vol. 1, p. 43.
184 Mayer, 'Studies', pp. 160–1.
185 'Continuatio Praemonstratensis', p. 454; William of Nangis, *Chronique*, vol. 1, p. 43.
186 See below under 'The second council of Tripoli and the return of royal authority'.
187 IQ, p. 300.
188 Min mulūki-him. IQ, pp. 297–8.
189 Pres lo malautia en la nau. *Biographies*, ed. Boutière and Schutz, p. 17.
190 See below under 'The Templars of Tripoli'.
191 Kamāl al-Dīn, *Zubdat al-ḥalab*, vol. 2, p. 292; IA, vol. 11, pp. 131–2. Cf. IQ, p. 300. Alfons's wife Faydide of Uzès probably did not accompany him. Devic and Vaissète, *Histoire*, vol. 3, p. 754. But cf. *Anonymi Auctoris Chronicon*, vol. 2, p. 111.
192 WT, vol. 1, pp. 623–4; vol. 2, p. 653. See Chapter 2.
193 Köhler, *Alliances*, *passim*.
194 Edbury and Rowe, *William*, pp. 159–61, 171–2 and *passim*.
195 WT, vol. 2, p. 849; John Kinnamos, *Deeds*, p. 143; *Anonymi Auctoris Chronicon*, vol. 2, p. 119; Richard, *Le comté*, p. 7. Cf. IQ, p. 358.
196 IQ, pp. 300–1; Abū Shāma, *Kitāb al-rawḍatayn*, vol. 1, p. 210.
197 Nikita Elisséeff, *Nūr ad-Dīn: un grand prince musulman de Syrie au temps des croisades (511–569 H./1118–1174)*, 3 vols (Damascus, 1967), vol. 2, pp. 24–426.
198 Alex Mallett, 'The battle of Inab', *Journal of Medieval History* 39.1 (2013), pp. 52–3.
199 Sivan, *L'Islam*, pp. 74–9.
200 Köhler, *Alliances*, pp. 158–9.

201 Hildefonsus comes {de} Sancti Egidii cum navali exercitu Palestin{-am}[-ae] applicuit, et cum magnum quid facturus speraretur, reginae [Jerosolymorum] ut aiunt dolo male potionatus, apud C[a]esaream Palæstinae moritur. [Tunc] filius ejus adolescens [sibi timens] quoddam castrum comitis Tripolitani {patruelis}[avunculi] sui ingreditur, sed dolo ejusdem [reginae] cum sorore a Turcis captivatur. 'Continuatio Praemonstratensis', p. 454; William of Nangis, *Chronique*, vol. 1, p. 43. Alternate readings found in Sigebert's continuator and William of Nangis are in curly and square brackets respectively.
202 Devic and Vaissète, *Histoire*, vol. 3, p. 758; Richard, *Le comté*, p. 7 n. 1.
203 Bruguière, p. 148 n. 12. See Chapter 5.
204 Mayer, 'Studies', pp. 93–182; Asbridge, 'Alice', pp. 29–47. Cf. Kevin Lewis, 'Countess Hodierna', pp. 1–22.
205 Cum laborantibus et ministrantibus tam domina comitissa Tripolitana Odierna, domine Milissendis sorore, quam domina Flandrensium comitissa Sibilla, domini regis itidem sorore. WT, vol. 2, pp. 840–1, at p. 840.
206 WT, vol. 1, p. 13. Cf. William of Tyre, 'Historia rerum in partibus transmarinis gestarum', *RHC Oc*, vol. 1, p. 854.
207 William of Tyre, 'Historia', *RHC Oc*, vol. 1, p. 854 n. 1.
208 William of Tyre, 'Historia', *RHC Oc*, vol. 1, p. 854.
209 Hamilton, *Latin Church*, pp. 75–6; William of Tyre, trans. Babcock and Krey, vol. 2, p. 271 n. 63.
210 Mayer, 'Studies', p. 174.
211 WT, vol. 1, pp. 623–4; Asbridge, 'Alice', p. 29.
212 Edbury and Rowe, *William*, pp. 80–3.
213 Bernard of Clairvaux, *Epistolae*, ed. J. Leclercq and H. Rochais, 2 vols, Sancti Bernardi Opera 7–8 (Rome, 1974–7), vol. 2, no. 289, pp. 205–6. Cf. Bernard of Clairvaux, *Epistolae*, vol. 2, no. 206, p. 65.
214 Richard, *Le comté*, p. 91. See Chapter 5.
215 La région toulousaine et provençale où, dans la seconde moitié du XIIe siècle, on se détournait de la Croisade. Le dernier croisé qui arriva de Toulouse, Alfonse-Jourdain. Richard, *Le comté*, p. 68.
216 See above under 'Medieval outsourcing', and Chapter 2.
217 *CGOH*, vol. 1, no. 72; *RRH*, no. 107. Berangar remained in the county until at least March 1126. *CGOH*, vol. 1, no. 75; *RRH Add.*, no. 113b.
218 Carraz, pp. 487–90.
219 Carraz, pp. 75, 76.
220 See Chapter 5.
221 Richard, 'Les Saint-Gilles', p. 71.
222 *Cartulaires des Templiers de Douzens*, ed. P. Gérard, E. Magnou and P. Wolff (Paris, 1965), nos 104, 105; *Le chartrier de l'Abbaye cistercienne de Fontfroide (894–1260)*, ed. V. de Becdelièvre, 2 vols (Paris, 2009), vol. 2, nos 804, 1685, 1687, 1695, 1727, 1728, 1758; *Rôles Gascons*, ed. F. Michel and C. Bémont, 3 vols + supplement (Paris, 1885–1906), vol. 3, no. 4033; *Enquêtes sur les droits et revenus de Charles Ier d'Anjou en Provence (1252 et 1278)*, ed. Edouard Baratier (Paris, 1969), p. 297.
223 *Layettes du Trésor des Chartes*, ed. A. Teulet *et al.*, 4 vols (Paris, 1863–1902), vol. 1, nos 287, 317, 323, 717.
224 Richard, *Le comté*, p. 76 n. 3.
225 *CGOH*, vol. 1, no. 253.
226 E. G. Rey, *Sommaire du supplément aux Familles d'Outremer* (Chartres, 1881), p. 11.
227 Richard, *Le comté*, p. 82; *RRH*, nos 191, 193, 198, 212, 217, 233, 236, 270, 527; *CCSSJ*, nos 81, 82, 83; *CGOH*, vol. 1, nos 144, 160, 199, 482; vol. 2, p. 828 n. 1, no. VII; Richard, 'Porcellet', no. 1; Riley-Smith, 'The Templars', pp. 287–8.
228 Riley-Smith, 'The Templars', p. 279.
229 See Chapter 2.

230 IQ, p. 318.
231 IQ, pp. 317–18.
232 Riley-Smith, 'The Templars', pp. 279–80, 282–3 and *passim*; Richard, *Le comté*, pp. 66–7. Cf. Kennedy, *Crusader Castles*, p. 138; Richard, *Le comté*, pp. 21–2, 67.
233 Carraz, pp. 117–18.
234 Luttrell, 'Earliest Hospitallers', pp. 44–6, 49–50.
235 Carraz, pp. 129–30 and *passim*.
236 Barber, *New Knighthood*, pp. 6–13.
237 Qurān 17:1.
238 See Chapter 2.
239 *Biographies*, ed. Boutière and Schutz, pp. 16–17.
240 Helen Nicholson, *Love, War and the Grail*, History of Warfare 4 (Leiden, 2001), p. 54.
241 See Conclusion.
242 Riley-Smith, 'The Templars', pp. 280–1 and *passim*.
243 Major, *Medieval Rural Settlements*, vol. 1, p. 76.
244 IQ, p. 288.
245 Catherine Holmes, 'Byzantium's Eastern Frontier in the Tenth and Eleventh Centuries', in *Medieval Frontiers*, ed. Abulafia and Berend, p. 88.
246 WT, vol. 2, pp. 781–2.
247 Mayer, 'Studies', pp. 157–8. Cf. Richard, *Le comté*, pp. 34–5.
248 WT, vol. 2, p. 780.
249 Ad partes [. . .] Tripolitanas. WT, vol. 2, p. 780.
250 See Chapter 2.
251 WT, vol. 2, pp. 782, 784–5.
252 MacEvitt, *passim*.
253 WT, vol. 2, p. 785.
254 Gérard Dédéyan, 'Les Arméniens au Liban (Xe-XIIIe siècle)', in *Le comté*, ed. Dédéyan and Rizk, pp. 73–99.
255 IQ, p. 315.
256 WT, vol. 2, pp. 776–7.
257 WT, vol. 2, pp. 794–5.
258 IQ, p. 315.
259 See Chapter 5.
260 Pseudo-Fretellus, 'Tractatus', p. 432.
261 Ernoul, p. 27. See Chapter 1.
262 *RRH*, no. 236; *CGOH*, vol. 1, no. 160.
263 Cf. Richard, *Le comté*, pp. 36, 40–1.
264 Mayer, 'Studies', p. 160.
265 WT, vol. 2, pp. 785–6.
266 WT, vol. 2, p. 786.
267 Mayer, 'Studies', p. 171.
268 John of Ibelin, *Le Livre*, p. 603.
269 Richard, *Le comté*, p. 35.
270 John of Ibelin, *Le Livre*, p. 600. See Chapter 1.
271 Richard, *Le comté*, p. 35.
272 Mayer, 'Studies', pp. 161, 169, 172.
273 Ex zelo maritali orta simultas. WT, vol. 2, p. 786.
274 See Chapter 4.
275 Ex parte patris erat uno gradu inferior. WT, vol. 2, p. 966.
276 John Kinnamos, *Deeds*, p. 159.
277 Translated from: *Biographies*, ed. Boutière and Schutz, pp. 16–17. See Appendix 2, no. 1.

278 Kevin Lewis, 'Countess Hodierna', pp. 11–16. Cf. William of Tyre, trans. Babcock and Krey, vol. 2, p. 292 n. 89.

279 Marcabru, *Marcabru: A Critical Edition*, ed. S. Gaunt, R. Harvey and L. M. Paterson (Cambridge, 2000), pp. 201, 205. See Appendix 2, no. 2.

280 R. Howard Bloch, *Medieval Misogyny and the Invention of Western Romantic Love* (Chicago, 1991), pp. 153–6.

281 Sarah Lambert, 'Queen or Consort: Rulership and Politics in the Latin East, 1118–1228', in *Queens and Queenship in Medieval Europe: Proceedings of a conference held at King's College London April 1995*, ed. Anne J. Duggan (Woodbridge, 1997), p. 158.

282 WT, vol. 2, p. 652.

283 Mayer, 'Studies', pp. 102–13. See Chapter 2.

284 WT, vol. 2, p. 786.

285 WT, vol. 2, pp. 786–7.

286 Benjamin of Tudela, *The Itinerary of Benjamin of Tudela: Travels in the Middle Ages*, trans. Michael A. Signer, Marcus Nathan Adler and A. Asher (New York, 2005), p. 77.

287 Smarandache, 'Franks', pp. 228–32.

288 Bernard Hamilton, 'The Templars, the Syrian Assassins and King Amalric of Jerusalem', in *The Hospitallers, the Mediterranean and Europe*, ed. Karl Borchardt, Nikolas Jaspert, Helen J. Nicholson (Aldershot, 2007), pp. 16–17; Bernard Lewis, *The Assassins: A Radical Sect in Islam*, new ed. (London, 2003), pp. viii–x, 129–31.

289 See Chapter 4.

290 Smarandache, 'Franks', pp. 231–2.

291 See Chapter 3.

292 Quemcumque alienum a lingua nostra vel habitu. WT, vol. 2, p. 787.

293 WT, vol. 2, p. 787.

294 Edmond Rostand, *La Princesse Lointaine*, ed. J. L. Borgerhoff (Boston, 1909), pp. viii–ix and *passim*; P. G. Wodehouse, *The Jeeves Omnibus*, 5 vols (London, 1989–93), vol. 1, pp. 229–30.

4 Count and captive

Count Raymond III (1152–74)

Introduction

Raymond III was thrust into power by the shocking public murder of his father. He had always been destined to become count of Tripoli, but the bloody circumstances that led to his succession could not have been foreseen. What is more, in later life Raymond seems to have treated his duties in Tripoli as something secondary to his career in the kingdom of Jerusalem. In this respect, he followed his mother, the princess Hodierna. Raymond would immerse himself in all the court intrigue and ambitious manoeuvring on offer in the thrilling yet volatile world of Jerusalemite politics. Unfortunately for the count, his circumstances, rivals and abilities – or lack thereof – conspired against him. Consequently he never quite managed to realise his ambitions in the south, seeming to follow the somewhat disappointing example set by his father rather than the more promising precedent of his mother. In some ways, his career proved less successful than his father's. True, Raymond III reigned much longer, but he spent almost ten years incarcerated in a Muslim prison in Aleppo and would acquire a highly controversial reputation after his death – arguably a worse legacy than Raymond II's posthumous obscurity.

No other count of Tripoli has been subject to as much historical attention as Raymond III. To some extent this is the result of a greater abundance of surviving source material. As the twelfth century entered its second half, the chronicler William of Tyre was able to rely more upon his own experiences and those of his contemporaries, with the result that his narrative becomes richer during this period. Raymond's place at the very centre of the major events leading to the eventual fall of the so-called 'first' kingdom of Jerusalem to Saladin in the 1180s has enhanced his visibility in surviving material, albeit through wildly differing lenses. William of Tyre held a generally favourable view of Raymond as his preferred, although perhaps not ideal, candidate to govern and thus save the kingdom from the brink of catastrophe in the 1170s and 1180s. Most medieval authors, however, cast the count in an extremely negative light. In many quarters, Raymond's reputation was forever sullied by his supposedly treacherous behaviour at this time.[1]

Modern historians have been just as varied in their evaluations of Raymond, especially regarding the extent to which he was culpable – or not – for the kingdom's collapse. They have also tended to approach Raymond III's life much as they have the Latin East as a whole: first by dividing it up territorially and then by focusing their attentions on events in the kingdom of Jerusalem to the detriment of those in the other crusader states. Marshall Baldwin prefaced his 1936 biography of Raymond with the following: 'With a few exceptions, Raymond's activities in Tripolis [*sic*] had no bearing upon his career in the kingdom of Jerusalem. It has consequently seemed advisable largely to omit local Tripolitan affairs from this biography.'[2] Less than a decade later, Richard decided to mirror Baldwin's approach: 'For the misadventures of Raymond III, candidate to the throne of Jerusalem, we simply referred to M. Baldwin's work, *Raymond III of Tripolis*.'[3]

This is a reasonable enough policy, for the historian is obliged to be selective at the best of times and it may have appeared fruitless to Richard to produce another study of Raymond III's role in Jerusalem less than a decade after the publication of Baldwin's monograph. Yet the obvious problem here is that Raymond himself did not live two separate lives. In the present work Raymond's life is divided chronologically, split between this and the following chapter. This ensures that Raymond's acts in both Tripoli and Jerusalem are analysed together in the same way that Raymond himself would have experienced them. New light is shed on how the count often pursued courses of action that are only fully comprehensible as part of a broader strategy, integrating his northern and southern interests. Raymond was many things to many people, but he was ultimately one man, not two.

A succession crisis averted

In 1152 Raymond II lay dead, likely before his fortieth year, and neither of his children were yet old enough to inherit the rule of the county in full. His son, the future Raymond III, was barely twelve years old, while his daughter Melisende – named for her famous aunt – was younger still. Raymond II's brother Philip was last recorded alive in the 1140s and his fate is unknown.[4] It thus fell to the royal house of Jerusalem to ensure stability in the county. Although most of the delegates gathered at the council of Tripoli in April or May 1152 seem to have departed by the time of Raymond's death immediately afterwards,[5] King Baldwin III had remained in the city to while away some time gambling, perhaps reluctant to travel home immediately with his fractious mother. It was fortunate that he did stay, because he was thus able to pacify the Latin Christians who rampaged through Tripoli killing easterners in revenge for the count's assassination. In addition, Baldwin was able to ensure that Raymond's premature death did not spark a dynastic crisis – all the greater a concern at a time when the principality of Antioch still lacked a male ruler, thanks to Princess Constance's intransigence on the issue of her marriage. The memory of Bertrand (II)'s attempted coup at ʿUrayma, possibly facilitated by members of the local Frankish aristocracy, must also have loomed large. Acutely aware of the danger to the county's stability, Baldwin immediately recalled his mother Melisende and aunt Hodierna to the city for Raymond's funeral. After the ceremony, the king ordered all of the county's nobility to swear fidelity to the countess and her two underage children, which they seem to have done without question.[6]

Marshall Baldwin evidently believed that Hodierna had effectively become regent, although Richard argued that this incident does not represent incontrovertible proof of a 'régence féminine'.[7] Since authority was to be shared by all three surviving members of the late Raymond II's immediate family – Hodierna, Raymond III and Melisende the younger – the resultant situation lay somewhere between these two extremes. King Baldwin had established a system of joint rule to cover what would otherwise have been a period of minority in the county of Tripoli. This had two important precedents. One was the minority of Count Pons in 1112, when a committee of noble guardians had governed the county.[8] More directly pertinent was the second precedent: King Baldwin had begun his own reign under a similar system of governance, crowned co-ruler with his mother Melisende and father King Fulk in 1131. Upon the death of the latter in 1143, the underage Baldwin continued to share power with his mother Melisende until the civil war in the spring of 1152.[9]

Hodierna's role in Tripoli's government was not unusual. There were plenty of other widows who ruled in the Latin East following the deaths of their husbands and the concomitant minorities of sons. Such arrangements were made on occasion in the great Jerusalemite baronies of Galilee, Tiberias and Transjordan.[10] In fact this was common practice for noble mothers throughout Latin Christendom, including in Europe.[11] If anything, the Franks of Syria experienced this arrangement with greater frequency than their western cousins, due to the nature of their war-torn society, where men were so often killed or thrown into captivity. It should be noted, nevertheless, that the Franks never regarded a period of female governance as an ideal situation or equal to male rule. King Baldwin had supposedly intervened to force Constance to marry in 1152 specifically because the houses of both Antioch and Edessa had been 'abandoned to feminine rule', in William of Tyre's memorable phrasing.[12] It was somewhat ironic, then, that the council of Tripoli had seen Baldwin fail to provide Antioch with a male ruler only then to hand Tripoli itself to a woman. Whatever imagined failings and dangers the concept of a female regency held for male contemporaries, it is surely wrong to share Richard's view that it was extraordinary for a woman to take charge of a Syro-Frankish lordship in the twelfth century. It was in fact a matter of routine.

Fortunately for Baldwin, choosing Hodierna to oversee the county was not just a matter of convenience or necessity, as she herself possessed demonstrable political skills. His aunt had already proven that she was more than capable of participating in the highest echelons of Latin society, unafraid to perform controversial acts when necessary to ensure the county's stability, exemplified by her involvement in the scandal at ʿUrayma. She was also an independent property-owner in Tripoli itself, possessing a garden named *La Gloriete.*[13] As Helen Nicholson has recently observed, 'Gloriettes' were found in many castles throughout Europe, serving as private domestic areas often reserved for the ladies of an aristocratic household and found mainly in texts from the thirteenth century.[14] It is possible then that Tripoli's *Gloriete* garden was part of Hodierna's own residence, perhaps within the fortified Pilgrims' Mount complex. Tripoli's *Gloriete* was one of the earliest recorded examples of a Gloriette in the entirety of Latin Christendom and the only one recorded in the Latin East. Pertinent here is the fact that Hodierna's property ownership in Tripoli suggests that she knew the city well.

Hodierna was also a strong choice for regent because she and her young son had already been actively lending their support to Raymond II in the routine tasks of government since at least 1151, when they both gave their consent to a donation to the Hospital.[15] Moreover, she was undeniably loyal to Jerusalem. In December 1138, which was well into the second year of Raymond II's reign, Hodierna could still be found at King Fulk's peripatetic court in Acre alongside her sister Melisende. Hodierna was identified already as the 'countess of Tripoli' but was not accompanied by her husband.[16] Had she remained in the south after her betrothal and subsequent marriage to Raymond *c.*1132, or was she simply accustomed to travel south on a regular basis to visit the land of her childhood and her family? Whatever the case, it would seem that she preferred the company of her southern family to that of her Tripolitan husband.

By insisting that the nobles of Tripoli swear allegiance to Hodierna and her daughter as well as to the male heir Raymond, King Baldwin apparently rejected one of the late count's own changes to Tripoli's laws. In his great donation to the Hospital in 1142, Raymond II had specified that in the event of a minority the 'master of the county and [the count's] son' would take responsibility for both the county and its underage heir until the latter reached the age of knighthood.[17] A 'master of the count' named Albert, possibly of Puylaurens, who appeared in a document in December 1139 may well be this otherwise mysterious functionary, even though there was no minority at the time.[18] Yet the role of 'master of the county' is wholly absent from proceedings after Raymond II's death. The late count had spent much of his life failing to live up to the achievements of the house of Jerusalem, either reliant upon King Fulk for military assistance at Montferrand in 1137 or overshadowed by his own wife. It was apt, then, that the crown of Jerusalem would also disregard the plans he had put in place for a minority.

Raymond II's sudden and violent death after little more than a decade of rule meant that he was to have only minimal influence upon his young son and namesake, who lived much of his later life following the example of his Jerusalemite mother. This began at an early stage, most notably when Raymond III was sent to live at the court of Jerusalem soon after his father's funeral. On 23 September 1152 or 1153, the thirteen-year-old Raymond witnessed one of King Baldwin's deeds in the kingdom.[19] His mother was not present, presumably seeing to affairs in Tripoli. It is almost certain that Baldwin had taken charge of his cousin's training and education as a knight, much as Tancred of Antioch had supervised Count Pons's entry into adulthood back in 1112. The key difference was that Tripoli's links with Jerusalem were now being strengthened rather than weakened in favour of Antioch. Raymond spent the formative years of his early teens immersed in life at the royal court and not at the somewhat parochial court of Tripoli, as would have been his fate had his father lived. This surely explains in large part why Raymond III would later expend so much energy attempting to secure and maintain high office in the kingdom, which had become for him his home, just as it had always been for his mother.

Hodierna's leading role in the administration of the county probably came to a close in 1155 when Raymond III attained his majority upon his fifteenth birthday.[20] Raymond had come into the fullness of his power but subsequent events would prove that the close entanglement of Jerusalem and Tripoli was far from over. Indeed, the extent to which Raymond would involve himself in southern affairs while permitting the intervention of the king of Jerusalem in Tripoli was unprecedented by any former count of Tripoli, except perhaps his short-reigning great-grandfather Bertrand, who had ruled when the distinction between kingdom and county was yet unclear. The county of Tripoli continued to be viewed as an independent crusader state, yet its history and that of the realm were now more closely intertwined than had been the case for decades.

Sole rule, seismic opportunism and a disappointing crusade

Home again in his patrimony of Tripoli, Raymond III took up his birthright and began to rule independently, even if his mother and advisors surely offered regular advice. His first few years as sole ruler of Tripoli followed a pattern not radically different from the reign of his father. On 11 June 1157, he confirmed one of his father's former donations, namely that of Tortosa to the Templars, originally made in 1152.[21] As his predecessors had done, Raymond III responded to 'la solidarité chrétienne' by continuing to offer military support in the Latin East's common interest.[22] His first confirmed military engagement – what Marshall Baldwin called his 'baptism of fire' – was in response to a request for aid from his cousin and mentor, Baldwin III.[23] The king had sent to the count and the new prince of Antioch, the controversial Raynald of Châtillon, seeking their help against Nūr al-Dīn, who had attacked Bāniyās. The Latins managed to scare off the Muslim general without bloodshed, simply by mustering their combined force within sight of him.[24] This helped to relieve the pressure Nūr al-Dīn had recently placed upon both the kingdom of Jerusalem and the county of Tripoli, by pushing into the Biqāʿ valley and occupying the formerly independent Islamic city of Baʿalbakk in April 1157 (Rabīʿ I AH 552).[25]

Nūr al-Dīn's invasion was nothing compared to the invincible and inhuman force that would soon wreak untold havoc on the crusader states just two months later. In August 1157, a major earthquake hit North Syria and inflicted widespread devastation upon cities and fortifications in Muslim and Christian territories alike. William of Tyre did not record the catastrophe, presumably because he was studying in the west at the time, but it is well documented in Arabic accounts. Ibn al-Athīr listed the ruin of three settlements in the county of Tripoli alone: Tripoli itself, ʿArqa and Crac des Chevaliers. Deaths ran high in the Muslim cities of the interior and surely in the Christian-controlled settlements of the coast as well.[26] Benjamin of Tudela passed through Tripoli just a few years later and recorded vividly how the city had collapsed on its inhabitants.[27] Roughly a century previously, the Persian traveller Nāṣir Khusraw had visited Tripoli and remarked on the extraordinary height of its buildings, some as tall as six storeys.[28] Since the time of the Ancient Phoenicians, the inhabitants of this part of the world had built upwards, using height to compensate for the lack of flat, dry land suitable for construction among the hills, valleys and rivers threading through this rugged land. These Phoenician high-rises had been as vulnerable to earthquakes as their Frankish successors.[29] It is these towering edifices and not the low urban structures of medieval Europe that must be imagined crashing down upon Tripoli's unwitting residents in 1157.

According to Ibn al-Qalānisī, the disaster of 1157 also had 'ugly effects' upon Jubayl, which was the southernmost point said to have been hit by this earthquake. Aftershocks continued to hit Syria and its cities for months after the initial incident, causing further damage still.[30] With castles reduced to rubble and people buried in their homes, serious military risks and opportunities presented themselves. Although silent on the earthquake, William of Tyre recorded that a Frankish expedition was launched around the same time to capitalise on the recent arrival of Count Thierry of Flanders on what was his third trip to the east. The count thus joined forces with the rulers of Antioch, Jerusalem and Tripoli.[31] According to Ibn al-Qalānisī, the Franks believed it opportune to attack Muslim Syria at this moment specifically because the tremors had devastated fortifications and houses.[32] Indeed, the very fact that Thierry's crusade targeted North Syria, where the shocks had been most damaging, corroborates this. Nūr al-Dīn was thus obliged to assemble a field army to defend his borders, striving all the while to rebuild the fortresses of Islamic Syria as quickly as possible.[33]

The earthquake had cracked open many of the buildings in the county of Tripoli and yet the timely arrival of the count of Flanders allowed Raymond III to go on an increasingly rare offensive to expand his borders. The Christian forces first assembled in the county of Tripoli itself, on the wide Buqayʿa plain, and the army's first target was the Muslim-held fortress of Chastel Rouge (*Castrum Rugium*).[34] The history of this castle prior to 1157 is somewhat obscure, but Richard suspected it was identical with Wādī Ibn al-Aḥmar, which had been attacked by the withdrawing Damascene army in 1137 following the death of Count Pons.[35] No contemporary authority specified who the Muslims of Chastel Rouge actually were and so it is unknown if the castle had spent the past twenty years in unbroken Damascene control or Muslim control more generally. Such a circumstance is not at all implausible given the dilapidated and ineffectual state of the Tripolitan military throughout Raymond II's reign.

Curiously, most historians have failed to mention altogether that the first stages of Thierry's expedition took place in and for the county of Tripoli.[36] This observation is surely important because it was unusual for Tripolitan priorities to dictate military objectives. Unfortunately for Raymond III, even the gift of Thierry's crusade was insufficient for him to reconquer Chastel Rouge. The assault failed for unknown reasons and so it fell to the prince of Antioch to dictate the rest of the expedition, leading the army out of the county and further north.[37] Christian control over Chastel Rouge was eventually restored, although perhaps not for another two decades – around the time Raymond III donated it to the Hospitallers in 1177.[38]

Thierry, Raymond of Tripoli and the various other Syro-Frankish barons reached the principality of Antioch shortly after their failure at Chastel Rouge. Here they received the welcome news that the feared Nūr al-Dīn had succumbed to a severe, seemingly terminal illness. Seizing upon the opportunity presented by this crisis in Muslim leadership, the Christians decided to besiege Shayzar. This town, ruled by the famous Munqidhid clan, was strategically important, with William of Tyre emphasising its prime location on the Orontes.[39] Such a valuable prize had already attracted plenty of Frankish attention in the past half-century, including from the counts of Tripoli, specifically Raymond IV of Saint-Gilles and William Jordan of Cerdanya.[40] Shayzar was nothing compared to the great Muslim metropoles of Aleppo and Damascus, but it had long been a thorn in the side of the Latin East. Its inhabitants had demonstrated both the will and the ability to disrupt Frankish travel between North and South Syria, as when they had slain hundreds of Christian pilgrims heading up from Jerusalem via Rafaniyya sometime between 1126 and 1137.[41]

The siege of Shayzar began well for the Christians. William of Tyre dismissed the residents as a pacific and mercantile bunch who were not up to mounting an adequate defence, and thus the city fell in a relatively short space of time save only its imposing citadel.[42] Judging by Ibn al-Qalānisī's account of this period, the crusaders were even able to launch some raids on the nearby cities of Homs and Hama, although these ultimately proved fruitless.[43] Despite this initial phase of confident Christian aggression, the crusade faltered. As had happened so many times before and was to occur many more times afterwards, the Christians began to argue among themselves. They all agreed that Shayzar's full capitulation was imminent, yet could not decide on the city's future. According to William of Tyre, the plan garnering the most support was to allow Count Thierry to hold the town as a hereditary possession, as his wealth and military resources would be ideal to protect this new acquisition against possible Muslim reconquest. The one dissenter among the generals was Raynald of Châtillon, who objected to the fact that the proud count of Flanders refused to swear fealty to anyone but King Baldwin of Jerusalem and certainly not to the 'mere' prince of Antioch. The entire crusade supposedly foundered on this one issue and the Franks withdrew, leaving Shayzar still unconquered. The crusade had not yet run its course and would eventually conquer a fortress near Antioch, probably Ḥārim, but this was a poor consolation prize.[44]

The exact nature of Raynald's complaint regarding Thierry's loyalties should Shayzar be conquered has a familiar ring to it. Raynald's opposition to the very suggestion that the king of Jerusalem exercise seigneurial rule over Shayzar was based on his assertion that 'the city with its dependencies had been part of the prince of Antioch's inheritance since the beginning and therefore whoever holds it must pledge fidelity to the prince of Antioch'.[45] Phillips has suggested that the exact legal precedent for this was John Komnenos's agreement with Raynald's predecessor in Antioch, Raymond of Poitiers, in 1137. According to this unrealised settlement, the emperor had promised to allow Prince Raymond to hold Shayzar in fief if the combined Byzantine–Latin army had been able to conquer it.[46] Of course, this had much earlier precedent in the form of the bipartite Latin East divided at Nahr al-ʿArqa or al-Nahr al-Kabīr al-Janūbī, which in turn was based on the bisection of the Levant by the Byzantine and Fāṭimid empires in the eleventh century.[47] Since Shayzar lay north of the former border, it should have been the rightful possession of the prince of Antioch and not the king of Jerusalem. Raynald of Châtillon's objection to Thierry's plans in 1157 was therefore another late reminiscence of a demarcation of territory that had been so dominant at the beginning of the twelfth century yet was now largely redundant.

The Cistercians of Syria

After Thierry's crusade fizzled out at Ḥārim the various participants headed home, with Raymond of Tripoli travelling south with the king of Jerusalem and count of Flanders as far as Tripoli itself.[48] For his part Thierry may have left a lasting legacy in Raymond's county. In the very same year as his disappointing expedition the Cistercian monastery of Belmont was founded, becoming the first of its kind in the whole Latin East. The origins of the Cistercians – dubbed 'white monks' after their undyed habits – are well known and need be recounted here only in summary. The Order had its origins in a group of Burgundian monks in the late eleventh century who had chosen to abandon the riches that had come to be associated with wealthy Benedictine monasteries. Instead they sought a simpler way of life defined by manual labour and strict notions of poverty, which they believed to be closer to the ideals of the original Benedictine Rule than the relatively comfortable lifestyles of the non-reformed Benedictine 'black monks'. Ironically, it was in attempting to conform so closely to St Benedict's regulatory code that the Cistercians introduced their defining novelty: the *Carta Caritatis*, a governing constitution intended to guarantee uniformity of practice within their first monastery at Cîteaux and across its family of dependent houses.

Many men from knightly families were drawn to the uncompromising, even puritanical message of the Cistercians. One of Cîteaux's earliest recruits was a certain Bernard, who soon led a mission of monks to establish in 1115 the abbey of Clairvaux – one of Cîteaux's four principal daughter-houses, alongside La Ferté, Morimond and Pontigny. Bernard of Clairvaux soon became one of the leading figures in the Order and the foremost epistolarian of his age, addressing letters to a staggering range of men and women in twelfth-century Europe. A man with such a wide network throughout Latin Christendom was naturally involved in the crusading movement. Bernard instructed the early Templars on matters of devotion and organisation; he helped to preach the Second Crusade, launched by his former student and fellow Cistercian, Pope Eugenius III; and he advised Queen Melisende of Jerusalem on her governance.

Bernard may have supported crusading in the broad sense but he opposed any Cistercians who wished to travel to the Latin East, either for the sake of establishing new monasteries or simply for pilgrimage. In December 1124 he criticised Abbot Arnold of Morimond for seeking to abandon his responsibilities and travel to the Holy Land with a group of his monks.[49] In fact, King Baldwin II of Jerusalem had invited Bernard himself to establish a house in the east only for the abbot to decline, advising the king to give the proposed site to the reformed Augustinian Premonstratensians instead.[50] Bernard viewed crusading and pilgrimage in much the same cautious, moralistic way as he viewed the use of elaborate images, decoration and liturgy in church: exercises in materialism that were acceptable for enhancing the religious lives of the laity, but to be avoided by monks whose cloistered lives and elevated spirituality ought to be close enough to the experience of the heavenly Jerusalem as to make the worldly Jerusalem unnecessary.[51]

Bernard died in 1153 and was canonised just two decades later in 1174. With Bernard's death, his intellectualist opposition to Cistercian adventures abroad was no longer a serious obstacle. Bernard had been dead and buried little more than four years by the time Thierry of Flanders visited Syria in 1157 and it was in this year that a colony of Cistercians was established in the county of Tripoli, specifically in al-Kūra – the hilly district immediately south of Tripoli, where countless eastern Christian monasteries already existed and where Count Pons had met his end in 1137.[52] Archaeological evidence suggests that the Cistercians settled here on the site of an older Byzantine-style Orthodox monastery, although the abbey's French name 'Belmont' (*bellus-mons*) was surely a new import.[53] Despite the undeniable friction between Christian communities in Syria at this time, it is unlikely that the Latins evicted the Orthodox with rash intolerance.[54] Indeed, Orthodox monasteries were not only tolerated under Latin rule but seem to have grown in both number and wealth.[55] It is probably the case then that Belmont's eastern antecedent had been abandoned sometime before the Latins arrived. According to Orderic Vitalis, Bohemond I of Antioch had earlier confirmed that eastern Christian monks in the Black Mountain could retain all their property, permitting Latin monks to settle there only in houses that had fallen into ruin before the Franks' arrival.[56] Such a carefully tolerant approach may well have been instituted in Lebanon, another area rich with eastern monasteries.

Controversial revisionist scholarship on the early growth of the Cistercians has contested the traditional narrative of a 'top-down' genesis whereby the precocious monks of young Cîteaux set up daughter-houses, which in turn established colonies of their own until a vast hierarchical network was created. Constance Berman believes that a 'bottom-up' process was at least as instrumental. Many 'Cistercian' abbeys began as independent reformed Benedictine institutions, which later agreed to affiliate themselves with Cîteaux, thereby becoming part of a full-fledged Order only from the third quarter of the twelfth century.[57] The timing of Belmont's foundation in the 1150s places it at the dawn of this phase of Cistercian consolidation. Indeed, the Black Mountain again is relevant. In the 1220s, Patriarch Peter II of Antioch – a Cistercian himself – sought pre-existing Latin monasteries in this area that were willing to convert into Cistercian abbeys and at least one house agreed to do so, that of St George of *Jubin*.[58] Extrapolating from the situation both in Europe and elsewhere in Syria, it is entirely plausible that the house later known as Belmont began as an Orthodox monastery, fell into disuse before the First Crusade, was occupied by an autonomous Latin monastic community sometime in the early twelfth century and was then re-established as an abbey affiliated to the great family of Cîteaux.

Whatever its primordial history, it is clear from surviving documentary evidence that Belmont entered the Cistercian family as early as May 1157, established or re-established as a daughter-house of Morimond. The Cistercian annalist to record this many years later made special note of the fact that the monks who established Belmont were precisely 'what

St Bernard had spurned: propagators of the Cistercians in the East'.[59] It is surely no coincidence then that Belmont's founders originated from Morimond – the same house once ruled by Abbot Arnold, whom Bernard had directly attacked for his desire to go to the Holy Land. The author of the thirteenth-century *Chronique de Terre Sainte* wrongly claimed that Belmont was not established until 1169, but archaeologists have thought that this later date may record when building work on the new abbey was completed.[60]

Indeed, the buildings of Belmont survive today in slightly altered form as a modern Orthodox monastery and university, which is still known as *Balamand* – an Arabic form of its original crusader French name.[61] Its medieval structures exhibit much the same architectural scheme and detail so characteristic of the Order of Cîteaux back in the west. Enlart thus judged it to be 'a precious witness to Cistercian colonial art'.[62] A sizeable abbey church dated to the twelfth century suggests the abbey housed a relatively large number of monks, while its even larger great hall could indicate that it was used to offer refuge in times of war to non-Cistercian locals or else shelter to pilgrims.[63] Even an outlying building some 50m to the south was built quite clearly in the mould of a classic Cistercian farm or grange, approximating quite closely such structures in France.[64] This implies that Belmont enjoyed the same cluster of agricultural benefices as did its sister-houses throughout Europe, where lower-class lay brothers known as 'converts' (*conversi*) or 'bearded ones' (*barbati*) tilled the land and collected tithes from tenants on behalf of the aristocratic 'choir monks'.[65] Indeed, over half of the abbey complex itself was given over to some aspect of agriculture or food storage – for example stables, cellars and barns.[66]

Institutions as well as buildings bound Lebanon to Cîteaux. Although located in Syria and thus distant from the Order's Burgundian core, Belmont nevertheless remained subject to the same rigid uniformity in style and practice that Cîteaux famously imposed upon its daughter-houses, however far-flung they may have been. Indeed, the abbot of Belmont was not exempt from the responsibility of attending regular General Chapter meetings at Cîteaux itself, even if he and other Syrian Cistercians were only required to make the trip on a five-, then six- then seven-year cycle, rather than annually as was expected of abbots closer to home.[67] Through this obligation to attend General Chapter, Belmont and the county of Tripoli were connected to what amounted to the most sophisticated and institutionalised network of communication in Christendom at the time – the most influential and important innovation of the *Carta Caritatis*.

Given the coincidence of the foundation of Belmont in 1157 and the visit of Thierry of Flanders, did this particular crusader prince help to establish the Latin East's first Cistercian monastery? No hard evidence links Thierry's visit and the establishment of Belmont, but the count of Flanders had been a keen patron of the Cistercians back in the west and an associate of Bernard of Clairvaux, so there may be more than coincidence

Figure 4.1 The abbey of Belmont (*Dayr Balamand*) © Denys Pringle

at play here. If so, then Thierry would not have been Belmont's only lay benefactor. Historians have assumed that the abbey was founded on land donated by Count Raymond III of Tripoli himself due to the proximity of the site to the capital.[68] Indeed, one seventeenth-century English traveller visited Belmont and claimed that 'one of the earls of Tripoli' had founded the abbey, perhaps deriving this information from the oral tradition of the Greek monks who then lived there and were his hosts.[69] Hamilton, who seems to think that Count Raymond remained in his minority until *c.*1157, suggests that negotiations with Morimond to establish Belmont were initiated by his mother and regent Hodierna, who in turn was perhaps influenced by her sister Queen Melisende, who had corresponded directly with St Bernard in the past.[70] Of course, the conflict between Clairvaux and Morimond over the specific issue of settlement in Syria casts doubt on this particular theory. Other historians have reached more eccentric conclusions regarding Belmont's earliest benefactors, listing also the western emperor Frederick Barbarossa and the eastern emperor Manuel Komnenos.[71]

Belmont was not to be the only Cistercian foundation either in the Latin East or in the county of Tripoli specifically. Just four years after its involvement in the establishment of Belmont, the great Burgundian abbey of Morimond instituted a second eastern daughter-house near Jerusalem, named Salvatio (possibly modern 'Allār al-Sufla).[72] Belmont itself founded a number of dependent monasteries: St John in the Woods near Jerusalem ('Ayn Karīm) in 1169;[73] Holy Trinity at a mysterious place called *Refech* in Syria, Cyprus or Sicily in 1187;[74] and the Cypriot house of Beaulieu in 1235.[75] Female houses were prevalent within the Cistercian Order from the beginning, even if their very existence in the historical record was obfuscated by a suspicious male hierarchy.[76] Belmont was already affiliated with the nunnery of St Mary Magdalene in Acre by 1222, although controversy with the other Syrian houses in the 1230s soon led Belmont to lose control over this convent. St Mary Magdalene itself had two further daughter-houses – both nunneries – in Tripoli and also in Nicosia, Cyprus.[77]

Morimond's success with Belmont motivated Cîteaux's other daughters to establish Syrian colonies, although the abbey of Clairvaux remained resistant. In the 1230s, Bishop Vassal of Jubayl permitted Cistercians from La Ferté to build an abbey in his diocese in the foothills of Lebanon. The new monastery near Jubayl probably had a non-Cistercian precedent, likely taking its dedicatory name – St Sergius (Mār Sarkīs) – from an earlier institution on the same site.[78] St Sergius was one of the military saints whose veneration was popular among local Christians and was adopted with enthusiasm by the Latins upon their arrival. The Embriaci of nearby Jubayl paid the canons of the Holy Sepulchre an annual stipend to pray for their souls on the vigil of St Sergius and his associate, St Bacchus.[79] A surviving icon at Mount Sinai suggests that a Frankish woman probably living in the county of Tripoli commissioned a Syrian Orthodox artist to paint an icon of St Sergius.[80]

The county of Tripoli's Cistercian abbeys survived and flourished well into the thirteenth century, although both Belmont and St Sergius were destroyed by the Mamluks *c.*1269 and their monks subsequently went into exile in Belmont's Cypriot daughter-house, Beaulieu.[81] Archaeological and charter evidence suggest that the monks returned to Belmont after a ten-year truce was signed with Baybars in 1271.[82] They were evicted a second and final time *c.*1289, when Tripoli itself and the surrounding region fell to the Mamluks. The Orthodox monks of twentieth-century 'Balamand' believed that their predecessors had acquired the monastery directly after the conquest and removal of the Latins, but there is no hard proof of such direct continuity or indeed of any Orthodox settlement there at all until 1602.[83]

International relations

With the establishment of the Cistercians in the county, new links between Tripoli and the lands of the west were forged. Ties between Tripoli and other 'foreign' lands were also renewed at this time. Ever since John Komnenos's Syrian campaign of 1137–8, the Byzantines had had little to do with the county. Over two decades later in 1158, John's son Manuel I arrived in Syria and stayed there until 1159. He used this opportunity to reassert imperial authority over recalcitrant Antioch and also to kindle a close friendship with Baldwin III of Jerusalem. This heralded a new phase of unusually amicable relations between Greeks and Latins – naturally a source of concern for Islamic onlookers such as Ibn al-Qalānisī, who beseeched God to turn the two reconciled groups of Christians against each other.[84] During his Syrian sojourn, Manuel largely avoided Tripoli. He was, however, able to use his diplomatic weight, military strength and immense wealth to pressure Nūr al-Dīn into releasing a number of Christian prisoners from Aleppo, including Bertrand of Toulouse – the man who had been Raymond II of Tripoli's would-be usurper back in 1148.[85]

After Manuel's return to Constantinople, another foreign visitor approached the crusader states. This was the cardinal-priest John, who had been sent by Pope Alexander III to seek the loyalties of the eastern patriarchates in the papal schism that had developed following the death of Hadrian IV in 1159. John had sailed in a Genoese ship, so it was appropriate that he landed at Jubayl in the county of Tripoli in 1160.[86] Jubayl was still Genoa's principal colony in Syria and remained in the hands of the Embriaci family, who had governed it since the first decade of the twelfth century. Interestingly, Merav Mack's study of Genoese interests in Syria has shown that the commune's grip on Jubayl had begun to slip by this point. As early as the 1140s, the consuls of Genoa had sought to confiscate the Embriaci family's property in Genoa itself precisely because their wealthy cousins in Syria had failed for over two decades to pay the lease for Jubayl, as agreed back when the city was first conquered. In 1154, the decision was taken to split the eastern Embriaci into two discrete administrative and financial parts, each owing the commune of Genoa different rents for their respective rights and lands in Syria: the fully Genoese city of Jubayl on the one hand and the limited Genoese quarters of Acre and Antioch on the other.[87]

The struggle between Genoa and the Embriaci of Syria highlights the extent to which Genoa and its colonies – Jubayl included – ought not to be viewed as 'a monolith with a single interest' as many historians have done, but rather a confederation of different families and autonomous agents with often conflicting interests.[88] By the late 1160s, Genoa's control over Jubayl had been eroded still further. According to Mack, the Embriaci were beginning to identify themselves less as Genoese agents and more as part of the 'Frankish' landowning class in Syria, who were free of any real legal obligation to Genoa.[89] The broad trend traced by Mack is that of an inexorable weakening of Genoa's direct rule over Jubayl to the point that the Embriaci of Syria ceased to view themselves as true Genoese, beholden no longer to the Italian homeland of their ancestors, fiscally or emotionally.

Of course, the demise of Genoa's power in Syria occurred neither in one single moment nor in a smooth, linear decline. Returning to John's arrival in Jubayl in 1160, this has been neglected by previous historians yet it suggests that Genoa continued to use Jubayl as its Syrian port of choice. Indeed, Benjamin of Tudela visited around the same time as this event and would describe Jubayl not as a Tripolitan fief ruled by a local baron, but as being 'under the rule of the Genoese, the name of the governor being (William) Embriacus'.[90] It is unlikely that Benjamin would have appreciated the fine distinction between local Syro-Frankish lords and Italian colonists, although his choice to emphasise the Embriaci's Genoese heritage is nonetheless noteworthy. Despite the trend of Genoa's lessening influence observed by Mack, the Italian city-state clearly remained active in Jubayl and relevant to its ruling family well into the second half of the twelfth century.

John's arrival also highlights the consolidation of the political frontier between the kingdom of Jerusalem and the county of Tripoli. According to William of Tyre, the legate landed at Jubayl because he had yet to secure permission to enter the kingdom. The secular and ecclesiastical magnates of Jerusalem instructed the legate to wait at Jubayl while they assembled in a synod at Nazareth to debate whether or not to welcome him into the realm. This was an important decision for those gathered at Nazareth, because they feared that allowing John ingress would give the impression that the patriarchate of Jerusalem had sided with Pope Alexander in the schism, thereby compromising the carefully guarded neutrality of both eastern patriarchates up to this point. It was far from clear in 1160 that Alexander would be triumphant over his rival Victor IV and so individual clergy in the east differed among themselves as to whom they supported.

It is telling that John went no further than Jubayl, as it was the southernmost city of the county of Tripoli in William of Tyre's influential quadripartite outline of the Latin East. The very ability of the Jerusalemites to block John at Jubayl recalls the importance of the pragmatic border at nearby Nahr al-Kalb, where geographical circumstances had made it extremely easy to forbid access in the past and would continue to do so in the future. Ultimately it was decided, against King Baldwin's judgement, to allow John into the kingdom, signalling the alignment of the Syrian Latins with Alexander against Victor.[91]

Matrimonial diplomacy

Around the same time that the Nazareth synod debated the papal schism, Raynald of Châtillon was captured by Majd al-Dīn, the Zankid governor of Aleppo, in a battle fought near Marash on 23 November 1161.[92] Once again the principality of Antioch was left without a prince, so Baldwin III of Jerusalem followed tradition by stepping in as regent, governing alongside the northern patriarch.[93] The extension of royal power into North Syria had created unease in Tripoli in the days of Count Pons, who had been opposed to the establishment of a Jerusalem-dominated 'Latin empire' even to the point of open rebellion.[94] No such sedition was evident under his grandson Raymond III, perhaps testifying to his personal sympathies towards Jerusalem. Indeed, it was around this time that the king was able to exert a considerable amount of influence over the house of Tripoli by arranging a politically motivated marriage with Byzantium.

The Byzantine emperor Manuel Komnenos, who had built profitable relationships with the Latins of Syria in 1158–9, now believed it was time to consolidate his achievements with a wedding. His first Latin wife – Bertha-Eirene of Sulzbach – had by this point died and so he sent an embassy, formed of the Greek John Kontostephanos and the Italian Theophylact, to Baldwin of Jerusalem, requesting that the king select for him a wife from among the noblewomen of the crusader states. As was customary, they carried a chrysobull with them, which William of Tyre seems to have reproduced verbatim in Latin translation. Through this document, Manuel suggested two of Baldwin's female relatives whom he thought suitable: Maria, sister of the late Bohemond III of Antioch, and Melisende, sister of Raymond III of Tripoli.[95]

Baldwin selected Melisende as the emperor's new bride and Manuel initially accepted. Suddenly the house of Tripoli found itself catapulted to the giddying heights of society, not just in the Latin East but throughout all of Christendom. Immediately Melisende's family began to prepare for the wedding. Melisende's mother Countess Hodierna and her aunt Queen Melisende of Jerusalem are reported to have spent no less than a year preparing the maiden for this illustrious marriage, purchasing vast quantities of jewellery at huge expense, 'above and beyond royal resources' (*supra vires regias*).

Young Melisende's brother contributed to this vast spending as well, managing to fund the construction of twelve galleys to escort his sister to Constantinople in a fashion worthy of an empress.[96] Count Raymond's gift to his sister is one of the earliest recorded instances of a ruler in the Latin East building his own domestic fleet. Late Islamic Tripoli had had its own fleet during the crusader siege some decades before, but there is no evidence that a permanent navy was maintained by the Franks at Tripoli.[97] By the 1160s the crusader states were still otherwise dependent upon the ships of European ports and in any case were no longer threatened seriously by Fāṭimid naval power, which had broadly deteriorated as the caliphate had lost its vital coastal outposts, including Tripoli.[98]

It is not wholly surprising that Tripoli was one of the first crusader ports to build its own fleet, given that the county was in close proximity to the historic timber-producing forests of Mount Lebanon.[99] True, the kingdom of Jerusalem also bordered on Lebanon but, as the Latin pilgrim Theoderic observed *c.*1172, it was difficult to access the trees from this direction 'because of the ambushes of the heathens' who lived there.[100] It will be remembered that the kingdom lay to the south-east of the mountain, so had to contend with the Druze and the Sunnī Muslims of the Biqāʿ valley. By contrast, Tripoli faced the north-western slopes, dominated by more amenable Christians. As a result, the county and not the kingdom came to dominate the timber trade of the Latin East. Indeed, the Frankish period coincided with and stimulated one of the last periods of intensive exploitation of Lebanese timber.[101]

In July 1161 Melisende of Tripoli, her brother, her mother and a handful of Tripolitan courtiers visited the royal family of Jerusalem at Nazareth where they witnessed a grant issued by Baldwin III. In this otherwise irrelevant document, Melisende already appears in appropriately grandiose style as 'the future empress of the throne of Constantinople'.[102] Richard is surely right to speculate that Count Raymond and his court had come south to discuss with the king their plans for the imminent marriage.[103] An additional reason was the deteriorating health of Melisende's namesake and aunt. Queen Melisende of Jerusalem had been on her deathbed for many months, cared for by her two surviving sisters Hodierna of Tripoli and the nun Yveta of Bethany. The queen was to draw her last breath on 11 September 1161.[104]

The marriage had still not taken place a year after young Melisende's betrothal to Manuel. Worrying rumours were starting to emanate from the Byzantine camp and William of Tyre reported how the emperor's agents were carefully scrutinising Melisende's conduct and physical characteristics down to the most intimate details. Throughout, the Greeks were in continuous contact with Manuel himself, keeping him abreast of their findings. The delay caused by these investigations began to irritate Melisende's family and friends, no doubt anxious that the emperor had developed cold feet. King Baldwin thus sent an ultimatum to Manuel in summer 1162 demanding an end to the prevarication – a characteristically Greek trait in William of Tyre's prejudiced opinion. The Byzantine court finally now came clean with the scandalous revelation that the marriage to Melisende was not to take place at all. Count Raymond was understandably outraged at this news and the Byzantine envoys quickly departed Syria for Cyprus to escape his fury.[105]

Despite the ambassadors' hasty departure, the count of Tripoli continued to seethe at this humiliation, made all the worse by the fact that he received the news just as his invited wedding guests were assembling at Tripoli to bid farewell to Melisende. In the heat of the moment, Raymond disregarded the fact that Manuel was, in William of Tyre's words, 'the most powerful amongst mortals', and decided to seek vengeance in any way he could. To effect his revenge, the count had the ships of his sister's bridal escort refitted for military use and crewed them with the worst criminals and pirates he could find. He then sent these corsairs out onto the Mediterranean for what he believed to be just cause, instructing them to raid the Byzantine empire's coastline and islands.[106] No doubt this included Cyprus, the imperial domain closest to Tripoli and the place where the Byzantine envoys had first fled. Indeed, Raynald of Châtillon had built ships five years before in 1156 in order to lead just such a piratical raid against Cyprus, so there was recent precedent.[107] William of Tyre was broadly sympathetic to Raymond's assault on Byzantine territory, but even he baulked at some of the excesses committed by the rogues in the count's service. The pirates of Tripoli ravaged and pillaged the empire's unwitting inhabitants as instructed, even to the extremes of attacking women and children, robbing merchants and pilgrims and looting churches and monasteries.[108]

While Raymond sought his revenge, King Baldwin headed north to Antioch to assume his responsibilities as regent, still reeling at the emperor's complete disregard for the bride he had chosen for him. Another shock came when the king arrived in Antioch, where he found the very same Byzantine envoys who had fled Raymond now negotiating a marriage between Manuel and Princess Maria, the other of the two brides proposed by the emperor back in 1160. The Greeks had with them a chrysobull detailing the new arrangement, suggesting that secret negotiations with the Antiochenes had begun long before Manuel's official repudiation of Melisende of Tripoli. The exasperated Baldwin could do little but agree. William of Tyre claimed the king saw the benefit of Maria's marriage to Manuel, since the princess was orphaned and lacked a male protector, unlike Melisende who had an elder brother. Here is a transparent attempt by William to gloss over what was an awkward moment for King Baldwin, thoroughly outmanoeuvred by the Byzantines and forced to agree to a settlement that cast him as a traitor to Raymond of Tripoli at worst and an unequal partner to Manuel Komnenos at best.[109] In truth, Baldwin had no real choice. He could never have hoped to challenge the emperor.

Writing close to the time, the Komnenian apologist John Kinnamos put forward a raft of excuses for why Manuel had chosen to disregard Baldwin's choice of bride in such a cruel and ostensibly deceptive fashion. One was that the imperial ambassadors' careful examination of Melisende's person had found her to be undeniably beautiful, but afflicted by violent seizures that were resulting in a noticeable deterioration of her health. Another reason was the rumour that the girl had been born out of wedlock. A third explanation was that the ambassador John Kontostephanos, wracked by doubt, had headed to a church in Tripoli to pray for guidance. Here he heard a divine disembodied voice recommend to him the termination of the marriage through a circumspect allusion to Scripture.[110] Obviously the miraculous revelation to John Kontostephanos reads suspiciously like an attempt to cover up an awkward truth with a fantastical story, as Richard observed.[111] It should not be thought, however, that Kinnamos's threefold explanation is entirely incredible. The rumour of illegitimacy may have a ring of truth, given the jealousy that had torn her presumed parents apart in 1152.[112] Moreover, Kinnamos's reference to Melisende's poor health may be corroborated by the testimony of a thirteenth-century French source, the *Lignages d'Outremer*, which claims that 'Melisende died whilst still an infant'.[113] Rumours of sickliness would have given Manuel's agents ample cause for concern, given that the emperor's first wife had herself died so recently and unexpectedly.

Most modern historians believe that the emperor never intended to marry Melisende. Magdalino is certain that Maria had always been Manuel's preferred choice of wife.[114] The restoration of imperial rule over Antioch had long been central to Byzantine strategy in Syria, while Tripoli was largely irrelevant. The emperor may only have offered King Baldwin the choice between her and Melisende in the first place as a diplomatic nicety to a man whose 'Byzantinophile' policies at this time were well known to the point that he himself had already married Manuel's niece Theodora Komnene in 1158.[115] Another possibility is that Manuel had only contacted the king for his help in choosing a bride because he thought that it was his best chance to marry Maria. The emperor's relations with the court of Antioch and especially with Raynald of Châtillon were exceptionally strained at the time, which would have dissuaded him from attempting any direct negotiations for Maria's hand. Perhaps Manuel had hoped that his intermediary and now kinsman, King Baldwin, would give him what he wanted.[116] Baldwin's selection of Melisende instead must have come as a surprise, since the king could not have been oblivious to the emperor's desire to restore Antioch to imperial rule. Runciman was likely correct to believe that Baldwin, for all his Byzantine sympathies, chose Melisende specifically because he feared the further growth of imperial influence in Antioch.[117]

Manuel had initially been forced to accept the king's choice, but his agents' prevarication for an entire year certainly hints at reluctance. In all likelihood the emperor had sent his ambassadors to Jerusalem in mid-1161, resigned to the fact that Prince Raynald of Antioch would not himself grant Maria's hand.[118] Fortunately for Manuel, the fiercely anti-Byzantine Raynald was captured in November 1161, which finally permitted the imperial ambassadors to open direct negotiations with Antioch – far more tempting a prize than Tripoli.[119] The emperor was still bound to his earlier agreement with the king, yet was able to delay his promised marriage to Melisende long enough for his envoys to secure Maria's hand. In the end, the emperor got what he had wanted but he had risked and lost his good relations with the Latins; relations between Jerusalem and Constantinople remained frosty for the better part of the next decade.[120] As for the count of Tripoli, it seems that Raymond never forgave this affront to his and his sister's honour, perhaps even actively undermining future Latin co-operation with the Byzantines.[121]

Battling and bluffing

In 1163, just a year after Raymond's assault on Cyprus, a Byzantine official and *doux* of Cilicia by the name of Constantine Kalamanos arrived in Syria with a Greek army. According to Ibn al-Athīr, 'they fought as those expecting reward in the hereafter in their reckoning'.[122] Constantine had not intended to visit the county of Tripoli specifically and had presumably been travelling back home after visiting the Holy Places of Jerusalem. Nevertheless, the *doux* proved instrumental in winning a battle against Nūr al-Dīn on its eastern marches: the so-called battle of Buqayʿa. Nūr al-Dīn only narrowly escaped the clash with his life, confronted not only by the Greeks but also by the Hospitaller garrison at Crac des Chevaliers and by a train of Latin pilgrims from Aquitaine, including Hugh VIII of Lusignan and equipped with a Templar escort.[123]

Having routed Nūr al-Dīn's army, the Christians debated pressing on into Islamic territory to take Homs. Showing his renowned strategic skill, Nūr al-Dīn decided to make a defiant stand at the lake of Homs, rallying what survived of his army despite the advice of his more flighty companions. The stoic Zankid general held position and waited for the Christians to make their move. Wary of heading through the Homs Gap past the county's natural mountainous defences, the Christians hung back and assumed that Nūr al-Dīn must have had more troops than they thought – more in fact than he actually did have. Nūr al-Dīn's bluff succeeded and the Christians chose to stay in the relative safety of the county. The Christians even requested a truce from Nūr al-Dīn, which the Muslim commander flatly refused, thereby obscuring his true weakness still further.[124] Through a display of military genius and dramatic courage, Nūr al-Dīn had transformed what had threatened to be a catastrophe into a favourable stalemate.

Richard has argued that Constantine Kalamanos's involvement in this whole incident is proof that the scandal over Melisende of Tripoli's abortive betrothal to Manuel Komnenos did not result in a permanent break in relations between the county and the Byzantine empire. Rather, he and Isabelle Augé have suggested that the matrimonial controversy of 1162 was a mere diplomatic spat, which could be – and was – forgotten by Tripoli and Constantinople whenever it seemed prosaic and necessary to do so.[125] Richard and Augé perhaps place too much import on Constantine's presence at Buqay'a. Crucially no contemporary recorded that Raymond III or any comital troops attended this battle. In other words, Raymond did not join forces with the Byzantine Constantine and the county was saved simply by a fortuitous coalition of troops – Latin and Greek pilgrims, joined by the brothers of the military orders – who happened to be passing through and had no known contact with the count of Tripoli himself.

The very fact that the military orders and especially the Hospitallers of Crac were so instrumental in the battle of Buqay'a acts as further proof that Constantine's presence meant nothing for Tripolitan relations with Byzantium. Count Raymond II of Tripoli had already granted the Hospitallers of Crac freedom in diplomatic issues back in the 1140s by allowing them to make and break truces with the Muslims independently of the count's own military policies.[126] The knights certainly did not refrain from exercising this independence from comital diplomacy. In 1169 they offered Duke Wladislaw II of Bohemia the keys of Crac itself as a symbolic gesture made in return for his generous donations to the Order.[127] When the Hospitallers agreed to fight alongside the Byzantines at Buqay'a, there were no grounds to construe this as a Tripolitan–Byzantine rapprochement in the general or official sense.

The king is dead

After settling business in Antioch, King Baldwin headed back south to Tripoli. He had left this city after the breakdown of Manuel's betrothal to Melisende in late summer 1162 and had taken with him a dose of pills to take before the onset of winter, presumably to stave off any number of seasonal illnesses. Count Raymond III's personal physician, a Syrian Christian named Barak (*Barac*), had prescribed this medication to the king while he had still been in Tripoli, instructing him to take a portion immediately and the remainder after a short interval.[128] It was only natural for the king to seek medical advice in Tripoli specifically, which under crusader rule possessed a medical school of wide renown among eastern Christians.[129] The existence of this centre of learning provides an important antidote to Usāma bin Munqidh's more famous account of the brutal Frankish physician who practised crude and deadly surgery at nearby al-Munayṭira.[130]

It should be noted that William of Tyre revealed his intellectual prejudices as a man educated in European schools by condemning the Latin rulers at the time for their reliance upon eastern physicians of all kinds, including Christians, Jews, Muslims and Samaritans. When the king began to feel ill at Antioch, William accused Barak of having poisoned the pills. Proof was allegedly forthcoming when the drugs were fed to an unfortunate dog, which promptly died. There is no way of verifying the archbishop's slanted testimony, although it is remarkable in light of this accusation that the supposed victim, King Baldwin, evidently felt confident enough in the abilities of Tripoli's medical practitioners to return there at the very end of 1162 in the hope of recuperating. The best treatment that Tripoli's famous medical practitioners could offer was not enough, however, to save the king, who steadily worsened as winter set in. After a few months convalescing in Tripoli, the king ordered that he be carried south. William of Tyre did not state explicitly what Baldwin's aim was in giving this order but the fact that the king stopped at Beirut, as soon as he was south of the border at Nahr al-Kalb, suggests that the king wanted to die in his own realm. This he promptly did on 10 February 1163.[131] In dramatic fashion, Baldwin's last act had signalled that Tripoli was not the king's homeland and thus was no longer within the kingdom of Jerusalem.

Captivity at Ḥārim

In 1163 Nūr al-Dīn had snatched victory from the jaws of defeat at the battle of Buqayʿa. After his courageous standoff against the Franks and Greeks near Homs, he managed to restore his army to full strength in a remarkably short space of time. In summer 1164 he marched north to besiege Ḥārim in the principality of Antioch, which had been most recently conquered for Christendom during the crusade of Thierry of Flanders in 1157. William of Tyre alleged that Nūr al-Dīn simply wanted revenge for the humiliation at Buqayʿa the previous year, but this reduces unjustly a master general's grand strategic vision to the level of unfocused petulance.[132] According to Ibn al-Athīr, Nūr al-Dīn attacked Ḥārim in order to draw the new king of Jerusalem, Baldwin III's brother Amalric, out of his invasion of Egypt.[133] At the same time, Ḥārim was an important fortress in its own right, guarding the approach to Antioch.

The defenders of Ḥārim formed an eclectic mix. The veterans of Buqayʿa still lingered in Syria, hence why Constantine Kalamanos, Hugh VIII of Lusignan and their fellow pilgrims found themselves arrayed once more against Nūr al-Dīn. Meanwhile, the rulers of all the crusader states save the Egypt-bound king of Jerusalem promptly assembled, including Prince Bohemond III of Antioch, the landless and purely titular Count Joscelin III of Edessa and Count Raymond III of Tripoli. Joining them was Prince Thoros of Cilician Armenia, a small independent Christian state that had emerged over the course of the twelfth century despite both Byzantine and Antiochene claims.[134] Naturally, the presence of so many disparate fighters proves more the strength of Christian solidarity in the face of invasion than it does any enduring bond between the various parties. Raymond of Tripoli's temporary alliance here with the *doux* Constantine among others can hardly be viewed as anything else, and certainly not as a Tripolitan–Byzantine rapprochement.

All the forces that Christianity could muster in Syria on short notice had been mobilised and personal differences had been set aside temporarily, yet the grand alliance proved in vain. Nūr al-Dīn won a resounding victory over the Christians on 10 August, killing many of them 'like sacrificial animals', in William of Tyre's florid language.[135] With the numerical exaggeration characteristic of medieval authors, Ibn al-Athīr reported that 10,000 Christians were killed and countless more taken captive.[136] Tactical blunders and poor discipline seem to have lain behind the Christian defeat, which Marshall Baldwin quite reasonably blamed on the youthful inexperience of both Bohemond of Antioch and Raymond of Tripoli.[137] Thoros of Armenia fled the field, leaving Bohemond, Raymond and Constantine to be captured and led off to Aleppo, where they joined Raynald of Châtillon, who had been captured back in 1160. Ḥārim itself fell a couple of days later on 12 August (21 Ramaḍān AH 559).[138] A great catastrophe had once again befallen the Latin East. Not for the first time, it was dangerously exposed to further attack, with its principal rulers either languishing in prison or on campaign in distant Egypt.

A royal regency

The Franks of Tripoli had endured the captivity of their counts before. On separate occasions back in 1137, both Pons and Raymond II had been captured, but these had been brief incarcerations lasting at most a few days, ending with death for the elder and swift release for the junior. Raymond III's imprisonment by contrast was much longer, lasting almost an entire decade and consuming much of his youth, from the age of twenty-four to approximately thirty-four.[139] Consequently, the count's forced absence was to have a greater impact on the county's history than the brief captivities of his predecessors.

William of Tyre's depiction of Raymond's experiences of imprisonment is inconsistent to say the least. On the one hand, the archbishop clearly wanted to highlight and even exaggerate the count's sufferings for literary effect, thus he described how Raymond and his fellow captives were 'bound up by chains pitifully as if the lowliest of slaves, led to Aleppo to be a spectacle for its infidel populace and then thrown into prison'.[140] It was, the archbishop later concluded, a period spent 'in beggary and iron'.[141] It is not clear whether William employed such evocative language to illustrate the count's strength of character and endurance, or to suggest that death in battle at Ḥārim – martyrdom, no less – would have been preferable to surrender and captivity.[142] At the same time William contradicted himself by claiming that Raymond had been able to spend much of his captivity in study, learning to read and thus acquiring a level of education unusual for a secular ruler of the time, which served to bolster his 'natural keenness of mind'.[143] Arabic authors would later confirm that Raymond was a remarkably clever, shrewd and capable leader among the Franks.[144] Some historians have believed that Raymond's studies in prison included learning Arabic, but there is no positive evidence to support this claim.[145] Indeed, it is significant that the precise word William of Tyre used to indicate that Raymond was 'literate' was *litteratus* – a term most often used in the Middle Ages to indicate literacy in Latin specifically.[146]

It is unfortunate that so little can be said with certainty regarding Raymond's time in Aleppo. Better attested are the arrangements for running the county during Raymond's involuntary absence. While Raymond learned or languished in prison, King Amalric of Jerusalem dutifully assumed responsibility for Tripoli's governance, fresh from his campaign in Egypt. In one of two rare documents issued by Amalric in the capacity of regent, he took the title 'administratór of the county of Tripoli'.[147] As his brother had done upon appointing Hodierna and her children to rule jointly over the county in 1152, Amalric had ignored Raymond II's provision for Tripoli to be governed by a 'master and caretaker' in the event of a minority, or in this case captivity.[148]

When appraising the regency, Richard was wary that Amalric's role in governing Tripoli might undermine his argument that the southern king had few seigneurial rights vis-à-vis the county. Thus he proposed that Amalric was entitled to the regency because he was Raymond's first cousin, not because of any notion that he was the count's feudal lord.[149] This attempt to determine the king's legal status led Richard to neglect Count Raymond's own alleged account of events, which he later gave to the court of Jerusalem in 1174, soon after his release. In what seems to have been a lengthy speech, the count revealed that he himself had sent instructions from his Aleppan prison, commanding his 'loyal vassals' (*fidelibus*) to transfer their loyalties, fortresses and territories to Amalric, placing the county under the king's sovereignty.[150] This chimes with the legal opinion shared by many historians of the mid-twentieth century, who assumed that the king of Jerusalem could only act as regent in another crusader state if invited to do so by the rightful ruler of the polity in question.[151] Whether such procedure was enshrined in law or an *ad hoc* custom at the time is uncertain. Raymond did not merely appoint Amalric his regent; he also designated his cousin as his heir in the event that he died in prison, childless as he was.[152] Indeed, Amalric himself later indicated the possibility that 'the county of Tripoli might remain held by me and my heirs as inheritance'.[153] Had this happened, the county of Tripoli would have been reunited with the realm proper, brought together under the permanent rule of the house of Jerusalem.

Having assumed responsibility for Tripoli, King Amalric was forced to expand the circuit and duties of Jerusalem's court, which was already highly peripatetic in the style of other royal courts in Latin Christendom. Amalric soon found himself dealing with Tripolitan affairs in the kingdom and Jerusalemite matters in the county. On 20 October 1168, Amalric confirmed one of Count Raymond's earlier donations to the citizens of Amalfi, originally made in June 1163. The royal deed was issued in Ascalon and witnessed only by the king's Jerusalemite courtiers.[154] On 14 March 1171 Amalric was in Tripoli, where he issued a document relating exclusively to the kingdom of Jerusalem in both content and witness list.[155] Between these two documents came the only surviving document issued by the king in Tripoli *for* Tripoli, around September 1170. This deed had a witness list comprised predominantly of Tripolitans, with only four drawn 'from the barons of the land of Jerusalem'.[156] These pertinent charters, few as they are, provide a remarkably broad and insightful cross-section of Amalric's strategy for governing both Tripoli and the realm.

Equally interesting is how Amalric enhanced Tripoli's role as a conduit for maritime travel between the kingdom of Jerusalem and the wider world, especially Byzantium. The years from 1167 to 1180 represented yet another new phase in Byzantine–Latin relations, with Emperor Manuel Komnenos enjoying an unprecedented level of influence over the crusader states after his earlier mistreatment of Melisende of Tripoli. Manuel employed familiar diplomatic tools such as gifts, marriages and alliances, while King Amalric and the Latins were willing to forget past controversies in return for necessary finances and military assistance.[157] During this period, the emperor funded extensive decoration and renovation programmes in many of the kingdom of Jerusalem's principal shrine-churches. In Bethlehem between 1167 and 1169, mosaics were erected to commemorate the provincial and ecumenical church councils of Late Antiquity, respected by the Latins and Greeks alike. The Latin authorities were even willing for the Niceno-Constantinopolitan creed of 381 to be written in Greek and, most surprisingly, *without* the controversial '*filioque*' clause. For the Latins, the *filioque* was key to understanding the Christian Trinity, as they insisted that the Holy Spirit proceeded from the Son as well as the Father. The Greeks, however, regarded this as a heresy, which was one of the many reasons why the churches had split back in the eleventh century. That the Latin hierarchy was willing to allow such an uncompromisingly Greek stance to be displayed in a Latin cathedral is one of the more striking instances of Latin–Byzantine rapprochement.[158]

In 1168 Emperor Manuel sent an embassy to King Amalric, with the intention being to organise a joint invasion of Egypt. The legation was led by two Italians in imperial service, Count Alexander of Gravina and Michael of Otranto. Where in Syria the legates' ship landed is unclear, but they met with the king in private audience at Tyre and departed from Tripoli for the Byzantine Balkans accompanied by a Latin embassy sent by Amalric and led by the famous chronicler William – as yet still archdeacon of Tyre. The ambassadors met the emperor at Ohrid in modern Macedonia, where they concluded with him a treaty over Egypt. They then left for home in October 1168, presumably sailing once more via Tripoli.[159]

What Raymond III would have thought of his own city becoming an integral part of Amalric's friendly diplomacy with the Byzantines less than a decade after the emperor had snubbed his sister is open to speculation. Evidently the king saw no problem in conducting his business through the port of Tripoli more frequently – or at least more visibly – than any preceding king of Jerusalem had.

Many questions regarding Amalric's regency still remain. Did the king enjoy all the profits ordinarily due to the count or were they redirected into a sort of trust fund in anticipation of Raymond's release? Did Amalric appoint his own loyal deputies to supervise the county's urban centres, as he is known to have done as regent of the principality of Antioch, or else trust Tripoli's own cadre of officers and barons?[160] On the latter point, William of Tyre noted that the king had been a man to delegate authority whenever and wherever possible, which sometimes proved a cause for concern among his contemporaries.[161] Amalric certainly fostered relations with individuals within the county, showing them special favour in return for their loyal assistance. When Amalric travelled to Constantinople in person in March 1171 to seek the emperor's support against Egypt, he was accompanied by a certain Raynald of Nephin.[162] Nephin was a settlement within the county of Tripoli, lying equidistant between Batrūn and Tripoli, close to the abbey of Belmont. The German traveller Wilbrand of Oldenburg sailed between Nephin and Tripoli in a storm in the 1210s – the firmest indication that the town possessed its own small port at this time.[163] The town is now known as Enfeh and possesses some remarkable crusader-era remains, including a church that is still in use today and a Frankish citadel on a stark narrow peninsula.[164]

Lilie quite credibly proposed that Raynald acted as Amalric's 'liaison man' with the Tripolitans during the king's regency.[165] He was most probably Lord Raynald I of Nephin, who had received this town from Raymond II as compensation for his former lordship of Tortosa – conquered temporarily by Nūr al-Dīn in 1152 and subsequently entrusted more to the Templars than to any secular power.[166] Raynald was thus one of the greatest of the local nobility. He had been lord of Tortosa, one of the county's principal cities, and even his consolation prize was a town of some middling importance. Although Nephin hardly compared to Tortosa, much less Tripoli itself, it nonetheless enjoyed a measure of prosperity under the Franks. Burchard of Mount Sion visited it in the thirteenth century and remarked on its flourishing economy, thriving viticulture, heavy fortifications and location on a jutting promontory – similar to the greater ports of Syria including Tripoli, Jubayl and Tyre.[167] The Embriaci of Jubayl owned some rights in the region of Nephin, which provided Lady Alice, widow of Hugh I Embriaco, with sufficient resources to institute a regular donation of gold *bezants* and oil to the canons of the Holy Sepulchre in 1135.[168] Raynald of Nephin must have seemed a sufficiently high-ranking candidate to assist King Amalric in governing the county.

Despite his penchant for delegation, King Amalric's ability to manage all three surviving crusader states was in doubt. The somewhat desperate situation was not at all helped by the king's insistence upon conducting invasions of Fāṭimid Egypt, which had already proved a dangerous distraction around the time of the disaster at Ḥārim in 1164. Egypt was central to Amalric's negotiations with the Byzantines in the late 1160s, yet plans for a Latin–Greek expedition ultimately failed, largely because the king was too impatient to wait for the completion of his diplomatic overtures and too greedy to contemplate sharing booty, so launched his invasion without Byzantine help.[169]

In a letter to King Louis VII of France dated as early as November 1164, the master of the Templars, Bertrand of Blancfort, warned that it was quite impossible for King Amalric alone to defend Jerusalem, Antioch, Tripoli and Egypt against Nūr al-Dīn.[170] This pessimism was soon justified by actual events. Sometime in 1165/66 (AH 561), Nūr al-Dīn led a light army into the county of Tripoli, catching the Franks off their guard and capturing al-Munayṭira, presumably by invading via the road traversing Lebanon from Baʿalbakk and the Biqāʿ valley.[171] Nūr al-Dīn was certainly not oblivious to broader concerns of grand strategy. Bahāʾ al-Dīn believed that Nūr al-Dīn had attacked al-Munayṭira in order to distract Amalric from Egypt, much as he had done by besieging Ḥārim in 1164.[172]

Just a year later, Nūr al-Dīn and his brother Quṭb al-Dīn the lord of Mosul raided the county again, this time via the Homs Gap and the eponymous city beyond. The Muslim army ravaged the very heartlands of the county, besieging ʿArqa and destroying the Templar fortresses of Castrum Album (Ḥalba), ʿUrayma and Chastel Blanc (Ṣāfīthā), before returning to Homs for the Ramaḍān fast (21 June–20 July 1167).[173] The timing of the invasion, which obliged Nūr al-Dīn and Quṭb al-Dīn to withdraw and suspend campaigning for Ramaḍān, suggests that permanent conquest was not their plan on this occcasion. That ʿArqa resisted conquest on this occasion was of great importance. The strategic value of this city remained as high as it always had – 'la clef de Tripoli' in Richard's assessment – and Nūr al-Dīn's failure to take it in 1167 may well have saved the county's capital itself.[174] Abū Shāma would later observe that 'if ʿArqa was conquered, Tripoli would be conquered'.[175]

Bertrand of Blancfort's fear that King Amalric was unable to bear the burden of his various responsibilities had more substance to it than mere scaremongering. Amalric's ambition surely exceeded the bounds of what he could practically achieve and it even threatened the security of the Latin East. In the king's defence, the tides of war were not entirely against the county of Tripoli during Amalric's regency. A military force, presumably from within the county itself, managed to re-capture Gibelacar in December 1169 or January 1170 (Rabīʿ II AH 565).[176] Richard credited 'les chevaliers tripolitains' with Gibelacar's reconquest, but both its location near Crac des Chevaliers and the fact that King Amalric gave responsibility for its reconstruction to the Hospitallers later the same year would point to the Knights of St John instead.[177]

Gibelacar was important to the county's defence, located on a spur of Lebanon overlooking the plain of ʿAkkār and thus a link in the chain of strongholds stretching from Crac des Chevaliers westward to Tripoli. Al-Dimashqī would later describe it as 'an impregnable stronghold ever since the creation of Islam'.[178] In fact, its history in the mid-twelfth century suggests it was anything but impregnable, moving between Christian and Muslim hands fairly regularly. It had probably been captured by Nūr al-Dīn during his raid in 1167, hence the need for reconquest.[179] According to Bahāʾ al-Dīn, the Franks succeeded in retaking Gibelacar from Nūr al-Dīn's deputy, the *mamlūk* Khutlukh the standard-bearer, primarily because their confidence had been buoyed by King Amalric's successes in his latest invasion of Egypt.[180] Nūr al-Dīn was evidently not alone in turning a war on multiple fronts to his advantage.

Freedom, orthodoxy and power in Antioch

Prince Bohemond III of Antioch was released from prison in 1165, just a year after Ḥārim. His liberation was secured largely through the intervention of Emperor Manuel Komnenos, who agreed to provide the finances necessary to pay the prince's ransom. It is significant that Manuel apparently did not help to secure the release of Raymond of Tripoli, who was to languish in captivity for another eight or so years. Historians have tended to assume that the emperor, by paying only for Bohemond's release and not Raymond's, sought to punish the latter for his vengeful actions after the scandal surrounding Manuel's abortive betrothal to his sister Melisende.[181]

Setting aside personal grudges, there were more positive reasons for Manuel to assist Bohemond rather than Raymond, recalling the perennial Byzantine obsession with controlling Antioch specifically. Indeed, the prince was quick to repay Manuel by inviting imperial influence back into the principality. In one of the more dramatic turns of the twelfth century, Bohemond agreed to allow the Greek patriarch of Antioch, Athanasios I, to move from Constantinople to Antioch itself in 1165, which forced the embittered Latin patriarch, Aimery of Limoges, into exile in his castle at al-Quṣayr (modern Kürsat) near Arzghān.[182] As is well known, the First Crusade had sought to liberate the Orthodox Christians of Syria, conquered in the late eleventh century by the Saljūqs. Quite quickly, however, antagonism between the Latins and the Greeks had arisen on campaign, culminating in the crusaders' controversial decision to institute a Latin hierarchy in all conquered cities, which was to be parallel to the Greek clergy who either lived as exiled titular patriarchs and bishops in Constantinople or else were subjected to Latin supremacy.[183] This matter of ecclesiastical jurisdiction was unsurprisingly a bone of contention for Latin–Greek relations, at least as important as the question of strictly political rule. It was thus a great coup for Manuel to facilitate the return of a Greek patriarch to what had always been the Byzantines' most treasured Syrian city.

In the event, Athanasios's reign at Antioch proved hugely unpopular among the predominantly hellenophobe Latins of the city itself and managed to do little more in the long term than to highlight just how poisonous the sectarian animosity between the Greeks and Latins had become. What it achieved in the short term was the re-establishment of the Orthodox episcopal hierarchy, not just in Antioch, but in a handful of other dioceses within the patriarchate. There is no definite evidence that Greek bishops returned to the sees of the county of Tripoli, although a Templar brother associated with Tortosa by the name of Salo seems to have lent his support to a 'Greek'[184] bishop who was installed in predominantly Orthodox Latakia at the expense of its exiled Latin bishop, Gerard of Nazareth. Surprisingly, this occurred as early as *c.*1159–61, *before* the installation of the Greek patriarch of Antioch – likely as a result of Manuel's triumph over Raynald of Châtillon back in 1159. Salo's support for a non-Latin bishop in this case probably stemmed from a dispute between the Templars and Bishop Gerard.[185] Whether Salo or any other Latin cleric from the county of Tripoli supported the installation of Orthodox clergy elsewhere, particularly in the county itself during the eventual residency of Athanasios in Antioch, is regrettably unknown.

In addition to furthering the Latin–Greek rapprochement of the 1160s and 1170s, Bohemond's liberation naturally relieved a great deal of the pressure on the Latin East and King Amalric personally. Now that the prince of Antioch could again assume governance of the second greatest crusader state, the king of Jerusalem only had to worry about the realm itself and the comparatively small county of Tripoli. The prince may even have assisted with the administration of the latter, specifically those northern territories that had been Antiochene fiefs in the days of Prince Tancred and Count Pons. In 1170, Bohemond reconfirmed Raymond II of Tripoli's earlier donation of Crac and long-lost Rafaniyya to the Hospitallers in 1142.[186] In light of this, it is most interesting to note that both of Amalric's surviving Tripoli-specific charters dealt exclusively with land south of the old border at al-Nahr al-Kabīr al-Janūbī – the city of Tripoli itself in one and ʿArqa and Gibelacar in the other.[187] Did the prince and king divide responsibility for the county according to the precedent set in the first decades of the twelfth century? Certainly it would appear from Bohemond's charter at least that the bipartite Latin East had resurfaced, albeit briefly.

Not all of Bohemond's actions at this time were to the house of Tripoli's benefit. Raymond's aunt Agnes, daughter to Count Pons, had given to her husband Raynald II Mazoir two fortresses in the principality of Antioch formerly in the possession of her own mother Cecilia: the castles of Arzghān and al-Rūj.[188] Recent years had seen Agnes's two dower forts subject to an worrying increase of military incursions. Arzghān had perhaps been conquered by Nūr al-Dīn as early as April 1148, recovered by Agnes's husband in 1157 or 1160 and lost once more to the Zankids in 1162/3.[189] By this point it would appear that Prince Bohemond no longer felt able to depend on the Mazoirs to provide military security in the east. In January 1168 Bohemond promised Arzghān to the Hospitallers, presumably hoping that they would be able to reconquer and hold this lost fortress, succeeding where the Mazoirs had failed.[190] This recalled what Raymond II of Tripoli had done over two decades before, handing Rafaniyya to the Hospital in 1142.[191] Ironically Bohemond was not to recover Arzghān until Saladin gave it to him in 1192.[192] What is particularly pertinent is that the Mazoirs never again held this fortress after the 1160s.

Bohemond also took the opportunity presented by his donation in 1168 to give the Hospital half of the estate of al-Rūj. Moreover he dramatically promised the Hospital the other half, 'which the Hospital will soon have to liberate and acquire from Raynald Mazoir and his heirs'.[193] Mayer sees this as an aggressive and centralising act, undermining the Mazoirs' landholding rights.[194] In the event, Raynald resisted for some six years before agreeing to concede his half of al-Rūj, and it would be another eight years before the estate was confirmed under Hospitaller control.[195] What seems to have happened in the 1160s, then, is that the prince of Antioch arbitrarily gave away two fortresses that belonged rightfully to the house of Mazoir, originally without the family's permission. Most intriguingly, this coincided closely with the power vacuum in Tripoli. Did Bohemond time his intervention to capitalise on the fact that Raynald and Agnes could not turn to their captive nephew to act as advocate on their behalf? Was Bohemond simply anxious that his eastern frontier desperately needed bolstering in the face of potential Muslim invasion? Indeed, it is noteworthy that the prince's distribution of Mazoir lands occurred just a couple of years before he dusted off Antioch's half-forgotten claims to the northern half of the county of Tripoli, reconfirming the Hospitallers' possession of Crac des Chevaliers. The prince evidently felt that only the Hospitallers could safeguard his principality's vast and exposed marches, the ineffective Mazoirs and the captive count of Tripoli both being unable to do so.

Whatever sensible reasons may have underpinned Bohemond's decisions in relation to Arzghān and al-Rūj, they surely constituted a blow for the house of Tripoli. By losing Arzghān and al-Rūj, the house of Tripoli – as represented by the line descending from Agnes – had lost what had once been their major outposts in the principality of Antioch, ever since Agnes's own parents had married half a century before. Count Raymond's later preference for Jerusalemite matters was surely encouraged by the fact his relatives no longer held as many Antiochene strongholds as they once had. Meanwhile Agnes's granddaughter by her son Bertrand, also named Agnes, would later seek to return to her ancestral home of Tripoli in 1240, with the Mazoirs having by then sold even their principal stronghold of Margat.[196] According to the *Lignages d'Outremer*, Agnes the elder also had a great-grandson named Hugh Angelier, born to her anonymous and otherwise obscure granddaughter. Little is known of Hugh, other than that he was killed at the gates of Tripoli in 1282.[197] Did Hugh, like his cousin Agnes the younger, seek to return to Tripoli, only to meet a fate tragically similar to that of his great-uncle Raymond II, assassinated in the very same place back in 1152?

Shaken and shattered

The greatest crisis faced by Tripoli in the absence of its count came on 29 June 1170, when another earthquake wreaked havoc throughout North Syria little more than a decade after the seismic event of 1157. William of Tyre, who had been safely studying in Europe in the 1150s, now suffered the effects of an earthquake and its aftershocks in person. He described vividly how the Christian and Muslim cities of North Syria were devastated in 1170, listing in particular his residence of Tyre together with Homs, Hama, Aleppo, Shayzar, Latakia, Jabala and Tripoli.[198] ʿImād al-Dīn (as cited by Abū Shāma) and Ibn al-Athīr added to this list a handful of military sites in the county of Tripoli in the vicinity of Baʿrīn (Montferrand): namely Crac, ʿUrayma, Ṣāfīthā and ʿArqa.[199] Archaeological surveys have revealed the scars of earthquake damage on the Cistercian abbey of Belmont near Tripoli, although whether or not this monastery suffered the shocks of 1170 specifically is impossible to tell.[200]

William of Tyre demonstrated his talents for incisive observation by noting that the earthquake only affected the ancient northern provinces, from Tyre up to Antioch, while southerly Palestine was spared by what he believed to be divine mercy.[201] Seismologists now know that North Syria and Palestine lie within two different rupture zones, dubbed the 'Syrian' and 'Dead Sea' fault systems respectively, with the Syrian system extending roughly from Tyre to Antioch and considerably more active than the Dead Sea zone.[202] No wonder then that North Syria was devastated so soon after the earthquake of 1157, whereas Palestine was spared on both occasions.

The best-known consequence of the earthquake of 1170 was the resultant collapse of Antioch's cathedral of St Peter. This great edifice fell and crushed the unpopular patriarch Athanasios beneath its rubble, which the Franks believed to be a sign of God's anger at the appointment of a Greek patriarch in the first place. Athanasios's death opened the way for the exiled Latin patriarch Aimery's eventual return.[203] As for Tripoli, William of Tyre wrote that the city was entirely destroyed with scarcely any survivors.[204] More contemporaneously, a letter sent by Tripoli's regent, King Amalric of Jerusalem, to King Louis VII of France within weeks of the tragedy described in awestruck terms how 'a sudden and hitherto unknown earthquake utterly destroyed Tripoli and suffocated almost everybody within it'.[205] Coming so soon after the fatalities and destruction witnessed in 1157, this must have been extremely harrowing to Tripoli's inhabitants. Indeed, some historically minded seismologists have estimated that Tripoli suffered more damage in 1170 than in 1157, which certainly corroborates King Amalric's implication that the scale of the later event was unprecedented.[206] Whatever the exactitude of such assessments, the earthquakes of 1157 and 1170 were certainly similar in having serious, albeit temporary, military consequences, as castles and fortifications were thrown to the ground. The main difference was that whereas 1157 had seen the crusaders go on the offensive thanks to the arrival of Thierry of Flanders, 1170 saw a decidedly more cautious defensive approach. In fact William of Tyre and Ibn al-Athīr both reported that the latter earthquake brought peace to Syria; Christians and Muslims alike were too fearful of their own defensive weaknesses to launch opportunistic attacks on each other from their cracked fortresses and crumbled cities.[207]

Military strategy was now directed towards repairing the damage as rapidly as possible. Nūr al-Dīn expended huge reserves of wealth and energy to rebuild cities and castles. Nor did he neglect mosques within this urgent reconstruction programme, sending the clear message that he had religious as well as military duties to uphold.[208] His Christian rivals also combined religious and military policy. It was after surveying the earthquake's impact on defensive structures that King Amalric sent his aforementioned desperately worded missive to Louis VII of France, warning that Tripoli, ʿArqa and a handful of cities in the principality of Antioch were at risk of being 'occupied by the enemies of the Cross of Christ'.[209] Acutely aware of the strain the necessary repairs would place upon the treasuries of Tripoli and Jerusalem, Amalric gave responsibility for the rebuilding of the shattered fortresses of ʿArqa and Gibelacar to the religio-military Hospitallers. Presumably only a wealthy religious order could afford such repairs. In return the Hospital received certain rights and privileges. Amalric clearly acted quickly, reaching this agreement within months of the earthquake. Desperate as he was, however, Amalric was careful not to give away too much of the county. In the relevant charter, Amalric made much of the fact that the agreement with the Hospital was ultimately dependent upon Count Raymond's consent, his imprisonment notwithstanding, and it seems that neither ʿArqa nor Gibelacar were transferred permanently to the Hospital at this time, remaining under secular control for the rest of the twelfth century at least.[210]

This moment in 1170, when a pragmatic peace descended over the collapsed castles of Syria, proved fleeting. In the holy month of Muḥarram AH 567 (September–October 1171), Nūr al-Dīn felt confident enough to attack the county of Tripoli, still reeling from the earthquake a year before. Nūr al-Dīn sought to punish the Franks for a recent controversy in the principality of Antioch, when the Christians had seized two Muslim merchant ships at Latakia despite a temporary truce then in place. Nūr al-Dīn had little interest in the finer political distinctions between the principality of Antioch and the county of Tripoli, so personally led his invasion force into the latter via the broad Homs Gap, heading straight for the familiar target of ʿArqa, which he besieged, destroying its outlying suburb. While Nūr al-Dīn remained at ʿArqa to supervise the siege, he sent a detachment of his soldiers to seize the lesser fortresses of Ṣāfīthā and ʿUrayma. Soon afterwards Nūr al-Dīn raised the stakes further by abandoning the siege of ʿArqa in order to march on Tripoli, plundering and ravaging as he went. Finally the Franks' resolve collapsed, they promptly returned the cargo of the seized ships and agreed to renew the broken truce. Nūr al-Dīn withdrew from Christian territory once this goal was achieved, again lacking any real desire to conquer the county permanently on this occasion.[211] The ease with which Nūr al-Dīn was able to enter the county and bring it to its knees underlined once again how weak the Franks of Tripoli had become.

The 'conversion' of the Assassins

Arguably the most dramatic incident during Amalric's regency of Tripoli was the overtures made to the king by the Nizārī Assassins in winter of 1173–4.[212] The Assassins' new leader in Syria was Rāshid al-Dīn Sinān, whom westerners dubbed the 'Old Man of the Mountain'. According to William of Tyre, Rāshid al-Dīn had developed a keen interest in Christianity and so sent an envoy named Abū ʿAbdullāh (Latin: *Boabdelle*) to treat with King Amalric. Through this ambassador the Nizārī leader offered to convert both himself and his entire sect to Christianity on the condition that they were freed of their obligation to pay a regular tribute to the Templars at Tortosa.[213]

Historians have long debated the substance behind William's belief that the Assassins wished to convert to Christianity in return for what seems like a fairly minor financial sacrifice on the part of a Christian religious order. The leading modern expert on medieval Ismāʿīlism, Farhad Daftary, suspects that the Assassins had no real intention to convert.[214] The earliest historian to express some measure of doubt was Walter Map, who wrote only a decade after William of Tyre's death and implied that the Assassins were characteristically perfidious.[215] Lundgreen was the first modern scholar to question the credibility of William's account, suggesting that the Nizārīs' desire to escape paying tribute to the Templars far exceeded their zeal for Christianity, if any existed at all.[216]

More recent historians have argued that the story of the Assassins' wish to convert was the result of William of Tyre's serious misunderstanding of Nizārī practices. In particular, Hauziński believes that William misunderstood two recent developments in the sect's religious practices and governance as having constituted a deliberate move towards Christianity. One was the Nizārīs' break from certain customs thought to be characteristically Islamic, such as the prohibition on eating pork and drinking alcohol.[217] William himself emphasised that the Assassins were now consuming pork and alcohol.[218] Latins at the time of the Crusades were fully aware that restrictions on the consumption of these two substances were symbolic of Islam. Almost a century later, in March 1260, Frankish soldiers were reported to have entered Damascus as part of a military coalition with the Mongols and Armenians. To signal their victory, the Latin Christians supposedly sprayed wine over the walls of the city's mosques and adorned them with slices of pork.[219] Although the historicity of this account has been doubted, the very fact that the author included it at all suggests that Latin Christians were (in)sensitive to the importance of such dietary symbols.[220]

Because eating pork and drinking alcohol were two of the main signs differentiating Christians from Muslims, it is not altogether surprising that William of Tyre was led to believe that the Nizārīs were moving away from Islam and towards Christianity on a more fundamental and comprehensive level. In truth, the liberalising of Nizārī practices meant nothing of the sort. The adoption of 'alien' religio-dietary customs in medieval Syria was far from unique to the Assassins. Some Latins curiously chose to perpetuate the Islamic ban on pork. One early settler in Antioch known to Usāma bin Munqidh ate only local Muslim-style food and refused to allow pork to enter his home.[221] It does not seem, however, that the Frank in question had become Muslim. Other Christians simply saw profit in the Islamic regulation of this meat. Riley-Smith writes that a particular 'absurdity' prevailed in Tyre: the Latin Christian continuation of a Fāṭimid tax of four *dīnār*s levied on the butchers of pigs, called the *tuazo* (*tawaḍḍu'*), meaning ritual ablutions.[222] Diet was an overt sign of religion, but a misleading one.

The second development among the Nizārīs to confuse William of Tyre was their pragmatic, even desperate desire for a temporary military alliance with the Franks against the staunchly Sunnī Nūr al-Dīn and later Saladin, who spent much time persecuting the Nizārīs and other Muslims for their perceived heterodoxies.[223] The Assassins were simply at a point in 1173–4 where they preferred to work with the Franks than with the Sunnīs, yet this was a fleeting military desire that would not have led to any permanent commitment and was certainly not the enduring religious fervour imagined by William of Tyre.[224] Hamilton has suggested that King Amalric himself was primarily concerned with the potential political and military ramifications of the alliance with the Nizārīs, which would imply that William's own emphasis on religion was secondary even to the main player on the Frankish side.[225]

Hauziński's two likely explanations for William's befuddlement, leading in turn to his mistaken belief that the Assassins were on the brink of conversion, should be supplemented by three further considerations. When describing how Rāshid al-Dīn had begun to take an interest in Christianity, William mentioned that he already owned Christian books, specifically the Gospels and an 'Apostolic codex'.[226] The latter may well find direct corroboration in John of Joinville's thirteenth-century account of a later 'Old Man of the Mountain', who owned a copy of a book containing Christ's sayings to St Peter.[227] William's assumption that the presence of ostensibly Christian books in a Muslim's library meant an interest in Christianity *per se* is based on a flawed understanding of Islam and its relationship to the wider Abrahamic tradition. Many Muslim scholars used the Gospels as a source for the life of the Prophet Jesus ('Īsā), despite technically believing that the available texts familiar to Christians were distortions of the lost 'true' Gospel (*Injīl*) given by God to Jesus.[228]

As for the book of sayings to St Peter that was possibly identical with the 'Apostolic tome', this could have roots in another peculiarity of Muslim and especially Nizārī belief at this time. The twelve Apostles of Christ are indicated vaguely in the Qurān, as devout Muslim followers of Jesus, so the concept of an 'Apostolic tome' related by Jesus to St Peter would hold interest even among the most rigidly orthodox Muslims.[229] Moreover, the Assassin lord himself explained that he loved St Peter greatly, as he believed him to be the reincarnation in turn of Abel, Noah and Abraham.[230] Some historians have believed this to be a garbled report of the genuine Nizārī belief in a cyclical succession of seven phases of revelation, each possessing its own 'speaking prophet' of God (*nāṭiq*) alongside the prophet's dedicated interpreter or 'foundation' (*asās*). The fifth revelatory cycle had had Jesus and Peter respectively in these roles.[231] More recently, Daftary has suggested that the Syrian branch of the Nizārīs actually did come to believe in the literal transmigration of souls, perhaps influenced by their radical Shī'a neighbours, the Nuṣayrī Alawites.[232] What is germane to the present discussion is that the Assassins' own belief system gave them plenty of reasons to exhibit an intellectual and spiritual interest in 'Christian' subjects, without borrowing from Christianity directly and certainly without wanting to convert.

The disputed meaning of baptism in medieval Syria was another cause for confusion. William of Tyre proudly noted the Assassins' desire to 'flock to the faith of Christ and to baptism', thereby associating the latter with the consumption of pork and alcohol that also served as outward signs of an inner desire to convert.[233] Yet, as with these dietary symbols, one's participation in Christian-led baptismal rites was not incontrovertible proof that one viewed oneself as a Christian, as some historians have thought.[234] Past Muslim rulers such as Jalāl al-Mulk bin 'Ammār, former *qāḍī* of Tripoli, had offered to be baptised as a sort of diplomatic bargaining in negotiations with the crusaders, but it was also a superstitious practice not unfamiliar to Muslims of lower status in more ordinary situations, who underwent baptism at churches such as Tortosa in order to attain health benefits – not to become Christian.[235] A sizeable if indeterminate number of the indigenous inhabitants of Syria and Lebanon agreed to be baptised en masse under the Franks. The thirteenth-century Dominican missionary William of Tripoli claimed he had personally 'baptised more than a thousand Muslims already'.[236] A young 'Saracen' convert to Christianity reportedly took to public preaching *c.*1201, baptising some two thousand of his former co-religionists in the process.[237] Given the known fashion of what could be called 'pseudo-baptism' among Muslims at this time, how reliable an indicator of genuine conversion are any of these reports of mass conversion – the Assassins' desire to be baptised included?

One final unappreciated factor that may have pushed William further into error on this matter was linguistic. Historians have differing opinions on how much Arabic William actually knew. Most have traditionally assumed that the archbishop had a fairly good, even advanced knowledge of the language in its written form, allowing him to use Arabic sources when writing his history.[238] More recent scholarship has argued instead that William probably knew little if any formal written Arabic, which even few Arabs would have known, but perhaps picked up some spoken colloquial during his childhood and later life in the east.[239] If this is the case, then it is entirely possible that the archbishop had heard the Assassins described by the Arabic name of their sect, *al-nizāriyya*, or else the term for their Alawite neighbours, *al-nuṣayriyya*, and had confused either or both of these with the Arabic word for 'Christians', *al-naṣārā* – 'Nazarenes' in reference to Jesus of Nazareth. The difference in the pronunciation of the three terms would have been obvious to native speakers, especially when the orthography was compared in written sources. This, however, would not have been readily apparent to a man like William with only rudimentary colloquial Arabic.

In short, the diplomacy between Amalric and the Assassins and the more general prospect of a wholesale conversion to Christianity certainly stemmed from mutual misunderstanding, rather than genuine religious conviction on the part of the Nizārīs. Nevertheless, according to William of Tyre, the king enthusiastically accepted the Assassins' alleged proposal, no doubt as excited by the prospect of a military alliance as by the alleged desire to convert. Amalric promptly sent the Nizārī envoy Abū ʿAbdullāh back to the sect's Syrian stronghold in Jabal al-Nuṣayriyya to finalise the arrangement. This naturally took the ambassador back up the coast road into the county of Tripoli and through the Templar-dominated area in its north, around Tortosa and Ṣāfīthā. As Abū ʿAbdullāh was completing the final part of his journey through Christian territory, the Templars attacked and killed him. The king had promised the man safe passage home, presumably confident in his authority as Tripoli's regent. That the Templars had ignored this and killed Abū ʿAbdullāh was construed by the court of Jerusalem as no less than an act of treason. Moreover, it supposedly led the Assassins to abandon their plans to convert to Christianity, King Amalric's personal apology notwithstanding.[240]

William of Tyre patently believed that the Templars had attacked the Assassin envoy because they were greedy, loathe to lose the highly lucrative source of income represented by the Nizārīs' tribute. This situation was all the worse because the king had supposedly offered to compensate the Templars fully for the annual payment of 2,000 gold coins, which they were set to lose.[241] Greed is certainly a credible motive, albeit characteristic of William's broad hostility towards the military orders, whom he – like many bishops – viewed as threatening the traditional hierarchies of the episcopacy and the monarchy through their acquisition of papal exemptions.[242] Clerical opposition to exempt religious orders would continue to swell until the early fourteenth century, when bishops and priests gave their support to King Philip IV of France in his infamous persecution of the Templars.[243] Already in the twelfth century, William of Tyre described with evident satisfaction how King Amalric, on the advice of his High Court, decided to ignore the Templars' exempt status in order to punish the particular knight responsible for Abū ʿAbdullāh's death, a one-eyed man named Walter of Le Mesnil, who was arrested at Sidon and thrown into prison in Tyre.[244]

William was evidently concerned more with questions of legitimate authority within the Church and so his dismissal of Templar motives as avaricious and money-driven is perhaps too simple an explanation. Hamilton suggests that the Templars were led to murder Abū ʿAbdullāh by their own chivalric code of honour, which was at odds with the Nizārīs' clandestine methods of political murder.[245] Some sort of knightly idealism may have motivated the Templars, but more pragmatic concerns are just as likely. Unlike the king of Jerusalem and the archbishop-chronicler of Tyre, the Templars of Tortosa were in regular contact with the Assassins, so were in a better place to judge the threat they posed and the sincerity of their promises to convert to Christianity. The Templars were closely involved with a couple of syncretic shrines in Syria and Lebanon, where Muslims and Christians alike went on pilgrimage and sought divine favour. The cathedral of Tortosa itself was one of the main Christian sites where Muslims brought their children to be baptised, not for the sake of conversion to Christianity, but to fulfil the folkloric belief that such a ritual brought health benefits.[246] Moreover, this church derived its popularity among Christians and Muslims alike because of its associations with the Virgin Mary, esteemed in both religious traditions.[247] The Templars were also closely associated with another Syrian shrine famous for syncretic Islamo-Christian Marian devotions, namely Ṣaydnāyā.[248]

When the Nizārīs showed signs of adopting quintessentially Christian practices – the consumption of pork and alcohol included – and then promised to undergo baptism, the Templars were experienced enough to know that these signs in no way meant a move towards Christianity *per se*, as William of Tyre assumed. By killing Abū ʿAbdullāh, the Templars may have hoped to retain a valuable tribute, but also to expose how spurious the rumours of conversion actually were. After all, it is surely suspicious that the Assassins so quickly abandoned their supposedly sincere plans to change religion after the mere killing of an envoy. The Templars were certainly to blame for undermining the hope of a beneficial alliance with the Assassins, not to mention making a mockery of royal authority in the process. They were not, however, responsible for preventing what would have been the most significant mass conversion of local Muslims to Latin Christianity ever seen in the crusader states, simply because this was never really a possibility in the first place.

Freedom once more

It is not clear when exactly Count Raymond was released. William of Tyre claimed the count had only been in prison for eight solar years, while Ibn Jubayr claimed 'twelve (Islamic lunar) years or more'.[249] Most historians reject both estimates, since Raymond's first recorded reappearance as a free man in the surviving written record does not occur until 18 April 1174 when he witnessed one of King Amalric's charters in Acre.[250] Captured in August 1164, it seems likely that Raymond's captivity lasted approximately ten years. No evidence permits Raymond's release to be dated more exactly than sometime before his reappearance on 18 April 1174. The count's absence from the controversial events surrounding the Assassins in winter 1173–4, together with King Amalric's prominent role in the same, strongly suggests that Raymond was released after this and not before.

Why the count was finally released is just as unclear as *when*. Ibn al-Athīr claimed decades later that Raymond had been released by the ambitious eunuch Saʿd al-Dīn Kumushtakīn, who had taken over the governance of Aleppo following Nūr al-Dīn's death in May 1174 and the succession of the sultan's underage son al-Ṣāliḥ Ismāʿīl al-Malik. Allegedly Saʿd al-Dīn wished to use the count as a ploy to distract Nūr al-Dīn's former lieutenant Saladin from besieging Aleppo itself as part of his own power grab, and it is true that Raymond would soon threaten Saladin's ambitions in Syria.[251] However, Raymond's recorded reappearance at Acre a month before Nūr al-Dīn's death makes Ibn al-Athīr's interpretation untenable.

At almost a full decade in duration, Raymond's captivity was shorter than Raynald of Châtillon's fifteen-year incarceration but much longer than that of his fellow captive at Ḥārim, Bohemond of Antioch, who was released within a single year. The greater length of Raymond's imprisonment is explained to some degree by Manuel Komnenos's preferential treatment towards Bohemond and his grievances against the openly anti-Byzantine Raymond and Raynald.[252] Without imperial assistance, Richard suspected that Tripoli's court simply could not afford the high ransom set for Raymond's release, especially after the huge expenditure it had been forced to make in repairs after the earthquake of 1170.[253] Medieval authors disagreed on how much Raymond's eventual freedom cost. It is tempting to accept the estimate of 80,000 gold pieces recorded by William of Tyre – Raymond's personal friend, chancellor of the kingdom and thus a man who more than most should have known the true figure. According to the archbishop, some 60,000 of the gold coins were not paid immediately. Instead Raymond had apparently given an unspecified number of Frankish hostages to Nūr al-Dīn as a guarantee for their eventual payment. Following Nūr al-Dīn's death in mid-1174, Saladin would free these same hostages, who were being held at Homs, in order to buy Raymond's neutrality in his war against the Zankid loyalists in North Syria.[254]

There is cause to doubt William's estimate of 80,000 *dīnārs* on the grounds that the sum paid seems to have been rather higher than this. Arab Muslim accounts set the sum as high as 150,000 'Tyrian' or 'Syrian' bezants together with the release of 1,000 Muslim prisoners held by the Christians.[255] 150,000 *dīnārs* is suspiciously identical with the purported ransoms for other Franks, including Baldwin of Ibelin in 1179, so this sum may reflect a literary *topos* rather than the actual amount paid.[256] Nevertheless, other evidence indicates that Raymond's release cost more than 80,000 gold pieces. On 21 August 1198, over twenty years after Raymond's release, his cousin and successor Bohemond III of Antioch issued a document revealing that Tripoli's treasury still owed the Hospital 37,000 bezants, which were to be repaid at a gradual rate of a thousand per year.[257]

Bohemond's charter permits at least three important observations regarding Raymond's ransom. Firstly, the count had relied upon Hospitaller finances, rather than Tripoli's own, which reveals again how indispensable this wealthy religious order had become to the counts. Indeed, Count Raymond himself acknowledged and rewarded the Hospitallers' financial assistance in this respect by giving them new liberties within the county in December 1174, only a matter of months after his eventual release.[258] Friedman has argued that the paying of ransoms became one of the many functions performed by the military orders in the Latin East, whereas in Iberia dedicated 'redemptionist' religious orders developed exclusively to meet this particular need.[259] Secondly, and assuming that Bohemond's schedule of repayments was followed, the debt was not settled fully until 1235, more than sixty years after Raymond's release and almost fifty after his death. Thirdly, if the outstanding amount of 37,000 bezants – not to mention whatever the counts had already been able to pay back to the Hospitallers *before* 1198 – is added to the *c.*60,000 written off by Saladin in 1174, then the total sum demanded for Raymond's release must have been at least 97,000 bezants. This is far in excess of William of Tyre's approximate figure of 80,000. The waters are muddied still further by William's related claim that King Amalric raised an unknown amount towards paying the count's ransom from his own nobles and clergy.[260] Friedman concludes that this – like the king's payment of other ransoms – was 'an instance of royal largesse', which perhaps signalled the Latin adoption of a custom common among eastern potentates rather than any instituted legal obligation upon the king to pay for the release of a 'vassal'.[261] The king's generosity in addition to the Hospital's charity certainly makes Ibn al-Athīr's estimate of 150,000 *dīnārs* seem less outlandish.

It is safe to assume that Raymond's ransom was exceedingly large. It thus comes as a surprise to learn that the amount demanded of the count was not necessarily beyond his means, as Richard assumed.[262] According to Abū Shāma, Raymond had asked Nūr al-Dīn to release him many times during his captivity. Money was reportedly not an issue, as the count had offered huge ransoms to no avail.[263] The reasons why Nūr al-Dīn initially opposed Raymond's release only to change his mind and free him when he did are today obscure. Arabic accounts that differ from Ibn al-Athīr's demonstrably flawed chronology do not help much in this respect. According to Abū Shāma, Nūr al-Dīn released Raymond because one of his high-ranking followers, Fakhr al-Dīn Masʿūd bin al-Zaʿfarānī, encouraged him to do so. No explanation was given for why Ibn al-Zaʿfarānī pushed for Raymond's release in the first place or why Nūr al-Dīn finally agreed to something he had resisted for so long.[264]

The most credible theory revolves around the internal politics of the Muslim world. At the time Raymond was released, Nūr al-Dīn was growing ever the more suspicious of his former servant Saladin, who had effectively been ruling Egypt semi-autonomously since 1169, abolishing the Fāṭimid caliphate in favour of the Sunnī ʿAbbāsids in 1171. A joint campaign waged by Nūr al-Dīn and Saladin against the kingdom of Jerusalem in autumn 1171 had underscored the growing gulf between the Zankid sultan in Syria and the precocious rogue in Egypt, as the latter had refused to meet his old suzerain in person at all during this war. Upon the moment of his sudden death in May 1174, Nūr al-Dīn was even preparing to attack Saladin.[265] Perhaps some of Nūr al-Dīn's advisors, Ibn al-Zaʿfarānī included, were wondering if it might be best to preserve the weakened crusader states as a buffer against Egypt, at least until Saladin was crushed. Releasing Raymond would have freed King Amalric from his obligations in the county of Tripoli, allowing him to focus more upon defending his southern frontier against Saladin and even upon pursuing yet another invasion of Egypt. This interpretation would partly explain Ibn al-Athīr's confused story that the Zankid eunuch Saʿd al-Dīn Kumushtakīn released Raymond to thwart Saladin's ambitions in Syria. Certainly one of the reasons Nūr al-Dīn had released Bohemond of Antioch back in 1165 had been to fill the power vacuum in North Syria with somebody other and *weaker* than the Byzantine emperor Manuel Komnenos.[266] There was thus precedent for Nūr al-Dīn's having freed rivals in order to prevent greater threats emerging. Indeed, this sort of reasoning is at the heart of what Köhler has identified as the 'no place doctrine': a policy followed fairly consistently by Frankish and Muslim rulers alike in the twelfth century, aimed at keeping Syria fragmented and thereby preventing the emergence of large power blocs.[267]

Upon his release Raymond was welcomed home by King Amalric, who showered the count with gifts.[268] Raymond was one of the greatest barons in the Latin East so this was wholly appropriate. As Ibn al-Athīr later put it, 'the Franks gathered to celebrate his safe return, for he was great among them, one of their prime devils'.[269] William of Tyre made special note that Amalric returned to Raymond the county of Tripoli 'without difficulty'.[270] Friedman thinks this phrasing implies that the king of Jerusalem was not necessarily obligated by law to return his vassals' fiefs but nonetheless did so on this particular occasion out of obedience to custom.[271] Setting aside the fine distinction between instituted law and non-instituted custom, not to mention the count of Tripoli's dubious 'feudal' status at this time, it is of course hard to see how the king could have raised objections in 1174 or would have wanted to, given that the county was rightfully Raymond's and had offered the king little enough benefit to compensate for the burdensome responsibilities it had given. After all, Amalric was famously fond of delegating his duties.[272] Yet again a king of Jerusalem had chosen to consolidate his rule in the kingdom proper rather than seek a restoration of direct rule over Tripoli.

Amalric gave Raymond more than his county and his freedom. According to Ernoul, King Amalric arranged for Raymond to marry Eschiva of Tiberias, heiress of the principality of Galilee, soon after the death of her first husband, Walter of Saint-Omer. Historians have hitherto neglected this passage, yet the author wrote clearly that 'when the lord of Tiberias died, the king gave the lady of Tiberias to the count of Tripoli'.[273] No doubt Amalric felt some responsibility for his bachelor cousin and recognised that Eschiva and Raymond made an ideal match, with the recently widowed princess of Galilee and the long-interred count of Tripoli being two of the most eligible figures in the whole Latin East. The precise dating of the marriage is unclear but it obviously happened sometime after Walter of Saint-Omer's death around early 1174, when Eschiva made a donation to the Hospital in his memory,[274] and before the death of King Amalric himself on 11 July. For Raymond it was a happy coincidence that he had won his freedom around the same time the prince of Galilee died. With his marriage to Eschiva, Raymond's life would become all the more oriented towards Jerusalem, where his interrupted political career was to reach new heights yet also sink to unprecedented depths.

Conclusion

Raymond was a man of two halves. His quarrelsome parents, Raymond II of Tripoli and Hodierna of Jerusalem, exerted somewhat contradictory influences upon his status, expectations, predilections and career path. It was his father's title he inherited, along with the bustling port of Tripoli and what remained in comital possession of the county as a whole, eroded as it was by Muslim reconquest and gifts to the military orders. Tripolitan matters thus consumed much of Raymond's life prior to his captivity. However, fate had ensured that Raymond's father, whom he surely remembered only as a shade of his childhood, would cease to be an active force early in his life. With Raymond II's death, his son was left as the only man in his immediate family – a position of significant responsibility in a patriarchal society like the Latin East. Raymond had barely turned twenty when he found himself looking out for his sickly little sister Melisende, who was to be married to no less a figure than Emperor Manuel Komnenos. In this first and arguably greatest test of Raymond's ability to fulfil the role of *pater familias*, the count and his family were humiliated – his sister spurned and their mother accused of adultery. This miserable outcome was in no way Raymond's own fault and rather the result of opaque Byzantine foreign policy. Raymond's vengeful yet futile assault on the innocent of Cyprus revealed the petulance of youth and was reminiscent also of his father's own act of misguided revenge for *his* father's death in 1137, inflicted upon Lebanese peasants.

Fortunately for Raymond, his mother Hodierna was more than capable of navigating the choppy seas of Frankish high society in the absence of his father. Indeed it was to be his mother and her Jerusalemite family, rather than his late father, who were to shape the young count beyond the age of twelve. Consequently he always looked south to the court of Jerusalem where his mother had flourished as a young woman, where she had returned during and after her unhappy marriage to Raymond's father, and where Raymond himself spent a number of years training to be a knight with his royal cousin, Baldwin III, after his father's brutal assassination in 1152. Raymond never restricted his ambitions to the county of Tripoli alone, as his father and namesake seems to have done, nor focused unduly upon the principality of Antioch, as his grandfather Pons had done. Raymond's captivity only strengthened his connections to the court of Jerusalem at the same time that it distanced him from events in Tripoli. This was largely because he appointed his first cousin, King Baldwin's brother and successor Amalric, as his regent and, although the king's many other duties and distractions often placed the county in greater danger than necessary, the whole affair ensured that Raymond would be all the more indebted to the king and thus aligned towards Jerusalem in future.

Raymond's modern biographer Marshall Baldwin wrote that the count's release in 1174 'closes the early period of [his] life'.[275] It is hard to disagree with this broad verdict and 1174 remains here the most appropriate point at which to divide Raymond's career. Yet the danger apparent is threefold: that the independent significance of the first phase of his life, which was spent predominantly in Tripoli, is neglected; that chronological continuity from the count's birth to his death is obscured; and that the opportunity to take a holistic approach to Raymond's life is ignored in favour of splitting analysis between Tripolitan affairs on the one hand and Jerusalemite matters, which became ever more important to Raymond from 1174, on the other. Together, such methodological oversights prevent a fuller understanding of how Raymond, the county of Tripoli and indeed the whole Latin East were shaped by the unique opportunities and pressures of the

Levant in the second half of the twelfth century. It is in light of this that the preceding conclusions must be read, as leading into and qualified by those in the chapter that now follows.

Notes

1 See Chapter 5.
2 Baldwin, *Raymond III* (1936), p. vii.
3 Pour les mésaventures de Raymond III, candidat au trône de Jérusalem, nous nous sommes contenté de renvoyer à l'ouvrage de M. Baldwin, *Raymond III of Tripolis*. Richard, *Le comté*, p. ii.
4 See Chapter 2.
5 For the exact dating of the council and thus Raymond's death, see: Mayer, 'Studies', pp. 159–60.
6 WT, vol. 2, p. 787.
7 Baldwin, *Raymond III* (1936), p. 9; Richard, *Le comté*, p. 47 and n. 3.
8 See Chapter 2.
9 Mayer, 'Studies', pp. 100–2, 113–15.
10 Sylvia Schein, 'Women in Medieval Colonial Society: The Latin Kingdom of Jerusalem in the Twelfth Century', in *Gendering the Crusades*, ed. Susan B. Edgington and Sarah Lambert (Cardiff, 2001), pp. 146–7.
11 Shulamith Shahar, *The Fourth Estate: A History of Women in the Middle Ages*, revised ed., trans. Chaya Galai (London, 2003), p. 96.
12 Femineo relicte moderamini. WT, vol. 2, p. 780.
13 *CGOH*, vol. 1, no. 871.
14 Helen Nicholson, '"La Damoisele del chastel": Women's Role in the Defence and Functioning of Castles in Medieval Writing from the Twelfth to the Fourteenth Centuries', in *Crusader Landscapes in the Medieval Levant: The Archaeology and History of the Latin East. A Festschrift in Honour of Denys Pringle*, ed. Micaela Sinibaldi, Kevin James Lewis, Jennifer Thompson and Balázs Major (forthcoming).
15 Richard, 'Porcellet', no. 1.
16 Hodierna Tripolis comitissa. *D.Jerus.*, vol. 1, no. 141; *CCSSJ*, no. 32; *RRH*, no. 179.
17 Magistro atque provisori comitatus meique filii [. . .] usque [. . .] ad etatem militie. *CGOH*, vol. 1, no. 144; *RRH*, no. 212.
18 Magistri comitis. *CGOH*, vol. 2, no. VII; *RRH*, no. 191; Richard, *Le comté*, pp. 47–8. Cf. *CCSSJ*, no. 82; *RRH*, no. 193.
19 *D.Jerus.*, vol. 1, no. †227; *RRH*, no. 276; W. Heyd, *Histoire du Commerce du Levant au Moyen-Âge*, 2 vols (Leipzig, 1885–6), vol. 1, 147 n. 1.
20 Baldwin, *Raymond III* (1936), p. 9.
21 Riley-Smith, 'The Templars', pp. 278–88. See Chapter 3.
22 Richard, *Le comté*, p. 35.
23 Baldwin, *Raymond III* (1936), p. 9.
24 WT, vol. 2, pp. 832–3; IQ, pp. 338–9.
25 IQ, p. 338; Stevenson, *Crusaders*, pp. 176–7.
26 IA, vol. 11, p. 218.
27 Benjamin of Tudela, p. 77.
28 Nāṣir Khusraw, p. 13.
29 Strabo, *The Geography of Strabo*, ed. and trans. Horace Leonard Jones, 8 vols (London, 1912–32), vol. 7, pp. 268–9.
30 IQ, pp. 334–6, 337, 343, 344–5, 346, 348.
31 WT, vol. 2, pp. 834–5; Phillips, *Defenders*, p. 274.
32 IQ, p. 348.
33 IQ, pp. 348–9; IA, vol. 11, 218.

34 WT, vol. 2, p. 835.
35 Richard, *Le comté*, p. 65 n. 2. See Chapter 2. But cf. Grousset, *Histoire*, vol. 2, p. 65.
36 Richard, *Le comté*, p. 18; Phillips, *Defenders*, pp. 277–8.
37 WT, vol. 2, p. 835.
38 *CGOH*, vol. 1, no. 519; *RRH*, no. 549. See also: *CGOH*, vol. 1, no. 549; *RRH Add.*, no. 562a.
39 WT, vol. 2, pp. 835–6. Cf. IQ, p. 355.
40 See Chapter 1.
41 See Chapter 2.
42 WT, vol. 2, pp. 836–7.
43 IQ, p. 338.
44 WT, vol. 2, pp. 837–40.
45 Princeps Rainaldus [. . .] dicens urbem illam cum suis pertinentiis ab initio hereditatis Antiocheni principis portionem esse ideoque oportere ut quicumque eam possideat, Antiocheno principi fidelitatem exhibeat. WT, vol. 2, p. 837.
46 Phillips, *Defenders*, p. 280. See Chapter 2.
47 See Chapter 1.
48 WT, vol. 2, p. 840.
49 Bernard of Clairvaux, *Epistolae*, vol. 1, nos 4, 5, pp. 24–7, 28–9.
50 Bernard of Clairvaux, *Epistolae*, vol. 2, no. 253, pp. 149–50.
51 James France, *The Cistercians in Medieval Art* (Stroud, 1998); Bernard Hamilton, 'The Impact of Crusader Jerusalem on Western Christendom', *CHR* 80.4 (1994), pp. 695–6.
52 See Chapter 2.
53 Enlart, 'L'abbaye cistercienne', pp. 4, 9; Breycha-Vauthier, 'Deir Balamand', p. 15. Cf. D. H. Williams, 'Cistercian Settlement in the Lebanon', *Cîteaux: commentarii cistercienses* 25 (1974), pp. 63–4.
54 Richard, 'Affrontement ou confrontation?' p. 23 n. 12.
55 Hamilton, *Latin Church*, pp. 166–9.
56 Orderic Vitalis, *Historia*, vol. 5, p. 278.
57 Constance Hoffman Berman, *The Cistercian Evolution: The Invention of a Religious Order in Twelfth-Century Europe* (Philadelphia, 2000). But cf. Chrysogonus Waddell, 'The Myth of Cistercian Origins: C. H. Berman and the Manuscript Sources', *Cîteaux* 51 (2000), pp. 319–86.
58 Jean Richard, 'L'abbaye cistercienne de Jubin et le prieuré Saint-Blaise de Nicosie', *Epeteris tou Kentrou Epistemonikon Ereunon* 3 (1969–70), pp. 63–7; Bernard Hamilton, 'The Cistercians in the Crusader States', in *One yet Two: Monastic Tradition East and West*, ed. M. Basil Pennington, Cistercian Studies 29 (Kalamazoo, 1976), pp. 408–9.
59 Quod respuisset Bernardus, Cistercium in Oriente propagaturos. *Cisterciensium, seu verius ecclesiasticorum Annalium a condito Cistercio*, ed. Angelo Manrique, 4 vols (Lyon, 1642–9), vol. 2, p. 302. The annalist also included the morsel that Belmont was known as Beaufont (*Bellus-fons*) in some registers.
60 'Chronique de Terre Sainte', in *Les gestes des Chiprois: Recueil de chroniques françaises écrites en Orient aux XIIIe & XIVe siècles (Philippe de Navarre & Gérard de Monréal)*, ed. Gaston Raynaud (Geneva, 1887), p. 7; Enlart, 'L'abbaye cistercienne', p. 1; Breycha-Vauthier, 'Deir Balamand', p. 8. Cf. Williams, 'Cistercian Settlement', p. 62.
61 Enlart, 'L'abbaye cistercienne', p. 4.
62 Un témoin précieux de l'art cistercien colonial. Enlart, 'L'abbaye cistercienne', pp. 2–20, 22.
63 Breycha-Vauthier, 'Deir Balamand', p. 16; Williams, 'Cistercian Settlement', p. 66.
64 Anis Chaaya, 'Observations sur l'abbaye de Belmond (monastère de Balamand) à partir des archives photographiques de la DGA', *Bulletin d'Archéologie et d'Architecture Libanaises* 14 (2010), pp. 394–5.

65 James France, *Separate but Equal: Cistercian Lay Brothers, 1120–1350*, Cistercian Studies 246 (Collegeville, MN, 2012).
66 Souad Slim, 'L'abbaye de Belmont: prototype cistercien et tête de pont des croisades', in *De Toulouse à Tripoli*, ed. Weber *et al.*, p. 266.
67 Hamilton, 'Cistercians', p. 410.
68 Bernard Hamilton, 'Ideals of Holiness: Crusaders, Contemplatives, and Mendicants', *The International History Review* 17.4 (1995), p. 700; Richard, 'Affrontement ou confrontation?' p. 23; Jidejian, *Tripoli*, p. 60.
69 Henry Maundrell, *A Journey from Aleppo to Jerusalem in 1697* (Beirut, 1963), pp. 35–6.
70 Hamilton, 'Cistercians', p. 406.
71 Breycha-Vauthier, 'Deir Balamand', p. 8; Slim, 'L'abbaye de Belmont', pp. 260–1.
72 Pringle, *Churches*, vol. 1, no. 9, pp. 47–51; Hamilton, 'Cistercians', pp. 405–7. Cf. Richard, *Le comté*, p. 61.
73 Hamilton, *Latin Church*, p. 102; Pringle, *Churches*, vol. 1, no. 8, pp. 38–47. Cf. Richard, *Le comté*, p. 61; Breycha-Vauthier, 'Deir Balamand', p. 8.
74 Leopold Janauschek, *Originum Cisterciensium: Tomus I* (Vienna, 1877), no. 482, p. 188; Hamilton, 'Cistercians', p. 407.
75 Breycha-Vauthier, 'Deir Balamand', p. 14; Williams, 'Cistercian Settlement', pp. 67–8.
76 Constance H. Berman, 'Were There Twelfth-Century Cistercian Nuns?' *Church History* 68.4 (1999), pp. 824–64.
77 Breycha-Vauthier, 'Deir Balamand', p. 14; Williams, 'Cistercian Settlement', p. 68.
78 Ernest Petit, 'Chartes de l'abbaye cistercienne de Saint-Serge de Giblet', *Mémoires de la société nationale des antiquaires de France*, 5th series, 8 (1887), pp. 20–2, 23–9; *RRH*, no. 1028, 1044, 1082; Hamilton, 'Cistercians', pp. 414–15; Breycha-Vauthier, 'Deir Balamand', p. 13.
79 *CCSSJ*, no. 84; *RRH*, no. 161.
80 Lucy-Anne Hunt, 'A Woman's Prayer to St. Sergios in Latin Syria: Interpreting a Thirteenth-Century Icon at Mount Sinai', in her *Byzantium, Eastern Christendom and Islam: Art at the Crossroads of the Medieval Mediterranean*, vol. 2 (London, 2000), pp. 78–126.
81 Williams, 'Cistercian Settlement', pp. 70–1; Breycha-Vauthier, 'Deir Balamand', p. 14.
82 L. de Mas Latrie, *Histoire de l'île de Chypre sous le règnes des princes de la maison de Lusignan*, 3 vols (Paris, 1852–61), vol. 3, pp. 662–8; *RRH*, no. 1444; Breycha-Vauthier, 'Deir Balamand', pp. 14, 18 n. 2, pl. II:1.
83 Enlart, 'L'abbaye cistercienne', pp. 1–2; Breycha-Vauthier, 'Deir Balamand', p. 14; Asmar, *L'Abbaye de Belmont*, p. 14.
84 IQ, p. 356.
85 WT, vol. 2, pp. 848–9; John Kinnamos, *Deeds*, p. 143; *Anonymi Auctoris Chronicon*, vol. 2, p. 119. Cf. IQ, p. 358. See Chapter 3.
86 WT, vol. 2, p. 852.
87 Mack, *Merchant*, pp. 115–16
88 David Abulafia, 'Marie-Luise Favreau-Lilie, *Die Italiener im Heiligen Land vom Ersten Kreuzzug bis zum Tode Heinrichs von Champagne (1098–1197)*', *Speculum* 67.1 (1992), p. 142; Mack, *Merchant*, p. 127. Cf. Favreau-Lilie, *Die Italianer*, *passim.*
89 Mack, *Merchant*, pp. 126–7, 131–2, 142–3.
90 Benjamin of Tudela, p. 77.
91 WT, vol. 2, pp. 852–4.
92 WT, vol. 2, p. 852. The chronology here follows: Mayer, *Varia*, pp. 45–54.
93 WT, vol. 2, pp. 854–5.
94 See Chapter 2.

95 WT, vol. 2, pp. 855–6; John Kinnamos, *Deeds*, p. 158; Paul Magdalino, *The Empire of Manuel I Komnenos, 1143–1180* (Cambridge, 1993), p. 72; Ferdinand Chalandon, *Les Comnène: Etudes sur l'Empire Byzantin, II: Jean II Comnène (1118–1143) et Manuel I Comnène (1143–1180)* (Paris, 1912), pp. 216 n. 7, 240, 461–2, 517, 567, 649 n. 4.
96 WT, vol. 2, pp. 856–7.
97 Richard, *Le comté*, p. 54. See Chapter 1.
98 Pryor, *Geography*, pp. 113–25.
99 Pryor, *Geography*, p. 123; David Abulafia, *The Great Sea: A Human History of the Mediterranean* (London, 2011), p. 293.
100 Propter gentilium insidias. Theoderich, 'Descriptio', p. 146.
101 Marvin W. Mikesell, 'The Deforestation of Mount Lebanon', *The Geographical Review* 59.1 (1969), pp. 23–4.
102 Future Constantinopolitane sedis imperatricis. *D.Jerus.*, vol. 1, no. 263; *RRH*, no. 366.
103 Richard, *Le comté*, p. 37.
104 WT, vol. 2, pp. 850–1, 858.
105 WT, vol. 2, p. 857.
106 Pro iusta causa. WT, vol. 2, pp. 858–9.
107 John Kinnamos, *Deeds*, pp. 136–7; WT, vol. 2, pp. 823–5; Michael the Syrian, 'Chronique', ed. and trans. J.-B. Chabot, 4 vols (Paris, 1899–1910), vol. 3, p. 315; Sempad the Constable, 'Chronique du Royaume de la Petite Arménie', *RHC Ar*, vol. 1, p. 621.
108 WT, vol. 2, p. 859.
109 WT, vol. 2, p. 857.
110 John Kinnamos, *Deeds*, p. 159.
111 Richard, *Le comté*, p. 8.
112 Steven Runciman, *A History of the Crusades, Volume II: The Kingdom of Jerusalem and the Frankish East, 1100–1187* (Cambridge, 1957), pp. 332, 359. See Chapter 3.
113 Melissent, qui morut enfant. *Lignages*, p. 96.
114 Magdalino, *The Empire*, p. 72.
115 La Monte, 'To What Extent', pp. 258–61; Lilie, *Byzantium*, pp. 175, 186.
116 Magdalino, *The Empire*, p. 72.
117 Runciman, *History*, vol. 2, p. 359.
118 Mayer, *Varia*, p. 53. Cf. Chalandon, *Les Comnène*, vol. 2, p. 517 n. 1; Lilie, *Byzantium*, p. 184 n. 176.
119 Lilie, *Byzantium*, pp. 185, 188.
120 La Monte, 'To What Extent', p. 261.
121 Lilie, *Byzantium*, p. 190; Hamilton, *Leper King*, p. 102; Phillips, *Defenders*, pp. 227–8, 235.
122 Qātalū muḥtasabīn fī za'm-him. IA, vol. 11, p. 295.
123 IA, vol. 11, 294–5; WT, vol. 2, pp. 873–4; Richard, *Le comté*, p. 30.
124 IA, vol. 11, p. 296.
125 Richard, *Le comté*, p. 30; Augé, 'Les Comnènes', pp. 148–52.
126 *CGOH*, vol. 1, no. 160; *RRH*, no. 236.
127 *CGOH*, vol. 1, no. 405; *RRH Add.*, no. 472a.
128 WT, vol. 2, p. 859.
129 Dorothea Weltecke, 'The Syriac Orthodox in the Principality during the Crusader Period', in *East and West: Antioch*, vol. 1, pp. 120–2. See also: Juliette Rāsī, "Kullīyat al-ṭibb' fī ṭarābulus 'alā 'ahd al-ṣalībiyyīn [The 'college of medicine' in Tripoli during the time of the crusaders]', *Chronos* 11 (2005), pp. 185–201.
130 Usāma, pp. 132–3.
131 WT, vol. 2, pp. 859–60; Mayer, *Varia*, p. 54.

132 WT, vol. 2, p. 874.
133 IA, vol. 11, pp. 301–2.
134 WT, vol. 2, p. 874.
135 More victimarum. WT, vol. 2, pp. 874–5.
136 IA, vol. 11, p. 303.
137 Baldwin, *Raymond III* (1936), p. 11.
138 Ibn al-Athīr, *Al-tārīkh al-bāhir*, p. 125; Ibn Wāṣil, *Mufarrij al-kurūb fī akhbār Banī Ayyūb*, ed. Jamāl al-Dīn al-Shayyāl *et al.*, 5 vols (Cairo, 1953–77), vol. 1, 145; WT, vol. 2, p. 875; John Kinnamos, *Deeds*, p. 164.
139 Baldwin, *Raymond III* (1936), p. 12.
140 Vinculis tanquam vilia mancipia miserabiliter alligantur et Halapiam traducti spectaculum facti sunt populis infidelibus et carceribus mancipati. WT, vol. 2, p. 875.
141 In mendicitate et ferro. WT, vol. 2, p. 952.
142 Yvonne Friedman, *Encounter Between Enemies: Captivity and Ransom in the Latin Kingdom of Jerusalem*, Cultures, Beliefs and Traditions: Medieval and Early Modern Peoples 10 (Leiden, 2002), pp. 216–17.
143 Naturali mentis vivacitate. WT, vol. 2, p. 967.
144 BD, p. 77; IA, vol. 11, p. 526.
145 Runciman, *History*, vol. 2, p. 405; Friedman, *Encounter*, p. 118. Cf. Kevin Lewis, 'Medieval Diglossia', p. 133.
146 WT, vol. 2, p. 967; Clanchy, *From Memory*, pp. 233–6.
147 Tripolitanum comitatum procurans. *D.Jerus.*, vol. 2, no. 346; *CGOH*, vol. 1, no. 411; *RRH*, no. 477.
148 See Chapter 3.
149 Richard, *Le comté*, pp. 33–4, 47. Cf. Friedman, *Encounter*, p. 81.
150 WT, vol. 2, p. 963.
151 La Monte, *Feudal Monarchy*, pp. 188, 197; Marshall Whithed Baldwin, 'The Latin States under Baldwin III and Amalric I, 1143–1174', in *A History of the Crusades*, ed. Setton, vol. 1, p. 529.
152 WT, vol. 2, p. 963.
153 Si Tripolitanus comitatus michi meisque heredibus hereditarie remanserit habendus. *D.Jerus.*, vol. 2, no. 346.
154 *D.Jerus.*, vol. 2, no. 337; *RRH*, no. 453. For Raymond's original donation, see: *RRH*, no. 380.
155 *D.Jerus.*, vol. 2, no. 349; *CCSSJ*, no. 156; *RRH*, no. 488.
156 Ex baronibus terrę Ierusalem. *D.Jerus.*, vol. 2, no. 346; *CGOH*, vol. 1, no. 411; *RRH*, no. 477.
157 La Monte, 'To what extent', p. 261; Lilie, *Byzantium*, pp. 208–9.
158 Andrew Jotischky, 'Manuel Comnenus and the Reunion of the Churches: the Evidence of the Conciliar Mosaics in the Church of the Nativity in Bethlehem', *Levant* 26 (1994), pp. 207–22.
159 WT, vol. 2, pp. 915–17. See also: Chalandon, *Les Comnène*, vol. 2, p. 536; Magdalino, *The Empire*, p. 222 n. 139.
160 WT, vol. 2, p. 878.
161 WT, vol. 2, pp. 865–6.
162 WT, vol. 2, p. 942.
163 Wilbrand of Oldenburg, p. 120.
164 Coupel, 'Trois petites églises', pp. 37–46; Jidejian, *Tripoli*, pp. 55–7, figs. 84–6.
165 Lilie, *Byzantium*, pp. 204–5.
166 Richard, *Le comté*, p. 74. See also: W. H. Rudt de Collenberg, 'Les « Raynouard », seigneurs de Nephin et de Maraclé en Terre Sainte, et leur parenté en Languedoc', *Cahiers de civilisation médiévale* 7 (1964), pp. 289–311.
167 Burchard of Mount Sion, pp. 27–8.

168 *CCSSJ*, nos 84, 85; *RRH*, nos 161, 218.
169 Lilie, *Byzantium*, pp. 198–200.
170 'Epistolae Regis Ludovici VII', *Recueil des historiens des Gaules et de la France*, 24 vols (Paris, 1738–1904), vol. 16, no. 244, 80.
171 IA, vol. 11, p. 322.
172 BD, p. 38. See also: Richard, *Le comté*, pp. 21–2.
173 IA, vol. 11, p. 327.
174 Richard, *Le comté*, p. 21.
175 Idhā mulikat [ʿarqa] mulikat ṭarābulus. Abū Shāma, *Kitāb al-rawḍatayn*, vol. 4, p. 8.
176 BD, p. 42; Abū Shāma, *Kitāb al-rawḍatayn*, vol. 2, p. 92; Stevenson, *Crusaders*, p. 198.
177 Richard, *Le comté*, p. 21 n. 4; *D.Jerus.*, vol. 2, no. 346; *CGOH*, vol. 1, no. 411; *RRH*, no. 477.
178 Ḥiṣn manbaʿ (corr. maniyaʿ) min bināʾ al-islām. Al-Dimashqī, *Nukhbat*, p. 208.
179 Richard, *Le comté*, p. 21 n. 4.
180 BD, pp. 41–42.
181 Lilie, *Byzantium*, p. 191; Augé, 'Les Comnènes', pp. 153–4.
182 Hamilton, *Latin Church*, pp. 45–6, 175–8; Cahen, *La Syrie*, pp. 167–8.
183 Hamilton, *Latin Church*, pp. 1–18, 172–81 and *passim*.
184 Although Gerard of Nazareth described his rival at Latakia as a '*Graecum episcopum*', it is likely that this term simply meant Orthodox, thus including the local Melkites, who spoke Arabic and used a Syriac liturgy rather than Greek, but nonetheless aligned themselves with the church of Constantinople.
185 Kedar, 'Gerard', pp. 61, 62–3, 77; Riley-Smith, 'The Templars', p. 288; *Codice diplomatico*, ed. Paoli, vol. 1, no. 39, p. 41; *RRH*, no. 381.
186 *CGOH*, vol. 1, no. 414; *RRH Add.*, no. 483a. Cf. Richard, *Le comté*, p. 41 n. 1.
187 *D.Jerus.*, vol. 2, nos 337, 346; *CGOH*, vol. 1, no. 411; *RRH*, nos 453, 477.
188 Cahen, *La Syrie*, 537–538. See Chapter 2.
189 Cahen, *La Syrie*, 382, 404, 541; Elisséeff, *Nūr ad-Dīn*, vol. 2, p. 551.
190 *CGOH*, vol. 1, no. 391; *RRH*, no. 428. Röhricht dated this to January 1167.
191 See Chapter 3.
192 Cahen, *La Syrie*, 432–433.
193 Quam cito liberaverit et aquitaverit eam a Reinaldo Masoerio et ab heredibus ejus. *CGOH*, vol. 1, no. 391.
194 Mayer, *Varia*, p. 180.
195 *CGOH*, vol. 1, nos 457, 623; *RRH*, nos 521, 612.
196 *CGOH*, vol. 2, no. 2249; *RRH Add.*, no. 1093b. See also: *CGOH*, vol. 2, nos 1579, 2223; *RRH*, no. 896; *RRH Add.*, no. 1088a; *Lignages*, pp. 118–19; de Briailles, 'Lignages', pp. 246–8; Burgtorf, 'Hospitaller Lordship', pp. 11–50.
197 *Lignages*, p. 118.
198 WT, vol. 2, pp. 934–5.
199 Abū Shāma, *Kitāb al-rawḍatayn*, vol. 2, p. 101; IA, vol. 11, p. 354.
200 Breycha-Vauthier, 'Deir Balamand', p. 15.
201 WT, vol. 2, p. 936.
202 J. Poirier *et al.*, 'Large Historical Earthquakes and Seismic Risk in Northwest Syria', *Nature*, 285 (1980), p. 218 and fig. 1; Gottfried Grünthal *et al.*, 'Compilation of the GSHAP Regional Seismic Hazard for Europe, Africa and the Middle East', *Annali di Geofisica* 42 (1999), fig. 2.
203 Hamilton, *Latin Church*, pp. 46, 176.
204 WT, vol. 2, p. 935.
205 Subitus et hactenus inauditus terre motus totam Tripolim funditus delevit et omnem fere in ea carnem suffocavit. Hans Eberhard Mayer, 'Das syrische Erdbeben von 1170. Ein unedierter Brief König Amalrichs von Jerusalem', *Deutsches Archiv für Erforschung des Mittelalters* 45 (1989), p. 484.

206 Mohamed Reda Sbeinati *et al.*, 'The Historical Earthquakes of Syria: An Analysis of Large and Moderate Earthquakes from 1365 B.C. to 1900 A.D.', *Annals of Geophysics* 48 (2005), pp. 371, 374 and fig. 9.
207 WT, vol. 2, p. 935; IA, vol. 11, pp. 354–5.
208 IA, vol. 11, p. 354.
209 Ab inimicis crucis Christi occupabuntur. Mayer, 'Das syrische Erdbeben', p. 484.
210 *D.Jerus.*, vol. 2, no. 346; *CGOH*, vol. 1, no. 411; *RRH*, no. 477; Richard, *Le comté*, pp. 64–5.
211 IA, vol. 11, pp. 373–4; BD, p. 45.
212 Hamilton, *Leper King*, p. 73.
213 WT, vol. 2, pp. 953–54.
214 Farhad Daftary, *The Assassin Legends: Myths of the Isma'ilis* (London, 1994), p. 68; Farhad Daftary, *The Ismāʿīlīs: Their History and Doctrines*, 2nd ed. (Cambridge, 2007), p. 369.
215 Walter Map, *De Nugis Curialium: Courtiers' Trifles*, ed. M. R. James, C. N. L. Brooke and R. A. B. Mynors (Oxford, 1983), p. 66.
216 F. Lundgreen, *Wilhelm von Tyrus und der Templerorden* (Berlin, 1911), p. 113.
217 Jerzy Hauziński, 'On Alleged Attempts at Converting the Assassins to Christianity in the Light of William of Tyre's Account', *Folia Orientalia* 15 (1974), pp. 240–4.
218 WT, vol. 2, p. 954.
219 'Chronique du Templier de Tyr', in *Les gestes des Chiprois*, ed. Raynaud, p. 162.
220 Concerning historicity, many scholars – mostly Mongol and Mamluk specialists – are sceptical. Peter Jackson, 'The Crisis in the Holy Land in 1260', *EHR* 95.376 (1980), p. 486; R. Amitai-Preiss, *Mongols and Mamluks: The Mamluk-Īlkhānid War, 1260–1281* (Cambridge, 1995), p. 31; Peter Thorau, *The Lion of Egypt: Sultan Baybars I and the Near East in the Thirteenth Century*, trans. P. M. Holt (London, 1992), pp. 68–9; Hans E. Mayer, *The Crusades*, trans. John Gillingham (Oxford, 1972), p. 276. Others, including most crusade historians, accept its validity. Prawer, *Histoire*, vol. 2, p. 426; Richard, *Royaume*, p. 305; David Morgan, *The Mongols*, 2nd edn (Oxford, 2007), p. 135; J. J. Saunders, *The History of the Mongol Conquests* (London, 1971), p. 113; Jaroslav Folda, 'The Figural Arts in Crusader Syria and Palestine, 1187–1291: Some New Realities', *DOP* 58 (2004), pp. 323–9.
221 Usāma, p. 140.
222 *Urkunden*, ed. Tafel and Thomas, vol. 2, no. 299, pp. 360, 385; Jonathan Riley-Smith, *Feudal Nobility*, p. 84; Riley-Smith, 'The survival', p. 13.
223 Hauziński, pp. 244–5.
224 Smarandache, 'Franks', pp. 222–3, 238–9.
225 Hamilton, *Leper King*, pp. 70, 74.
226 WT, vol. 2, p. 953.
227 John of Joinville, *Vie de saint Louis*, ed. Jacques Monfrin (Paris, 2010), p. 228; Smarandache, 'Franks', p. 235. Hamilton believes the Petrine book was somehow related to an obscure text known as the '*Kerygmata Petrou*'. Hamilton, 'Knowing', p. 377 n. 18.
228 David Thomas, 'Gospel, Muslim conception of', *The Encyclopaedia of Islam: Three* (Leiden, 2007–), 2014.4.
229 Qurān 3:52–3; 5:114–18; 61:14.
230 John of Joinville, *Vie*, p. 228.
231 Nasseh Ahmad Mirza, *Syrian Ismailism: The Ever Living Line of the Imamate, AD 1100–1260* (Richmond, 1997), pp. 52, 76–8; Charles E. Nowell, 'The Old Man of the Mountain', *Speculum* 22.4 (1947), p. 514; Hamilton, 'Knowing', p. 377.
232 Daftary, *Ismāʿīlīs*, 371–2.
233 Ad fidem Christi et baptisma convolarent. WT, vol. 2, p. 954.

234 Cf. Hamilton, 'Knowing', p. 380; Mallett, *Popular Muslim Reactions*, pp. 106–7.
235 See Chapter 1.
236 Plus quam mille iam baptizavit. William of Tripoli, *Notitia de Machometo; De statu Sarracenorum*, ed. Peter Engels (Würzburg, 1992), p. 370; Thomas F. O'Meara, 'The Theology and Times of William of Tripoli, O. P.: A Different View of Islam', *Theological Studies* 69 (2008), p. 96.
237 *CGOH*, vol. 2, no. 1131; *RRH*, no. 787.
238 William of Tyre, trans. Babcock and Krey, vol. 1, pp. 16, 63 n. 9; vol. 2, p. 324 n. 46; Baldwin, *Raymond* (1936), p. 161; Philip K. Hitti, *History of the Arabs from the Earliest Times to the Present*, 10th ed. (Basingstoke, 2002), p. 667; Edbury and Rowe, *William*, p. 23; Hussein M. Attiya, 'Knowledge of Arabic in the Crusader States in the Twelfth and Thirteenth centuries', *Journal of Medieval History* 25 (1999), pp. 205–6, 211.
239 Hannes Möhring, 'Zu der Geschichte der orientalischen Herrscher des Wilhelm von Tyrus: Die Frage der Quellenabhängigkeiten', *Mittelalteinisches Jahrbuch* 19 (1984), p. 174 and n. 7; WT, vol. 1, pp. 2–3; Kevin Lewis, 'Medieval Diglossia', pp. 133–4.
240 WT, vol. 2, pp. 954–5.
241 WT, vol. 2, p. 954.
242 Edbury and Rowe, *William*, pp. 123–8.
243 William Chester Jordan, *Unceasing Strife, Unending Fear: Jacques de Thérines and the Freedom of the Church in the Age of the Last Capetians* (Princeton, 2005).
244 WT, vol. 2, p. 955.
245 Hamilton, *Leper King*, p. 74.
246 See Chapter 1.
247 Michael O'Carroll, 'Islam', in his *Theotokos: A Theological Encyclopedia of the Blessed Virgin Mary* (Wilmington, 1982), pp. 192–3; Jane I. Smith and Yvonne Y. Haddad, 'The Virgin Mary in Islamic Tradition and Commentary', *The Muslim World* 79.3–4 (1989), pp. 162–84, 186–7; Kevin James Lewis, *Rule and Identity in a Diverse Mediterranean Society: Aspects of the County of Tripoli during the Twelfth Century* (Unpublished DPhil thesis: University of Oxford, 2014), pp. 300–1.
248 Benjamin Z. Kedar, 'Convergences of Oriental Christian, Muslim and Frankish worshippers: The Case of Saydnaya and the Knights Templar', in *The Crusades and the Military Orders: Expanding the Frontiers of Medieval Latin Christianity*, ed. Zsolt Hunyadi and József Laszlovszky (Budapest, 2001), pp. 95–7; Hamilton, 'Our Lady', p. 211. See also: Kevin James Lewis, 'Friend or Foe: Islamic Views of the Military Orders in the Latin East as Drawn from Arabic Sources', in *The Military Orders, 6.1: Culture and Conflict in the Mediterranean World*, ed. Jochen Schenk and Mike Carr (Abingdon, 2017), pp. 20–7.
249 WT, vol. 2, p. 952; IJ, p. 309.
250 *D.Jerus.*, vol. 2, no. 362; *CGOH*, vol. 1, no. 463; *RRH*, no. 514; William of Tyre, trans. Babcock and Krey, vol. 2, p. 390 n. 54; Baldwin, *Raymond III* (1936), p. 14 and n. 23; Richard, *Le comté*, pp. 56, 68, 72.
251 IA, vol. 11, p. 419. See Chapter 5.
252 See above under 'Freedom, orthodoxy and power in Antioch'.
253 Richard, *Le comté*, pp. 56–7.
254 WT, vol. 2, pp. 972–3. See Chapter 5.
255 IA, vol. 11, p. 419; Abū Shāma, *Kitāb al-rawḍatayn*, vol. 2, p. 229; Richard, *Le comté*, p. 56. The term *dhahab Ṣūrī/danānīr Ṣūriyya*, as employed by medieval Arabic authors, should probably be understood as a corruption of 'Syrian *dīnārs*', rather than '*dīnārs* of Tyre' as sometimes believed.
256 IA, vol. 11, p. 456.
257 *CGOH*, vol. 1, no. 1031; *RRH*, no. 742.

258 *CGOH*, vol. 1, no. 467; *RRH*, no. 519.
259 Friedman, *Encounter*, pp. 200–6.
260 WT, vol. 2, p. 952. Cf. Baldwin, *Raymond III* (1936), p. 15; Richard, *Le comté*, p. 72.
261 Friedman, *Encounter*, p. 83.
262 Cf. Richard, *Le comté*, pp. 56–7.
263 Abū Shāma, *Kitāb al-rawḍatayn*, vol. 2, p. 229.
264 Abū Shāma, *Kitāb al-rawḍatayn*, vol. 2, p. 229.
265 Malcolm Cameron Lyons and D. E. Jackson, *Saladin: The Politics of Holy War* (Cambridge, 1982), pp. 48–9, 68–9.
266 WT, vol. 2, p. 878; IA, vol. 11, pp. 303–4.
267 Köhler, *Alliances*, *passim*.
268 WT, vol. 2, p. 952.
269 Ijtamaʿa al-firanj ʿalay-hi yuhanniʾūna-hu bi-l-salāma, wa-kāna ʿaẓīman fī-hum min aʿyān shayāṭīn-him. IA, vol. 11, p. 419.
270 Sine difficultate. WT, vol. 2, p. 952.
271 Friedman, *Encounter*, p. 81.
272 WT, vol. 2, pp. 865–66.
273 Quant li sires de Tabarie fu mors, li rois donna le dame de Tabarie au conte de Triple. Ernoul, p. 32. See Chapter 5.
274 *CGOH*, vol. 1, no. 459; *RRH*, no. 522.
275 Baldwin, *Raymond III* (1936), p. 14.

5 The regent thwarted

Count Raymond III (1174–87)

Introduction

Upon his release from prison, Raymond's life changed dramatically. No longer incarcerated in Aleppo, he threw himself into political intrigue amid the highest echelons of Frankish society. Within mere months, Syria itself was transformed radically. In May 1174, the great Muslim general Nūr al-Dīn died, leaving as heir the eleven-year-old al-Ṣāliḥ Ismāʿīl al-Malik. The young al-Ṣāliḥ was soon surrounded by his late father's courtiers and former generals, not all of whom had the boy's best interests at heart. Nūr al-Dīn's less-than-loyal lieutenant in Egypt, Saladin, seized upon the instability of the Zankid regime at large to invade Syria, alleging that he did so to restore peace on behalf of al-Ṣāliḥ. In truth, he intended to shed his superficial allegiance to Nūr al-Dīn's heir at the earliest opportunity. Ever since ʿImād al-Dīn Zankī's campaigns in the 1120s and 1130s, the Zankids had been the major power arrayed against Frankish interests, albeit not without some opposition from rival Muslim groups and the Franks. With Nūr al-Dīn's death in mid-1174, the fledgling empire itself was reduced to civil war as Saladin vied for control and legitimacy with the remaining Zankid loyalists. One outcome of this was that the war against the Franks fell as a strategic priority of local Islamic leaders for approximately the next decade.[1]

The fragmentation of Islamic Syria in the past had allowed the armies of the First Crusade to divide and conquer the cities of the Levantine coastline, but in 1174 the Latins were unable to capitalise on the opportunity offered by the Zankid meltdown. In a remarkable coincidence, King Amalric died in July 1174, just two months after Nūr al-Dīn. Like Nūr al-Dīn, Amalric left only an underage son, Baldwin IV, as heir. Worse still, it was already becoming apparent that the boy king was sickly. Symptoms of the leprosy that would blight his body had probably been suspected, if not identified unequivocally, before his father's death. Regarded by many in the Middle Ages as an incurable and foul sickness tied to sin, the king's disease threatened to be an evil omen for the kingdom of Jerusalem.[2] Into this uncertainty strode Raymond of Tripoli, as much an opportunist as Saladin, although by no means as wise or capable. Saladin would enjoy unparalleled renown in posterity – ironically more so in the Christian West than the Islamic East.[3] Meanwhile, Raymond was fated to leave a disappointing, bitter legacy in Christendom and was all but forgotten by Muslims.

Given that contemporaries and historians alike have tended to judge Raymond by the impact he had on the kingdom of Jerusalem, it is all the more important to continue assessing him here as a man whose Tripolitan career was just as instrumental to his life as any of his activities in the south. If nothing else, this helps to avoid falling into the same trap of anachronism that captured many contemporary authors and modern historians, by focusing on what Hamilton calls 'the seeds of future Frankish weakness': judging the count's acts with the retrospective knowledge that the kingdom of Jerusalem did eventually fall, which by no means seemed inevitable at the time.[4]

The claim to regency

With King Amalric dead and succeeded by the underage Baldwin, the High Court of Jerusalem had to decide on the best course of action. Raymond of Tripoli, by then married to the princess of Galilee, was naturally entitled to take part in such discussions. In August 1174, Raymond travelled to Jerusalem to voice his opinion before his fellow barons at a time of growing dissatisfaction with the *de facto* regent, the kingdom's seneschal Miles of Plancy.[5] The count's preferred solution was simple, arguing that he himself should act as regent until Baldwin IV came of age. Raymond was able to present no fewer than three different quasi-legalistic reasons why he should be selected for such a position of responsibility and honour, recounted in detail by William of Tyre, who famously supported the count's candidacy in both this and a second regency a decade later.

Raymond's first justification was that he was the closest male relative to young King Baldwin, whose father had been the count's first cousin.[6] Certainly, proximity of blood carried a lot of weight. William of Tyre made sure to emphasise the count's royal blood, acquired both from his mother Hodierna of Jerusalem and from his grandmother Cecilia of France – the latter giving him an additional, albeit weak link to King Fulk of Jerusalem.[7] Nevertheless, Raymond clearly felt it necessary to give two further reasons to support his assumption of the regency. His second argument was that he was 'the wealthiest and most powerful of all the king's *fideles*'.[8] Perplexingly, William of Tyre chose not to specify whether Raymond viewed himself as the king's vassal as count of Tripoli or as prince of Galilee. Some have assumed the former, thus using this incident as proof that the county of Tripoli was still regarded as a 'vassal state' or barony of the kingdom of Jerusalem, even at this late stage.[9] Indeed, William of Tyre elsewhere noted that the pledge of fealty sworn by Count Bertrand of Tripoli to King

Baldwin I of Jerusalem back in 1109 was still valid in the days of Count Raymond III and King Baldwin IV.[10]

Whatever personal ties still bound the count to the king in theory, the county was no longer regarded as part of the kingdom in territorial terms, as William of Tyre's own description of the four discrete crusader 'principalities' at the Second Crusade unequivocally suggests. Within a decade of Raymond's attempt to claim the regency, a new tax – the so-called 'Saladin tithe' – was levied across the realm, which was defined as extending only as far north as Beirut.[11] With doubts thus hanging over the county's status vis-à-vis the kingdom, some historians have preferred to assume that Raymond III in 1174 claimed to be the king's vassal on the basis of his recent acquisition of the principality of Galilee through his marriage to Eschiva of Tiberias.[12] This would seem reasonable, but uncertainty lingered in the minds of many modern scholars because they were unable to find certain proof that Raymond was indeed married by August 1174.[13] William of Tyre indicated merely that the wedding took place 'in the same year that (Raymond) assumed the regency of the kingdom'.[14] Eschiva's earliest appearance as Raymond's wife in charter evidence is equally unhelpful, coming only in October 1177.[15] Riley-Smith seems confident that Raymond was married before he made his claim to the regency, but Hamilton and Barber believe the count was married only *after* this – even after he had actually taken office as regent in October or November.[16] Curiously, no historian seems to have noticed the vital piece of evidence preserved in the Chronicle of Ernoul, that King Amalric personally gave Raymond Eschiva's hand in marriage, so this must have happened before the king's death on 11 July 1174.[17] Thus, the count was married, or at least betrothed, to the widowed heiress of Galilee before he made his claim to the regency, removing any need to assume that Raymond viewed himself as the king's vassal because he was the count of Tripoli.

Returning to Raymond's threefold claim to the regency, his third argument was less legalistic still and more anecdotal. He reminded his audience that, during his own captivity in Aleppo, he had given Baldwin's father Amalric 'authority' (*dicio*) over the county of Tripoli 'in every way' (*omnimode*) and therefore should receive the same honour in return. When Raymond did eventually assume the regency, were the exact same terms once applied to King Amalric during his regency of the county of Tripoli now applied to the count himself? If so, this would have invited the possibility of Raymond's becoming king of Jerusalem. Back in 1164, the childless Raymond had supposedly appointed King Amalric as his 'heir' (*heredem*), with the king presumably inheriting the county fully had the count died in prison.[18] Raymond may well have thought the same conditions should apply to his regency in Jerusalem, should Baldwin IV meet a premature end. Indeed, many during the last years of the kingdom of Jerusalem suspected Raymond of wanting more than the regency, but the throne itself.[19] Mayer even suspects that the royal-blooded Raymond and his cousin Bohemond of Antioch may have been mooted as possible successors to Baldwin III back in 1163, when many of the barons of Jerusalem opposed Amalric's candidature on the grounds of an obscure marital irregularity.[20] If Raymond did seek the throne of Jerusalem as early as 1174, then the underage and – as might already have been apparent even to the count – sickly Baldwin IV may have seemed a promising opportunity to realise this particular ambition.

Riley-Smith observes that Raymond's triple claim to the regency in 1174 was elaborated by later jurists to form the basis of the kingdom of Jerusalem's written law of succession.[21] It is important to remember this when attempting to evaluate which of the claims was the stronger. Historians have favoured the first, kinship-based claim as the strongest, dismissing the second as 'irrelevant' and the third as 'an appeal to sentiment'.[22] Yet it is unlikely that people at the time – least of all Raymond – were as quick to dismiss the count's second and third claims outright. After all, William of Tyre saw fit to record all three and gave special attention to the supposedly sentimental third justification, which he described as 'very strong reasoning'.[23] Without written law, there seem to have been no clear guidelines on what actually constituted a 'strong' claim to the regency.

Many historians, not least Marshall Baldwin, fell for William of Tyre's preferential depiction of Raymond, by assuming that the count of Tripoli was the best candidate available to steer the kingdom at the time.[24] Not all of Jerusalem's courtiers in 1174 actually subscribed to this view. One might have thought that, if Raymond was such a desirable regent, he would have been appointed to the position almost immediately after he made his appeal in the aftermath of Amalric's death in July. Instead, it would be a number of months, during which time Raymond headed back to Tripoli. In the meantime, the controversial Miles of Plancy continued to oversee the kingdom's affairs, implying that Jerusalem's court was relatively content to accept his rule in the meantime, at least tacitly.[25] William of Tyre attempted to explain the barons' delay in as innocuous a way as possible, by noting that it took time to summon them all together to make their decision.[26] This is unconvincing, not least because Raymond himself managed to return all the way to Tripoli before the decision was finally announced, making this a longer trip than that taken by any other member of Jerusalem's High Court.

Miles of Plancy was murdered in October, although William of Tyre remained silent regarding the culprit.[27] Some at the time pointed the finger of blame at Walter III of Brisebarre, formerly lord of Beirut, and his brother Guy.[28] Smail, however, noted with suspicion that Raymond of Tripoli benefited most from Miles's death.[29] If the count did have a hand in this assassination, it would follow something of a family tradition. Raymond's great-grandfather Bertrand of Tripoli had reaped the rewards after the mysterious death of William Jordan in 1109, while his parents had gone to extreme lengths to rid themselves of Bertrand (II) in 1148.[30]

Even with Miles conveniently dispatched and Raymond invited back to Jerusalem at the end of October, it took a further two days of deliberation after the count's arrival before he was finally invested as regent.[31] The consistent prevarication of the Jerusalemite nobility suggests strongly that Raymond was not a universally popular choice, perhaps supported only by a minority of the barons. William of Tyre listed Raymond's principal advocates in 1174 as follows: the royal constable Humphrey II of Toron, Baldwin of Ramla and his brother Balian of Ibelin, Raynald of Sidon and all the bishops – presumably including William himself, as yet a mere archdeacon.[32] Beyond these, however, Raymond likely faced staunch opposition, or else lukewarm ambivalence.

Friends, factions and land

It was once common for historians to explain the political bickering that contributed to the eventual fall of the kingdom of Jerusalem in 1187 by reference to two distinct and identifiable factions within the realm's nobility, which supposedly coalesced in the 1170s and 1180s. Broadly speaking, the groups were defined against each other by two interlinked factors: where their members originated and whether they preferred a bellicose or pacific approach to the kingdom's Muslim neighbours, especially Saladin. Those who were 'native' to Syria – that is to say, the descendants of those Latin Christians who had settled in the east after the First Crusade – were said to favour peaceful policies, such as truces and alliances with local Islamic powers. Those who were not part of this native Frankish aristocracy – that is, first-generation European immigrants – were believed to be zealously intolerant of Muslims and quicker to provoke war. The natives were led by Count Raymond III of Tripoli, while their rivals were a motley bunch of bitter conspirators and incompetents – collectively dubbed the 'court party' – including Raynald of Châtillon, Guy of Lusignan, Patriarch Heraclius of Jerusalem (r. 1180–*c.*1190), Baldwin IV's mother Agnes of Courtenay and her brother Count Joscelin III of Edessa.[33]

Contemporary sources do indicate such stereotyped groups in the general sense. At some point in the twelfth century, Latin Christians living in Europe had taken to calling the 'native' Franks of Syria by the sobriquet *pullani*, which most likely originated as neutral nickname for the offspring of crusaders – literally, the 'colts' – but mutated into a term carrying pejorative connotations, especially after the Second Crusade faltered at Damascus in 1148 when the local Franks chose to do a deal with the city's Muslim inhabitants.[34] The modern historians most responsible for promoting the factionalist interpretation, namely Marshall Baldwin and Steven Runciman, were just as inclined to make value judgements as their medieval predecessors, although they generally sided with the dovish *pullani* and criticised the supposedly unnecessary, even counterproductive warmongering of the newcomers.

More recent historians have questioned the 'orthodoxy' of the traditional factional view, mainly because the theory simply does not withstand close inspection.[35] Like all generalising stereotypes, the dichotomy of native-newcomer is rather too simplistic and reductive an explanation and more often than not a gross distortion of what was a complex historical situation. Hamilton for one has questioned whether the *pullani*'s supposed policy of appeasing Saladin was even wise in light of the sultan's actual deeds in life, as opposed to the praise he garnered in the west posthumously. It is uncertain that Saladin, a man who seems to have had genuine zeal to flush the Franks from the Holy Land, would have spared the kingdom if only the Latins had left him alone in return.[36] Historians have also done much to rehabilitate individual members of the 'court party', including Guy of Lusignan, Agnes of Courtenay and Patriarch Heraclius.[37]

Edbury has launched what is arguably the most damaging critique of the traditional interpretation. He notes that the contemporary evidence reveals 'no clear pattern' for believing that the newcomers were bellicose 'hawks' and the natives pacifist 'doves', with both sides seeking treaties and war in equal measure. Edbury has also shown that the supposed factions lacked either the consistent membership or the unanimous opinion that they are traditionally assumed to have had. Certain people banded together around particular *causes célèbres* at different times – for example, the appointment of Raymond III as regent in 1174 and *c.*1185, or the coronation of Guy of Lusignan in 1186 – but never formed permanent, unchanging 'factions'.[38] Even the fundamental distinction between 'natives' and 'newcomers' dissolves when it is considered that Agnes of Courtenay and her brother Joscelin were hardly 'newcomers', but the survivors of the house of Edessa, tracing their ancestry back to one of the first crusaders, their grandfather Joscelin I. These two were as much 'native' barons as their rivals, Raymond of Tripoli or Bohemond of Antioch. For this very reason, Hamilton writes that, if any factions existed, then they only emerged in 1180 and were divided, 'not between native barons and newcomers from the West, but between the king's maternal and paternal kin'.[39]

Returning to 1174, the various Jerusalemite barons eventually did set aside their reluctance and accepted Raymond as their regent in late October.[40] Once their decision had been made, the count was invested with power in a lavish ceremony. The extravagance of Raymond's formal investiture seems to be unique among surviving accounts of other regencies in the Latin East. Raymond received his authority in a manner that was surely designed to emphasise again his royal credentials. The ceremony was held in the cathedral of the Holy Sepulchre – site of many a royal baptism, coronation, marriage and funeral. As William of Tyre wrote, 'all the administration and power of the realm – second only to the lord king – was bequeathed to the count'.[41] Raymond was not quite king, but it was the closest he would ever come. In an appropriate nod to his late mother, whose bloodline and political example very much underpinned his regency, one of the count's first documents issued in his new office made an unusual acknowledgement of his matrilineal as well as patrilineal heritage. He was 'Raymond, count of Tripoli, son of Count Raymond (II) and Countess Hodierna'.[42]

Ill-advised negotiations

Hamilton suspects that the main reason the barons of Jerusalem finally decided to appoint Raymond as regent, any qualms notwithstanding, was because of the looming threat posed by Saladin, who was seeking to unite the Muslim world of the Near East under his sole rule – a manifestation of political unity never before seen by the Franks.[43] By the time Raymond entered office in late autumn, Saladin had brazenly managed to seize Damascus, Baʿalbakk, Shayzar and Hama from those claiming to represent Nūr al-Dīn's son, al-Ṣāliḥ Ismāʿīl al-Malik. His most recent act was to besiege Homs, which he had occupied fully with the exception of the citadel, and he had reasonable hopes of securing the great city of Aleppo shortly.[44] Thus it was that Raymond's first act as regent was to lead a joint army from Jerusalem and Tripoli to derail Saladin's imperialist ambitions at Homs, located on the county of Tripoli's eastern border. This army left Jerusalem at the very beginning of January 1175 and travelled first to ʿArqa, where they made camp in a district known as *terra Galifa* – a latinisation of Arabic *Tall Khalīfa* (Hill of the Caliph).[45]

While the Christian army mustered near ʿArqa, William of Tyre reported that the beleaguered Muslims of Homs sent a desperate message to Count Raymond, seeking his help against Saladin and promising various rewards. These inducements included the offer to release those Christian hostages handed to Nūr al-Dīn some months before as guarantees for the payment of 60,000 *dīnār*s of Raymond's own ransom. Raymond was keen to have this debt written off, so led his army eastwards towards Homs.[46] Ibn al-Athīr later corroborated that Raymond had common cause with those Muslims ranged against Saladin, although he claimed instead that it was the Muslims of Aleppo who sought the count's aid, beseeching him to attack Homs in order to distract Saladin from his simultaneous siege of Aleppo itself.[47] Although Ibn al-Athīr's account shows errors of chronology, it seems fair to accept that the people of Aleppo did request Raymond's aid. Saladin's own secretary, the *qāḍī* Fāḍil, would later condemn the Aleppans for 'seeking the aid of [the Franks'] crosses and attacking Islam [or rather Saladin] aggressively', in a letter to Saladin's brother Al-ʿĀdil Sayf al-Dīn (Saphadin).[48] Supposedly, the Aleppans were also calling upon the 'heretic' Ismāʿīlī Assassins at this time, in addition to the 'infidel' Christians: testament to their desperation to resist Saladin.[49]

In early 1175, the Franks led by Count Raymond had a real opportunity to disrupt Saladin's ambitions and perhaps send Muslim Syria spiralling back down into the political fragmentation and petty warring that had dominated it before the Zankid ascendancy. In the event, however, Raymond demurred on the chance to curtail Saladin's expansion, withdrawing the army from Homs. William of Tyre explained that the Christians had retreated back to ʿArqa because they could not trust that the Muslims of Homs would uphold their promise to release the hostages. Although William was presumably keen to rationalise an action that proved controversial in hindsight, it must be said that Raymond comes across as obsessed with his own selfish concerns, rather than the grander strategic issues that would ultimately lead to disaster for the Latin East. This was underscored by Raymond's next act, when he agreed to commit the Latin East to neutrality in Saladin's wars with the Zankids – an invaluable truce Saladin bought by releasing the Christian prisoners at Homs himself. Not only was Homs lost to Saladin's expanding empire as a result of Raymond's appeasement of Saladin, but the Franks were now bound to stand by and watch as Syria and Egypt were united under one man. In the shorter term, with Homs having fallen to Saladin and with the Franks having achieved nothing in four months other than the release of Raymond's hostages, the Christian army returned home in May 1175.[50]

Criticisms of Raymond on the grounds that Saladin was soon to unite the Islamic Near East, only to lay waste to the kingdom of Jerusalem in the 1180s, are naturally made with the benefit of hindsight. Marshall Baldwin suggested that Raymond's trilateral negotiations with Saladin and Zankid Aleppo actually bought the Latin East time, by permitting Aleppo to remain independent of Saladin for a short while longer.[51] In Raymond's defence, Ibn al-Athīr was probably correct to attribute the initial Christian withdrawal from Homs, not to the count's selfish obsession with freeing his hostages, but to their fear at the approach of Saladin's army.[52] Encountering a hostile army in the field, as opposed to a siege, was a notoriously dangerous and unpredictable affair in the Middle Ages, as the Franks of the Latin East learned on more than one occasion – to their joy in some cases and their sorrow in others.[53]

Nevertheless, there are good reasons to question Raymond's choices even without recourse to hindsight. For one thing, it cannot be said that Saladin's rise was wholly unpredictable by this stage, if not necessarily inexorable. Saladin's conquest of various Muslim towns bordering on all three surviving crusader states was surely a cause for alarm even at the time. Around the same time that Saladin took Homs, he also managed to acquire Baʿrīn – formerly the county of Tripoli's eastern stronghold of Montferrand. From Baʿalbakk in the Biqāʿ valley, round to Homs and Baʿrīn, Saladin's empire now enclosed the county almost entirely, were it not for the Nizārīs in the Alawite mountains. Just as worrying were the reports, which must have reached the Franks, that Saladin was now shedding his superficial allegiance to al-Ṣāliḥ bin Nūr al-Dīn: by dropping the young Zankid's name from the *khuṭba* at Friday prayers, by minting coins in his own name and by receiving from the ʿAbbāsid caliph at Baghdad robes of investiture as sultan in his own right.[54]

It is therefore hard to look upon Christian inaction at Homs as Raymond's finest hour. Put to his first real test as regent, Raymond had led the army on a pointless campaign to the frontiers of Christendom, to watch impotently as a Muslim army posing no direct threat to Christian territory at the time conquered a Muslim city – helpless spectators to an Islamic civil war, which ended only in the strengthening of Saladin's rule in North Syria.[55] When he had been given the choice to intervene, by confronting Saladin's army and potentially disrupting his ambitions, the count had chosen discretion over valour. The wisdom behind Raymond's avoidance of a military confrontation with Saladin would only grow ever the more questionable with hindsight. Even William of Tyre seemed somewhat embarrassed by Raymond's strategic choices at Homs, as he attempted to blame the royal constable Humphrey II of Toron for negotiating such a self-defeating truce with Saladin.[56]

The remainder of Raymond's regency proved just as inauspicious. Within a few months of the incident at Homs, in July/August 1175 (Muḥarram 571), the count apparently negotiated yet another general truce with Saladin – seemingly a formal enhancement of the earlier pact of neutrality.[57] The Franks were again bound to neutrality in the Muslims' civil war, which permitted the new sultan to consolidate his power still further over Mosul and other areas of North Syria.[58] Hamilton argues that the general peace prevented the kingdom from intervening at the 'excellent opportunity' offered by increasing internal strife within Saladin's empire. In fact, he exacerbated the situation by alienating two potential allies – Sicily and Byzantium. He achieved this when he helped to arrange a marriage between Baldwin IV's sister Sybil and William V of Montferrat, a vassal of the German emperor Frederick Barbarossa, who in turn was a great rival of the Sicilians and the aging Greek emperor Manuel Komnenos alike.[59] It has been suggested that Raymond was motivated to do this for the selfish reason that he still resented Emperor Manuel's treatment of his sister many years before.[60]

The count seems to have done so little of worth in his regency that William of Tyre was forced to invent deeds. William erroneously dated two raids launched against the region around Damascus and the Biqāʿ valley respectively to 1175 and thus Raymond's regency.[61] Ibn al-Athīr stated that these assaults actually took place in 1176/77 (AH 572), after Raymond's time as regent had come to its scheduled end on 15 July 1176 – Baldwin IV's fifteenth birthday.[62] According to Hamilton, William's misdating of these events was done deliberately to give the impression that the count-regent continued to apply pressure to Saladin, the earlier truces notwithstanding.[63] When Raymond's regency did finally come to a close, he had achieved very little, beyond what proved to be harmful in the long run.

Despite his shortcomings, it cannot be denied that Raymond was an exceptionally busy man during his first regency of Jerusalem. In order to fulfil both his ambitions in Jerusalem and his duties in Tripoli, Raymond dedicated a lot of energy to travelling around the Latin East. His movements between April 1174 and May 1175 are remarkably well attested in surviving sources, as he travelled back and forth between Acre, Tripoli, Jerusalem, ʿArqa and Homs in the space of a year. Raymond continued to pursue a fairly peripatetic lifestyle throughout the remainder of his life, moving between Tripoli, Jerusalem and his wife's principality of Galilee. He would discover, however, that such a nomadic existence was not necessarily conducive to maintaining these lands. Any absences threatened his losing influence at court or else losing land, as later events were to demonstrate. It is telling that, when he acquired a fourth responsibility in the form of Beirut in 1185, he was only able to hold this city for a year.[64] Raymond's later failures resulted from the simple fact he overstretched himself.

Crusading controversy

After Raymond's regency came to an underwhelming end on 15 July 1176, he returned to Tripoli. Little more than a year later, the count found himself back at the forefront of another military controversy. In August 1177, Count Philip of Flanders – son of Count Thierry, who had fought alongside Raymond back in 1157[65] – arrived at Acre on crusade. At this time, yet another Latin–Byzantine alliance against Egypt was being planned and William of Tyre evidently expected Philip to support this mooted invasion. Instead, the plans came to nothing, allegedly because Count Raymond and Prince Bohemond III of Antioch selfishly convinced Philip to help bring about 'the increase of their own domains'.[66] William was of course an uncompromising partisan – happy to see the participants of the Second Crusade favour the southern realm at the expense of the northern crusader states, but envious and critical when the tables were turned.[67] Thus it was that William depicted Philip as the quintessential meddling European, whose interventions caused more harm than good. So too did William condemn the prince of Antioch and count of Tripoli, showing that his support for the latter had its limits.[68]

The northern expedition in late 1177 proved to be as ill-advised a move as Raymond's earlier confrontation with Saladin at Homs in January 1175. Latin and Arabic accounts agree that the intent was to take advantage of the fact that Saladin was far away in Egypt by attacking distant North Syria. However, this logic worked both ways. With the prince of Antioch and the counts of Tripoli and Flanders engaged in the north, the kingdom of Jerusalem lacked the valuable protection their armies would have offered. So it was that Saladin was able to invade the kingdom of Jerusalem from the south with great effect, threatening even the Holy City itself.[69] This placed the realm in precipitous danger, hence William of Tyre's severe criticism of the prince and counts.

In a manner reminiscent of Thierry of Flanders's expedition in 1157, the northern expedition began by attacking Homs and Hama, but ended by besieging Ḥārim. Although of undeniable strategic import, Ḥārim was not held by Saladin at the time, but by a faction of his lingering Zankid opponents – led either by al-Malik al-Ṣāliḥ himself, or by the eunuch Sa'd al-Dīn Kumushtakīn.[70] Did Raymond and Bohemond simply have an unhealthy obsession with Ḥārim, still smarting over their defeat in 1164? Fortunately for the northerners, they did at least manage to take Ḥārim on this occasion, with Bohemond negotiating the surrender of its Muslim garrison.[71] However, the northern campaign was described as a 'tactical error' by the usually sympathetic Marshall Baldwin.[72] The count and his allies had done nothing but to strengthen Saladin, by undermining what little remained of his Zankid opponents and by shunning the Byzantine assault on Egypt and thereby alienating Manuel Komnenos – the last truly powerful Byzantine emperor to look with any favour on the Latins. Indeed, it was the latter that rankled most with William of Tyre, who had evidently pinned high hopes on the expedition against Egypt. This had allegedly collapsed as soon as the emperor had learned that the plan did not enjoy unanimous support among the Franks.

As Hamilton argues, it is difficult to tell 'what really happened' because William of Tyre obfuscated the events of 1177 to such a considerable degree in order to point the finger of blame at Philip.[73] In fact, many at the time blamed Bohemond and Raymond, as William himself acknowledged: 'There were some who attributed it to the lord prince of Antioch and the lord count of Tripoli that the count (of Flanders) was so averse to the expedition into Egypt.'[74] Moreover, at the siege of Ḥārim, Philip supposedly complained that he had been strung along by Bohemond and Raymond, which again suggests he was not the primary agent of the northern campaign.[75]

Indications that Raymond specifically bore much of the responsibility can be found in the fact that the expedition went first to Tripoli, where Raymond and Philip spent almost a month between October and November making the necessary arrangements before attacking nearby Homs and Hama. Meanwhile, Bohemond came north to meet them 'by another road' (*alia via*) – probably the inland route along the Biqā' valley, rather than the awkwardly narrow *Passus Canis* by the coast, which Raymond and Philip had presumably taken.[76] Just as noteworthy is the fact that the army began by attacking Homs – a city that had long been a target of the counts of Tripoli's ambitions for conquest.[77]

Ultimately, even William of Tyre could not resist gloating at the northern lords' expense, by comparing their disappointing performance in the north with Baldwin IV's famous victory over Saladin at the battle of Montgisard in November 1177.[78] Interestingly, this battle marked the first recorded time that two of Raymond's four stepsons by Eschiva of Tiberias, Hugh and William, went to war – still 'young knights', but evidently old enough to make up for their stepfather's absence.[79] Remarkably, William of Tyre went so far as to praise King Baldwin's decision to appoint Raynald of Châtillon – a man rarely favoured by the archbishop – as 'executive regent' of the kingdom around the same time, which Hamilton regards as an implicit criticism of how Raymond of Tripoli had managed the king's minority back in 1174–6, not to mention Raymond's folly with the count of Flanders.[80] After his release in 1174, Raymond had thrown himself with great enthusiasm back into the churning politics of the Latin East, but as late as 1177 he had yet to make much of a positive impact.

Subversion and raiding from Tripoli

Raymond's failure to live up to his or anyone else's expectations continued in the years that followed Philip of Flanders's crusade. During this time he embarked upon a handful of military escapades, few of which were successful and none of which were of profound significance. In 1178–9 (AH 574), he raided a gathering of Türkmens, capturing their flocks, although Saladin was quickly able to shore up his border against any further incursions.[81] Shortly afterwards, Saladin invaded the lordship of Sidon for the third time in recent months. On this occasion, King Baldwin chose to engage the sultan, mustering his forces as he moved through the kingdom, including Raymond's lordship of Galilee.[82] It was presumably here that Raymond himself joined the army, having issued a document at Tiberias just a month before.[83] The Christians eventually met the Muslim army near Bāniyās on 10 June 1179. It would seem that Raymond's entourage at this battle included his stepson Hugh of Tiberias and 'the brother of the lord (Hugh II Embriaco) of Jubayl', probably Raymond (fl. 1174–80).[84]

Despite meeting with initial success against Saladin's vanguard, the Christian army soon collapsed under pressure from the Muslims' main forces. From their elevated position, Raymond of Tripoli and Odo, master of the Templars, watched with despair as the battle unfolded. After fighting bravely if briefly, the count and the Templar fled the field in a manner condemned by William of Tyre as 'disgraceful' (*turpiter*). Raynald of Sidon arrived with his reinforcements, but these too quickly retreated, taking shelter in caves, whence they were soon rooted out and captured. Raymond of Tripoli managed to reach Tyre 'with only a few men' (*cum paucis*) and was evidently back in Tripoli by 9 August, when he issued a charter there.[85] However, neither his stepson nor the man from Jubayl were so lucky. They were both thrown into captivity, along with the rest of the Frankish prisoners.[86] This was not the first time the count of Tripoli experienced the ignominy of defeat and it was far from being the last.

The unwelcome wedding guests

One of the major occasions when Raymond of Tripoli was outmanoeuvred by his political opponents in Jerusalem came at Easter 1180, when Baldwin IV arranged for his sister to marry Guy of Lusignan, who had arrived in the kingdom relatively recently in the 1170s, as a crusader travelling from his Poitevin homeland.[87] It is clear that William of Tyre struggled to report the important events surrounding Guy's marriage to Sybil, as the whole incident threatened to cast Raymond of Tripoli and Bohemond of Antioch in an even less favourable light than had the controversy over Philip of Flanders' crusade in 1177. As Easter approached, Raymond and Bohemond arrived in the kingdom with a large army, which met not with King Baldwin's warm welcome but with his suspicion and fear. According to William, their presence forced Baldwin to take the surprising step of marrying his sister to Guy. Upon reaching Jerusalem, the prince of Antioch and count of Tripoli continued to be held suspect by the king and his men and soon departed for their northern homes.[88]

As in 1177, William's account is again oddly framed, lacking adequate explanation, not least for why Baldwin became so anxious upon hearing of the northerners' arrival, or why the king chose to marry Sybil to Guy so quickly – even to the point of rejecting custom by arranging the marriage for Easter week. The best William had to offer was that the king was suffering so severely from his leprosy that he was growing ever more paranoid and was thus unable to act with the best wisdom. At the same time, the chronicler was reticent regarding why Bohemond and Raymond had come south in force at all – at most implying that they came merely for the Easter festivities.[89] Exacerbating the situation, William was not actually present in Jerusalem at this time, having been sent to Rome to attend the Third Lateran Council in 1179 and then to Constantinople to negotiate with Manuel Komnenos on behalf of the kingdom. He only arrived back in the realm in May, so was reliant upon hearsay.[90]

The curious nature of William's account has led historians to assume that he was covering up the truth: that Raymond and Bohemond were marching south to stop Baldwin IV from marrying Sybil to Guy at all costs, only to be thwarted by the king's swift action in holding the wedding so unexpectedly early.[91] Why else should they have been accompanied by armed men – a *militia*, in William of Tyre's words? Such a revisionist interpretation is not only likely, but reframes both Raymond and Bohemond as reckless would-be traitors, who were willing to threaten war simply because they disagreed with Baldwin's choice of husband for his sister. Already the so-called 'doves' of the supposed *pullani* faction, especially Raymond of Tripoli, were showing that they were more than willing to use violence to disrupt the peaceful actions of the alleged 'hawks'. The question then arises as to why William of Tyre should have felt compelled to protect Raymond and Bohemond from potential criticism, in his portrayal of this sequence of events and others. It is instructive at this point to defer to Edbury and Rowe, who emphasised William's commitment to the principle of legitimate descent through royal blood, often setting this above more pragmatic concerns.[92] So strong was William's loyalty to the royal house of Jerusalem that he was willing to overlook the shortcomings of the otherwise poor crop of candidates who presented themselves in his lifetime, in this case Raymond of Tripoli and Bohemond of Antioch – direct descendants of King Baldwin II.

Invasion and incompetence

After the débâcle at Easter, Raymond and Bohemond headed north, first sojourning for a few days at Tiberias. At this juncture, Saladin happened to attack the principality of Galilee, although swiftly withdrew as soon as he realised that both the prince and count were in the area. Raymond and Bohemond then marched to their respective North Syrian homes and thus it fell to Baldwin IV to negotiate a peace with Saladin, whose army hovered near the kingdom's frontier at Baʿalbakk. This truce was to apply 'through both land and sea, to both foreigners and residents alike'.[93] It evidently did not apply, however, to the county of Tripoli, as Saladin quickly took the opportunity presented by his temporary pacification of Jerusalem to attack this northern crusader state.

First, the sultan invaded the county – presumably via the Homs Gap – and then established himself in the plain of ʿAkkār between ʿArqa and Crac des Chevaliers. The county's available soldiery proved inadequate to the task of resisting Saladin. Count Raymond hid himself away in ʿArqa, the Hospitallers remained holed up in Crac and the Templars took refuge in one of their nearby castles – probably Ṣāfīthā or ʿUrayma.[94] With just one army, Saladin had outmanoeuvred the county's three principal military forces and forced them all into hiding, cut off from one another with no hope of co-ordinating a counterattack. Marshall Baldwin, who chose to ignore Tripolitan affairs, argued that 'Raymond became a capable leader after 1180', that is to say after the fiasco at Easter.[95] Despite this verdict, the initial signs in Tripoli were not promising. The Muslim soldiers were now free to ravage the valuable ʿAkkār plain, burning the crops they found growing in fields and stored in granaries and driving the cattle off as booty. A drought had sorely affected Damascus's agriculture for the last five years, so destroying and seizing the Christians' food supplies was surely intended to level the playing field.[96]

As if Saladin's achievements on land were not damaging enough, he co-ordinated his invasion from the east with a naval assault from the west. 1180 marked the end of a period when Saladin had made huge investments to improve the strength of the Egyptian fleet, doubling the number of ships after years of neglect under the Fāṭimids.[97] It was this reinvigorated fleet that he sent up the Frankish coast. His sailors' first conquest in the county was the ancient Phoenician island of Arwād, where they harboured their ships.[98] There was apparently a grand church on Arwād fortified 'with iron gates like a guardhouse' in the mid-twelfth century, although this seemingly proved of little use in 1180.[99] Meanwhile, the small fleet built by Raymond of Tripoli to celebrate his sister's abortive imperial wedding two decades before was nowhere to be seen.[100] From Arwād, the unchallenged Muslim navy sailed the short distance to the mainland and set fire to a house in the port of Tortosa. Saladin's militarily brilliant amphibious assault on the county understandably struck fear into its Frankish inhabitants. Fortunately for them, however, Saladin chose not to pursue permanent occupation, withdrawing as soon as Count Raymond agreed to a truce.[101] This was, in Hamilton's opinion, the main reason Saladin had invaded the county in the first place: to neutralise Tripoli just as he had neutralised Jerusalem through a similar treaty just months before.[102]

A 'multiplicity of affairs'

After the scandal at Easter 1180, Raymond was a *persona non grata* in the kingdom of Jerusalem and did not return until two years later, in April 1182. William of Tyre explained this long absence in mundane terms. Allegedly, the count had been 'impeded by a multiplicity of affairs in the area of Tripoli for a continuous two years'.[103] One might be inclined to suspect, as did Marshall Baldwin, that William was being disingenuous, concealing the lasting impact of Raymond's actions at Sybil's and Guy's wedding in order to protect the count's reputation.[104] This is a reasonable enough theory, although there is evidence to suggest that Raymond had to handle an unusually large number of issues in the county of Tripoli in the years 1180–2. Whether these various problems were significant or numerous enough to justify his prolonged absence from Jerusalem is less clear.

Saladin's invasion of the county almost immediately after Raymond's return represented a serious military crisis. Although the county was spared occupation or conquest, Raymond had to deal with the consequences of a nonetheless damaging incursion. In August 1180, Raymond confirmed a donation made by one of his vassals, Wiliam of Maraqiyya, who had surrendered to the Hospital three small forts (*casalia*) in the vicinity of Crac, namely *Marmoniza* (Marmarīṭa), *Erbenambra* (Ḥabnimra) and *Lebeizar* (al-Biṭār).[105] These were located either in or near what is now called the Wādī al-Naṣārā (Valley of the Christians), in reference to the high proportion of Christians still living in the area. More pertinently, all three were close to where Saladin raided the ʿAkkār plain and it is likely that Lord William no longer felt confident in his ability to hold these *casalia* after such a shocking invasion. Raymond himself extended the Hospitallers' lordship up to the Orontes in March 1181 and later donated the nearby fortress of Lo Camel to the Hospitallers in June 1184, with further concessions following in 1186.[106] Bolstering the county's defences with the assistance of the military orders thus constituted the first of the count's many distractions throughout this period.

In 1179, the commune of Genoa had resurrected its old claim to Jubayl, asking Pope Alexander III to assist. The pope obliged and wrote to Hugh II of Jubayl on 25 April 1179, demanding that the recalcitrant Embriaco lord respect the rights that Genoa had held in his city since the days it was first conquered.[107] Just a day later, the pope addressed a second letter in support of Genoese interests in the county of Tripoli, this time favouring them in a dispute over buildings erected illegally by the Templars at ʿArqa.[108] Perhaps Alexander remembered how instrumental Genoa's control over Jubayl had been when securing the loyalty of the eastern patriarchates back in 1160 and now sought to reward the Italian commune by supporting their ambitions in Syria.[109] It had taken until the late 1170s for the papal schism to be resolved in Alexander's favour, so it was only now that he was in a position to reward Genoa's past assistance.[110] As it happened, the Embriaci stubbornly resisted both the pope's and Genoa's claims to Jubayl, preferring henceforth to align themselves with other 'native' Latin settlers in Syria. Nevertheless, the affair concerning Genoese rights in Jubayl lasted right up until Saladin conquered the city in 1187, rendering the whole matter moot.[111] It is thus entirely plausible that Genoa's renewed interest in Jubayl had been one of the causes for concern distracting Raymond into the early years of the 1180s, arguably posing a threat to the count's own authority over perhaps his most independently minded vassals, the Embriaci. Indeed, numerous papal bulls were addressed to the bishop and count of Tripoli throughout this time, asking them all to put pressure on the Embriaci and even reminding Raymond that Genoa was still entitled to a third of Tripoli itself, according to the half-forgotten agreement reached with Count Bertrand some eighty years before.[112]

In addition to the worrying resurgence of Genoese interest in Jubayl, Raymond no doubt played some part in securing the release of his stepson Hugh of Tiberias, captured by Saladin near Bāniyās back in 1179. It is not clear when or how Hugh regained his freedom, but by September 1181 he was in Tripoli with his stepfather and possibly brother William.[113] Hugh's co-captive, Hugh Embriaco's brother, was perhaps released as early as August 1180, when Hugh's brother Raymond is named in a charter.[114]

The next matter to concern Count Raymond was not in the county of Tripoli at all, although it too continued to distract him from Jerusalem. Around the time Emperor Manuel Komnenos died on 24 September 1180, Bohemond of Antioch put aside his Greek wife Theodora Komnene in favour of a mistress named Sybil, whom William of Tyre accused of being a witch. The principality's clergy excommunicated the prince for this marital infidelity, which led Bohemond to seize and violate church possessions. Even relations between the prince and his secular magnates began to sour, perhaps because of the ecclesiastical interdict upon the entire province, and there were growing fears that this discord would invite and facilitate Muslim conquest. With the situation seemingly intractable, the king and patriarch of Jerusalem felt justified to intervene in this Antiochene controversy, calling together a wide range of people from the highest echelons of Frankish society, including Raynald of Châtillon – a former prince of

Antioch, not to mention Bohemond's stepfather – and the masters of the Temple and Hospital.[115]

This grand delegation of Jerusalemite nobles travelled north to confront Bohemond in his principality, stopping in the county of Tripoli on the way. This was apparently the first time since Easter that the barons of Jerusalem had deigned to meet with Raymond. They did so seemingly because the count of Tripoli's word was thought to carry more weight with the prince than anyone else's, by virtue of the close relationship between the two men. The magnates continued towards Antioch and met the prince at Latakia, where they concluded a temporary peace, whereby the prince would respect ecclesiastical property in return for the interdict on the principality to be lifted. Bohemond himself would remain excommunicated unless he abandoned his mistress and returned to Theodora. Although the prince soon thereafter returned to his old ways, forcing many of the Franks of Antioch to flee to Armenia, the various grandees and clerics at Latakia seemed satisfied for the moment and headed home.[116]

In 1181, William of Tyre proudly reported that some 40,000 Maronites living near Jubayl, Batrūn and Tripoli had sought official union with the Roman Church.[117] Like so much of Maronite history, this event has been disputed. Patriarch al-Duwayhī believed that the Maronites had unified with Rome as soon as the Franks had arrived in the area at the turn of the eleventh to the twelfth century, although this can safely be dismissed as anachronistic propaganda. One of the main things the Maronites supposedly did to symbolise this early union was abandon their wooden *semantra* in favour of copper bells, but James of Vitry complained that they were still using their eastern-style percussive instruments over a century later.[118] Meanwhile, Hiestand has argued that even the event in 1181 was somewhat more restricted than historians have sometimes assumed: being only the opening of negotiations over doctrine and involving only the Maronites who lived near the coast in the county of Tripoli. Thus it neither constituted a formal union nor included the many Maronites who lived higher in the mountains and in the north of the kingdom of Jerusalem, especially around Beirut.[119] According to Salibi, the Maronite–Latin negotiations of 1181 constituted 'the major step towards union', although he agreed that the Maronites remained divided in their attitude to this ecumenical matter for a long time afterwards, perhaps as late as 1515.[120] Although the discussions in 1181 may not have been the great watershed that some – not least William of Tyre – have heralded it as, even this was presumably of sufficient demographic, social and military significance to have involved secular figures on both sides, including the count of Tripoli himself, in whose armies the Maronites sometimes fought.[121]

The years 1180–2 were crucial to Count Raymond for another, arguably more significant reason, as he also found himself embroiled in an infamous internal dispute with one of his courtiers over the important town of Batrūn. According to the *Eracles*, Raymond III had promised Gerard of Ridefort – who was himself a new arrival in the east, described by Ernoul as a *clerc de Flandres* – the hand in marriage of the first available heiress in the county. However, when one did become available – the heiress of William Dorel, lord of Batrūn – Raymond instead sold her to a Pisan merchant named Plivain in return for gold. Raymond accepted the bribe and so Plivain became lord of Batrūn. Gerard was stunned by the count's treachery, but allegedly also because a noble Frenchman like himself had lost out to a base Italian.[122] Offended and betrayed, Gerard then stormed off to Jerusalem to become a celibate Templar, swiftly reaching the rank of master.[123]

Raymond may have had his reasons for accepting Plivain's money, not least the huge amount he still owed on the ransom paid to secure his release from prison a few years earlier.[124] Nevertheless, this feud soon gained notoriety, as many came to blame the mutual hatred that developed between Raymond and Gerard for no less than the downfall of the kingdom of Jerusalem in 1187.[125] Even Marshall Baldwin had to admit that Raymond was partly at fault here for initiating this damaging conflict with Gerard of Ridefort.[126]

Much debate surrounds the veracity of this story. Neither Baldwin nor Richard questioned the Old French sources, with Richard finding some corroborating evidence in the thirteenth-century *Lignages d'Outremer*.[127] Morgan dismissed the story in the *Eracles* for its 'caractère folklorique', although Hamilton believes that 'this story may have been true', since Plivain was both a real person and lord of Batrūn from March 1181.[128] Barber has pointed to a charter from the county of Tripoli, in which Gerard appears as a witness, as proof that Gerard and Raymond were at least onetime associates.[129] The charter lacks a complete dating clause, but Delaville le Roulx dated it to *c.*1175, primarily on the basis of the witnesses.[130] As for the Batrūn scandal itself, historians have offered speculative dates ranging between late 1179 and early 1181.[131] In other words, this best known of Raymond's controversies was yet another of the 'multiplicity of affairs' that prevented him from returning to Jerusalem between 1180 and 1182.

More broadly, the Batrūn incident also proves two of Richard's theories regarding the county of Tripoli under Raymond III. The first is that Raymond III was the first count to favour the Pisans over their longer established Italian rivals, the Genoese and the Venetians.[132] The Pisans had assisted in the conquest of the county back in the first decade of the twelfth century, partly because Count Bertrand was married to a woman from Lombardy, near Pisa.[133] However, unlike the Genoese who had acquired the city of Jubayl, or the Venetians who had gained a handful of properties in Tripoli, the Pisans never seemed to capitalise on the opportunities on offer in the county. It was only in the 1170s that Pisan representatives made serious efforts to enter Tripolitan high society,

Figure 5.1 The seal of the lord of Batrūn incorporating his castle: *CASTELLVM BOTRONI* © Jonathan Phillips

not merely as mercantile consuls but as members of the settled nobility. Thus it was that Plivain the Pisan made his first attested appearance in the county alongside a number of his Pisan fellows in a comital donation to the commune of Pisa on 9 August 1179.[134] One may wonder if the late King Amalric's regency a few years before had played some part in Pisa's ascendancy in Tripoli and the Latin East more generally, as the Pisans had earlier found favour with the king in Jerusalem, due in part to the support they offered him in his 1167 invasion of Egypt.[135] From 1182, Pisan interest in the Latin East only increased, as anti-Latin riots in Constantinople forced many merchants out of the city.[136] Indeed, the same tensions in Byzantium encouraged Genoa also to take a more active interest in Jubayl and Syria generally.[137] Perhaps Count Raymond even favoured the Pisans because he desired a counterbalance to Genoa's papal-backed claims to Jubayl and Tripoli.

The second of Richard's theories is that Raymond more than any previous count of Tripoli was forced to seek non-Occitan immigrants to replenish the county's Latin society. As the twelfth century had worn on, certain old Occitan families – descendants of the southern French crusaders in Raymond of Saint-Gilles's train decades before – had become extinct, including the Languedocian families of Puylaurens and Agout. The Puylaurens had been lords of Gibelacar, but were replaced by the obscure Astafortis. Meanwhile, the Agouts had been lords of Batrūn, until Count Raymond had arranged for the family's sole heiress to be betrothed first to Gerard of Ridefort, a man from Flanders, and then to a Pisan, Plivain. Richard thought that fewer Occitans were travelling to the Latin East and the county of Tripoli, especially after the acrimony that had supposedly arisen between the houses of Tripoli and Toulouse during the Second Crusade, hence Raymond III's greater reliance upon other Europeans.[138] Although the extent to which Occitan immigration dried up in the second half of the twelfth century is uncertain, there seems little reason to object to the basic observation that a greater variety of non-Occitans did enter the ranks of the Tripolitan nobility during Raymond's reign.[139]

The 'multiplicity of affairs' in Tripoli was manipulated by William of Tyre to conceal the controversy surrounding Raymond's march on Jerusalem in Easter 1180, but it was not an outright fabrication. Evidently Raymond found himself in these years stretched beyond his abilities, unable to make any serious attempts at returning to Jerusalem after the crisis of 1180 because he was overburdened by his responsibilities in Tripoli. It is thus no longer possible to agree with Marshall Baldwin, who wrote that 'Raymond's activities in Tripolis had no bearing upon his career in the kingdom of Jerusalem'.[140] The count's deeds in the north were intimately connected with his actions in the south. Raymond could not dedicate himself fully to one while the other made competing demands on his time.

A cold welcome

By April 1182, Raymond's embarrassment or Tripolitan responsibilities had abated enough that he was able to make his belated return to the kingdom. Raymond had not only avoided the lofty politicking at the court of Jerusalem for these two years, but had apparently not visited his wife's domain in Tiberias either, which Raymond had presumably left in the hands of Eschiva, her sons, or Galilee's constable – as indeed he did on future occasions.[141] As Raymond approached Jubayl with his sights set on entering the kingdom at Beirut, certain advisors to Baldwin IV warned against allowing the count to return and so he had to head back to Tripoli. These advisors, whose leaders William of Tyre identified as the queen mother Agnes of Courtenay and her brother Joscelin the royal seneschal, were said to have feared losing their influence at court, which they had been able to build during Raymond's years of unavoidable exile. With characteristic partisanship, William condemned the Courtenays and their supporters as 'seducers' and 'wicked people'.[142] It was ironic that Raymond was prevented from travelling any further south than Jubayl. This was, after all, the *Passus Canis*, which had allowed the restriction of travel between the county and kingdom many times before, most importantly during Pons's rebellion against King Fulk in 1132.[143] The count of Tripoli had fallen victim to the very same geographical obstacle that had been so instrumental to his domain's independence.

Fortunately for Raymond, it was not long before other 'princes and greater men of the realm' convinced the king to permit the count to enter.[144] William gave no indication as to whom the 'greater men of the realm' actually were. Marshall Baldwin suspected that the latter were surviving members of those who had supported Raymond's candidacy for the regency in 1174, namely Raynald of Sidon and the Ibelin brothers, Baldwin of Ramla and Balian.[145] William of Tyre's implication was, of course, that the Courtenays were wrong to block the count's return to the kingdom. Riley-Smith and Hamilton both caution against following William's propaganda, suspecting instead that many of the kingdom's elite, including Baldwin IV himself, viewed Raymond as a dangerously ambitious and undesirable 'pretender' to the throne, whom the king had consistently avoided giving any position of power if he could help it – kinship and status notwithstanding.[146] The count's behaviour up to this point was hardly encouraging, especially after his ill-advised attempted rebellion alongside Bohemond of Antioch at Easter 1180, his inability to stave off Saladin's invasion of his county shortly afterwards and his unscrupulous treatment of Gerard of Ridefort at the first sniff of Pisan gold. It is certainly hard to see in Raymond's demonstrations of greed and incompetence the man whom Marshall Baldwin described as 'by 1182 generally respected and admired'.[147]

With Jerusalem's government having set aside their serious misgivings about Raymond, the count accompanied King Baldwin on a military expedition to the south of the kingdom, specifically to the ancient Nabatean city of Petra, with the intention being to protect the lordship of Transjordan against Saladin. Petra was the site of a Latin archbishopric from 1168 and archaeological explorations have uncovered a fortress and signs of settlement there dating back to the twelfth century, attesting to the locale's strategic importance in the crusader period.[148] According to William of Tyre, the expedition to Petra in summer 1182 was against Raymond of Tripoli's better judgement, as it left the rest of the kingdom without an army. At the time, however, Raymond's voice was drowned out by the other barons, who preferred to lend their support to Raynald of Châtillon, lord of Transjordan, in one of his personal feuds with Saladin, rather than ensure the security of the kingdom as a whole.[149] More recently, historians have reassessed this expedition, arguing that it was in fact 'strategically correct' to attempt disrupting Saladin in the south while keeping the kingdom's army intact, whatever Raymond of Tripoli and William of Tyre might have thought.[150]

Nevertheless, Raymond was the one vindicated when the Muslims of Damascus, Homs, Bostrum (Buṣrā) and Baʿalbakk launched an opportunistic raid into the north of the kingdom, plundering the fortress of *Buria* (modern Dabbūriyya) in Raymond's own principality of Galilee and capturing 500 women.[151] Around the same time, in June 1182 (Ṣafar AH 578), another fortress near Tiberias – a cave-fortress called Ḥabis Jaldak – fell to the Muslims.[152] According to William of Tyre, Ḥabis Jaldak was betrayed by 'Syrians, who "we" believe to be effeminate and weak', although the real blame lay with Fulk, the constable of Tiberias, who had left the fortress in their hands.[153] William apparently did not think any responsibility passed to Raymond of Tripoli for deputising Fulk in the first place.

Tantamount to treachery

As the 1180s progressed, Raymond's military and political career continued on much the same underwhelming, even controversial trajectory it had been following since at least 1174. In July 1182, Raymond fell seriously ill at Tiberias and so it was left to his stepson Hugh to take command of Galilee's army, winning a great victory at the battle of Forbelet.[154] Marshall Baldwin argued that this incident proved that the count was 'rapidly becoming indispensable', but it is hard to agree since the Christians won the day at Forbelet despite Raymond's incapacitation.[155] In early December 1182, Raymond led a crack team of knights on a stealthy raid into Muslim territory around Buṣrā, where they seized livestock and slaves alike. He was given this command, not so much because of any innate talent, but because the mission was led from his lordship of Tiberias.[156] No permanent conquests were made and Hamilton suspects that the real purpose of this scouting party was reconnaissance, specifically directed at discerning whether or not the Muslims of Damascus had reinforced the fortress of Aylāt.[157] It is very probable that Raymond accompanied the large-scale military expedition led by Baldwin IV against Damascus itself in the immediate aftermath of this intelligence-gathering exercise, not least because this too was launched from Tiberias. Like so many Frankish attempts on Damascus, this latest campaign failed, this time with the Christians losing their nerve in a dramatic standoff with the massed inhabitants of this Muslim-dominated city. The Latins were back home by Christmas, having achieved nothing yet again.[158]

In late September 1183, Saladin looked poised to lead a huge invasion of the kingdom of Jerusalem. The Frankish armies of Jerusalem, Antioch and Tripoli all assembled at the kingdom's traditional mustering point of the springs of Ṣaffūriyya, together with a large number of visiting pilgrims from Aquitaine, Louvain and North Italy. According to William of Tyre, the combined forces constituted the largest Latin Christian army on record. During the long, tense wait that followed, King Baldwin languished at Nazareth, his health rapidly deteriorating. From this distance he chose to appoint Guy of Lusignan as his regent. William of Tyre was as hostile as ever towards Guy, describing him as 'indiscreet and thoroughly useless' (*indiscretus et penitus inutilis*), supported only by selfish advisors who wished to derive some personal advantage from such a manifestly poor appointment. It is Guy then whom William blamed for the fact the Christian army at Ṣaffūriyya did nothing more than to stand and watch as Saladin's army was left free to ravage the countryside continuously for seven or eight days.[159]

Interestingly, William of Tyre admitted that there were two explanations for the failure to engage the Muslims, although he was willing to commit to neither: an official reason originating among the barons and an unofficial one that circulated among the 'simple folk', who William wrote were blissfully unaware of the subtler points of military planning. The barons believed that, although the Christians enjoyed numerical superiority, the Muslims held strategically favourable and easily defensible rocky land. The popular theory was that Guy's political opponents had refused to support him, effectively crippling the army simply because they did not want their rival to win a great victory over Saladin.[160] If this is true, and many recent historians believe it to be so, then the fault for the inaction at Ṣaffūriyya lay not with Guy but with his political enemies, including Raymond of Tripoli, whose petty, self-serving objections to the regent's authority were tantamount to treachery.[161] Most shocking was that these men were the same who immediately turned Guy's perceived failure to their political advantage. Raymond, Bohemond of Antioch, Raynald of Sidon and the Ibelin brothers led the call for Baldwin IV to strip Guy of the regency and to appoint his own infant nephew Baldwin V as co-ruler, presumably with the intention of preventing Guy from ever becoming king himself via his marriage to Princess Sybil.[162] The image of the court party as the selfish, volatile firebrands and the *pullani* barons as the selfless, far-sighted diplomats is thus completely inverted.

Raymond's second regency

What happened after Guy's loss of favour has a confused chronology. It has sometimes been thought that King Baldwin heeded Raymond of Tripoli and his supporters, sacking Guy of Lusignan as regent soon after the incident at Ṣaffūriyya and immediately appointing Count Raymond in his place following the coronation of Baldwin V as co-king.[163] Indeed, William of Tyre implied that Raymond's assumption of the regency of Jerusalem, for what was the second time in his life, took place the very same day as Baldwin V's coronation, 20 November 1183, as the people of Jerusalem thought it advisable that the count govern on behalf of both the terminally ill Baldwin IV and the six-year-old Baldwin V.[164] Confusing matters, however, is that William of Tyre seemingly contradicted himself by implying that Raymond actually became regent at a later date. At the very end of his great chronicle, the archbishop wrote that the dying King Baldwin IV 'committed the care and general administration of the kingdom to the count of Tripoli', but only *after* Guy of Lusignan had proven himself recklessly inappropriate by launching a contentious raid against a crown-protected Bedouin tribe near Daron (Dayr al-Balaḥ) in the far south of the kingdom of Jerusalem.[165] Current thinking is that Guy's assault on these nomads happened on 6 October 1184, almost a year after Baldwin V's coronation, and that Raymond was not appointed to the regency until early 1185, when the disease-wracked Baldwin IV finally passed away at the age of twenty-three.[166] When Raymond finally became regent in 1185, he was, in Hamilton's words, 'an unexpected choice', coming only in desperate circumstances and only after Guy of Lusignan had already been seen to fail in his duties.[167]

As when the count had been appointed to his first regency back in 1174, it seems that Raymond continued to lack unanimous support at court. According to the so-called Chronicle of Ernoul and the Old French continuations of William of Tyre, four conditions were set before Raymond took up the regency in the mid-1180s: first, that a personal guardian be appointed to look after Baldwin V lest Raymond be accused of causing his death, should it occur while the young king remained a minor; second, that the military orders take control of the royal castles instead of Raymond; third, that Raymond be given Beirut to defray his expenses; and four, that the great rulers of western Europe – the pope, the German emperor, the king of France and the king of England – ought to make the final decision on whether to crown the young king's mother Sybil or her half-sister Isabel, King Amalric's daughter by Maria Komnene, in the event of Baldwin V's death.[168]

The Old French sources imply that Raymond of Tripoli himself requested these four conditions, yet the very nature of at least three suggests otherwise, implying that influential courtiers wished to place restrictions upon the new regent's authority.[169] For instance, the appointment of somebody else, in the event Joscelin of Edessa, to look after the person of the king while Raymond managed the kingdom represents a novel separation of the duties of a regent, perhaps indicating a fear that the count might otherwise commit infanti-regicide. At least one contemporary, William of Newburgh, accused Raymond of poisoning Baldwin V when the young king did eventually die.[170] Similar rumours included the claim that the count used his second regency to embezzle the crown's money.[171] As for the second and fourth conditions on Raymond's regency, these were equally restrictive. By transferring the royal castles to the military orders, the count's burden was lessened, but so too was his power. Meanwhile, the decision to defer to European monarchs on the question of the future succession was very possibly a way of preventing Raymond of Tripoli from claiming the crown for himself.

According to Hamilton, the only condition upon Raymond's regency that was 'in any way favourable to him' was his acquisition of Beirut, since it provided him with economic compensation for his efforts.[172] To this should be added an important geo-strategic consideration. Unlike Galilee, Beirut was contiguous with the county of Tripoli. Despite Richard's claim that 'Raymond III eut uni à son comté la principauté de Galilée', it seems that these two polities had remained separate since Raymond's marriage to Eschiva, with discrete social and administrative frameworks.[173] It may well be that greater union was effectively prevented by the distance between Galilee and Tripoli, divided by Christian- and Muslim-controlled lands, not to mention Mount Lebanon and the Biqāʿ valley. Had Raymond been successful in holding Beirut in the long term, however, then he may have been able to unite the lordships of Tripoli and Beirut, as his grandfather Pons had managed to do with the discrete but contiguous fiefs north and south of al-Nahr al-Kabīr al-Janūbī.[174]

More immediately, Beirut controlled the main thoroughfare between the county and the kingdom, a point that would not have been lost on Raymond, who had been prevented from entering the county at this very location in 1182. Indeed, the count's opponents in the kingdom of Jerusalem were clearly aware that control over Beirut was key. When relations between Raymond and Baldwin IV had reached their lowest ebb in the years 1180–2, Beirut and its environs had been central to royal policy. Riley-Smith argues that Baldwin IV, by acquiring in October 1180 the fiefs of Toron and Chastelneuf through his half-sister Isabel's arranged betrothal to Humphrey IV of Toron, had hoped to create a buffer zone against Raymond III of Tripoli specifically.[175] Baldwin's new acquisitions had created a large crown-controlled territory stretching from Beirut and Sidon to Chastelneuf and Toron. This would have allowed communication to be cut between Raymond's two power-bases of Tripoli and Galilee, no doubt explaining why the count was unable to enter even his own Jerusalemite principality, let alone the realm at large, during this period. By controlling Beirut, Raymond no longer had to fear such humiliating treatment.

It is in the context of continuing suspicion of Raymond that the chronology of his career between 1183 and 1185 must be understood. Very soon after the coronation of his nephew in November 1183, Baldwin IV had led an army south to Karak, accompanied by Raymond III, with the intention being to dislodge Saladin from Petra, which he was besieging. Saladin allegedly retreated as soon as he heard that the Christian army was approaching under Raymond's command. Crucially, however, Baldwin had not agreed to appoint Raymond as his general until the army had reached the Dead Sea and then only 'after many deliberations' (*post multas deliberationes*).[176] This sequence of events again suggests that Raymond had not yet been made regent, as he would otherwise have held military primacy without such question or delay. Thus Raymond attained power only gradually and in the face of clear reluctance on the part of others, first by being granted control of the military but not the civil government in late 1183 and then by receiving responsibility for the latter but not the person of King Baldwin V in early 1185.

Crowning controversy

Baldwin V died in Acre in the summer of 1186, at the age of just nine.[177] A succession crisis loomed once more in the kingdom of Jerusalem, little more than a year after Baldwin IV's death. According to the conditions set upon Raymond of Tripoli's regency, there was a clear course of action to follow in such a case as this, namely to contact the greatest of Europe's rulers, seeking their opinion on which of King Amalric's surviving children to crown: Sybil or Isabel.[178] Nobody in the kingdom seriously attempted to follow this quasi-legal agreement, however, and thus different parties within the kingdom began vying for control. The latest squabble began when Joscelin of Courtenay convinced Raymond of Tripoli to head to Tiberias while arrangements were made for Baldwin V's burial in Jerusalem. It quickly became apparent that this was a ruse, as Joscelin seized Raymond's valuable new fief of Beirut. The count, who was still acting regent, was enraged and humiliated. As Smail put it, he had exhibited 'unbelievable political ineptitude' in falling for Joscelin's trick.[179]

Keen to recover from this disgrace, Raymond summoned the barons of the kingdom to gather at Nablus. Those who came most likely included some or all of his Galilean stepsons, Princess Isabel, her husband Humphrey IV of Toron and the Ibelin brothers. Not all answered his call, with a sizeable group of magnates heading instead to attend young Baldwin's funeral. These included Guy of Lusignan, Sybil of Jerusalem, Raynald of Châtillon, the Templar master Gerard of Ridefort and Patriarch Heraclius.[180] In truth, Raymond had no good reason to absent himself and his allies from the king's funeral, less to summon a baronial meeting timed to compete directly with it. Modern historians suspect that the count intended to gather support for his own candidacy to succeed Baldwin V as king.[181]

No fewer than three medieval authors claimed that Raymond was seeking to become king in 1186: Ibn al-Athīr, the German Benedictine Arnold of Lübeck and the anonymous Genoese author of the *Regni Iherosolymitani Brevis Historia*.[182]

The Genoese anonymous offers the most remarkable report, namely that Raymond believed himself to be more entitled to the throne than even the late Baldwin V on the basis of porphyrogeniture. The count allegedly argued that, although Baldwin's grandmother Queen Melisende was indeed Baldwin II's eldest daughter, she had been born when he had remained merely count of Edessa. By contrast, Raymond's mother Hodierna had been born after Baldwin II's coronation in 1118 and thus her descendants – principally Raymond himself – were the more legitimate candidates for kingship.[183] It is doubtful that the count did make this argument, since there was precious little precedent for succession by porphyrogeniture in the Latin East, except for the patently inappropriate case of Alfons Jordan and his son Bertrand, who may have used it against Raymond's father in 1148.[184] Moreover, the argument was fallacious, as Hodierna was actually born before her father ascended the throne in 1118.[185] It would be surprising if Raymond made such a glaring mistake and expected it to be accepted as truth.

As Hamilton observes, the various writers who reported Raymond's ambitions to be king were 'widely separated in space and time', which at least suggests a widespread *belief* that Raymond had his sights set on the throne, even if it does not necessarily prove that the suspicion in its manifold intricacies and variations was accurate.[186] Such rumours dated back a few years at least. The author of the pro-Lusignan Latin continuation of William of Tyre alleged that, around the time Raymond became regent for the second time, he had insisted upon his royal lineage and thus greater suitability for the crown than Guy of Lusignan.[187] The Andalusian Muslim Ibn Jubayr had passed through the realm in 1184 and heard enough local gossip to conclude that Raymond was 'the one qualified for kingship and also a candidate for the position'.[188] Ironically, this was one of the most positive, not to mention highly contemporary assessments ever made of Raymond's abilities, free of the heavy criticism that lay in store for the count's posthumous reputation in European sources.

Not for the first time in his life, Raymond misjudged the extent to which the Jerusalemite nobility were willing to support him. As at Easter 1180 or in April 1182, Raymond found himself unable to win over a controlling majority of the High Court. The many magnates who ignored his summons to Nablus decided to politicise Baldwin V's funeral further by crowning the bereaved queen mother Sybil as queen regnant, albeit on the condition that she divorce the controversial Guy of Lusignan – much as Sybil's own father Amalric had had his marriage to Agnes of Courtenay annulled before becoming king in 1163. Sybil seems to have tricked her barons by agreeing to the divorce only if she had the right to pick a new husband of her own choice. Once this condition was granted and Sybil crowned by Patriarch Heraclius, the new queen appointed Guy as her new husband and thus king.[189] Legend soon thereafter claimed that Gerard of Ridefort, who witnessed this coronation, exclaimed triumphantly that 'this crown was well worth the marriage of Batrūn', referencing his former betrayal at the hands of Raymond of Tripoli.[190] This was why so many contemporaries blamed the Batrūn scandal for the realm's eventual collapse.[191]

Throughout these proceedings, Raymond and his supporters remained stubbornly at Nablus, refusing to attend the coronation after their envoys forbidding it proved to no avail. These messengers were two Cistercian abbots, accompanied by one of Raymond's sergeants dressed as a monk to spy in the Holy City.[192] It is tempting to think that one of these Cistercians was the abbot of Belmont in Raymond's own county of Tripoli. It is more likely that they were the abbots of Belmont's daughter-house of St John in the Woods and of Salvatio – a daughter of Morimond and thus Belmont's 'sister'. Both of these monasteries were located near Jerusalem.[193] When the news arrived that not only Sybil but also Guy had been crowned, Raymond's court at Nablus was thrown into disarray. The count of Tripoli decided then to crown Sybil's sister Isabel and her husband Humphrey of Toron as rivals to the monarchs at Jerusalem. Even in view of Raymond's personal history of political errors, this was an exceptionally reckless move, threatening to tear the kingdom apart in a civil war. Conflict was averted, however, when the king-elect Humphrey refused to be party to such an overtly treasonable act, escaping Nablus by night and fleeing to Jerusalem, where he submitted himself to King Guy.[194]

Support for Raymond quickly evaporated after Humphrey's defection. The barons who had been with the count at Nablus now went to Jerusalem to do homage to the new king. Other than Raymond himself, the only one to refuse to do so was Baldwin of Ibelin, who nevertheless neutralised his own personal objections: not least by placing his lands under Guy's control and by heading into self-imposed exile in Antioch.[195] Seeing that his erstwhile allies had abandoned him so completely in such a short space of time must have come as a shocking disappointment to Raymond, who until recently had regarded himself as regent and a possible candidate for the throne itself. Indeed, Edbury believes that the speed with which the count's onetime supporters defected undermines the assumption that Raymond was 'the head of a baronial faction' at all.[196] Unable to bring himself to surrender meekly like the rest, Raymond departed Nablus for Tiberias.[197]

A troubadour's nostalgia

The count of Tripoli was now completely alienated from the other barons of the kingdom, his schemes for power in tatters. It was at this point that he chose to revive the one potential alliance he had remaining to him, namely his ancestral link to the county of Toulouse. Richard believed that Raymond II's supposed betrayal of Alfons Jordan and Bertrand in 1148 had effectively severed the ties between Tripoli and Occitania, but the surviving source material is simply too scant to bestow any certainty upon this theory.[198] What there is, however, is curiously neglected evidence to suggest that Raymond III made a deliberate effort to unite Tripoli and Toulouse once again in the later years of his reign. The crux of this is poetry composed by the Occitan troubadour Peire Vidal, who visited Syria in the 1180s, likely on pilgrimage.[199]

Upon his arrival in the east, Vidal sought and received the patronage of Raymond III of Tripoli, about whom he wrote the following praise in one of his *chansons*:

> But upon Tripoli I rely,
> Because whereas the other barons
> Chase away glory, he retains it
> And does not let it depart from him.[200]

At least one other troubadour had been in contact with the comital family of Tripoli before, when Jaufré Rudel had supposedly died in the arms of Countess Hodierna during the Second Crusade.[201] Of course, Rudel had accompanied the pretenders Alfons Jordan and Bertrand (II) and in any case died almost as soon as he stepped ashore. By contrast, Vidal, who served Raymond III directly, serves as a better demonstration of the Tripolitan dynasty's enduring cultural and emotional attachment to their distant Occitan heritage.

Vidal was an adventurous troubadour, plying his trade not only in the unusual marketplace of the Latin East, but also in León, which otherwise 'attracted few troubadours'.[202] Paterson has summarised the Occitan literary output of the Latin East, albeit with an overriding focus upon Raymond of Poitiers – prince of Antioch, son of Duke William IX of Aquitaine the 'first troubadour' and great literary patron in North Syria, overseeing the composition of the surviving *Chanson des Chétifs* among other lost works.[203] Her general conclusion is that Antioch's literary output – specifically in *langue d'oc* – left 'the court of the count of Tripoli, wherever this was, very much in second place'.[204] This corroborates the observation that the county of Tripoli had no monopoly on Occitan settlement and culture in the Latin East.[205]

Despite her focus upon Antioch, Paterson does discuss Vidal's employment with Raymond, if only briefly, and observes that it is unclear whether Vidal attended Raymond's court at Tripoli, Jerusalem during one of his regencies, or Tiberias.[206] Paterson's chronology is vague, but Hoepffner uses the dedication to Raymond to provide the song – and thus Vidal's voyage eastwards – with two possible *termini post quem*: Raymond's own death in the second half of 1187 or the earlier battle of Ḥaṭṭīn, 4 July 1187, of which Vidal makes no mention.[207] Certainly Vidal's praise for Raymond's retention of glory, while other barons chased it away, would be incongruous had the song been composed after this battle. As it happened, it was Raymond who was to flee Ḥaṭṭīn, abandoning the other Frankish lords to captivity and death.[208]

As for the *terminus ante quem*, Hoepffner believes that Vidal travelled to Syria after a disagreement in 1185 with his lord and Raymond III's cousin, Count Raymond V of Toulouse (r.1148–94). This dispute had forced Vidal into exile from his lands and into the camp of Raymond V's great rival, Alfonso II of Aragon, Barcelona and Provence.[209] Hoepffner proposes that Vidal then travelled east in the spring passage of 1186, returning west probably in autumn. He had certainly returned by late 1187, when he was reconciled with Raymond V after some two years in exile.[210] Hoepffner's precise chronology makes it more likely that Vidal attended Raymond in Jerusalem during his regency for Baldwin V, or Tiberias after the coronation of Guy of Lusignan and Sybil of Jerusalem, or even his temporary holding of Beirut, rather than in Tripoli.

The content of the song Vidal composed at Raymond's court suggests that he wrote in response to the specific political circumstances in which the count found himself after Sybil's and Guy's coronation, sometime between 20 July and mid-September 1186. This would explain why Vidal's eulogy of Raymond makes the loaded point that his patron retained glory while the other barons did not. The main themes explored by the song itself are the frustrated love that had supposedly forced Vidal to travel east in the first place – a poetic device to conceal the true, political reason for his exile – and his concomitant homesickness for Provence:[211]

> I wish to return and go,
> To a place
> Between Arles and Toulon
> In secret, because there
> I would like better a small field,
> Than to have here Daron,
> Or to have Toron
> Or Ibelin . . .[212]

That the only eastern castles named by Vidal were Daron, Toron and Ibelin – all located within the kingdom of Jerusalem – further suggests that he attended Raymond in the kingdom, rather than the county of Tripoli. Moreover, the choice of these castles in particular could be coded criticism of the *autre baro* who had 'chased away glory' by abandoning Raymond's cause in favour of making peace with the recently crowned Guy of Lusignan. Among these were the lords of Toron and Ibelin, Humphrey and Baldwin respectively. As for Daron, this was a royal fief in which the very incident that had led to Raymond's appointment as regent *c.*1185, namely Guy of

Lusignan's scandalous attack upon crown-protected Bedouin, had taken place.[213] Thus Vidal's inclusion of *Lo Daro* not only permitted a convenient rhyme with *Lo Toro,* but also recalled both Guy's greatest blunder to date and the poisoned chalice that was Raymond's second regency.

If the preceding interpretation is correct, then Vidal's song would have been composed at Tiberias in late summer 1186 or early 1187. The writing of this troubadour's verses thus coincided with the composition of another political song sung by southern Frenchmen in the kingdom at this time, except in this case by Guy of Lusignan's supporters. According to the *Eracles,* Guy's followers from Poitou chanted the following inflammatory verses in Jerusalem to celebrate their man's controversial coronation: 'despite the *pullani,* we have a Poitevin king'.[214] The realm's political convulsions were set to music on both sides.

Returning to Vidal, the fact that this disgruntled follower of Raymond V of Toulouse had taken up service with his erstwhile lord's distant cousin, Raymond of Tripoli, could be taken as proof that relations between the houses of Tripoli and Toulouse had been soured by the events of the Second Crusade. However, Hoepffner makes the interesting observation that the poem composed under Raymond of Tripoli's patronage also represents a marked softening of Vidal's attitude towards Raymond of Toulouse. The troubadour's earlier poems contain angry outbursts of criticism directed at the count of Toulouse, but this one blames anonymous enemies for his exile and was perhaps composed out of a desire to be reconciled with his former lord.[215]

It may be that Vidal's time in the east set the scene for Raymond III to offer his kin in the house of Toulouse the opportunity to inherit from him Tripoli. According to one recension of the *Lignages d'Outremer* (*c.*1312), Raymond offered his county to any of 'les héritiers du comté de Toulouse' who would be willing to travel east, since he himself lacked any heirs upon his death in 1187.[216] Mayer is sceptical of this account on account of its late composition.[217] Nevertheless, it is a credible claim. Raymond was not the only ruler of the Latin East to offer his domains to distant western cousins around this time. A few years earlier, the dying Baldwin IV had sent an embassy to the west, hoping in particular that his kinsman, King Henry II of England, would act as regent for the infant Baldwin V.[218] Just as King Henry never went to the Holy Land, neither did any Toulousan ever take up Raymond's offer, which ultimately led the count to offer Tripoli to his cousins in Antioch instead.[219] Bruguière suggests that Raymond III did not put enough effort into contacting his western cousins, speculating that Raymond V's third son, Baldwin, would have relished the opportunity to escape a meagre inheritance by becoming count of Tripoli, an 'aventure orientale'.[220] It is Richard's belief that Raymond V and Raymond VI (r.1194–1222) of Toulouse, together with their immediate families, were simply too preoccupied by their own affairs, not least the rise of the Cathar heresy and the threat posed by persistent Angevin claims to Toulouse.[221]

Conceivably, Vidal acted as the mediator during Raymond III's attempts to pass the county to his Toulousan cousins. Vidal's own poetry suggests that he was at least sympathetic to the principle of keeping Tripoli a Toulousan patrimony. In another of his songs, Vidal wrote the following:

> Although he stole
> Saint-Félix [Languedoc] and Mornas [Provence],
> Tripoli, know this,
> Was nobly conquered by him.[222]

Some scholars believed that this was a simple reference to Raymond IV of Saint-Gilles's conquest of Tripoli in 1109 [*sic*], but Crescini went further and suggested that Vidal intended this historical recollection as coded criticism of Raymond V of Toulouse, whose inaction had allowed Tripoli to pass from the house of Toulouse to the house of Antioch without challenge.[223]

Crescini was apparently unaware of the *Lignages d'Outremer* and its claim that Raymond III had actually offered Tripoli to his Toulousan cousin.[224] Nevertheless, his theory regarding the meaning of Vidal's verses and the testimony of the *Lignages* are complementary, with the possibility that the once-exiled Vidal was the messenger who brought Raymond III's offer of Tripoli to his cousin Raymond V *c.*1186. This renders him similar to Guy of Lusignan, who had been favoured upon first arriving at the court of Jerusalem a decade before, when it was thought that the then-exiled Poitevin might nevertheless convince his lord, King Henry of England, to come east to help the beleaguered kingdom.[225] More generally, Vidal's employment at Raymond III's court represents the last and arguably greatest occasion when a count of Tripoli actively engaged with Occitan culture.

High treason

Even if he had wanted to, Raymond could not wallow forever in self-pity at Tiberias, listening to songs about Provence and hoping for a Toulousan renaissance in the east. Shortly after the count had retreated from Nablus, King Guy acted on advice proffered by Gerard of Ridefort and marched on Tiberias, aiming to disseize Raymond for refusing to do him homage. Confronted by this new threat yet lacking any realistic means of defending himself, Raymond decided to embark on a plan of action that would garner him notoriety for centuries to come, by placing himself under the protection of Saladin and inviting the sultan's Muslim troops into the principality of Galilee. Guy then had no option but to withdraw.[226]

The vast majority of medieval reporters, not to mention current thinking among modern historians, agreed that Raymond's latest act was an outrageous act of treason.[227] Authors as diverse as Arnold of Lübeck, James of Vitry and Ibn al-Athīr claimed that Raymond allied with Saladin in order to become king.[228] According to Ibn al-Athīr, Saladin even promised

Figure 5.2 Twelfth-century Toulousan-style silver *denier* in the name of Raymond II/III of Tripoli (Metcalf no. 509) © Ashmolean Museum, University of Oxford

Raymond that 'he would make him independent king for the Franks one and all'.[229] This implies that Raymond was willing to sacrifice the Latin East's sovereignty in return for becoming a sort of client ruler within the Islamic Ayyūbid empire, with special oversight of the particular religio-ethnic group of the Franks. This arrangement would have been reminiscent of the *ruʾasāʾ*, whom Frankish and Muslim rulers used as intermediaries with the locals of Syria. It also recalls the situation in the early twelfth century, when the king of Jerusalem viewed himself in non-territorial terms as 'king of the Latins', with the count of Tripoli ruler of a subordinate Occitan *Staatsvolk*.[230] The broadly critical Ibn al-Athīr claimed that Saladin was so keen for an alliance with Raymond that he released some of the count's captured men.[231] Raymond was expected to reciprocate, as Ibn Jubayr claimed that Raymond already owed Saladin his 'homage' (*ʿubūdiyya*) in 1184, beholden to the sultan ever since he had facilitated the count's freedom a decade before.[232] Thus he liberated the brother of the fiercely anti-Latin, pro-Ayyūbid Byzantine emperor Isaac II Angelos (r. 1185–95) upon Saladin's request.[233]

In the short term, Raymond's perceived betrayal of Christendom itself only managed to alienate further his erstwhile supporters and rivals alike, confirming that Guy was indeed the best – or at least better – man for the job of king.[234] Raymond's imprudent alliance with Saladin was not without precedent and Raymond's own parents had allied with Nūr al-Dīn in order to remove Bertrand of Toulouse in 1148. William of Tyre's reticence in reporting this earlier incident may well have been calculated to avoid the harm it could do to Raymond III's reputation, especially in the west where alliances with Muslims were neither common nor accepted as they were for the pragmatic politicians of the Latin East.[235] William of Tyre did not live long enough to see Raymond III's treachery in 1186, but Marshall Baldwin made the intriguing suggestion that the count was consciously inspired by the precedent established by his father – and mother – when seeking another Muslim's assistance in his own inter-Christian dispute.[236] Of course, this makes rather too much of the family connection and not enough of the basic fact that Syrian Franks generally did not share the ideological distaste at alliances with Muslims exhibited by their western cousins. Finding himself in dire straits, Raymond III no doubt had in mind his parents' success in ridding themselves of Bertrand some forty years previous, but also the much more widespread and long-established Syro-Frankish tradition of seeking assistance from their Muslim neighbours when a greater threat presented itself.

It must be said that Raymond's alliance with Saladin remained foolhardy for two reasons, the first being that Guy himself and many of his entourage were westerners with less direct experience and thus tolerance of such inter-faith co-operation, and the second being that Saladin – the Kurdish imperialist from the Islamic East – was himself the greatest current threat to the very system of autonomous lordships in Syria that had made such alliances advisable in the earlier twelfth century. By the 1180s, after the gradual erosion of the liberties of individual cities and towns and their subordination to imperialistic rule, enough of the Islamic Middle East had been united that there remained very few advisable and truly local Muslim allies, and Saladin the sultan was most emphatically not one of them.[237]

Raymond's poor strategic judgement can be assessed further by means of comparison, as he was not the only Jerusalemite baron to be conducting his own foreign policies at this time. In the winter of 1186–7, Raynald of Châtillon, lord of Transjordan, chose to attack a Muslim caravan passing from Cairo to Damascus, thereby threatening the truce between Saladin and Jerusalem that had been in place ever since 1180.[238] Raynald's seemingly reckless act was long believed to be the reason why Saladin resumed his hostilities against the Franks, choosing not to renew the truce when it came to its scheduled end on 5 April 1187. However, recent historians have done much to revise this, arguing that Saladin was looking for any excuse – however thin – to begin his final conquest of the Holy Land, while Raynald's seizure of the caravan was a relatively sensible attempt at disrupting the sultan's logistical network at a time when war seemed all but inevitable.[239] The current consensus then is that Raynald acted with far greater, if flawed, strategic wisdom in attacking the Muslim caravan than Raymond of Tripoli did by allying with Saladin against Guy: another neat inversion of the traditional view of the 'dovish' *pullani* and 'hawkish' newcomers. Furthermore, despite his immigrant status, Raynald seems to have appreciated the need to undermine Saladin's empire-building in the style of the Syrian autonomous rulers of decades past far more than did Raymond of Tripoli.

Events soon proved all the more just how disastrous was Raymond's appeasement of Saladin. As the Christian–Muslim truce lapsed and Saladin pressed hard on Raynald's Transjordanian castle of Karak, the High Court decided it was time to make peace with the count of Tripoli. A delegation consisting of Raynald of Sidon, Balian of Ibelin, Archbishop Joscius of Tyre and the masters of the Temple and Hospital was dispatched to meet with Raymond at Tiberias on 1 May 1187. The ecclesiastical party, led by the archbishop and the masters of the military orders, arrived at the Templar stronghold of La Fève near Nazareth the night before the planned meeting, while the secular lords headed north via different routes. Meanwhile, Saladin's son al-Afḍal led a raiding party into the kingdom of Jerusalem. Upon receiving an appeal for help from watchmen at Nazareth, the Templars and Hospitallers set out to intercept these Muslims. On the very day scheduled for the negotiations with the count of Tripoli, battle was joined at the springs of Cresson. The outcome was one of the most notorious bloodbaths in the history of the Latin East, with the entire Frankish force reduced to just four knights – the Templar master Gerard of Ridefort and three companions. The Hospitaller master, Roger of Moulins, was killed with the rest. Although some tried to blame Gerard and exonerate Raymond of Tripoli, it is hard to deny that the count had at least facilitated this disaster. Al-Afḍal had only been able to penetrate so deeply into the kingdom because he had passed right through Raymond's fief of Galilee without encountering the slightest opposition.[240]

Raymond's career to date had been marred by numerous misjudgements in both the military and the political spheres. The springs of Cresson, however, secured his infamy among his fellow Latin Christians. Cowed and shocked by what had transpired, Raymond immediately realised the mistake he had made by allying with Saladin and finally surrendered to Guy, accepting him as his king.[241] According to Arab chroniclers, Raymond was motivated in part by the threats made against him by his fellow Franks, including mooted rebellions by his soldiers, and excommunication and the forced annulment of his marriage to Eschiva by Christian clerics.[242] Even after the king had formally accepted Raymond's submission, the count found himself the target of much suspicion. Worse, the threat posed by Raymond's former ally Saladin was looming larger by the day.

Ḥaṭṭīn

As May 1187 progressed, the sultan gathered his forces to the east of the kingdom while Türkmens far to the north distracted Bohemond of Antioch. King Guy mustered all the forces he could at Ṣaffūriyya, draining the realm's cities and castles of their defenders almost completely and hiring mercenaries with funds raised by King Henry II of England. When the anticipated invasion finally came, Saladin targeted Raymond's own principality of Galilee.[243] On 2 July 1187, Saladin besieged Tiberias, hoping to draw the Christians into battle. Countess Eschiva, who had remained in the city when her husband had left to join the king's army, dispatched letters to the Frankish generals, warning them of what had happened.[244] The Christian high command immediately debated the best plan of action, making arguments both for and against direct military intervention. As had proved crippling before, the commanders of the Frankish army could not agree on a plan of action and a fierce debate quickly took place in the king's presence.

Raymond of Tripoli urged against a direct attack, arguing that Saladin had too great an army and in any case only threatened Tiberias, which was well-protected by its fortifications and garrison. Raymond was willing to risk both his city and his wife, as he believed that open battle would place the kingdom as a whole in unnecessary danger. Gerard of Ridefort and Raynald of Châtillon condemned Raymond's caution as cowardly and unchivalrous, as it left the count's wife Eschiva and her attendant ladies at the mercy of Saladin's army. Gerard dismissed Raymond's proposal as having about it something 'of the hair of the wolf' – a bizarre idiom that likely carried connotations of skittish behaviour or else deception, evocative of a sheep in wolf's clothing.[245] The Templar master also engaged in a candid *ad hominem* attack by reminding King Guy that Raymond was a traitor.[246] Marshall Baldwin blamed Gerard for his bitterness, but Smail noted that the Templar master's advice was 'very much to the point', with the count's recent actions having constituted nothing less than treason.[247] As the king contemplated these arguments and recriminations, he was undoubtedly mindful of the criticism he had received for his inaction at Ṣaffūriyya back in 1183, which had been largely Raymond of Tripoli's fault.[248] It is perhaps no surprise then that Guy sided with the bellicose Gerard and thus the Christian army headed eastwards towards Tiberias.[249]

As contemporaries later reflected on this posturing at Ṣaffūriyya, they came to believe that the decision taken in 1187 to attempt to relieve Tiberias led directly to the disastrous defeat that followed at Ḥaṭṭīn and thus the fall of Christian Jerusalem.[250] Much has been written about the battle of Ḥaṭṭīn and it does not require a detailed rehearsal here.[251] The Frankish army left Ṣaffūriyya on 3 July and marched towards Tiberias for a few miles, before they stopped to camp near the spring of Ṭurʿān. As the afternoon wore on, King Guy led the army away from this spring and further towards Tiberias, yet this proved misguided and too hasty, as Muslim raiding and the scorching sun gradually eroded the Christians' strength and confidence. Raymond of Tripoli's advice then to seek the springs of Ḥaṭṭīn for the sake of water made sense given the desperate circumstances, yet persistent raids prevented the Franks from reaching their intended destination, and forced them to camp away from water, surrounded by a Muslim army. The Christians spent a sleepless night becoming steadily more fearful and dehydrated, and woke to find themselves surrounded by fires ignited on Saladin's orders. Choking as the smoke filled the dry summer air, the Franks finally joined battle with Saladin's numerous host on 4 July. The Christians put up a brave effort, showing remarkable endurance for hours in the face of extremely unfavourable odds, but the Muslims eventually won the day when, finally, the king's tent collapsed and Guy himself was captured, together with numerous other survivors and the holy relic of the True Cross – symbol of the kingdom itself, now lost forever.

Some historians have thought that the county of Tripoli remained neutral in the conflict with Saladin up to and beyond Ḥaṭṭīn, with Raymond participating in the battle as prince of Galilee rather than as count of Tripoli, thereby preserving the truce with Saladin that he had sealed to protect his independent crusader state back in summer 1180.[252] Again this tendency to divide Raymond's life neatly into discrete Jerusalemite and Tripolitan spheres does not withstand close scrutiny. It is true that Raymond was accompanied by warriors from Galilee, most notably all four of his stepsons. So thorough was the Galilean levy that Raymond's wife Eschiva was left in Tiberias without any knights to protect her, only a garrison.[253] Ḥaṭṭīn itself was within the principality of Galilee, so the mobilisation of so many local knights is hardly surprising. Nevertheless, Tripolitans were in attendance as well, with Ibn al-Athīr describing Raymond's men as 'soldiers of Tiberias and Tripoli'.[254] Some of these Tripolitans can be identified in the sources: Hugh II Embriaco of Jubayl and probably his brother Raymond, Melioret of Maraqiyya and Plivain of Batrūn, each of whom presumably brought troops of his own.[255] The fact is that the county did not maintain neutrality. Raymond was doubted for his loyalty, but in the end he was willing to sacrifice his county's security for the defence of the Latin East. Saladin would soon enough make the county pay for this breach of trust.

Raymond's own actions in the battle of Ḥaṭṭīn itself were as controversial as any other in his life. According to the Old French narratives, Raymond of Tripoli fled the field upon seeing that the king had been taken. The count and a cavalry escort rode away through the ranks of Muslim soldiers, who parted before him.[256] According to Bahā' al-Dīn bin Shaddād, Raymond had actually left the battle sometime before this bitter climax – even before the fighting grew fierce, having already recognised that the Christian cause was doomed.[257] Lyons and Jackson have argued that the count's ostensibly dishonourable retreat was actually a brave cavalry charge that went awry in the face of superior Muslim manoeuvring, yet this still leaves Raymond's gifts as a soldier in doubt.[258] Unfortunately there is no way of reconstructing an accurate chronology, let alone determining whether Raymond meant to flee or fight, but such concerns are largely irrelevant.[259] What is important is that Raymond's departure only served to damage the morale of those Christians who remained, as Ibn al-Athīr noted.[260]

Baldwin framed Raymond's retreat as a 'sensible move' in the circumstances.[261] The fact is that the count had proven himself once again to be an ineffectual warrior, either incapable of a successful cavalry charge or cautious to the point of cowardice. Indeed, his behaviour at Ḥaṭṭīn follows a pattern observable in his actions at Ḥārim in 1164 – choosing captivity over death – and at Homs in 1175, preferring to appease rather than confront Saladin. Friedman suggests that Raymond's experiences of prison in Aleppo underlay the 'dovish policies he pursued after his return', becoming close to his captors in a way not dissimilar to some modern prisoners.[262] Of course, the count may simply have learned from Ḥārim and his subsequent decade of incarceration that, just as captivity was preferable to death, so too was freedom better than prison – even when bought pusillanimously. Modern historians, in their pursuit of objectivity, ought not to judge Raymond for retreating from Ḥaṭṭīn, yet contemporaries naturally did just that, believing that his withdrawal confirmed his treacherous nature beyond doubt.[263]

Death of a count

The Latin East was changed irrevocably after the battle of Ḥaṭṭīn. The True Cross was lost, never to be recovered. Countless Franks were taken prisoners, including high-ranking nobility. Among these were King Guy and Gerard of Ridefort, who would remain helplessly incarcerated until the following year. In a famous scene in his tent, Saladin made good on his promise to slay Raynald of Châtillon with his own hands. Within a few short months, the Palestinian holy cities of Jerusalem and Hebron were restored to Muslim control for the first time in almost a century, together with settlements of more mundane value, such as Acre, Jaffa and Ascalon. Never again would the kingdom of Jerusalem enjoy the same territorial extent that it had in the twelfth century, even after the armies of the Third Crusade (1189–92) relieved Tyre and recaptured Acre and Jaffa.

Many of those who had marched to Ḥaṭṭīn with Raymond of Tripoli were presumably killed or captured, abandoned by their count. A handful of those who were taken prisoner are known. Among them were Melioret – lord of Maraqiyya and son-in-law to Agnes of Tripoli, Count Raymond's paternal aunt[264] – and Plivain of Batrūn, the Pisan merchant-turned-nobleman, now joining his onetime rival Gerard of Ridefort in prison.[265] According to Bahā' al-Dīn bin Shaddād, at least one of Raymond's stepsons was also captured.[266] It is not known which of the four this was, but his brothers fled with Raymond and at least one – William – was recorded in Tyre a matter of days later.[267] Arguably the most important of Saladin's Tripolitan prisoners was Hugh II Embriaco, lord of Jubayl, who – unlike his lord Raymond – remained on the field: captured at the Christians' last stand, together with King Guy.[268]

According to some contemporaries, Saladin sent a small force to invade the southern county of Tripoli and capture Jubayl in early August 1187, while he was besieging Beirut.[269] According to Ibn al-Athīr, however,

Saladin only managed to acquire Jubayl because Hugh Embriaco surrendered it to buy his freedom.[270] After Jubayl was yielded on 4 August 1187, the sultan sent only a small garrison to Jubayl, comprised of his fellow Kurds and led by a religious jurist (*faqīh*).[271] No doubt this individual played a part in the long-anticipated restoration of Islam to this town, which still possessed a sizeable Muslim population after a century of Christian rule. As ʿImād al-Dīn recalled fondly, 'the church bells fell silent and the Christian laws became void; the Muslims elevated their own leaders and discovered their souls'.[272]

Saladin may also have reached a similar agreement with the captive Plivain of Batrūn as with Hugh Embriaco, although only a few of recensions of the *Ernoul-Eracles* narrative record Saladin's conquest of Batrūn at all.[273] Moreover, these late and augmented narratives emphasised the loss of Batrūn primarily to lend poetic justice to the long-running scandal concerning this city and the way in which Plivain had acquired it in the first place. It is possible that the fall of Batrūn in these narratives was one of the *Ernoul-Eracles*' many fictional interpolations. It may have been one of the smaller fortifications in the county, but it also happened to be north of the *Passus Canis*, which may have dissuaded Saladin from sending a sufficiently sizeable army to Batrūn. After all Jubayl – also north of the *Passus Canis* – was surrendered through mere diplomacy, with Salaldin having sent only a nominal force to garrison it. In all likelihood, the sultan recognised that he could not afford to risk sending his whole army through a dangerous bottleneck. Returning to Batrūn, then, its wealthy lord Plivain most probably could have afforded to buy his way out of prison with his famous gold, without also having to surrender his town, and he was indeed released soon after Ḥaṭṭīn, remaining lord of Batrūn until at least 1206.[274]

While many Tripolitans like Hugh of Jubayl and Plivain of Batrūn were left to negotiate and buy their own way out of captivity, the count of Tripoli himself and a small entourage of men, including his free stepsons, had headed first to Tyre after fleeing Ḥaṭṭīn, unable to take refuge with his wife in Tiberias.[275] Raymond joined other barons and bishops of the kingdom, who had for various reasons avoided capture and were now sheltering in Tyre. Within a month of Ḥaṭṭīn, these Franks granted generous liberties to Genoa. This so-called 'barons' charter' was also witnessed by Raymond of Byblos (Jubayl), who was presumably there because he had marched to Ḥaṭṭīn with the count of Tripoli and his own now-captive brother Hugh Embriaco.[276] Being himself a man of Genoese descent, Raymond Embriaco perhaps had a special interest in witnessing this particular concession. At a time of cataclysm for the Syrian Franks, the barons' charter was to initiate a surprising renaissance for Genoese interests in the east, except captured Jubayl itself.[277]

Raymond of Tripoli stayed in Tyre for approximately a month. His nerve soon failed him again, as he grew concerned that the city was vulnerable to conquest. Following the news that Beirut had fallen to Saladin on

6 August, Raymond departed Tyre and sailed north to Tripoli, believing it to be more secure.[278] The count could only trust that he would be protected beyond the mountains of Lebanon, hoping that Saladin would remain reluctant to risk a full invasion along the narrow coastal road from Beirut – his recent acquisition of Jubayl and perhaps Batrūn notwithstanding.

According to the *Estoires d'Outremer*, Countess Eschiva had joined Raymond at Tyre shortly after surrendering Tiberias to the victorious Saladin.[279] Meanwhile, ʿImād al-Dīn claimed that Eschiva did not reunite with her husband until he had already reached Tripoli, but this interpretation would require the lady to have taken an inexplicably long time to travel the narrow breadth of the kingdom of Jerusalem.[280] A close reading of the French and Arabic sources suggests that she had 'her children' with her at Tiberias during the battle of Ḥaṭṭīn.[281] These were apparently not her four adult sons by her late husband Walter of Saint-Omer, as these had accompanied Raymond to war. Ernoul made this clear by stating categorically that 'the countess had no knights with her'.[282] Who were these mysterious children? Since they did not fight, they may have been Eschiva's daughters with Walter or otherwise undocumented younger sons. William of Tyre had asserted not long before that Eschiva and Raymond had no children of their own.[283] Taken with Eschiva's fairly advanced age at this point, not to mention the fact that the county of Tripoli passed to the Antiochene dynasty shortly afterwards, it seems doubtful that these children were Raymond's. Indeed, the author of the *Eracles* claimed that Raymond referred to them specifically as 'her children', that is Eschiva's and not his.[284]

Other refugees soon followed the count and countess, including Raymond's old friend Balian of Ibelin, who requested and received permission from Saladin at Ascalon to take his own wife and children to Tripoli.[285] Shortly after the disputatious Conrad of Montferrat arrived at Tyre, another of Raymond's erstwhile allies, Raynald of Sidon, travelled from here to Tripoli in a boat by night.[286] Raynald's stealthy voyage illustrates the importance in such uncertain times of avoiding Muslim-controlled Beirut and Jubayl, not to mention the narrow mountain pass that linked them.

The *Ernoul-Eracles* tradition claims that the count of Tripoli treated a group of Jerusalemite refugees with outrageous cruelty, by denying them access to the city of Tripoli and by permitting brigands to attack them. The count's behaviour was compared unfavourably to the way in which the Muslims of Alexandria treated other Frankish refugees at this time.[287] One wonders if the poor treatment of these unfortunate individuals was less the result of deliberate malice on the part of the count and more an unavoidable consequence of the county's government being unable to cope with such a huge influx of people.

The chronology of this particular tale makes it highly unlikely, if not impossible, for Raymond to have been the count responsible.[288] Saladin did not capture Jerusalem, thereby driving its inhabitants to seek refuge elsewhere, until 2 October 1187, by which point Raymond III was most likely dead. Since the count was identified by title alone rather than name, it could be that the original author had in mind one of Raymond's Antiochene successors, as indeed James of Vitry assumed.[289] Contemporaries reported that, in the short weeks between the battle of Ḥaṭṭīn in July 1187 and Raymond of Tripoli's death in September, he had been forced to offer the county to his namesake and godson Raymond, eldest son of his maternal cousin Bohemond III of Antioch.[290] The count had no heirs of his own and his overtures to the house of Toulouse had proven fruitless. Bohemond would later ignore his cousin's choice of Raymond (IV) of Tripoli and instead gave the county to his second son, Bohemond IV, while the principality of Antioch passed to Raymond. The latter's premature death in 1199 opened the way for the two lordships to be united henceforth under a single dynast. However, it is unlikely that the Antiochene dynasty was actually ensconced in Tripoli as early as summer 1187.

According to the Lyon recension of the *Eracles*, it was not the count of Tripoli but Renoard, lord of Nephin, who bore chief responsibility for attacking the Jerusalemite refugees. God allegedly punished Renoard for his crimes on earth, ensuring both that he went blind before he died and that his successors were disinherited of Nephin.[291] Edbury has cautioned that the Lyon *Eracles* as a whole is a late and unreliable redaction, but nevertheless concedes that it contains some unique information derived from lost sources.[292] Perhaps then there was truth to the claim that Renoard was the one responsible for the refugees' sufferings. Alternatively, perhaps the Lyon author wished to shift the blame from Bohemond of Antioch onto Renoard, who by the time he was writing decades later was out of favour. In any case, it is highly likely that Raymond of Tripoli was not at fault, despite how neatly the mistreatment of the refugees fitted into the emerging narrative tradition that condemned him as a traitor, even apostate.[293] Indeed, the reference to how the Muslims had treated the refugees better than the Christians had, fed into a parallel tradition in western sources, eulogising Saladin as the 'noble pagan'.[294]

Fate caught up with Raymond rather more quickly than it did Renoard of Nephin, as the count died at Tripoli in late summer 1187, probably in September. A number of French and Arabic sources alike claimed that he 'died of sorrow or hurt', deeply depressed by the disasters for which he bore some responsibility, not least the outcome of events at Ḥaṭṭīn.[295] Bahā' al-Dīn simply claimed that he died of pleurisy.[296] Of course, at forty-eight years of age, Raymond was older than any count of Tripoli since Raymond of Saint-Gilles and perhaps Bertrand. It is entirely possible that the physical exertions and emotional tragedies of recent months had weakened Raymond and exacerbated an underlying respiratory problem that eventually killed him.

An evil reputation

The Christians' defeat at Ḥaṭṭīn and their subsequent loss of vast swathes of territory in the kingdom of Jerusalem, including the Holy City itself, sent shockwaves throughout Europe, leading soon to the launching of the Third Crusade and centuries of retrospection. Raymond, the man who had allied with Saladin and later fled Ḥaṭṭīn, attracted the particular ire of his co-religionists. Within a few years of Raymond's death, Christian authors were accusing Raymond of treachery for allying with Saladin prior to the battle of Cresson.[297] In the 1240s, the Cistercian Alberic of Trois-Fontaines alleged that Raymond and Saladin had drunk each other's blood in a wicked ritual to cement their alliance.[298] A contemporary French minstrel described the words Saladin purportedly used to convince Raymond to abandon the battle of Ḥaṭṭīn in a way befitting of a scene in a modern pantomime: 'count of Tripoli, count of Tripoli, remember your oath'.[299]

Western authors were soon bold enough to claim that Raymond had not simply betrayed his fellow Christians, but had apostatised – abandoning Christianity to become Muslim.[300] Various authors writing in the thirteenth century even told a fanciful story about how God had killed the count in his bed one night, as he had supposedly planned to betray the city to Saladin. When Raymond's body was examined the next day, it was discovered that he had recently been circumcised.[301] This is patently salacious nonsense, although the focus on such a visual symbol of Islam as circumcision – and one loathed by Christians ever since their primordial rejection of this and other originally Jewish customs – is noteworthy. Back when Pope Urban II had launched the First Crusade at Clermont in 1095, his Muslim targets were accused of forcibly circumcising Christians, spreading their blood on altars and in baptismal fonts.[302] That Raymond III, a descendant of one of the First Crusade's leading participants, was accused of undergoing this particular rite voluntarily thus illustrates how far his reputation in Europe had fallen.

Intriguingly, Islamic accounts do record that Raymond's fellow Franks during his lifetime accused him of 'becoming Muslim' (*aslamta*), with ʿImād al-Dīn even claiming that 'had it not been for fear of the people of his religion, [Raymond] would have become Muslim'.[303] Baldwin rightly observed that it is highly unlikely that Raymond did convert, since none of these Muslim accounts went so far as to claim that he actually did, even though such an incident would surely have been a noteworthy coup for Islamic propagandists. Moreover, the Christian sources that claimed he did convert were composed later than those that did not.[304] It should also be remembered that Raymond III ultimately did fight alongside his fellow Christians at Ḥaṭṭīn, against and not with Saladin. The claims of both French and Arab authors that Raymond died of a broken heart shortly after the defeat – Islam's victory – would make no sense whatsoever if Raymond himself was a Muslim.

Nor were Muslim authors particularly fond of Raymond, equating him with Satan (*al-shayṭān*), as when Ibn al-Athīr said that 'he was the Satan of the Franks and the unyieldingly harshest of them against the Muslims', or when ʿImād al-Dīn described Conrad of Montferrat's succession of him at

Tyre in 1187 as 'like one substituting Satan with a devil'.[305] Some Muslims even placed Raymond on a par with the notorious Raynald of Châtillon. One of Saladin's courtiers recommended that the sultan, were he to capture the two men, ought to 'seek God's favour by the shedding of their blood'.[306] None of this suggests that Raymond was anything other than a loyal Christian, even if his actions and policies of appeasement often came across as self-serving to the point of cowardice and treachery. Nevertheless, his posthumous reputation was to be sullied for centuries to come.

Conclusion

It was as a broken man and political failure that Raymond concluded his reign – by a whole decade the longest in the history of the so-called Toulousan dynasty of Tripoli. William of Tyre praised him for having 'much foresight' in politics and warfare.[307] Marshall Baldwin agreed, judging William's words to be 'more a statement of fact than an expression of opinion'.[308] Upon closer inspection, it is clear that Raymond's life both before and after his captivity was one defined more by personal failure and an astonishing lack of judgement both in battle and at court. Despite the high expectations of what the wealthy, ambitious and high-status Raymond might have achieved, the count's career reads as a veritable litany of inconsequential, misguided, or downright disastrous endeavours. To list the most serious examples, there was the humiliation suffered by his sister on his watch at the hands of Manuel Komnenos in 1162, his captivity at Ḥārim in 1164 and the ill-advised campaign to North Syria with Bohemond of Antioch and Philip of Flanders in 1177. He and Bohemond were soon thereafter outwitted at Guy's and Sybil's wedding in Easter 1180, which led to Raymond's subsequent two-year absence from the kingdom. He sank to petty levels when he and his allies undermined Guy's rightful authority at Ṣaffūriyya in 1183 and made a serious error of judgement when he failed to prevent Joscelin of Edessa's ruse to seize Beirut in 1186. It is little wonder then that the barons of Jerusalem appointed him to the regency in both 1174 and *c.*1185 with only great reluctance and lengthy prevarication, or that his allies abandoned his cause so quickly after Guy's and Sybil's coronation in 1186.

Raymond's mother, who had inspired him so much, lived on in troubadour fantasy for centuries to come, while his father had entered into an obscurity that spared him posthumous criticism. By contrast, Raymond's own fate was much worse – maligned as a traitor and an apostate by his fellow Christians, a devil and demon by his Islamic foes. Even William of Tyre's guarded praise for the count convinced only a handful of modern historians, principally Marshall Baldwin, before Raymond's reputation sank again in recent revisionist literature. On some level, Raymond himself must have appreciated that he had achieved frustratingly little in his life to leave the legacy he might have hoped. Raymond approached the end of his life dreaming of Toulouse and Provence – the very lands his great-great-grandfather had left almost a century before, never to see again. Unconsciously reflecting the last Toulousan count of Tripoli's lingering nostalgia for distant Occitania, Ibn al-Athīr would describe him as 'Raymond, son of Raymond, the man of Saint-Gilles'.[309] Perhaps at times in his life, incarcerated in Aleppo or outmanoeuvred in Jerusalem, Raymond III had shared the same opinion surely held by his Muslim rivals, critics and victims: that it would have been better if the sons of Saint-Gilles had never left the west at all, remaining far from the valleys of Syria and the mountains of Lebanon.

Notes

1 Hillenbrand, *Crusades*, pp. 171–2.
2 Barber, *Crusader States*, pp. 262–4.
3 Carole Hillenbrand, 'The Evolution of the Saladin Legend in the West', *Mélanges de l'Université de Saint-Joseph* 58 (2005), pp. 1–13.
4 Hamilton, *Leper King*, p. 235.
5 Hamilton, *Leper King*, pp. 84–8; Barber, *Crusader States*, pp. 264–5.
6 WT, vol. 2, p. 963.
7 WT, vol. 2, pp. 966–77.
8 Ditissimus et potentissimus erat omnium regis fidelium. WT, vol. 2, p. 963.
9 William of Tyre, trans. Babcock and Krey, vol. 2, p. 400 n. 7.
10 WT, vol. 1, p. 510. See Chapter 1.
11 WT, vol. 2, pp. 1043–6; Benjamin Z. Kedar, 'The General Tax of 1183 in the Crusading Kingdom of Jerusalem: Innovation or Adaptation?' *EHR* 89 (1974), pp. 340–5; Barber, *Crusader States*, p. 279.
12 Baldwin, *Raymond III* (1936), p. 25; La Monte, *Feudal Monarchy*, p. 27 n. 2. Cf. La Monte, *Feudal Monarchy*, p. 188.
13 Baldwin, *Raymond III* (1936), p. 25 n. 26.
14 Eodem anno quo regni procurationem suscepit. WT, vol. 2, p. 967.
15 *RRH*, no. 549.
16 Riley-Smith, *Feudal Nobility*, p. 102; Hamilton, *Leper King*, p. 94; Barber, *Crusader States*, p. 265.
17 Ernoul, p. 32. See Chapter 4.
18 WT, vol. 2, p. 963.
19 See below under 'Crowning controversy'.
20 Hans Eberhard Mayer, 'The Beginnings of King Amalric of Jerusalem', in *The Horns of Ḥaṭṭīn*, ed. Benjamin Z. Kedar (Jerusalem, 1992), p. 135.
21 Riley-Smith, *Feudal Nobility*, p. 102.
22 La Monte, *Feudal Monarchy*, pp. 27, 50 n. 1, 52 n. 1, 199; Baldwin, *Raymond III* (1936), p. 17; Richard, *Le comté*, p. 34; Hamilton, *Leper King*, p. 89.
23 Ratio validissima. WT, vol. 2, p. 963.
24 Baldwin, *Raymond III* (1936), p. 145.
25 Hamilton, *Leper King*, pp. 90, 93.
26 WT, vol. 2, p. 964.
27 WT, vol. 2, p. 965.
28 'Regni Iherosolymitani Brevis Historia', in *Annali Genovesi*, ed. Belgrano, vol. 1, p. 135; Hamilton, *Leper King*, pp. 90–3.
29 R. C. Smail, 'The Predicaments of Guy of Lusignan, 1183–87', in *Outremer*, p. 174. Cf. Baldwin, *Raymond III* (1936), p. 26.

30 See Chapters 1 and 3.
31 WT, vol. 2, pp. 965–6.
32 WT, vol. 2, 964.
33 Baldwin, *Raymond III* (1936), pp. 21–3 and *passim*; Runciman, *History*, vol. 2, p. 405.
34 M. R. Morgan, 'The Meanings of Old French *Polain*, Latin *Pullanus*', *Medium Aevum* 48 (1979), pp. 40–53.
35 Peter W. Edbury, 'Propaganda and Faction in the Kingdom of Jerusalem: The Background to Hattin', in *Crusaders and Muslims in Twelfth-Century Syria*, ed. Maya Shatzmiller (Leiden, 1993), pp. 174–5.
36 Hamilton, *Leper King*, pp. 2–3 and *passim*.
37 Smail, 'Predicaments', pp. 159–76; Hamilton, *Leper King*, pp. 95–6; Benjamin Z. Kedar, 'The Patriarch Eraclius', in *Outremer*, pp. 177–204; P. W. Edbury and John Gordon Rowe, 'William of Tyre and the Patriarchal Election of 1180', *EHR* 93 (1978), p. 25; Edbury and Rowe, *William*, pp. 21–2.
38 Edbury, 'Propaganda', pp. 173–89.
39 Hamilton, *Leper King*, p. 158.
40 Hamilton, *Leper King*, pp. 93–4; Barber, *Crusader States*, p. 265.
41 Tradita est ei universa regni post dominum regem [...] procuratio et potestas. WT, vol. 2, p. 966.
42 Raimundus, Tripolis comes, Raimundi comitis et Hodierne comitisse filius. *CGOH*, vol. 1, no. 467. Cf. *RRH*, no. 519.
43 Hamilton, *Leper King*, pp. 93–4.
44 WT, vol. 2, pp. 967–8, 972–3.
45 WT, vol. 2, p. 971; Major, *Medieval Rural Settlements*, vol. 1, p. 265.
46 WT, vol. 2, pp. 972–3. See Chapter 4.
47 IA, vol. 11, p. 419.
48 Istanjadū bi-ṣulbān-him wa-istaṣālū ʿalā al-islām bi-ʿudwān-him. Abū Shāma, 'Le Livre des Deux Jardins. Histoire des Deux Règnes, celui de Nour ed-Dîn et celui de Salah ed-Dîn', ed. B. de Meynard, *RHC Or*, vol. 4, p. 168.
49 IA, vol. 11, p. 419.
50 WT, vol. 2, p. 973.
51 Baldwin, *Raymond III* (1936), p. 29.
52 IA, vol. 11, pp. 419–20.
53 R. C. Smail, *Crusading Warfare, 1097–1193*, 2nd edn (Cambridge, 1995), p. 198 and *passim*.
54 IA, vol. 11, pp. 422–3.
55 Hamilton, *Leper King*, pp. 99–100.
56 WT, vol. 2, p. 973.
57 IA, vol. 11, p. 435.
58 Hamilton Gibb, *The Life of Saladin: From the Works of 'Imād ad-Dīn and Bahā' ad-Dīn* (Oxford, 1973), pp. 41, 46
59 Hamilton, *Leper King*, pp. 101–2, 215.
60 Barber, *Crusader States*, pp. 266–7. See Chapter 4.
61 WT, vol. 2, pp. 974, 975–6
62 IA, vol. 11, p. 437; Barber, *Crusader States*, p. 267.
63 Hamilton, *Leper King*, p. 100.
64 See below under 'Crowning controversy'.
65 See Chapter 4.
66 Ad incrementum regionum suarum. WT, vol. 2, p. 985.
67 See Chapter 3.
68 WT, vol. 2, pp. 979–96.
69 WT, vol. 2, pp. 986–8.
70 WT, vol. 2, pp. 986–7; IA, vol. 11, pp. 445–6.
71 WT, vol. 2, pp. 995–6.

72 Baldwin, *Raymond III* (1936), p. 33.
73 Hamilton, *Leper King*, p. 7.
74 Erant nonnulli qui domino principi Antiocheno [. . .] et domino comiti Tripolitano imputabant quod comes ita erat adversus profectioni in Egyptum. WT, vol. 2, p. 985.
75 WT, vol. 2, p. 995.
76 WT, vol. 2, pp. 985, 986.
77 Richard, *Le comté*, pp. 17–18.
78 WT, vol. 2, pp. 987–94.
79 Jouene chevalier. Ernoul, pp. 44–5.
80 Hamilton, *Leper King*, p. 118.
81 IA, vol. 11, p. 453.
82 WT, vol. 2, pp. 1000–1.
83 *CGOH*, vol. 4, no. 563*bis*.; *RRH*, no. 583.
84 IA, vol. 11, pp. 455–6. Cf. *RRH*, nos 519, 595.
85 WT, vol. 2, pp. 1001–2; *Documenti*, ed. Müller, I, no. 15, pp. 17–18; *RRH*, no. 585.
86 IA, vol. 11, pp. 455–6; WT, vol. 2, p. 1002.
87 Hamilton, *Leper King*, p. 157.
88 WT, vol. 2, p. 1007.
89 WT, vol. 2, p. 1007.
90 WT, vol. 2, p. 1009; Edbury and Rowe, *William*, pp. 147–8; Hamilton, *Leper King*, pp. 147–9.
91 Hamilton, *Leper King*, p. 155; Riley-Smith, *Feudal Nobility*, p. 106; Barber, *Crusader States*, pp. 274–5.
92 Edbury and Rowe, *William*, pp. 63–5.
93 Tam per mare quam per terras tam advenis quam indigenis. WT, vol. 2, pp. 1007–8.
94 WT, vol. 2, p. 1008.
95 Baldwin, *Raymond III* (1936), p. 45.
96 WT, vol. 2, pp. 1007, 1008.
97 A. S. Ehrenkreutz, 'The Place of Saladin in the Naval History of the Mediterranean Sea in the Middle Ages', *Journal of the American Oriental Society* 75.2 (1955), pp. 100–2, 105–8.
98 WT, vol. 2, pp. 1008–9.
99 Dhāta abwāb ḥadīd wa-hiya ka-al-muḥras. Al-Idrīsī, p. 375.
100 See Chapter 4.
101 WT, vol. 2, pp. 1008–9.
102 Hamilton, *Leper King*, p. 159.
103 Comes Tripolitanus quasi per continuum biennium circa partes Tripolitanas, multiplicitate negociorum impeditus. WT, vol. 2, p. 1019.
104 Baldwin, *Raymond III* (1936), p. 36.
105 *CGOH*, vol. 1, no. 589; *RRH*, no. 595. Cf. Deschamps, *Les Châteaux*, vol. 3, p. 19; Richard, 'Questions', p. 54 n. 1.
106 *CGOH*, vol. 1, nos 596, 676, 801, 804; *RRH*, nos 602, 637; *RRH Add.*, nos 651a, 651b; Richard, *Le comté*, p. 65.
107 *CDRG*, vol. 2, no. 118; *RRH*, no. 580; Mack, *Merchant*, p. 132.
108 L. T. Belgrano and A. Neri, 'Due bolle pontificie', *Giornale ligustico di archeologia, storia e letteratura* 10 (1883), no. 2, pp. 164–5; *RRH*, no. 581.
109 See Chapter 4.
110 Anne J. Duggan, '*Alexander ille meus*: The Papacy of Alexander III', in *Pope Alexander III (1159–81): The Art of Survival*, ed. Peter D. Clarke and Anne J. Duggan (Farnham, 2012), pp. 13–49.
111 Mack, *Merchant*, pp. 132–4.
112 *CDRG*, vol. 2, nos 161, 162; *RRH*, no. 580.

113 *CGOH*, vol. 2, no. XXI; *RRH*, no. 605.
114 *RRH*, no. 595.
115 WT, vol. 2, pp. 1013–16.
116 WT, vol. 2, p. 1016.
117 WT, vol. 2, pp. 1018–19.
118 Iṣṭifān al-Duwayhī, *Tārīkh*, p. 104; JV, p. 318.
119 Rudolf Hiestand, 'Die integration der Maroniten in der römische Kirche', *Orientalia Christiana Periodica* 54 (1988), pp. 119–52.
120 Kamal S. Salibi, 'The Maronite Church in the Middle Ages and its Union with Rome', *Oriens Christianus: Hefte für die Kunde des christlichen Orients* 42 (1958), pp. 92–104.
121 See Chapter 3.
122 Cf. Malcolm Barber, 'The Reputation of Gerard of Ridefort', in *The Military Orders. Volume 4: On Land and by Sea*, ed. Judi Upton-Ward (Aldershot, 2008), pp. 116–17.
123 *La continuation de Guillaume de Tyre (1184–1197)*, ed. M. R. Morgan, Documents relatifs à l'histoire des Croisades publiés par l'Académie des Inscriptions et Belles-Lettres 14 (Paris, 1982) (*Cont.*), pp. 45–6; 'L'Estoire de Eracles empereur et la conquest de la terre d'Outremer: C'est la continuation de l'estoire de Guillaume archevesque de Sur', *RHC Oc*, vol. 2, pp. 1–481 (*Eracles*), pp. 50–2. Plivain and his gold do not appear in all the French narratives. Cf. Ernoul, p. 114.
124 Barber, 'Reputation', p. 115.
125 Ernoul, pp. 114, 178. See below under 'Crowning controversy'.
126 Baldwin, *Raymond III* (1936), p. 41.
127 Baldwin, *Raymond III* (1936), p. 41; Richard, *Le comté*, pp. 75, 80; *Lignages*, pp. 83, 119.
128 *Cont.*, p. 46 n. 1; Hamilton, *Leper King*, pp. 146–7; *RRH*, no. 602.
129 Barber, 'Reputation', p. 114; J. Delaville le Roulx, 'Chartes de Terre Sainte', *Revue de l'Orient latin* 11 (1905–8), no. IV.
130 Delaville le Roulx, 'Chartes', no. IV.
131 Baldwin, *Raymond III* (1936), p. 41 n. 41; Hamilton, *Leper King*, pp. 146–7; Barber, 'Reputation', pp. 114–15.
132 Richard, *Le comté*, p. 85.
133 See Chapter 1.
134 *RRH*, no. 585; Richard, *Le comté*, p. 75 n. 2.
135 Barber, *Crusader States*, p. 245.
136 Hamilton, *Leper King*, pp. 175–6.
137 Gerald W. Day, *Genoa's Response to Byzantium, 1155–1204: Commercial Expansion and Factionalism in a Medieval City* (Urbana, 1988), p. 165.
138 Richard, *Le comté*, p. 91; Richard, 'Les comtes', p. 213. Cf. Richard, 'Les Saint-Gilles', pp. 70–1.
139 See Chapter 3.
140 Baldwin, *Raymond III* (1936), p. vii.
141 See below under 'A cold welcome'.
142 Seductorum [. . .] viris impiis. WT, vol. 2, p. 1019.
143 See Chapter 2.
144 Regni principibus [. . .] regni maiores. WT, vol. 2, pp. 1019–20.
145 Baldwin, *Raymond III* (1936), p. 44.
146 Riley-Smith, *Feudal Nobility*, pp. 104–5; Hamilton, *Leper King*, p. 205.
147 Baldwin, *Raymond III* (1936), p. 45.
148 Hamilton, *Latin Church*, p. 77; Guido Vannini and Michele Nucciotti, 'Petra a Shawbak. Archeologia di una frontiera. La missione in Giordania dell'Università di Firenze', in *La Giordania che abbiamo attraversato. Voci e immagini da un viaggio*, eds Silvia Lusuardi Siena and Claudia Perassi (Scilla, 2012), pp. 55–73; Mohammed al-Nasarat and Abd alrzaq Al-Maani, 'Petra during the

Crusader period from the evidence of al-Wuayra castle: a review', *Mediterranean Archaeology and Archaeometry* 14.1 (2014), pp. 222–32.
149 WT, vol. 2, pp. 1026–7.
150 Lyons and Jackson, *Saladin*, p. 166; Hamilton, *Leper King*, p. 172.
151 WT, vol. 2, pp. 1026–8.
152 IA, vol. 11, p. 479.
153 Syri, qui apud nos effeminati et molles habentur. WT, vol. 2, pp. 1028–9. See also: *CGOH*, vol. 4, no. 563*bis.*; *RRH*, no. 583.
154 WT, vol. 2, pp. 1030–2; Stevenson, *Crusaders*, pp. 228–9.
155 Baldwin, *Raymond III* (1936), p. 48.
156 WT, vol. 2, p. 1042.
157 Hamilton, *Leper King*, p. 179.
158 WT, vol. 2, pp. 1042–3.
159 WT, vol. 2, 1048–50, 1053–4.
160 WT, vol. 2, 1054–5.
161 R. C. Smail, 'Predicaments', pp. 170–2.
162 WT, vol. 2, p. 1058.
163 Grousset, *Histoire*, vol. 2, p. 731; Baldwin, *Raymond III* (1936), p. 57; Prawer, *Histoire*, vol. 1, p. 624.
164 WT, vol. 2, pp. 1058–59.
165 Tripolitano comiti regni curam et generalem administrationem committit. WT, vol. 2, pp. 1063–4; Hamilton, *Leper King*, pp. 198, 204.
166 Hamilton, *Leper King*, pp. 198, 204–5; Riley-Smith, *Feudal Nobility*, pp. 106–8.
167 Hamilton, *Leper King*, p. 205.
168 Ernoul, pp. 116–17; *Eracles*, pp. 6–7.
169 Hamilton, *Leper King*, pp. 206–7.
170 William of Newburgh, *Historia Rerum Anglicarum*, 3.16, in *Chronicles of the Reigns of Stephen, Henry II., and Richard I.*, ed. Richard Howlett, 4 vols, Rolls Series 82 (London, 1884–9), vol. 1, p. 255.
171 IA, vol. 11, p. 527.
172 Hamilton, *Leper King*, p. 207.
173 *CGOH*, vol. 4, no. 563*bis.*; *RRH*, no. 583. Cf. Richard, *Le comté*, p. 72.
174 See Chapter 2.
175 Riley-Smith, *Feudal Nobility*, p. 105.
176 WT, vol. 2, pp. 1059–60.
177 Hamilton, *Leper King*, p. 216.
178 Ernoul, pp. 116–17; *Eracles*, p. 7.
179 R. C. Smail, 'Predicaments', p. 175.
180 *Cont.*, pp. 30–2; Ernoul, pp. 129–31; *Eracles*, pp. 25–7; Hamilton, *Leper King*, pp. 217–18.
181 Hamilton, *Leper King*, p. 217; Barber, *Crusader States*, p. 293.
182 IA, vol. 11, p. 526; Arnold of Lübeck, 'Chronica Slavorum', ed. I. M. Lappenberg, *MGH SS*, vol. 21, p. 165; 'Regni Iherosolymitani Brevis Historia', p. 136.
183 'Regni Iherosolymitani Brevis Historia', pp. 136–7.
184 See Chapter 3.
185 Mayer, *Bistümer*, pp. 253, 254–6; Hamilton, *Leper King*, p. 217 n. 30.
186 Hamilton, *Leper King*, p. 217.
187 *Die lateinische Fortsetzung Wilhelms von Tyrus*, ed. Marianne Salloch (Leipzig, 1934), p. 51.
188 Muʾahhal li-l-mulk wa-murashshaḥ la-hu. IJ, p. 309.
189 *Cont.*, pp. 32–3; Ernoul, pp. 131–5; *Eracles*, pp. 27–9; Kedar, 'Patriarch Eraclius', pp. 195–8; Hamilton, *Leper King*, pp. 218–21.
190 Ceste corone vaut bien le marriage dou Botron. Cont., pp. 33, 46; *Eracles*, pp. 29, 52.

191 See above under 'A "multiplicity of affairs"'.
192 *Cont.*, pp. 32–3; Ernoul, pp. 131–2, 134; *Eracles*, pp. 27–8, 29.
193 Hamilton, *Latin Church*, p. 102 n. 5. See Chapter 4.
194 *Cont.*, pp. 33–4; Ernoul, pp. 135–6; *Eracles*, pp. 30–1; Hamilton, *Leper King*, p. 221.
195 *Cont.*, pp. 34–5; Ernoul, pp. 136–9; *Eracles*, pp. 31–4; Hamilton, *Leper King*, pp. 221–2.
196 Edbury, 'Propaganda', pp. 185–6.
197 *Cont.*, p. 35; Ernoul, p. 137; *Eracles*, p. 32.
198 Richard, *Le comté*, p. 91. See Chapter 4.
199 E. Hoepffner, *Le troubadour Peire Vidal, sa vie et son œuvre*, Publications de la Faculté des lettres de l'Université de Strasbourg 141 (Paris, 1961), pp. 52–4, 71.
200 Translated from: Peire Vidal, *Poésie: Edizione Critica e Commento*, ed. D'A. S. Avalle, 2 vols, Documenti di Filologia 4 (Milan and Naples, 1960), vol. 1, p. 43. See Appendix 2, no. 3.
201 See Chapters 3–4.
202 Paterson, *World*, p. 94.
203 Linda M. Paterson, 'Occitan Literature and the Holy Land', in *The World of Eleanor of Aquitaine: Literature and Society in Southern France between the Eleventh and Thirteenth Centuries*, ed. Marcus Bull and Catherine Léglu (Woodbridge, 2005), pp. 85–9. See also: Paterson, *World*, p. 30; Cahen, *La Syrie*, pp. 569–76; *Canso d'Antioca*, eds Sweetenham and Paterson, p. 52.
204 Paterson, 'Occitan Literature', p. 96.
205 See Chapter 2.
206 Paterson, 'Occitan Literature', p. 95.
207 Hoepffner, pp. 57, 69.
208 See below under 'Ḥaṭṭīn'.
209 Hoepffner, pp. 50, 52, 69–71.
210 Hoepffner, p. 69.
211 Hoepffner, pp. 54, 55–6, 69; Paterson, 'Occitan Literature', p. 92.
212 Translated from: Peire Vidal, vol. 1, pp. 41–2. See Appendix 2, no. 4.
213 See above under 'Raymond's second regency'.
214 Maugré li Polein, Avrons nous roi poitevin. *Cont.*, p. 53.
215 Hoepffner, pp. 56–7.
216 *Lignages*, p. 145; Richard, *Le comté*, pp. 8, 90–1; Richard, 'Les Saint-Gilles', pp. 70–1.
217 Mayer, *Varia*, p. 185.
218 Hamilton, *Leper King*, p. 209.
219 See below under 'Death of a count'.
220 Bruguière, p. 149.
221 Richard, *Le comté*, p. 91.
222 Translated from: Peire Vidal, vol. 2, p. 236. See Appendix 2, no. 5.
223 Vincenzo Crescini, 'Canzone-sirventese di Peire Vidal', in his *Románica Fragmenta, scritti scelti dall'autore* (Turin, 1932), pp. 479–80; Peire Vidal, vol. 2, pp. 231–2.
224 Crescini, 'Canzone-sirventese', p. 480. Cf. *Lignages*, p. 145.
225 Hamilton, *Latin Church*, pp. 156–7.
226 *Cont.*, pp. 36–7; Ernoul, pp. 141–3; *Eracles*, pp. 34–6.
227 Hamilton, *Leper King*, pp. 223–4; Barber, *Crusader States*, p. 296.
228 Arnold of Lübeck, 'Chronica', pp. 165, 166; JV, p. 430; IA, vol. 11, p. 526.
229 Yajʿalu-hu malikan mustaqillān li-l-firanj qāṭibatan. IA, vol. 11, p. 527.
230 See Chapter 2.
231 IA, vol. 11, p. 527.
232 IJ, p. 309.

233 Lyons and Jackson, *Saladin*, p. 251.
234 Smail, 'Predicaments', p. 175.
235 See Chapter 3.
236 Baldwin, *Raymond III* (1936), pp. 8–9.
237 Köhler, *Alliances*, *passim*.
238 Riley-Smith, *Feudal Nobility*, p. 27. See above under 'Invasion and incompetence'.
239 Lyons and Jackson, *Saladin*, p. 248; Hamilton, *Leper King*, pp. 225–7.
240 *Cont.*, pp. 37–40; Ernoul, pp. 143–50; *Eracles*, pp. 36–44; IA, vol. 11, pp. 530–1; Hamilton, *Leper King*, pp. 227–8.
241 Ernoul, p. 153; *Eracles*, pp. 44–5.
242 IA, vol. 11, p. 532; Kamāl al-Dīn, *Zubdat al-ḥalab*, vol. 3, p. 93; Hamilton, *Leper King*, pp. 228–9.
243 Hamilton, *Leper King*, pp. 229–30.
244 Ernoul, p. 158; *Eracles*, pp. 47–50.
245 Dou poil dou loup. Ernoul, pp. 158–62; *Eracles*, pp. 48–50.
246 Ernoul, p. 161; *Eracles*, pp. 52–3.
247 Baldwin, *Raymond III* (1936), pp. 94–135 *passim*; Smail, 'Predicaments', p. 173.
248 See above under 'Tantamount to treachery'.
249 Smail, 'Predicaments', pp. 168–73; Edbury, 'Propaganda', pp. 177–8.
250 *Eracles*, p. 52.
251 Benjamin Z. Kedar, 'The Battle of Ḥaṭṭīn Revisited', in *Horns*, ed. Kedar, pp. 190–207; Lyons and Jackson, *Saladin*, pp. 255–66.
252 La Monte, *Feudal Monarchy*, p. 199; Richard, *Le comté*, pp. 23, 37. Cf. Baldwin, *Raymond III* (1936), p. 102. See above under 'Invasion and incompetence'.
253 Ernoul, pp. 157–8.
254 ʿAskar ṭabariyya wa-ṭarābulus. IA, vol. 11, p. 532.
255 See below under 'Death of a count'.
256 Ernoul, pp. 169–70; *Eracles*, p. 65.
257 BD, p. 77.
258 Lyons and Jackson, *Saladin*, pp. 262–3.
259 Kedar, 'Battle of Ḥaṭṭīn', p. 204.
260 IA, vol. 11, p. 535.
261 Baldwin, *Raymond III* (1936), p. 125.
262 Friedman, *Encounter*, p. 6.
263 See below under 'An evil reputation'.
264 Richard, *Le comté*, p. 74; Rudt de Collenberg, 'Les « Raynouard »,' p. 296. Melioret was also a nephew of Raynald I of Nephin, who had assisted King Amalric in governing the county of Tripoli, 1164–*c*.1174. See Chapter 4.
265 *Eracles*, pp. 65–6.
266 BD, p. 77.
267 Cf. Ernoul, p. 170; *Eracles*, p. 65; *D.Jerus.*, vol. 3, no. 769; *RRH*, no. 659.
268 BD, p. 77; IA, vol. 11, p. 537.
269 Ernoul, p. 178; *Eracles*, p. 71 n. 30; BD, p. 80.
270 IA, vol. 11, p. 543.
271 These Kurds were to be blamed for the later Frankish reoccupation of the city, perhaps representing coded criticism of the Kurdish sultan himself. Abū Shāma, *Tarājim rijāl al-qarnayn al-sādis wa-al-sābiʿ, al-maʿrūf bi-al-dhayl ʿalā al-rawḍatayn*, ed. Ibrāhīm Shams al-Dīn (Beirut, 2002), p. 4.
272 ʿImād, p. 42; Abū Shāma, *Kitāb al-rawḍatayn*, vol. 3, p. 208. See Chapter 1.
273 Ernoul, p. 178; *Eracles*, p. 71.
274 Charles du Fresne du Cange and E. G. Rey, *Les Familles d'Outremer* (Paris, 1869), p. 258.
275 Ernoul, p. 170; *Eracles*, p. 65.
276 *D.Jerus.*, vol. 3, no. 769; *RRH*, no. 659.

277 Mack, *Merchant*, pp. 150–1; Merav Mack, 'A Genoese Perspective on the Third Crusade', *Crusades* 10 (2011), pp. 45–62.
278 IA, vol. 11, pp. 537–8, 543; BD, p. 77; Abū Shāma, *Kitāb al-rawḍatayn*, vol. 3, p. 189; Ernoul, pp. 170, 178; *Cont.*, p. 54; *Eracles*, pp. 65, 71; Magister Tolosanus, *Chronicon Faventinum*, ed. Giuseppe Rossini (Bologna, 1936–47), p. 106.
279 *Estoires d'Outremer et de la naissance Salehadin*, ed. Margaret A. Jubb, Westfield Publications in Medieval Studies 4 (London, 1990), p. 198.
280 ʿImād, p. 28; Abū Shāma, *Kitāb al-rawḍatayn*, vol. 3, pp. 185–6.
281 Awlād-hā. IA, vol. 11, pp. 533, 538. Si enfant. *Eracles*, p. 49.
282 Li contesse [...] n'avoit nul chevalier aveuc li. Ernoul, pp. 157–8.
283 WT, vol. 2, p. 967.
284 Si enfant. *Eracles*, p. 49.
285 Ernoul, pp. 186–7.
286 Ernoul, p. 182.
287 Ernoul, pp. 231–2; *Eracles*, pp. 100–1.
288 Barber, *Crusader States*, p. 312.
289 JV, p. 438.
290 *Lignages*, pp. 66, 94, 97, 145; *Eracles*, pp. 71–2; Ernoul, p. 178; Richard, *Le comté*, p. 8; Bruguière, pp. 149–50. Cf. *Lignages*, p. 173.
291 *Eracles*, pp. 100–1. Note that the editors of the *Recueil des historiens des croisades* chose to privilege the expanded *Colbert-Fontainebleau* recension and duly relegated all other versions to the literal margins of their edition. P. W. Edbury, 'New Perspectives on the Old French Continuations of William of Tyre', *Crusades* 9 (2010), pp. 110–11.
292 Peter W. Edbury, 'The Lyon *Eracles* and the Old French Continuations of William of Tyre', in *Montjoie*, pp. 139–53.
293 See below under 'An evil reputation'.
294 John France, 'Saladin, from Memory towards Myth in the Continuations', in *Deeds Done Beyond the Sea: Essays on William of Tyre, Cyprus and the Military Orders Presented to Peter Edbury*, ed. Susan B. Edgington and Helen J. Nicholson (Farnham, 2014), p. 75.
295 Ernoul, p. 178; *Eracles*, pp. 72–3; Abū al-Fidāʾ, *Kitāb al-mukhtaṣar*, vol. 3, p. 71; IA, vol. 11, p. 538. See also: *Anonymi Auctoris Chronicon*, vol. 2, p. 149.
296 Dhāt al-junab. BD, p. 77. Neither Baldwin nor Richard could reach a conclusive judgement between the two possible causes of death. Baldwin, *Raymond III* (1936), p. 138 and n. 17; Richard, *Le comté*, pp. 7–8.
297 Ernoul, pp. 141, 161–2, 167–9; *Cont.*, p. 46; *Eracles*, pp. 52–3; Benedict de Accoltis, 'Historia Gotefridi', *RHC Oc*, vol. 5, pp. 619–20.
298 Alberic of Trois-Fontaines, 'Chronica', ed. P. Scheffer-Boichorst, *MGH SS*, vol. 23, p. 860.
299 Cuens de Tripe, cuens de Trîpe [*sic*], tenez vo serement [alt. vostre convenenche]. *Récits d'un ménestrel de Reims au treizième siècle*, ed. Natalis de Wailly (Paris, 1876), p. 23.
300 Robert of Auxerre, 'Chronicon', ed. O. Holder-Egger, MGH SS, vol. 26, p. 251; William of Nangis, *Chronique*, vol. 1, p. 87; Joannes Iperii, 'Chronico Sythiensi Sancti-Bertini', *Recueil des Historiens des Gaules et de la France*, 24 vols (Paris, 1738–1904), vol. 18, p. 595; Marino Sanudo, 'Liber Secretorum', p. 194.
301 Robert of Auxerre, 'Chronicon', pp. 250–1; Vincent of Beauvais, 'Speculum Historiale', in his *Speculum Maius*, 4 vols (Douai, 1624), vol. 4, p. 1200; William of Nangis, *Chronique*, vol. 1, p. 87; Marino Sanudo, 'Liber Secretorum', p. 194. Cf. Ralph of Coggeshall, *Chronicon Anglicanum*, ed. Joseph Stephenson, Rolls Series 66 (London, 1875), p. 22; Roger of Howden, *Chronica*, ed. William Stubbs, 4 vols, Rolls Series 51 (London, 1868–71), vol. 2, p. 322. The earliest

version was also the most detailed, namely Robert of Auxerre's. Baldwin, *Raymond III* (1934), vol. 2, p. 353 n. 15.

302 Robert the Monk, *Historia Iherosolimitana*, ed. D. Kempf and M. G. Bull (Woodbridge, 2013), p. 5.

303 Kāna lawlā khawf ahl millat-hi yuslim. Abū Shāma, *Kitāb al-rawḍatayn*, vol. 3, p. 176; IA vol. 11, p. 532; Al-Fatḥ bin ʿAlī al-Bundārī, *Ikhtiṣār min kitāb al-barq al-shāmī li-l-ʿImād, al-kātib al-ʾIṣfahānī*, ed. Fatḥiyya al-Nabarāwī (Cairo, 1979), p. 289. Al-Bundārī's work is an abridgement of ʿImād al-Dīn's. Hillenbrand, *Crusades*, p. 155.

304 Baldwin, *Raymond III* (1936), pp. 84 n. 35, 159. See also: Baldwin, *Raymond III* (1934), vol. 2, pp. 347–54.

305 Kāna shayṭān al-franj, wa-ashadd-hum shakīma ʿalā al-muslimīn. IA, vol. 11, p. 303. Kamā yataʿawwaḍu ʿan al-shayṭān bi-iblīs. Abū Shāma, *Kitāb al-rawḍatayn*, vol. 3, p. 208. See also: IA, vol. 11, pp. 419, 531.

306 Tataqarrab ilā Allāh bi-irāqat dam-himā. Abū Shāma, *Kitāb al-rawḍatayn*, vol. 3, p. 187.

307 Providus multum. WT, vol. 2, p. 967.

308 Baldwin, *Raymond III* (1936), p. 139.

309 IA, vol. 11, pp. 419, 526.

Conclusion

Alien and native

The 'dynastie antiochénienne', like its Toulousan predecessor, prevailed through assassinations and war, earthquakes and rebellions, until finally it too died out, first evicted from its principal metropolis of Antioch by the Mamluks of Egypt in 1268 and then from Tripoli itself in 1288, this time by a communalist rebellion against Countess Lucia. Less than a year later, in 1289, the Mamluk sultan Qalawūn captured Tripoli, sweeping away the claims of commune and countess alike. Fearful that the European Christians would return, perhaps from their base of Cyprus, the Mamluks destroyed old Tripoli. They relocated the city away from the site it had long occupied, ever since the Phoenicians first founded it in the first century BC as a triple colony of Arados (Arwād/Ruad), Sidon and Tyre, hence the very name *Tripolis*. To avoid Frankish naval assaults, the Mamlūks abandoned the old city and rebuilt it further inland, around the fortress of the Pilgrims' Mount, which had been built by Raymond IV of Toulouse two centuries previously and which had since grown to be an important settlement in its own right, the true centre of Latin Christian political and economic life in the county.[1] In 1697, Henry Maundrell visited the area and observed the impressive ruins of the old city, left to decay on the shore.[2] After 1289, then, the county was no more, notwithstanding some minor outposts such as the Templar Knights' short-lived headquarters on the tiny island of Arwād, which fell to the Mamluks in 1303, or the Franks of Jubayl, permitted to remain under Muslim rule until *c.*1302. The title of count of Tripoli became an anachronistic honorific granted by the kings of Cyprus, with the last titular count being the Catalan pirate Juan Tafures in the fifteenth century.[3]

Each of the four so-called 'crusader states' had characteristics familiar to one another and to other regions within medieval western Christendom, from the dominant presence of religious orders – especially the military orders – to the use of Latin as the principal administrative language. Yet each also had a set of unique characteristics, found nowhere else. These did not derive from the cultural essence particular to each European dynasty that imposed itself upon each state, as past historians have thought, but rather from a history peculiar to its precise location within the Middle

East and the character of its inhabitants, including indigenous as well as European immigrants. The kingdom of Jerusalem had its sacred ground and holy cities, its deserts stretching down to touch Egypt and Arabia. The principality of Antioch was defined by the immense ridges of land that rippled out towards the Syrian interior and by the rich Romano-Byzantine heritage of its wealthy and ancient cities. The county of Edessa was a landlocked and vulnerable region that nonetheless managed to survive for a few decades thanks to the extent to which its Latin rulers were able to ingratiate themselves into a vibrant Armenian Christian society. What, then, did the county of Tripoli have?

Nestled in a coastal plain where the slopes of Jabal al-Nuṣayriyya and Mount Lebanon approached one another, the county enjoyed a surprising amount of military security compared to the other crusader states. Unlike the broad open frontiers of Jerusalem, Antioch and Edessa, Tripoli's main weakness in regard to the field armies of neighbouring Muslim powers was the Homs Gap – the trough where the Alawite and Lebanon mountains just failed to meet. A number of Islamic raids entered the county through this route during the twelfth century, including those led by the famous generals Nūr al-Dīn and Saladin. The counts of Tripoli could not fail to recognise this strategic vulnerability, not least as one – Pons – died in battle with just such an easterly invasion in 1137. However, lacking the resources of money and manpower, not to mention the sacred appeal of the kingdom of Jerusalem, they were forced to rely more heavily upon the military orders for their defence and at an earlier stage in history than any other ruler in the Latin East. Thus it was that the Templars and Hospitallers came to dominate the rich, fertile plains of Tripoli, managing castles that dwarfed most of their fortifications anywhere else in Syria.

Of course, the county of Tripoli was shaped by more than the threat of invasion from Muslim quarters beyond the mountains. The region's geography also determined the course that would be taken by the county in relation to its Christian neighbours, particularly the kingdom of Jerusalem and the principality of Antioch. The earliest settlers entered into negotiations with local powers as well as with each other, with the concept of a bipartite Levant looming large in their minds. Thus many of the leading Latins, including Tancred of Antioch and the first rulers of Jerusalem, attempted to divide the Middle East into northern and southern spheres in emulation of the political precedent set by the Byzantines and Fāṭimids a generation before. What would become the county of Tripoli was split along the middle, with the northern towns of Tortosa and the future Crac des Chevaliers subject to Antiochene suzerainty and the southern settlements of Tripoli itself and ʿArqa incorporated into the fledgling kingdom of Jerusalem. As the twelfth century wore on, however, it became increasingly difficult for either the princes of Antioch or (especially) the kings of Jerusalem to assert their authority over Tripoli, protected as it was by treacherous mountain roads. Thus, geographical obstacles to human power gave rise to the county of Tripoli, and with it the four crusader states familiar to every historian of the Latin East since William of Tyre.

The counts of Tripoli and the various peoples – both Christian and Muslim – who came into contact with them never forgot that they were indeed 'sons of Saint-Gilles', heirs to a dynasty that had arisen in the distant land of Occitania, where troubadours plied their trade and where the counts of Toulouse continued to rule their domains despite all the odds. Yet they were also very much Lebanese rulers, minting coins in Arabic, appointing locals to positions of responsibility and articulating their own power vis-à-vis others through the great mountain itself. Their success in balancing this duality was limited. On the one hand, they were content to ally with eastern potentates when in their interests to do so. On the other, they directed brutal violence against their local subjects on a number of occasions. By the end they were both alien and native, demonstrated by the fact that the dynasty of Toulouse disappeared from Tripoli accompanied by the harsh criticism of westerners and easterners alike: Raymond III, the traitor and devil both.

Notes

1 Piana, pp. 307–54.
2 Maundrell, *Journey*, p. 42.
3 Richard, 'Pairie', pp. 85, 86.

Appendix 1
Sources

Compared to historians of the contemporary Islamic world, the historian of the crusader states enjoys a disproportionate abundance and variety of source material, for what was a relatively small area of the Near East. If compared to historians of the contemporary Latin West, however, the historian of the Latin East has only a meagre body of surviving sources. Of course, this latter observation does not hold true for all areas of Europe. In the south of France, whence the county of Tripoli's ruling dynasty originated, the archives of the period have almost entirely disappeared, with few documents surviving even for great magnates like the counts of Toulouse.[1] Extant historical narratives are similarly sparse when compared to northern France, although some consolation is to be found in the relatively extensive and early body of literature composed in the vernacular *langue d'oc*, principally being the songs of troubadours.[2] To compensate for the relative paucity of evidence for the counts of Tripoli, their Islamic neighbours and their western cousins, an extremely wide range of source material has been used in this present work: primarily in Latin and Arabic, but also in Old French and *langue d'oc*, as well as modern translations of Greek, Persian, Syriac and Armenian texts. These sources, rarely concerned with the county or its rulers directly, must be read closely and cross-examined carefully in order to yield useful information.

Latin chronicles

The county of Tripoli produced no Latin historical narratives of its own. This renders it unlike the principality of Antioch, with Ralph of Caen's *Gesta Tancredi* and Walter the Chancellor's *Bella Antiochena*, or the kingdom of Jerusalem, with Fulcher of Chartres's *Historia Hierosolymitana* and William of Tyre's *Historia Ierosolimitana*. A fairly large number of the surviving Latin narratives concern the events of the First Crusade. Ostensibly the most relevant is Raymond of Aguilers's *Historia Francorum qui ceperunt Iherusalem*.[3] Raymond was a canon of Le Puy and became chaplain to Raymond of Saint-Gilles during the First Crusade, seeking thenceforth to document the count's achievements in his chronicle.[4] Raymond's chronicle is not wholly original, but closely related to other contemporary 'eyewitness' accounts of the First Crusade, namely the *Gesta Francorum* and Peter Tudebode's *Historia de Hierosolymitano Itinere.*[5] Each generation of historians has evaluated these related sources differently, but such shifting debates are of little direct relevance to this present study.[6] The *Gesta* and Peter Tudebode's *Historia,* together with subsequent revisions by authors such as Robert the Monk, add little of relevance that cannot also be found in Raymond of Aguilers's *Historia.*

The major problem with the early narratives is their limited chronological scope: all concluding with the battle of Ascalon, 13 August 1099, and thus furnishing no direct information on the county itself, only the historical background to its foundation. Other, often derivative narratives do survive to follow events beyond Ascalon. Fulcher of Chartres was chaplain to Baldwin of Boulogne, first count of Edessa and then king of Jerusalem, on the First Crusade. In the three decades following the expedition, Fulcher wrote his *Historia Hierosolymitana,* which in its initial chapters owes much to the *Gesta* or an associated text, before becoming an independent account of the early kingdom of Jerusalem.[7] Like Raymond of Aguilers, Fulcher wrote largely to eulogise his lord, Baldwin. As Baldwin became king, so too did Fulcher's narrative tend towards aggrandising the power of the crown of Jerusalem. This proves to be an important consideration to bear in mind when attempting to establish the early constitutional status of the county of Tripoli vis-à-vis its southern neighbour.[8]

Other sources that move beyond the battle of Ascalon include narratives more fully separate from the *Gesta* tradition. Walter the Chancellor's history of the principality of Antioch from 1114 to 1122, the *Bella Antiochena,* is essentially independent, as are the narratives composed by the Genoese Caffaro of Caschifellone.[9] A lengthier chronicle is Albert of Aachen's *Historia Ierosolimitana,* which covers the First Crusade and its aftermath up to 1120.[10] Albert was a cleric who wrote in the Rhineland and never visited the east, starting his chronicle sometime between 1100 and 1119 and finishing between the 1120s and 1140s.[11] Albert's *Historia* was once valued less than the accounts of the so-called 'eyewitnesses', but recent historiography has viewed Albert's text more favourably, as preserving accurate details and traditions derived from lost oral sources.[12]

After the conclusion of Fulcher's *Historia* in 1127, no substantial narratives were produced in the Latin East for a number of decades, until Archbishop William II of Tyre began to write. William's *magnum opus* is his famous narrative history of the kingdom of Jerusalem, which spans the period 1095 to 1184 and was written between *c.*1170 and 1184.[13] He drew upon a wide range of sources, including personal experience, the kingdom's archival records and earlier chronicles by authors such as Fulcher of Chartres and Albert of Aachen.[14] William's account is undeniably valuable but has certain limitations for this present study, not least the author's heavy focus upon his own *patria,* the kingdom of Jerusalem.

William rarely dealt with the other crusader states, even less the Muslim principalities, except when their histories directly impacted upon that of the kingdom. Although the county of Tripoli was regarded by many as part of the kingdom of Jerusalem in the early twelfth century, few adhered to this interpretation by the time William was writing. Furthermore, William's narration of events between 1127 and 1165 is notoriously thin and frequently erroneous.[15] The county of Tripoli in the middle years of the twelfth century is thus poorly served by William's chronicle.

William did compose another narrative, an overview of Islamic history, entitled *Gesta Orientalium Principum*.[16] Unfortunately this potential treasure trove does not survive, but it may have influenced the works of later authors, including James of Vitry and the Dominican missionary William of Tripoli.[17] James of Vitry excelled in his career as a churchman, reaching the rank of cardinal-bishop of Tusculum by the time of his death in 1240. His early life and origins are obscure; he was probably born between 1160 and 1170 and studied at Paris, soon becoming a talented preacher.[18] It was during his time as bishop of Acre that he wrote a handful of works dealing with the Latin East, particularly his *Historia Hierosolimitana* or *Historia Orientalis*, which is part history, part polemic and part geography.[19] James wrote this lengthy and popular piece between 1216 and *c.*1223/4, during his residence in the east and around the time of the Fifth Crusade (1213–21).[20] James's efforts in documenting and classifying the everyday activities, religious beliefs and cultural mores of communities throughout the Levant offer some intriguing insights into the lives of the county's ordinary non-Latin residents, albeit coloured by the author's unshakeable confidence in the supreme rectitude of the Roman Catholic Church.

Latin itineraries

Descriptions of the Holy Land produced by and for Latin Christian pilgrims prove useful as repositories of contemporary legends about the region, as well as providing geographic and demographic details. There is evident similarity between many of these itineraries, which regularly repeat the same information and stories about the region and its sites of interest, often verbatim. Scholars have thus assumed that the authors of these works used at least one lost ur-text or 'old compendium', generally dated to some point in the eleventh century but potentially incorporating older material.[21] One of the earliest crusader-era itineraries is that of Rorgo Fretellus, a chaplain and archdeacon of the cathedral of Nazareth, who wrote his *Descriptio Terrae Sanctae* in 1137.[22] Elements of Fretellus's work are evident in a great number of subsequent itineraries.[23] John of Würzburg, who wrote about his journey to the Holy Land *c.*1170, used one of Fretellus's sources for the places he did not visit in person.[24] John wrote for a friend or acquaintance named Dietrich, who may be identical with Theoderic, the author of another similar itinerary, 1169–74.[25]

Much of the content of these twelfth-century works found its way into sources outside the genre of itinerary, most notably James of Vitry's *Historia Orientalis.*[26] In turn, the pilgrim Burchard of Mount Sion used James's *Historia* when writing his *Descriptio Terrae Sanctae,* as he freely admitted.[27] Burchard was a German Dominican who visited the Holy Land between 1274 and 1284, probably composing a first draft of his *Descriptio* between 1280 and 1283. Other geographical treatises do exist, independent of the 'old compendium' tradition. Most notably, a canon of Hildesheim, Wilbrand of Oldenburg, left an account of his journey along the entire Levantine coast, the county of Tripoli included, in 1211–12.[28]

Vernacular Romance sources

Increasingly historians have recognised that the divide between Latin 'histories' and vernacular 'literature' was not as stark as once thought. Latin authors used vernacular sources – oral and written – and vice versa, and authors from the two categories did not necessarily write with markedly different goals or audiences in mind. The most important French sources used here are the Chronicle of Ernoul and the Old French Continuations of William of Tyre, or *Eracles,* which together comprise a bewilderingly complex textual tradition. The Chronicle of Ernoul was an independent narrative written in part by a squire of Balian of Ibelin soon after 1187. It does not survive in its original form, but was reworked and extended by another author or authors in the 1220s and 1230s, producing a related family of surviving variants, dubbed *Ernoul-Bernard.*[29] The narrative actually written by Ernoul the squire probably does not go beyond 1187. In the 1230s, an anonymous author grafted the post-1184 narrative of *Ernoul-Bernard* – henceforth simply Ernoul – on to the end of the Old French translation of William of Tyre's Latin chronicle, which concluded in 1184, thus creating the Old French Continuation.[30] In turn, these were reworked and extended further by others, leaving to posterity a great array of recensions: 'broadly similar in tone and content', sharing a range of narrative 'fragments', but each one containing unique information of variable reliability.[31] At present, the most comprehensive edition of the Old French Continuations remains that found in the *Recueil des Historiens des Croisades.*[32] Edbury has criticised the editors for emphasising the late and unusual *Colbert-Fontainebleau* variant, written around the 1240s.[33] Building on this, Guy Perry has recently underlined the thirteenth-century political context of the text's composition, but adds the important caveat that the *Recueil* edition remains the definitive, most accessible version at present.[34]

Arabic narratives

Whereas crusading inspired dedicated 'crusades chronicles' in Latin Christendom, the crusaders' main targets, the Muslims of Syria, produced no such works. Instead, information on these Christian wars was worked into various Arabic historical narratives. Broadly speaking, the works used here can be broken down into local chronicles, dynastic panegyrics and anthologies of extracts. The earliest surviving of the local chronicles to mention the Franks is Muḥammad bin ʿAlī al-ʿAẓīmī's *Tārīkh ḥalab* (History of Aleppo).[35] Abū Yaʿlā Ḥamza bin al-Qalānisī's *Dhayl tārīkh dimashq* (Continuation of the History of Damascus) is a more substantial work, with its author – the hereditary *raʾīs* of Damascus (d. 1160) – doing for his city's historiography what al-ʿAẓīmī had done for his.[36] The *Dhayl* is an important source, not least because it served as the basis for many later narratives and compilations, including those of Ibn al-Athīr and Abū Shāma. Moreover, its later sections incorporate accounts of the Franks, although Ibn al-Qalānisī's focus on the city of Damascus means that his source is restricted in much the same way as William of Tyre's Latin Jerusalemite chronicle, recording these activities only when they directly impacted upon Damascene history. Another useful local Arabic chronicle, like al-ʿAẓīmī's focusing on Aleppo, is the *Zubdat al-ḥalab min ṭārīkh ḥalab* (Cream of Aleppo from the History of Aleppo), written by Aleppo's *qāḍī* Kamāl al-Dīn (d. 1262).[37] This is a fairly late source, but one compiled by a well-connected intellectual and politician with access to earlier, often lost accounts and thus retains great value if used with caution.[38]

Dynastic panegyrics began to be produced under Saladin to glorify the personal achievements of the individual ruler and conqueror rather than to record the events that befell a particular city. Two men in Saladin's service, ʿImād al-Dīn al-Iṣfahānī (d. 1201) and Bahāʾ al-Dīn bin Shaddād (d. 1234), produced biographies of their master after his death, which incorporate some important material regarding the county of Tripoli, particularly during Saladin's invasion in 1188. ʿImād al-Dīn served as Saladin's secretary right up until the sultan's death and his *Al-fatḥ al-qussī fī al-fatḥ al-qudsī* (The Loosing of Bows in the Conquest of Jerusalem) is most useful, not least because he was an eyewitness to many of Saladin's military campaigns in the late 1180s and early 1190s.[39] Meanwhile, Bahāʾ al-Dīn entered Saladin's service as 'judge of the army' (*qāḍī al-ʿaskar*) while the sultan was besieging Crac des Chevaliers in the county of Tripoli in 1188. He is best known today for his biography of Saladin, *Al-nawādir al-sulṭāniyya wa-al-maḥāsin al-yūsufiyya* (the Extraordinary Things of the Sultan and the Meritorious Qualities of Yūsuf).[40] This biography is based partly on that of his colleague ʿImād al-Dīn, although it is more concise, less elaborate and contains some independent information.

The early thirteenth century produced more than mere dynastic historiography. Ibn al-Athīr (d. 1233) was born to a family associated with the Zankid dynasty and wrote a lengthy work of history, *Al-kāmil fī al-tārīkh* (Perfection in History), of which the later sections are invaluable to the historian of the crusades.[41] His narrative is late yet incorporates information from lost Arabic accounts. That said, the distortions he introduced mean that historians should always be alert when reading *Al-kāmil*.[42] Abū Shāma's *Kitāb al-rawḍatayn* (Book of Two Gardens) – a metaphor for the reigns of Nūr al-Dīn and Saladin – was composed in the mid-thirteenth century, constituting a compilation of letters and extracts from earlier authorities, whom Abū Shāma himself diligently cited.[43] The principal value of the *Kitāb* therefore is for preserving extracts from otherwise lost works, especially additional writings by ʿImād al-Dīn.

Miscellaneous Arabic sources

Some Arabic sources prove difficult to classify either for their genre or language. Usāma bin Munqidh was a scion of the ruling family of Shayzar. He was born in 1095, was expelled from Shayzar by his uncle in 1138, became a diplomat and courtier in Syria and Egypt, fell out of favour with Saladin in 1176 and died in 1188.[44] His most famous work is *Kitāb al-iʿtibār* (Book of Learning by Example).[45] Irwin believes that this was written for his son, while Cobb believes Usāma wrote it for Saladin.[46] Some have described it as an autobiography – a rare genre within medieval Islamic writing – whereas Irwin has stressed that it is a piece of literature, guided by an exploration of likenesses and antitheses, and of fatalism before the inscrutable will of God.[47] This raises doubts as to whether what Usāma wrote should be taken as an honest or accurate depiction of events. Cobb is insistent that what Usāma described should not be discarded simply because of his literary and didactic intentions, and certainly *Kitāb al-iʿtibār* contains precious details regarding everyday life in medieval Syria.[48] Usāma's writings include a small handful of anecdotes relating to the county's inhabitants. Despite Shayzar's proximity to the county of Tripoli, Usāma never stated that he himself visited Tripoli, although one of his slaves did.[49] The closest Usāma came to the county personally was to accompany Zankī of Mosul during the latter's siege of Rafaniyya on the county's easternmost frontier in 1137.[50]

Biographical dictionaries are a major genre within medieval Arabic literature although tend only to include Muslim figures, with 'biographies de princes francs [. . .] exceptionnelles'.[51] These works do prove relevant sometimes, such as Ibn Khallikān's (d. 1282) biography of the Shīʿite poet, Ibn Munīr, who was evicted from Tripoli by the crusader conquest.[52] Alongside biographical dictionaries are geographic encyclopaedias, which have not been utilised extensively by crusade historians but nonetheless incorporate valuable information regarding sites of religious and historical significance in the region. For example, Yāqūt al-Rūmī al-Ḥamawī composed his *Muʿjam al-buldān* (Encyclopaedia of Lands) between *c.*1218/19 and his death in 1229.[53] A handful of Arabophone Muslim travellers left accounts of their voyages to the Latin East or the region it occupied. Most famous is Ibn Jubayr, an Andalusian Muslim who visited the kingdom of Jerusalem and various other locales in the Mediterranean between 1183 and 1185 during a pilgrimage to Mecca. His travelogue or *riḥla* survives today.[54]

Charters

Charter evidence survives for the county, overwhelmingly in Latin for the period under study. The loss of the county's domestic archives means that such evidence is highly diffuse and subject to certain distortions. Most surviving charters pertain to the Hospitaller military order, giving the misleading impression that this institution possessed a greater share of property in the county than it probably did. Occasionally, contemporary sources indicate the existence of many more documents, now lost. On 2 June 1271, the Hospitallers returned to Guy II of Jubayl forty-four charters (*privillegia*) originally deposited with the Order by Guy's father Henry for safekeeping.[55] They were presumably lost with the Mamluk conquest a few years later. In the nineteenth century, Lord Lindsay reported a tantalising story that a French traveller had discovered 'a bundle of old parchments' in the possession of the *shaykh* of the village of Ghosta, Lebanon, and that these parchments were proof of the *shaykh*'s descent from 'one of the oldest crusading families in France'. The *shaykh* had set out for Paris with the documents, but had fallen ill at Alexandria and had returned home, where he still lived in the 1830s.[56] The fate of these documents, if they ever existed, is unknown. Whatever the veracity of this particular story, it is not inconceivable that local landowners held on to Frankish-era documents for centuries. Indeed, this is suggested by the incorporation of summaries of thirteenth-century Frankish Arabic documents pertaining to local lords into Ṣāliḥ bin Yaḥyā's fifteenth-century *Tārīkh bayrūt* (History of Beirut).[57] These are among the scant few documents issued in Arabic under Frankish rule that survive and none are known for the county of Tripoli, although it is highly likely that Arabic document production was prevalent in all the crusader states.[58]

Modern registers and editions enable the identification of those charters that do survive. Foremost among the registers for comprehensiveness is Reinhold Röhricht's *Regesta Regni Hierosolymitani* and supplementary *Additamentum*, although its age means that it does not include any discoveries or editions subsequent to 1904.[59] Among these later findings are a number of charters from the Latin East, including one from the county of Tripoli edited by Delaville le Roulx in 1905–8.[60] Richard has usefully edited and published a handful of previously unedited charters relevant to the county: one issued by Raymond of Saint-Gilles, two by Pons of Tripoli and six relevant *acta* from the archives of the Porcelet family of Arles.[61] In 1969, Riley-Smith edited an episcopal deed dated to 1157, which confirmed an earlier donation to the Templars of rights and property in the diocese of Tortosa, 1152.[62] Mayer's *Die Urkunden der lateinischen Könige von Jerusalem* is useful for its recent and thorough analysis of charters relating to the kings and queens of Jerusalem, but proves largely irrelevant to a study of the county of Tripoli.[63] Delaville le Roulx's four-volume edition of Hospitaller documents from 1100 to 1310, primarily preserved in Marseille and Valletta, is extremely helpful.[64] The incorporation of some Templar documents into the Hospitaller archives of Malta led Delaville le Roulx to produce also his *Documents concernant les Templiers*, which includes a few formerly unedited charters.[65] Aside from the military religious orders, the surviving recensions of the cartulary of the canons of the Holy Sepulchre in Jerusalem contain a number of charters detailing property in the county, for which Bresc-Bautier's edition is the best.[66]

Other sources

A range of sources written in languages other than Latin, French, Occitan and Arabic shed light on the county's history. The most important Greek narrative is Anna Komnene's *Alexiad*.[67] As the title suggests, the author wrote primarily to eulogise her father, Emperor Alexios I Komnenos, and did so many years after the events she described, with the outcome being that historians often doubt her reliability. Among the most useful sources written in Syriac is a chronicle by an anonymous Edessan (fl.1187–1237), extending up to the year 1234 and available in a French translation for the later sections relevant to the crusader period.[68] Armenian sources can provide helpful additional information, although are generally more useful for events in North Syria and especially the county of Edessa.

Moving away from written texts, there is also a reasonable quantity of relevant archaeological and art historical evidence. One particularly rich seam of evidence is numismatic. Although fairly formulaic in their designs, the coins that survive from the county of Tripoli are nonetheless crucial evidence, not least of the continued use of Arabic as an administrative language.[69] Since the nineteenth century, numismatists have produced studies of extant crusader coins, most of which are presently housed in western collections.[70] As for archaeological sites and artefacts that remain *in situ*, these – like crusading history more broadly – have not been studied as extensively in modern Syria and Lebanon as in Israel. That said, research in Syria and Lebanon has continued to reveal tantalising clues as to the material environment of the county of Tripoli.

Beginning with the capital, Oleg Grabar described the city of Tripoli as 'a Mamluk creation', on account of the fact the old city was abandoned following its conquest in 1289 and rebuilt further inland.[71] Crusader Tripoli is now buried by the modern district of al-Mīnā, 'the Port', or else incorporated as *spolia* into the buildings of the 'new' Mamluk city.[72] The fortress at the heart of the modern city is none other than that built by Raymond of Saint-Gilles with Byzantine assistance to besiege the city in 1103, and although it incorporates earlier Islamic structures and was substantially rebuilt by later Muslim governments, it still bears Raymond's name as the 'Citadel of Saint-Gilles' (*qalʿat ṣanjīl*).[73] On the other hand, the Frankish cathedral survives only as architectural fragments incorporated into the city's main mosque.[74]

Other settlements in the former county bear traces of the Frankish period, such as the cathedral – now a museum – at Tortosa and its counterpart at Jubayl.[75] Balázs Major has carried out an extensive survey of the above-ground remains – mainly stone towers and churches – of minor rural settlements in what is now the modern Republic of Syria, that is to say the southern half of the principality of Antioch and the northern half of the county of Tripoli.[76] Major's work is an important complement to the earlier work carried out on monumental edifices by predominantly French scholars in the nineteenth and early twentieth centuries, particularly during France's League of Nations Mandate of Syria and Lebanon (1923–43). For example, the county's greatest archaeological monument, the former Hospitaller stronghold of Crac des Chevaliers, was surveyed most comprehensively by Deschamps in the 1930s, framing his study within the context of 'colonisation'.[77] In more recent years, German-led research has expanded our understanding of this formidable structure.[78] Deschamps's impressive work on Crac was followed by two related volumes, *La défense du royaume de Jérusalem* and *La défense du comté de Tripoli et de la principauté d'Antioche.*[79] These books are accompanied by fairly shallow historical overviews, but their real value to the historian lies in their localisation of specific places in the Levant, as well as Deschamps's extensive illustrations, photographs and surveys. The third volume in particular covers the principal surviving edifices in the county of Tripoli, including the citadels of Tripoli and Jubayl, the castle of Ṣāfītā (*Chastel Blanc*) and numerous lesser, ruined or rebuilt sites.

The former chapel of Crac des Chevaliers is – or was, prior to damage sustained during the Syrian civil war (2011–present) – adorned with famous wall paintings, analysed by Jaroslav Folda as an example of 'crusader art', a uniquely Levantine fusion of western, Byzantine, Syrian and Islamic art styles.[80] This chapel is not the only structure to bear medieval wall paintings, with many other decorated churches scattered throughout West Syria and Lebanon. Many of the paintings have not survived the centuries, with decay still occurring on a regular basis. Paintings have fallen foul of manifold scourges including weather, earthquakes, deliberate iconoclasm, graffiti, bombs, amateur attempts at restoration and ill-advised 'modernisation' of church buildings.[81] Fortunately, art historians have worked to record and analyse many of the paintings prior to their destruction. The best modern works are by Erica Dodd and Mat Immerzeel.[82] The foremost scholarly outlet for art historians working on medieval Lebanon is the journal *Chronos*, published by the University of Balamand in Lebanon itself, near the site of the county of Tripoli's principal and still-extant Cistercian abbey Belmont, which is now an Orthodox monastery.[83]

Notes

1 Thomas N. Bisson, 'Some Characteristics of Mediterranean Territorial Power in the Twelfth Century', in his *Medieval France*, p. 259; Pierre Bonnassie, 'From the Rhône to Galicia: Origins and Modalities of the Feudal Order', in his *From Slavery to Feudalism in South-Western Europe*, trans. Jean Birrell (Cambridge, 1991), p. 127.

2 Thomas N. Bisson, 'Unheroed Pasts: History and Commemoration in South Frankland before the Albigensian Crusades', *Speculum* 65.2 (1990), pp. 281–2 and *passim*.
3 RA.
4 But cf. Pryor, 'The oaths', p. 127.
5 *GF*; PT; Pryor and Jeffreys, 'Alexios, Bohemond', pp. 85–6.
6 See, for example: Jay Rubenstein, 'What is the *Gesta Francorum*, and who was Peter Tudebode?' *Revue Mabillon: Revue internationale d'histoire et de littérature religieuses*, n.s. 16.77 (2005), pp. 179–204; Jean Flori, 'De l'Anonyme normand à Tudebode et aux *Gesta Francorum*: L'impact de la propagande de Bohémond sur la critique textuelle des sources de la première croisade', *Revue d'histoire ecclésiastique* 102.3–4 (2007), pp. 717–45; Samu Niskanen, 'The origins of the *Gesta Francorum* and two related texts: their textual and literary character', *Sacris Erudiri: A Journal on the Inheritance of Late Antique and Medieval Christianity* 51 (2012), pp. 287–316.
7 FC.
8 See Chapter 2.
9 Walter the Chancellor, *Bella*; Caffaro, 'De Liberatione', pp. 95–124.
10 AA.
11 Edgington, 'First Crusade', p. 61; Peter Lock, *The Routledge Companion to the Crusades* (Oxford, 2006), p. 228.
12 Flori, *Pierre l'Ermite*, pp. 51–66; Edgington, 'First Crusade', pp. 61–73.
13 Edbury and Rowe, *William*, pp. 1, 26.
14 Edbury and Rowe, *William*, pp. 44–58.
15 Murray, 'Mighty', pp. 222–3.
16 Edbury and Rowe, *William*, p. 23.
17 R. H. C. Davis, 'William of Tyre', in *Relations between East and West in the Middle Ages*, ed. Derek Baker (Edinburgh, 1973), p. 71; Edbury and Rowe, *William*, p. 24.
18 John F. Benton, 'Qui étaient les parents de Jacques de Vitry?' in his *Culture, Power and Personality in Medieval France*, ed. Thomas N. Bisson (London, 1991), pp. 89–91.
19 JV.
20 JV, pp. 10–12.
21 Fretellus, *Rorgo Fretellus de Nazareth et sa description de la Terre Sainte: Histoire et édition du texte*, ed. P. C. Boeren (Amsterdam, 1980), p. xxxi; Theoderich, *Description of the Holy Places. (Circa 1172 A.D.)*, trans. Aubrey Stewart, Palestine Pilgrims' Text Society 5 (London, 1896), pp. iii–iv; Wilkinson, p. 3.
22 Fretellus, pp. vii, viii–xiii.
23 Wilkinson, p. 15.
24 John of Würzburg, 'Peregrinatio', pp. 78–141; Wilkinson, p. 21.
25 Theoderich, 'Descriptio', pp. 142–97; Wilkinson, pp. 21, 22.
26 JV, p. 28.
27 Burchard of Mount Sion, pp. 1–100.
28 Wilbrand of Oldenburg, pp. 109–37.
29 Edbury, 'New Perspectives', pp. 108–9.
30 Edbury, 'New Perspectives', pp. 108, 109; Ernoul.
31 Edbury, 'Lyon *Eracles*', p. 140; Edbury, 'New Perspectives', pp. 110–13; M. R. Morgan, *The Chronicle of Ernoul and the Continuations of William of Tyre* (London, 1973), pp. 177–8.
32 *Eracles*. See also: *Cont*.
33 Edbury, 'New Perspectives', pp. 110–11.
34 Guy Perry, *John of Brienne: King of Jerusalem, Emperor of Constantinople*, c. *1175–1237* (Cambridge, 2013), pp. 14–15.
35 Al-ʿAẓīmī, *Tārīkh ḥalab.*

36 IQ, pp. 6–7; Ibn al-Qalānisī, trans. Gibb, pp. 9–10.
37 Kamāl al-Dīn, *Zubdat al-ḥalab.*
38 H. A. R. Gibb, 'Notes on the Arabic Materials for the History of the Early Crusades', *Bulletin of the School of Oriental and African Studies* 7.4 (1935), p. 753. See also: Anne-Marie Eddé, 'Kamāl al-Dīn ʿUmar Ibn al-ʿAdīm', in *Medieval Muslim Historians and the Franks in the Levant,* ed. Alex Mallett (Leiden, 2014), pp. 109–35.
39 ʿImād.
40 BD.
41 IA.
42 Gibb, 'Notes', pp. 746–53.
43 Abū Shāma, *Kitāb al-rawḍatayn.*
44 Irwin, 'Usamah', pp. 71–2, 77–82; Cobb, *Usama, passim.*
45 Usāma.
46 Irwin, 'Usamah', p. 72; Usāma, trans. Cobb, p. xxx.
47 *L'Orient au temps des croisades,* ed. Anne-Marie Eddé and Françoise Micheau (Paris, 2002), p. 16. Cf. Irwin, 'Usamah', pp. 73–5.
48 Paul M. Cobb, 'Infidel Dogs: Hunting Crusaders with Usama ibn Munqidh', *Crusades* 6 (2007), p. 57.
49 Usāma, pp. 79–80.
50 Usāma, p. 46.
51 *L'Orient,* ed. Eddé and Micheau, p. 100.
52 Ibn Khallikān, *Wafayāt,* vol. 1, pp. 156–60.
53 Yāqūt, *Muʿjam al-buldān.*
54 IJ.
55 *CGOH.*
56 Lord Lindsay, *Letters on Egypt, Edom, and the Holy Land,* 5th edn (London, 1858), p. 346.
57 Ṣāliḥ bin Yaḥyā, *Tārīḫ Bayrūt: Récits des anciens de la famille de Buḥtur b. ʿAlī, émir du Gharb de Beyrouth,* ed. Francis Hours, Kamal S. Salibi *et al.* (Beirut, 1969), pp. 47–8, 73–4.
58 Kevin Lewis, 'Medieval Diglossia', pp. 138–46.
59 *RRH Add.*
60 Delaville le Roulx, 'Chartes', pp. 181–91.
61 Richard, 'Le chartrier', pp. 605–12; Richard, 'Porcellet', pp. 339–82.
62 Riley-Smith, 'The Templars', pp. 278–88.
63 *D.Jerus.*
64 *CGOH.*
65 *Documents concernant les Templiers,* ed. Delaville le Roulx.
66 *CCSSJ.*
67 AK.
68 *Anonymi Auctoris Chronicon.*
69 See Chapter 2.
70 See, for example: Gustave Schlumberger, *Numismatique de l'Orient latin* (Paris, 1878); Blancard, *Le besant*; D. M. Metcalf, *Coinage of the Crusades and the Latin East,* 2nd edn (London, 1995).
71 Oleg Grabar, 'Art of the Mamluks: Some Questions of Methodology', *Art Journal* 41.4 (1981), p. 365.
72 Piana, pp. 307–34.
73 Jidejian, *Tripoli,* p. 59.
74 T. S. R. Boase, 'Ecclesiastical Art in the Crusader States in Palestine and Syria: A. Architecture and Sculpture', in *A History of the Crusades,* ed. Setton, vol. 4, p. 108.
75 Boase, 'Ecclesiastical Art', pp. 107–10.

76 Major, *Medieval Rural Settlements.*
77 Deschamps, *Les Châteaux*, vol. 1.
78 See, for example: *Der Crac des Chevaliers: Die Baugeschichte einer Ordensburg der Kreuzfahrerzeit*, ed. Thomas Biller (Regensburg, 2006).
79 Deschamps, *Les Châteaux*, vols 2–3.
80 Jaroslav Folda *et al.*, 'Crusader Frescoes at Crac des Chevaliers and Marqab Castle', *DOP* 36 (1982), pp. 178–96.
81 Youhanna Sader, *Painted Churches and Rock-Cut Chapels of Lebanon*, trans. Deirdre Baker (Beirut, 1997), *passim.*
82 Dodd, *Medieval Painting*; Immerzeel, *Identity Puzzles*; Mahmoud Zibawi, *Images chrétiens du Levant: les décors peints des églises syro-libanaises au Moyen Âge* (Paris, 2009).
83 *Chronos: Revue d'Histoire de l'Université de Balamand* (1998–present). See Chapter 4.

Appendix 2
Troubadour poetry and Tripoli

The anonymous *vida* of Jaufré Rudel (*c.*1200)

Jaufres Rudels de Blaia si fo mout gentils hom, princes de Blaia.	Jaufré Rudel of Blaye was a very noble man, the prince of Blaye.
Et enamoret se de la comtessa de Tripol, ses vezer, per lo [gran] ben [e per la gran cortesia] qu'el n'auzi dire als pelerins que venguen d'Antiocha.	And he fell in love with the countess of Tripoli, without seeing her, due to the [very] good [and the very courteous] things that he heard said about her by pilgrims who were coming from Antioch.
E fez de leis mains vers ab bons sons, ab paubres motz.	And he composed about her many songs with good tunes, [albeit] with poor words.
E per voluntat de leis vezer, et se croset e se mes en mar [per anar lieis vezer], e pres lo malautia en la nau, e fo condug a Tripol, en un alberc, per mort.	And because of the desire to see her, he took the cross and set to sea [in order to see her], and a sickness seized him in the ship and he was brought to Tripoli, into a hospice, near death.
E fo fait saber a la comtessa et ella venc ad el, al son leit e pres lo antre sos bratz.	And this was made known to the countess and she came to him, to his bed, and took him in her arms.
E saup qu'ella era la comtessa, e mantenent recobret l'auzir e·l flairar, e lauzet Dieu, que l'avia la vida sostenguda tro qu'el l'agues vista; et enaissi el mori entre sos bratz {entre·ls braz de la comtessa}.	And he realised that she was the countess and immediately regained his senses [lit. 'sense of hearing and sense of smell'] and praised God that He had sustained his life until he had seen her; and he then died in her arms {in the arms of the countess}.
Et ella lo fez a gran honor {honradamenz} sepellir en la maison del Temple; e pois, en aquel dia, ella se rendet morga, per la dolor qu'ella n'ac de la mort de lui.	And she had him buried with great honour {honourably} in the house of the Temple; and then, on the same day, she became a nun, for the sorrow that she felt for his death.
[*E aqui son escriutas de las soas chanssos.*][1]	[And here are written some of his songs.]

Marcabru mentions Jaufré Rudel and the Second Crusade (*c*.1147–8)[2]

Lo vers e·l son voill enviar	I want to send the song and the melody
a·n Jaufre Rudel oltramar,	to Sir Jaufré Rudel, in Outremer,
e voill que l'aion li Frances	and I want the French[4] to have it,
per lor coratges alegrar,	to cheer their hearts,
que Dieus lor o pot perdonar,	for God can pardon them,
o sia peccaz o merces.[3]	whether it is a sin or a good deed.[5]

Peire Vidal dedicates a eulogy to Count Raymond III of Tripoli (*c*.1186)

Mas a Tripol m'ado,	But upon Tripoli I rely,
Que quan l'autre baro	Because whereas the other barons
Caço prez, et el lo rete	Chase away glory, he retains it
E no·l laissa partir de se.	And does not let it depart from him.

Peire Vidal compares the kingdom of Jerusalem unfavourably to Provence (*c*.1186)

Retornar et anar	I wish to return and go,
M'en vuelh ad espero	To a place
Entr'Arle e Tolo	Between Arles and Toulon
A tapi, quar aqui	In secret, because there
Am mais un pauc cambo,	I would like better a small field,
Qu'aver sai Lo Daro,	Than to have here Daron,
Ni aver Lo Toro	Or to have Toron
N'Ibeli . . .	Or Ibelin . . .

Peire Vidal references Raymond IV of Toulouse's conquest of Tripoli in 1109 [*sic*] as coded criticism of Raymond V of Toulouse's failure to reclaim Tripoli from the Antiochene dynasty (*c*.1187–94)

Pero si n'a raubatz	Although he stole
Sain Felitz e Mornatz,	Saint-Félix (Languedoc) and Mornas (Provence),
Mas Tripol, so sapchatz,	Tripoli, know this,
Fo gen d'el conqistatz.[6]	Was nobly conquered by him.

Notes

1 *Biographies*, ed. Boutière and Schutz, pp. 16–17. Two main versions of this text survive, with the shortest most likely the earliest. Where the longer text contains significant additions, these are provided above in square brackets, with notable variant readings in curly brackets.
2 The poem has been dated *c.*1147–8 on the assumption that Rudel participated in the Second Crusade and because of the song's apparent reference to (northern) French crusaders. Marcabru, p. 201; *Biographies*, ed. Boutière and Schutz, p. 19 n. 4.
3 Marcabru, p. 204.
4 That is, the northern French participants in the Second Crusade, especially after the scandal caused on this expedition by the alleged antics of the queen of France, Eleanor of Aquitaine.
5 Translated in: Marcabru, p. 205.
6 Peire Vidal, vol. 2, p. 236.

Bibliography

Manuscripts

Vatican City, Biblioteca Apostolica Vaticana, MS Vat. lat. 1345
Vatican City, Biblioteca Apostolica Vaticana, MS Vat. lat. 7241

Primary sources

Abbot Daniel, *The Pilgrimage of the Russian Abbot Daniel in the Holy Land. 1106–1107 A.D.*, trans. C. W. Wilson, Palestine Pilgrims' Text Society 4 (London, 1895)

Abū al-Fidā', *Kitāb taqwīm al-buldān*, ed. J. T. Reinaud and W. Mac Guckin de Slane (Paris, 1840)

Abū al-Fidā', *Kitāb al-mukhtaṣar fī akhbār al-bashar (al-Tārīkh)*, 4 vols (Cairo, 1907)

Abū Shāma, 'Le Livre des Deux Jardins. Histoire des Deux Règnes, celui de Nour ed-Dîn et celui de Salah ed-Dîn', ed. B. de Meynard, in *Recueil des Historiens des Croisades: Historiens Orientaux*, 5 vols (Paris, 1872–1906), vol. 4, pp. 1–525

Abū Shāma, *Kitāb al-rawḍatayn fī akhbār al-dawlatayn al-nūriyya wa-al-ṣalāḥiyya*, ed. Ibrāhīm Shams al-Dīn, 4 vols-in-2 (Beirut, 2002)

Abū Shāma, *Tarājim rijāl al-qarnayn al-sādis wa-al-sābi', al-ma'rūf bi-al-dhayl 'alā al-rawḍatayn*, ed. Ibrāhīm Shams al-Dīn (Beirut, 2002)

Al-'Aẓīmī, Muḥammad bin 'Alī al-Ḥalabī, *Tārīkh ḥalab*, ed. Ibrāhīm Za'rūr (Damascus, 1984)

Al-Dimashqī, *Nukhbat al-dahr fī 'ajā'ib al-barr wa-al-baḥr*, ed. A. F. Mehren (Jubayl, 2008)

Al-Fatḥ bin 'Alī al-Bundārī, *Ikhtiṣār min kitāb al-barq al-shāmī li-l-'Imād, al-kātib al-'Iṣfahānī*, ed. Fatḥiyya al-Nabarāwī (Cairo, 1979)

Al-Idrīsī, *Opus Geographicum sive «Liber ad eorum delectationem qui terras peragrare studeant»*, ed. E. Cerulli *et al.*, 2nd ed., 9 vols (Leiden, 1971–84)

Alberic of Trois-Fontaines, 'Chronica', ed. P. Scheffer-Boichorst, *Monumenta Germaniae Historica: Scriptores*, 39 vols (Hannover, 1826–), vol. 23, pp. 631–950

Albert of Aachen, *Historia Ierosolimitana: History of the Journey to Jerusalem*, ed. Susan B. Edgington (Oxford, 2007)

'Alī bin Abī Bakr al-Harawī, *Kitāb al-Ishārāt ilā Ma'rifat al-Ziyārāt*, ed. Josef W. Meri, Studies in Late Antiquity and Early Islam 19 (Princeton, NJ, 2004)

Anna Komnene, *Alexias*, 13.12, ed. Diether R. Reinsch and Athanasios Kambylis, 2 vols, Corpus Fontium Historiae Byzantinae 40.1–2 (Berlin, 2001)

Anna Komnene, *The Alexiad*, trans. E. R. A. Sewter and Peter Frankopan (London, 2009)

Anonymi Auctoris Chronicon ad A.C. 1234 pertinens, trans. J.-B. Chabot *et al.*, 2 vols, Corpus Scriptorum Christianorum Orientalium, 109, 354 (Louvain, 1965–74)

Arnold of Lübeck, 'Chronica Slavorum', ed. I. M. Lappenberg, *Monumenta Germaniae Historica: Scriptores*, 39 vols (Hannover, 1826–), vol. 21, pp. 100–250

Bahā' al-Dīn bin Shaddād, *Sīrat Ṣalāḥ al-Dīn: «al-sīra al-yūsufiyya»*, ed. Jamāl al-Dīn al-Shayyāl (Cairo, 1962)

Baratier, Edouard, ed., *Enquêtes sur les droits et revenus de Charles Ier d'Anjou en Provence (1252 et 1278)* (Paris, 1969)

de Becdelièvre, V., *Le chartrier de l'Abbaye cistercienne de Fontfroide (894–1260)*, 2 vols (Paris, 2009)

Belgrano, L. T. and A. Neri, 'Due bolle pontificie', *Giornale ligustico di archeologia, storia e letteratura* 10 (1883), pp. 161–5

Benedict de Accoltis, 'Historia Gotefridi', *Recueil des Historiens des Croisades: Historiens Occidentaux*, 5 vols (Paris, 1844–95), vol. 5, pp. 525–620

Benjamin of Tudela, *The Itinerary of Benjamin of Tudela: Travels in the Middle Ages*, trans. Michael A. Signer, Marcus Nathan Adler and A. Asher (New York, 2005)

Berger, E., ed., *Les Registres d'Innocent IV publiés ou analysés d'après les manuscrits originaux du Vatican et de la Bibliothèque Nationale*, 4 vols (1884–1919)

Bernard of Clairvaux, *Epistolae*, ed. J. Leclercq and H. Rochais, 2 vols, Sancti Bernardi Opera 7–8 (Rome, 1974–7)

Bongars, Jacques, ed., *Gesta Dei per Francos* (Hanover, 1611)

Boutière, J. and A. H. Schutz, eds, *Biographies des troubadours: textes provençaux des XIIIe et XIVe siècles*, 2nd ed. (Paris, 1973)

Bresc-Bautier, Geneviève, ed., *Le Cartulaire du Chapitre du Saint-Sépulcre de Jérusalem* (Paris, 1984)

Burchard of Mount Sion, 'Descriptio Terrae Sanctae', in *Peregrinatores Medii Aevi Quatuor*, ed. J. C. M. Laurent, 2nd ed. (Leipzig, 1873), pp. 1–100

Caffaro of Caschifellone, 'De Liberatione Ciuitatum Orientis Liber', in *Annali Genovesi di Caffaro e de' suoi continuatori dal MXCIX al MCCXCIII*, ed. Luigi Tommaso Belgrano, 5 vols (Genoa, 1890–1929), vol. 1, pp. 95–124

'Chronique de Terre Sainte', in *Les gestes des Chiprois: Recueil de chroniques françaises écrites en Orient aux XIIIe & XIVe siècles (Philippe de Navarre & Gérard de Monréal)*, ed. Gaston Raynaud (Geneva, 1887), pp. 1–24

'Chronique du Templier de Tyr', in *Les gestes des Chiprois: Recueil de chroniques françaises écrites en Orient aux XIIIe & XIVe siècles (Philippe de Navarre & Gérard de Monréal)*, ed. Gaston Raynaud (Geneva, 1887), pp. 139–334

Chroniques d'Amadi et de Strambaldi, ed. René de Mas Latrie, 2 vols (Paris, 1891–3)

'Continuatio Praemonstratensis', in 'Sigeberti Gemblacensis Chronographia', ed. L. C. Bethmann, *Monumenta Germaniae Historica: Scriptores*, 39 vols (Hannover, 1826–), vol. 6, pp. 447–56

'De Miraculis S. Roberti, Auctore Bertrando monacho Casæ-Dei', ed. Philippe Labbe, in *Acta Sanctorum Aprilis*, ed. Godefridus Henschenius and Davidus Papebrochius, 3 vols (Antwerp, 1675), vol. 3, pp. 326–33

Delaville le Roulx, J., 'Chartes de Terre Sainte', *Revue de l'Orient latin* 11 (1905–8), pp. 181–91

Delaville le Roulx, J., ed., *Documents concernant les Templiers: extraits des archives de Malte* (Paris, 1882)

Delaville le Roulx, J., ed., *Les Archives, la Bibliothèque et le Trésor de l'Ordre de Saint-Jean de Jérusalem à Malte*, Bibliothèque des Ecoles françaises d'Athènes et de Rome 32 (Paris, 1883)

Delaville le Roulx, J., ed., *Cartulaire général de l'Ordre des Hospitaliers de S. Jean de Jérusalem (1100–1310)*, 4 vols (Paris, 1894–1906)

Delaville le Roulx, J., ed., *Inventaire de pièces de Terre Sainte de l'ordre de l'Hôpital* (Paris, 1895)

Die lateinische Fortsetzung Wilhelms von Tyrus, ed. Marianne Salloch (Leipzig, 1934)

'Epistolae Regis Ludovici VII', *Recueil des historiens des Gaules et de la France*, 24 vols (Paris, 1738–1904), vol. 16

Ernoul, *Chronique d'Ernoul et de Bernard le Trésorier*, ed. L. de Mas Latrie (Paris, 1871)

Estoires d'Outremer et de la naissance Salehadin, ed. Margaret A. Jubb, Westfield Publications in Medieval Studies 4 (London, 1990)

Flavius Josephus, *The Jewish War*, ed. and trans. H. St. J. Thackeray, 3 vols, The Loeb Classical Library: Josephus 2–3 (London, 1961)

Fretellus, *Rorgo Fretellus de Nazareth et sa description de la Terre Sainte: Histoire et édition du texte*, ed. P. C. Boeren (Amsterdam, 1980)

Fulcher of Chartres, *Historia Hierosolymitana (1095–1127)*, ed. Heinrich Hagenmeyer (Heidelberg, 1913)

Gérard, P., E. Magnou and P. Wolff, eds, *Cartulaires des Templiers de Douzens* (Paris, 1965)

Gesta Francorum et aliorum Hierosolimitanorum, ed. Heinrich Hagenmeyer (Heidelberg, 1890)

Guérard, *Cartulaire de l'Abbaye de Saint-Victor de Marseille*, 2 vols (Paris, 1857)

Hayton of Gorgios, 'Flos Historiarum Terre Orientis', ed. C. Köhler, in *Recueil des Historiens des Croisades: Documents Arméniens*, 2 vols (Paris, 1869–1906), vol. 2, pp. 255–363

Huygens, R. B. C, 'Un nouveau texte du traité "De constructione castri Saphet"', *Studi Medievali*, 3rd series, 6.1 (1965), pp. 355–87

Ibn al-Athīr, *Al-kāmil fī al-tārīkh*, ed. C. J. Tornberg, rev. ed., 12 vols + index (Beirut, 1965–7)

Ibn al-Athīr, *Al-tārīkh al-bāhir fī al-dawla al-atābakiyya bi-l-mūṣul*, ed. ʿAbd al-Qādir Aḥmad Ṭulaymāt (Cairo, 1963)

Ibn al-Furāt, *Ayyubids, Mamlukes and Crusaders*, ed. U. Lyons and M. C. Lyons, 2 vols (Cambridge, 1971)

Ibn al-Qalānisī, Abū Yaʿlā Ḥamza, *History of Damascus, 363–555 a. h., by Ibn al-Qalānisī from the Bodleian Ms. Hunt. 125, being a continuation of Hilâl al-Sâbi*, ed. H. F. Amedroz (Leiden, 1908)

Ibn al-Qalānisī, Abū Yaʿlā Ḥamza, *The Damascus Chronicle of the Crusades: Extracted and Translated from the Chronicle of* Ibn al-Qalānisī, trans. H. A. R. Gibb (London, 1932)

Ibn Jubayr, *Riḥla*, ed. William Wright and M. J. de Goeje (Leiden, 1907)

Ibn Khallikān, *Wafayāt al-aʿyān*, ed. Iḥsān ʿAbbās, 8 vols (Beirut, 1968–72)

Ibn Khurdādhba, *Kitāb al-masālik al-mamālik*, ed. M. J. de Goeje, Bibliotheca Geographorum Arabicorum 6 (Leiden, 1889)

Ibn Taymiyya, *Iqtiḍāʾ al-ṣirāṭ al-mustaqīm mukhālafat aṣḥāb al-jaḥīm*, ed. Muḥammad Ḥāmid al-Fiqī (Cairo, 1950)

Ibn Wāṣil, *Mufarrij al-kurūb fī akhbār Banī Ayyūb*, ed. Jamāl al-Dīn al-Shayyāl *et al.*, 5 vols (Cairo, 1953–77)

ʿImād al-Dīn al-Iṣfahānī, *Kitāb al-fatḥ al-qussī fī al-fatḥ al-qudsī*, ed. Carlo de Landberg (Leiden, 1888)
Imperiale di Sant'Angelo, Cesare, *Codice Diplomatico della Repubblica di Genova dal DCCCCLVIII al MCLXIII*, 3 vols (Rome, 1936–42)
Joannes Iperii, 'Chronico Sythiensi Sancti-Bertini', *Recueil des Historiens des Gaules et de la France*, 24 vols (Paris, 1738–1904), vol. 18, pp. 593–610
Isṭifān al-Duwayhī, *Tārīkh al-azmina*, ed. Buṭrus Fahd, 3rd ed. (Beirut, 198–)
Jabre-Mouawad, Ray, 'Un témoin melkite de la prise de Tripoli par les Mameluks (27 avril 1287)', in *Studies on the Christian Arabic Heritage in Honour of Father Prof. Dr. Samir Khalil Samir S. I. at the Occasion of his Sixty-Fifth Birthday*, ed. Rifaat Ebied and Herman Teule, Eastern Christian Studies 5 (Leuven, 2004), pp. 133–61
Jacobus a Voragine, *Legenda Aurea Vulgo Historia Lombardica Dicta*, ed. Th. Graesse, 2nd ed. (Leipzig, 1850)
James of Vitry, *Historia orientalis*, ed. Jean Donnadieu (Turnhout, 2008)
James of Vitry, *Lettres de Jacques de Vitry (1160/1170–1240), évêque de Saint-Jean-d'Acre*, ed. R. B. C. Huygens (Leiden, 1960)
Janauschek, Leopold, *Originum Cisterciensium: Tomus I* (Vienna, 1877)
Jibrāʾīl bin al-Qilāʿī, *Zajaliyyāt*, ed. Baṭrus al-Jamīl, Uṣūl wa-marājiʿ tārīkhiyya 2 (Beirut, 1982)
Jōḥannān of Mardē, 'Canons', in *The Synodicon in the West Syrian Tradition*, ed. Arthur Vööbus, 2 vols, Corpus Scriptorum Christianorum Orientalium 375–6 (Louvain, 1975–6)
John Kinnamos, *Deeds of John and Manuel Comnenus*, trans C. M. Brand (New York, 1976)
John of Ibelin, *Le Livre des Assises*, ed. Peter W. Edbury, The Medieval Mediterranean: Peoples, Economies and Cultures, 400–1500, 50 (Leiden, 2003)
John of Joinville, *Vie de saint Louis*, ed. Jacques Monfrin (Paris, 2010)
John of Würzburg, 'Peregrinatio', in *Peregrinationes Tres: Saewulf, John of Würzburg, Theodericus*, ed. R. B. C. Huygens (Turnhout, 1994), pp. 78–141
John Phocas, *The Pilgrimage of Joannes Phocas in the Holy Land (In the Year 1185 A.D.)*, trans. Aubrey Stewart, Palestine Pilgrims' Text Society (London, 1889)
Kamāl al-Dīn, *Zubdat al-ḥalab min tārīkh ḥalab*, ed. Sāmī al-Dahhān, 3 vols (Damascus, 1951–68)
Kehr, Paul, ed., *Papsturkunden in Spanien, Vorarbeiten zur Hispania Pontificia, I. Katalanien, II. Urkunden und Regesten* (Berlin, 1926)
'L'Estoire de Eracles empereur et la conquest de la terre d'Outremer: C'est la continuation de l'estoire de Guillaume archevesque de Sur', in *Recueil des Historiens des Croisades: Historiens Occidentaux*, 5 vols (Paris, 1844–95), vol. 2, pp. 1–481
Les Miracles de Saint Privat suivis des opuscules d'Aldebert III, évêque de Mende, ed. C. Brunel (Paris, 1912)
'Li Estoire de Jerusalem et d'Antioche', in *Recueil des Historiens des Croisades: Historiens Occidentaux*, 5 vols (Paris, 1844–95), vol. 5, pp. 621–48
Lisiard of Tours, 'Secunda Pars Historiae Iherosolimitanae', in *Recueil des Historiens des Croisades: Historiens Occidentaux*, 5 vols (Paris, 1844–95), vol. 3, pp. 545–85
Magister Tolosanus, *Chronicon Faventinum*, ed. Giuseppe Rossini (Bologna, 1936–47)
Manrique, Angelo, ed., *Cisterciensium, seu verius ecclesiasticorum Annalium a condito Cistercio*, 4 vols (Lyon, 1642–9)
Marcabru, *Marcabru: A Critical Edition*, ed. S. Gaunt, R. Harvey and L. M. Paterson (Cambridge, 2000)

Marino Sanudo, 'Liber Secretorum Fidelium Crucis', in *Gesta Dei per Francos*, ed. Jacques Bongars (Hanover, 1611), vol. 2, pp. 1–281
Matthew of Edessa, 'Extraits de la chronique de Matthieu d'Édesse', in *Recueil des Historiens des Croisades: Documents Arméniens*, 2 vols (Paris, 1869–1906), vol. 1, pp. 1–150
Maundrell, Henry, *A Journey from Aleppo to Jerusalem in 1697* (Beirut, 1963)
Mayer, Hans Eberhard, ed., *Die Urkunden der lateinischen Könige von Jerusalem*, 4 vols, Monumenta Germaniae Historica: Diplomata Regum Latinorum Hierosolymitanorum (Hannover, 2010)
Michael Italikos, *Michel Italikos lettres et discours*, ed. Paul Gautier (Paris, 1972)
Michael the Syrian, 'Chronique', ed. and trans. J.-B. Chabot, 4 vols (Paris, 1899–1910)
Michel, F. and C. Bémont, ed., *Rôles Gascons*, 3 vols + supplement (Paris, 1885–1906)
Monachus Anonymus Littorensis, 'Historia de Translatione Sanctorum Magni Nicolai Terra Marique Miraculis Gloriosi', in *Recueil des Historiens des Croisades: Historiens Occidentaux*, 5 vols (Paris, 1844–95), vol. 5, pp. 253–92
Morgan, M. R., ed., *La continuation de Guillaume de Tyre (1184–1197)*, Documents relatifs à l'histoire des Croisades publiés par l'Académie des Inscriptions et Belles-Lettres 14 (Paris, 1982)
Mujīr al-Dīn, *Kitāb al-uns al-jalīl bi-tārīkh al-quds wa-al-khalīl*, 2 vols (Cairo, 1866)
Müller, Giuseppe, ed., *Documenti sulle Relazioni delle Città Toscane coll'Oriente Cristiano e coi Turchi fino all'anno MDXXXI* (Florence, 1879)
Muṣliḥ al-Dīn Sa'dī Shīrāzī, *The Gulistan (Rose Garden)*, ed. and trans. Wheeler M. Thackston (Bethesda, MD, 2008)
Nāṣir Khusraw, *Nāṣer-e Khosraw's Book of Travels (Safarnāma)*, trans. W. M. Thackston, Persian Heritage Series 36 (Albany, 1986)
Nielen, Marie-Adélaïde, ed., *Lignages d'Outremer*, Documents relatifs à l'histoire des croisades publiés par l'Académie des Inscriptions et Belles-Lettres 18 (Paris, 2003)
Niketas Choniates, *Historia*, ed. Jan-Louis van Dieten, Corpus Fontium Historiae Byzantinae 11 (Berlin, 1975)
Niketas Choniates, *O City of Byzantium, Annals of Niketas Choniatēs*, trans. Harry J. Magoulias (Detroit, 1984)
Orderic Vitalis, *Historia Æcclesiastica*, ed. Marjorie Chibnall, 6 vols (Oxford, 1969–80)
Otto of Freising, 'Chronica sive Historia de Duabus Civitatibus', ed. Adolf Hofmeister, in *Monumenta Germaniae Historica: Scriptores rerum Germanicarum*, 78 vols (Hanover, 1871–2007), vol. 45
Paoli, Sebastiano, ed., *Codice diplomatico del Sacro Militare Ordine Gerosolimitano oggi di Malta*, 2 vols (Lucca, 1733)
Peire Vidal, *Poésie: Edizione Critica e Commento*, ed. D'A. S. Avalle, 2 vols, Documenti di Filologia 4 (Milan and Naples, 1960)
Petit, Ernest, 'Chartes de l'abbaye cistercienne de Saint-Serge de Giblet', *Mémoires de la société nationale des antiquaires de France*, 5th series, 8 (1887), pp. 20–30
Petrus Tudebodus, *Historia de Hierosolymitano Itinere*, ed. John Hugh Hill and Laurita L. Hill, Documents relatifs à l'histoire des croisades publiés par l'Académie des Inscriptions et Belles-Lettres 12 (Paris, 1977)
von Pflugk-Harttung, J., ed., *Acta Pontificum Romanorum Inedita*, 2 vols (Stuttgart, 1880–4)

Pseudo-Fretellus, *Fetellus (Circa 1130 A.D.)*, trans. J. R. MacPherson, Palestine Pilgrims' Text Society (London, 1892)

Pseudo-Fretellus, 'Tractatus de Locis circa Hierusalem', in Melchior de Vogüé, *Les Eglises de la Terre Sainte* (Paris, 1860), pp. 407–51, no. 1

Pseudo-James of Vitry, 'Historiae Orientalis Liber Tertius', in *Gesta Dei per Francos*, ed. Jacques Bongars (Hanover, 1611), vol. 1, pp. 1125–45

Ralph of Caen, *Tancredus*, ed. Edoardo D'Angelo (Brepols, 2011)

Ralph of Coggeshall, *Chronicon Anglicanum*, ed. Joseph Stephenson, Rolls Series 66 (London, 1875)

Raymond of Aguilers, *Liber*, ed. John Hugh Hill and Laurita L. Hill, Documents relatifs à l'histoire des croisades publiés par l'Académie des Inscriptions et Belles-Lettres 9 (Paris, 1969)

Récits d'un ménestrel de Reims au treizième siècle, ed. Natalis de Wailly (Paris, 1876)

'Regni Iherosolymitani Brevis Historia', in *Annali Genovesi di Caffaro e de' suoi continuatori dal MXCIX al MCCXCIII*, ed. Luigi Tommaso Belgrano, 5 vols (Genoa, 1890–1929), vol. 1, pp. 125–49

Richard, Jean, 'Le chartrier de Sainte-Marie Latine et l'établissement de Raymond de Saint-Gilles à Mont-Pèlerin', in *Mélanges d'histoire du Moyen Âge dédiés à la mémoire de Louis Halphen* (Paris, 1951), pp. 605–12

Richard, Jean, 'Le comté de Tripoli dans les chartes du fonds des Porcellet', *Bibliothèque de l'école des chartes* 130.2 (1972), pp. 339–82

Riley-Smith, Jonathan, 'The Templars and the Castle of Tortosa in Syria: An Unknown Document concerning the Acquisition of the Fortress', *The English Historical Review* 84.331 (1969), pp. 278–88

Robert of Auxerre, 'Chronicon', ed. O. Holder-Egger, *Monumenta Germaniae Historica: Scriptores*, 39 vols (Hannover, 1826–), vol. 26, pp. 219–87

Robert the Monk, *Historia Iherosolimitana*, ed. D. Kempf and M. G. Bull (Woodbridge, 2013)

Roger of Howden, *Chronica*, ed. William Stubbs, 4 vols, Rolls Series 51 (London, 1868–71)

Röhricht, Reinhold, ed., *Regesta Regni Hierosolymitani (MXCVII–MCCXCI)* (Innsbrück, 1893)

Röhricht, Reinhold, ed., *Regesta Regni Hierosolymitani (MXCVII–MCCXCI): Additamentum* (Innsbrück, 1904)

Rostand, Edmond, *La Princesse Lointaine*, ed. J. L. Borgerhoff (Boston, 1909)

Round, J. Horace, ed., *Calendar of Documents preserved in France, Illustrative of the History of Great Britain and Ireland. Vol. I. A.D. 918–1206* (London, 1899)

Saewulf, 'Peregrinatio', in *Peregrinationes Tres: Saewulf, John of Würzburg, Theodericus*, ed. R. B. C. Huygens (Turnhout, 1994), pp. 58–77

Ṣāliḥ bin Yaḥyā, *Tārīḫ Bayrūt: Récits des anciens de la famille de Buḥtur b. ʿAlī, émir du Gharb de Beyrouth*, ed. Francis Hours, Kamal S. Salibi *et al.* (Beirut, 1969)

Sempad the Constable, 'Chronique du Royaume de la Petite Arménie', in *Recueil des Historiens des Croisades: Documents Arméniens*, 2 vols (Paris, 1869–1906), vol. 1, pp. 605–72

Sibṭ bin al-Jawzī, 'Extraits du Mirât ez-Zèmân', in *Recueil des Historiens des Croisades: Historiens Orientaux*, 5 vols (Paris, 1872–1906), vol. 3, pp. 511–70

Strabo, *The Geography of Strabo*, ed. and trans. Horace Leonard Jones, 8 vols (London, 1912–32)

Strehlke, Ernest, ed., *Tabulae Ordinis Theutonici* (Berlin, 1869)

Sweetenham, Carol and Linda M. Paterson, *The* Canso d'Antioca*: An Occitan Epic Chronicle of the First Crusade* (Aldershot, 2003)

Tafel, G. L. F. and G. M. Thomas, eds, *Urkunden zur Älteren Handels- und Staatsgeschichte der Republik Venedig mit Besonderer Beziehung auf Byzanz und die Levante vom Neunten bis zum Ausgang des Fünfzehnten Jahrhunderts*, 3 vols (Vienna, 1856–7)

Teulet, A., ed., *Layettes du Trésor des Chartes*, 4 vols (Paris, 1863–1902)

Theoderich, 'Descriptio', in *Peregrinationes Tres: Saewulf, John of Würzburg, Theodericus*, ed. R. B. C. Huygens (Turnhout, 1994), pp. 142–97

Theoderich, *Description of the Holy Places. (Circa 1172 A.D.)*, trans. Aubrey Stewart, Palestine Pilgrims' Text Society (London, 1896)

Theodore Prodromos, *Theodore Prodromos: historische Gedichte*, ed. Wolfram Hörandner (Vienna, 1984)

Usāma bin Munqidh, *An Arab-Syrian gentleman and warrior in the period of the Crusades: memoirs of Usāmah ibn-Munqidh (*Kitāb al-I'tibār*)*, trans. Philip K. Hitti (New York, 2000)

Usāma bin Munqidh, *The Book of Contemplation: Islam and the Crusades*, trans. Paul M. Cobb (London, 2008)

Usāma bin Munqidh, *Usāmah's Memoirs entitled* Kitāb al-I'tibār, ed. Philip K. Hitti, Princeton Oriental Texts 1 (Princeton, NJ, 1930)

Van Houts, Elisabeth M. C., *Gesta Normannorum Ducum*, 2 vols (Oxford, 1992–5)

Vincent of Beauvais, *Speculum Maius*, 4 vols (Douai, 1624)

Walter Map, *De Nugis Curialium: Courtiers' Trifles*, ed. M. R. James, C. N. L. Brooke and R. A. B. Mynors (Oxford, 1983)

Walter the Chancellor, *Bella Antiochena*, ed. Heinrich Hagenmeyer (Innsbrück, 1896)

Weiland, Ludwig, ed., 'Gesta Episcoporum Halberstadensium', *Monumenta Germaniae Historica: Scriptores*, 39 vols (Hannover, 1826–), vol. 23, pp. 73–123

Wilbrand of Oldenburg, 'Journey to Syria, Lesser Armenia, Cyprus, and the Holy Land (1211–1212): A New Edition', ed. Denys Pringle, *Crusades* 11 (2012), pp. 109–37

William of Malmesbury, *Gesta Regum Anglorum: The History of the English Kings, Volume I*, ed. R. A. B. Mynors, Rodney M. Thomson and Michael Winterbottom (Oxford, 1998)

William of Nangis, *Chronique latine de Guillaume de Nangis, de 1113 à 1300, avec les continuations de cette chronique, de 1300 à 1368*, ed. H. Géraud, 2 vols (Paris, 1843)

William of Newburgh, *Historia Rerum Anglicarum*, 3.16, in *Chronicles of the Reigns of Stephen, Henry II., and Richard I.*, ed. Richard Howlett, 4 vols, Rolls Series 82 (London, 1884–9)

William of Tripoli, *Notitia de Machometo; De statu Sarracenorum*, ed. Peter Engels (Würzburg, 1992)

William of Tyre, *Chronicon*, ed. R. B. C. Huygens, 2 vols, Corpus Christianorum Continuatio Mediaevalis 63, 63A (Turnhout, 1986)

William of Tyre, 'Historia rerum in partibus transmarinis gestarum', in *Recueil des Historiens des Croisades: Historiens Occidentaux*, 5 vols (Paris, 1844–95), vol. 1

William of Tyre, *A History of Deeds Done Beyond the Sea*, trans. E. A. Babcock and A. C. Krey, 2 vols (New York, 1976)

Wodehouse, P. G., *The Jeeves Omnibus*, 5 vols (London, 1989–93)

Yāqūt bin 'Abd Allāh al-Ḥamawī, *Mu'jam al-buldān*, 5 vols (Beirut, 1955–7)

Secondary sources

'Abana', in *The Encyclopædia Britannica*, 11th ed., 29 vols (Cambridge, 1910–11), vol. 1, p. 6

Abulafia, David, 'Marie-Luise Favreau-Lilie, *Die Italiener im Heiligen Land vom Ersten Kreuzzug bis zum Tode Heinrichs von Champagne (1098–1197)*', *Speculum* 67.1 (1992), pp. 141–3

Abulafia, David, *The Great Sea: A Human History of the Mediterranean* (London, 2011)

Abulafia, David and Nora Berend, ed., *Medieval Frontiers: Concepts and Practices* (Aldershot, 2002)

al-Nasarat, Mohammed and Abd alrzaq Al-Maani, 'Petra during the Crusader period from the evidence of al-Wuayra castle: a review', *Mediterranean Archaeology and Archaeometry* 14.1 (2014), pp. 221–34

Ambrose, Kirk, *The Nave Sculpture of Vézelay: The Art of Monastic Viewing* (Toronto, 2006)

Amitai-Preiss, R., *Mongols and Mamluks: The Mamluk-Īlkhānid War, 1260–1281* (Cambridge, 1995)

Amouroux-Mourad, Monique, *Le comté d'Edesse 1098–1150* (Paris, 1988)

Antweiler, Wolfgang, *Das Bistum Tripolis im 12. und 13. Jahrhundert. Personengeschichtliche und strukturelle Probleme*, Studia humaniora 20 (Düsseldorf, 1991)

Asbridge, T., 'The Principality of Antioch and the Jabal as-Summāq', in *The First Crusade: Origins and Impact*, ed. Jonathan Phillips (Manchester, 1997), pp. 142–151

Asbridge, Thomas S., *The Creation of the Principality of Antioch, 1098–1130* (Woodbridge, 2000)

Asbridge, Thomas, 'Alice of Antioch: A Case Study of Female Power in the Twelfth Century', in *The Experience of Crusading. Volume Two: Defining the Crusader Kingdom*, ed. Peter W. Edbury and Jonathan Phillips (Cambridge, 2003), pp. 29–47

Asbridge, Thomas, *The First Crusade: A New History* (Oxford, 2004)

Asmar, Camille, 'L'Abbaye de Belmont dite Deir el Balamend', *Bulletin du Musée de Beyrouth* 25 (Paris, 1972)

Attiya, Hussein M., 'Knowledge of Arabic in the Crusader States in the Twelfth and Thirteenth centuries', *Journal of Medieval History* 25 (1999), pp. 203–13

Augé, Isabelle, 'Les Comnènes et le comté de Tripoli: une collaboration efficace?' in *Le comté de Tripoli: État multiculturel et multiconfessionnel (1102–1289)*, ed. Gérard Dédéyan and Karam Rizk (Paris, 2010), pp. 141–56

Aurell, Martin, *Une famille de la noblesse provençale au Moyen Âge: les Porcelet* (Avignon, 1986)

Bachrach, Bernard S., 'Review Article: Medieval Identity: People and Place', *The International History Review* 25 (2003), pp. 866–70

Baker, Derek, ed., *Relations between East and West in the Middle Ages* (Edinburgh, 1973)

Baldwin, Marshall Whithed, *Raymond III of Tripoli (1140–87) and the Fall of the Kingdom of Jerusalem*, 2 vols (Unpublished PhD thesis: Princeton University, 1934)

Baldwin, Marshall Whithed, 'Ecclesiastical Developments in the Twelfth Century Crusaders' State of Tripolis', *The Catholic Historical Review* 22.2 (1936), pp. 149–71

Baldwin, Marshall Whithed, *Raymond III of Tripolis and the Fall of Jerusalem (1140–1187)* (Princeton, NJ, 1936)

Baldwin, Marshall Whithed, 'The Latin States under Baldwin III and Amalric I, 1143–1174', in *A History of the Crusades*, ed. Kenneth M. Setton, 6 vols (Madison, WI, 1969–89), vol. 1, pp. 528–61

Baratier, Edouard, 'Marquisat et comtés en Provence', in *Histoire de la Provence*, ed. Edouard Baratier (Toulouse, 1969), pp. 123–67

Baratier, Edouard, ed., *Histoire de la Provence* (Toulouse, 1969)

Barber, Malcolm, 'The Reputation of Gerard of Ridefort', in *The Military Orders. Volume 4: On Land and by Sea*, ed. Judi Upton-Ward (Aldershot, 2008), pp. 111–19

Barber, Malcolm, *The Crusader States* (London, 2012)

Barber, Malcolm, *The New Knighthood: A History of the Order of the Temple* (Cambridge, 2012)

Barber, Malcolm, ed., *The Military Orders: Fighting for the Faith and Caring for the Sick* (Aldershot, 1994)

Beech, George T., 'The Crusader Lordship of Marash in Armenian Cilicia, 1104–1149', *Viator* 27 (1996), pp. 35–52

Bellomo, Elena, 'The First Crusade and the Latin East as Seen from Venice: The Account of the *Translatio sancti Nicolai*', *Early Medieval Europe* 17.4 (2009), pp. 420–43

Beltz, W., ed., *Die Folgen der Kreuzzüge für die orientalische Religionsgemeinschaft: Internationales Kolloquium vom 16.–18.10.1996 in Halle/Saale* (Halle-Saale, 1996)

Benjamin, Richard, 'A Forty Years War: Toulouse and the Plantagenets, 1156–96', *Historical Research* 61 (1988), pp. 270–85

Benton, John F., *Culture, Power and Personality in Medieval France*, ed. Thomas N. Bisson (London, 1991)

Benton, John F., 'Qui étaient les parents de Jacques de Vitry?' in his *Culture, Power and Personality in Medieval France*, ed. Thomas N. Bisson (London, 1991), pp. 89–98

Berend, Nora, 'Preface', in *Medieval Frontiers: Concepts and Practices*, ed. David Abulafia and Nora Berend (Aldershot, 2002), pp. x–xv

Berman, Constance H., 'Were There Twelfth-Century Cistercian Nuns?' *Church History* 68.4 (1999), pp. 824–64

Berman, Constance Hoffman, *The Cistercian Evolution: The Invention of a Religious Order in Twelfth-Century Europe* (Philadelphia, 2000)

Biller, Thomas, ed., *Der Crac des Chevaliers: Die Baugeschichte einer Ordensburg der Kreuzfahrerzeit* (Regensburg, 2006)

Bisson, Thomas N., *Medieval France and Her Pyrenean Neighbours: Studies in Early Institutional History* (London, 1989)

Bisson, Thomas N., 'The Rise of Catalonia: Identity, Power, and Ideology in a Twelfth-Century Society', in his *Medieval France and Her Pyrenean Neighbours: Studies in Early Institutional History* (London, 1989), pp. 125–52

Bisson, Thomas N., 'Some Characteristics of Mediterranean Territorial Power in the Twelfth Century', in his *Medieval France and Her Pyrenean Neighbours: Studies in Early Institutional History* (London, 1989), pp. 257–64

Bisson, Thomas N. ,'Unheroed Pasts: History and Commemoration in South Frankland before the Albigensian Crusades', *Speculum* 65.2 (1990), pp. 281–308

Blancard, Louis, *Le besant d'or sarrazinas pendant les croisades: Etude comparée sur les monnaies d'or, arabes et d'imitation arabe, frappées en Egypte et en Syrie, aux XIIme et XIIIme siècles* (Marseille, 1880)

Bloch, R. Howard, *Medieval Misogyny and the Invention of Western Romantic Love* (Chicago, 1991)

Boas, Adrian J., 'The Frankish Period: A Unique Medieval Society Emerges', *Near Eastern Archaeology* 61.3 (1998), pp. 138–73

Boase, T. S. R., 'Ecclesiastical Art in the Crusader States in Palestine and Syria: A. Architecture and Sculpture', in *A History of the Crusades*, ed. Kenneth M. Setton, 6 vols (Madison, WI, 1969–89), vol. 4, pp. 69–139

Bonnassie, Pierre, 'From the Rhône to Galicia: Origins and Modalities of the Feudal Order', in his *From Slavery to Feudalism in South-Western Europe*, trans. Jean Birrell (Cambridge, 1991), pp. 104–31

Borchardt, Karl, Nikolas Jaspert and Helen J. Nicholson, eds, *The Hospitallers, the Mediterranean and Europe* (Aldershot, 2007)

Brauer, Ralph W., *Boundaries and Frontiers in Medieval Muslim Geography*, Transactions of the American Philosophical Society 85.6 (Philadelphia, 1995)

Breycha-Vauthier, A. C., 'Deir Balamand: Témoin de Cîteaux en terre libanaise', *Bulletin du Musée de Beyrouth* 20 (1967), pp. 7–20

de Briailles, Chandon, 'Lignages d'Outre-Mer: les seigneurs de Margat', *Syria* 25.3–4 (1946), pp. 231–58

Bruguière, Marie-Bernadette, 'Un precedent à la loi salique? L'exclusion des femmes dans la maison de Toulouse et de Tripoli', *Mémoires de l'Académie des Sciences, Inscriptions et Belles-Lettres de Toulouse* 141 (1979), pp. 141–52

Buck, Andrew D., *The Principality of Antioch and its Frontiers in the Twelfth Century* (Woodbridge, 2017)

Bull, Marcus, 'Overlapping and Competing Identities in the Frankish First Crusade', in *Le Concile de Clermont de 1095 et l'Appel à la Croisade: Actes du Colloque Universitaire International de Clermont-Ferrand (23–25 juin 1995) organisé et publié avec le concours du Conseil Régional d'Auvergne* (Rome, 1997), pp. 195–211

Bull, Marcus, 'Introduction', in *France in the Central Middle Ages 900–1200*, ed. Marcus Bull (Oxford, 2002), pp. 1–14

Bull, Marcus, ed., *France in the Central Middle Ages 900–1200* (Oxford, 2002)

Bull, Marcus and Catherine Léglu, eds, *The World of Eleanor of Aquitaine: Literature and Society in Southern France between the Eleventh and Thirteenth Centuries* (Woodbridge, 2005)

Burgtorf, Jochen, 'The Hospitaller Lordship of Margat', in *East and West in the Medieval Eastern Mediterranean: Antioch from the Byzantine Reconquest until the End of the Crusader Principality*, ed. Krijnie Ciggaar *et al.*, 2 vols, Orientalia Lovaniensia Analecta 147, 199 (Leuven, 2006–13), vol. 2, pp. 11–50

Cahen, Claude, *La Syrie du Nord à l'époque des croisades et la principauté franque d'Antioche* (Paris, 1940)

Cahen, Claude, *Orient et Occident au temps des Croisades* (Paris, 1983)

Cahen, Claude, 'Préface à la réimpression de sa thèse', *Arabica*, 43.1 (1996), pp. 85–8

Carraz, Damien, *L'Ordre du Temple dans la basse vallée du Rhône (1124–1312): Ordres militaires, croisades et sociétés méridionales*, Collection d'histoire et d'archéologie médiévales 17 (Lyon, 2005)

Chaaya, Anis, 'Les fortifications des entrées du château Saint-Gilles de Tripoli', *Archaeology & History in the Lebanon* 26–7 (2007–8), pp. 385–98

Chaaya, Anis, 'Observations sur l'abbaye de Belmond (monastère de Balamand) à partir des archives photographiques de la DGA', *Bulletin d'Archéologie et d'Architecture Libanaises* 14 (2010), pp. 385–98

Chalandon, Ferdinand, *Les Comnène: Etudes sur l'Empire Byzantin, II: Jean II Comnène (1118–1143) et Manuel I Comnène (1143–1180)* (Paris, 1912)

Charaf, Hanan and Anis Chaaya, 'Syriac Cult Places in Wadi Qadisha in Lebanon', in *Ideologies as Intercultural Phenomena: Proceedings of the Third Annual Symposium of the Assyrian and Babylonian Intellectual Heritage Project, Held in Chicago, USA, October 27–31, 2000* (Milan, 2002), pp. 45–52

Charaf, Jean, 'Les Maronites et le comté de Tripoli d'après Duwayhi: essai critique', in *Le comté de Tripoli: État multiculturel et multiconfessionnel (1102–1289)*, ed. Gérard Dédéyan and Karam Rizk (Paris, 2010), pp. 57–72

Cheynet, Jean-Claude, 'La conception militaire de la frontière orientale (IXe–XIIIe siècle)', in *Eastern Approaches to Byzantium: Papers from the Thirty-third Spring Symposium of Byzantine Studies, University of Warwick, Coventry, March 1999*, ed. Antony Eastmond (Aldershot, 2001), pp. 57–69

Cheynet, Jean-Claude, 'The Duchy of Antioch during the Second Period of Byzantine Rule', in *East and West in the Medieval Eastern Mediterranean: Antioch from the Byzantine Reconquest until the End of the Crusader Principality*, ed. Krijnie Ciggaar *et al.*, 2 vols, Orientalia Lovaniensia Analecta 147, 199 (Leuven, 2006–13), vol 1, pp. 1–16

Chléirigh, Léan Ní, '*Gesta Normannorum*? Normans in the Latin Chronicles of the First Crusade', in *Norman Expansion: Connections, Continuities and Contrasts*, ed. Keith J. Stringer and Andrew Jotischky (Farnham, 2013), pp. 207–26

Ciggaar, Krijnie, *et al.*, eds, *East and West in the Medieval Eastern Mediterranean: Antioch from the Byzantine Reconquest until the End of the Crusader Principality*, 2 vols, Orientalia Lovaniensia Analecta 147, 199 (Leuven, 2006–13)

Ciggaar, Krijnie, Herman Teule *et al.*, eds, *East and West in the Crusader States: Context – Contacts – Confrontations*, Orientalia Lovaniensia Analecta, 75, 92, 125 (Leuven, 1996–2003)

Clanchy, Michael T., *From Memory to Written Record: England 1066–1307*, 3rd ed. (Oxford, 2013)

Clarke, Peter D. and Anne J. Duggan, eds, *Pope Alexander III (1159–81): The Art of Survival* (Farnham, 2012)

Cobb, Paul M., *Usama ibn Munqidh: Warrior-Poet of the Age of Crusades* (Oxford, 2005)

Cobb, Paul M., 'Infidel Dogs: Hunting Crusaders with Usama ibn Munqidh', *Crusades* 6 (2007), pp. 57–68

Coupel, Pierre, 'Trois petites églises du comté de Tripoli', *Bulletin du Musée de Beyrouth* 5 (Paris, 1941), pp. 35–55

Cowdrey, H. E. J., *Pope Gregory VII, 1073–1085* (Oxford, 1998)

Crawford, Robert W., 'William of Tyre and the Maronites', *Speculum* 30.2 (1955), pp. 222–8

Crescini, Vincenzo, *Románica Fragmenta, scritti scelti dall'autore* (Turin, 1932)

Crescini, Vincenzo, 'Canzone-sirventese di Peire Vidal', in his *Románica Fragmenta, scritti scelti dall'autore* (Turin, 1932), pp. 464–93

Crouch, David, 'A Norman "conventio" and Bonds of Lordship in the Middle Ages', in *Law and Government in Medieval England and Normandy: Essays in honour of Sir James Holt*, ed. George Garnett and John Hudson (Cambridge, 1994), pp. 299–324

Cuffel, Alexandra, 'From Practice to Polemic: Shared Saints and Festivals as "Women's Religion" in the Medieval Mediterranean', *Bulletin of the School of Oriental and African Studies* 68.3 (2005), pp. 401–19

Curiel, Raoul and Rika Gyselen, eds, *Itinéraires d'Orient: Hommages à Claude Cahen*, Res Orientales 6 (Burs-sur-Yvette, 1994)

Daftary, Farhad, *The Assassin Legends: Myths of the Isma'ilis* (London, 1994)
Daftary, Farhad, *The Ismā'īlīs: Their History and Doctrines*, 2nd ed. (Cambridge, 2007)
Davis, R. H. C., 'William of Tyre', in *Relations between East and West in the Middle Ages*, ed. Derek Baker (Edinburgh, 1973), pp. 64–76
Day, Gerald W., *Genoa's Response to Byzantium, 1155–1204: Commercial Expansion and Factionalism in a Medieval City* (Urbana, 1988)
Dédéyan, Gérard, 'Les Arméniens au Liban (Xe-XIIIe siècle)', in *Le comté de Tripoli: État multiculturel et multiconfessionnel (1102–1289)*, ed. Gérard Dédéyan and Karam Rizk (Paris, 2010), pp. 73–99
Dédéyan, Gérard and Karam Rizk, eds, *Le comté de Tripoli: État multiculturel et multiconfessionnel (1102–1289)* (Paris, 2010)
Deschamps, Paul, *Les Châteaux des Croisés en Terre Sainte*, 3 vols (Paris, 1934–73)
Deschamps, Paul, 'Raymond de Saint-Gilles et sa sépulture au château de Tripoli (Liban)', in *Etudes de civilisation médiévale (IXe-XIIe siècles). Mélanges offerts à Edmond-René Labande à l'occasion de son départ à la retraite et du XXe anniversaire du C.E.S.C.M. par ses amis, ses collègues, ses élèves* (Poitiers, 1974), pp. 209–16
Devic, C. and J. Vaissète, *Histoire Générale de Languedoc avec des notes et les pièces justificatives*, 2nd ed., 16 vols (Toulouse, 1872–1904)
Devos, Paul, 'Les premières versions occidentales de la légende de Saïdnaia', *Analecta Bollandiana* 65 (1947), pp. 245–78
Dodd, Erica Cruikshank, *Medieval Painting in the Lebanon* (Wiesbaden, 2004)
Duggan, Anne J., '*Alexander ille meus*: The Papacy of Alexander III', in *Pope Alexander III (1159–81): The Art of Survival*, ed. Peter D. Clarke and Anne J. Duggan (Farnham, 2012), pp. 13–50
Duggan, Anne J., ed., *Queens and Queenship in Medieval Europe: Proceedings of a Conference held at King's College London April 1995* (Woodbridge, 1997)
Dunbabin, Jean, 'Discovering a Past for the French Aristocracy', in *The Perception of the Past in Twelfth-Century Europe*, ed. Paul Magdalino (London, 1992), pp. 1–14
Dunbabin, Jean, *France in the Making, 843–1180*, 2nd ed. (Oxford, 2005)
Dussaud, René, *Topographie historique de la Syrie antique et médiévale* (Paris, 1927)
Eastmond, Antony, ed., *Eastern Approaches to Byzantium: Papers from the Thirty-third Spring Symposium of Byzantine Studies, University of Warwick, Coventry, March 1999* (Aldershot, 2001)
Ebied, Rifaat and Herman Teule, eds, *Studies on the Christian Arabic Heritage in Honour of Father Prof. Dr. Samir Khalil Samir S. I. at the Occasion of his Sixty-Fifth Birthday*, Eastern Christian Studies 5 (Leuven, 2004)
Edbury, Peter W., 'Propaganda and Faction in the Kingdom of Jerusalem: The Background to Hattin', in *Crusaders and Muslims in Twelfth-Century Syria*, ed. Maya Shatzmiller (Leiden, 1993), pp. 173–89
Edbury, Peter W., *John of Ibelin and the Kingdom of Jerusalem* (Woodbridge, 1997)
Edbury, Peter W., 'The Lyon *Eracles* and the Old French Continuations of William of Tyre', in *Montjoie: Studies in Crusade History in Honour of Hans Eberhard Mayer*, ed. Benjamin Z. Kedar, Jonathan Riley-Smith and Rudolf Hiestand (Aldershot, 1997), pp. 139–53
Edbury, P. W., 'New Perspectives on the Old French Continuations of William of Tyre', *Crusades* 9 (2010), pp. 107–13
Edbury, Peter W., ed., *Crusade and Settlement: Papers Read at the First Conference of the Society for the Study of the Crusades and the Latin East and Presented to R. C. Smail* (Cardiff, 1985)

Edbury, P. W. and John Gordon Rowe, 'William of Tyre and the Patriarchal Election of 1180', *The English Historical Review* 93 (1978), pp. 1–25

Edbury, P. W. and John Gordon Rowe, *William of Tyre: Historian of the Latin East* (Cambridge, 1990)

Edbury, Peter W. and Jonathan Phillips, eds, *The Experience of Crusading. Volume Two: Defining the Crusader Kingdom* (Cambridge, 2003)

Eddé, Anne-Marie, 'Kamāl al-Dīn ʿUmar Ibn al-ʿAdīm', in *Medieval Muslim Historians and the Franks in the Levant*, ed. Alex Mallett (Leiden, 2014), pp. 109–35

Eddé, Anne-Marie and Françoise Micheau, eds, *L'Orient au temps des croisades* (Paris, 2002)

Edgington, Susan, 'The First Crusade: Reviewing the Evidence', in *The First Crusade: Origins and Impact*, ed. Jonathan Phillips (Manchester, 1997), pp. 55–77

Edgington, Susan B. and Sarah Lambert, eds, *Gendering the Crusades* (Cardiff, 2001)

Edgington, Susan B. and Helen J. Nicholson, eds, *Deeds Done Beyond the Sea: Essays on William of Tyre, Cyprus and the Military Orders Presented to Peter Edbury* (Farnham, 2014)

Ehrenkreutz, A. S., 'The Place of Saladin in the Naval History of the Mediterranean Sea in the Middle Ages', *Journal of the American Oriental Society* 75.2 (1955), pp. 100–16

Ellenblum, Ronnie, *Frankish Rural Settlement in the Latin Kingdom of Jerusalem* (Cambridge, 1998)

Ellenblum, Ronnie, 'Were There Borders and Borderlines in the Middle Ages? The Example of the Latin Kingdom of Jerusalem', in *Medieval Frontiers: Concepts and Practices*, ed. David Abulafia and Nora Berend (Aldershot, 2002), pp. 105–19

Ellenblum, Ronnie, *Crusader Castles and Modern Histories* (Cambridge, 2007)

Ellenblum, Ronnie, Jonathan Riley-Smith and Iris Shagrir, eds, *In Laudem Hierosolymitani: Studies in Crusades and Medieval Culture in Honour of Benjamin Z. Kedar* (Aldershot, 2007)

Elisséeff, Nikita, *Nūr ad-Dīn: un grand prince musulman de Syrie au temps des croisades (511–569 H./1118–1174)*, 3 vols (Damascus, 1967)

Enlart, Camille, 'L'abbaye cistercienne de Belmont en Syrie', *Syria* 4.1 (1923), pp. 1–22

Enlart, Camille, *Les Monuments des Croisés dans le Royaume de Jérusalem*, 2 vols (Paris, 1925–8)

Epp, Verena, *Fulcher von Chartres. Studien zur Geschichtsschreibung des ersten Kreuzzuges*, Studia humaniora 15 (Düsseldorf, 1990)

Fattal, Antoine, *Le Statut Légal des non-Musulmans en pays d'Islam* (Beirut, 1958)

Favreau-Lilie, Marie-Luise, *Die Italiener im Heiligen Land vom ersten Kreuzzug bis zum Tode Heinrichs von Champagne (1098–1197)* (Amsterdam, 1989)

Fiey, Jean Maurice, 'Un grand sanctuaire perdu? Le Martyrion de Saint Léonce à Tripoli', *Le Muséon: Revue d'études orientales* 95.1–2 (1982), pp. 77–98

Fink, Harold S., 'The Foundation of the Latin States, 1099–1118', in *A History of the Crusades*, 6 vols (Madison, WI, 1969–89), vol. 1, pp. 368–409

Flori, Jean, *Pierre l'Ermite et la première croisade* (Paris, 1999)

Flori, Jean, 'De l'Anonyme normand à Tudebode et aux *Gesta Francorum*: L'impact de la propagande de Bohémond sur la critique textuelle des sources de la première croisade', *Revue d'histoire ecclésiastique* 102.3–4 (2007), pp. 717–46

Folda, Jaroslav, 'The Figural Arts in Crusader Syria and Palestine, 1187–1291: Some New Realities', *Dumbarton Oaks Papers* 58 (2004), pp. 315–31

Folda, Jaroslav, *et al.*, 'Crusader Frescoes at Crac des Chevaliers and Marqab Castle', *Dumbarton Oaks Papers* 36 (1982), pp. 177–210

Forde, Simon, Lesley Johnson and Alan V. Murray, eds, *Concepts of National Identity in the Middle Ages* (Leeds, 1995)

France, James, *The Cistercians in Medieval Art* (Stroud, 1998)

France, James, *Separate but Equal: Cistercian Lay Brothers, 1120–1350*, Cistercian Studies 246 (Collegeville, MN, 2012)

France, John, 'The First Crusade and Islam', *The Muslim World* 67.4 (1977), pp. 247–57

France, John, 'Saladin, from Memory towards Myth in the Continuations', in *Deeds Done Beyond the Sea: Essays on William of Tyre, Cyprus and the Military Orders Presented to Peter Edbury*, ed. Susan B. Edgington and Helen J. Nicholson (Farnham, 2014), pp. 69–82

France, John and William G. Zajac, eds, *The Crusades and their Sources: Essays Presented to Bernard Hamilton* (Aldershot, 1998)

Frankopan, Peter, *The First Crusade: The Call from the East* (London, 2012)

du Fresne du Cange, Charles and E. G. Rey, *Les Familles d'Outremer* (Paris, 1869)

Friedman, Yvonne, *Encounter Between Enemies: Captivity and Ransom in the Latin Kingdom of Jerusalem*, Cultures, Beliefs and Traditions: Medieval and Early Modern Peoples 10 (Leiden, 2002)

Garnett, George and John Hudson, eds, *Law and Government in Medieval England and Normandy: Essays in Honour of Sir James Holt* (Cambridge, 1994)

Gaussin, Pierre Roger, *L'Abbaye de la Chaise-Dieu (1043–1518)* (Paris, 1962)

Gerish, Deborah, 'The True Cross and the Kings of Jerusalem', *The Haskins Society Journal* 8 (1996), pp. 137–55

Gervers, Michael, ed., *The Second Crusade and the Cistercians* (New York, 1992)

Gibb, H. A. R., 'Notes on the Arabic Materials for the History of the Early Crusades', *Bulletin of the School of Oriental and African Studies* 7.4 (1935), pp. 739–54

Gibb, H. A. R., 'The Caliphate and the Arab States', in *A History of the Crusades*, ed. Kenneth M. Setton, 6 vols (Madison, WI, 1969–1989), vol. 1, pp. 81–98

Gibb, Hamilton, *The Life of Saladin: From the Works of 'Imād ad-Dīn and Bahā' ad-Dīn* (Oxford, 1973)

Grabar, Oleg, 'Art of the Mamluks: Some Questions of Methodology', *Art Journal* 41.4 (1981), pp. 365–6

Grabois, Aryeh, 'Christian Pilgrims in the Thirteenth Century and the Latin Kingdom of Jerusalem: Burchard of Mount Sion', in *Outremer: Studies in the History of the Crusading Kingdom of Jerusalem Presented to Joshua Prawer*, ed. B. Z. Kedar, H. E. Mayer and R. C. Smail (Jerusalem, 1982), pp. 285–96

Grousset, René, *Histoire des Croisades et du royaume franc de Jérusalem*, 3 vols (Paris, 1934–6)

Grünthal, Gottfried, *et al.*, 'Compilation of the GSHAP regional seismic hazard for Europe, Africa and the Middle East', *Annali di Geofisica* 42 (1999), pp. 1215–23

Hall, Martin and Jonathan Phillips, *Caffaro, Genoa and the Twelfth-Century Crusades*, Crusade Texts in Translation 24 (Ashgate, 2013)

Hamilton, Bernard, 'The Cistercians in the Crusader States', in *One yet Two: Monastic Tradition East and West*, ed. M. Basil Pennington, Cistercian Studies 29 (Kalamazoo, 1976), pp. 405–22

Hamilton, Bernard, *The Latin Church in the Crusader States: The Secular Church* (London, 1980)

Hamilton, Bernard, 'The Impact of Crusader Jerusalem on Western Christendom', *The Catholic Historical Review* 80.4 (1994), pp. 695–713

Hamilton, Bernard, 'Ideals of Holiness: Crusaders, Contemplatives, and Mendicants', *The International History Review* 17.4 (1995), pp. 693–712

Hamilton, Bernard, 'Knowing the Enemy: Western Understanding of Islam at the Time of the Crusades', *Journal of the Royal Asiatic Society of Great Britain and Ireland*, 3rd series, 7.3 (1997), pp. 373–87

Hamilton, Bernard, *The Leper King and his Heirs: Baldwin IV and the Crusader Kingdom of Jerusalem* (Cambridge, 2000)

Hamilton, Bernard, 'Our Lady of Saidnaiya: an Orthodox Shrine Revered by Muslims and Knights Templar at the Time of the Crusades', in *The Holy Land, Holy Lands, and Christian History: Papers read at the 1998 Summer Meeting and the 1999 Winter Meeting of the Ecclesiastical History Society*, ed. R. N. Swanson, Studies in Church History 36 (Woodbridge, 2000), pp. 207–15

Hamilton, Bernard, 'The Templars, the Syrian Assassins and King Amalric of Jerusalem', in *The Hospitallers, the Mediterranean and Europe*, ed. Karl Borchardt, Nikolas Jaspert and Helen J. Nicholson (Aldershot, 2007), pp. 13–24

Harris, Jonathan, *Byzantium and the Crusades* (London, 2003)

Hasluck, F. W., *Christianity and Islam under the Sultans*, 2 vols (Oxford, 1929)

Hauziński, Jerzy, 'On Alleged Attempts at Converting the Assassins to Christianity in the Light of William of Tyre's Account', *Folia Orientalia* 15 (1974), pp. 229–46

Havemann, Axel, 'The Vizier and the Raʾīs in Saljuq Syria: The Struggle for Urban Self-Representation', *International Journal of Middle East Studies* 21.2 (1989), pp. 233–42

Heyd, W., *Histoire du Commerce du Levant au Moyen-Âge*, 2 vols (Leipzig, 1885–6)

Hiestand, Rudolf, 'Die integration der Maroniten in der römische Kirche', *Orientalia Christiana Periodica* 54 (1988), pp. 119–52

Hoepffner, E., *Le troubadour Peire Vidal, sa vie et son œuvre*, Publications de la Faculté des lettres de l'Université de Strasbourg 141 (Paris, 1961)

Holt, P. M., ed., in *The Eastern Mediterranean Lands in the Period of the Crusades* (Warminster, 1977)

Hill, John Hugh and Laurita Lyttleton Hill, *Raymond IV, Count of Toulouse* (Syracuse, 1962)

Hillenbrand, Carole, 'The First Crusade: The Muslim Perspective', in *The First Crusade: Origins and Impact*, ed. Jonathan Phillips (Manchester, 1997), pp. 130–41

Hillenbrand, Carole, *The Crusades: Islamic Perspectives* (Edinburgh, 1999)

Hillenbrand, Carole, 'The Evolution of the Saladin Legend in the West', *Mélanges de l'Université de Saint-Joseph* 58 (2005), pp. 1–13

Hirschler, Konrad, 'The Jerusalem Conquest of 492/1099 in the Medieval Arabic Historiography of the Crusades: From Regional Plurality to Islamic Narrative', *Crusades* 13 (2014), pp. 37–76

Hitti, Philip K., *Origins of the Druze People and Religion: With Extracts from their Sacred Writings* (New York, 1928)

Hitti, Philip K., *History of the Arabs from the Earliest Times to the Present*, 10th ed. (Basingstoke, 2002)

Holmes, Catherine, 'Byzantium's Eastern Frontier in the Tenth and Eleventh Centuries', in *Medieval Frontiers: Concepts and Practices*, ed. David Abulafia and Nora Berend (Aldershot, 2002), pp. 83–104

Horden, Peregrine and Nicholas Purcell, *The Corrupting Sea: A Study of Mediterranean History* (Oxford, 2000)

Hoteit, Ahmad, 'Influence des Croisades sur les diverses Communautés religieuses libanaises', in *Die Folgen der Kreuzzüge für die orientalische Religionsgemeinschaft: Internationales Kolloquium vom 16.–18.10.1996 in Halle/Saale*, ed. W. Beltz (Halle-Saale, 1996), pp. 63–74

Hoteit, Ahmad, 'Les différentes communautés de Tripoli et leur attitude envers les croisés', in *De Toulouse à Tripoli: Itinéraires de cultures croisées*, ed. Edgar Weber *et al.* (Toulouse, 1997), pp. 41–58

Huizinga, Johan, *Men and Ideas: History, the Middle Ages, the Renaissance*, trans. James S. Holmes and Hans van Marle (London, 1960)

Huizinga, Johan, 'Patriotism and Nationalism in European History', in his *Men and Ideas: History, the Middle Ages, the Renaissance*, trans. James S. Holmes and Hans van Marle (London, 1960), pp. 97–155

Hunt, Lucy-Anne, *Byzantium, Eastern Christendom and Islam: Art at the Crossroads of the Medieval Mediterranean*, vol. 2 (London, 2000)

Hunt, Lucy-Anne, 'A Woman's Prayer to St. Sergios in Latin Syria: Interpreting a Thirteenth-Century Icon at Mount Sinai', in her *Byzantium, Eastern Christendom and Islam: Art at the Crossroads of the Medieval Mediterranean*, vol. 2 (London, 2000), pp. 78–126

Hunyadi, Zsolt and József Laszlovszky, eds, *The Crusades and the Military Orders: Expanding the Frontiers of Medieval Latin Christianity* (Budapest, 2001)

Immerzeel, Mat, 'Divine Cavalry: Mounted Saints in Middle Eastern Christian Art', in *East and West in the Crusader States: Context – Contacts – Confrontations*, ed. Krijnie Ciggaar, Herman Teule *et al.*, Orientalia Lovaniensia Analecta, 75, 92, 125 (Leuven, 1996–2003), vol. 3, pp. 265–86

Immerzeel, Mat, 'Medieval Wall Paintings in Lebanon: Donors and Artists', *Chronos: Revue d'Histoire de l'Université de Balamand* 10 (2004), pp. 7–47

Immerzeel, Mat, *Identity Puzzles: Medieval Christian Art in Syria and Lebanon* (Leuven, 2009)

Irwin, Robert, 'The Mamlūk Conquest of the County of Tripoli', in *Crusade and Settlement: Papers Read at the First Conference of the Society for the Study of the Crusades and the Latin East and Presented to R. C. Smail*, ed. Peter W. Edbury (Cardiff, 1985), pp. 246–50

Irwin, Robert, 'Usamah ibn Munqidh: An Arab-Syrian Gentleman at the Time of the Crusades Reconsidered', in *The Crusades and their Sources: Essays Presented to Bernard Hamilton*, ed. John France and William G. Zajac (Aldershot, 1998), pp. 71–87

Iskenderian, D. Ter-Gregorian, *Die Kreuzfahrer und ihre Beziehungen zu den armenischen Nachbarfürsten bis zum Untergange der Grafschaft Edessa* (Leipzig, 1915)

Jackson, Peter, 'The Crisis in the Holy Land in 1260', *The English Historical Review* 95.376 (1980), pp. 481–513

Jidejian, Nina, *Tripoli through the Ages* (Beirut, 1980)

Johns, Jeremy, *Arabic Administration in Norman Sicily: The Royal Dīwān* (Cambridge, 2002)

Jordan, William Chester, *Unceasing Strife, Unending Fear: Jacques de Thérines and the Freedom of the Church in the Age of the Last Capetians* (Princeton, 2005)

Jotischky, Andrew, 'Manuel Comnenus and the Reunion of the Churches: the Evidence of the Conciliar Mosaics in the Church of the Nativity in Bethlehem', *Levant* 26 (1994), pp. 207–25

Kedar, Benjamin Z., 'The General Tax of 1183 in the Crusading Kingdom of Jerusalem: Innovation or Adaptation?' *The English Historical Review* 89 (1974), pp. 339–45

Kedar, Benjamin Z., 'The Patriarch Eraclius', in *Outremer: Studies in the History of the Crusading Kingdom of Jerusalem Presented to Joshua Prawer*, ed. B. Z. Kedar, H. E. Mayer and R. C. Smail (Jerusalem, 1982), pp. 177–204

Kedar, Benjamin Z., 'Gerard of Nazareth: A Neglected Twelfth-Century Writer in the Latin East: A Contribution to the Intellectual and Monastic History of the Crusader States', *Dumbarton Oaks Papers* 37 (1983), pp. 55–77

Kedar, Benjamin Z., *Crusade and Mission: European Approaches toward the Muslims* (Princeton, NJ, 1984)

Kedar, Benjamin Z., 'The Subjected Muslims of the Frankish Levant', in *Muslims under Latin Rule, 1100–1300*, ed. James M. Powell (Princeton, NJ, 1990), pp. 135–74

Kedar, B. Z., '*De Iudeis et Sarracenis*: On the Categorization of Muslims in Medieval Canon Law', in *Studia in honorem ementissimi cardinalis Alphonsi M. Stickler*, ed. R. I. Castillo Lara (Rome, 1992), pp. 207–13

Kedar, Benjamin Z., 'The Battle of Ḥaṭṭīn Revisited', in *The Horns of Ḥaṭṭīn*, ed. B. Z. Kedar (Jerusalem, 1992), pp. 190–207

Kedar, Benjamin Z., 'Some New Sources on Palestinian Muslims before and during the Crusades', in *Die Kreuzfahrerstaaten als multikulturelle Gesellschaft*, ed. Hans Eberhard Mayer, Schriften des Historischen Kollegs, Kolloquien, 37 (Munich, 1997), pp. 129–40

Kedar, Benjamin Z., 'On the Origins of the Earliest Laws of Frankish Jerusalem: The Canons of the Council of Nablus, 1120', *Speculum* 74.2 (1999), pp. 310–35

Kedar, Benjamin Z., 'Convergences of Oriental Christian, Muslim and Frankish Worshippers: The Case of Saydnaya and the Knights Templar', in *The Crusades and the Military Orders: Expanding the Frontiers of Medieval Latin Christianity*, ed. Zsolt Hunyadi and József Laszlovszky (Budapest, 2001), pp. 89–100

Kedar, Benjamin Z., ed., *The Horns of Ḥaṭṭīn* (Jerusalem, 1992)

Kedar, B. Z., H. E. Mayer and R. C. Smail, eds, *Outremer: Studies in the History of the Crusading Kingdom of Jerusalem Presented to Joshua Prawer* (Jerusalem, 1982)

Kedar, Benjamin Z., Jonathan Riley-Smith and Rudolf Hiestand, eds, *Montjoie: Studies in Crusade History in Honour of Hans Eberhard Mayer* (Aldershot, 1997)

Kennedy, Hugh, *Crusader Castles* (Cambridge, 1994)

Knobler, Adam, 'Pseudo-Conversions and Patchwork Pedigrees: The Christianization of Muslim Princes and the Diplomacy of Holy War', *Journal of World History* 7 (1996), pp. 181–97

Köhler, Michael A., *Alliances and Treaties between Frankish and Muslim Rulers in the Middle East: Cross-Cultural Diplomacy in the Period of the Crusades*, trans. P. M. Holt and Konrad Hirschler (Leiden, 2013)

Kostick, Conor, ed., *The Crusades and the Near East* (London, 2011)

Kropáček, Luboš, 'Les *Ifrandj* dans les sources arabes', in *Clovis: histoire & mémoire, II: Le baptême de Clovis, son écho à travers l'histoire*, ed. Michel Rouche (Paris, 1997), pp. 461–72

Kuttner, Stephan and J. Joseph Ryan, eds, *Proceedings of the Second International Congress of Medieval Canon Law: Boston College, 12–16 August 1963* (Vatican City, 1965)

La Monte, John L., *Feudal Monarchy in the Latin Kingdom of Jerusalem, 1100 to 1291* (Cambridge, MA, 1932)

La Monte, John L., 'To What Extent was the Byzantine Empire the Suzerain of the Latin Crusading States?' *Byzantion* 7 (1932), pp. 253–64

Labbe, Philippe, *Tableaux genealogiques de la maison royale de France. Et des six Pairies Laïques; Bourgogne, Normandie, Guyenne, Tolose, Flandre, Champagne,* 2nd ed. (Paris, 1664)

Lambert, Sarah, 'Queen or Consort: Rulership and Politics in the Latin East, 1118–1228', in *Queens and Queenship in Medieval Europe: Proceedings of a Conference held at King's College London April* 1995, ed. Anne J. Duggan (Woodbridge, 1997), pp. 153–69

Lamonthe-Langon, Etienne Léon, *Biographie toulousaine,* 2 vols (Paris, 1823)

Lapina, Elizabeth, 'Gambling and Gaming in the Holy Land: Chess, Dice and Other Games in the Sources of the Crusades', *Crusades* 12 (2013), pp. 121–32

Lawrence, T. E., *Crusader Castles,* ed. Denys Pringle (Oxford, 1988)

Lev, Yaacov, 'The Fatimid Navy and the Crusades, 1099–1171', in *Tropis II: 2nd International Symposium on Ship Construction in Antiquity, Delphi, 1987: Proceedings,* ed. Harry E. Tzalas (Athens, 1990), pp. 257–8

Lewis, Bernard, 'The Sources for the History of the Syrian Assassins', *Speculum* 27.4 (1952), pp. 475–89

Lewis, Bernard, *The Assassins: A Radical Sect in Islam,* new ed. (London, 2003)

Lewis, Kevin James, 'Countess Hodierna of Tripoli: From Crusader Politician to "Princesse Lointaine"', *Assuming Gender* 3.1 (2013), pp. 1–26

Lewis, Kevin James, *Rule and Identity in a Diverse Mediterranean Society: Aspects of the County of Tripoli during the Twelfth Century* (Unpublished DPhil thesis: University of Oxford, 2014)

Lewis, Kevin James, 'Medieval Diglossia: The Diversity of the Latin Christian Encounter with Written and Spoken Arabic in the "Crusader" County of Tripoli, with a Hitherto Unpublished Arabic Note from the Principality of Antioch (MS, AOM 3, Valletta: National Library of Malta, no. 51v)', *Al-Masāq: Islam and the Medieval Mediterranean* 27.2 (2015), pp. 119–52

Lewis, Kevin James, 'Friend or Foe: Islamic Views of the Military Orders in the Latin East as Drawn from Arabic Sources', in *The Military Orders,* 6.1: *Culture and Conflict in the Mediterranean World,* ed. Jochen Schenk and Mike Carr (Abingdon, 2017), pp. 20–9.

Lilie, Ralph-Johannes, *Byzantium and the Crusader States 1096–1204,* trans. J. C. Morris and Jean E. Ridings (Oxford, 1988)

Lindsay, Lord, *Letters on Egypt, Edom, and the Holy Land,* 5th ed. (London, 1858)

Lock, Peter, *The Routledge Companion to the Crusades* (Oxford, 2006)

Loud, Graham A., 'Some Reflections on the Failure of the Second Crusade', *Crusades* 4 (2005), pp. 1–14

Lundgreen, F., *Wilhelm von Tyrus und der Templerorden* (Berlin, 1911)

Luscombe, David and Jonathan Riley-Smith, eds, *The New Cambridge Medieval History. Volume IV: c. 1024–c. 1198. Part II* (Cambridge, 2004)

Lusuardi Siena, Silvia and Claudia Perassi, eds, *La Giordania che abbiamo attraversato. Voci e immagini da un viaggio* (Scilla, 2012)

Luttrell, Anthony, 'The Earliest Hospitallers', in *Montjoie: Studies in Crusade History in Honour of Hans Eberhard Mayer,* ed. Benjamin Z. Kedar, Jonathan Riley-Smith and Rudolf Hiestand (Aldershot, 1997), pp. 37–54

Lyons, Malcolm Cameron and D. E. Jackson, *Saladin: The Politics of Holy War* (Cambridge, 1982)

MacEvitt, Christopher, *The Crusades and the Christian World of the East: Rough Tolerance* (Philadelphia, 2008)

Mack, Merav, *The Merchant of Genoa: The Crusades, the Genoese and the Latin East, 1187–1220s* (Unpublished PhD thesis: University of Cambridge, 2003)
Mack, Merav, 'A Genoese Perspective on the Third Crusade', *Crusades* 10 (2011), pp. 45–62
Magdalino, Paul, *The Empire of Manuel I Komnenos, 1143–1180* (Cambridge, 1993)
Magdalino, Paul, *The Byzantine Background to the First Crusade* (Toronto, 1996)
Magdalino, Paul, ed., *The Perception of the Past in Twelfth-Century Europe* (London, 1992)
Magnou-Nortier, Elisabeth, *La société laïque et l'Église dans la province ecclésiastique de Narbonne (zone cispyrénéenne) de la fin du VIIIe à la fin du XIe siècle*, Publications de l'Université de Toulouse-Le Mirail A.20 (Toulouse, 1974)
Major, Balázs, *Medieval Rural Settlements in the Syrian Coastal Region (12th and 13th Centuries)*, 2 vols (Unpublished PhD thesis: Cardiff University, 2008)
Mallett, Alex, 'The Battle of Inab', *Journal of Medieval History* 39.1 (2013), pp. 48–60
Mallett, Alex, *Popular Muslim Reactions to the Franks in the Levant, 1097–1291* (Farnham, 2014)
Mallett, Alex, ed., *Medieval Muslim Historians and the Franks in the Levant* (Leiden, 2014)
Mann, Michael, *The Sources of Social Power. Volume 1: A History of Power from the Beginning to AD 1760*, new ed. (Cambridge, 2012)
de Mas Latrie, L., *Histoire de l'île de Chypre sous le règnes des princes de la maison de Lusignan*, 3 vols (Paris, 1852–61)
Mayer, Hans E., *The Crusades*, trans. John Gillingham (Oxford, 1972)
Mayer, Hans Eberhard, 'Studies in the History of Queen Melisende of Jerusalem', *Dumbarton Oaks Papers*, 26 (1972), pp. 93–182
Mayer, Hans Eberhard, *Bistümer, Klöster und Stifte im Königreich Jerusalem* (Stuttgart, 1977)
Mayer, Hans Eberhard, 'Latins, Muslims and Greeks in the Latin Kingdom of Jerusalem', *History* 63 (1978), pp. 175–92
Mayer, H. E., 'Carving Up Crusaders: The Early Ibelins and Ramlas', in *Outremer: Studies in the History of the Crusading Kingdom of Jerusalem Presented to Joshua Prawer*, ed. B. Z. Kedar, H. E. Mayer and R. C. Smail (Jerusalem, 1982), pp. 101–18
Mayer, Hans Eberhard, 'The Concordat of Nablus', *Journal of Ecclesiastical History* 33.4 (1982), pp. 531–43
Mayer, Hans E., *Mélanges sur l'histoire du royaume latin de Jérusalem* (Paris, 1984)
Mayer, Hans E., 'Etudes sur l'histoire de Baudouin 1er roi de Jérusalem', in his *Mélanges sur l'histoire du royaume latin de Jérusalem* (Paris, 1984), pp. 10–91
Mayer, Hans Eberhard, 'The Origins of the Lordships of Ramla and Lydda in the Latin Kingdom of Jerusalem', *Speculum* 60.3 (1985), pp. 537–52
Mayer, Hans Eberhard, 'The Succession to Baldwin II of Jerusalem: English Impact on the East', *Dumbarton Oaks Papers* 39 (1985), pp. 139–47
Mayer, Hans Eberhard, 'Angevins *versus* Normans: The New Men of King Fulk of Jerusalem', *Proceedings of the American Philosophical Society* 133 (1989), pp. 1–25
Mayer, Hans Eberhard, 'Das syrische Erdbeben von 1170. Ein unedierter Brief König Amalrichs von Jerusalem', *Deutsches Archiv für Erforschung des Mittelalters* 45 (1989), pp. 474–84
Mayer, Hans Eberhard, 'The Beginnings of King Amalric of Jerusalem', in *The Horns of Ḥaṭṭīn*, ed. Benjamin Z. Kedar (Jerusalem, 1992), pp. 121–35
Mayer, Hans Eberhard, *Varia Antiochena. Studien zum Kreuzfahrerfürstentum Antiochia im 12. und frühen 13. Jahrhundert*, Monumenta Germaniae Historica: Studien und Texte 6 (Hannover, 1993)

Mayer, Hans Eberhard, 'The Latin East, 1098–1205', in *The New Cambridge Medieval History. Volume IV: c. 1024–c. 1198. Part II*, ed. David Luscombe and Jonathan Riley-Smith (Cambridge, 2004), pp. 644–74

Mayer, Hans Eberhard, ed., *Die Kreuzfahrerstaaten als multikulturelle Gesellschaft*, Schriften des Historischen Kollegs, Kolloquien, 37 (Munich, 1997)

Meri, Josef W., *The Cult of Saints among Muslims and Jews in Medieval Syria* (Oxford, 2002)

Metcalf, D. M., *Coinage of the Crusades and the Latin East*, 2nd ed. (London, 1995)

Metcalfe, Alex, *Muslims and Christians in Norman Sicily: Arabic Speakers and the End of Islam* (London, 2003)

Mikesell, Marvin W., 'The Deforestation of Mount Lebanon', *The Geographical Review* 59.1 (1969), pp. 1–28

Mirza, Nasseh Ahmad, *Syrian Ismailism: The Ever Living Line of the Imamate, AD 1100–1260* (Richmond, 1997)

Möhring, Hannes, 'Zu der Geschichte der orientalischen Herrscher des Wilhelm von Tyrus: Die Frage der Quellenabhängigkeiten', *Mittelalteinisches Jahrbuch* 19 (1984), pp. 170–83

Molyneaux, George, 'Why Were Some Tenth-Century English Kings Presented as Rulers of Britain?' *Transactions of the Royal Historical Society* 21 (2011), pp. 59–91

Morgan, David, *The Mongols*, 2nd ed. (Oxford, 2007)

Morgan, M. R., *The Chronicle of Ernoul and the Continuations of William of Tyre* (London, 1973)

Morgan, M. R., 'The Meanings of Old French *Polain*, Latin *Pullanus*', *Medium Aevum* 48 (1979), pp. 40–54

Murray, Alan V., 'Baldwin II and His Nobles: Baronial Factionalism and Dissent in the Kingdom of Jerusalem, 1118–1134', *Nottingham Medieval Studies* 38 (1994), pp. 60–85

Murray, Alan V., 'Ethnic Identity in the Crusader States: The Frankish Race and the Settlement of Outremer', in *Concepts of National Identity in the Middle Ages*, ed. Simon Forde, Lesley Johnson and Alan V. Murray (Leed., 1995), pp. 59–73

Murray, A. V., '"Mighty Against the Enemies of Christ": The Relic of the True Cross in the Armies of the Kingdom of Jerusalem', in *The Crusades and their Sources: Essays Presented to Bernard Hamilton*, ed. John France and William G. Zajac (Aldershot, 1998), pp. 217–38

Murray, A. V., *The Crusader Kingdom of Jerusalem: A Dynastic History 1099–1125* (Oxford, 2000)

Murray, A. V., 'National Identity, Language and Conflict in the Crusades to the Holy Land, 1096–1192', in *The Crusades and the Near East*, ed. Conor Kostick (London, 2011), pp. 107–30

Nicholson, Helen, *The Knights Hospitaller* (Woodbridge, 2001)

Nicholson, Helen, *Love, War and the Grail*, History of Warfare 4 (Leiden, 2001)

Nicholson, Helen, '"La Damoisele del chastel": Women's Role in the Defence and Functioning of Castles in Medieval Writing from the Twelfth to the Fourteenth Centuries', in *Crusader Landscapes in the Medieval Levant: The Archaeology and History of the Latin East. A Festschrift in Honour of Denys Pringle*, ed. Micaela Sinibaldi, Kevin James Lewis, Jennifer Thompson and Balázs Major (forthcoming)

Nicholson, R. L., *Joscelyn I, Prince of Edessa*, Illinois Studies in the Social Sciences 34.4 (Urbana, IL, 1954)

Niskanen, Samu, 'The origins of the *Gesta Francorum* and two related texts: their textual and literary character', *Sacris Erudiri: A Journal on the Inheritance of Late Antique and Medieval Christianity* 51 (2012), pp. 287–316

Nordiguian, Lévon, 'La chapelle de Saydet Al-Kharayeb à Kfâr Heldâ (Caza de Batrûn)', in *Le comté de Tripoli: État multiculturel et multiconfessionnel (1102–1289)*, ed. Gérard Dédéyan and Karam Rizk (Paris, 2010), pp. 67–91

Nowell, Charles E., 'The Old Man of the Mountain', *Speculum* 22.4 (1947), pp. 497–519

O'Carroll, Michael, *Theotokos: A Theological Encyclopedia of the Blessed Virgin Mary* (Wilmington, 1982)

O'Carroll, Michael, 'Islam', in his *Theotokos: A Theological Encyclopedia of the Blessed Virgin Mary* (Wilmington, 1982), pp. 192–3

O'Meara, Thomas F., 'The Theology and Times of William of Tripoli, O. P.: A Different View of Islam', *Theological Studies* 69 (2008), pp. 80–98

Olmo, Olivia, 'Les chrétiens orientaux dans le comté de Tripoli: localisation et positions sociales', in *Le comté de Tripoli: État multiculturel et multiconfessionnel (1102–1289)*, ed. Gérard Dédéyan and Karam Rizk (Paris, 2010), pp. 157–68

Onclin, W., 'L'Âge requis pour le mariage dans la doctrine canonique médiévale', in *Proceedings of the Second International Congress of Medieval Canon Law: Boston College, 12–16 August 1963*, ed. Stephan Kuttner and J. Joseph Ryan (Vatican City, 1965), pp. 237–47

Paterson, Linda M., *The World of the Troubadours: Medieval Occitan Society, c. 1100–c. 1300* (Cambridge, 1993)

Paterson, Linda M., 'Occitan Literature and the Holy Land', in *The World of Eleanor of Aquitaine: Literature and Society in Southern France between the Eleventh and Thirteenth Centuries*, ed. Marcus Bull and Catherine Léglu (Woodbridge, 2005), pp. 83–99

Paterson, Linda M., *Culture and Society in Medieval Occitania* (Farnham, 2011)

Paterson, Linda M., 'Was there an Occitan Identity in the Middle Ages?' in her *Culture and Society in Medieval Occitania* (Farnham, 2011), §I, pp. 1–11

Peacock, A. C. S., *The Great Seljuk Empire* (Edinburgh, 2015)

Pennington, M. Basil, ed., *One Yet Two: Monastic Tradition East and West*, Cistercian Studies 29 (Kalamazoo, 1976)

Perry, Guy, *John of Brienne: King of Jerusalem, Emperor of Constantinople,* c. *1175–1237* (Cambridge, 2013)

Phillips, Jonathan, *Defenders of the Holy Land: Relations Between the Latin East and the West, 1119–1187* (Oxford, 1996)

Phillips, Jonathan, *The Second Crusade: Extending the Frontiers of Christendom* (London, 2007)

Phillips, Jonathan, ed., *The First Crusade: Origins and Impact* (Manchester, 1997)

Piana, Mathias, 'From Montpèlerin to Ṭarābulus al-Mustajadda: The Frankish-Mamluk Succession in Old Tripoli', in *Egypt and Syria in the Fatimid, Ayyubid and Mamluk Eras, VI: Proceedings of the 14th and 15th International Colloquium Organized at the Katholieke Universiteit Leuven in May 2005 and May 2006*, ed. U. Vermeulen and K. D'Hulster, Orientalia Lovaniensia Analecta 183 (Leuven, 2010), pp. 293–301

de Planhol, Xavier, *An Historical Geography of France*, trans. Janet Lloyd, Cambridge Studies in Historical Geography 21 (Cambridge, 1994)

de Planhol, Xavier, *Minorités en Islam: géographie politique et sociale* (Paris, 1997)

Poirier, J., *et al.*, 'Large Historical Earthquakes and Seismic Risk in Northwest Syria', *Nature*, 285 (1980), pp. 217–20

Poly, Jean-Pierre, *La Provence et la Société féodale (879–1166): Contribution à l'étude des structures dites féodales dans le Midi* (Paris, 1976)

Powell, James M., ed., *Muslims under Latin Rule, 1100–1300* (Princeton, NJ, 1990)

Prawer, Joshua, 'Colonization Activities in the Latin Kingdom of Jerusalem', *Revue belge de philologie et d'histoire* 29 (1951), pp. 1063–118

Prawer, Joshua, *Histoire du Royaume Latin de Jérusalem*, 2 vols (Paris, 1969–70)

Prawer, Joshua, 'Social Classes in the Crusader States: The "Minorities"', in *A History of the Crusades*, ed. Kenneth M. Setton, 6 vols (Madison, WI, 1969–89), vol. 5, pp. 59–115

Prawer, Joshua, *The Latin Kingdom of Jerusalem: European Colonialism in the Middle Ages* (London, 1972)

Prawer, Joshua, *Crusader Institutions* (Oxford, 1980)

Pringle, Denys, 'Magna Mahumeria (al-Bīra): the Archaeology of a Frankish New Town in Palestine', in *Crusade and Settlement: Papers Read at the First Conference of the Society for the Study of the Crusades and the Latin East and Presented to R. C. Smail*, ed. Peter W. Edbury (Cardiff, 1985), pp. 147–68

Pringle, Denys, *The Churches of the Crusader Kingdom of Jerusalem: A Corpus*, 4 vols (Cambridge, 1993–2009)

Pringle, Denys, 'The Church of the Holy Sepulchre in the Castle of Tripoli (Mont-Pèlerin)', in *Egypt and Syria in the Fatimid, Ayyubid and Mamluk Eras V: Proceedings of the 11th, 12th and 13th International Colloquium Organized at the Katholieke Universiteit Leuven in May 2001, 2002 and 2003*, ed. U. Vermeulen and K. D'Hulster, Orientalia Lovaniensia Analecta, 169 (Leuven, 2007), pp. 167–82

Pringle, Denys, 'Castles and Frontiers in the Latin East', in *Norman Expansion: Connections, Continuities and Contrasts*, ed. Keith J. Stringer and Andrew Jotischky (Farnham, 2013), pp. 227–39

Pryor, J. H., 'The Oaths of the Leaders of the First Crusade to Emperor Alexius I Comnenus: Fealty, Homage – πίστις, δουλεία', *Parergon: Bulletin of the Australian and New Zealand Association for Medieval & Renaissance Studies*, new series, 2 (1984), pp. 111–41

Pryor, John H., *Geography, Technology, and War: Studies in the Maritime History of the Mediterranean, 649–1571* (Cambridge, 1988)

Pryor, John H. and Michael J. Jeffreys, 'Alexios, Bohemond, and Byzantium's Euphrates Frontier: A Tale of Two Cretans', *Crusades* 11 (2012), pp. 31–86

Rāsī, Juliette, '"Kullīyat al-ṭibb" fī ṭarābulus ʿalā ʿahd al-ṣalībiyyīn [The "college of medicine" in Tripoli during the time of the crusaders]', *Chronos* 11 (2005), pp. 185–201

Rey, E. G., *Sommaire du supplément aux Familles d'Outremer* (Chartres, 1881)

Rey, E. G., *Les colonies franques de Syrie aux XIIme et XIIIme siècles* (Paris, 1883)

Richard, Jean, *Le comté de Tripoli sous la dynastie toulousaine (1102–1187)*, Bibliothèque archéologique et historique 39 (Paris, 1945)

Richard, Jean, 'Note sur l'archidiocèse d'Apamée et les conquêtes de Raymond de Saint-Gilles en Syrie du nord', *Syria* 25.1–2 (1946–8), pp. 103–8

Richard, Jean, 'Questions de topographie tripolitaine', *Journal Asiatique* 236 (1948), pp. 53–59

Richard, Jean, 'Pairie d'Orient latin: les quatre baronnies des royaumes de Jérusalem et de Chypre', *Revue historique de droit français et étranger*, 4th series, 28 (1950), pp. 67–88

Richard, Jean, *Le royaume Latin de Jérusalem* (Paris, 1953)

Richard, Jean, 'L'abbaye cistercienne de Jubin et le prieuré Saint-Blaise de Nicosie', *Epeteris tou Kentrou Epistemonikon Ereunon* 3 (1969–70), pp. 63–74

Richard, Jean, 'Les Saint-Gilles et le comté de Tripoli', *Islam et chrétiens du Midi (XIIe-XIVe s.)*, Cahiers de Fanjeaux 18 (Toulouse, 1983), pp. 65–75

Richard, Jean, 'Les comtes de Tripoli et leurs vassaux sous la dynastie antiochénienne', in *Crusade and Settlement: Papers Read at the First Conference of the Society for the Study of the Crusades and the Latin East and Presented to R. C. Smail*, ed. Peter W. Edbury (Cardiff, 1985), pp. 213–21

Richard, Jean, '*Cum omni raisagio montanee* ... À propos de la cession du Crac aux Hospitaliers', in *Itinéraires d'Orient: Hommages à Claude Cahen*, ed. Raoul Curiel and Rika Gyselen, Res Orientales 6 (Burs-sur-Yvette, 1994), pp. 187–92

Richard, Jean, 'Affrontement ou confrontation? Les contacts entre deux mondes au pays de Tripoli au temps des Croisades', *Chronos* 2 (1999), pp. 7–25

Richard, Jean, 'Les familles féodales franques dans le comté de Tripoli', in *Le comté de Tripoli: État multiculturel et multiconfessionnel (1102–1289)*, ed. Gérard Dédéyan and Karam Rizk (Paris, 2010), pp. 7–30

Richard, Jean, 'Préface', in *Le comté de Tripoli: État multiculturel et multiconfessionnel (1102–1289)*, ed. Gérard Dédéyan and Karam Rizk (Paris, 2010), pp. 1–2

Riley-Smith, Jonathan, *The Knights of St. John in Jerusalem and Cyprus, c. 1050–1310* (London, 1967)

Riley-Smith, Jonathan, *The Feudal Nobility and the Kingdom of Jerusalem, 1174–1277* (London, 1973)

Riley-Smith, Jonathan, 'The survival in Latin Palestine of Muslim administration', in *The Eastern Mediterranean Lands in the Period of the Crusades*, ed. P. M. Holt (Warminster, 1977), pp. 9–22

Riley-Smith, Jonathan, 'The Title of Godfrey of Bouillon', *Bulletin of the Institute of Historical Research* 52.125 (1979), pp. 83–6

Riley-Smith, Jonathan, 'The Latin Clergy and the Settlement in Palestine and Syria, 1098–1100', *The Catholic Historical Review* 74.4 (1988), pp. 539–57

Riley-Smith, Jonathan, 'Family Traditions and Participation in the Second Crusade', in *The Second Crusade and the Cistercians*, ed. Michael Gervers (New York, 1992), pp. 101–8

Riley-Smith, Jonathan, *The First Crusaders, 1095–1131* (Cambridge, 1997)

Riley-Smith, Jonathan, 'Raymond IV of St Gilles, Achard of Arles and the conquest of Lebanon', in *The Crusades and their Sources: Essays Presented to Bernard Hamilton*, ed. John France and William G. Zajac (Aldershot, 1998), pp. 1–8

Riley-Smith, Jonathan, *The First Crusade and the Idea of Crusading* (London, 2003)

Riley-Smith, Jonathan, *The Knights Hospitaller in the Levant, c.1070–1309* (Basingstoke, 2012)

Rizk, Karam, 'Avant-propos', in *Le comté de Tripoli: État multiculturel et multiconfessionnel (1102–1289)*, ed. Gérard Dédéyan and Karam Rizk (Paris, 2010), pp. 3–5

Roach, Andrew, 'Occitania Past and Present: Southern Consciousness in Medieval and Modern French Politics', *History Workshop Journal* 43 (1997), pp. 1–22

Röhricht, Reinhold, *Geschichte der Königreichs Jerusalem (1100–1291)* (Innsbrück, 1898)

Rouche, Michel, ed., *Clovis: histoire & mémoire, II: Le baptême de Clovis, son écho à travers l'histoire* (Paris, 1997)

Rowe, John Gordon, 'The Papacy and the Ecclesiastical Province of Tyre (1100–1187)', *Bulletin of the John Rylands Library* 43 (1960–1), pp. 160–89

Rubenstein, Jay, 'What is the *Gesta Francorum*, and who was Peter Tudebode?' *Revue Mabillon: Revue internationale d'histoire et de littérature religieuses*, n.s. 16.77 (2005), pp. 179–204

Rudt de Collenberg, W. H., 'Les « Raynouard », seigneurs de Nephin et de Maraclé en Terre Sainte, et leur parenté en Languedoc', *Cahiers de civilisation médiévale* 7 (1964), pp. 289–311

Runciman, Steven, *A History of the Crusades, Volume II: The Kingdom of Jerusalem and the Frankish East, 1100–1187* (Cambridge, 1957)

Sabine, C. J., 'The Billon and Copper Coinage of the Crusader County of Tripoli, *c.*1102–1268', *The Numismatic Chronicle*, 7th series, 20 (1980), pp. 71–112

Sader, Youhanna, *Painted Churches and Rock-Cut Chapels of Lebanon*, trans. Deirdre Baker (Beirut, 1997)

Salamé-Sarkis, Ḥassān, *Contribution à l'histoire de Tripoli et de sa région à l'époque des croisades: problèmes d'histoire, d'architecture et de céramique*, Bibliothèque archéologique et historique 106 (Paris, 1980)

Salibi, Kamal S., 'The Maronites of Lebanon under Frankish and Mamluk Rule (1099–1516)', *Arabica* 4:3 (1957), pp. 288–303

Salibi, Kamal S., 'The Maronite Church in the Middle Ages and its Union with Rome', *Oriens Christianus: Hefte für die Kunde des christlichen Orients* 42 (1958), pp. 92–104

Salibi, Kamal S., *Maronite Historians of Mediæval Lebanon* (Beirut, 1959)

Salvat, J., 'Provençal ou occitan?' *Annales du Midi* 66.3 (1954), pp. 229–41

Saunders, J. J., *The History of the Mongol Conquests* (London, 1971)

Sbeinati, Mohamed Reda, *et al.*, 'The Historical Earthquakes of Syria: An Analysis of Large and Moderate Earthquakes from 1365 B.C. to 1900 A.D.', *Annals of Geophysics* 48 (2005), pp. 347–435

Schein, Sylvia, 'Women in Medieval Colonial Society: The Latin Kingdom of Jerusalem in the Twelfth Century', in *Gendering the Crusades*, ed. Susan B. Edgington and Sarah Lambert (Cardiff, 2001), pp. 140–53

Schlumberger, Gustave, *Numismatique de l'Orient latin* (Paris, 1878)

Schwennicke, Detlev, ed., *Europäische Stammtafeln: Stammtafeln zur Geschichte der Europäischen Staaten. Neue Folge, Band III, Teilband 4: Das Feudale Frankreich und sein Einfluss auf die Welt des Mittelalters* (Marburg, 1989)

Setton, Kenneth M., ed., *A History of the Crusades*, 6 vols (Madison, WI, 1969–89)

Shagrir, Iris, 'The Medieval Evolution of By-naming: Notions from the Latin Kingdom of Jerusalem', in *In Laudem Hierosolymitani: Studies in Crusades and Medieval Culture in Honour of Benjamin Z. Kedar*, ed. Ronnie Ellenblum, Jonathan Riley-Smith and Iris Shagrir (Aldershot, 2007), pp. 49–59

Shahar, Shulamith, *The Fourth Estate: A History of Women in the Middle Ages*, revised ed., trans. Chaya Galai (London, 2003)

Shatzmiller, Maya, ed., *Crusaders and Muslims in Twelfth-Century Syria* (Leiden, 1993)

Shepard, Jonathan, 'When Greek meets Greek: Alexius Comnenus and Bohemond in 1097–98', *Byzantine and Modern Greek Studies* 12 (1988), pp. 185–277

Simpson, Alicia, *Niketas Choniates: A Historiographical Study* (Oxford, 2013)

Sinibaldi, Micaela, Kevin James Lewis, Jennifer Thompson and Balázs Major, eds, *Crusader Landscapes in the Medieval Levant: The Archaeology and History of the Latin East. A Festschrift in Honour of Denys Pringle* (forthcoming)

Sire, H. J. A., 'The Character of the Hospitaller Properties in Spain in the Middle Ages', in *The Military Orders: Fighting for the Faith and Caring for the Sick*, ed. Malcolm Barber (Aldershot, 1994), pp. 21–7

Sivan, Emmanuel, *L'Islam et la Croisade: Idéologie et Propagande dans les Réactions Musulmanes aux Croisades* (Paris, 1968)

Slim, Souad, 'L'abbaye de Belmont: prototype cistercien et tête de pont des croisades', in *De Toulouse à Tripoli: Itinéraires de cultures croisées*, ed. Edgard Weber *et al.* (Toulouse, 1997), pp. 257–68

Smail, R. C., 'The Predicaments of Guy of Lusignan, 1183–87', in *Outremer: Studies in the History of the Crusading Kingdom of Jerusalem Presented to Joshua Prawer*, ed. B. Z. Kedar, H. E. Mayer and R. C. Smail (Jerusalem, 1982), pp. 159–76

Smail, R. C., *Crusading Warfare, 1097–1193*, 2nd ed. (Cambridge, 1995)

Smarandache, Bogdan, 'The Franks and the Nizārī Ismāʿīlīs in the Early Crusade Period', *Al-Masāq: Islam and the Medieval Mediterranean* 24.3 (2012), pp. 221–39

Smith, Jane I. and Yvonne Y. Haddad, 'The Virgin Mary in Islamic Tradition and Commentary', *The Muslim World* 79.3–4 (1989), pp. 161–87

Stafford, Ned, 'How Geology Came to Help Alexander the Great', *Nature*. Uploaded 14 May 2007. Accessed 17 August 2014. http://www.nature.com/news/2007/070514/full/news070514-2.html

Stevenson, W. B., *The Crusaders in the East: A Brief History of the Wars of Islam with the Latins in Syria during the Twelfth and Thirteenth Centuries* (Cambridge, 1907)

Stringer, Keith J. and Andrew Jotischky, eds, *Norman Expansion: Connections, Continuities and Contrasts* (Farnham, 2013)

Swanson, R. N., ed., *The Holy Land, Holy Lands, and Christian History: Papers Read at the 1998 Summer Meeting and the 1999 Winter Meeting of the Ecclesiastical History Society*, Studies in Church History 36 (Woodbridge, 2000)

Tannous, Jack Boulos Victor, *Syria Between Byzantium and Islam: Making Incommensurables Speak. Volume 1* (Unpublished PhD thesis: Princeton University, 2010)

Thomas, David, 'Gospel, Muslim conception of', *The Encyclopaedia of Islam*, 3rd ed. (Leiden, 2007–), 2014.4

Thomson, Rodney M. and Michael Winterbottom, *William of Malmesbury, Gesta Regum Anglorum: The History of the English Kings, Volume II. General Introduction and Commentary* (Oxford, 1999)

Thorau, Peter, *The Lion of Egypt: Sultan Baybars I and the Near East in the Thirteenth Century*, trans. P. M. Holt (London, 1992)

Tibble, Steven, *Monarchy and Lordships in the Latin Kingdom of Jerusalem 1099–1291* (Oxford, 1989)

Todt, Klaus-Peter, 'Antioch and Edessa in to [*sic*] so-called Treaty of Deabolis (September 1108)', *ARAM* 11–12 (1999–2000), pp. 485–501

Tonghini, Cristina, *Shayzar I: The Fortification of the Citadel* (Leiden, 2012)

Treadgold, Warren, *A History of the Byzantine State and Society* (Stanford, CA, 1997)

Turner, Ralph V., *Eleanor of Aquitaine: Queen of France, Queen of England* (London, 2009)

Tzalas, Harry E., ed., *Tropis II: 2nd International Symposium on Ship Construction in Antiquity, Delphi, 1987: Proceedings* (Athens, 1990)

Upton-Ward, Judi, ed., *The Military Orders. Volume 4: On Land and by Sea* (Aldershot, 2008)

Vannini, Guido and Michele Nucciotti, 'Petra a Shawbak. Archeologia di una frontiera. La missione in Giordania dell'Università di Firenze', in *La Giordania che abbiamo attraversato. Voci e immagini da un viaggio*, ed. Silvia Lusuardi Siena and Claudia Perassi (Scilla, 2012), pp. 55–73

Vermeulen, U. and K. D'Hulster, eds, *Egypt and Syria in the Fatimid, Ayyubid and Mamluk Eras, V: Proceedings of the 11th, 12th and 13th International Colloquium Organized at the Katholieke Universiteit Leuven in May 2001, 2002 and 2003*, Orientalia Lovaniensia Analecta 169 (Leuven, 2007)

Vermeulen, U. and K. D'Hulster, eds, *Egypt and Syria in the Fatimid, Ayyubid and Mamluk Eras, VI: Proceedings of the 14th and 15th International Colloquium Organized at the Katholieke Universiteit Leuven in May 2005 and May 2006*, Orientalia Lovaniensia Analecta 183 (Leuven, 2010)

Vryonis, Speros, *The Decline of Medieval Hellenism in Asia Minor and the Process of Islamization from the Eleventh through the Fifteenth Century* (Berkeley, CA, 1971)

Waddell, Chrysogonus, 'The Myth of Cistercian Origins: C. H. Berman and the Manuscript Sources', *Cîteaux* 51 (2000), pp. 299–386

Walker, Paul E., *Exploring an Islamic Empire: Fatimid History and its Sources* (London, 2002)

Weber, Edgar, *et al.*, eds, *De Toulouse à Tripoli: Itinéraires de cultures croisées* (Toulouse, 1997)

Weltecke, Dorothea, 'The Syriac Orthodox in the Principality during the Crusader Period', in *East and West in the Medieval Eastern Mediterranean: Antioch from the Byzantine Reconquest until the End of the Crusader Principality*, ed. Krijnie Ciggaar *et al.*, 2 vols, Orientalia Lovaniensia Analecta 147, 199 (Leuven, 2006–13), vol. 1, pp. 95–124

Whittow, Mark, *The Making of Orthodox Byzantium, 600–1025* (Basingstoke, 1996)

Wilkinson, John, *Jerusalem Pilgrimage 1099–1185*, Works Issued by the Hakluyt Society, 2nd series, 167 (London, 1988)

Williams, D. H., 'Cistercian Settlement in the Lebanon', *Cîteaux: commentarii cistercienses* 25 (1974), pp. 61–74

Zibawi, Mahmoud, *Images chrétiens du Levant: les décors peints des églises syro-libanaises au Moyen Âge* (Paris 2009)

Index

Printed in the USA
CPSIA information can be obtained
at www.ICGtesting.com
LVHW021754061223
765867LV00011B/530